INFAMOUS CRIMES

...that *shocked* the world

BLACK CAT

CONTENTS

INTRODUCTION

Each day our newspapers tell stories of crime and violence – stories which have a powerful fascination for many readers. Yet each of these enthralling cases is essentially the story of a personal tragedy for its victim or victims. What is it, then, about crime that so fascinates us, despite our repugnance?

The accounts of crimes we have gathered together here go a long way towards answering that question. They are much more than merely an absorbing read; they also paint an intricate, if horrifying, portrait of the society in which we live. The book comprises articles on a variety of themes, from robber barons and kidnappers to mass murderers and rapists: each theme is exemplified by a typical case and trial. Here you will find all the classic crime stories – the Great Train Robbery, Al Capone, the Moors Murderers, the Lindbergh Kidnapping, Jack the Ripper – but here too are many lesser-known cases, which were briefly in the public eye but have been largely forgotten. The same threads, however, occur time and again, and together these cases provide a telling commentary on society and its attitude towards crime, the criminal and the victim. Much can be learnt from the public reaction to crimes, the way the criminals are brought to trial, and the attitudes of the judges and detectives involved, as well as the criminals themselves.

Perhaps the most striking feature reflected in these pages is the way attitudes have changed over the years, pure sensationalism alternating with moral revulsion. Today, however, both seem to be giving way to a better understanding of the psychology of crime, coupled with a new determination on the behalf of society to ensure that crime simply will not pay.

The material in this book originally appeared in *Crimes and Punishment*

first published in Great Britain in 1989
by Macdonald & Co (Publishers) Ltd.
Reprinted 1989 by Macdonald & Co (Publishers) Ltd under the Black Cat imprint

Reprinted 1991

Macdonald & Co (Publishers) Ltd
Orbit House
1 New Fetter Lane
London EC4A 1AR

A member of Maxwell Macmillan Pergamon Publishing Corporation

ISBN 0-7481-0260-4

Printed and bound in Czechoslovakia by Aventinum

50828

Rodney Shackell

AN OFFICER AND A GENTLEMAN...

A tall, handsome young Air Force hero, home from the war . . . to women his easy charm was utterly fatal. Neville Heath was more than a fraud . . . he was a suave sex-maniac, one of the most violently depraved men the world has known. In a few summer days, he haunted England's genteel South coast.

POLICE GAZETTE

PUBLISHED BY AUTHORITY.

NEW SERIES.   TUESDAY, JUNE 25, 1946.   No. 147, VOL. XXXIII.

Manuscript for publication should be addressed "THE COMMISSIONER OF POLICE, NEW SCOTLAND YARD. S.W.1." with "C.R.O. (P.G.)" in top left corner.

HAROLD SCOTT
The Commissioner of Police of the Metropolis.

Special Notice

MURDER

M.P. (FH).—It is desired to trace the after-described for interview respecting the death of MARGERY GARDNER, during the night of 20th-21st inst.—NEVILLE GEORGE CLEVELY HEATH, alias ARMSTRONG, BLYTH, DENVERS and GRAHAM, C.R.O. No. 28142-37, b. 1917, 5ft. 11½in., c. fresh, e. blue, believed small fair moustache, h. and eyebrows fair, square face, broad forehead and nose, firm chin, good teeth, military gait ; dress, lt. grey d.b. suit with pin stripe, dk. brown trilby, brown suede shoes, cream shirt with collar attached or fawn and white check sports jacket and grey flannel trousers. Nat. Reg. No. CNP/2147191.

Has recent conviction for posing as Lt.-Col. of South African Air Force. A pilot and believed to possess an "A" licence, has stated his intention of going abroad and may endeavour to secure passage on ship or plane as passenger or pilot. May stay at hotels accompanied by woman.

Enquiries are also requested to trace the owner of gent's white handkerchief with brown check border, bearing "L. Kearns" in black ink on hem and stitched with large "K" in blue cotton in centre.

LUNCHTIME had come and gone, yet there was still no sign of life from Room No. 4 at the Pembridge Court Hotel in Notting Hill, London. The maid responsible for the room, eager to get on with her cleaning and tidying, was understandably irritated. She peeped through the keyhole. The room was in darkness and there was nothing to be seen. She knocked at the door again. Still there was no answer.

Perhaps she should inform someone. She sought out Mrs. Alice Wyatt, who helped her father-in-law to run the 19-bedroomed hotel, and explained the situation. Mrs. Wyatt looked at the clock. It was 2 p.m. She thought it was time to investigate. She let herself into the bedroom with her pass key and drew back the curtains. In one of the single beds, the sheets and blankets pulled up around her neck, lay a young, dark-haired woman. It was hardly necessary to move the bedclothes to establish that she was dead. The red bloodstains all over the second bed told their own story.

The police arrived within minutes. Beneath the bedclothes they found a badly mutilated body. The dead woman's nipples had been practically bitten off. There were 17 weals, apparently made by the plaited thong of a whip with a metal tip, across her back, chest, stomach, and face. Her ankles were bound together with a handkerchief and she had bled from the vagina. It was clear that her face had been washed, but there were still traces of blood on her cheeks and in her nostrils. The blood on the second bed suggested that she had been killed there and her body moved after death — while interlacing markings on the pillow-case pointed to a bloodstained whip having lain there.

Female companion

The victim's body was removed to Hammersmith Mortuary where Dr. Keith Simpson, the pathologist, carried out a post-mortem. He found the woman had died from suffocation, probably caused by a gag or by having her face pressed into a pillow.

Meantime, the police had started the hunt for the killer. The trail did not prove difficult to follow. The woman's body was found on Friday, June 21, 1946. Room No. 4 had been let the previous Sunday to a man with a female companion (not the dead woman), who had signed the register "Mr. and Mrs. N. G. C. Heath", giving an address in Hampshire.

"FIANCÉE" Yvonne Symonds (right): "Yvonne, there's been a nasty murder in London . . . in the room where we stayed last weekend." Police soon pinpointed Heath, but the use of his photograph (left) placed them in a fatal dilemma.

VICTIM: Film extra Margery Gardner liked the "bohemian" life. At the Panama Club, she drank and danced her way to a dreadful death with debonair Heath.

Within hours, Superintendent Thomas Barratt, who was in charge of the case, had established that Mr. N. G. C. Heath was Neville George Clevely Heath, a handsome, 29-year-old former officer, six feet tall and the possessor of a criminal record, although not for violence. The police had also uncovered the identity of the dead woman. She was 32-year-old Mrs. Margery Gardner, occasionally a film extra, separated from her husband and fond of the gay, bohemian life.

On the night before the killing, she drank and danced with Heath at the Panama Club in South Kensington. Around midnight they left the club together, hailed a cruising taxicab and directed it to the Pembridge Court Hotel. Harry Harter, the cabdriver, remembered the journey well. "I picked them up in

the Old Brompton Road and put them down about 50 yards from the Pembridge Court Hotel," he told detectives. "The man asked me how much the fare was. I said it was 1s. 9d. and he gave me 2s. 2d. Then they walked towards the hotel. He put his arm round the woman's waist and I saw them enter the hotel gate."

The police were well pleased with their progress. It was beginning to look as if an arrest was merely a matter of days. It was decided to release Heath's name and description to the newspapers as a man who, in the cautious legal phrase, the police would like "to assist them with their inquiries". At this point, however, the police faced a dilemma. They had collected four photographs of Heath from his home in Merton Hall Road, Wimbledon. Should these photographs be published along with Heath's name and description? It seemed on the one hand that identification would prove a critical issue in Heath's trial if, as expected, he proved to be the murderer, and widespread publication of his likeness might easily prejudice the chances of a conviction. If, on the other hand, Heath's suave and easy charm masked a sex maniac, he might easily kill again unless he were captured quickly. In the end the decision was taken not to release the photographs. As a result, another woman was to die.

Name and description

While his name and description was being flashed to police stations and newspapers all over the country, Heath was in the Sussex seaside resort of Worthing. He had travelled down to the South Coast on the day Margery Gardner's mutilated body was found, and booked in under his own name at the Ocean Hotel. The purpose of his visit was to look up yet another of the many women in his life,

A RAKE'S PROGRESS...THAT ENDED IN MULTIPLE MURDER

Police pieced together details of Heath's extraordinary career of crime and service in the armed forces, during which, in the course of ten years, he managed to get himself commissioned and dishonourably discharged on three occasions. In outline, his dossier reads:

February 1936. Obtained short-service commission in R.A.F.

August 1937. Court-martialled for being absent without leave for nearly five months. Other charges included escaping while under arrest and "borrowing" a non-commissioned officer's car without permission. Sentenced to be cashiered. Commuted subsequently to dismissal.

November 1937. Placed on probation on charges of fraudulently obtaining credit at a Nottingham hotel and attempting to obtain a car by false pretences. Eight other offences, including posing as "Lord Dudley", taken into account.

July 1938. Sentenced to three years' Borstal treatment for housebreaking and stealing jewellery worth £51 from a friend, and for obtaining clothing worth £27 by means of a forged bankers' order. Ten other offences taken into account.

September 1939. Released from Hollesley Bay Colony because of the outbreak of the war.

October 1939. Enlisted in Royal Army Service Corps.

March 1940. Commissioned and posted to the Middle East.

July 1941. Placed under arrest after a dispute with a brigadier. Went absent without leave. Court-martialled for these offences and for obtaining a second pay-book by making a false statement; making a false statement to his commanding officer, enabling him to be absent from his unit; and on five charges relating to dishonoured cheques. Sentenced to be cashiered.

Keystone

November 1941. Absconded from the troopship that was bringing him to England when it docked at Durban in South Africa. Went to Johannesburg where he passed himself off as a Captain Selway, M.C., of the Argyll and Sutherland Highlanders.

December 1941. Enlisted in South African Air Force under the name of Armstrong. Commissioned.

May 1944. Seconded to Royal Air Force. Shot down on the Dutch-German border while piloting a Mitchell bomber.

August 1945. Court-martialled and dismissed the service in South Africa on six charges, three of conduct prejudicial to good order and military discipline and three of wearing military decorations without authority.

February 1946. Arrived back in Britain.

April 1946. Fined at Wimbledon Magistrates' Court in South London for wearing a military uniform and decorations to which he was not entitled.

Yvonne Symonds, whom he had met at a dance in Chelsea the previous Saturday. After the dance he took her to the Panama Club. "Let's find a hotel and sleep together," Heath suggested. His new companion refused.

Heath spent the whole of the next day with her. He was at his most debonair and charming. Yvonne Symonds found him fascinating. When he proposed, she gladly accepted—although she had known him for only a few hours. Once again Heath suggested: "Let's spend the night together." This time she agreed, and she was the "Mrs. N. G. C. Heath" who had occupied Room No. 4 at the Pembridge Court Hotel the previous Sunday night. Heath phoned her several times in the course of the week. Now, down in Worthing, he phoned again and arranged to take her out to lunch on the Saturday.

Utmost courtliness

By then the news of Margery Gardner's killing was out, and, in the course of the meal, Heath suddenly said: "Yvonne, there's been a nasty murder in London. Have you read about it in the papers?" Miss Symonds said she hadn't. "I'll tell you all about it later," Heath promised. He returned to the subject that night when he took her to dine and dance at the Blue Peter Club in Angmering. "That murder I mentioned," he said. "It took place in the room we stayed in last weekend. I knew the girl. She was with some man who had nowhere to stay so I gave him the key to the room and went and slept somewhere else. The police—an Inspector (it should have been Superintendent) Barratt—got on to me and took me round to the room. I saw the body. It was a pretty gruesome sight."

Miss Symonds did not doubt Heath's story for a moment. This, after all, was the man who had swept her off her feet, who, in their brief time together, had always treated her with the utmost courtliness and consideration. How had the girl died? "A poker was stuck up her," replied Heath bluntly. "I think that's what killed her—although Inspector Barratt seems to believe she might have been suffocated."

Miss Symonds was horrified. "What sort of person could commit a brutal crime like that?" she asked.

"A sex maniac, I suppose," shrugged Heath.

He took her home safely at the end of the evening and chastely kissed her goodnight. She was to speak to him only once again. That was the following morning after she and her parents had read Sunday newspaper accounts of the murder and a renewed appeal by the police—the first one had been published on the Saturday—for Heath to come forward. Miss Symonds immediately rang

HEATH'S
ROOM

BUILDER'S
LADDER HERE

Popperfoto

"A LITTLE DECEPTION": After savagely murdering Doreen Marshall, Heath returned to his hotel room by way of a fire escape and a ladder.

her fiancé at his hotel.

"My parents are very worried about the story in the papers," she told him.

Heath remained the cool man-of-the-world. "I thought they would be," he said laconically. Then he added: "I've got a car and I'm driving back to London to sort things out. I'll probably give you a ring this evening." But he did not ring. Nor did he return to London. Instead he caught a train to Bournemouth where he booked into the Tollard Royal Hotel, using the improbable name of Group-Captain Rupert Brooke — Brooke being the brilliant young English poet who died in Greece in the First World War.

Until now, Heath had acted in a careless, almost reckless, manner for a killer who, presumably, did not want to be caught. Margery Gardner had been found in a room rented to him, and, in describing the murder to Yvonne Symonds, he had revealed an intimate knowledge of the crime. His claim that "Inspector" Barratt had taken him to the scene was quite untrue and would not withstand investigation if Miss Symonds talked. Before leaving Worthing, Heath therefore took his first positive step to try to point the

finger of suspicion away from him. He wrote to "Chief Inspector" Barratt. The letter arrived on the police officer's desk at New Scotland Yard on the Monday morning. It read:

"Sir, I feel it to be my duty to inform you of certain facts in connection with the death of Mrs. Gardner at Notting Hill Gate. I booked in at the hotel last Sunday, but not with Mrs. Gardner, whom I met for the first time during the week. I had drinks with her on Friday evening, and whilst I was with her she met an acquaintance with whom she was obliged to sleep. The reasons, as I understand them, were mainly financial.

Invidious position

"It was then that Mrs. Gardner asked if she could use my hotel room until two o'clock and intimated that, if I returned after that, I might spend the remainder of the night with her. I gave her my keys and told her to leave the hotel door open. It must have been almost 3 a.m. when I returned to the hotel and found her in the condition of which you are aware. I realised I was in an invidious position, and rather than notify the police I packed my belongings and left.

"Since then I have been in several minds whether to come forward or not, but in view of the circumstances I have been afraid to. I can give you a descrip-

tion of the man. He was aged approximately 30, dark hair (black), with a small moustache. Height about 5ft. 9ins., slim build. His name was Jack and I gathered that he was a friend of Mrs. Gardner's of some long standing.

"The personal column of the *Daily Telegraph* will find me, but at the moment I have assumed another name. I should like to come forward and help, but I cannot face the music of a fraud charge which will obviously be preferred against me if I should do so. I have the instrument with which Mrs. Gardner was beaten and am forwarding this to you today. You will find my fingerprints on it, but you should also find others as well. N. G. C. Heath."

The parcel containing the instrument never arrived, and for the next 13 days — from Sunday, June 23, until Saturday, July 6 — Heath lived what was apparently the life of a carefree holidaymaker in Bournemouth. The guests, and the staff, at the Tollard Royal Hotel found him pleasant and amusing company. His entire wardrobe seemed to consist of grey flannel trousers and a mustard-coloured sports jacket, and during most of his stay he appeared to have no cash, putting all his drinks on the bill, but nobody was particularly concerned. The man they knew as Group-Captain Rupert Brooke was obviously an officer and a gentleman.

It was also established that, while in South Africa, Heath was married in 1942 and had a son. His wife had divorced him in October 1945, on the grounds of desertion.

Within a couple of days of Heath's arrival in Bournemouth, every police force in the country, including the local one, had a copy of his photograph as a wanted man. The decision not to release pictures to the newspapers was adhered to, however, even as the days passed, producing nothing but the inevitable crop of frustrating false leads as to Heath's whereabouts. With each 24 hours that passed, death came a day nearer to 21-year-old Doreen Marshall.

Doreen Marshall was a pert and pretty ex-Wren (the Women's Royal Naval Service), the daughter of a Pinner, Middlesex, company director. After being demobilized she suffered a severe attack of influenza, and her father decided that a few days by the sea would help to put her on her feet again. He packed her off to Bournemouth where she booked in at the Norfolk Hotel.

It is not exactly clear how her path crossed with Heath's. His own account, written later, said: "On Wednesday, July 3, during the morning, I was seated on the promenade on Westcliff when I saw two young ladies walking along the front. One of these two was a casual acquaintance whom I had met at a dance at the Pavilion during the latter half of the preceding week (her Christian name was Peggy but I was unaware of her surname). Although I was not formally introduced to the other I gathered that her name was "Doo" or something similar. The girl Peggy left after about half-an-hour and I walked along the front with the other girl whom I now know to be Miss Marshall. I invited her to have tea with me in the afternoon and she accepted.

Smilingly agreed

In the course of tea at the Tollard Royal Hotel that afternoon, Heath asked: "Would you care to join me for dinner tonight?" Miss Marshall smilingly agreed. After dinner they sat in the hotel lounge until shortly after midnight. Other guests noted that Heath seemed to be slightly drunk and, as the evening wore on, his companion appeared unhappy. At one point she begged one of the men present to order her a taxi. Soon afterwards, Heath cancelled it and said: "My guest has decided to walk home." He left the hotel with Miss Marshall about 12.15 a.m.

"I'll be back in about half-an-hour," he told the porter.

"A quarter-of-an-hour," snapped Miss Marshall.

Nobody saw her alive again. As for Heath, it was never established at what time he returned to the hotel. He regained his room by climbing a ladder and getting in through a window. It was, he explained later, "a little deception" on his friend the night porter. The mystified porter confessed subsequently that at 4.30 a.m. he had peeped into Heath's bedroom to see if he was there. The guest was fast asleep.

Thursday passed apparently normally. So did most of Friday. Then the manager of the Tollard Royal Hotel, Ivor Relf, received a phone call from the manager of the Norfolk Hotel. "One of our guests appears to be missing," he said, "and we believe she dined at your place on Wednesday." He added that the missing guest, Miss Marshall, had come from Pinner, outside London.

Suave demeanour

Heath, in the meantime, showed no signs of agitation or excitement. The only changes in him—both significant, it was to turn out—was that he now seemed to have money in his pockets and had taken to wearing a silk scarf to hide a couple of scratches on his neck. There was nothing else about the demeanour of Group-Captain Rupert Brooke to arouse suspicion, and it was not until the Saturday morning that Mr. Relf got around to mentioning the phone call from the Norfolk Hotel.

Heath, playing it as coolly as ever, laughed off the notion that the missing woman might have been his dinner guest. "I believe she came from Pinner," said Mr. Relf. "I have known that lady for a long while, and she certainly doesn't come from Pinner," replied Heath airily.

But he was now to take a step as extraordinary as his decision to write to Superintendent Barratt. He telephoned the police and asked if they had a photograph of the missing woman. The officer in charge of the case was out and Heath said he would ring again later. He phoned for a second time at 3.30 and, on hearing that the police did have a photograph of Miss Marshall, offered to come round a couple of hours later to have a look at it and see if he could be of any help.

He can hardly have suspected it, but the step he took through the door of the police station was to be his last as a free man. Heath identified himself as Brooke, but he was almost immediately recognised from the photographs circulated to police stations throughout the country as the man wanted for questioning about the death of Margery Gardner. Heath still insisted that he was Brooke. However at

VICTIM: "Miss Marshall did not wish me to accompany her." Not far from the beach, police with bloodhounds searched for the body of Doreen Marshall in wooded Branksome Chine.

Popperfoto

9.45 that evening, Detective-Inspector George Gates told him: "I am satisfied that you are Neville George Clevely Heath and I am going to detain you pending the arrival of officers of the Metropolitan police."

"Oh, all right," murmured Heath, not, it seemed, particularly concerned.

Now the evidence began to pile up on all sides. Heath, who had gone to the police station without a coat, apparently believing that he would not be there long, asked if his sports jacket could be brought from the hotel. In a pocket the police found a cloakroom ticket issued at Bournemouth West station on the Sunday Heath arrived in the town. The ticket led the police to a suitcase which, on being opened, was found to contain a blood-stained scarf and a leather riding-whip with a plaited thong. The tip had worn away, exposing the metal underneath.

Artificial pearl

Detectives also found in the sports jacket the return half of a London-Bournemouth rail ticket, subsequently proved to have been the one issued to Miss Marshall, and an artificial pearl. In a drawer in Heath's hotel room was a soiled, blood-stained handkerchief, tightly knotted, with human hairs adhering to it. It was established also that, in the previous 36 hours, Heath had pawned a ring belonging to Miss Marshall for £5 and a fob watch for £3. But where was Miss Marshall herself?

A statement written by Heath after he was detained at Bournemouth hinted that she had probably left the town. After

SPECTATORS, attracted by one of the most horrifying murder stories the world has known, gather to see Heath at his trial in London's famous Old Bailey court.

walking out of the hotel in the early hours of Thursday morning, it continued, they had "sat on a seat near the hotel overlooking the sea. We must have talked for at least an hour, probably longer, and then we walked down the slope towards the Pavilion. Miss Marshall did not wish me to accompany her but I insisted on doing so—at least some of the way. I left her at the Pier and watched her cross the road and enter the gardens. Before leaving her I asked her if she would come round the following day, but she said she would be busy for the next few days, but would telephone me on Sunday if she could manage it. I have not seen her to speak to since then although I thought I saw her entering Bobby's Ltd., on Thursday morning."

The body of Doreen Marshall was discovered in Branksome Chine on the Monday, two days later. It was the circling flies that led a passer-by, who had heard about a missing woman, to her. Her body

had been dragged into some rhododendron bushes. She was naked except for her left shoe, but she was covered with her own clothing—underwear, a black frock and a yellow swagger coat—and some boughs of fir trees. Twenty-seven artificial pearls, which came from her broken necklace and matched the one found in Heath's pocket, lay nearby. Her powder compact and stockings were some distance away and her empty handbag was found at the bottom of the chine.

Like Margery Gardner, she had been savagely mutilated. Her throat had been cut, causing her death. In places the wound was three-quarters-of-an-inch deep. Before that, her hands had been pinioned, but there were cuts on them suggesting that she had tried to fight off an assailant with a knife.

Question of sanity

Heath was charged with both murders. but his trial, which opened at the Central Criminal Court on September 24, dealt only with the murder of Margery Gardner. The horrifying details of Doreen Marshall's death came out in evidence, however. It was quickly clear that the real question was not whether Heath had killed the two women but whether he was sane. The defence did not bother to put him into the witness-box. They pinned all their hopes for cheating the gallows on insanity, and the debate about whether Heath was or was not in his right senses proved the only interesting part of the short, three-day trial.

At the end, however, the jury took only 59 minutes to find him guilty. He was sentenced on September 26 and executed on October 26. To the very last he remained the debonair playboy, completely in control of himself, ordering a grey, pin-striped suit, grey socks, grey shirt and polka-dot blue tie for his trial, asking for his diaries and address books to be destroyed once the verdict was known: "I have caused enough trouble in this world already without causing more."

He refused to see any members of his family, but the day before he hanged he wrote two letters to his mother. The first said: "My only regret at leaving the world is that I have been so damned unworthy of you both." In the second he wrote: "I shall probably stay up reading tonight because I'd like to see the dawn again. So much in my memory is associated with the dawn—early morning patrols and coming home from nightclubs. Well, it wasn't really a bad life while it lasted . . . Please don't mourn my going—I should hate it —and don't wear black."

It was said that his last wish to the governor of the prison was for a whisky. Then, on reflection, he added: "In the circumstances, you might make that a double!"

He loved 283 women . . . and killed ten of them. In a country famed for its lovers, he was the most famous. His name was Henri Landru, but they called him . . .

BLUEBEARD.

THROUGHOUT the morning of November 7, 1921, a curious crowd of spectators gathered outside the Court of Assize in the Palais de Justice at Versailles. The entrance was guarded by police and troops, who turned away almost everyone who tried to gain admission to the small and shabby courtroom, since there was only accommodation for a handful of people inside apart from the court officials and lawyers concerned with the trial. It was a case which had already attracted world-wide interest, since the accused man was said to have had relations of one sort or another with no less than 283 women and to have murdered ten of them, having previously seduced them and persuaded them to hand over their money and property to him for safekeeping or investment.

Enormous indictment

Punctually at one o'clock in the afternoon President Gilbert in red robes and gold-braided hat took his place on the bench accompanied by two assessors. The uniformed soldiers on duty in their steel helmets presented arms smartly and the usher rang his bell calling everyone in court to order. Immediately below the judicial bench was a table containing the grim exhibits in the case, pieces of charred clothing and human bones. At a sign from the President, a little door at the side of the courtroom opened and the prisoner appeared, escorted by three gendarmes, two of whom stood on either side of him and one behind as he stepped into the appointed place in court which served as a dock. A tall red-bearded figure, he looked a rather weary old man, although in truth he was only 52. His complexion wore the familiar prison pallor, since he had been in custody for more than two years.

The President's first duty was to establish the prisoner's identity. "Your name is Landru?" he asked the man on whom every eye in court was firmly fixed. "Henri Désiré, son of Alexandre Julien and Henriette Floré Landru? You were born in Paris on 12 April 1869, and your last residence was 76 Rue de Rochechouart?"

"Yes," Landru quietly replied.

The Clerk of the Court thereupon rose to his feet and proceeded to read the indictment, a document of enormous length, which it took the Clerk three hours to do and which occupied the greater part of the first day of the trial. It was an extraordinary story of forgery, swindling, seduction and multiple murder. For the most part Landru listened to this appalling account with an air of apparent unconcern, his bearded face bent forward between his shoulders. Only once did he look up and scowl in the course of the lengthy recitation of his misdeeds. That was when the Clerk uttered the phrase, "exploitation of women". An audible titter ran round the courtroom at the mention of the 283 women with whom Landru was stated to have had "relations".

Landru's usual technique was the familiar one of the matrimonial advertisement. A typical example of this "come into my parlour" technique appeared in *Le Journal*, a Paris morning newspaper, on May 11, 1915:

Widower with two children, aged forty-three, with comfortable income, affectionate, serious, and moving in good society, desires to meet widow with a view to matrimony.

Among the women who replied to this advertisement was a 44-year-old widow named Madame Anna Collomb, who gave full particulars of her family and fortune, discreetly giving her age as 29. In due course she received a letter from a Monsieur Cuchet, who described himself as a director of a factory in Montmartre. At the meeting which followed Cuchet told Anna Collomb that he was a war refugee, an engineer from Rocroi, who had left everything before the advancing Germans and had come to Paris to build up his business afresh.

He added that he had a car, a little apartment in town and a modest house, the Villa Ermitage, at Gambais, near the forest of Rambouillet, not far from Paris. He now wished to marry and settle down, he said. The result was that Madame Collomb found Monsieur Cuchet most attractive and loved him "because he is a real gentleman and says such beautiful things to me".

Wife and children

After a while, however, Landru's ardour for the lady began to cool. The truth was that he had several other affairs on hand since there had been many replies to his advertisement and he could not spare all the time that the infatuated Anna Collomb demanded. However, they eventually came together again, she gave up her own apartment and went to live with her lover in his flat in the Rue Chateaudun, while she gave him her furniture to put into store. She also visited the villa at Gambais where Landru was known as Monsieur Fremyet.

Elsewhere and with other women he had different aliases: Petit, Dupont, Diard and Guillet. He had another villa at Vernouillet on the river Seine near Paris. He also had a second apartment in Paris, 76 Rue de Rochechouart, not to mention a wife and four children who lived at Clichy, where he ran a garage.

SURROUNDED BY WOMEN right to the end . . . Henri 'Bluebeard' Landru, some of his victims, and the garden at Gambais, where their bodies were burned . . .

Mme. COLOMB

Mme. LABORDE LINE

Mme. BUISSON.

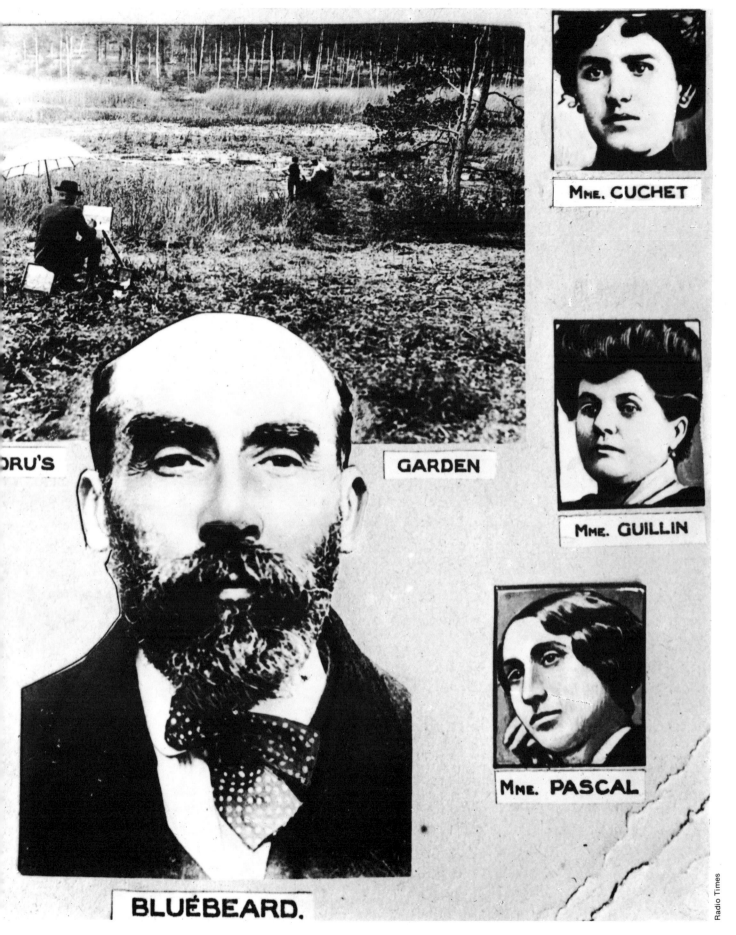

Mme. CUCHET

GARDEN

Mme. GUILLIN

DRU'S

Mme. PASCAL

BLUÉBEARD.

On Christmas Eve 1916, the court was told, Mme. Collomb invited her sister Mme. Pelat to Gambais to meet her lover. M. Fremyet ingratiated himself by saying that he would soon regularise their position by marrying his mistress, after which they would be moving to Nice. That was the last Mme. Pelat saw of her sister and M. Fremyet. After writing to both of them at Gambais and receiving no reply, she addressed a letter to the local Mayor, asking him if he could tell her where M. Fremyet was and how to get into touch with him.

It so happened that not long before this the Mayor had received a similar request from a certain Mlle. Lacoste about her sister Mme. Celestine Buisson, who had also visited the villa in Gambais and had disappeared. On making inquiries the Mayor learned that the Villa Ermitage was occupied by a M. Dupont, of whom there was likewise no trace. The Mayor suggested that Mlle. Lacoste and Mme. Pelat should get into touch with one another. In due course they met and compared notes. Both women had seen the occupier of the villa and they agreed that Cuchet-Fremyet and Dupont were singularly alike. Meanwhile the police were investigating another disappearance, that of a genuine Mme. Cuchet. It appeared that Jeanne Cuchet and her son André had gone to live with a certain M. Diard in his house at Vernouillet in December 1914 and had not been seen or heard of since. After making further inquiries, the police were satisfied that Cuchet, Fremyet, Dupont and Diard were one and the same person. On April 10, 1919, a warrant was issued for the arrest of the individual whose identity corresponded with any of these aliases.

Unmistakable figure

Next day, the court was told, Mlle. Lacoste happened to be walking along the Rue de Rivoli when she suddenly saw the unmistakable figure of the man she recognized as M. Dupont. He had a smartly-dressed young woman on his arm and Mlle. Lacoste saw them enter a shop. She followed them inside where she heard the man order a white china dinner service to be sent to his apartment. After the two had left the shop Mlle. Lacoste continued

"THE WOMEN never reproached me . . . perhaps some of them will turn up for the trial." The only people who turned up for Bluebeard's trial were a string of witnesses testifying that the missing women had last been seen with him. As the accused man gave evidence, the judge had to suppress laughter in court. When Bluebeard finally faced the guillotine, his humour could only be described as deadpan.

to follow them but eventually lost them in the crowd. She thereupon went to the nearest police station and reported her suspicions. On following up this clue, the police learned that the dinner service had been ordered by M. Lucien Guillet, an engineer, of 76 Rue de Rochechouart.

The following morning Landru was arrested in his apartment and told he would be charged with murder. He protested that he was Lucien Guillet, born at Rocroi, in 1874, and seemed shocked that he should be accused of a capital crime. He was then searched and the police discovered a black loose-leaved note-book in his pocket which he made an unsuccessful attempt to dispose of by throwing it out of the window.

Meticulous account

The note-book revealed that Landru kept a meticulous account of his daily expenses. For instance, on the day he invited Anna Collomb to Gambais, he had recorded one return ticket and one single ticket to the local station, similarly with Celestine Buisson. The note-book also showed that the replies to his matrimonial advertisements had been carefully classified and information had been filed about their fortunes, children, relations and so on. The names were briefly marked under the following heads:

1. To be answered *poste restante*.
2. Without money.
3. Without furniture.
4. No reply.
5. To be answered to initials *poste restante*.
6. Possible fortune.
7. To be further investigated.

The first police searches of the Villa Ermitage and the house at Vernouillet revealed nothing of importance, but later a stove was discovered in which Landru was alleged to have burnt the bodies of his victims after he had cut them up.

Afterwards 295 bone fragments of human bodies were discovered. These were believed to belong to three corpses; there was also a miscellaneous collection of women's clothing, buttons, and trinkets of various kinds.

Besides the Mesdames Buisson, Collomb and Cuchet and the latter's 18-year-old son, seven more women whom Landru knew were stated to have disappeared without trace. Their names were given to the court as Mme. Thérèse Laborde-Line, widow, aged 47, and a native of Buenos Aires, whom Landru called 'Brésil'; Mme. Desirée Guillin, a widow, aged 59, formerly a governess, who had inherited 22,000 francs which Landru drew out of her bank account with a forged signature, having also sold her furniture; Andrée Babelay, a servant girl, aged 19, whom Landru met in the Metro; Mme. Louise Jaume, a married woman, aged 38, who was separated from her husband, and whose money and furniture Landru appropriated after he had taken her to Gambais; Mme. Anne-Marie Pascal, a divorcée, aged 33, and a struggling dressmaker of easy morals, whose furniture and personal belongings were found in Landru's garage; and Mme. Marie-Thérèse Marchadier, a prostitute turned brothel-keeper, who gave up her establishment and went with Landru to Gambais, after parting with her furniture.

All the names with accompanying particulars appeared in the sinister black note-book which Landru had tried to hide from the police when he was arrested.

On the second day of the trial, President Gilbert examined the prisoner on his past record. "You have received seven sentences for fraud, Landru," he remarked. "Your parents were honest and decent folk. Your father was for a long time a fireman in the Vulcain Ironworks. Your mother worked at home as a dressmaker. After her death, your father who had retired to the Dordogne, came to Paris to see you but found you were in prison. He was so upset by your conduct that in 1912 he committed suicide in the Bois de Boulogne."

As the prisoner did not dispute these facts, the judge went on: "You were a clever boy at school and earned high praise from your teachers. On leaving school you were admitted as a subdeacon to a religious establishment?"

"Only for a short time," Landru added.

"Perhaps it was there," said the judge, "that you learned that unctuous manner which has been one of your chief methods of seduction, and which has helped you to capture the trust and affections of so many woman."

President Gilbert paused, but the prisoner remained silent. "Then," continued the judge, "you took up more profane occupations. Not far from you there lived your cousin Mme Remy, who had a young daughter."

"She had two," Landru interrupted.

"Very well. One of them became your mistress, and you had a daughter born in 1891. Two years later you regularized the position, married her and acknowledged the child. In all you had four children?" Landru nodded his agreement.

"You had a lot of different jobs," said the judge. "Clerk in an architect's office,

TRIAL BY PRESIDENT

PROCEDURE in French criminal trials differs from that in other national courts in several important respects. For one thing, the presiding judge, who sits with two legally qualified assessors and is called the President, takes a much more prominent part in the proceedings than, say, his British counterpart, whose function broadly speaking is limited to seeing that the rules of evidence and the rights of the accused are observed, to summing up the evidence to the jury, and in the event of the jury returning a verdict of guilty to passing sentence.

On the other hand, the President of a French assize court has the full record of the case in front of him which he has read, and he interrogates the prisoner on every detail of the charges during the proceedings. The basis of his interrogation is the dossier which has been compiled by the pre-trial investigating magistrate known as the *juge d'instruction*; this is usually the result of prolonged questioning by this official while the prisoner is in custody.

In French courts the whole of the prisoner's past criminal record forms an essential part of the indictment and is read out at the beginning of the trial. This also contrasts with British courts, where a witness of fact is only permitted to testify to matters of which he has direct and personal knowledge, but in France hearsay evidence is admissible – i.e. witnesses may repeat what they have been told by others.

Finally, in France the President of the Court must consult with the two assessors and take into account their views on the punishment due.

agent, toy salesman and so on. In fact you had no definite, stable occupation."

"Which proves how inadequate were the inquiries which were made about me," Landru again broke in. "The police are often inefficient."

"Yet," said the judge, "when the magistrate confronted you with this information you had nothing to say?"

Flattered conceit

The prisoner threw up his hands as if amazed at such official stupidity. "It was not my business to guide the police," he exclaimed. "Have they not been accusing me for the past three years of deeds which the women who disappeared never for one moment reproached me with?"

These words produced some laughter among the onlookers in court which the judge suppressed by calling for silence. "It is you," he emphasised his words by pointing a finger at the prisoner, "it is you who have made it impossible for these women to complain. That is as clear as anything."

Asked to explain to the jury why the names of so many women were in his note-book, at first he was evasive. Finally when pressed by the judge, he said: *"Eh bien! Voila!* It is the list of a business man, who entered the names of his clients with whom he did business." He had bought these women's furniture from them to help them during the war, he explained, intending to sell it back to them when the German armies had been driven out of France.

"Why then recruit your clients by means of matrimonial advertisements?" the judge asked.

"Just a little business ruse, very innocent," Landru replied. "It flattered their conceit." The prisoner let his gaze wander in the direction of the jury, as if to say what a clever answer he had given. But they did not look at all convinced. Then he turned again to the judge and said: "You say that some of these women have not been found. Perhaps they will turn up during the trial." However, none of them did so.

During the succeeding days a string of relatives of the ten women who had vanished came forward to testify to the occasions when they had last seen the women in question, usually in Landru's company. Others testified having seen dense smoke coming out of the chimneys of the houses which Landru had occupied at Gambais and Vernouillet, accompanied by a most offensive stench. Indeed one of the neighbours complained about it to the police at Vernouillet. This was at a critical stage of the First World War, and though the police did call at the house they eventually dropped the matter as they had more serious matters to think about at that time than malodorous smoke from a domestic chimney—particularly when Landru assured them that he had only been burning some refuse. There were also stories of portions of putrefied human flesh being recovered from a lake near Gambais by fishermen.

One witness who attracted particular attention was the pretty young woman who had been with Landru when he went shopping in the Rue de Rivola, and as events fortunately turned out for her was "the one that got away". She gave her name as Fernande Segret, her age as 29,

"BE BRAVE? But I *am* brave," replied Bluebeard, refusing confession or Mass, rum or cigarettes. The execution was to be a public one, in the square outside . . .

Le Petit Journal

HEBDOMADAIRE
61, rue Lafayette, Paris

illustré

PRIX : 0 fr. 30
5 Mars 1922

Avant l'heure suprême

Dans sa cellule de la prison de Versailles, la veille même de son exécution, Landru, parfaitement calme et toujours méthodique, a passé des heures à compulser ses dossiers — Espérait-il y trouver un dernier moyen de retarder la minute fatale... ou bien pensait-il au sort mystérieux de ses fiancées ?

THE FINAL HOURS: Did Bluebeard hope for a last-minute stay of execution? Cool as ever, he achieved the celebrity of a star at his trial.

and her occupation as "lyric artist". She described how she had become engaged to Landru whom she knew as Roger Guillet, how her mother had described him as an imposter and an adventurer, and how despite this warning she had insisted on going to live with him as his mistress. She was deeply in love with him, she said, and wished to marry him.

Rather disappointed

"I went to Gambais seven or eight times," said the love hungry Fernande Segret. "The villa was not what you would call well furnished. In one room there were some guns and cartridges which he knew well how to use."

"Do you know what means your fiancé had?" the judge asked her. "How did you live?"

"Landru told me his garage brought in a good deal, enough for our needs. I went there one day, and was rather disappoint-

ed, as there was only one apprentice working in the place, for he had told me he had a considerable business there."

Asked if they ever had any quarrels, pretty Mademoiselle Segret replied that they had two she remembered in particular. One was when a letter came for him addressed in another name. The other was when she began to look through some of his papers in their flat in the Rue de Rochechouart and he flew into a great rage. "I promised not to do it again," she added, "but I showed my astonishment since all my correspondence was read by him."

There was "a delicate point" he wished to clear up, said the judge to this witness. She had told the examining magistrate that in her sexual relations with the accused she had found him extremely passionate but at the same time quite normal.

"Is that right?"

"Oh, yes!" replied Mademoiselle Segret. "Very normal." What President Gilbert was trying to ascertain was whether Landru was a sadist and pervert. Apparently he was not, though the medical evidence pointed to his being a

dangerous psychopath, though well aware of what he was doing.

In his speech to the court, the chief prosecutor declared: "I demand the extreme punishment—death for Landru, the murderer of Vernouillet and Gambais. He is entirely responsible for his deeds. The doctors have certified this, and the ability which he has shown here is proof of his sanity. He had no pity on his victims. Why then should you have pity on him?"

It took the jury an hour and a half to find Landru guilty on all charges except two. Only in respect of those of defrauding the domestic servant Andree Babelay of her property (she had virtually none) was he acquitted.

Mercy recommendation

Prompted by Landru's defence counsel, the jury surprisingly added a recommendation to mercy, calling upon the President of the Republic to reprieve the condemned man. However, the judge sentenced him to death by the guillotine, to be carried out publicly in front of the prison where he was confined.

"Be brave!" one of the officials said when they came to fetch him, as was customary, between five and six o'clock in the morning. "I *am* brave," replied Landru. Asked if he would make his confession to the priest and hear Mass, he exclaimed, "Never on your life!" "Anyhow," he added, "I cannot think of keeping these gentlemen waiting." He also refused the usual offer of a glass of rum and a cigarette.

As he was led out into the prison yard, he shivered a little in the cold early morning air, since he was wearing thin trousers and an open-necked shirt. Then the prison gates were flung open and for a minute or two he faced a cordon of troops holding back the spectators who had gathered in front of the guillotine which had been erected in the square outside the prison.

In a matter of seconds the executioner and his assistant strapped him face downwards on the platform of the guillotine.

Curious tailpiece

The Landru story has a curious tailpiece. More than sixty years later a film entitled *Landru,* scripted by the bestselling novelist Françoise Sagan, was made and publicly shown. Fernande Segret, whom everyone thought was dead as she had not been heard of for years—in fact she had been working as a governess in the Lebanon—suddenly turned up and sued the film company for 200,000 francs damages. She got 10,000. She then retired to an old people's home in Normandy where she eventually drowned herself, saying she was tired of people pointing to her as "the woman in the Landru case".

THE GRANITE WOMAN AND THE PUTTY MAN

It had been a passionate affair. "You are my Queen, my Momsie, my Mommie," he told her. "And you are my Baby, my 'Bud,' my Lover Boy." Ruth Snyder was a powerful woman, and she dominated the weak Judd Gray. They loved together and died together . . . when Ruth Snyder finally got the meanness off her ample chest.

HOUSE OF DEATH:
The three-storey clapboard home in Queens, New York State, where Ruth Snyder tried half a dozen times to arrange fatal "accidents" for her husband. Cheerful Albert Snyder, a "good, solid, silent man", apparently suspected nothing, even when she gave him poisoned whiskey (below).

DOUBLE INDEMNITY:
"Mommie" Ruth Snyder used daughter Lorraine to ensure respect-ability when she had hotel assig-nations with her lover. She was keen on insurance . . . and took out a policy worth the best part of $100,000 (left) on her husband's precarious life.

She wanted a slave, he wanted a mother . . . and they met on a blind date

HE WAS nothing to look at as he entered the little Swedish restaurant, peered myopically around, and went nervously up to a booth at the back of the room. With his cleft chin, round wire-rimmed glasses, slight build, and eyes that were constantly blinking, he resembled nothing more than what he was—a drummer (or commercial traveller) who would never earn more than his current salary of some $5000 a year. But to his blind date in the booth —gum-chewing Mrs. Ruth May Snyder— he represented everything she had looked for in life and marriage and so far failed to find: an adoring, full-time slave.

It was in June 1925—the fifth year of Prohibition in the United States, the year in which Charlie Chaplin appeared in *The Gold Rush,* and the year when Anita Loos published her "gold-diggers" novel, *Gentlemen Prefer Blondes*—that Judd Gray and Ruth Snyder formed a liaison that was to bring about the murder of Mrs. Snyder's husband, Albert, and eventually take her and Gray to the electric chair in Sing Sing prison. But on that hot summer's afternoon in Henry's restaurant in New York City they were too busy sizing each other up, eating *smörgasbord* and drinking bootleg gin to sense that fate—and mutual friends—had done them a tragic disservice in bringing them together.

Ignoring the couple with them in the booth, they took turns to relate the sad and hopeless stories of their marriages; the fact that neither of them had the spouse that he or she had yearned for; the atmosphere of bitterness and tension that pervades a home with no love, respect or understanding in it. It was Ruth —her thick blonde hair set off by a grey fox fur draped over her shoulders, her wrists clanking with the cheap copper trinkets she habitually wore, her firm thrusting jaw aimed at Judd like a pistol —who, first of all, as she put it, "got the meanness" off her ample chest. What she had to say was not novel, but it made Gray—whose job was selling ladies' corsets—lean sympathetically forward.

According to herself, Ruth Snyder— then aged 30 and of Swedish-Norwegian stock—had been the victim of a man, Albert Snyder, who ten years earlier had taken advantage of her youth, innocence and naïvety and manoeuvred her into a marriage she did not really want. "He was so mean, that guy," she told Judd, taking his hand in hers beneath the table.

"He took me out dining and dancing, then got real angry when I wouldn't come across and get into the sack with him. I was a self-respecting girl then and so he changed his line. He bought me a box of chocolates with a diamond solitaire in them. Picture that! I was all of 19 then— 13 years younger than him. He had this good job as art editor of *Motor Boating*— that's a Hearst magazine, you know—and the day we got married I was too weak and faint to go to bed with him. He had to wait till I was better before he got his way. But to him I was never any better than the ex-switchboard operator who worked in the typing pool."

A quiet, honest man

As he listened to this lament—which could have come straight from one of the silent picture melodramas of the time— Judd Gray felt' nothing wrong, nothing false about her words. Even at 19 Ruth must have been a strapping, full-figured girl, and the thought of anyone pushing her around—let alone pushing her into marriage—was more than somewhat absurd. Albert Snyder—curly-haired, cheerful, and wind- and suntanned from long solitary hours of boating and fishing—was just not the sort of man to bully anyone, and certainly not an inexperienced girl who claimed to be religious, God-fearing, and a virgin. Later, after Albert's death, his editor and publisher, C. F. Chapman, was to say of him: "He was a man's man . . . a quiet, honest, upright man, ready to play his part in the drama of life without seeking the spotlight or trying to fill the leading role. Our world is made up of good, solid, silent men like this."

Gray, however, knew and cared nothing for this as the lunch-hour wore on and three and then four o'clock passed. In comparison with Ruth's marriage—a relationship that alternated between blazing rows and frozen silences—his own domestic background was of peace, tranquility and eternal boredom. His wife, Isabel, was so seldom seen or heard by anyone that she had taken on the aspect of an "invisible woman". Few of Gray's colleagues at the Bien Jolie Corset Company had ever met or spoken to her, and some of them did not even know that the 32-year-old salesman had a wife at all. In his autobiography written in the Death House, Gray said frankly:

"Isabel, I suppose, one would call a home girl; she had never trained for a career of any kind, she was learning to cook and was a careful and exceptionally exact housekeeper. As I think it over searchingly I am not sure, and we were married these many years, of her ambitions, hopes, her fears or her ideals— we made our home, drove our car, played bridge with our friends, danced, raised our child—ostensibly together—married.

Never could I seem to attain with her the comradeship that formed the bond between my mother and myself . . ."

It took nearly four hours for Snyder and Gray to exchange marital and emotional histories. They said goodbye to their mutual friends in the booth at Henry's and arranged to meet again in August—after Ruth, Albert, and their seven-year-old daughter Lorraine had returned from a boating holiday on Shelter Island. Although Judd Gray did not then know it, he was the latest in a string of "men friends" with whom Ruth had gone dancing, beer-drinking, and who had helped her to devour plates of her favourite pretzels. On the evening of August 4 Gray rang the Snyder residence—a three-story clapboard house in Queens Village, New York City—and asked Ruth to have dinner with him at "their place"—Henry's Swedish restaurant.

After the meal and drinks Gray— with a daring that came more from the rye than any personal quality—invited Ruth to come back to his office on 34th Street and Fifth Avenue. "I have to collect a case of samples," he said lamely. "The latest thing in 'corselets'." Ruth smiled at his modesty—the word "corset" never crossed his lips—and agreed to his suggestion. Once inside the office she took off her scarf, ostensibly because she was suffering from holiday sunburn. "I've some camphor oil in my desk," said Gray solicitously. "Let me get it for you." He did so and proceeded to dab the oil over Ruth's blistered neck and shoulders. "Oh, that's so good!" she exclaimed. "No one is ever kind to me like this!" Gray flushed at her words. "I've something else for you," he murmured. "A new corselet. Please let me fit it on for you." Ruth shrugged. "Okay," she said, "you can do that. And from now you can call me 'Momsie'."

Lust and indiscretion

So in the deserted offices of the Bien Jolie Corset Company Ruth Snyder and Judd Gray began their affair—which was to burn with increasing ardour until March 1927, when they were trapped, arrested, and then turned on each other like warring rats. In the meantime, however, their lust and their indiscretion knew few limits. As often as they could they spent the night—or part of the night —in Manhattan hotel bedrooms, when Gray would sink to his knees and caress Ruth's feet and ankles. "You are my queen, my Momsie, my Mommie!" he declared, looking up at her imperious face. "And you are my baby, my 'Bud', my Lover Boy," she replied. Sometimes, by way of "respectability", little Lorraine Snyder would be taken along and left in the lobby while her "parents" retired upstairs. It was at this stage that Mrs.

Snyder first told Gray of the strange series of "accidents" that had befallen her husband in the summer of 1925 – shortly after she and Gray had first met.

The first incident occurred when Albert Snyder was jacking up the family Buick in order to change a tire. Suddenly, as he lay by the hub, the jack slipped, the car toppled sideways, and he only just missed being badly injured. A few evenings later he had a mishap with the crank, struck himself on the forehead and fell down unconscious. Some men might have felt that two such near escapes were enough, and that it might be a case of third time unlucky. But not Snyder. Later that August he again entered the garage of his salmon-painted house at 9327, 222nd Street, Queens, and stretched beneath the car with the engine running. Like a dutiful wife Ruth brought him a glass of whiskey to keep out the cold and praised his skill as a mechanic. She went back into the house and within a few minutes of drinking the whiskey Albert felt strangely sleepy. Just in time he noticed that the garage doors had somehow swung shut and that he was inhaling carbon monoxide fumes. He just managed to wriggle from under the car and reach the fresh air before being poisoned.

Ruth was desperate

If Snyder saw nothing ominous or significant in these happenings, then Judd Gray certainly did. "What are you trying to do?" he gasped, as Ruth ended her story. "Kill the poor guy?" She hesitated. "Momsie can't do it alone," she answered. "She needs help. Lover Boy will have to help her." At the time it is doubtful if Gray took her seriously. After all, they had both been drinking more than they should and had spouted more "big talk" than was wise. He only realized she was in earnest when she next met him and said triumphantly: "We'll be okay for money. I've just tricked Albert into taking out some hefty life insurance. He thinks it's only for 1000 dollars, but it's really for 96 thousand – if he dies by accident. I put three different policies in front of him, only let him see the space where you sign, and told him it was the thousand buck policy in triplicate. He's covered for 1000, 5000, and 45 thousand with a double indemnity accident clause!"

After this Snyder had three more close shaves with death – in July 1926 when he fell asleep on the living room couch and was almost gassed; in January 1927 when he was taken violently ill after Ruth had given him bichloride of mercury to "cure" an attack of hiccoughs; and in February when Ruth "unwittingly" turned on the gas tap in the living room. More by good luck than caution or commonsense Snyder survived all these attempts on his

life. Ruth was now desperate and was determined there would be no "miraculous escape" from her seventh attempt.

"My husband's turned into a brute – a killer!" she claimed. "He's even bought a gun and says he'll shoot me with it!" This time, she continued sternly, there would be no slip-up – Albert would die and she and Judd would live richly ever after. One night in February 1927 they booked into the Waldorf-Astoria Hotel and there Ruth gave Judd his instructions. He was to buy some chloroform on his next trip out of town – to Kingston, New York – and also purchase a sash weight and some picture wire. "That way," she explained, "we have three means of killing him. One of them must surely work!" For a moment Gray raised objections to her plan, but he became obediently silent when she threatened: "If you don't do as I say then that's the end of us in the bed. You can find yourself another 'Momsie' to sleep with – only nobody else would have you but me!"

To prepare him for his coming role, she invited him round to Queens one night when Albert and Lorraine were away. She got drunk with him and then – as Gray later testified – "We went upstairs to her daughter's room, where we had intercourse." After that – encouraged by erotic love-play and fearful that it would abruptly end – Gray agreed to everything Ruth said as, stage by stage, she masterminded the "accidental" death of her still unsuspecting husband. One such "planning meeting" took place over lunch at Henry's, with Lorraine as an inquisitive witness as slips of paper outlining the imminent death of her father were handed back and forth across the table. She overheard some of the guarded conversation, but not enough for her to warn her father about what to expect in the early hours of Sunday, March 20.

At a bridge party

It was then that Gray – reinforcing his resolution with sips of whiskey from a flask – took a bus from downtown Manhattan to Queens Village and let himself into the Snyder house through an unlocked side door. The time was just after midnight and Ruth, Albert, and Lorraine were out at a bridge party in the home of one of their neighbours, Mrs. Milton Fidgeon. They returned tired but as happy as they ever were at about two o'clock – with Gray then hidden in the upstairs spare bedroom. The chloroform, sash weight, and picture wire were already concealed under the pillow of the bed, and he sat steadily drinking and staring at the blue "immigrants" handkerchief and Italian newspaper which he had brought with him as false "clues".

Gray was not the only person who had been drinking that night. Albert Snyder

had consumed more alcohol than he was used to, and after putting the car away he lurched upstairs, seconds after a snatched conversation between his wife, in the corridor, and Gray in the middle bedroom. With Lorraine put to bed and Albert lying in their room in a drunken haze, Ruth slipped along the hall and rejoined her lover. She was wearing slippers, a nightgown and negligee, and after kissing Gray she hissed: "Have you found the sash weight?" "Sure," he nodded. "Keep quiet, then. I'll be back as quick as I can."

Whispered consultation

Half-an-hour later Ruth left the master bedroom and held another whispered consultation with Gray. Together they finished the last of the whiskey and at three o'clock they were ready to act. There was no sound in the house, nor in the street outside, and apart from being tight Albert Snyder was also deaf in one ear. It is debatable if he would have heard the conspirators had they resorted to shouting at each other. "Okay," breathed Ruth. "This is it." Taking Gray by the hand she led him out of the spare bedroom and along the darkened corridor. He was wearing long rubber gloves so as to leave no fingerprints on the sash weight. It was she who carried the chloroform, wire, handkerchief, and some cotton waste.

They entered the front bedroom quietly, furtively. There, for the first and last time, Gray saw Albert Snyder – the man he had been ordered to kill. He paused for a moment, as if appalled by the reason for his being there. Then as Ruth opened her mouth to say something, he raised the weight with both hands and brought it crashing down on Snyder's exposed head. The blow was a strong one – but not strong enough to kill the sleeping man. Snyder awoke, sat up, and began to fight for his life. He clenched his hands and struck out at the half-seen intruder. Again Gray smashed the weight against Snyder's skull – this time drawing blood. The injured man caught hold of Gray's necktie and as he did so the weight fell to the floor. "Help, Momsie!" cried Albert pitifully. "For God's sake help me!" Whether or not he saw his wife in the room was never established. But Ruth answered him by retrieving the weight, lifting it with her strong and muscular arms and battering him on the top of the head with it.

Incredibly, Albert was still alive. He remained so until Grey clambered over his twitching body . . . until Ruth stuffed the chloroform-soaked cotton waste into his mouth and nostrils . . . until finally she tied his hands and feet and then methodically strangled him with the picture wire. There was blood everywhere – but mostly

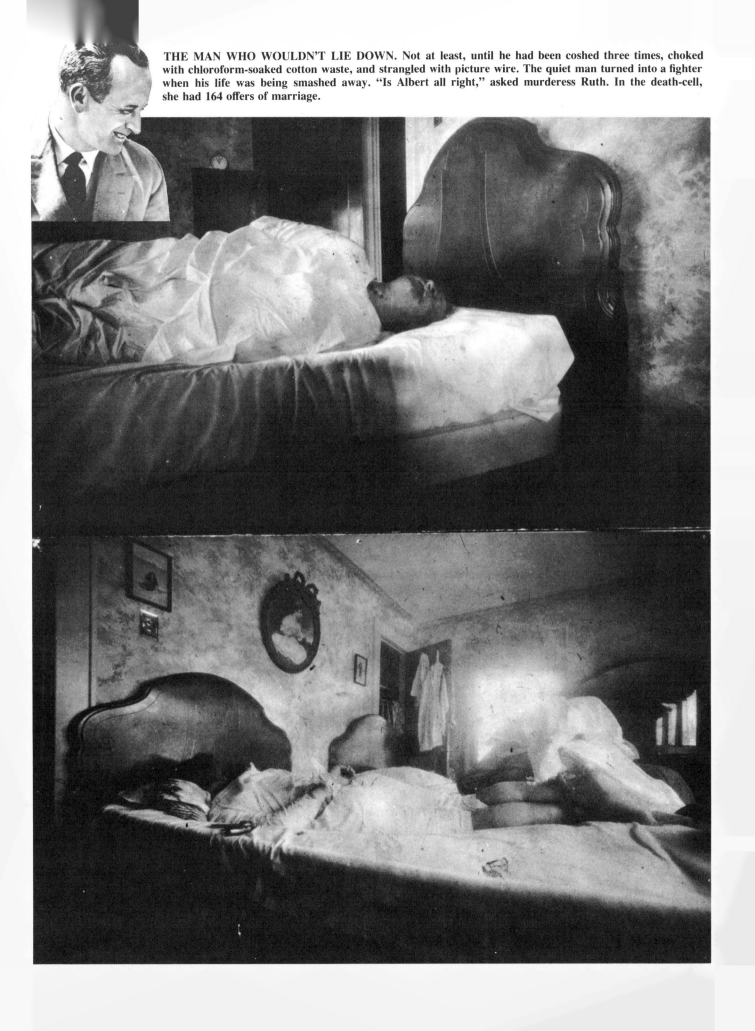

THE MAN WHO WOULDN'T LIE DOWN. Not at least, until he had been coshed three times, choked with chloroform-soaked cotton waste, and strangled with picture wire. The quiet man turned into a fighter when his life was being smashed away. "Is Albert all right," asked murderess Ruth. In the death-cell, she had 164 offers of marriage.

on Ruth's nightgown and the buckskin gloves she had borrowed from Gray, and on the salesman's freshly laundered shirt. For the next hour they washed themselves, sponged or changed their clothes (Gray put on a clean blue shirt of Albert's), hid the sash weight in the cellar, removed her jewellery and furs, and disarranged the ground floor furniture and cushions to make it seem as if a burglary had taken place. Only then did Gray tie his mistress up, fasten cheesecloth over her mouth and leave her lying in the spare bedroom, together with the Italian newspaper. He was ready to travel to the Onondaga Hotel in Syracuse, Kansas, and resume his corset selling activities first thing on Monday morning. As he left he looked back at Ruth Snyder—possibly for the first time with disgust and loathing—and said: "It may be two months, it may be a year, and it may be never before you'll see me again." One thing was sure: he and Snyder were never to drink, dance, make love, or even speak to each other again.

Curious tapping

Dawn broke gently in Queens Village on the morning of March 20. Young Lorraine Snyder was tired after her late night at the grown-ups' party and would have slept in had it not been for the curious tapping she heard at her bedroom door. Puzzled, she called out to her father and then her mother. Getting no reply she jumped out of bed and ran bare-footed to open the door—from where she saw her mother lying gagged and bound in the corridor. Lorraine bent and untied the cheesecloth and her mother told her to run and get help. The girl did so and a few minutes later Ruth was babbling out her story to her neighbours, Harriet and Louis Mulhauser. "It was dreadful, just dreadful!" she cried hysterically. "I was attacked by a prowler . . . He tied me up . . . He must have been after my jewels . . . Is Albert all right?" Mr. Mulhauser went to the main bedroom and came back white-faced with the news that Albert had two gaping head wounds and was dead.

Twice more that morning Mrs. Snyder repeated her thin and preposterous story of being attacked by "a big, rough-looking guy of about 35 with a black moustache. He was a foreigner, I guess. Some kind of Eyetalian." She gasped this out to Dr. Harry Hansen of Queens, who was called to the house to examine the body and check Ruth for any sign of assault. He found none and was convinced that her account was "a fabrication of lies". This opinion was shared by Police Commissioner George McLaughlin, who headed the 60 policemen who converged on the Snyder house before breakfast. Ruth—pale and trembling and far from being

"The Granite Woman" she was to be dubbed by the press—was grilled for 12 hours by McLaughlin and Inspector Arthur Carey.

Their suspicions had first been aroused by the frantic disorder of the downstairs rooms. "This doesn't look like a professional burglary to me," growled Carey. Ruth looked resentfully at him. "What do you mean?" He indicated to the turned over chairs and cushions. "It just doesn't look right." "How do you mean?" "I've seen lots of burglaries," he replied. "And they are not done this way. Not with killing." A search of the house soon revealed Ruth's rings and necklaces stuffed beneath a mattress, and a fur coat hanging in a closet. No one then had any doubts about it being an "inside" job.

After examining an address book containing the names of 28 men—including that of Judd Gray—and on discovering a cancelled check made out to Gray for $200, Ruth Snyder was taken to the Jamaica precinct police station, where she was tricked into making a partial confession. Told that Gray had already been arrested and had "told all", she admitted that she and the corset salesman had plotted to kill her husband and then fake a break in. "But I didn't aim a single blow at Albert," she protested. "That was all Judd's doing. At the last moment I tried to stop him—but it was too late!"

Terrified, snivelling

By then detectives had found the blood-stained sash weight in the basement and had come across the insurance policies which made Albert Snyder a rich man—once he was dead. The next move—acting on information provided by Ruth—was to arrest the terrified and snivelling Judd Gray at his Syracuse hotel. The officers who brought him to New York City intimated that Snyder had not, in fact, died of his head wounds. He had been doped with chloroform and then strangled while unconscious. By the time the train pulled into 125th Street station, and Gray was taken from the private compartment to a waiting police car, he, too, had given his version of the night's deed. Faced with a murder charge he unexpectedly showed more courage than his "Granite Woman" lover and freely admitted to his part in the slaying of Snyder. He did not, however, cover up for Ruth and recounted everything she had said and done in the house in Queens. "I would never have killed Snyder but for her," he wept when he had completed his statement. "She had this power over me. She told me what to do and I just did it."

From then on the case against Gray and Snyder proceeded with all the implacability of the law. On April 18, 1927, their trial opened in Queens County

Courthouse and continued there for the next 18 days. Ruth appeared dressed in a black coat and hat, with a black rosary and crucifix conspicuously dangling at her throat—while Gray wore a double-breasted blue pinstripe suit with knife-edged creases in the trousers. Among the many star reporters and sob sisters who packed the press box was Peggy Hopkins Joyce, who gushed in the New York *Daily Mirror*: "Poor Judd Gray! He hasn't IT, he hasn't anything. He is just a sap who kissed and was told on! . . ."

Passionate vampire

"This putty man was wonderful modeling material for the Swedish-Norwegian vampire . . . She was passionate and she was cold-blooded, if anybody can imagine such a combination. Her passion was for Gray; her cold-bloodedness for her husband . . . You know women can do things to men that make men crazy. I mean, they can exert their influence over them in such a way that men will do almost anything for them. And I guess that is what Ruth did to Judd."

On May 9 Snyder and Gray were duly found guilty as charged. Both their subsequent appeals were refused and they were sentenced to die in the electric chair in Sing Sing at 11 o'clock on the night of January 12, 1928. While in the Death House they both wrote their autobiographies, and Ruth received 164 offers of marriage from men who—in the event of her being reprieved—were eager to exist humbly beneath her dominance. But there was no reprieve, and "Momsie" and "Lover Boy" perished within four minutes of each other. They kept their last rendezvous when they were laid out in the prison's autopsy room on a pair of stone slabs. However, if Ruth's religious convictions were anything to go by, it was not quite the end of their relationship—or of their triangle with Albert. In a poem published shortly before her death, and apparently addressed to all those of the police, press, and public who had "sullied" her name as a loving wife and mother, she said:

"You've blackened and besmeared a
    mother,
Once a man's plaything—A Toy—
What have you gained by all you've
    said,
And has it—brought you Joy?

And the hours when 'Babe' needed my
    love,
You've seen fit to send me away—
I'm going to God's home in heaven,
Ne'er more my feet to stray.

Someday—we'll all meet together,
Happy and smiling again,
Far above this earthly span
Everlastingly—in His reign."

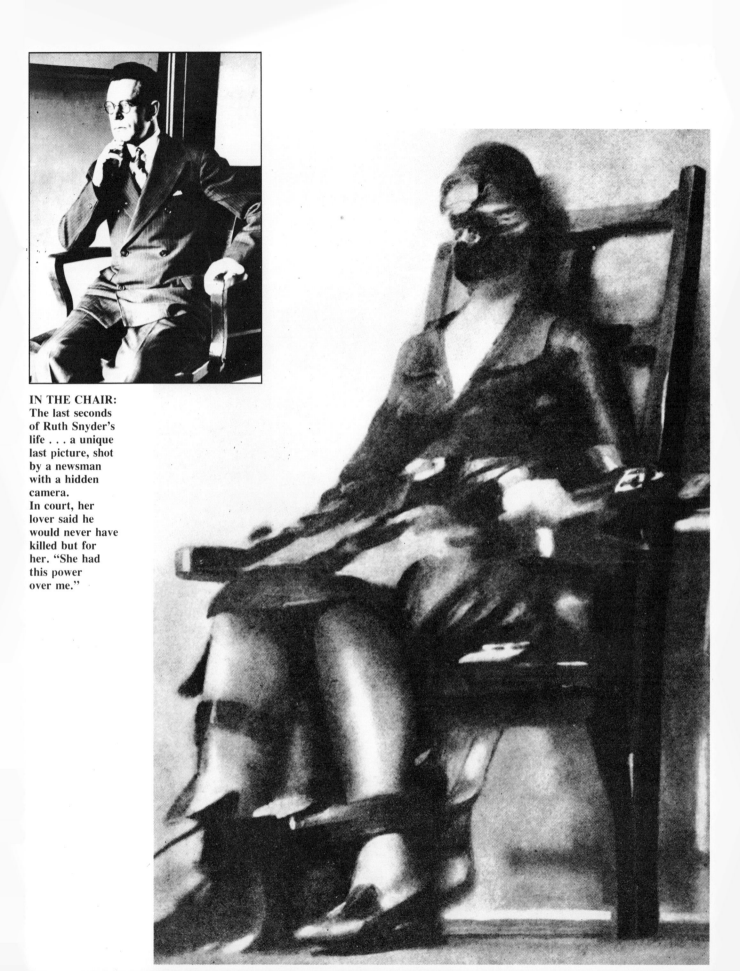

IN THE CHAIR:
The last seconds
of Ruth Snyder's
life . . . a unique
last picture, shot
by a newsman
with a hidden
camera.
In court, her
lover said he
would never have
killed but for
her. "She had
this power
over me."

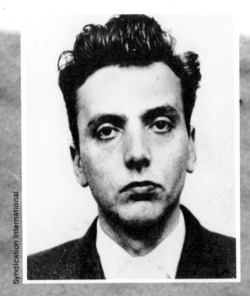

BRADY AND HINDLEY
THE MURDERERS OF THE MOORS

"All over the place . . . we have been practically all over the place," said Myra Hindley. With Ian Brady, she had haunted the bleak Pennine moorlands of Northern England. Their ghoulish journeys ended when shallow graves were discovered on the moors. For the dominant Brady and his worshipping mistress, the next journey was to the courtroom. Some called it, "The Trial of the Century".

Brady and Hindley...
"I love him," she croaked
"And I still... I love him"

THE DOCK, surrounded on three sides by four-inch thick bulletproof glass, dominated the courtroom. It had been specially altered and strengthened at the request of the British police, who, weeks before the trial began, feared that an attempt might be made to assassinate the prisoners— 28-year-old Ian Brady and his worshipping mistress, Myra Hindley. As they sat behind the glass—safe from any guns there might be in court, but exposed to the public's hostility—they sucked mints, passed copious notes to their counsels, and occasionally nudged one another— especially if an adjournment was due. Once, losing her composure for a moment, Hindley stuck her tongue out at a reporter who stared too nakedly at her. But Brady's impassiveness never faltered; he appeared to regard the proceedings as a tiresome formality, a charade to be enacted before he was found guilty and sent to prison for life. "They smell blood," he told a policeman stoically. "I'll be convicted whatever happens out there."

The trial of Brady and Hindley—an event which the judge, Mr. Justice Fenton Atkinson, said had been called "the trial of the century"—opened at Chester Assizes on Tuesday, April 19, 1966. In its own perverse and macabre way, it was just as impressive an occasion as a theatrical first night or a fashionable film première. Hundreds of journalists and television reporters from every part of the world descended on Chester Castle, and the Post Office installed a special cable and rows of telephones to handle their calls. Although only 60 seats were available to the public, scores of spectators—mainly middle-aged women in floral hats or silk headscarves—scrambled to get a place in the gallery of No. 2 Court. A corps of

VICTIM: Homosexual Edward Evans (far left). He was picked up at a railroad station snack bar by Ian Brady, and taken home. At the house Brady shared with Myra Hindley, Evans was battered to death with an axe. Brady asked Myra's brother-in-law, Smith, to help in the killing, but he was frozen by the horror of what he saw. He reported Brady to the police, and is pictured (right) going to court with his wife. Evidence given by Mr. and Mrs. David Smith helped send Ian Brady to jail for life. Their sister-in-law Myra Hindley also received a life sentence... a deadly partnership was finally broken by prison walls.

MURDERER'S HOME: Myra Hindley grew up in a city slum... a child of World War II, daughter of a paratrooper. Her lover's hero was Hitler.

five well-known authors was present, hoping to concoct bestsellers from the affair, and in the distinguished visitors' gallery another 23 people looked down on the crowded courtroom, or arena.

There were few citizens in Chester— or indeed in Britain—who did not know why Brady, a £12-a-week stock clerk, and Hindley, her hair dyed a startling shade of lilac, were in the reinforced dock. They were accused of murdering three young people—Edward Evans, a 17-year-old homosexual, Lesley Ann Downey, a child of 10, and John Kilbride, aged 12. It was common knowledge that the sexually-assaulted bodies of John and Lesley

had been discovered by the Lancashire police in shallow graves on Saddleworth Moor, near Manchester, and that Evans had been found in a bedroom of Hindley's council house home with his head smashed in by an axe. There appeared to be no rational explanation for the crimes, and in the 14 days that followed those in the court listened to a twentieth-century horror story as Sir Elwyn Jones, the Attorney-General, submitted that, "In association with all these killings there was present not only a sexual element but an abnormal sexual element, a perverted sexual element."

Hushed courtroom

The main prosecution witness was Hindley's brother-in-law, David Smith, 18, a delinquent with an unenviable police record of violence and brutality. Despite his conduct in the past, it was Smith who had informed the police the morning after he had seen Brady beat Edward Evans to death. The murder took place on the evening of October 6, 1965, after Brady had picked up the youth outside the buffet of Manchester Central Station and brought him to 16 Wardle Brook Avenue, Hattersley—the box-like house in which he shared a bedroom with Myra Hindley and living quarters with her grandmother. Wearing tight-fitting blue jeans, and with his dark brown hair falling over his forehead in the manner of the late James Dean, Smith told a hushed court how he had been summoned round to Hindley's house ostensibly to drink some miniature bottles of wine. A minute or so later he heard "a hell of a scream", followed by Hindley shouting "Dave, help him!" Clutching a stick he had brought with him, he ran from the kitchen and into the living room where he saw a scene that made him "freeze".

"My first thoughts were that Ian had hold of a life-sized rag doll and was just

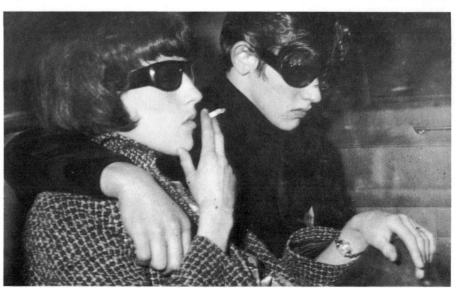

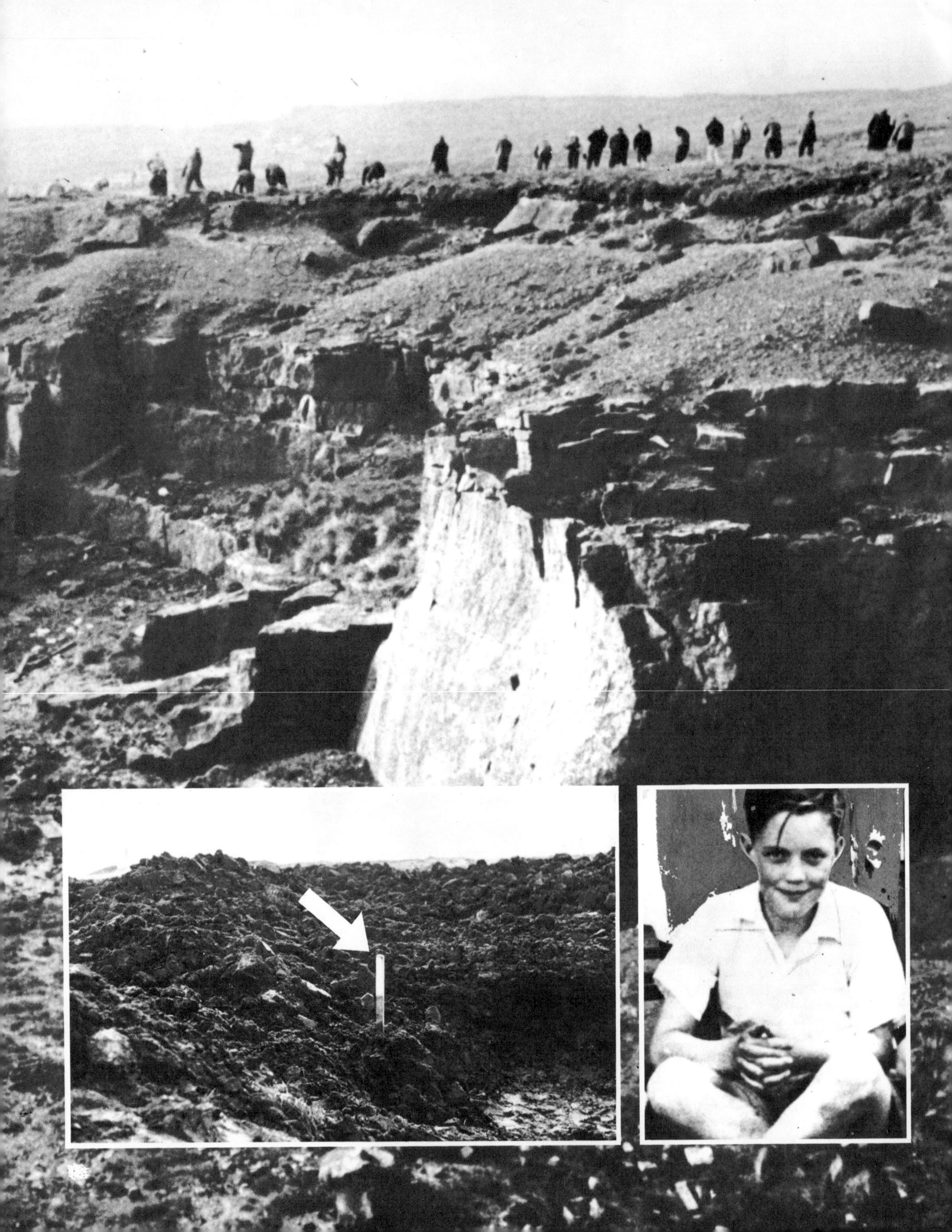

waving it about," he said tightly. "The arms were going all over. Then it dawned on me that it was not a rag doll. It fell against the couch not more than two feet away from me. My stomach turned over. It was half screaming and groaning. The lad was laid out on his front and Ian stood over him with his legs apart with an axe in his right hand. The lad groaned and Ian just lifted the axe over his head and brought it down upon the lad's head. There were a couple of seconds of silence and the lad groaned again, only very much lower. Ian lifted the axe way above his head again and brought it down. The lad stopped groaning then. He was making a gurgling noise like when you brush your teeth and gargle with water. Ian placed a cover over his head. He had a piece of electric wire, and he wrapped it round the lad's neck and began to pull it; and he was saying: 'You f . . . ing dirty bastard', over and over again. The lad just stopped making this noise, and Ian looked up and said to Myra: 'That's it. It is the messiest yet!'"

Supreme pleasure

As Smith left the witness stand—after admitting to Brady's counsel, Mr. Emlyn Hooson, Q.C., M.P. that he had written in a notebook that, "People are like maggots, small, blind, worthless, fish bait. Rape is not a crime. It is a state of mind. Murder is a hobby and a supreme pleasure"—the spectators in the court relaxed. Surely, they told themselves, they had heard the cruellest, the bloodiest, the most chilling details. But, unbelievably enough, there was worse, far worse, to come. Turning to the killing of Lesley Downey—who had disappeared after visiting a fairground at Hattersley on December 26, 1964—the judge had to decide whether or not to allow a tape recording to be played, a recording made by Brady and Hindley in which the terrified youngster pleaded for safety, for her mother, for her life.

Leaning gravely forward, Mr. Justice Atkinson said: "There is a question whether this piece of evidence should be heard in camera or not. There has been so much talk, that in my opinion we have no right to exclude the public. Anyone who wishes not to listen should leave now. During it I request complete silence. The Attorney-General will beforehand read out the transcript, at dictation speed."

It was at this stage, as the transcript

VICTIM: John Kilbride, aged 12 (left) was sexually assaulted. His body was found in a shallow grave (arrowed) by police searchers on the moors. Brady denied all knowledge of his death, but the Attorney-General said that Kilbride was "killed by the same hands" as the other Moors victims.

POLICE CHIEF Joe Mounsey discovered the bodies. After arresting Brady and Hindley, police became their protectors against any assassination bid.

was read out and the tape played, that the assassination attempt—if there was to be one—would be made. Police closed in and formed a protective semicircle in front of the dock, their eyes roving from face to face as they scanned those in the press box, the well of the court, and the galleries. As the spool began to revolve—and the words and then the screams were heard—a number of women in the public gallery shuddered and closed their eyes. The all-male jurors (half of whom appeared to be under 30) lowered their heads, a man in the distinguished visitors' gallery put his hand over his face, and a policeman attended to another man who slumped forward in distress.

It was the screams punctuating the tape which turned most people's stomachs—and then there was Lesley's voice, shrill with panic and fear, as she begged, whispered, and sobbed. "Please God, help me!" she cried. ". . . Can I just tell you summat? I must tell you summat. Please take your hands off me a minute, please . . . I can't breathe . . . What are you going to do with me? . . . Don't undress me, will you? . . . It hurts me. I want to see mummy, honest to God . . . I have to get home before eight o'clock . . . Or I'll get killed if I don't. Honest to God . . . It hurts me neck . . ."

In a way the most appalling section of the tape came towards the end when a radio was turned on, bells rang out, and two Christmas-style songs were heard: *Jolly St. Nicholas,* and *The Little Drummer Boy.* Later, opening Brady's defence, Mr. Hooson was to say: "It is terribly, terribly important that you dispose from your minds all the natural revulsion one has in reading or hearing evidence connected with the death of children." But as, after 16 minutes and 21 seconds, the tape whirred to a close there was no one in the court—with the possible exception of the two accused—who did not sit stun-

ned and sickened, and who found it hard not to allow their "feelings to be aroused to the exclusion of dispassionate justice."

The evidence of the recording was more monstrous even than the photographs Brady had taken of Lesley, showing her naked and with a scarf over her mouth, posing obscenely in the shoddily furnished bedroom. It was not until the ninth day of the trial that Brady was escorted by two prison officers from the dock to the witness stand. People craned forward to look at him as, sallow-faced and lanky, he affirmed rather than take the oath on the *Bible.* In appearance he seemed neither better nor worse than any of the young men who lived in Hattersley—a drab estate which acts as an overspill for Manchester. He wore an ordinary grey suit, plain white shirt and had a neatly-folded handkerchief in his breast pocket. He might boast of worshipping Hitler, agree with the French writer the Marquis de Sade that inflicting pain upon others was the ultimate thrill, and believe in the Germanic philosophy of the superman who was "beyond good and evil". But none of this was apparent until the illegitimate son of a Glasgow waitress arrogantly answered questions put to him by Hooson.

Despite an accent that veered between a thick Scottish brogue and a Lancashire drawl, he spoke out firmly and loudly. Yes, he had spent the autumn of 1964 discussing a "perfect payroll robbery" with his disciple David Smith. As he spoke, his cold, pale eyes were as blank and lifeless as stones seen under water, and a ray of animosity seemed to stretch between him and the public. It was a two-way band of hatred and it broadened and intensified when he admitted to offering Lesley Downey ten shillings to pose for him and Hindley in the nude, and to unintentionally killing Evans as part of "a bit of practice".

Insolent contempt

During this stage, and throughout the cross-examination that followed, he showed his wholesale contempt for the trial and all its trappings, and displayed his insolence towards the judge and the Attorney-General (he never addressed them as "My Lord", or "Sir"). In contrast to this, Sir Elwyn Jones spoke to him in polite, restrained tones, as if interviewing a somewhat sullen and disinterested job applicant. "You never intended Evans to leave that room alive?"—"Yes," came the answer. "The right side of his skull was smashed to pieces and some of his brains were on the floor?" Brady nodded. "Yes—in fact Smith made a joke about it. He said, 'He was a brainy swine, wasn't he!'" And—how did he feel when he had heard Lesley Downey's screams filling the courtroom?

MOTHERS: Mrs. Kilbride (left) and Mrs. Downey. Their children were victims. Friend Linda Clark (inset) was with Lesley Downey the day she vanished.

The answer was he found it "embarrassing".

Later on Brady demonstrated some of the reasoning power and misplaced "brilliance" which had dominated Smith and made Hindley his eager slave. The exchange came when Elwyn Jones asked him about his library: "This was the diet you were consuming. Pornographic books, books on violence and murder?" — "Not pornographic books. You can buy them at any bookstall . . ." "they are dirty books, Brady" — "It depends on the dirty mind. It depends on your mind . . . Let me give you the names of just two." (Here the judge intervened saying: "*Uses of the Torture Chamber, Sexual Anomalies and Perversions*.") Brady shrugged. "These are written by doctors. They are supposed to be social . . ." "Was your interest in them on a high social plane?" — "No, for erotic reasons . . ." "Of course. This is the atmosphere of your mind. A sink of pornography, was it not?" — "No. There are better collections than that in lords' manors all over the country."

Warped philosophy

Although Brady admitted that he had murdered Evans, he denied any knowledge as to how Lesley Downey had died, and said he knew nothing of the disappearance and death of young John Kilbride. Both the children were found in graves on the moors only 400 yards apart. Lesley had been stripped of her tartan skirt and pink cardigan, and John's trousers and underpants had been rolled down to the thighs, indicating sexual interference. After spending 8¾ hours in the box Brady was allowed to return to the dock, to sit next to Hindley — the typist who had worked for the same chemical distributing firm as himself, and who had adored him for a year before he spoke to her, writing in her redbound diary:

"Ian looked at me today . . . He smiled at me today . . . The pig . . . he didn't look at me . . . He ignored me today . . . I wonder if he'll ever take me out . . . I almost got a smile out of him today . . . Ian wore a black shirt and looked smashing . . . He is a loud-mouthed pig . . . I love him." Then, shortly before Christmas 1961, she was able to record: "Eureka! Today we have our first date. We are going to the cinema."

The movie Brady took her to see was *Trial at Nuremburg*, which dealt with Nazi war criminals and atrocities, and he chose this as an introduction to his warped and secondhand philosophy of "power over others". They were both children of the slums (she was a war baby, the daughter of a paratrooper), but there their early resemblance ended. Brady had been a boy who enjoyed torturing cats, flashing the flick-knife he habitually carried, and viewing as many horror movies as he could get into. His boyhood nickname in the Glasgow Gorbals had been "Dracula", whereas Hindley had been of slightly above average I.Q. as a schoolgirl, had always had religious tendencies and was later to return to the Roman Catholic church in which she had been raised.

Expressionless voice

Interrupted from her note-taking and the scowls she delivered across the court, she was led to the witness stand, leaving Brady to resume sketching the brutal looking thugs with fierce black eyes and low foreheads — which was his way of killing time during the long and repetitive hours of the trial. By then, the 11th day of the proceedings, Hindley's lilac hair

had undergone a bizarre change. It was now dyed a banana-yellow with tell-tale black zigzags at the roots. It looked as if she was wearing a grotesque raffia wig — a squat figure in a speckled tweed suit, pale blue blouse, a pair of white high-heeled shoes belonging to her mother, and giving every indication as to why she was called "square-arse" by the local youths.

Like Brady, she affirmed instead of taking the oath. With her hooked, parrot nose and thick lips there was nothing outwardly attractive about her, and this impression was heightened when she spoke. Her expressionless voice was low-pitched and hoarse as she answered her counsel, Mr. Godfrey Heilpern, as to her feelings towards Brady. "I loved him," she croaked, "and I still . . . I love him." She then explained that she was suffering from a sore throat, and told how she had passed her driving test in November 1963 — when she was aged 21 — and had driven Brady around the moors and countryside of Lancashire in an Austin Mini Traveller. "All over the place . . . we have been practically all over the place," she said.

Frightened, upset

Although she lacked Brady's surly self-confidence, she maintained her poise until Mr. Heilpern brought up the subject of the tape recording. She frowned and clenched her hands as he said: "You have heard that recording played and you have had a copy of the transcript? — Yes . . . What are your feelings about that?" — "I am ashamed." The lawyer nodded and went on to the night when Lesley Downey had been taken to the house in Wardle Brook Avenue. "What was the child like at the beginning?" he asked. "Willing or reluctant or what?" There was a pause, then Hindley replied that the little girl had been quiet at first, and then frightened and upset when she was taken upstairs.

She added: "As soon as she started crying I started to panic because I was worried. That is why I was so brusque and cruel in my attitude, because I wanted her to be quiet. I didn't expect her to start making such a noise . . . The front door was wide open. The bedroom door was open and the bedroom window was open. I was frightened that anyone would hear. I just wanted her to be quiet and I said, 'Be quiet until we get things sorted out.' The girl sat on the bed. I switched on the radio then because I was hoping she would remain quiet and that the radio would help to alleviate her fears."

After that, claimed Hindley, Lesley left the house with Smith and she and Brady did not see the child again. In answer to Mr. Heilpern she also said she had nothing at all to do with the

Syndication International

VICTIM: Lesley Ann Downey, aged 10 (top). She went to a Christmas fair . . . and vanished. Brady and Hindley taped her screams for mercy before murdering her. Lesley's body was also found in a shallow grave on the moors by police. At the trial, the horrifying tape was played back to a stunned court, and obscene photographs of Lesley taken by Brady and Hindley were shown. "Dispose from your minds all natural revulsion," said the defence Queen's Counsel.

Syndication International

35

killing and burying of John Kilbride, and it was not until she was cross-examined by the Attorney-General that her role in the two other murders became more apparent. Hardening his voice, Sir Elwyn asked her how she had reacted to the scream made by Edward Evans as he was attacked by Brady: "You could not stand the scream?" "The noise was so loud I put my hands over my ears." "This Court has heard of another scream, more than one, in a room where you were?" "Yes." "The screams of a little child of ten, of your sex, madam?" "Yes." "Did you put your hands over your ears when you heard the screams of Lesley Ann Downey?" "No." "Why not?" "I wanted her to be quiet." "Or get the child out and see that she was treated as a woman should treat a female child, or any child?" "I should have done and I didn't. I have no defence for that. No defence. It was indefensible. I was cruel." "Cruel and pitiless?" "I was cruel." "And pitiless?" "I was cruel."

Depraved killers

Finally, after 5 hours and 46 minutes, she came to the end of her evidence and rejoined Brady—who pointedly looked away from her—in the dock. The trial of

A MOTHER'S FAREWELL to a child whose last cries for help had been in vain. "I was cruel," Myra Hindley told the court. "I am ashamed."

the century was now in its closing stages and in winding-up his final address the Attorney-General said dramatically: "My submission is that the same hands killed all three of these victims, Evans, Downey, and Kilbride—and these are the hands of the two accused in the dock." The two defence counsel followed by asserting that—although Brady was patently guilty of murdering Evans—there was no evidence to show that he, or Hindley, had been responsible for the deaths of the other two victims. And, although nothing had been openly stated, there was a feeling in the court that the accused were not normal, not balanced, not sane. Aware of this, Mr. Justice Atkinson warned the jury: "I suppose that hearing and reading about these allegations, the first reaction of kindly, charitable people is to say this is so terrible that anyone doing anything like that might be mentally afflicted. You must put that aside at once . . . It is a presumption of our law that anyone who comes into the dock is sane. There has not been the smallest suggestion that either of these two are mentally abnormal or not fully and completely responsible for their actions. If, and I underline if, the prosecution is right, you are dealing with two sadistic killers of the utmost depravity . . ."

The jurors listened attentively to the careful summing-up. Then, at 2.40 p.m. on Friday, May 6, they retired to consider their verdict. They were out until

five o'clock, when they returned and pronounced Brady guilty of all three murders, and Hindley guilty of the murders of Edward Evans and Lesley Ann Downey; she was found not guilty of the murder of John Kilbride, but guilty of harbouring Brady knowing that he had committed the crime.

Equally horrible

Once the judge heard that the trial came to an abrupt, almost anticlimactic end. "Ian Brady," he said coldly, "these were three calculated, cruel, cold-blooded murders. I pass the only sentence which the law now allows, which is three concurrent sentences of life imprisonment." Brady did not flinch and the judge said dismissively to the prison officer in the dock, "Put him down." Hindley now stood alone as Brady left her without a glance. She nervously thrust another mint into her mouth and chewed on it as the judge said: "In your case, Hindley, you have been found guilty of two equally horrible murders and in the third as an accessory after the fact. On the two murders the sentence is two concurrent sentences of life imprisonment. On the accessory charge a concurrent sentence of seven years' imprisonment."

She paled, swayed as if to fall and was supported by a woman jailer who helped her down the steep flight of steps to the cells below.

Syndication International

The illustration shows four Bank of England cheques bearing portraits labelled Edwin Noyes, George Bidwell, George Macdonnell, and Austin Bidwell. The cheque reads: *Bank of England / Pay I A Warren / The Sum of £ 100,000 / M Johnson / CHIEF CASHIER*. Artist credit: Rodney Shackell.

THEY SWINDLED THE BANK OF ENGLAND...

From the shadier side of Wall Street, they came with an audacious plan to make themselves richer by £100,000*. The Old Lady of Threadneedle Street was to be rudely conned. A wealthy American customer would turn out to be nothing better than a disgusting foreigner. He would commit an affront to a Great British Institution famed for its impregnability ...

*By current money standards, £1 million or $2½ million.

IT WAS with a routine flourish that Colonel Peregrine Madgwick Francis, manager of London's Western Branch of the Bank of England, signed the note to his wealthy American customer, Mr. Warren. After all, the note was purely routine; just an acknowledgement of another satisfactory piece of business with a gentleman of substance. The message itself had been penned in immaculate copperplate by one of his senior clerks:

"Your favour of the 21st enclosing £4,250 in bills for discount is received and the proceeds of same passed to your credit as requested."

An hour or so later, that January day in 1873, the note was on its way to the flourishing Midlands city of Birmingham, where busy Mr. Warren was so clearly making commendable progress in selling some of the new Pullman's Palace Sleeping Cars to British railway companies. Since Mr. Warren was a typical go-getting American, with no time to have a permanent residence in Britain, it was addressed, as ordered, care of the Central Post Office, Birmingham.

Pure invention

So far as Colonel Francis was concerned, the acknowledgment in the note meant simply that the Bank of England had promptly and properly honoured payment on bills of exchange issued by no less a merchant bank than the illustrious House of Rothschild in Paris—furthermore, Mr. Lionel Rothschild was one of the Bank of England's 24 directors.

But Colonel Francis would not have turned with contentment to the other business of the day if he had known the alarming truth about his "impressive" customer. For Mr. Warren and his bills of exchange were both phoney. The name Warren was fictitious, the story of the Pullman business trip to Britain was pure invention.

Worst of all for the Colonel, however, was the fact that the Rothschild bills were brilliant but worthless forgeries, and the "impregnable" 179-year-old Bank of England had been neatly swindled, and would soon be swindled again.

The following morning, January 23, a cabdriver, taking two passengers from Birmingham's Queen's Hotel to New Street railway station was ordered to stop on the way at the Post Office and collect any mail addressed to Mr. Warren. There was just one letter. The cabbie took it and duly handed it to his passengers, who leapt from the cab at the station and sprinted to catch the London train.

Only when they were certain that they

TEEMING with activity, as it is today, the bank (right in the big picture) was given even more to think about by the four cunning men on the right.

208 Edwin Noyes Hills
Bank Forger.
Age 29.
5ft 9 high.
Hair auburn.
Eyes hazel.
Complexion pale.

Convicted at C.C. Court
August 1873.
Sentence P.S. for Life

AUSTIN B. BIDWELL

209 Austin B. Bidwell
Bank Forger.
Age 27.
6ft high.
Hair dark.
Eyes hazel.
Complexion dark.

Convicted at C.C. Court
August 1873.
Sentence P.S. for Life

Mansell

210 George Macdonnell
Bank Forger.
Age 28 high
5ft 10 in high
Hair brown
Eyes grey
Complexion sallow
Convicted at C.C. Court
August 1873.
Sentence P.S. for Life.

211 George Bidwell
Bank Forger
Age 34 high
5ft 8 in high
Hair dark
Eyes dark
Complexion dark.
Convicted at C.C. Court
August 1873.
Sentence P.S. for Life.

Commissioner of the City of London Police

were alone in the compartment, and the train was pulling out, did one of the men, George Bidwell, rip open the envelope and greedily read through the enclosed note.

Then, eyes shining with triumph, he handed it to his companion, Edwin Noyes, stabbing his finger as he did so at the signature: "Yours faithfully, P. M. Francis". Noyes gave a gasp of relief and excitement. "My God, George," he cried, "we're rich men!"

Rich indeed, it seemed, were Bidwell and Noyes. And not only themselves but George Bidwell's brother, Austin (alias Mr. Warren) and a fourth man, George Macdonnell. For with that note from Colonel Francis the four Americans had succeeded in the first phase of an audacious plan to rob the "Old Lady of Threadneedle Street" by forgery, and to go on to an ultimate target that would overshadow any other recent fraud—a staggering target of £100,000.

Swollen with pride

George Bidwell and Noyes could hardly wait to rejoin their fellow conspirators in London, and pass on their tremendous news. They were swollen with pride at the thought of how much their crooked syndicate had achieved in so short a time.

The Bidwell brothers and Macdonnell had arrived in England in April of the previous year, 1872, with the specific intention of "taking" the Bank—but with no fixed idea of how to set about the coup.

Both the Bidwells, George, then 33, and Austin, 25, had dabbled for some years in shady Wall Street finance, and were fascinated by the Bank of England's much-vaunted reputation for total security. They were sure that, somehow, they could change all that, and so they had invited the 26-year-old Macdonnell to join them.

To them, Macdonnell was a highly attractive proposition. The son of wealthy Bostonians, he had turned his back on family respectability and enrolled as the talented "apprentice" to a forger named George Engels—whose highly damaging and spurious financial documents had earned him the nickname of "The Terror of Wall Street"

Each man had put up £400 in sterling as working capital to finance the enterprise—a substantial total, and one that would allow them to present a "cover" as well-heeled gentlemen. Their manners suited their pocket books. They had engaging personalities, were elegantly polite, and there was a certain romanticism about their strong American accents which might—and did—disarm the most stolid and cautious of English bankers.

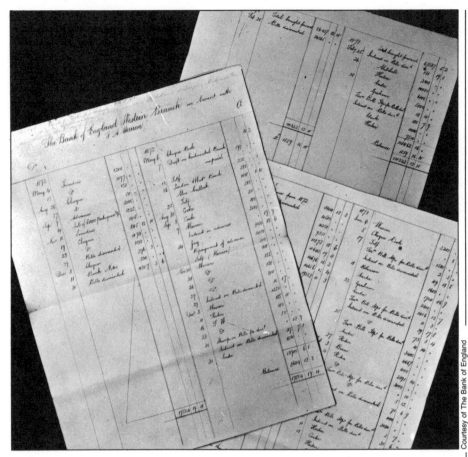

As soon as they reached London they took modest lodgings in the anonymous North London suburb of Haggerston. They selected Austin Bidwell as the syndicate member who would become the Bank of England's "customer", and booked him a room at the respectable Golden Cross Hotel at Charing Cross—which, from then on, he would use purely as an accommodation address.

Austin was the most experienced and travelled man of the three. Only a few years before he had visited Europe, as courier for a criminal organization, and had successfully disposed of a batch of stolen bonds for a "commission" of $13,000.

Opulent district

The prospects for the Bank of England job looked good from the start. The trio found that, for the convenience of businessmen living or working in the opulent district of Mayfair, the bank had opened its Western Branch in Burlington Gardens, just off Piccadilly. From there, they reasoned, it should be easier to make a "sound impression", and build up close financial contacts, than in the more impersonal headquarters of the bank in Threadneedle Street.

It only remained for the three to keep watch on the Western Branch, follow some of the customers back to their business premises, and decide who could best "assist" Austin Bidwell with an introduction to the manager. The choice fell upon a certain Mr. Green.

Edward Hamilton Green was, at the age of 55, one of London's most fashionable tailors. He had a business at 35 Savile Row, and his ears were acutely tuned to the voices of lavish spenders. It was not surprising, therefore, that one morning strong American tones drew him from his office into his dim, gaslit store. There, for the first time, he saw the six-foot form of Austin Bidwell, adorned with a large Stetson hat and a choice Havana cigar.

"I require a fashionable city suit," Austin demanded, and Mr. Green was eagerly helpful. "Allow me to suggest this large-pattern worsted," he purred, unrolling a length of cloth. Graciously Austin accepted his recommendation and, to the tailor's delight, nonchalantly ordered five suits and two formal frock coats.

Mr. Green reached across the counter and opened a large leather-bound volume. "If you would fill in the customers' signature book, please," he said, "there is room for your references beneath."

As Austin Bidwell took the tailor's proferred pen, and scribbled "Frederick Albert Warren, Golden Cross Hotel, London," he thought swiftly about the problem of references. "There is no need for an account," he said, airily. "I shall

pay cash for everything. I am not a resident." Mr. Green bowed, arranged the dates for "Mr. Warren's" fittings, and sent an assistant scuttling to summon a cab for his impressive new customer.

During the fittings over the next few weeks, Austin built up a close and confidential relationship with Mr. Green, and on May 4 he arrived to collect his impeccably tailored clothes. While they were being placed in his leather travelling case—ostentatiously marked with the initials "F.A.W."—he flourished a £500 banknote and told Mr. Green:

"I would like to settle my account now, if you please." His bill came to £150, and he was therefore invited into the office while the tailor found the change in his safe.

Delighted to oblige

The safe apparently impressed "Mr. Warren", who remarked: "How advantageous! I have more money than I care to carry. Perhaps I could leave it with you?" Mr. Green was delighted to oblige —until he observed that his customer was counting out a series of notes of large denominations, and had still not stopped when he reached a total of £1000.

This sum was too great a responsibility even for a wealthy tailor. A bank, he suggested, would be a safer place. "Mr. Warren" hesitated, then confided: "I have no bank account here." Mr. Green smiled. "I'm sure we can attend to that Mr. Warren. I will be delighted to introduce you to my bank. It is just at the end of the street!"

True to his word, Mr. Green made the personal introduction to Mr. Fenwick, the assistant manager of the Western Branch, and Bidwell duly deposited £1200, describing himself, after the signature "F. A. Warren", as "Commission Agent".

Mr. Fenwick could not have been more helpful. He said not a word about written references, and added the encouraging information: "You may now make remittances and withdrawals as you wish." He handed "Mr. Warren" a book of 50 Bank of England cheques.

So far, it appeared, so good. But just how was the big "killing" to be worked? Forged letters of credit might succeed in some foreign banks. But surely they would not pass undetected through the mighty Bank of England? The crucial questions seemed unanswerable until everything was suddenly solved by a most happy accident.

While Austin had been busy with Mr. Green, George Bidwell and Macdonnell had slipped across to the Continent to

STATEMENTS OF ACCOUNT...
Little by little, the forged bills of exchange were paid in, and accepted. It was greed that betrayed the gang.

Both courtesy of The Bank of England

raise more capital. In Rotterdam Macdonnell had converted some foreign currency into a perfectly legitimate bill of exchange drawn on Baring Brothers, the famous city of London merchant banking firm.

Back in London he presented it to the London and Westminster Bank, where he expected to be told it would be honoured after it had been checked. But, unbelievably, the money was paid out there and then, at the counter, with no questions asked.

Fortune's gates

Bills of exchange are a special system of transferring money between different countries, which came into popular use in Western Europe in the Middle Ages. In the earliest days they worked accordingly: a trader in one country ordering large consignments of goods which took a long time to deliver would give his supplier in the other country a note promising payment three or four months later.

As time passed the "bills of exchange" came to be accepted as legal tender, like banknotes. If a person to whom the bill was made out presented it *before* the stated settlement date, the bank would hand over the face value, less a discount for early payment.

Then, when the date arrived, the bank would reclaim the full amount from the banking house or individual who accepted

STATEMENT OF PROSECUTION . . .
It was a unique trial. Incredibly, for Britain, the judge was armed. He talked of "a blow to confidence in this country".

Peter Jackson Collection

responsibility for the bill — the "Acceptor", in financial language.

This, to the Bidwell group, seemed like the opening of fortune's gates. Clearly, unlike United States banks, British banks made no check with "acceptors" before making early payment on bills. All the syndicate had to do, therefore, was to produce authentic-looking forgeries dated for settlement at least three months ahead.

They would then present these, collect immediate payment, and be out of the

country before the bills eventually found their way back to the acceptors.

Blank bills of exchange, printed in a variety of languages, were not difficult to obtain. With these, some wood block engravings, and his mastery in copying signatures, Macdonnell produced documents in which, even after intensive scrutiny, the Bidwell brothers could detect no differences from genuine bills. First of all, however, a little more caution was needed. They had to be absolutely sure that the Bank of England was as trusting as the other banks.

Reputable firm

On November 29, "Mr. Warren" went to the Western Branch, met his manager, Colonel Francis, and handed him two perfectly legal bills bearing the name of the reputable City of London firm of Suse and Sibeth as acceptors. They were dated for settlement on February 3, 1873 — nearly three months hence.

When he looked at them Colonel Francis was disconcerted. "Ah, but Mr. Warren," he apologized, "we never accept bills of exchange for discount at the Western Branch." Mr. Warren was visibly annoyed. Could the Bank of England question the credentials of Suse and Sibeth? Colonel Francis was loath to fail this very businesslike American. He would make personal inquiries at the bank's headquarters. "Perhaps," he said

41

hopefully, "they will make an exception in this case."

An exception *was* made, and the next day the money was credited to "Mr. Warren's" account. The Bidwell syndicate realized it had succeeded beyond its most avaricious hopes. After that incident, Colonel Francis would never dream of questioning any of "Mr. Warren's" future demands. It remained now only to tie up one or two minor ends in the scheme.

"We can now syphon funds from the Bank of England into a new account at another bank on cheques from Mr. Warren," George Bidwell proposed. "But we must have a fourth man to withdraw cash from this new account. We'll send for Edwin Noyes."

Noyes, from Hartford, Connecticut, was an old friend of the Bidwells, a minor-league criminal who had dabbled in forgery and served time in the New Jersey State Penitentiary. He had a simple faith in the Bidwell brothers, and an unfailing readiness to share in any easy money wherever it might be found. He welcomed his invitation and accordingly arrived in London on December 17.

By then, Austin Bidwell had opened an account at the Continental Bank in Lombard Street in the name of Charles Johnson Horton, and Noyes was "appointed" his confidential clerk. The final act of the drama was about to unfold. Austin, as "Mr. Warren", would regularly convert forged bills into credit at the Western branch, and then transfer that money, sum by sum, to "Mr. Horton" at the Continental.

From the Continental, Noyes, acting on "Mr. Horton's" instructions, would draw the money in cash. All four syndicate members would then share it out, take it back to the States and live richly ever after.

Syndicate delighted

Still with an eye to caution, the syndicate decided it would be safer for Austin Bidwell not to hand forged bills to Colonel Francis in person. Consequently, he explained to the manager that he would be in Birmingham "on Pullman's business", and that any forthcoming bills from European customers should be forwarded to the bank by registered letter. Colonel Francis accepted the arrangement and the syndicate was delighted when a first receipt for credit of £4250 reached Birmingham.

George Bidwell spent a busy time as "postman", hurrying every few days from London to Birmingham to dispatch the bills on which Macdonnell had worked with loving care. So "Mr. Warren's" credit gradually mounted. One day's batch of bills totalled £9850, another day's £11,072. Before long the

"income" from the forgeries had reached £45,000, and was still rising.

"Mr. Horton" did well, too. Cheques to his credit flowed in a steady stream from the Bank of England to the Continental Bank, and poor Noyes, the cash-collecting courier, began to feel the strain. At one point he complained:

"I have carried 400 lbs. of gold from the Bank of England, 40 times I have visited the Continental Bank under threat of awkward questions or even sudden arrest and I have been buying U.S. bonds in thicker and thicker bundles!"

By Wednesday, February 26, the syndicate had cashed close to £100,000, and the time had come to burn all the evidence and vanish. Everything went into the fire in their lodgings – Mr. Warren's cheque books, Mr. Horton's credit slips, wood engraving blocks.

George Bidwell, however, felt dissatisfied. He was unwilling to wind up the coup when they had not quite reached the magical target figure. "Are these bills good enough to send in, Mac?" he asked, fondling a batch of paper about to be tossed into the flames. "We've only the details to fill in," Macdonnell replied. "Right then, fill them in," Bidwell commanded.

Working rapidly Macdonnell completed three bills which reached Colonel Francis on Friday morning, February 28. With only a cursory glance, the manager handed them to his discount clerk. But an hour later the clerk returned, looking puzzled. "Excuse me, sir," he said, "the dates of issue on these bills seem to be missing."

Colonel Francis examined the items and agreed. Obviously, he supposed, it

---

BIDWELL'S TRAVELS.

FROM

Wall Street
To London Prison

Fifteen Years in Solitude.

FREED A HUMAN WRECK, A WONDERFUL SURVIVAL AND A MORE WONDERFUL RISE IN THE WORLD.
TO-DAY HE HAS A NATIONAL REPUTATION AS A WRITER, SPEAKER AND IS CONSIDERED AN AUTHORITY ON ALL SOCIAL PROBLEMS. HE WAS TRIED AT THE OLD BAILEY AND SENTENCED FOR LIFE, CHARGED WITH THE £1,000,000 FORGERY ON THE BANK OF ENGLAND.
THIS STORY SHOWS THAT THE EVENTS OF HIS LIFE SURPASS THE IMAGINATIONS OF OUR FAMOUS NOVELISTS, ITS THRILLING SCENES, HAIR-BREADTH ESCAPES AND MARVELOUS ADVENTURES ARE NOT A RECORD OF CRIME, BUT ARE PROOFS OF THAT

IN THE WORLD OF WRONGDOING SUCCESS IS FAILURE.

---

490 Pages. 80 Graphic Illustrations.

Copyrighted 1897 by
BIDWELL PUBLISHING COMPANY,
HARTFORD, CONN.

CHEAT TO THE END . . . swindler George Bidwell got out of prison on the grounds of ill-health, then embarked on a vigorous career doing lecture-tours.

---

was an oversight on the part of the banking house whose name appeared as the acceptors, B. W. Blydenstein and Company. It was a matter easily rectified. "Send them down to Blydenstein's for correction," he instructed.

Later that day Colonel Francis received the most appalling shock of his life. He had completely dismissed the minor problem of the bills from his mind, when a messenger gave him an envelope marked "Urgent and Confidential". Inside it were the bills and a single sheet of paper, bearing a brief message of doom from Blydenstein and Company:

"We have no record of these bills and can only assume they are forgeries. – William Henry Trumpler, Member."

The unfortunate Colonel, sick with anxiety, took a close look at "Mr. Warren's" file, sped to Threadneedle Street and panted out his dreadful news to Mr. May, the Bank's deputy chief cashier. Mr. May seemed most shocked that the fraudulent customer was a foreigner, an American.

Excited headlines

"Disgusting!" he gasped, and went off personally to make inquiries at Rothschild's, and at the Continental Bank where "Mr. Warren" had passed so many cheques.

Next day the machinery of the law began to move. Edwin Noyes, arriving with an order to collect the last batch of cash for "Mr. Horton" was arrested at the Continental Bank. The other members of the syndicate were warned by the excited headlines in the newspapers and, too late, they learned that the greedy haste of those final, incomplete bills had brought their "perfect" plan crumbling about them. Panic-stricken, they split up and fled.

In New York the Pinkerton Detective Agency went immediately to work. It produced a list of 20 forgers known to deal in financial documents, eliminated 16 and noted the name of Austin Bidwell among the remaining four. It was an important lead and a finely-meshed net was spread, into which Macdonnell was the first man to walk – as he prepared to land in New York on a liner from France.

He was extradited to England and was followed, a few weeks later, by Austin Bidwell who had been arrested in Havana, Cuba. Only George Bidwell was unaccounted for. He had a long run, dodging across first to Ireland, where close watch on the ports prevented him from boarding a ship, and thence to Scotland. Finally he was captured in Edinburgh.

At the swindlers' trial at London's Old Bailey, in August 1873, there were fears of an escape plot. Armed guards surrounded the court, and even the judge himself carried a gun in his pocket – an

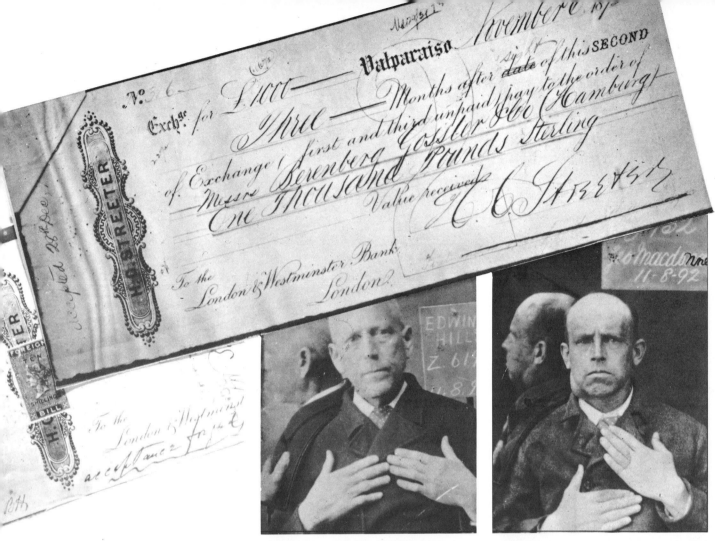

unprecedented and never-repeated occurrence in a British court of law.

There was little hope for the unrepentant prisoners. Even so, the sentence — penal servitude for life — came as a shock to many people in the United States and Britain. No doubt the affront to the Bank of England added to the severity for the judge told the four men:

"It is not the least atrocious part of your crime that you have given a severe blow to the confidence which has been so long maintained in this country."

As it turned out, Austin Bidwell served 17 years and Noyes and Macdonnell 18 years. The strangest and most stubborn of the prisoners was George Bidwell. He refused to undertake any work in the fortress prison of Dartmoor, took to his cell bed and stayed there for 14 long years. All attempts to make him walk failed. He wasted away until he was reduced almost to a skeleton, and was hardly able to use his legs. The prison governor felt certain he could not last long.

On July 18, 1887, George Bidwell was released on the grounds that he was close to death. But he had one final trick in his cheating hand. He returned to the States, recovered his health and made a very comfortable living out of lecturing on the evils of crime.

EDWIN NOYES HILLS, better known to the Bank of England by his first two names, was already a small-time criminal, and had been in prison in New Jersey.

GEORGE MACDONNELL, the son of a wealthy Bostonian, turned his back on the life of respectability . . . and became an "apprentice" to a forger.

AUSTIN BIDWELL had dabbled for some years in shady Wall Street deals. What fascinated him about the Bank of England was its reputation for security.

GEORGE BIDWELL . . . his eyes shone with triumph as he greedily read the note. "My God, we're rich men . . ." He made a strange and stubborn prisoner.

THE GREAT TRAIN ROBBERY

THE BIGGEST HEIST of all time . . .
it had to be that classic of crime, a mail-train
raid. The haul: a staggering £2½ million, or
nearer $7 million in the language of Jesse James.
It happened in the slumbering softness of England's
countryside . . . the silent night disturbed only by the
Royal Mail, bound by dawn for millions of London
letter-boxes. An unscheduled stop . . . the signals
had been rigged. A well-drilled team of crooks
had planned this moment for months. By morning,
they had written the world's headlines . . .

TWELVE MEN IN DOCK, THE MAN WHO HELPED P

William Boal ... *reduced to 14 years*

Charles Wilson

Thomas Wisbey

James Hussey

Leonard Field ... *reduced to five years*

Douglas Goody

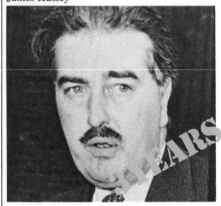

John Wheater

Brian Field

Robert Welch

Roy James

Ronald Biggs

John Daly

ICE...AND THE ONE THAT GOT AWAY

IN THE courtroom the twelve major defendants were seated in two rows in the dock. The eldest, William Boal, aged 50, came first: he was a small, red-faced man with defective eyesight. Married with three children, he lived in Fulham and was just working up a nice little business in aircraft components and precision work when he became involved with criminal types right outside his class.

Next, 31-year-old Charles Frederick Wilson, a dark, good-looking, and amiable bookmaker, who also ran a greengrocery business and came from Clapham. He was married to a pretty young wife and had three daughters. Then there was Thomas William Wisbey, aged 34. He appeared to be a jovial character, also married with children; he too ran a betting shop in London. He had been a private in the Royal Army Service Corps and had been discharged with a good character.

After him came James Hussey, aged 31, a painter and decorator. He was a bachelor and looked rather stupid, which was said to be the result of nervousness. He was reputed to be good company and popular among his friends. Another 31-year-old was Leonard Dennis Field, a florist who had previously been a shore side waiter with the merchant navy. Last in the front row was Douglas Gordon Goody, a hairdresser from Putney, always immaculately dressed. He was 34 and was about to marry a pretty redhead named Patricia Cooper, who lodged in the Goody house.

Leading the second row of defendants was the only one with a public school and university education, John Denby Wheater, a London solicitor, 42-years old, with a dark, heavy impassive face and a moustache. He lived in a prosperous commuter belt in Surrey with a pretty wife and two young daughters. He had a good wartime record and had been awarded a decoration, Member of the British Empire, for "personal courage of a very high order" while serving as an officer with his regiment in Italy.

Next to him sat Brian Arthur Field, aged 29, Wheater's managing clerk who lived in Oxfordshire with his good-looking second wife Karin, who was German. Then there was Robert Alfred Welch, aged 35, a club proprietor, who was pale and tense and was said to look more like a research student than a criminal. After him came Roy John James (28), a silversmith, unmarried but very attractive to women; he was much addicted to motor racing and was nicknamed "The Weasel".

Next came Ronald Arthur Biggs, a 34-year-old carpenter from Redhill, Surrey, tall, dark and mild-mannered, a kindly husband and father to his wife and two children. He had previously served in the RAF and prior to the trial was working up a lucrative business in the building trade.

Finally, there was John Thomas Daly, aged 32, an Irish antique dealer and skilled craftsman. His wife Frances was the sister of another antique dealer in London, Bruce Reynolds, the acknowledged leader of the robber gang, whom the police had failed to apprehend.

THE TRIAL which opened in the Aylesbury assize court in Buckinghamshire on January 20, 1964, was unique in British criminal annals. Twenty people filed into the dock under strong police guard—seventeen men and three women—accused of what has every claim to be regarded as the biggest and most daring robbery in history. The unusually large number of accused, coupled with the length of time the proceedings were expected to take, made it impracticable for the trial to be held in the normal assize court. Consequently a part of the local Rural District Council offices was converted into a courtroom which was specially equipped for the occasion, and included a very large dock with a spike-topped mahogany surround.

The prisoners who faced trial were charged with conspiring to rob a mail train of 120 mail bags containing over £2½ million, of carrying out the robbery with the use of offensive weapons, and of receiving specific sums of money in the knowledge that they had been stolen.

Sheer effrontery

It was a crime which for its magnitude and sheer effrontery made the exploits of train robbers in the past, such as the legendary Jesse James in America's "Wild West", appear almost child's play. Indeed one American newspaper, the *New York Herald Tribune,* printed an account of the opening of the trial on its front page and devoted six columns to the story under the headline: "History's Greatest Robbery—there'll always be an England." However, as this amazing trial unfolded in the temporary courtroom in Aylesbury, it became evident that the crime and its perpetrators were not quite

Roger Cordrey . . . *paroled after serving half of a 14-year sentence*

Bruce Reynolds . . . *caught after four years*

SEARS CROSSING,
SIGNAL FAKED
AT RED

TO LEIGHTON
BUZZARD

TO TRING

TO LONDON

GANG'S LORRY
PARKED HERE

DRIVER FORCED TO
BRING TRAIN HERE

ESCAPE ROAD

RAILWAYMEN'S
CAPS STOLEN
FROM THIS HUT

TO CHEDDINGTON
STATION

BRIDEGO BRIDGE

Camera Press

Syndication International

so efficient as the American press credited them with being.

As soon as the presiding judge, portly Mr. Justice Edmund Davies, had taken his place on the bench, and before the jury was sworn, the decision was taken to "put down" seven of the accused—including the three women—who were charged with the lesser offence of receiving stolen property, for subsequent trial.

Of the remaining thirteen, one, 41-year-old Roger Cordrey, who lived at East Molesey, in Surrey, and had a florist's shop, had pleaded guilty to conspiracy to rob and also to two charges of receiving. The Crown accepted his plea and he was taken out of court.

Cordrey was a somewhat neurotic individual, with a very protuberant forehead, and was a heavy gambler. In due course it was to appear that "the help" which he had given the police with their "inquiries" was considerable. In fact it had led to the recovery of £141,000 of the stolen money.

Extraordinary narrative

Altogether 40 barristers were engaged in the case. Leader of the prosecution team was Mr. Arthur James, Q.C., who took ten hours to open the case for the Crown. His extraordinary narrative centred round the postal train which travels nightly from Glasgow to London, making scheduled stops on the way to pick up additional mail.

On the night of the robbery it comprised a diesel engine and 12 coaches, which were exclusively concerned with the carriage and sorting of mail. The coach second from the engine was known as the high value package coach. On this occasion it contained 128 mail bags filled with

AN INCREDIBLY efficient bit of larceny? The fireman sensed there was something wrong. The phone wires had been cut. He saw a figure by the track.

Mirrorpic

money in the shape of banknotes, most of them in denominations of £5 and £1, which were being sent by banks, mainly in Scotland, to their branches or head offices in London.

The man in charge of the high value package coach was a post office official named Frank Dewhurst, a taciturn 49-year-old Londoner, who had other post office personnel helping him to sort the mail in that and the other coaches. The fact that an unusually large consignment of money was being carried was due to the fact that it was just after the August Bank Holiday spending spree.

On the footplate of the powerful diesel was the driver Jack Mills, aged 58, and the fireman David Whitby, aged 26. They both boarded the train at Crewe, where they lived, about half-an-hour after midnight on August 8, 1963. It was about 2 a.m. when the driver and his mate had downed their final brew of tea and the train, travelling at 70 miles an hour, had just passed through Leighton Buzzard, in Bedfordshire, and they might normally expect to pull into Euston station in

INSIDE THE £2½ million train . . . sorters worked on mail as they sped through the night towards London. Then the night became a nightmare for the crew. Fireman David Whitby (left) was threatened with death by one of the gang.

London within half an hour.

Just after Leighton Buzzard there is a dwarf signal known as the Distant signal. If this signal shows green it means that the driver can proceed at full speed, but if it shows amber, it means that he must slow down since he must expect that the next signal, known as the Home signal—which in this case was at a point called Sears Crossing, about 1300 yards along the lines—may show red against him when he would have to bring the train to a halt.

The Distant signal now showed amber, and the Home signal, which was on a gantry at Sears Crossing, showed red. Driver Mills accordingly stopped the train at Sears Crossing and said to his mate, pointing off the track with his hand as he did so: "There should be a telephone to the signal box just down there; phone through and ask them how long the delay's going to be."

What's up, mate?

The fireman jumped down and went along to the foot of the signal gantry. When he got there, he immediately sensed that something was wrong, since the telephone wires had been neatly severed and he was unable to speak to the man in the signal box which was some distance farther along the line. "Jack, the wires are cut!" he shouted to the driver. Whitby then made his way back to the engine and in the darkness was just able to make out the figure of a man at the rear of the high value package coach.

Thinking it was one of the post office sorters who had got down on to the track, he approached the figure and asked, "What's up, mate?" The man did not reply

but beckoned Whitby to the nearby embankment, where he was suddenly pushed down the slope and overpowered by two men who were waiting at the bottom. One of them put a hand over the fireman's mouth, while at the same time he brandished a cosh with the other. "If you shout, I'll kill you," he hissed. "All right, mate," the terrified Whitby answered when he had recovered his breath, "I'm on your side."

Whitby was then taken back to the train, where he saw Mills in the driver's cab on his knees bleeding profusely from the head. He also saw that the cab was full of men in boiler suits and balaclavas — woollen head and shoulders coverings — with holes just showing their eyes. Then, because the diesel was a new type with which the gang's railway expert was unfamiliar, and which he was consequently unable to operate, Mills was forced to drive the engine and the first two coaches — which the gang had uncoupled from the rest of the train — a distance of about half-a-mile to Bridego Bridge, where the track crosses a road.

Here the windows of the high value package coach were smashed with coshes and an axe. Dewhurst and the other postal workers inside were quickly overpowered and were made to lie on the floor at the side of the coach, face downwards. All but eight of the mail bags with their valuable contents were then removed from the coach and loaded onto a truck — which was then driven to Leatherslade Farm, the gang's hideout about 20 miles away.

Before the gang took off, Mills and Whitby, who had been handcuffed to each other, were pushed into the coach and told to keep quiet for half-an-hour, and that any movement they made would be observed. This was a piece of bluff, since no observer was there. When he judged it was safe to move, Dewhurst sent two of his men to raise the alarm, which they were eventually able to do by telephone from the village of Linslade.

Remarkably careless

Inquiries set in motion by the local police, aided by detectives sent down from Scotland Yard, led five days later to the farm. This was mainly due to the reports given by neighbours when they were questioned. A herdsman named Maris said that he saw vehicles coming to the farm on various dates between July 29 and August 11. A Mrs. Nappin was able to give some useful particulars of the movements of the vehicles on the night of the robbery. Then, another neighbour, Mr. Wyatt, had noticed dirty curtains being put up at the farm to cover the windows and had some conversation with several of the occupants who described themselves as "decorators". Finally there was Mrs. Brooke, who had delivered the keys of the farm to its putative buyers.

From these and other local inhabitants the police were gradually able to identify the farm and some of its occupants. They were helped too by the remarkable carelessness of the gang — who left their fingerprints everywhere as well as a miscellaneous collection of other clues including a can of paint and two Land Rovers with the same number plate.

Ironically enough, it was over-scrupulousness rather than any lack of scruple or overt dishonesty that led the police to make the first arrests. When two men turned up at Bournemouth in an Austin A35 van, and spoke to Mrs. Ethel Clark, a policeman's widow, about renting her lock-up garage in Tweedale Road, there was no thought in her mind that the two had anything to do with the train robbery. But when they offered to pay three months' rent in advance and pulled out a large wad of notes to do so, her suspicions were aroused — since unlike London, Bournemouth at that time had no overnight parking problem.

As the two men were actually putting

Syndication International

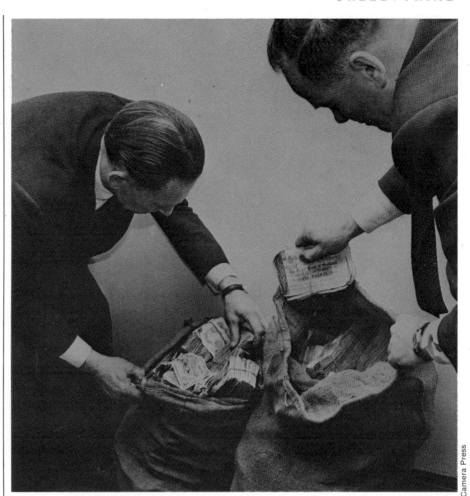

Camera Press

THE DRAGNET closes in . . . led by Scotland Yard's Detective-Superintendent Fewtrell (inset). A focal point was the gang's hideout at Leatherslade Farm. Money was found in various places, some in sacks . . . but £2 million is still missing.

the van into the garage, Mrs. Clark telephoned the Bournemouth police. In a matter of minutes two plain clothes detectives arrived in Tweedale Road. The detectives were questioning the men, when one of them made a dash for it and was brought down with a smart rugby tackle. The other likewise made off, but was quickly overtaken. He then agreed to come quietly to the police station. The two men were Cordrey and Boal, and while they were "helping the police with their inquiries", their van was subjected to a thorough search—as a result of which notes to the face value of £141,000 were discovered. A further sum of £300 in notes was discovered at Boal's house in Fulham, where it was handed over to the police by Mrs. Boal.

About the same time a young man and woman were walking through Redlands Wood, a beauty spot near Dorking, Surrey, and happened to see two holdalls and a briefcase lying just off a pathway. There was nothing inside any of the abandoned articles to identify the owner, but the contents consisted of thousands of banknotes. Rightly convinced that they had stumbled on some of the loot of the robbery, the couple immediately telephoned the police who arrived on the scene shortly afterwards with tracker dogs, which nosed out another case also filled with notes. The total recovered in this operation was £101,000.

The police now believed that the robbers had panicked when they realized the heat was on, and that they had stacked the money away in various hiding places. At all events further arrests quickly followed.

Brian Field and Leonard Field—who were not related—Goody, Wheater, and Daly followed Wilson into custody. Wheater, the solicitor, was charged with conspiracy and harbouring Leonard Field, the conspiracy charge being concerned with Leatherslade Farm and the negotiations leading up to its sale.

Dramatic roof chase

Finally Roy ("The Weasel") James, who had disguised himself by growing a beard, was arrested after a dramatic rooftop chase by the police in St. John's Wood, where he had been living in a flat with Bruce Reynolds. Also recovered was another holdall containing more than £12,000 in notes. However, Reynolds, who was thought to be the chief planner of the robbery, happened to be out at the time the flat was raided and he did not return. It was four years before he was caught and sentenced to 25 years' jail.

The evidence for the prosecution took most of three weeks to present, since there were over 200 Crown witnesses. Most unforgettable was the unfortunate driver of the train, Jack Mills, unsteady on his feet, sometimes inaudible in his speech, gripping the top of the witness stand and plainly showing the traces of the terrible beating he had received and from which he never recovered. (The total compensation he received from British Railways was £25.) Due to the helmets the robbers had worn he was unable to identify any of the men.

Most of the defendants then took the stand and testified in their own defence, although Wilson and James did not do so. It was difficult, if not impossible, to give any convincing answer to the Crown's circumstantial evidence—for example Hussey's palm print on the lorry in the yard at the farm; Wisbey's finger prints on the bathroom rail; Welch's palm print on a beer can, Wilson's on the window sill, and James's on a cat's dish.

Only Daly was lucky—his fingerprints had been found at the farm on a box of cards and tokens for playing Monopoly. But when his counsel submitted that there was no evidence to show when and where the prints got on to the Monopoly set—or, for that matter where the set was at the time the impression was made—the judge accepted the submission and Daly was discharged.

Another of the defendants, Ronald Biggs, had already been discharged by now—but only on a technicality which involved his being tried separately at a later date.

The trial occupied 48 working days, six of which the judge took to sum up the evidence, after which the jury were kept in seclusion for three days and three nights in a secret place. The verdict was delivered by the foreman at 10.30 a.m. on March 26, 1964. Boal, Wilson, Wisbey, Welch, Hussey, James, and Goody were each found guilty of conspiracy and armed robbery. The remaining three defendants were convicted of conspiracy.

Astonished gasp

First to be sentenced by Judge Edmund Davies was Cordrey, who got 20 years. This announcement caused a gasp of astonishment in the public gallery, particularly since Cordrey had been a considerable help to the police. Wilson, Wisbey, Welch, Hussey, James, and Goody were all sent to prison for 30 years; while Brian Field, Leonard Field, and Boal each received 24 years. Wheater, whom the judge said had served his country gallantly in war and faithfully in peace, was sentenced to three years.

The Court of Criminal Appeal allowed the appeals of the two Fields against conviction for conspiracy to rob the mail train, but held that the charges of conspiracy to obstruct the course of justice must stand: this meant that their sentences were in effect reduced from 24 to 5 years. The sentences passed on Cordrey and Boal were reduced to 14 years each.

Public reaction to the sentences was to some extent one of shocked astonishment, as indeed had been expressed in court. Journalist James Cameron, writing in the *Daily Herald,* pointed out that the gang would have been much more lightly punished if they had been convicted of non-capital murder, blackmail, and breaking a baby's leg.

However, the story of the Great Train Robbery did not end with the trial. Two years later, in 1966, another member of the gang, James White, was sentenced to 18 years' imprisonment.

That same year Buster Edwards was also arrested and then given 15 years. Bruce Reynolds, one of the key masterminds of the operation, had only £6,500 left when he was arrested in 1969—and

Sunday Times

Syndication International

he was sentenced to 25 years.

Later, Charlie Wilson escaped from prison and stayed on the run for three-and-a-half years before being recaptured. Ronald Biggs also escaped and is currently living with a girl friend in Brazil—apparently no longer a wealthy man.

William Boal spent seven years in

POSTSCRIPT . . . victim driver Mills, who was coshed in the raid, died a broken man some years later. Robber Ronald Biggs regained his freedom by climbing a prison wall and jumping on to a parked van.

prison before he died. All he got out of his participation in the robbery was a short-lived spending spree. Train driver Jack Mills died six-and-a-half years after the coup. He had suffered severely as a result of his head injuries—but, at the inquest, these were not linked with the cause of his death.

Today, almost 12 years after the raid, it is still not certain how many people were involved in it or its organization. A detective recently stated that at least three men directly involved have not yet been brought to justice. One of them is thought to be the man who attacked Mr. Mills with the metal bar.

Only some £400,000 of the total haul has so far been recovered. Even so, the Great Train Robbery was a disaster for most of those involved in the daringly conceived but finally unsuccessful "big job".

THE LINDBERGH BABY

Fame followed the pioneer aviator . . .
and the headlines grew when his child was snatched

Anthony Cobb

53

IT WAS an odd sound, a sharp crack. Colonel Charles A. Lindbergh, the aviator who had made his name a household word around the world by becoming the first man to fly the Atlantic non-stop, paused as he read in the library of his luxurious retreat on Sourland Mountain, a remote, forested peak in New Jersey. The sound was not repeated. The Colonel went back to his book. A few minutes later, Betty Gow, the Lindbergh's nursemaid, decided to look in on Charles, Jr., their golden-haired, 20-month-old baby son. She went into the nursery, turned up the electric heater in his darkened room and went over to the crib. She could hear no sound of breathing. She felt with her hand. The crib was empty.

She dashed out to the landing where she met Mrs. Lindbergh. "Have you got the baby?" she panted anxiously. "No," said Mrs. Lindbergh. The nursemaid rushed downstairs to the library. "Colonel," she gasped, "have *you* got the baby?" "No," he answered. "Isn't he in his crib?"

He didn't wait for her answer. Suddenly he recalled the mysterious sound he had heard. He took the stairs two at a time and switched on the light in the nursery. He was standing in front of the empty crib as his wife joined him in the room. "Anne," he said sorrowfully, "they have stolen our baby."

The possibility of kidnapping had always been in the Lindberghs' minds. They were obvious targets, both rich and famous. The Colonel first hit the headlines with his Transatlantic flight in May 1927, covering the 3600 miles from Long Island to Le Bourget airport outside Paris in 33½ hours.

His next long-distance solo trip was

THE SPIRIT OF ST. LOUIS . . .
Adventurous, romantic, the flying Lindberghs were an ideal match, but their hour of triumph turned to tragedy.

the 2100 mile hop from New York to Mexico City in 27 hours 10 minutes. There he met and fell in love with Anne Morrow, daughter of the U.S. ambassador. It was an ideal match. Mrs. Lindbergh quickly became an accomplished radio operator and joined her husband on a series of flights, pioneering what have developed into America's modern airline routes.

Their first flight as a team was from Los Angeles to New York in 14 hours 45 minutes. To the newspapers of the era

they became "the most romantic and adventurous couple of all time". They seemed to have everything—money, happiness, a satisfying purpose in life. To all those gifts was added in 1930 the joy of the birth of the son they named Charles Augustus Lindbergh, Jr.

Among the precautions they took to avoid a kidnapping was never to reveal in newspaper interviews which bedroom their little son occupied in the Sourland Mountain retreat. Yet now, on this dark night at the beginning of March 1932, someone had found the room and kidnapped him.

Characteristically, in this moment of crisis the Colonel did not lose his calm. "Get the butler to call the police and don't touch anything," he ordered. From a closet he took a Springfield rifle which he had carried with him on many of his flights. He went out into the dark night, but there was nothing to be seen and no sound except the wind whistling through the bare branches of the trees. He went back into the house to console his wife while the first police message flashed out along the whole Eastern seaboard of the United States: "Lindbergh baby kidnapped from his home near Hopewell, New Jersey. Stop and search all cars."

At the house on Sourland Mountain, the police found few clues. Beneath the nursery window were a few footprints, indistinct, as if the kidnapper had either removed his shoes altogether or bound them with sacking. Nearby police found a chisel and a crude ladder in three

THE LINDBERGH BABY (below, left) and the note demanding $50,000 ransom in a mixture of different denominations . . . signed with interlocking circles.

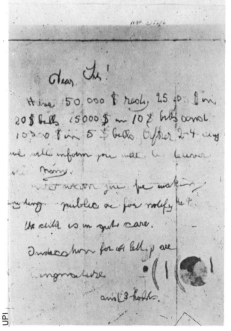

WANTED

INFORMATION AS TO THE WHEREABOUTS OF

CHAS. A. LINDBERGH, Jr.

OF HOPEWELL, N. J.

SON OF COL. CHAS. A. LINDBERGH

World-Famous Aviator

This child was kidnaped from his home in Hopewell, N. J., between 8 and 10 p.m. on Tuesday, March 1, 1932.

DESCRIPTION:

Age, 20 months   Hair, blond, curly
Weight, 27 to 30 lbs.
Height, 29 inches
    Deep dimple in
    Dressed in one-piec

ADDRESS ALL COMMUNICATI
COL. H. N. SCHWARZKO
COL. CHAS. A. LINDBER

ALL COMMUNICATIONS WILL

March 11, 1932   Supt.

sections. The ladder was broken at the point where the top section joined the middle one. From the start it was believed that it broke as the kidnapper made his escape, and that this was the cracking sound the Colonel heard as he read in the library.

The final clue was the misspelt ransom note, lying on the nursery window sill. It read: *"Dear Sir, Have 50,000 dollars redy, 25,000 in 20-dollar bills, 15,000 in 10-dollar bills and 10,000 in five-dollar bills. After 2-4 days we will inform you were to deliver the mony. We warn you for making anyding public or for notify the police. The child is in gut care. Instruction for the letters are singnature."*

In good care?

The "singnature" referred to, which was kept secret for months to prevent cranks from duplicating it and confusing the trail, consisted of two interlocking circles, one red and one blue. In the centre of each circle was a hole with a third hole equidistant between them. The inference drawn from the note was that it had been written by a German, but that was not much to go on.

The world shared the agony of the Lindberghs as they waited, red-eyed with weeping and fatigue, sustained only by the hope that their son really was "in gut care" and would be restored to them unharmed. Two hundred thousand letters and postcards of sympathy arrived by the sackful at their home. Carloads of police, F.B.I. agents, secret servicemen, reporters and photographers descended on Sourland Mountain, plus some of America's top private detectives, hired by newspapers who hoped they might crack the case before the authorities.

WANTING AND WAITING . . . the world shared the agony of the Lindberghs. Letters of sympathy by the thousand, F.B.I. agents by the carload, but a house which had once been a retreat told the story of the Lindberghs' new emptiness . . . the ladder led from the nursery.

55

Extra telephone lines were strung to cope with the traffic. From his prison cell, "Scarface" Al Capone, former king of the Chicago underworld, issued a statement promising to recover the missing child if he were granted his freedom. Mrs. Lindbergh made a broadcast to the whole of the United States, Canada, and Mexico, giving instructions on how to mix her baby's feed. "Take care of him," she pleaded. Her poignant words drew a note from the kidnapper, assuring her that her son was well.

The hunt for the kidnapper spread throughout America and from there to Canada, Mexico, Europe, and ships at sea. Yet the first man to make contact with him proved to be Dr. John F. Condon, an elderly educator who had taught and lectured for 50 years in the Bronx district of New York. Moved, like millions more throughout the world, by the Lindberghs' sorrow, he sent a letter to his local newspaper, the *Bronx Home News*, appealing for the return of the baby. The letter, addressed to the kidnapper, said in part:

"For the sake of his own mother, that he may offer restitution for his crime, I offer all that I could scrape together, 1,000 dollars of my own money, so that a loving mother may again have her darling child, so that people will know that the greatest criminal in the world has a bright spot in his heart, and that Colonel Charles A. Lindbergh may know that the American people are grateful for the honor he has bestowed upon the United States by his pluck and daring.

"Let the kidnapper know that I write of my own free will, that no testimony of mine or coming from me will be used against him, and that this is an appeal for the sake of humanity . . ."

The letter was published on March 8,

exactly a week after the disappearance of the baby. By the first post next morning, Dr. Condon received a letter from the kidnapper, identified by the familiar red and blue circles. After contacting the Lindberghs, Dr. Condon made a rendezvous for March 12, late at night on a lonely road bordering Woodlawn Cemetery. He was driven to the spot by a friend, Al Reich, a former heavy-weight boxer. As he went to meet the kidnapper, Dr. Condon said: "Al, if I should never return, remember a child's life is at stake. Forget me. Remember Colonel Lindbergh's baby."

The meeting was a success. The kidnapper, who gave his name as John, accepted that Dr. Condon was acting in

MOMENT OF DESPAIR . . . Mrs Lindbergh arrives at the funeral parlour (top left) to identify the remains of her child (left). The baby's body was found in an area of dense woodland (top, right), not far from the Lindberghs' home. The ransom of $50,000 (above) had proved useless.

good faith. He obligingly took his hat off to let Dr. Condon see his face so that, if they met again, the Doctor would know he was talking to the right person. For his part, Dr. Condon was satisfied that he was speaking with the man who had abducted the Lindbergh child. He showed "John" safety pins of an uncommon design which had been used in the Lind-

bergh nursery and asked if he knew what they were. "Sure I know," said "John". "They were used to pin the blankets to the crib."

A series of communications now began between "John" and Dr. Condon, "John" sending notes, the Doctor replying through the advertisement columns of newspapers. "John" provided further proof of his authenticity by sending a sleeping suit which was positively identified as the one Charles Lindbergh Jr. had worn on the night of the kidnapping. He also upped his demands from 50,000 to 70,000 dollars, and he threatened to increase it to 100,000 dollars unless the money was paid by April 8.

A second rendezvous was made at an-

other cemetery, St. Raymond's, for the night of April 2. On this occasion, Colonel Lindbergh himself accompanied the Doctor, and, convinced that he was dealing with the genuine kidnapper, took 70,000 dollars with him in a cardboard box. Unknown to the Colonel, the U.S. Treasury had listed the serial numbers of every note — a precaution which was later to prove critical.

The Colonel sat in the car while the Doctor walked towards a voice in the darkness that kept calling: "Here, Dr. Condon, here." It was darker than at the first meeting, but Dr. Condon recognized the kidnapper's voice. He had left the ransom money in the car, hoping to persuade the kidnapper to hand over the missing baby. "John" refused to lead him to the child. "But I will give you full instructions as soon as I have the money," he promised.

Getaway plans

Dr. Condon decided, in the circumstances, that he would at least try to save Colonel Lindbergh the extra 20,000 dollars that had been demanded. "Look, John," he said, "Colonel Lindbergh is not as rich as they say he is. He has been able to raise only 50,000 dollars. Of course, he could have asked his friends for the money but he is not that kind of man. You know that and I know it." The kidnapper was not at first convinced, but ultimately he agreed: "All right, we'll take the 50,000 dollars."

Dr. Condon went back to the car to get the money. As he did so the kidnapper shouted: "Hey, Doctor," as if he feared he was about to be tricked. Colonel Lindbergh heard the call and the man's voice burned itself into his memory, never to be forgotten. Dr. Condon removed the extra 20,000 dollars, then went back to hand the balance over to the kidnapper. Once again he saw "John's" face clearly as he took the money.

The arrangement was that the kidnapper and his accomplices should have eight hours to make their getaway before revealing the whereabouts of the missing baby. The details arrived by post next day. The note said:

"The boy is on the boad (boat) Nelly. It is a small boad 28 feet long. Two persons are on the boad. They are innocent. You will find the boad between Horseneck Beach and Gay Head, near Elizabeth Island."

The Colonel, his personal friend Colonel Henry Breckinridge and Dr. Condon flew to the spot off the coast of Massachusetts. There, however, no one had heard of the *Nelly*. The Colonel flew low over the adjacent waters. There was no sign of the boat or his baby. He realized then that he had been tricked. Embittered, he

returned home and released for the first time details of the negotiations and the serial numbers of the ransom notes.

There could now be little chance that his son was still alive, and what hope there was vanished altogether on May 12. William Allen, a Negro teamster walking in the woods a few miles from the Colonel's home, and only a few yards from the spot where telephone workers had been busy ten weeks earlier rigging emergency lines, stumbled upon a shallow leaf-covered grave. In the grave was the body of a child. There could be no doubt about the identity. The golden curls and the little homemade shirt, stitched together by Betty Gow from one of his long flannel petticoats to keep him warm, told their own story. The Lindbergh baby had been dead since the night of the kidnapping, and he had died from severe head injuries.

The world grieved for the Lindberghs anew and, in the backlash that followed, there was a renewed outburst of earlier charges that the kidnapping must have been "an inside job". Betty Gow, although

strongly defended by the Lindberghs, came under suspicion. So did Violet Sharpe, a maid in the Morrow home at Englewood, who went up to her room and committed suicide when police called to requestion her.

Meanwhile there had been several indications that the kidnapper probably lived, like Dr. Condon, in the Bronx. In the first place, there was the prompt reply from the kidnapper to Dr. Condon's appeal, published in the local Bronx newspaper. Then, from time to time, bills from the ransom money had turned up in the area. The issue was settled virtually beyond doubt by a remarkable piece of detection, carried out not by a policeman but by a member of the U.S. Forestry

Service, Arthur Koehler. To Koehler fell the task of identifying and tracing the source of the wood used to make the sectional ladder featured in the crime.

Nobody, except Koehler himself, had much faith in the assignment. It was cheap, ordinary lumber of the type sold all over the country. It seemed almost impossible to trace it to the lumber yard that had sold it. But Koehler, who had worked with wood since childhood, was quietly confident. "I can find it," he said. Although it took 18 months, he traced the lumber yard concerned.

They were at the kidnapper's doorstep. But there the trail might easily have ended. Although the company kept a record of purchases, it did not note what sort of

A NEW FIND: Two years had passed since the kidnapping, and again attention was focussed on the Lindbergh case. $13,000 of the ransom money was found at the home (top left) of Bruno Hauptmann. Money was hidden with a gun in a hollowed-out joist (left). Hauptmann was arrested (above) and convicted of murder. He protested his innocence . . .

material it bought. Koehler had traced the lumber from the forest where it had grown, to the mill where it was processed, to the yard that sold it to the kidnapper. That, however, was as far as the telltale marks in the wood could take him.

But "John's" luck was about to run out. What proved his undoing was nothing to do with Koehler, or the police, or the private detectives, or the skilled reporters who had been assigned to track the kidnapper down. He was the victim of an international monetary crisis. On May 1, 1934, more than two years after the kidnapping, President Roosevelt abandoned the gold standard.

At the time, in addition to ordinary currency, the United States had notes known as gold certificates which were freely convertible into bullion. The effect of abandoning the gold standard was that gold certificates were called in and became illegal as currency. For the kidnapper it was about the worst thing that could have happened. Of the 50,000 dollars ransom money, 35,000 had been in gold certificates.

At 10 a.m. one day in mid-September, a Dodge sedan pulled into a Bronx gas station and the driver asked for five gallons of gasoline. He gave the manager, Walter Lyle, a ten-dollar gold certificate in payment. "You don't see many of these any more," said Lyle. "No," replied the motorist, "I've only got a hundred more left." Lyle had forgotten about the Lindbergh case but, as a precaution, took a note of the car's registration number. Then he went to a bank to exchange the certificate for two five-dollar bills. He explained how he came to be in possession of the bill. The teller looked up the serial number. It was part

of the Lindbergh ransom money.

Again the trail was warm. Police checked on the car. It was registered to Bruno Richard Hauptmann, 36, a former German soldier who, inquiries revealed, had entered the United States illegally in 1923.

Hauptmann was arrested outside his Bronx home on September 19. In one pocket he had a 20-dollar bill, also part of the ransom money. Police took him into a rear bedroom to question him. Special agent Thomas Fisk noticed that Hauptmann kept glancing furtively out of the window. "What are you looking at?" he asked.

"Nothing," said Hauptmann.

Gold certificates

Fisk went over to the window. Outside there was a garage. "Is that where you have the money?" he asked.

"I have no money," Hauptmann shouted angrily.

Despite his denial, the police decided to concentrate their search on the garage. In a shellac can, under some old rags and wrapped in newspapers, they found 11,930 dollars in gold certificates, all from the Lindbergh ransom. Police carpenters took the garage to pieces. In a hollowed-out joist they found another 840 dollars of the ransom money. Another 20-dollar certificate was traced to a shoe store where Hauptmann had bought a pair of shoes for his wife, Anna. By the end of the police search, 31,000 dollars were still missing. It never turned up. Nor were any more of the ransom bills passed after Hauptmann's arrest.

His trial for the murder of the Lindbergh baby began at Flemington, New Jersey, on January 2, 1935. Hauptmann pleaded "not guilty" but, although the case dragged on for five weeks, there was never any serious doubt about the outcome. Over and above the ransom money, which he claimed to have been "minding" for someone else, all the evidence pointed to Hauptmann's guilt.

The one thing which did not emerge from the trial was whether the Lindbergh baby had been deliberately killed in his cot, or had died accidentally by falling to the ground when the ladder broke. Hauptmann never talked and still protested his innocence, even after the jury had brought in a unanimous verdict of guilty and New Jersey High Court had rejected every argument in his appeal.

The news that his appeal had failed was brought to Hauptmann in the death house, where he was waiting to pay the penalty for the crime which had shocked the world. It was the eve of his tenth wedding anniversary and his first thought was for his wife. "My God," he exclaimed, "what a fine anniversary present for Anna!"

ROOKS FARM, at Stocking Pelham, in the green English county of Hertfordshire, was the home of two unique kidnappers. But what did the Hosein brothers do with Mrs. Muriel McKay? Where is the body that was never found?

STOCKING PELHAM

On this farm, a woman was imprisoned for more than a month... then she vanished without trace.

Syndication International

Two brothers were charged with her murder. They had planned to seize the wife of a newspaper millionaire, and demand a £1 million ransom. They got the wrong woman...

The Mrs. McKay "missing body" trial ... it was unique in British legal history

NO trial in Britain since the abolition of hanging for murder received more advance publicity than the court room drama which opened in London's Old Bailey on September 14, 1970. The two men who were brought up from the cells below the building to take their places in the dock of the historic No. 1 Court were brothers from Trinidad named Arthur and Nizamodeen Hosein. Although born in the former British colony, they were strictly speaking not West Indians but Indian Moslems whose family had originally come from the sub-continent of India.

Their father Shaffi Hosein was a respectable, hard-working tailor who had settled in Trinidad and owned the house where the family lived near Port of Spain. A deeply religious man, Shaffi also officiated as Imam in the Mosque which served the needs of the local Indian Moslem community in his village. The two boys, Arthur aged 34, and Nizamodeen, 12 years younger, had been brought up according to the teachings of the Koran, the Moslem bible.

The local squire

Together with their sister Hafiza and Arthur's wife Elsa and her two children, they lived at Rooks Farm, Stocking Pelham, near Epping, in Hertfordshire. This was a small property of some 12 acres, which Arthur had bought for £14,000 with the aid of a mortgage in May 1968. It was largely uncultivated and the only livestock consisted of a few pigs, calves, and chickens. Incidentally, pig keeping hardly commended itself to Arthur's father, since the pig is considered unclean by good Moslems. For finance Arthur depended on his sewing machine with which he used to produce trousers for London's East End tailors. Nevertheless, Arthur Hosein, who possessed delusions of grandeur, fancied himself as the local squire and spent freely in the neighbouring bars. He even tried, without success, to join the local hunt. At his trial he gave his occupation as "fashion designer". He was known in the neighbourhood as "King Hosein".

Both brothers were charged with murder, kidnapping, blackmail, and sending threatening letters. Their victims were an attractive, 56-year-old Australian married woman named Muriel Frieda McKay and her husband Alick. One reason, the principal one, why the trial had already received such extensive press coverage was that Alick McKay was the Deputy Chairman of the *News of the World*, which

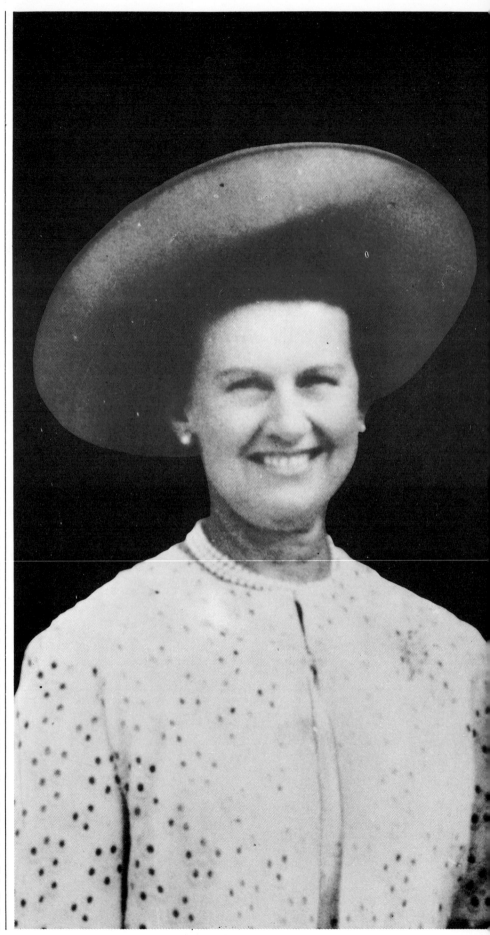

Press Association

Syndication International

"ALICK, DARLING" . . . the wife of Alick McKay was snatched from her home, and never seen again. Mr. McKay was Deputy Chairman of the biggest-selling newspaper in Britain.

has the largest circulation of any English newspaper. The *News of the World* had recently been bought by another Australian. the young millionaire Rupert Murdoch.

The story which the stern and tight-lipped Attorney-General Sir Peter Rawlinson, who led the prosecution, recounted to the jury of nine men and three women was an extraordinary one. The Hosein brothers, he said, had devised "a brutal and ruthless scheme to kidnap a wife and by menaces to extort from her husband a vast sum of money."

Chauffeured Rolls

Arthur Hosein had noticed a luxurious chauffeur-driven Rolls Royce driving round London. He took a note of the registration number ULO 18F and determined to trace its owner. This he was able to do at County Hall, the headquarters of the Greater London Council where particulars of all motor vehicles in the metropolitan area are filed. At his brother's prompting, Nizamodeen made the inquiry in person, giving a false name in the application form he filled out. The reason for his inquiry, he told the counter clerk, was that the Rolls had sustained minor damage in a collision with his own vehicle and he was anxious to get into touch with its owner. As a result he learned that the car belonged to the *News of the World* and was allotted to the chairman for his use.

The brothers then proceeded to follow the Rolls one evening from the *News of the World* offices off Fleet Street to the prosperous London suburb of Wimbledon, where it deposited its occupant, whom they took to be Rupert Murdoch, at the door of a fine Georgian-style house in Arthur Road, No. 20, known as St. Mary House. However, the man in the Rolls was not Rupert Murdoch. Rupert Murdoch had left England with his wife a short time before on a business trip to Australia and lent the car to the deputy-chairman, who was in charge of the paper during his absence. The man in the Rolls was Alick McKay, and he owned St. Mary House.

Gagged and trussed

During the late afternoon of Monday, December 29, 1969, the Hosein brothers used some pretext to get into the McKay house, since Muriel McKay always left the door on the safety chain. Having overpowered her, they took her away with them. "It was obvious," said the Attorney-General, "that they thought they were abducting Mrs. Rupert Murdoch, but she was safe and at home in Australia."

When Alick McKay returned an hour or so later, he found several articles which the intruders had left behind. They were some sheets of a newspaper, a roll of twine, a piece of sticking plaster tape, and a billhook. This latter is an implement resembling a small axe, which is used by farmers for hedging and ditching work. The telephone was on the floor, but had not been ripped away from the wall. Muriel McKay's reading glasses, hand-bag, wallet, keys, and cheque book were lying scattered about the stairs. Some short time before, the house had been burgled, and Alick McKay now thought that the burglars had returned and used some of the twine to tie up his wife before abducting her.

The picture which Sir Peter Rawlinson presented to the jury was a horrifying one. "Can you imagine the horror of a woman, one minute beside the fire waiting for her husband to return, and minutes later —gagged and trussed—then driven away in the darkness?"

Five hours later the phone rang in St. Mary House. Alick McKay heard a voice at the other end of the line identifying himself with "Mafia Group Three from America," or M3 for short. "We tried to get Rupert Murdoch's wife," said the caller. "We could not get her so we took yours instead. Have one million pounds by Wednesday night or we will kill her!"

During the next few weeks there were 18 calls from the kidnappers, most of which were taken by Alick McKay's son Ian—who moved into the house in order to spare his father, who was suffering from a serious heart condition, since the excitement of continuing to speak to the kidnappers on the telephone might prove fatal.

"Frankly we want to know if she is alive and well," said Ian McKay in response to one call. "We have the money. But why should we give you the money if we do not know if she is alive?"

"I have told you what she is wearing," M3 replied. "What do you want me to do? Take her clothes off and send them to you? If you do not cooperate you will get her dead on your doorstep."

A request by Ian McKay to speak to his mother, or have her voice taped as proof of her continued existence, was ignored. Three letters had been received from her, Sir Peter went on, two addressed to her husband and one to her daughter Dianne. ("Alick darling, I am blindfolded and cold. Only blankets. Please do something to get me home.") But when Ian McKay continued to press for proof that she was still alive, he was told that she would not be allowed to write again.

Never murdered

"It's because you have not got her," Ian shouted over the telephone to M3. "You have got a corpse. You are trying to trick us. How many other people have you kidnapped before?"

"We have never murdered anyone as yet," was the ominous reply, "but there will always be a first time."

A further letter, postmarked January 9, 1970, was addressed to the editor of the *News of the World*. Written in block letters on a single sheet of white lined paper,

Press Association

the message, which bore no signature, asked the editor to inform Mr. Alick McKay that they had his wife, that he would get some proof, that they wanted a million pounds, and that if Mr. McKay failed to cooperate his wife "would be disposed off" [SIC]. In fact some pieces of the dress, coat, and shoes, she was wearing at the time were later sent to the unfortunate husband.

Meanwhile, a sheet of paper similar to that on which the *News of the World* letter was written had been found by the police in Nizamodeen's bedroom at Rooks Farm. The sheet had been torn from an exercise book and exactly matched the letter. In addition, there were two ransom notes which a handwriting expert stated were in Arthur Hosein's disguised handwriting, and one of these notes had impressions of Arthur's thumb and one of his fingers. Apart from this, a palm print found on the newspaper lying on the floor of St. Mary House on the night of the kidnapping was positively identified as being that of Arthur Hosein.

In this instance the English police were up against a completely novel kind of crime. In no case since that of King Richard the Lion Heart in the twelfth century had the kidnapped person been held to ransom.

It was otherwise in America and the European continent where the F.B.I. and the police authorities have learned from

"I APPEAL" . . . Mr. McKay pleaded with the kidnappers for news of his wife, at a Press conference. With him, daughter Dianne. Son Ian (above) rallied the family during the search.

experience to put the safety of the kidnapped person first, and the capture of the abductors second, and do not usually take action against the kidnappers until after the ransom money has been paid and the victim released. This procedure has as a rule worked well in practice, although there have been exceptions, of which the case of the Lindbergh baby in 1932 is the best known. But in America and the continent the kidnapping is normally the work of professionals who leave notes plainly stating their ransom requirements at the time the victim is taken away.

The amateurish Hosein brothers left no such message behind at St. Mary House, and with hoaxers frequently calling up the house as a result of the newspaper publicity, the police were hampered in their investigations through being unable to say whether Muriel McKay had, in fact, been abducted at all. Indeed, there was a suggestion that she had gone off to Australia on her own.

Enormous publicity

Furthermore, for the first two weeks in January 1970 no word was heard from the kidnappers, who were no doubt alarmed by the enormous publicity which Muriel McKay's disappearance had attracted. Then, on January 14, the telephone calls from M 3 were resumed. Six days later Alick McKay received a letter containing directions for his son Ian to go to a certain telephone call box outside London on the Cambridge Road on the evening of February 1, where he would get a call at 10 p.m. telling him where to proceed with the money. This was followed by a second letter on January 26 repeating the directions, and enclosing a letter from Muriel McKay with the pieces of her clothing. In this letter M 3 threatened that she would be "executed" if her son failed to keep "our business date without any error".

The date was kept—by Detective Sergeant Street who posed as Ian McKay. He took the call and was told to proceed to another telephone box on the road and wait for another call. The second call duly came through at 10.45, and "Ian" was told to look on the floor where he would find a used packet of Piccadilly cigarettes with further instructions. A note inside the packet ordered "Ian" to travel to a place called High Cross, beyond which he would see a road junction. At the side of the road there was a bank marked by some paper flowers, and this was the point where he was to leave the suitcase with the ransom money.

The Detective Sergeant did as he was instructed, while another police officer kept watch. But no one came to collect the suitcase, although the paper flowers were there. The result was that the police

eventually collected it themselves and took it back to Wimbledon.

Next day Ian McKay had a call from M 3 accusing him of doublecrossing the kidnappers by going to the police, since they had seen a police car in the High Cross area the previous night. Later the same day M 3 called again, this time saying he would do no more business with Ian McKay, but must deal with his father—who was instructed to pack the money into two smaller suitcases on February 6, and follow a similar call box procedure. This eventually led the police to Bishop's Stortford in Hertfordshire, where the suitcases were to be placed near a hedge by the side of a road leading into the town.

Here the kidnappers' luck ran out. A security officer, who had nothing to do with the investigation, happened to be driving past with his wife, and his suspicions were aroused by the sight of the two suitcases at the side of the road. He went to a call box and telephoned the local police, after which he returned and kept watch over the two cases. Meanwhile the Hosein brothers had been cruising round in Arthur's Volvo car, and noticing several police in the area, they thought it too risky to stop and pick up the suitcases. Thereupon they drove off—but not before the police had noted the Volvo's registration number. The number was checked; it was found to belong to Arthur Hosein, and it led the police to Rooks Farm.

No trace of Muriel McKay was found at the farm, but there were various articles there which connected the brothers with the abduction. These included paper flowers, which corresponded with those left at High Cross. It appeared that

THE MOST thorough and prolonged searches . . . whether Mrs. McKay died on the farm, and how she met her death, remains a mystery.

Nizamodeen's girl friend, Liley Moham-med, who worked as a hospital nurse, had shown Arthur's sister Hafiza how to make them—a process Liley had learned from a patient in the hospital. All this amounted to enough to incriminate the brothers as the kidnappers, and they were consequently arrested.

The first prosecution witness was Alick McKay, who looked very pale and shaky. He described the last time he saw his wife, which was the morning of her dis-appearance. "She was a very bright per-son."

Alick McKay was followed by a string of other witnesses who confirmed every point in the Attorney-General's story. Everyone who had spoken to M3 on the telephone—the operator who connected the first call, the editor of the *News of the World,* and various members of the McKay family—all testified.

Then the fingerprint and handwriting experts identified the prints and writing on the various articles exhibited in court as belonging either to Arthur or Niza-modeen Hosein. Finally, a neighbour-ing farmer in Hertfordshire swore that he had missed his billhook after visiting Rooks Farm in October 1969. When shown the billhook which had been found in the McKay house, he waved it from the witness box and exclaimed: "That's my bill. I defy anyone to say it's not!"

Both brothers gave evidence in their own defence, and denied all knowledge of the charges. But each tried to put the blame on the other for any suspicious happening or circumstance on which he was questioned.

Questioned about the billhook, Arthur said he could not recognize it and he thought the farmer had made up the story about it. However, he did admit, on being pressed, that he had borrowed a bill-hook to cut up a calf which had been brought to the farm. From time to time Arthur burst out into wild accusations against the police, who he said had fre-quently beaten him up after his arrest.

Nizamodeen, on the other hand, said he had been "scared stiff" of his brother.

He admitted going to County Hall and making inquiries about the Rolls, of which Arthur, he said, had supplied him with the registration number. It was Arthur, too, who told him to give the counter clerk a false name and address. His brother did not say why he wanted this information, Nizamodeen added, and he "did not give it another thought".

In his summing up of the evidence, the judge (Mr. Justice Sebag Shaw) mentioned every relevant point. "Each one perhaps is small in itself," he told the jury, "but from them it may be that an edifice is slowly erected by one tiny brick after another tiny brick."

It was clear that the jury thought so too. After an absence of just over four hours, they returned a verdict of guilty on all counts, but they recommended Nizamodeen to leniency.

Denounced judge

Asked by the judge whether they had anything to say before sentence was passed, Nizamodeen remained silent. But Arthur burst into a hysterical denunciation of the judge for his partiality. In

passing sentence, the judge addressed grave words to the men in the dock: "The kidnapping and detention of Mrs. McKay was cold-blooded and abominable. She was snatched from the security and comfort of her home and so long as she remained alive she was reduced to terrified despair.

"The crime will shock and revolt any right-minded citizen and the punishment must be sanguine so that law-abiding citizens will be safe in their homes. There cannot have been a worse case of blackmail. You put Mrs. McKay's family on the rack for weeks and months in an attempt to extort money from them by monstrous demands."

Both brothers were then sentenced to life imprisonment for murder. On the other charges, Arthur got 25 years and Nizamodeen 15 years for kidnapping, and both got 14 years and 10 years respectively for blackmail and sending threatening letters—all the sentences to run concurrently.

Among the spectators in the crowded court was old Shaffi Hosein, who had come over from Trinidad for the trial. "I still cannot believe my boys would have done this," he said with a stupefied look. "I am sure they are not guilty."

However, it is abundantly clear that both brothers were convicted on overwhelming circumstantial evidence. Yet there is one puzzling factor about the case. Muriel McKay's body was never found. Not the slightest trace of her was discovered at the farm, or in the large surrounding area, in spite of the most thorough and prolonged searches.

There was a gruesome story current at the time that after they killed her the brothers cut up her body into pieces which they then fed to the pigs on the farm. But this is entirely unsupported by the evidence. Had it been so, some bones must have remained, but nothing of this kind was ever forthcoming. Nor was anything in the way of bones found in the large stove and chimney in the farm house, where it was likewise suggested that she had been cremated.

On the other hand, she may have died

from exposure during the bitterly cold weather at the time of her kidnapping, and her death may have been accelerated by lack of the drugs which she had been taking under medical prescription. It is possible too that she may never have been at the farm at all, but held in some hideout, perhaps in nearby Epping Forest, and after her death her body was weighted and dumped in a river or the sea.

Reprisals danger

Exactly how Muriel McKay met her death remains a mystery. How long it will remain so depends largely on Nizamodeen Hosein, who may conceivably be persuaded to solve it in return for an early parole by the prison authorities. Asked by Elsa Hosein, when she visited him in prison whether there was a third party in the case, Nizamodeen replied enigmatically:

"Arthur says that we must never talk about that, because if we do the children will be in great danger. There would be reprisals."

Keystone

THE MEN WHO WALK ALONE: A lost wife, a shattered life . . . Alick McKay (centre), pictured leaving court. Parted, prisoners . . . the brothers Nizamodeen (far left) and Arthur Hosein (above). Was there another person involved in the puzzling case of Mrs. McKay? The brothers remained enigmatic . . .

Both Syndication International

THE ACID BATH BLOOD-DRINKER

Totally emotionless killers are rarer than is generally supposed. But John George Haigh was more than this: he also drank the blood of his victims . . .

TO THE permanent residents, and especially the elderly ladies, at the genteel Onslow Court Hotel, in London's South Kensington, Mr. John George Haigh was the epitome of charm and well-bred good manners. At meal times he never failed to acknowledge his fellow guests with a warm smile and the hint of a formal bow as he threaded his way between the separate tables to his own reserved corner of the dining room. In the eyes of the widowed ladies, comfortably, if sometimes tediously, counting off the days in quiet seclusion, he was something of a favourite handsome nephew.

One of these widows, a Mrs. Durand-Deacon, was already enjoying a growing friendship with the 39-year-old, and apparently successful, self-employed engineer. They occupied adjoining tables and, as a result of mutual confidence, Haigh already knew a good deal about her. Olive Henrietta Helen Olivia Robarts Durand-Deacon was 69, a well-preserved, well-dressed, buxom woman, who was a devoted Christian Scientist and whose late husband—a colonel in the Gloucestershire Regiment—had left her a legacy of some £40,000.

She was not the sort of person who could spend her final years in total idleness. To amuse herself, and add to her invested capital, she had made some paper designs of artificial fingernails which, she hoped, could be manufactured in plastic. To her delight, the kindly Mr. Haigh suggested that he might be able to help, and they could choose the materials at his factory at Crawley, in Sussex.

Elaborate preparations

On the afternoon of Friday, February 18, 1949, Haigh drove Mrs. Durand-Deacon the 30 miles south to Crawley in his Alvis car, and at around four o'clock they were seen together in the George Hotel. From the hotel they went to a small factory in Leopold Road, Crawley—a factory that Haigh did not own, as he had said, but where he was allowed the use of a storeroom for his "experimental engineering" work.

There in the factory he had made elaborate preparations for Mrs. Durand-Deacon's visit. He had bought a carboy of sulphuric acid and a 45-gallon drum specially lined to hold corrosive chemicals. He had laid out, on a bench, a stirrup pump, of the type used for firefighting during the days of the German air raids on Britain, gloves, and a rubber apron.

It was strange equipment to assemble for what was supposed to be a discussion about artificial fingernails. But, whatever Mrs. Durand-Deacon might have thought, that was not the purpose for which Haigh had brought her to the deserted workshop.

As the elderly widow turned her back to him to search in her handbag for her

paper designs, Haigh slipped a revolver from his coat pocket and killed her with a single shot through the nape of the neck. Stooping beside the body he took a knife, made an incision in an artery, gathered a few inches of the still-coursing blood in a glass, and drank it at a gulp.

Haigh then began the real work for which he had lured his victim to the factory. He stripped the body and carefully placed on one side the widow's Persian lamb coat, rings, necklace, ear-rings, and a cruciform, which had hung around the neck. That done, he moved to the second part of his plan, in which he had the benefit of previous experience: the disposal of the body by dissolving it in acid.

His own later description of the operation illustrated the workmanlike way in which this 10-stone murderer put his 15-stone victim into an acid bath.

He took an anticorrosive drum, or barrel, as he called it, laid it down lengthwise on the floor "and with a minimum of effort pushed the head and shoulders in. I then tipped the barrel up by placing my feet on the forward edge and grasping the top of the barrel with my gloved hands. By throwing my weight backwards the barrel containing the body rocked to a vertical position fairly easily and I found I could raise a 15-stone body easily.

"You may think that a 40-gallon drum standing only four feet high would be too

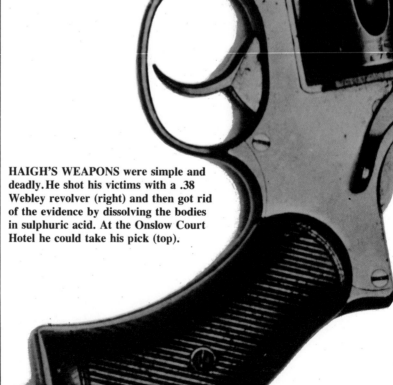

HAIGH'S WEAPONS were simple and deadly. He shot his victims with a .38 Webley revolver (right) and then got rid of the evidence by dissolving the bodies in sulphuric acid. At the Onslow Court Hotel he could take his pick (top).

F. Wilkinson

small for such a body," Haigh went on, "but my experiments showed that as the drum tipped, the body slumped down to the shoulders and the legs disappeared below the surface of the drum."

Having stowed the body neatly in the drum, Haigh poured in the sulphuric acid ("the question of getting the right amount was only learned by experience," he loftily explained) and then added more to make up the correct solution by pumping it in with the stirrup pump. When that was done, he had to wait until, slowly, the acid destroyed every trace of the body.

Tired after his efforts, however, Haigh left the workshop, slipped into his car, and drove to Ye Olde Ancient Priors Restaurant, in Crawley. There he ordered a pot of tea and poached eggs on toast, which he consumed with relish while exchanging good-natured banter with Mr. Outram, the proprietor.

Since this was the beginning of a weekend, during which the small factory would be closed, Haigh left the body in its dreadful bath and returned to the Onslow Court Hotel. There, at breakfast the following morning, Mrs. Durand-Deacon's absence was noticed by some of the other guests —and particularly by a Mrs. Constance

Lane who was a close friend of hers.

To Haigh's alarm, it transpired that Mrs. Lane had known of his proposed visit to Crawley with Mrs. Durand-Deacon. While he had been fetching his car, the previous afternoon, the two women had met in the hotel lounge and Mrs. Durand-Deacon had told her friend about her imminent "business trip".

For Haigh it was a devastating piece of information. The masterstroke in his plan had been his expectation that Mrs. Durand-Deacon would want to keep the promising deal over the artificial finger-nails a "company secret". Furthermore, at his suggestion, they had met for the start of their journey to Crawley not outside the hotel, but by the entrance to a large London store, some little distance away in Victoria Street. His subtle plan had now been undermined by Mrs. Lane's knowledge, and Haigh knew he would be involved in the questions following Mrs. Durand-Deacon's disappearance.

Little profit

With his nagging fears locked within him, he spent a busy Saturday putting into practice the purpose for which he had murdered the avaricious widow. In the course of a journey which took him to South London, Surrey, and Sussex, he disposed of Mrs. Durand-Deacon's jewellery for around £150. Her Persian lamb coat—which was blood-stained and not yet ready to realize its secondhand purchase price of £50—he left for cleaning at a shop in Reigate. But, since Haigh had pressing debts—including £350 to a bookmaker—which he could no longer avoid paying, his total "gain" was a reduction of his bank overdraft to £78.

Death had brought the blood-drinking criminal little financial profit. By the next day it seemed certain that it would bring him catastrophic personal loss. For Mrs. Lane, now thoroughly disturbed by her friend's failure to return, insisted that she and Haigh should go to the police and make out a missing person report. Haigh had no choice but to agree, attempting outwardly to express a "correct" measure of solicitude and concern.

The report he made, at Chelsea Police Station, appeared plausible enough. He had arrived at the Army and Navy Stores in Victoria Street, on Friday at 2.30, to keep his prearranged appointment with Mrs. Durand-Deacon. When, an hour later, she had failed to arrive he assumed her plans had changed and drove down to Crawley alone. He was thanked for his assistance and returned with Mrs. Lane to the Onslow Court Hotel—still a free man and still not under official suspicion.

But the last grains of sand in his criminal hourglass were flowing fast, and Woman Police-Sergeant Alexandra Maude Lambourne helped to speed them on their

Daily Mirror

FORWARD WITH THE PEOPLE

FRI MAR. 4 1949

ONE PENNY

No. 14,095

Registered at GPO as a Newspaper.

VAMPIRE— A MAN HELD

THE Vampire Killer will never strike again. He is safely behind bars, powerless to lure victims to a hideous death.

This is the assurance which the *Daily Mirror* can give today. It is the considered conclusion of the finest detective brains in the country.

The full tally of the Vampire's crimes is still not known.

It may take squads of police many weeks yet to piece together full details of the murderer and his ghastly practices. So far five murders are attributed to him. They are:—

Dr. Archibald Henderson; Mrs. Rosalie Mercy Henderson, his wife; Mr. Donald McSwan; Mrs. Amy McSwan, his wife; and Mr. Donald John McSwan, their son.

The police believe that Donald McSwan, junior, was the first of the Vampire's victims—in 1945—followed two months later by his parents.

Dr. and Mrs. Henderson are known to have disappeared in February of last year.

Held captive for a month?

Made to sign alibi notes, says brother

AFTER killing Dr. Henderson, the Vampire is believed to have kept Mrs. Henderson alive for at least a month writing letters—and signing typewritten letters—to relatives and friends.

When the Vampire thought himself safe, Rosalie Mercy Henderson followed her husband to a ghastly death.

This theory is held by her brother, Mr. Arnold Henry Burlin, 35, hotelier, of Arnfield-road, Withington, Manchester.

"I am convinced," he told the *Daily Mirror* last night, "that my sister was under duress for at least a month ... was shot and her body dis—...

... believe she was ... ...ters posted ... ...llay

Mrs. Rosalie Henderson

Advertiser's Announcement

★ No. 79—room of horror

In tins, bags and little parcels, detectives bring specimens from 79, back-basement of 79, Gloucester-road, London, S.W., in which the McSwans are believed to have been slain. Police, digging, found false teeth in the floor.

3 thirsty Rus... rush the bar...

His booby trap tripped the wrong man

THREE of the eight Russian repatriation officials ... by American troops broke from the building ... Ignoring calls to halt and the glare of searchlight... hind the building and tried to start up a car. A... ...ind the building and sto... ...back into the building...

The officials have ... authorities to retur... said last night.

Gas and water se... off. The phones ha... being allowed in.

One of the Rus... terday asked th... guards for n... "We are cut of... world," he said.

He was give... *Stars and Stri...* Army newspa...

According ... radio the R... officer has ... can Supre... that Russia wil... allow American offic... search in the Soviet Zone ... for American subjects who ... wish to go home ...

The wrong man — a motorist—fell into the trap which Alfred Hatcher, 26, admitted he had set one night for his rival in love, Reg Moore, 34.

Hatcher had tied a piece of twine across the road ... ...it was fined £2 at Ashford when he was ... Edith Scott, 16, said last night she thought Hatcher ... Moore was meet... ...

Reduced P... of FRY... Chocol...

As fre... all Fry's chocolat... price or increased in w... Quality unchanged.

FRY'S NEW P...
- Sandwich Assortme...
- Silver Lining Assor...
- Crunchie
- Chocolate Crea...
- Sandwich Block...
- Quality ¼lb. B...

FRY'S

way. She was sent to the hotel to gather additional information about the missing widow; but, unlike the elderly guests at Onslow Court, she did not succumb to Haigh's glib tongue and superficial charm. On the contrary, her combination of police experience and feminine intuition aroused a vague but nevertheless persistent feeling of suspicion.

After talking to Haigh she returned to Chelsea Police Station and wrote a report to Divisional Detective-Inspector Shelley Symes in which she said: "Apart from the fact that I do not like the man Haigh, with his mannerisms, I have a sense that he is 'wrong' and that there may be a case behind the whole business."

Symes respected her judgment sufficiently to ask Scotland Yard's Criminal Record Office to check on whether there was, in the British police phrase, "anything known" about John George Haigh. Within a few hours he learned that something *was* "known", and that Haigh had served three prison sentences—two for fraud and one for theft.

Notorious asylum

On Saturday, February 26, the police forced an entry into the storeroom attached to the Crawley factory and found the stirrup pump, carboys of acid, and a rubber apron bearing traces of blood. From a holster they took a .38 Webley revolver which, after being tested by a firearms expert, was shown to have been recently fired.

Haigh was then "invited" back to the police station to answer further questions. However, before many had been put to him, he, himself, asked one which was to set the pattern of subsequent events. "Tell me frankly," he asked his interrogators. "What are the chances of anybody being released from Broadmoor?"

Realizing he hoped to gain "sanctuary" in the notorious asylum for the criminally insane, the detectives refused to answer him. Haigh then drew heavily on the cigarette he was smoking and said dramatically: "If I tell you the truth you would not believe it. It sounds too fantastic."

Having thus set the scene he continued: "I will tell you all about it. Mrs. Durand-Deacon no longer exists. She has disappeared completely and no trace of her can ever be found again. I have destroyed her with acid. You will find the sludge that remains at Leopold Road, Crawley. Every trace has gone. How can you prove murder if there is no body? . . .

"I shot her in the back of the head. Then I went out to the car and fetched a drinking glass and made an incision, I think with a penknife, in the side of the throat and collected a glass of blood which I then drank."

Two days after putting the body into the acid drum Haigh returned to Crawley, he said, "to find the reaction almost complete" with nothing left of the body but a residue composed of the chemically reduced remains of flesh and bone.

"I emptied off the sludge with a bucket and tipped it on to the ground opposite the storeroom," Haigh explained in careful detail. Then he added: "I should have said that after putting her in the tank and pouring in the acid I went round to the Ancient Priors for tea."

Once more the police returned to Crawley and dug up and removed the patch of soil on to which Haigh said he had emptied the "sludge". When this was methodically sifted and examined at Scotland Yard's laboratory, it became clear that Haigh's assertion that no trace of Mrs. Durand-Deacon would ever be found was ill-based.

Among the 28 lbs. of melted body fat, the pathologists found 18 fragments of human bone, partly eroded by acid but still sufficiently preserved to exhibit traces of arthritis—and thus point to the victim having been an elderly person. In addition, a piece of hipbone was positively identified as female. But, most decisive of all, upper and lower dentures were discovered in an undamaged state, and were proved to have been made for Mrs. Durand-Deacon.

Even though Haigh had failed to "completely erase" the widow's body, his work looked like that of someone experienced in acid baths and killings. Indeed, the police soon learned that he had murdered and similarly disposed of five previous victims in recent years. The first was William Donald McSwann, a young amusement arcade operator, killed in 1944, whose mother and father Haigh shortly afterwards also dispatched. The others were a doctor and his wife, Archibald and Rosalie Henderson, done to death and destroyed in February 1948.

Scandalous case

In each case Haigh acquired the money and other property of his victims by highly skilful forgery. Long after their acid-burned remains had been buried, he wrote business and private letters in impeccable facsimiles of their handwriting, successfully staving off inquiries from relatives and friends.

In a letter postmarked Glasgow, Haigh wrote in a forged hand to Mrs. Henderson's housekeeper in London: "Dear Daisy: We are going to South Africa. Mr. John Haigh has the property now and you will hear from my brother, Arnold Burlin. I want to thank you for the splendid help you have always been and I am sure you must have been while we have been away. If you would like to write, our address until we settle down will be c/o the GPO, Durban, South Africa. Shall always be glad to hear from you. Yours sincerely, Rose Henderson."

In recalling the murders Haigh claimed that "in each case I had my glass of blood after I killed them." It soon became evident that his vampirish ritual would play an important part in his trial—on the charge of murdering Mrs. Durand-Deacon—as "proof" of his insanity. He was duly detained on remand at London's Brixton Prison, and it was then that the London *Daily Mirror* told its 15 million readers of Haigh's supposed activities.

On March 4, 1949, the tabloid appeared with the blazoning front page headline: "Vampire—A Man Held." Underneath, the story began: "The Vampire Killer will never strike again. He is safely behind bars, powerless to lure his victims to a hideous death . . ."

Silvester Bolam, the then editor of the *Mirror,* was brought—in the King's Bench Division of the High Court—before Lord Goddard, the Lord Chief Justice, and Judges Humphreys and Birkett and told: "In the long history of this class of case there has, in the opinion of this Court, never been a case approaching such gravity as this one of such a scandalous and wicked character."

Imposing what they described as "Severe punishment", the High Court judges sentenced Mr. Bolam to three months' imprisonment—in another part of that same jail in which Haigh was being held—and fined the newspaper £10,000, plus the costs of the case.

Once this had been settled, the law once again turned its attention to Haigh. On July 18, 1949, he was put on trial at Lewes, in Sussex. The prosecution was led by Sir Hartley Shawcross, the Attorney-General, and the defence by

EXHIBITS—pieces of bone and the decisive dentures—were carried to and from a pre-trial hearing in a syrup box.

Sir David Maxwell Fyfe—two eminent lawyers who had earned high international reputations for their work at the trial of Nazi war criminals in Nuremberg after World War II.

Despite lengthy legal wranglings over the definition of insanity and the alleged blood-drinking rites, Haigh was found guilty after only a 15-minute retirement by the jury, and sentenced to death.

There were no public expressions of pity for the departed John George Haigh, but there were many of curiosity. How was it, people wondered, that an intelligent boy from a good home should have grown up into such a hideous creature? At the age of 12 he had been an angelic-looking choirboy at Wakefield Cathedral, in Yorkshire, and his parents were devoutly religious Plymouth Brethren.

Brand of Satan

While awaiting execution Haigh wrote: "Although my parents were kind and loving, I had none of the joys, or the companionship, which small children usually have. From my earliest years my recollection is of my father saying: 'Do not' or 'Thou shalt not.' Any form of sport or light entertainment was frowned upon and regarded as not edifying. There was only condemnation and prohibition . . .

"It is true to say that I was nurtured on Bible stories but mostly concerned with sacrifice. If by some mischance I did, or said, anything which my father regarded as improper, he would say: 'Do

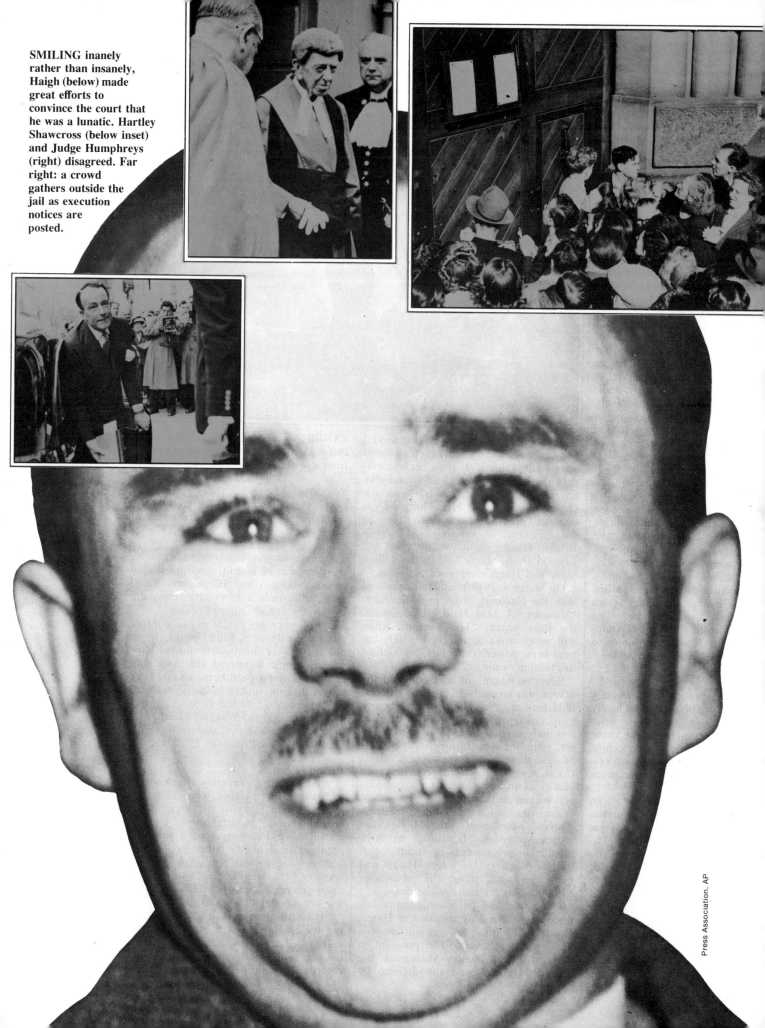

SMILING inanely rather than insanely, Haigh (below) made great efforts to convince the court that he was a lunatic. Hartley Shawcross (below inset) and Judge Humphreys (right) disagreed. Far right: a crowd gathers outside the jail as execution notices are posted.

not grieve the Lord by behaving so.' And if I suggested that I wanted to go somewhere, or meet somebody, he would say: 'It will not please the Lord.' "

According to the same statement, Haigh's father told him that his mother was, literally, "an angel". So that no outside worldly evil might penetrate the sacred home, the couple had built a high wall around the garden of their tiny house in Outwood, Yorkshire. Mr. Haigh, who was a foreman electrician at a nearby colliery, had been struck by a piece of flying coal and, as a result, bore a blue scar on his forehead.

This, the father had explained to the son, was the brand of Satan. "I have sinned and Satan has punished me. If you ever sin, Satan will mark you with a blue pencil likewise." After that, in the night, before sleep came, young John George would pass his fingers, tremulously, across his own forehead to see if he, too, had yet been stamped by Satan's mark.

During his younger days, Haigh asserted, he suffered from dreams in which flowing blood figured prominently. After a car accident in March 1944, in which blood had streamed down his face and into his mouth, the dreams recurred.

"I saw before me," he said, "a forest of crucifixes which gradually turned into trees. At first there appeared to be dew, or rain, dripping from the branches, but as I approached I realized it was blood. Suddenly the whole forest began to writhe and the trees, stark and erect, to ooze blood . . . A man went to each tree catching the blood . . . When the cup was full he approached me. 'Drink,' he said, but I was unable to move."

The dream faded, later to become a waking nightmare for Haigh . . . and to bring eternal sleep to his victims.

THE IMAGINATION of a vampire . . . Haigh's weird, religious background may have turned him into a twisted killer.

Deutsche Presse

THE VAMPIRE OF DUSSELDORF

His mild manners and soft-spoken courteousness placed him above suspicion,
and to most people he appeared to be totally harmless. Yet his bourgeois
exterior concealed one of the most brutal sadists of modern times . . .

AS NIGHT fell across the city that had lived through a year of terror, the streets rapidly emptied. People hurried through the narrow lanes to their homes. Children were plucked from playgrounds and sent to bed. Doors were bolted and curtains drawn. The people were in dread of a creature — a vampire — which had no face, no name, no shape. Already, it had committed 46 violent crimes, displaying every kind of perversion. Five bodies had been taken to the mortuary. But still it remained little more than a spectre.

As the lights went out on the night of August 23, 1929, the people of Düsseldorf, in the German Rhineland, felt almost inured to horror. Nothing more, they thought, could shock them now. As they slept fitfully, they little foresaw that the next few hours would demonstrate the full bestiality of the man they had labelled The Düsseldorf Vampire.

There was one bright and cheerful patch of light that evening. In the suburb of Flehe, hundreds of people were enjoying the annual fair: Old-fashioned merry-go-rounds revolved to the heavy rhythm of German march tunes, stalls dispensed beer and *würst*, there was a comforting feeling of safety and warmth in the closely-packed crowd.

A shadow

At around 10.30, two foster sisters, 5-year-old Gertrude Hamacher and 14-year-old Louise Lenzen, left the fair and started walking through the adjoining allotments to their home. As they did so a shadow broke away from among the beansticks and followed them along a footpath. Louise stopped and turned as a gentle voice said:

"Oh dear, I've forgotten to buy some cigarettes. Look, would you be very kind and go to one of the booths and get some for me? I'll look after the little girl."

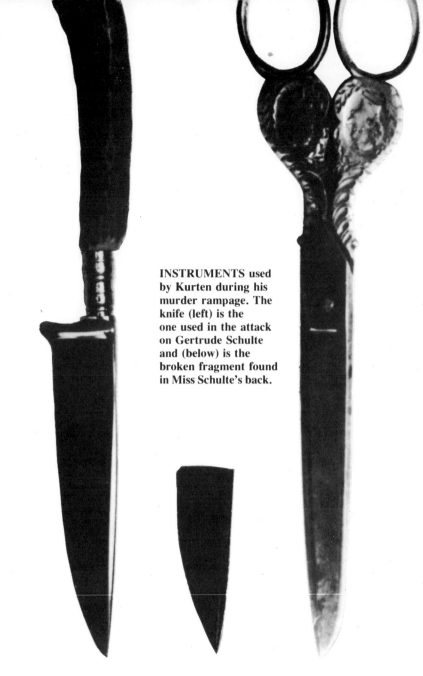

INSTRUMENTS used by Kurten during his murder rampage. The knife (left) is the one used in the attack on Gertrude Schulte and (below) is the broken fragment found in Miss Schulte's back.

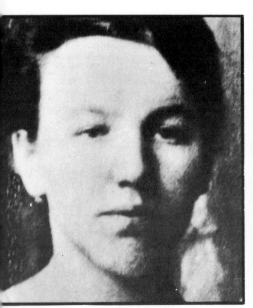

Louise took the man's money and ran back towards the fairground. Quietly, the man picked up Gertrude in his arms and carried her behind the beanpoles. There was no sound as he strangled her and then slowly cut her throat with a Bavarian clasp knife. Louise returned a few moments later and handed over the cigarettes. The man seized her in a stranglehold and started dragging her off the footpath. Louise managed to break away and screamed "Mama! Mama!" The man grabbed her again, strangled her and cut her throat. Then he vanished.

Twelve hours later, Gertrude Schulte, a 26-year-old servant girl, was stopped by a man who offered to take her to the fair at the neighbouring town of Neuss. Foolishly, she agreed. The man introduced himself as Fritz Baumgart and suggested they take a stroll through the woods. Suddenly, he stopped and roughly attempted sexual intercourse. Terrified, Gertrude Schulte pushed him away and screamed, "I'd rather die!"

The man cried "Well, die then!" and began stabbing her frenziedly with a knife. She felt searing pains in her neck and shoulder and a terrific thrust in her back. "Now you can die!" said the man and hurled her away with such force that the knife broke and the blade was left sticking in her back. But Gertrude Schulte didn't die. A passer-by heard her screams and called the police and an ambulance. By then, the attacker had disappeared.

In barely more than half a day, the Düsseldorf maniac had killed two children and attempted to rape and kill another woman. The citizens were stunned as they read their morning papers. Day by day, the attacks continued. Their increasing frequency and ferocity convinced medical experts that the Vampire had lost all control of his sadistic impulses.

In one half-hour, he attacked and wounded a girl of 18, a man of 30, and a woman of 37. The Bavarian dagger gave way to a sharper, thinner blade and then to some kind of blunt instrument. It was the bludgeon that hammered to death two more servant girls, Ida Reuter and Elisabeth Dorrier; the thin blade that killed five-year-old Gertrude Albermann, her body shredded with 36 wounds.

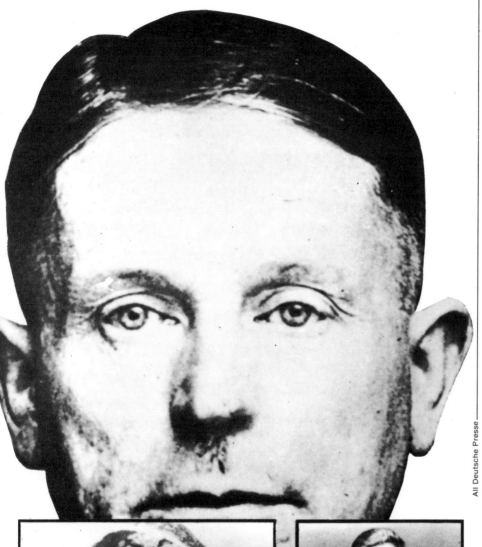

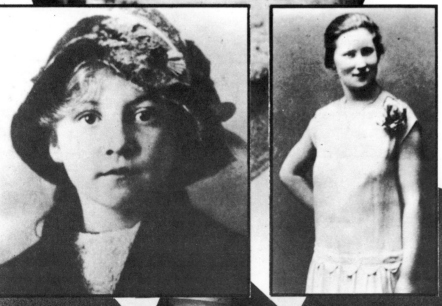

SAVAGED by the Vampire . . . (below from left to right) Ida Reuter, Frau Meurer, Gertrude Albermann, Christine Klein, Maria Hahn and Gertrude Schulte. The latter survived but Kurten (left) fled before her rescuers could spot him.

All Deutsche Presse

·Mettmannerstrasse

Twenty miles away, in the cathedral city of Cologne, a 21-year-old "domestic" named Maria Budlick read the anguished headlines and said to a friend: "Isn't it shocking? Thank goodness we're not in Düsseldorf."

A few weeks later, Maria Budlick lost her job. On May 14, she set out to look for work and boarded a train for Düsseldorf . . . and an unwitting rendezvous with the Vampire.

On the platform at Düsseldorf station, she was accosted by a man who offered to show her the way to a girls' hostel. They followed the brightly-lit streets for a while, but when he started leading her towards the dark trees of the Volksgarten Park she suddenly remembered the stories of the Monster, and refused to go any farther. The man insisted and it was while they were arguing that a second man appeared, as if from nowhere, and inquired softly: "Is everything all right?" The man from the railway station slunk away and Maria Budlick was left alone with her rescuer.

Walk in the woods

Tired and hungry, she agreed to accompany him to his one-room flat in Mettmannerstrasse, where she had a glass of milk and a ham sandwich. The man offered to take her to the hostel, but after a tram ride to the northeastern edge of the city, she realized they were walking deeper and deeper into the Grafenburg Woods. Her companion stopped suddenly and said:

"Do you know now where you are? I can tell you! You are alone with me in the middle of the woods. Now you scream as much as you like and nobody will hear you!"

The man lunged forward, seized her by the throat and tried to have sexual intercourse up against a tree. Maria Budlick struggled violently and was about to lose consciousness when she felt the man's grip relax. "Do you remember

GENTLE vampire's apartment . . . It was to this humdrum room that Kurten led Maria Budlick for a sandwich and a glass of milk before attacking her.

Deutsche Presse

where I live?" he asked. "In case you're ever in need and want my help?" "No," gasped Maria, and in one word saved her own life and signed the death warrant of the Düsseldorf Vampire. The man let her go and showed her out of the woods.

Misdirected letter

But Maria Budlick *had* remembered the address. She vividly recalled the nameplate "Mettmannerstrasse" under the flickering gaslight. And in a letter to a friend the next day, she told of her terrifying experience in the Grafenburg Woods with the quiet, soft-spoken man. The letter never reached her friend. It was misdirected and opened by a Frau Brugman, who took one look at the contents and called the police.

Twenty-four hours later, accompanied by plainclothes detectives, Maria Budlick was walking up and down Mettmannerstrasse trying to pinpoint the quiet man's house. She stopped at No. 71. It looked familiar and she asked the landlady if "a fair-haired, rather sedate man" lived there. The woman took her up to the fourth floor and unlocked a room.

It was the same one in which she had drunk her milk and eaten her sandwich two nights earlier.

She turned round to face even more conclusive proof. The quiet man was coming up the stairs towards her. He looked startled, but carried on to his room and shut the door behind him. A few moments later, he left the house with his hat pulled down over his eyes, passed the two plainclothes men standing in the street and disappeared round a corner.

Maria Budlick ran out and told the officers: "That's the man who assaulted me in the woods. His name is Peter Kurten." So far, nothing linked Kurten with the Vampire. His only crime was suspected rape. But he knew there was no longer any hope of concealing his identity. Early the following morning—after meeting his wife as usual at the restaurant where she worked late—he confessed: "I am the Monster of Düsseldorf."

On May 24, 1930, Frau Kurten told the story to the police, adding that she had arranged to meet her husband outside St. Rochus Church at three o'clock

that afternoon. By that time the whole area was surrounded by armed police. The moment Peter Kurten appeared, four officers rushed forward with loaded revolvers. The man smiled and offered no resistance. "There is no need to be afraid," he said.

Grisly exhibits

After exhaustive questioning, during which he admitted 68 crimes—not including convictions for theft and assault, for which he had already spent a total of 20 years in prison—the trial of the Düsseldorf Vampire opened on April 13, 1931. He was charged with a total of nine murders and seven attempted murders.

Thousands of people crowded round the converted drillhall of the Düsseldorf police headquarters waiting to catch their first glimpse of the depraved creature who had terrorized the city. A special shoulder-

SIXTEEN names appeared on the police list of vampire victims of whom nine were murdered. At the trial, Kurten related the details with obvious relish.

Straftaten und Urteil im Mordprozeß gegen Peter Kürten 13.4.–22.4.1931.

Lfd. Nr.	Name des Opfers	Anklagebehörde — Straftat	Beantragte Strafe	Anträge des Verteidigers	Urteil des Schwurgerichts	Gesamturteil
1	Kind Christine Klein	Mord — Die unzüchtigen Handlungen sind verjährt	Todesstrafe	Totschlag daher bereits verjährt	Todesstrafe	
2	Frau Berta Kühn	Mordversuch in Tateinheit mit versuchter Vornahme unzüchtiger Handlungen	10 Jahre Zuchthaus	gefährliche Körperverletzung	10 Jahre Zuchthaus	
3	Kind Rosa Ohliger	Mord in Tateinheit mit gewaltsamer Vornahme unzüchtiger Handlungen	Todesstrafe	Totschlag	Todesstrafe	
4	Maschinist Rudolf Scheer	Mord	Todesstrafe	Totschlag keine Überlegung	Todesstrafe	
5	Hausangestellte Maria Hahn	Mord in Tateinheit mit gewaltsamer Vornahme unzüchtiger Handlungen	Todesstrafe	Totschlag keine Überlegung	Todesstrafe	
6	Fräulein Anna Goldhausen	Mordversuch	10 Jahre Zuchthaus	gefährliche Körperverletzung	10 Jahre Zuchthaus	
7	Frau Mantel	Mordversuch	5 Jahre Zuchthaus	gefährliche Körperverletzung	5 Jahre Zuchthaus	
8	Arbeiter Kornblum	Mordversuch	5 Jahre Zuchthaus	gefährliche Körperverletzung	5 Jahre Zuchthaus	
9	Kind Hamacher	Mord in Tateinheit mit gewaltsamer Vornahme unzüchtiger Handlungen	Todesstrafe	keine Überlegung Totschlag	Todesstrafe	
10	Kind Luise Lenzen	Mord in Tateinheit mit gewaltsamer Vornahme unzüchtiger Handlungen	Todesstrafe	keine Überlegung Totschlag	Todesstrafe	
11	Gertrud Schulte	Mordversuch in Tateinheit mit versuchter Notzucht	15 Jahre Zuchthaus			
12	Hausangestellte Ida Reuter	Mord in Tateinheit mit vollendeter Notzucht	Todesstrafe			
13	Hausangestellte Elisabeth Dörrier	Mord in Tateinheit mit gewaltsamer Vornahme unzüchtiger Handlungen	Todesstrafe			
14	Frau Meurer	Mordversuch in Tateinheit mit versuchter Vornahme unzüchtiger Handlungen	10 Jahre Zuch...			
15	Frau Wanders	Mordversuch in Tateinheit mit vollendeter Vornahme unzüchtiger Handlungen	5 Jahre Zuch...			
16	Kind Traudchen Albermann	Mord in Tateinheit mit gewaltsamer Vornahme unzüchtiger Handlungen	Todesstrafe			

Urteil:
9 × zum Tode, 15 Jahre Zuchthaus, Stellung unter Polizeiaufsicht und Aberkennung der bürgerlichen Ehrenrechte auf Lebzeit.

Gesamte beantragte Strafe siehe Urteil.

Gesamtstrafe: 9 × zum Tode 60 Jahre Zuchthaus

Deutsche Presse, Hauptstaatsarchiv Düsseldorf

high "cage" had been built inside the courtroom to prevent his escape and behind it were arranged the grisly exhibits of the "Kurten Museum" – the prepared skulls of his victims, showing the various injuries, knives, scissors and a hammer, articles of clothing, and a spade he had used to bury a woman.

The first shock was the physical appearance of the Monster. Despite his appalling crimes, 48-year-old Peter Kurten was far from the maniac of the conventional horror film. He was no Count Dracula with snarling teeth and wild eyes, no lumbering, stitched-together Frankenstein's Monster. There was no sign of the brutal sadist or the weak-lipped degenerate. With his sleek, meticulously parted hair, cloud of Eau de Cologne, immaculate suit, and well-polished shoes, he looked like a prim shopkeeper or minor civil servant.

It was when he started talking that a chill settled over the court. In a quiet, matter-of-fact voice, as if listing the stock of a haberdasher's shop, he described his life of perversion and bloodlust in such clinical detail that even the most hardened courtroom officials paled.

Drunken brute

His crimes were more monstrous than anyone had imagined. The man wasn't a mere psychopath, but a walking textbook of perverted crime: sex maniac, sadist, rapist, vampire, strangler, stabber, hammer-killer, arsonist, a man who committed bestiality with animals, and derived sexual satisfaction from witnessing street accidents and planning disasters involving the deaths of hundreds of people.

And yet he was quite sane. The most brilliant doctors in Germany testified that Kurten had been perfectly responsible for his actions at all times. Further proof of his awareness was provided by the premeditated manner of his crimes, his ability to leave off in the middle of an attack if disturbed, and his astonishing memory for every detail.

How did this inoffensive-looking man become a Vampire? In his flat, unemotional voice, Kurten described a life in which a luckless combination of factors – heredity, environment, the faults of the German penal system – had conspired to bring out and foster the latent sadistic streak with which he had been born.

Kurten described how his childhood was spent in a poverty-stricken, one-room apartment; one of a family of 13 whose father was a drunken brute. There was a long history of alcoholism and mental trouble on the father's side of the family, and his father frequently arrived home drunk, assaulted the children and forced intercourse on his mother. "If they hadn't been married, it would have

been rape," he said. His father was later jailed for three years for committing incest with Kurten's sister, aged 13.

Bestiality

Kurten's sadistic impulses were awakened by the violent scenes in his own home. At the age of nine, a worse influence took over. Kurten became apprenticed to a dogcatcher who lived in the same house, a degenerate who showed him how to torture animals and encouraged him to masturbate them. Around the same time, he drowned a boy while playing on a raft in the Rhine. When the boy's friend dived in to rescue him, Kurten pushed him under the raft and held him down until he suffocated, too.

His sexual urges developed rapidly, and within five years he was committing bestiality with sheep and goats in nearby stables. It was soon after that he "be-

came aware of the pleasure of the sight of blood" and he began to torture animals, achieving orgasm stabbing pigs and sheep.

The terrible pattern of his life was forming. It only needed one more depraved influence to transfer his sadistic urges from animals to human beings. He found it in a prostitute, twice his age, a masochist who enjoyed being ill-treated and abused. His sadistic education was complete and they lived together for some time.

Far from straightening him out, a two-year prison sentence for theft left him bitter and angry at inhuman penal conditions – particularly for adolescents – and introduced him to yet another sadistic refinement, a fantasy world where he

ENCAGED in court, Peter Kurten looked anything but a savage killer. He was smartly dressed, polite and tranquil.

could achieve orgasm by imagining brutal sexual acts. He became so obsessed with these fantasies that he deliberately broke minor prison rules so that he could be sentenced to solitary confinement. It was the ideal atmosphere for sadistic daydreaming.

Shortly after being released from prison, he made his first murderous attack on a girl during sexual intercourse, leaving her for dead in the Grafenburg Woods. No body was ever found and the girl probably crawled away, keeping her terrible secret to herself. More prison sentences followed, for assault and theft. After each jail term, Kurten's feelings of injustice were strengthened. His sexual and sadistic fantasies now involved revenge on society.

THE EVIDENCE . . . Kurten, it turned out, was also a dab hand at arson and police had managed, in several cases, to recover the matches he had used (below). But the killer himself supplied most of evidence, like the map (right) which he drew to show where he buried a victim.

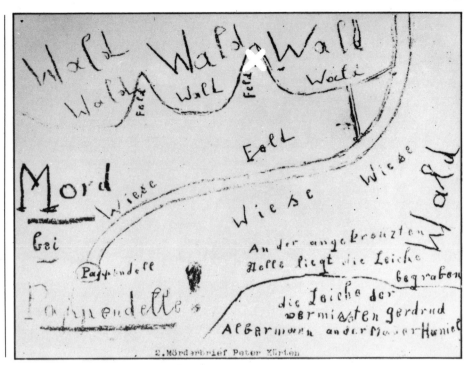

"I thought of myself causing accidents affecting thousands of people and invented a number of crazy fantasies such as smashing bridges and boring through bridge piers," he explained. "Then I spun a number of fantasies with regard to bacilli which I might be able to introduce into the drinking water and so cause a great calamity.

"I imagined myself using schools or orphanages for the purpose, where I could carry out murders by giving away chocolate samples containing arsenic which I could have obtained through housebreaking. I derived the sort of pleasure from these visions that other people would get from thinking about a naked woman."

The court was hypnotized by the revelations. To them, Kurten's narrative sounded like the voice of Satan. It was almost impossible to associate it with the mild figure in the wooden cage. While hysteria and demands for lynching—and worse—reigned outside the court, the trial itself was a model of decorum and humanity, mainly due to the courteous and civilized manner of the Presiding Judge, Dr. Rose. Quietly, he prompted Kurten to describe his bouts of arson and fire-raising . . .

"Yes. When my desire for injuring people awoke, the love of setting fire to things awoke as well. The sight of the flames delighted me, but above all it was the excitement of the attempts to extinguish the fire and the agitation of those who saw their property being destroyed."

The court was deathly quiet, sensing that the almost unspeakable had at last arrived. Gently, Dr. Rose asked, *"Now tell us about Christine Klein . . ."* Kurten pursed his lips for a second as if mentally organizing the details and then—in the unemotional tones of a man recalling a minor business transaction—described the horrible circumstances of his first sex-killing.

"It was on May 25, 1913. I had been stealing, specializing in public bars or inns where the owners lived on the floor above. In a room above an inn at Köln-Mülheim, I discovered a child of 13 asleep. Her head was facing the window. I seized it with my left hand and strangled her for about a minute and a half. The child woke up and struggled but lost consciousness.

"I had a small but sharp pocketknife with me and I held the child's head and cut her throat. I heard the blood spurt and drip on the mat beside the bed. It spurted in an arch, right over my hand. The whole thing lasted about three minutes. Then I locked the door again and went back home to Düsseldorf.

"Next day I went back to Mülheim. There is a cafe opposite the Kleins' place and I sat there and drank a glass of beer and read all about the murder in the papers. People were talking about it all round me. All this amount of indignation and horror did me good."

In the courtroom, the horrors were piling up like bodies in a charnel house. Describing his sexual aberrations, Kurten admitted that the sight of his victims' blood was enough to bring on an orgasm. On several occasions, he drank the blood —once gulping so much that he vomited. He admitted drinking blood from the throat of one victim and from the wound on the temple of another. In another attack, he licked the blood from a victim's hands. He also had an ejaculation after decapitating a swan in a park and placing his mouth over the severed neck.

Everyone in the courtroom realized they were not just attending a sensational trial, but experiencing a unique legal precedent. The prosecution hardly bothered to present any evidence. Kurten's detailed, almost fussy, confession was the most damning evidence of all. Never before had a prisoner convicted himself so utterly; and never before had a courtroom audience been given the opportunity to gaze so deeply into the mind of a maniac.

Bitter sting

Every tiny detail built up a picture of a soul twisted beyond all recognition. Kurten described with enthusiasm how he enjoyed reading *Jack the Ripper* as a child, how he had visited a waxwork Chamber of Horrors and boasted "I'll be in there one day!" The whole court shuddered when, in answer to one question, Kurten pointed to his heart and said: "Gentlemen, you must look in here!"

When the long, ghastly recital was over, Kurten's counsel, Dr. Wehner, had the hopeless task of trying to prove insanity in the face of unbreakable evidence by several distinguished psychiatrists. During Professor Sioli's testimony, Dr. Wehner pleaded:

"Kurten is the king of sexual delinquents because he unites nearly all perversions in one person. Can that not change your opinion about insanity? Is it possible for the Kurten case to persuade psychiatry to adopt another opinion?"

Professor Sioli: "No."

Dr. Wehner: "That is the dreadful thing! The man Kurten is a riddle to me. I cannot solve it. The criminal Haarman only killed men, Landru only women, Grossmann only women, but Kurten killed men, women, children, and animals, killed anything he found!"

Professor Sioli: "And was at the same time a clever man and quite a nice one."

Here was the final twist to the conundrum. The face peeping over the wooden cage was recognizably only too human. Witnesses had spoken of his courteousness and mild manners. Neighbours had refused flatly to believe he was the Vampire. Employers testified to his honesty and reliability. He could charm women to their deaths, indeed was regarded as a local Casanova. His wife had been completely unaware of his double life and had only betrayed him on his insistence, so she could share in the reward for his arrest. Right at the beginning of the Düsseldorf Terror, a former girlfriend who suggested he might be the Vampire was fined by the police for making a malicious accusation.

Some of the bourgeois puritanism which made Kurten so plausible burst out in his final statement before sentence was passed. Speaking hurriedly and gripping the rail, he said:

"My actions as I see them today are so terrible and so horrible that I do not even make an attempt to excuse them. But one bitter sting remains in my mind. When I think of Dr. Wolf and the woman doctor — the two Socialist doctors accused recently of abortions performed on working-class mothers who sought their advice—when I think of the 500 murders they have committed, then I cannot help feeling bitter.

"The real reason for my conviction is that there comes a time in the life of every criminal when he can go no further. And this spiritual collapse is what I experienced. But I do feel that I must make one statement: some of my victims made things very easy for me. Manhunting on the part of women today has taken on such forms that . . ."

At such self-righteousness, Dr. Rose's patience snapped. "Stop these remarks!" he ordered, banging his desk. The jury then took only 1½ hours to reach their verdict: Guilty on all counts. Dr. Rose sentenced him to death nine times.

On the evening of July 1, 1932, Peter Kurten was given the traditional *Henkers-Mahlzeit*, or condemned man's last meal. He asked for Wienerschnitzel, fried potatoes, and a bottle of white wine—which he enjoyed so much that he had it all over again. At six o'clock the following morning, the Vampire of Düsseldorf, a priest on either side, walked briskly to the guillotine erected in the yard of Klingelputz Prison. "Have you any last wish to express?" asked the Attorney-General. Without emotion, almost cheerfully, Kurten replied "No."

For in the few minutes before that walk, and the blow that separated his head from his body, he had already expressed his last, earthly desire. "Tell me," he asked the prison psychiatrist, "after my head has been chopped off, will I still be able to hear, at least for a moment, the sound of my own blood gushing from the stump of my neck?" He savoured the thought for a moment, then added: "That would be the pleasure to end all pleasures."

THE DEADLY TWINS

Protection was their evil
game. But when anyone crossed
them, the Kray Firm, led by
boxing twins Reg and Ronnie and
their brother Charlie, killed
without mercy. Yet for
years the code of silence
in London's East End (above)
helped them to escape
the law. Eventually
that code was broken . . .

BUSINESS was quiet in the bars of the Blind Beggar pub in the East End of London's Whitechapel Road on the evening of March 8, 1966. It was close to 8.30 and there was an hour to go before trade was likely to build up. Almost as a gesture of confidence the barmaid put a record—"The Sun Ain't Gonna Shine Any More"—on the juke box and its brassy notes created the illusion that the pub was about to come to life.

But the pounding beat was no distraction to a dark, pouting customer, George Cornell, absorbed in conversation with two other men in the private bar. Occasionally the talk between the trio was interrupted by short bursts of coarse, tough laughter.

Cornell, perched on a bar stool, sipped slowly at a glass of light ale. He was relaxed, enjoying his hour or so away from his "work" as a more brutal type of petty gangster. His glass was almost empty, and ready for the refill that was never to come, when the door to the bar opened and two men stalked in.

Cornell half turned on his stool and his

THE PUB of death . . . The Blind Beggar, in London's East End. Here, Ronnie Kray (below) mercilessly executed small-time crook George Cornell (inset). With Kray was Ian Barrie (below, right), another of The Firm's gunmen. But people who saw the killing told police nothing.

dark eyes lit with a falsely welcoming smile as he recognized one of the two newcomers, a brooding, boxer-framed man with thick eyebrows that almost collided on the bridge of his long, flared nose. His name was Ronald Kray.

"Well, just look who's here!" cried Cornell, with mock surprise. Neither man answered him, but Kray's companion, a one-time safeblower from Scotland named Ian Barrie, drew a revolver and fired two shots into the ceiling. The barmaid screamed and fled. Cornell and his friends sat frozen, unspeaking. Then, with a melo-dramatic gesture, Ronald Kray pulled a 9-mm Mauser automatic from a shoulder holster and pointed it at Cornell's head.

At the instant that Kray squeezed the trigger, Cornell's mouth sagged in a sudden reaction of disbelief and fear. Then, as the blast of the shot momen-tarily obliterated the racket of the juke box, he toppled from his stool, his fore-head torn open.

Scared barmaid

As quickly as they had arrived, Kray and his henchman disappeared. The frightened barmaid ran back to help the wounded man, but he was beyond all hope. When the summoned ambulance arrived at the hospital there was nothing for the doctors to do but scribble down on their record sheets the letters DOA— dead on arrival.

Within a few hours the whole of the East End of London had heard the whis-pered news that "Ronnie Kray has 'done' a bloke in a pub". It was a fearful piece of information to possess, and however swiftly it passed along the grapevines of Whitechapel, Poplar and Bethnal Green, it was not for the ears of outsiders.

When Superintendent Tommy Butler, the outstanding and almost legendary Scotland Yard detective, arrived to begin his investigations he was met by an Iron Curtain of silence. No one had seen or heard anything. Customers in the pub in-sisted that they had "not been paying any attention".

Butler knew the identity of the killer well enough. He and his men had their own "ears" along the grapevine. But their problem remained what it had been in the East End for so long; the problem that no one with first-hand evidence would dare go into court and testify against 32-year-old Ronnie Kray or his twin brother, Reggie.

In what he was sure would be a fruit-less move, but nevertheless one he must try, Butler put Ronnie Kray into an identi-fication parade at Commercial Street police station.

The unhappy and worried barmaid from the Blind Beggar went through the motions of walking along the line of men and studying their faces. At the end she apologized to Butler. Her memory for faces was not good, and she could not swear that she had seen any of the men in the pub at the time of the murder.

Tommy Butler returned to Scotland Yard, and the newspapers ran the story of the "mystery slaying" for a few days, and then moved on to other headline subjects. The East End, its "villains" and its decent, hardworking people alike, accepted the fact of its life; the fact that The Firm had "got away with it again".

A plague of gangsterism

The Firm was the Kray twins, Ronnie and Reggie. With violence, "protection" and corruption they ruled, from Aldgate Pump to the sprawling docklands, as underworld monarchs, relying on a charter of fear.

In the seventeenth century families had fled from the plague-ridden City of Lon-don to the safe meadows and hamlets that lay to the eastwards. Now, a new plague of gangsterism and vicious greed had come to the vestiges of the slums, and the municipal housing estates and high-rise working-class flats that stretched across the miles where forgotten generations had tended their sheep. The name of the plague was Kray.

Kray is an Austrian name, and no one knows for sure when the founders of the East End branch of the family first arrived in London. But in the pre-war years Charles Kray, a travelling dealer, and his attractive wife, Violet, were living in a modest degree of comfort in Bethnal Green. In 1929 Violet delivered their first-born, Charles David. Four years later, on October 24, 1933, she produced twin boys, Reggie and Ronnie, with Reggie the elder by almost an hour.

Mindless gang

By the time they reached the age of 17 Reggie and Ronnie had developed a taste for brawling which they satisfied partly as leaders of mindless teenage gang war-fare, and partly as lower-grade pro-fessional boxers. It was then already clear that their joint course was pointing away from all the normal social disciplines— and the final, decisive break came in 1952 when they were called up to do their national service.

After a very brief encounter with the Royal Fusiliers they deserted and ended their service period in military prisons, where experience confirmed them in their conviction that they could dominate others through fear. In their own brutish way they were fearless, and nothing excited them so much as to savour the glassy look of fear in other men's eyes.

Their first experimental foray into organized crime on their return to the East End centred on "protection", a small-scale form of the Chicago gangland

activities of the 1920s and 1930s which Ronnie so fervently admired. Knives and cutlasses were among their most favoured weapons, and the twins acquired a following of obedient henchmen by a series of "power demonstrations" in which drinking club or billiard hall managers, reluctant to part with a weekly "pension" for the twins, had themselves or their premises — or both — "done up".

For the twins the highest accolade was that fearful and superstitious East Enders soon found the word "Kray" too ominous to pronounce. So, by universal consent, Ronnie, Reggie and their gang became known by the less oppressive title of The Firm. Ronnie, recognizing that their established "business" must expand, moved on from knives to guns. His first exploit in this new and more exciting realm of weaponry was to lie in wait for a docker who had spoken disrespectfully to a friend, and shoot the man in the leg.

Identity parade

In the investigation that followed, the Krays were able, for the first time, to make good use of their remarkably close physical resemblance. The police, who, like everyone else, had heard that The Firm was involved, arrested Ronnie Kray on suspicion and put him into an identity parade. Without hesitation the docker picked him out as his assailant and the police warned that "you, Ronald Kray" would now be charged with another and more serious offence.

"Yeah? But I'm not Ronnie Kray," said the arrested man. "I'm Reggie Kray, and what's more, I wasn't nowhere near where this bloke says he was shot."

The police grudgingly apologized, released him, and waited for the day when the real Ronnie, now clearly the more violent of the twins, would fall securely into their hands. That day came in 1956. Ronnie decided that a trader named Terry Martin was "taking liberties" — his favourite phrase for anyone who offended him. With a companion's help he dragged Martin from an East End pub and stabbed him in the neck and back with a bayonet. When the police arrived to question him and took possession of a bloodstained shirt, Ronnie quipped: "Well, I 'ad a nose-bleed, din' I?"

He was confident that Martin would not "sing". By that time no one in the East End would risk bringing the wrath of the Krays on themselves or their families. But he fatally miscalculated in this case. Martin appeared at the Old Bailey as the Crown's principal witness, and on November 5 a shocked Ronnie Kray was sentenced to three years' imprisonment.

It was the first major parting between the twins, but, despite some East End predictions, The Firm did not collapse. Instead, Reggie combined a degree of legiti-

Popperfoto

THE MAD AXEMAN . . . Frank Mitchell is led back to jail after trying to escape. But when the Krays (opposite) sprang him from Dartmoor there was no going back. Below left, the twins toast Reggie's bride. But she, too, was to die after two years of unhappy marriage . . .

mate business with crime by renting an empty shop in the Bow Road and converting it into a drinking club he called the Double R — in honour of himself and his absent brother.

Surprisingly content in jail at first, Ronnie soon began to develop marked symptoms of mental instability. He began to hear voices, to imagine that he was surrounded by informers and spies, and he injured several fellow prisoners before being removed to the psychiatric wing of Winchester Jail.

The climax to his mental breakdown followed directly on the news of the death of a favourite aunt — for the Krays, who spared no feelings for the victims they maimed, retained all the sentimentality of a close-knit Cockney family. Two days after the news was delivered, Mrs. Violet Kray, the twins' mother, received an official prison telegram announcing: "Your son, Ronald, certified insane."

From Winchester Ronnie was sent to a security ward in Long Grove Hospital, near Epsom, in Surrey. From there he escaped by working the same identity-

switch plan with Reggie that had rescued him after shooting the docker. One visiting day Reg arrived at the hospital dressed exactly the same as Ron. Reg went out of the ward to fetch the afternoon tea — except that it was not Reg but Ron. When the nurses called upon "Ron" to say goodbye to his visitors he replied: "Ron's gone, I'm Reg."

While on the run, Ronnie found a perfectly respectable Harley Street psychiatrist who, unaware of the true identity of the curious patient worried about his health, pronounced him sane. But the Kray family, resigned to the fact that he obviously needed treatment, decided on the unthinkable and called the police.

Urge to kill

Ronnie was arrested at the family home — known as "The Fort" — in Vallance Road, Bethnal Green, and returned to jail to complete his sentence. By the spring of 1969 he was back in his old haunts, no longer officially certified as insane. All he wanted, to give him a sense of importance and prestige, was to kill someone. He was paranoiac, homosexual and homicidal.

Meanwhile, under Reggie's control, The Firm flourished. Anxious to extend its province and move into the more luscious pastures of the West End, it acquired a profitable and fashionable gaming club, Esmeralda's Barn, in Belgravia's Wilton Place. In the East End the twins contributed to charity as part of a carefully designed move by Reggie to gain "respectability".

They seemed to hold a fascination for the famous. Television personalities, ex-world champion boxers such as Ted "Kid" Lewis, movie stars (including Judy Garland), politicians and local dignitaries supported their charity events and joined in the festivities at their clubs.

The Krays could have had what Reggie wanted: a profitable but trouble-free life with legitimate business as the cream on their criminal cake. But then Ronnie Kray slaked his thirst for blood in the bar of the Blind Beggar by killing George Cornell, hatchet man for the rival south London gang headed by the Richardson brothers, Charles and Eddie. It was a glorious draught he desperately needed his brother to share. After all, they were inseparable twins. In his frequent rages he screamed at Reggie: "I done my one. When are you going to do yours? Are you too soft?"

Ronnie's obsession with death hung over The Firm like a black pall. Pretty little East Ender Frances Shea killed herself in June, 1967, at the age of 23, and after less than two years of unhappy marriage to Reggie. The depressing aura the twins had created around themselves was too much for her. But her death served

only to thrust Reggie further under Ronnie's dark spell. He drove early one morning to the flat of a former friend whom he suspected of making disdainful comments about his late wife and, in front of the man's terrified wife and children, shot him through the leg.

All reason now seemed to leave the megalomaniac twins, and one of their most brutal and bizarre escapades involved the Dartmoor prisoner, Frank Mitchell, dubbed by the press as the "Mad Axe Man" for threatening an elderly couple with a woodsman's axe. Mitchell, a simple-minded man and an old friend of the Krays, was allowed out on the moors on working parties.

Strong-arm man

The Krays, ostensibly because they needed a superior strong-arm man, decided to help him to escape and whisked him away from the moors by car to Barking, near London. There they secreted him in a flat and helped him to write a half-coherent letter to the London *Times* asserting that his escape was intended to draw attention to the fact that he had been held in Dartmoor "during Her Majesty's pleasure"—officialese for an indefinite sentence—and that he would return if granted a specific date of release.

To ease the boredom of Mitchell's days under cover the Krays provided him with a night-club hostess who later declared: "His virility was greater than that of any man I have ever known!" But they very soon tired of the burden of being saddled with the great bear of a man who, in physique and childlike character, was reminiscent of Lennie in John Steinbeck's novel *Of Mice and Men*. Like Lennie, who needed in his confused way to cling to some other human being, Mitchell complicated the situation by falling in love with the girl who was being paid by the Krays to comfort him.

As a final, desperate solution the Krays told Mitchell he was being moved to a "safe" farm in Kent, and, for security's sake, the girl would follow within a few hours. So, after dark on Christmas Eve, 1966, Mitchell was bundled into the back of a van which sped off down the Barking Road, taking him to an unmarked grave. Subsequently at the Old Bailey, Albert Donaghue, Mitchell's escort, alleged that, as soon as the van moved off, two men, waiting inside, poured a fusillade of shots into the axe man's body. Later Donaghue telephoned Reggie Kray with the brief message: "The geezer's gone!"

Still Ronnie criticized his brother because he had not yet personally killed a man. Repeatedly he pointed out that there was no shortage of people "taking liberties". At the top of his list was a squalid, small-time hoodlum named Jack McVitie who, because of vanity about his baldness, was never seen without a hat and had thereby earned the nickname of "Jack the Hat".

Black marks

McVitie had two black marks against him: one for cheating Ronnie over money collected in one of the Krays' enterprises, and the other for failing to fulfil The Firm's orders to kill a former associate. This was to be Reggie's "job". Drunk and sadistic when his boy lovers were absent, Ronnie extolled to Reggie the delight of watching a man's head burst open under a bullet's impact as Cornell's head had done.

Nagged by Ronnie, dispirited by a declining "business"—Esmeralda's Barn had long since collapsed in debt—Reggie gave in. Jack the Hat was lured to a basement flat in Cazenove Road, Stoke Newington, in north London, with the promise of a lively party and all needs catered for. Just before midnight, buoyant and breezy, McVitie arrived demanding: "Where's all the birds and booze?"

THE END . . . the newspaper page that tells of the Krays' downfall. One of the men they killed was Jack McVitie (inset, left). He died at a "party" in a house in Stoke Newington, London (left), stabbed again and again with a carving knife.

Daily Mirror

5d. Wednesday, March 5, 1969   No. 20,276

GUILTY OF MURDER

The Kray Firm's 'directors'.. Reginald, left, and his twin brother Ronald. Picture by DAVID BAILEY

By GEORGE GLENTON and
BRIAN McCONNELL

THE Kray Firm is finally out of business. The twin "directors," Ronald and Reginald Kray, were convicted last night of murder.

Today, the 35-year-old twins and eight henchmen will be sentenced at the Old Bailey after a 39-day trial.

Ronald Kray was convicted of two killings.

One was the murder of 38-year-old George Cornell, who was shot dead in

The Kray twins will be sentenced today

March, 1966, at the Blind Beggar pub, Whitechapel. The other was the stabbing of Jack "The Hat" McVitie in a North London flat in October, 1967.

Reginald Kray was convicted of the McVitie murder. He was also found guilty of being an accessory to the Cornell killing.

The twins' 41-year-old brother, Charles —the judge called him a "consultant" to the Firm—was convicted as an accessory in the McVitie case. His wife Dolly had earlier collapsed in the court's public gallery. She was not there when the verdict was announced. Of the ten men

who had denied being involved in murder, only one was acquitted — club owner Anthony Barry, 30.

He had admitted taking a gun to the flat where Jack McVitie died. But, he said, he did so only through fear of being killed himself.

The nine men convicted yesterday— another had pleaded guilty—were brought up to the dock one at a time to hear the decisions of the twelve-man jury.

As the "guilty" verdicts were announced, there were sounds of weeping from the public gallery.

First to be brought up was Ronald Kray.

He stood, sullen-faced, as the jury foreman—stocky, middle-aged, wearing glasses —delivered the two "guilty" verdicts.

Ronald Kray did not speak. Nor did his twin Reginald.

Gallery

Nor did the other convicted Kray associates — except Christopher Lambrianou, 29, one of McVitie's killers.

He turned and looked up at the public gallery.

"I'll be seeing you," Lambrianou said.

The judge, Mr. Justice Melford Stevenson, ordered: "Let him stand down." Lambrianou was hurried downstairs to the cells below the court.

His brother, Anthony, 26 — also convicted of murdering McVitie — gave a thumbs-up sign to the gallery before leaving the dock.

As the only "not guilty" verdict—on

Turn to Back Page

BACKGROUND TO MURDER

See Pages 4 and 5

and

MIRRORSCOPE Pages 15-18

John Frost

91

Popperfoto

As Ronnie Kray greeted him from his place on the living-room sofa, Reggie sprang from behind the door, pressing the trigger of his .32 automatic. The gun clicked but refused to fire. Reggie threw it away and leapt upon McVitie, who struggled, shouting: "Reg, why are you doing this to me?"

His plea and Reggie's oaths were drowned by the hysterical screaming of Ronnie. "Kill him, Reg! Do him!" he screeched. "Don't stop now!" The terrified McVitie leapt for the window, lost his hat in his failure to get through and, trembling and pale, backed away with sweat pouring from his hairless head. "Be a man, Jack," Ronnie urged. "I'll be a man, but I don't want to die like one," sobbed McVitie.

Those were his last words. In a frenzy Reggie snatched a carving knife and plunged it repeatedly into the helpless victim — into the face, chest and stomach — until, in a deluge of blood, the shattered body of McVitie slid to the floor. From that moment the corpse, like that of Mitchell, disappeared and was never found.

The next day the best-informed East Enders knew that Reggie had evened the score with Ronnie and "done his one". Word seeped through to Scotland Yard, where plans for a swoop on The Firm were nearing completion. At 6 a.m. on May 9, 1968, a specially recruited team of detectives, led by Inspector (later Superintendent) Leonard "Nipper" Read, raided the homes of 24 members of The Firm. Read personally arrested the twins, and when he burst into the flat they were using in Braithwaite House, Shoreditch, east London, Reggie was in bed with a girl, Ronnie with a boy.

A LAST LOOK at the outside world . . . members of the Kray gang peer from the prison van taking them to jail. At last justice is done. The code of silence has been broken. The Firm is out of business.

On March 8, 1969, at the Old Bailey, the Kray twins, together with other members of their gang, including their elder brother, Charles, were charged in the cases of Cornell and McVitie. At last the curtain of East End silence was drawn apart. Specially protected witnesses came forward and told what they had so long feared to tell and, at the age of 35, the Kray twins reached the end of their "business" career.

In sentencing them to life imprisonment, Mr. Justice Melford Stevenson added: "I would recommend that this should be not less than 30 years."

For years the Richardson brothers and their gang of vicious hoodlums terrorized all south London with their remorseless violence. For the sake of "security" they beat and mutilated all potential informers — calmly munching fish and chips as their victims bled and writhed in agony. Any juror would have been brave indeed to vote for conviction. . . .

THE FRATERNITY OF TORTURE

THE most notable factor about the appearance of 32-year-old Charles William Richardson in the prisoner's dock of London's Central Criminal Court was that it ever happened at all. Many people —especially senior officers of Scotland Yard—had long thought it the proper place for Richardson to be. But most had suffered the frustrating belief that he would never be seen there—and Charles William Richardson himself had held it, as a matter of faith, that he would never cross the Old Bailey's threshold.

Not only was he among the most vicious of London's criminal thugs, but he was one of a select underworld band who had taken almost total security measures to ensure that no witness would dare to point a finger at them and say: "These men are evil—and I can prove them to be so."

In Richardson's case the "security measures" involved torture to "persuade" the would-be informers to maintain their silence. So it was that Richardson was as much surprised as the authorities, that

TORTURE CHAMBER and "office", this seedy warehouse in a remote south London suburb was often the end of the line for victims of the Richardson gang who were recruited in the Astor Club (below).

April day in 1967, when he found himself arraigned for trial.

With seven of his henchmen—the "Richardson Gang"—he stood charged with the violence and intimidation with which he had built, over several years, a criminal empire in the densely packed tenement and high-rise housing estate areas of London that stretch south from the Thames.

On the charge sheet he was described as a "company director". But, as the evidence was to show, his "company" consisted of a motley collection of executives who made their profits from shady deals, and whose "labour relations" were based upon the theory that dissident employees or business associates were best kept in line by being stripped naked and given electric shock treatment.

Latter-day Capone

Richardson moved in a criminal world that was a scaled-down replica of the Prohibition era of Chicago and its mobs, and he liked to think of himself as a kind of latter-day Al Capone. As he stepped into the dock in his £50 suit there was an air of arrogance on his chubby features. This was reinforced by the deliberately careless manner in which he bore his stocky, boxerlike frame. When the charges of violence were put to him he snapped out: "Not guilty."

The Crown had decided to concentrate on the torture and other forms of violence, and not upon the actual criminal activities of the Richardson gang. Mr. Sebag Shaw, leading the prosecution, made that clear to the jury in the first few moments of his opening speech. Charles Richardson, he told the 11 men and one woman in the jurybox, was the dominant leader of a "somewhat disreputable business fraternity" who operated through a number of phoney companies.

"But," he said, with a wave of his arm, "this case is not about dishonesty or fraud; it is about violence and threats of violence. Not, let me say, casual acts of violence, committed in sudden anger—but vicious and brutal violence systematically inflicted, deliberately and cold-bloodedly and with utter and callous ruthlessness."

Beatings and torture of people who upset Richardson—or who were even suspected of jeopardizing his "business" career—ensured that no one ever complained to the authorities about south London gangsterism. Such methods had succeeded for years until, finally, some of the sufferers had told their disgruntled stories to the police.

The first of the alleged victims to be seen by the jury was Jack Duval, born in Russia in 1919, and a one-time French legionnaire. He acknowledged that he had come to the Old Bailey that day from

prison, where he was serving a three-year sentence for an airline tickets fraud.

Duval was asked to recall a day in 1960, and did so in tones that suggested it was the unluckiest day of his life. That was the day on which he was first introduced to Richardson—in the Astor Club, off London's Berkeley Square. Very soon he was serving his apprenticeship as European representative for one of the gang's "companies"—whose main purpose was to import Italian-made nylon stockings on credit and then omit to pay the bills. His efforts were not of a high standard, and he was recalled to London.

He duly reported to the Richardson headquarters in south London's Camberwell, where he was greeted by Edward Richardson, the gang leader's younger brother, who "punched me in the face. Then, when I fell down, I was beaten with golf clubs. When I asked what I had done to deserve that, Edward Richardson said, 'You just do as Charlie tells you.'"

Later, still serving as a loyal employee, he was sent to Germany to order goods on credit for the Common Market Merchants Ltd.—another of the Richardsons' concerns.

"I was in Germany for about eight weeks," said Duval wistfully. Then, once again, his return to "head office" turned out to be a far from festive occasion. The greeting he received from Charles Richardson was in the traditional gang fashion. "As I entered the Camberwell office," said Duval, "Mr. Richardson hit me with his fist, and I still have the mark on the side of my nose from his ring."

Relating his ordeal

Members of the jury peered at Duval to see the scar. But, in the excitement of relating his ordeal, he was moving his head too rapidly from side to side. "When I came to," he recalled, "I found I had been relieved of my watch, ring and wallet containing 200 dollars. Mr. Richardson was sitting behind his big desk with chairs all around, like a court."

But "Mr. Richardson" was far from behaving with the decorum of a judge. He was, in fact, selecting knives from a canteen of cutlery, and throwing them in the direction of a Mr. Alfred Blore—the manager of Common Market Merchants. The knives, some of which were striking Blore in the arm, were intended to draw Blore's attention to his business failings.

According to Duval, Richardson "kept saying to Blore: 'I'm the boss and if I tell you what to do you will do it.' Mr. Blore asked, 'What have I done, Charlie?' Naturally, I was quiet; sitting in my corner. Mr. Blore was screaming: 'Don't do it to me!'" The crux of the matter, Duval explained to the jury, was that "Mr. Blore came in as a director of Common Market Merchants and he did not

want to run the company under the orders of Mr. Charles Richardson."

Other cronies of Richardson, minor "executives" of the company, had been lurking on the fringes of the bizarre Camberwell office-cum-courtroom, and two were ordered to go to Common Market Merchants' office in Cannon Street (in the square-mile business section of London called "the City") "and collect the stock and books and make it look as if there had been a robbery". The reason for that, Duval drily testified, was that by then Mr. Blore "was covered in blood", and if any questions were asked it would be said that he had been attacked during the supposed robbery.

Mr. Geoffrey Crispin, defending Richardson, suggested that it was Duval, and *not* Charles Richardson, who was the real gang leader. Duval agreed that he had lived a life of fraud, involving large sums of money. But he denied that in the fraudulent companies run by the gang he was, as Mr. Crispin put it, "the guvnor".

A guest of Her Majesty

Sharply, Duval told the lawyer: "I have never been the boss. I have worked for Charles Richardson because I had to." But, continued Mr. Crispin, Duval was hoping to receive a large sum of money by selling his life story to the newspapers. Duval had a swift answer to that. "I am," he said, haughtily, "at present a guest of Her Majesty and cannot indulge in any business activities while I am in prison."

Duval was followed into the witness box by a nervous, 38-year-old Polish-born businessman, Bernard Wajcenberg, whose dealings with Richardson and his "firm" had also been of an unhappy nature. He, it appeared, had sought business "references" about Richardson from the police—a move which had met with Richardson's disapproval. At a meeting in the notorious Camberwell office—at which Wajcenberg was "so paralyzed with fear I could not speak"—Richardson told him: "You have ratted by making inquiries about me from the police. If you don't pay £5000 you will not get out of this office alive."

To add weight to his threat, Richardson showed Wajcenberg a cupboard stocked with knives, axes, and a shotgun. Hoarsely, the witness told the jury: "Richardson grabbed me by the lapels and said, 'When I go berserk you know what happens.'" Wajcenberg did know and took swift steps to borrow £3000, which Richardson accepted in settlement.

ARROGANCE characterized the tough appearance of Charles Richardson (left), which was reinforced by the careless way he carried himself. Charles was sentenced to 25 years, his brother Edward, who was already in prison, 10.

Derek John Lucien Harris, another business associate of Richardson's, was not so fortunate as Wajcenberg. He had been selected as victim for the most sophisticated form of torture employed by the "firm"—torture by electric shock. Harris testified that this had happened in June, 1964, when he was negotiating the sale of a company to Richardson, and called at the Camberwell office to collect money owing to him.

Since Richardson was in the habit of receiving, rather than paying, money, this was an unwise approach by Harris—who was taken by some of the gang's gorillas to a nearby warehouse. There Richardson greeted him with the pained comment: "I like you, Lucien, and I don't want to hurt you." Then, aided by another member of the gang, he proceeded to beat Harris up. On tiring of that, the gang boss muttered orders to a couple of his men, who left and returned a few minutes later. One carried a parcel of scampi; the other a hand-operated electric generator of the type used for testing car spark-plugs.

Bound and gagged

"Everyone," Harris recalled, "began eating. After he had finished, Charles Richardson screwed his thumbs in my eyes. It was very painful, and I could not see for some moments. On Richardson's instructions my shoes were removed, and my toes were wired up to the generator. Roy Hall [another member of the gang] turned the handle, and the shock caused me to jump out of my chair, and I fell to the floor.

"After that I was stripped except for my shirt, and the shock treatment was repeated. As I rolled on the floor Richardson said the generator wasn't working very well and orange squash was poured over my feet. Then I was bound and gagged and given further electric shocks to various parts of my body. Finally, Richardson said I was to be taken to the marshes where I gathered I would be killed and dumped under a pile of refuse."

As he was dressing after the "treatment", Harris said, Richardson pinned his left foot to the floor with a knife. On the instructions of the judge, Mr. Justice Lawton, Harris then removed the shoe and sock from his left foot and rested the foot on a chair in the witness box. For the next 10 minutes the attention in the courtroom was wholly concentrated on the Harris foot. First the judge came down from his bench to examine it, then the members of the jury filed past it, in pairs. Finally, it was surrounded by the barristers on both sides of the trial, Crown and defence.

Two scars were visible on the foot, and Harris pointed to each during the inspections and repeated, again and again: "The knife went in there and came out here."

Altogether, he said, his session in the warehouse torture chamber lasted for six hours—at the end of which the mercurial Richardson "apologized and then gave me £150".

Next another victim of the shock treatment, a man named Benjamin Coulston, told the court that he, too, had undergone a six-hour torture ordeal. He was stripped naked, some of his teeth were torn out with a pair of pliers, lighted cigars were stubbed out on his arms and legs, and he was "toasted" on face and body by a closely held electric heater. As an endpiece to the session he was bundled into a tarpaulin sheet, along with two 14-lb. weights, and from inside the shroud he heard Richardson say: "Get rid of him."

Coulston stared at the jury with saddened eyes. "I thought I was going to be dumped in the river," he said. "And all the time this was happening Richardson and the others were drinking, laughing, smoking and enjoying the fun." But, luckily for him, Richardson wearied of the episode once the victim's terror had been savoured and ordered him to be released. "He gave me a new shirt," said Coulston, "and his brother, Edward, drove me home."

Other victims came to the witness box to recount similar experiences in the firm's office and warehouse. One man—who had been beaten and burned and had his toes broken—heard the screams of another sufferer as he lay in a hole,

16 men and a[ ]
accused in Lor[ ]
TORTUR[E]
CHAIR[S]

THE 17 ACCUSED

THE accused are:

Charles William Richardson, aged 32, company director, of Acland Crescent, Denmark Hill. His wife, Mrs. Jean Richardson.

Roy Hall, aged 25, metal sorter of Rangefield Road, Bromley, Kent.

Derek Brian Mottram, aged 32, caterer, of Somers Road, Balham.

Albert John Longman, aged 40, director of no settled address.

Thomas Clarke, aged 33, unemployed, of Fulham Road, Fulham.

James Henry Kensitt, aged 51, salesman, of Homer Road, Croydon.

James Thomas Fraser, aged 24, porter, of Midwell Street, Walworth.

Robert Geoffrey St. Leger, aged 44, dealer, of Broomhill

Counsel tell[s]
pattern of vic[ ]

'.. WHEN ANYONE INCURRED [THE DISPLEASURE]
OF CHARLES WILLIAM RIC[HARDSON]

Evening News repo[rters]
Stephen Claypole, John [ ]
Aldo Nicolotti[ ]

woman

lon

IN ELECTRIC CROWN

YOUR WEATHER

The Meteorological Office states:

6 A.M. TO MIDNIGHT TOMORROW: Rather cloudy but some sunny intervals, scattered showers, moderate north-westerly winds, temperatures near or a little below normal, maximum 18 degrees C., 64 degrees F. OUTLOOK: Changeable with further rain or showers at times, but some sunny intervals especially in the south-east. CHANNEL: Sea moderate. BAROMETER (2 p.m.): 29.56in., steady.

Lighting-up time 8.22 p.m. until 5.40 a.m. tomorrow. Sun sets 7.52 p.m., rises tomorrow 6.10 a.m. Moon rises 8.14 p.m., sets tomorrow 6.12 a.m. Full moon tomorrow. High water London Bridge 2.42 a.m., 2.49 p.m. Tomorrow 3.20 a.m., 3.21 p.m.

**FIRST WITH THE NEWS
RING FLEET ST 6000**

Epoque

John Frost

of

ence

*'PLEASURE
DSON'*

rs

by and

'I won't be at talks' —Kaunda snub for Wilson

By MAURICE ROMILLY

MR. WILSON was snubbed today by President Kaunda of Zambia, who let it be known that he is staying away from next week's Commonwealth

TOWN HALL
URGENT STAFF VACANCIES

Gus

" I could put in four hours' clerical work every week-end until I'd worked off my rates."

ROCKS
SITY

LAUGHING, drinking, smoking and enjoying the fun . . . while the victim suffered the agony of shock treatment and "toasting" with an electric heater. Then Charles (right) would give the victim a new shirt, and brother Edward would drive him home.

beneath a trap door, into which he had been thrown when his torturers had finished with him.

The highlight of the trial came on the morning on which Richardson himself finally entered the box to tell his own story. Tough and self-assured, his defence was based on the simple line that all the evidence against him was perjured. Duval's story was an example, and he blandly told the jury: "It is something out of a storybook and never happened at any time. It is a ridiculous allegation that I should beat him up just to do what I told him to."

Had he ever attacked anyone? he was asked. He looked around the courtroom with the smile of a man who would endeavour, patiently, to answer all nonsensical questions. Of course he had never attacked anyone. "Never had a cross word," he declared. "They are a lot of clever fraudsmen, putting these allegations and getting out of their own frauds by blaming me for these incidents."

On a table in the well of the court stood the electric generator said to have been the principal torture machine. But Richardson eyed it as though it were some totally mysterious piece of equipment. "That's the only one of those I've ever seen," he insisted. "I have never owned one, and I don't know anyone who has." He looked at the machine again. "It's a conspiracy," he said. "It's a tissue of lies. These people have ganged up against me."

Alive and well

One moment of humour came when prosecuting counsel, seeking information about a potential witness whom the police had been unable to trace, asked Richardson: "Is this man alive and well?" With mock exasperation, Richardson retorted: "You keep asking me all the time if people are alive and well, and I object to it. It has a very serious inference!"

Richardson was followed into the stand by his henchman Roy Hall, who was alleged to have operated the electric generator. But, like his boss, he firmly declared that he had never before seen such a machine. What was more, he added, he had never seen the two victims, Harris and Coulston, "never in my life before I saw them in the magistrate's court. I am an innocent, hard-working man. Prosecution witnesses have tried to frame me."

The jury witnessed a parade of other gang members alleged to have acted as assistants to the chief torturer. One was the man said to have attempted to draw a victim's teeth with pliers, and who succeeded only in tearing the man's gums. Again, he had done nothing, seen nothing, knew nobody. On the day that the loudest screams were being enjoyed by the scampi-eating gang—and the electric generator was emitting its agonizing stream of current—he was busy putting flowers on the grave of his wife's father.

For the Crown, Mr. Sebag Shaw summed up this, and similar defence evidence, as "poppycock produced in the hope of creating a smokescreen through which you, the members of the jury, would not be able to see. But this trial is concerned with matters of the gravest import to society. If the charges made out are well founded, it reveals a canker in our midst which, if unchecked, would undermine the civilized society in which we live." Of Richardson, he said: "He was the man of power who could get things done and who could succeed by his methods where other methods had failed."

But it was on the 38th day of the trial—the longest trial so far in British criminal history—that an important and significant announcement came from the judge. He had been informed, he said, that threats had been made to members of the jury that "there had better be a disagreement in the Richardson case". One threat had been hastily whispered to a juryman's 75-year-old mother as she waited at a bus stop. Similar "warnings" had been given to other jurymen by telephone.

Mr. Justice Lawton, careful to preserve the fair-trial rights of the prisoners, told the jury: "Whatever has happened must have been done without the co-operation of the defendants, most of whom have been in custody since last July.

"But, unfortunately, whenever there is a trial of this kind it attracts publicity, and there are busybodies, evil-wishers, misguided acquaintances and friends who will interfere. When they do interfere there is a danger that a jury might take the view that what did happen came about as the result of the intervention of the defendants. Now that I have pointed out the position to you I am confident that no such view will be taken by you."

All the same, the judge went on, a special police telephone post had been set up with a secret number for jurymen to ring immediately, at any hour, if they were approached again. "A police patrol car will be on the scene within minutes," Mr. Lawton added.

New trial threat

The judge repeated his concern over the issue in his detailed summing up of the trial. There was "not a scrap of evidence," he warned, that Richardson and his fellow defendants had been parties to the jury threats, and the jurors must put the matter out of their minds in reaching their verdicts. He reminded the jury of the importance of a unanimous decision. "If you cannot agree, there will have to be a new trial," he told them. "Just think what that will mean."

Mr. Justice Lawton spent three days on his summing up—one of the longest addresses ever made from the bench—and on June 7 the jurors retired for nine hours and 26 minutes. As they finally filed back into court, many of them showing signs of fatigue, the eight men in the dock stared anxiously at them. The list of charges was long, and it took time for the foreman to deliver the several verdicts. Richardson and five other gang members were found guilty of some—although not all—of the charges against them.

Richardson, pronounced guilty on nine counts, told the judge, "I am completely innocent of these charges." But he and the rest still had to wait before hearing their sentences. Mr. Justice Lawton said he would hand down verdicts the following day. Meanwhile he discharged the jury "from your long, wearisome and worrying time" but added: "You are not concerned with sentencing, but having regard to your long connection with the case you might like to be in court to-morrow."

The jury accepted his invitation and were back at the Old Bailey the next morning to hear the judge sentence Charles Richardson to 25 years' imprisonment. Mr. Justice Lawton told him: "I have come to the conclusion that no known penal system will cure you but time. The only thing that will cure you is the passing of the years.

Sadistic disgrace

"I am satisfied that over a period of years you were the leader of a large, disciplined, well led, well organized gang, and that for purposes of your own material interests, and on occasions for purposes of your criminal desires, you terrorized those who crossed your path, terrorized them in a way that was vicious, sadistic and a disgrace to society.

"When I remember some of the evidence of your brutality I am ashamed to think that one lives in a society that contains men like you. It must be clear to all those who set themselves up as gang leaders that they will be struck down by the law as you are struck down."

Richardson stared, tight-lipped, at the judge as the sentence was delivered. Then, as three police officers formed a guard around him to take him to the cells below the courtroom, he turned to the jury and snarled: "Thank you—very much!" Sentences ranging from eight to ten years were given to the other guilty defendants. Edward Richardson, the gang boss's brother, collected one of the 10-year sentences, which was to follow the five years he was currently serving for other offences.

It was the end of the notorious Richardson gang, and it had been achieved through the concentrated efforts of a team of 100 policemen. As his last duty in the trial the judge called before him the dozen senior detectives of the team—including young, blonde Woman Police-Constable Gillian Hoptroff.

Mr. Justice Lawton told the police team: "I want to thank all of you on behalf of the court—and I think I am speaking on behalf of every law-abiding citizen in this country—for the work you have done in breaking up one of the most dangerous gangs I have ever heard of."

THE SOCIALITE AND THE PLAYBOY

Thaw and White . . . and the champagne murder at Madison Square Garden

New York socialites had packed into Madison Square Garden for the opening of a new musical, *Mamzelle Champagne*. The show was not going well. In the informal atmosphere of the roof garden, where everyone sat at tables instead of in conventional theatre seats, people moved about, chatting with friends. Suddenly there was a gunshot, followed by two more. Every eye turned to Stanford White, at 52 America's most distinguished architect. Slowly his elbow slipped from the table at which he had been sitting alone. The table overturned with a tinkle

of breaking glass, and White slumped to the floor with a bullet in his brain and two more in his left shoulder.

Over him, unmoved, a smoking pistol in his hand, stood Harry Kendall Thaw, 34-year-old playboy and wastrel son of a Pittsburgh railroad and coke magnate. There was silence for a moment. Then Thaw, the pistol held above his head, made his way out of the roof garden to join his wife, Evelyn, and two guests in the elevator lobby.

They had all got up to leave a few moments earlier at Evelyn's instigation

SENSATIONAL SHOOTING: The gunman was the son of a railroad magnate . . . the victim was the most famous architect in all America.

because the show was so boring. She had reached the lobby with the guests before realizing that her husband was not with them. Then came the shots. "Good God, Harry, what have you done?" she asked in bewilderment as he joined them with the pistol still clutched over his head.

Meantime, back in the roof garden, screaming women fought their way to the

101

HER BEAUTY was as vague and intangible as that of a lily, or any other frail or delicate thing. It lay over her face like a gossamer veil . . . and she haunted Harry Thaw even in his cell, according to a newspaper cartoonist on the New York "Evening Journal". But (right) he did not forego all his pleasures in prison—breakfast was still a lavish occasion.

Culver

exit. The manager tried to restore order by jumping on a table and shouting: "Go on playing. Bring on the chorus." The shock of having a murder committed before their eyes, however, seemed to have paralyzed both musicians and chorus girls. Then a doctor fought his way through the stampeding audience to White's side. He lay in a pool of blood, his face blackened and unrecognizable from powder burns. He was already dead.

Out in the elevator lobby, a fireman disarmed Thaw, who did not offer any resistance. A few moments later a policeman arrived and arrested him. Together they walked to the nearest police station in the Tenderloin—a district notorious for its prostitution, lawlessness, and graft. There Thaw identified himself as "John Smith", a student, of 18 Lafayette Square, Philadelphia. A visiting card found on him when he was searched, however, revealed his real name.

Great party-goer

Thaw made no comment. "Why did you do this?" the sergeant in charge asked him. "I can't say," Thaw answered laconically. Several reporters had tracked him down by this time, but Thaw—at least until he had consulted his lawyer—refused to make any further statement.

The shooting took place on the night of June 25, 1906. The next day it dominated the front pages of newspapers across

the United States. Even the New York *Times,* not given to sensationalism, ran the heading:

THAW MURDERS STANFORD WHITE

Shoots Him on the Madison Square Garden Roof

ABOUT EVELYN NESBIT

"You've Ruined My Life," He Cries and Fires

AUDIENCE IN A PANIC

Chairs and Tables Are Overturned in a Wild Scramble For the Exits

Stanford White, a big man with a thatch of red hair and a moustache to match, was a national figure. He has been credited with being the greatest single influence in beautifying the rather drab, brownstone New York City of the nineteenth century. Madison Square Garden itself, with its amphitheatre for horse shows and prize fights, and its theatre, roof garden, restaurant, and arcade of fashionable shops, was his creation. So were the memorial arch at Washington Square and the Hall of Fame at New York university.

But there was another side to the dignified architect. He enjoyed mixing in theatrical and Bohemian circles, was a great party-goer, and, although married, had a quick eye for a pretty girl. In fact, it was only the stage manager's promise to introduce him to a chorus girl who

had taken his fancy, that kept him sitting through the dull *Mamzelle Champagne.*

For his part, Thaw's life had consisted of one notorious escapade after another. During a brief spell at Harvard, he had devoted himself almost exclusively to studying the finer points of poker. Later, he tried to ride a horse into one of several exclusive New York clubs which had barred him. He had also driven a car through a display window, lost $40,000 in a single poker game, and thrown a party in Paris at which his guests were the French capital's leading whores.

Unspecified services

The bill for the Paris party, including jewellery and trinkets handed out to his guests for unspecified services rendered, was said to be $50,000. It was hardly surprising, therefore, that on the death of his father, Thaw found himself cut off with an allowance of $200 a month until such time as he showed himself responsible enough to handle his $5 million share of the $40 million estate. However, his doting mother, Mrs. William Thaw, enabled him to resume the wastrel's life he enjoyed by upping his allowance again to $80,000 a year.

As might be expected, it was sex that led to the tragic crossing of the paths of White and Thaw. Thaw's wife was the former Evelyn Nesbit, a photographer's model who graduated to the chorus of the famous musical *Floradora*. She was one of the beauties asked nightly: "Tell me, pretty maiden, are there any more at home like you?"

She had an oval face, copper curls, hazel eyes, a voluptuous mouth, and a splendid figure. When Thaw eventually came to trial, and his wife was called to give evidence, columnist Dorothy Dix, wrote: "Her beauty consists in something as vague and intangible as that of a lily or any other frail or delicate thing. It is something that lies over her face like a gossamer veil, infinitely appealing . . ."

Despite, or possibly because of, her apparent frailty, White had seduced her when she was just 16. Thaw had married her on April 4, 1905 – 14 months before the shooting – when she was 20. In the interval, he had twice lived with her as man and wife on trips to Europe, and had caused a major New York scandal when the two of them were evicted from a hotel where they were again cohabiting.

In the events which followed the shooting, the principals fell into roles as clearly defined as those in an old-fashioned melodrama. White was the aging roué, seducer of young girls . . . Thaw the chivalrous avenger, who dwelt so long on his wife's dishonouring that he eventually had a "brainstorm" and killed the man who had wronged her . . . Evelyn, the young innocent, brought to a life of shame by a man she looked upon almost as a father, now standing loyally by the man she loved, the man who had made an honest woman of her.

Mrs. Thaw, Senr., who was in England visiting her daughter, the Countess of Yarmouth, also announced that she was returning to the United States to stand by her son. "I am prepared to pay a million dollars to save his life," she said.

Thaw's trial did not begin until January 21, 1907. In the intervening seven months, White underwent a character assassination in the newspapers that was unprecedented for an American of distinction moving in respectable society. There were so many tales about his amorous activities that, for even half to be true, he would have had to have slept with a large proportion of the women and teenage girls in New York.

A typical story concerned a 15-year-old model, Susie Johnson, who had been the highlight of a Bohemian party which White attended. She had risen out of a giant pie and exhibited her charms – "lilliputian, tender, rose-coloured breasts, and evasive hips, proclaiming precocious puberty" – clad only in a wisp of chiffon.

White was so taken with her, the story in the New York *Evening Journal* went on, that he plied her with champagne and, when she was in a stupefied condition, took her back to his apartment – "furnished with Oriental splendour" – and seduced her. Later, he turned her out penniless. "Girls, if you are poor, stay in the safe factory or kitchen," were the last words of the story which, it was said, Susie had told to a friend before dying at the age of 23 and being buried in a pauper's grave.

The campaign of slander and vilification against White was masterminded by Ben Atwell, a press agent hired by Thaw's mother. Mrs. Thaw Senr. also backed a play based loosely on the construction which the yellow press put on the known events.

Gave girls swings

It featured three characters named Harold Daw, Emeline Hudspeth Daw, and Stanford Black. On his first appearance, Black brutally assaulted a blind man who was asking for news of his beautiful young daughter. The Girl in the Pie incident was featured in another lurid scene. The play ended with Daw shooting Black during a performance in a roof garden theatre, then declaring from his cell at The Tombs (where Thaw was being held awaiting trial):

"No jury on earth will send me to the

chair, no matter what I have done or what I have been, for killing the man who defamed my wife. That is the unwritten law made by men themselves, and upon its virtue I will stake my life."

There is evidence that the episode with Susie Johnson did take place at a party, given by an artist friend, which White attended. It seems probable, however, that the seduction part of the tale was inspired by what happened to Evelyn Nesbit before she became Mrs. Harry Thaw, and was seen as a useful overture to the story she would tell in court.

Evelyn first met White in the summer of 1901 when she was 16 and a girlfriend took her to lunch at the architect's apartment on West 24th Street. A second man was there but left after the meal. White then took the two girls upstairs to a room where there was a red velvet swing. He gave the girls swings in turn. "Right up to the ceiling," Evelyn recalled. "They had a big Japanese umbrella on the ceiling, so when we were swung up very high our feet passed through it."

White did not lose touch with his new discovery. He met her mother by arrangement and suggested that Evelyn should have some dental treatment. He sent her a hat, a feather boa, and a long red cape.

Throughout, he always behaved with the utmost correctness. "At supper," said Evelyn, "he wouldn't let me have but one glass of champagne, and he said

I mustn't stay up late. He took me home himself to the Arlington Hotel, where we were staying, and knocked at my mother's door."

Then came the day when Evelyn's mother decided to visit friends in Pittsburgh, but did not like to leave her daughter alone in New York. When he heard of this, White immediately offered his services. "You may leave her with me in perfect safety," he said. "I will take care of her." He also made Evelyn promise that she would not go out with anyone but him while her mother was away.

Mirrors round bed

White paid for her mother's trip and, the second night after her departure, sent a note to the theatre – Evelyn by this time was appearing in *Floradora* – asking her to a party at the West 24th Street apartment. When she got there, however, there were just the two of them. "The others have turned us down," White explained somewhat lamely.

He suggested they should have something to eat nevertheless, and afterwards offered to show her the rooms she hadn't seen on her previous visit. He took her up some tiny back stairs to a bedroom. "He poured me a glass of champagne," said Evelyn. "I don't know whether it was a minute after or two minutes after, but a pounding began in my ears, then the whole room seemed to go round."

When she came to, she said, she was in bed. All her clothes had been torn off. White, naked, lay beside her. There were mirrors all round the bed. "I started to scream," she said. "Mr. White tried to quieten me. I don't remember how I got my clothes on or how I went home, but he took me home. Then he went away and left me, and I sat up all night."

White called the next day and found her still sitting in a chair, staring out of the window. "Why don't you look at me, child?" he asked. "Because I can't," she replied. Then he told her not to worry because "everyone does those things". She asked if the *Floradora* sextet, and various people she had met with White, made love. "They all do," he said, adding that the most important thing was not to be found out, and making her promise not to say a word to her mother about what had happened.

Amid all the subsequent mudslinging, Thaw, the "chivalrous avenger", did not escape. Before the trial one enterprising reporter unearthed details of a suit brought against him by a girl named Ethel Thomas in 1902. She told how, at the start of their relationship, Thaw had lavished affection upon her and bought her flowers and jewellery.

"But one day," she went on, "I met him by appointment, and, while we were walking towards his apartment at the

Bedford, 304 Fifth Avenue, he stopped at a store and bought a dog whip. I asked him what that was for and he replied laughingly: 'That's for you, dear.' I thought he was joking, but no sooner were we in his apartment and the door locked than his entire demeanour changed. A wild expression came into his eyes, and he seized me and with his whip beat me until my clothes hung in tatters.' "

Evelyn, too, it was said, had undergone a similar experience during the first of her two European holidays with Thaw. She had suffered so much at his hands, in fact, that, on her return, she had gone to Abe Hummel, a celebrated lawyer, and sworn an affidavit about the way Thaw had treated her.

The trouble had begun while they were staying at Schloss Katzenstein, a castle Thaw had rented in the Austrian Tyrol. One morning she had come down to breakfast wearing only a bathrobe. After the meal Thaw accompanied her to her bedroom where, "without any provocation, he grasped me by the throat and tore the bathrobe from my body, leaving me entirely nude except for my slippers.

". . . His eyes were glaring and he had in his right hand a cowhide whip. He seized hold of me and threw me on the bed. I was powerless and attempted to scream, but Thaw placed his fingers in my mouth and tried to choke me. He then, without any provocation, and without the slightest reason, began to inflict on me several severe and violent blows with the cowhide whip.

Besought him to desist

"So brutally did he assault me that my skin was cut and bruised. I besought him to desist, but he refused. I was so exhausted that I shouted and cried. He stopped every minute or so to rest, and then renewed his attack upon me, which he continued for about seven minutes. He acted like a demented man. I was absolutely in fear of my life . . . It was nearly three weeks before I was sufficiently recovered to be able to get out of my bed and walk.

"During all the time I travelled with Thaw, he would make the slightest pretext an excuse for a terrific assault on me . . . He also entered my bed and, without any consent, repeatedly wronged me. I reproved him for his conduct, but he compelled me to submit, threatening to beat and kill me if I did not do so . . ." It was on this trip, she also claimed, that she had discovered Thaw was a cocaine addict.

Why, people wondered, had she married a man who treated her so badly? Evelyn's motives seem clear – the desire for wealth and position. Thaw, it appears, was "persuaded" to marry her by White at

her family's instigation. The alternative to this was a charge – backed up by the affidavit – of corrupting a minor (Evelyn had been only 18 at the time of her first European holiday with Thaw).

The trial, which began on January 21, 1907, did not end until April 11. Then, after being out for more than 24 hours while an inquisitive crowd of 10,000 milled around under the courtroom windows, the jury announced that they had been unable to reach a verdict. On the final ballot, it was later learned, seven had voted Thaw guilty of first-degree murder, five had voted him not guilty by reason of insanity.

Thaw was kept in custody until his second trial started early in January 1908. This time his "ordeal" was shorter. On February 1 the jury – after again being out for more than 24 hours – found him not guilty by reason of insanity, and he was committed to the New York state asylum for the criminal insane.

Escape by limousine

Attempts by his lawyers to get him released were protracted and unsuccessful, and, on the morning of August 17, 1913, Thaw escaped from the asylum. With the aid of a limousine waiting outside the gates, he then sought refuge in Canada. The next month, under heavy pressure from the U.S. government, the Canadian Minister of Justice agreed to return him to the United States.

Put in jail in Concord, New Hampshire, Thaw fought a long legal battle against being returned to New York. It was not until December 1914 – over a year later – that the U.S. Supreme Court decided that this should happen. Back in New York, Thaw faced another long trial at which most of the evidence given at the two previous hearings was repeated. Finally, on July 16, 1915, he was declared sane and not guilty of all charges.

It was a victory of money over justice, and over commonsense for, only 18 months later, he was indicted for kidnapping and brutally whipping Frederick Gump Junr., a 19-year-old Kansas City youth. Once again Thaw was declared insane, but a week-long court hearing reversed the decision.

His bizarre behaviour periodically made the headlines until his death in February 1947, at the age of 76, after a heart attack. A photograph at the time showed him bespectacled and shrunken, looking more like a retired business executive than the sadistic paranoic that he was.

FINAL TRIANGLE: Was the appealing Evelyn really a young innocent? Was White a father-figure turned seducer? Was young Thaw a chivalrous avenger? It was melodrama in the old-fashioned style.

DO SOMETHING DESPERATE, DARLING

She died for her vanity . . . and a nation's morals. But did she really persuade her masterful lover to kill her "cad" of a husband? The fatal passion of Edith Thompson and Frederick Bywaters was writ large in love letters. They caused a sensation in court . . . a story of love and murder in the suburbs.

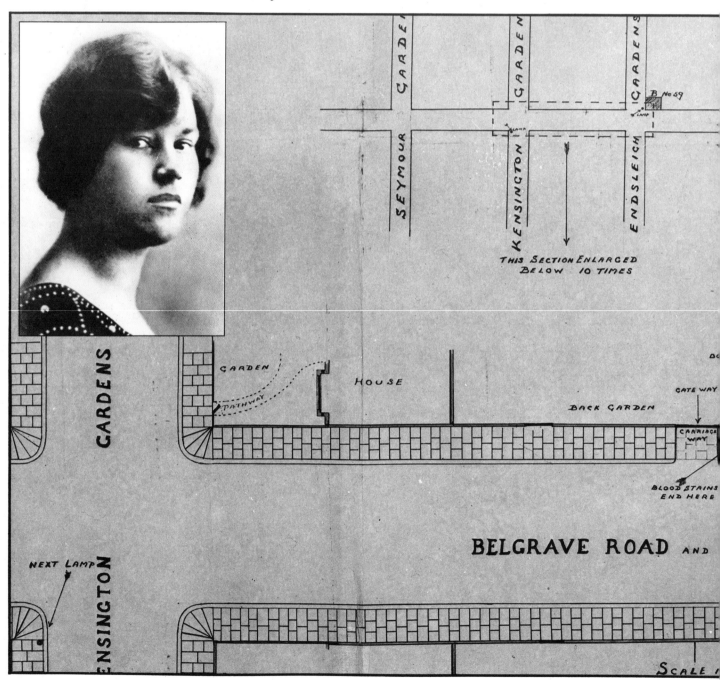

THE TRIAL which began in No. 1 Court at the Old Bailey in London on the morning of December 6, 1922, before a jury of eleven men and one woman was unquestionably the most sensational one of the year in England if not for the whole period between the two World Wars. It aroused nationwide interest, so much so that when the court doors were opened there was a queue outside of more than 50 people which had formed during the previous afternoon and throughout the night for the few seats available in the public gallery.

The accused were Frederick ("Freddy") Bywaters, a 20-year-old laundry steward on an ocean liner, and his mistress Edith ("Edie") Thompson, a mar-ried woman, who worked as manageress-bookkeeper in a firm of wholesale milliners in the City of London and was eight years older than her lover. Just over two months previously, Edith's husband Percy Thompson, a 32-year-old shipping clerk, had been killed near his home at Ilford, a small town in London's commuter belt, when returning late one night with his wife. Bywaters was charged with his murder, while Edith Thompson was charged with inciting her lover to carry out the killing after she had unsuccessfully tried to kill him herself by giving him poison and mixing powdered glass with his food.

As soon as the judge, the venerable-looking Mr. Justice Shearman, had taken his place on the Bench in the historic wood-panelled courtroom, the accused were brought up by a policeman and a female wardress from the cells below where they had been anxiously waiting. As they took their places in the dock, Bywaters, a good-looking youth with curly dark hair, gave the impression of being a virile almost animal type, essentially a

MURDERER: Youthful seaman (below), Frederick Bywaters was a man of action. His mistress's life was being "made hell" by her husband. So Bywaters stabbed the husband, while Edith cried, "Oh, don't, oh, don't!" In the death cell, Bywaters insisted: "She never planned it. She's innocent."

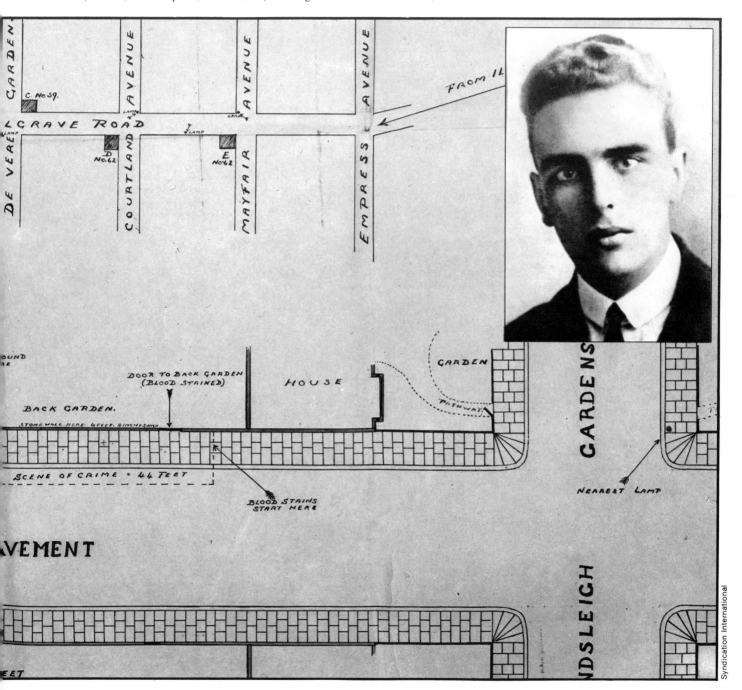

man of action, determined and masterful. His companion, however, looked pale, and she trembled slightly as she followed Bywaters and gave her plea to the Clerk of the Court as he had done: "Not guilty".

Edith Thompson's defence was in the hands of Sir Henry Curtis-Bennett, King's Counsel, who was a fashionable leading advocate of the day in criminal cases. As his counsel Bywaters had Mr. Cecil Whiteley, another eminent K.C. and a prominent criminal lawyer. The prosecuting team was led by the Solicitor-General, Sir Thomas Inskip, since it was customary for a Law Officer of the Crown to prosecute in any case involving a poison charge. Sir Thomas was a stern Sabbatarian and no criminal could expect any mercy at his hands.

Enough for an elephant

On the table in front of the Solicitor-General was a large bundle of letters, 62 in all, which Edith Thompson had written to Bywaters in the course of their love affair and which had been recovered by the police, some in the house in London where Bywaters had lived with his mother and others in his locker on his ship. Some of them were to be described by the judge as "gush". Certainly Edith analyzed her feelings and emotions in remarkable detail. Her favourite term of endearment for her lover was "Darlingest", contracted to "Darlint". The letters breathed a curious passion, in which the writer depicted herself as half mother and half slave-mistress. She also described how she had tried to do away with her husband on several occasions.

"You said it was enough for an elephant," she wrote in one letter. "Perhaps it was. But you don't allow for the taste making it possible for only a small quantity to be taken." And again: "I'm going to try the glass again occasionally – when it's safe. I've got an electric light globe this time." In fact, according to her, she used the light bulb three times in his food, "but the third time he found a piece – so I've given it up – until you come home."

Be jealous, darling

They were foolish letters to write and even more foolish to keep. Incidentally Edith Thompson never referred to her husband in them by his Christian name, but always as "he" or "him". In one letter she wrote:

"Yes, darlint, you are jealous of *him* – but I want you to be – he has the right by law to all that you have the right by nature and love – yes, darlint, be jealous, so much that you will do something desperate."

In this letter she enclosed a cutting from a newspaper which described how a

Conway

VICTIM (left and above) with wife. "Is marriage improper because the law acknowledges it? Is illicit love noble?" A "wicked affection" ended in a fatal stabbing. The knife was found in a grate at the side of Belgrave Road. "Right-minded persons will be filled with disgust," said the judge.

woman's death had been caused by taking a bowl of broth made from the carcass of a chicken which had been killed by rat poison. Other cuttings enclosed in Edith's letters contained headings like "Patient Killed by an Overdose", "The Poisoner Curate", "Poisoned Chocolates", "Masterful Men", and "Woman the Consoler".

Compromising passages

Edith Thompson's counsel had been shown these highly compromising letters before the trial opened, since under the rules of criminal procedure the prosecution was bound to disclose them to the defence if it was intended to introduce them as evidence against her. Not only did they contain passages suggesting on the face of them that Edith had tried to kill her husband with poison and powdered glass, but they also plainly indicated that that on at least one occasion she had aborted herself and had a miscarriage after becoming pregnant by her lover.

Thus Sir Henry Curtis-Bennett had to reckon with the prosecution showing that she was not merely an adulteress but also

Syndication International

a self-abortionist as well as a potential murderess. The nature of her relations with her husband were also reflected in certain passages in the letters describing how, after Bywaters first went to sea, she rejected her husband's sexual approaches. Eventually, however, she yielded to him and became "the dutiful wife" which she thought was the best way to allay his suspicions if she and Bywaters had to take what she called "drastic measures".

Realizing that the letters were dynamite, Sir Henry did his best to persuade the judge to rule that they were inadmissible as evidence against his client. Therefore, as soon as the jury had been sworn, Sir Henry jumped to his feet and with a glance in the direction of the bundle of letters informed the judge that he had an objection to make to certain evidence which he understood the Solicitor-General proposed to put before the jury. The jury were then sent out of the court room while Curtis-Bennett and Inskip argued the point with the judge.

Admissible evidence

Briefly Curtis-Bennett's argument was that the letters could not and should not be admitted until the prosecution had shown that Mrs. Thompson took some active part in the murder – if it was murder – of her husband. The Solicitor-General replied by submitting that they were admissible because she was being charged as a principal in the second degree, although she did not strike the

fatal blow. "The crime is one where one hand struck the blow," said Inskip, "and we want to show by these letters that her mind conceived it and incited it – the evidence of that is the letters that Mrs. Thompson wrote to the man who struck the blow."

After listening patiently to the argument, the judge then gave his ruling. "I think these letters are admissible as evidence of intention and motive," he said, "and I shall admit them." Turning towards Edith Thompson's counsel, he added: "I do not think you can contest the letters, showing the affectionate relations between the parties, are not evidence of motive in so far as they show affection."

Sir Henry was overruled. He had done everything he could to exclude the damning letters; now he knew that the task before him was all the more difficult. He glanced at his client in the dock. Her face, almost hidden by the brim of her black velour hat, looked anxious and drawn.

The jury were then brought back to court, and the Solicitor-General proceeded to open the case for the Crown. "May it please your lordship, members of the jury," he began, "on October 4, a little after midnight, Percy Thompson was stabbed to death on his way home from Ilford station. He was in a dark part of the road, not over-well lit at the best of times, when he was struck, first of all, apparently from behind, and then in front, by some assailant. The only person

present was his wife, Mrs. Thompson, who is now in the dock. She is charged with Bywaters, who is said by the prosecution to have been the assailant, with the murder of Percy Thompson."

It was a sombre tale which the Solicitor-General went on to relate. Husband and wife had been to the theatre, and as they were walking along the road from Ilford station to the terraced row of suburban houses in Kensington Gardens where they lived, a man suddenly jumped out of the shadows. Seizing Percy Thompson by the arm, he said, "Why don't you get a divorce from your wife, you cad?"

Thompson, who appeared to recognize the man, replied, "I've got her, I'll keep her, and I'll shoot you."

Strange attacker

The assailant then pulled out a knife from his coat pocket. With it he stabbed Thompson several times, while Edith Thompson shouted, "Oh, don't! Oh, don't!" The attacker turned, ran off, and disappeared into the darkness. Meanwhile Percy Thompson fell to the ground, blood pouring from his mouth. He was dead before a doctor, who had been summoned, arrived on the scene followed by the police.

Edith Thompson was still in too hysterical a condition to tell the police very much except that her husband had been "attacked by a strange man". However, a woman named Mrs. Fanny Lester, who lived in the same house with the Thomp-

Both Radio Times Hulton Picture Library

NATIONWIDE INTEREST: The result is awaited outside the court. After two hours, the verdict was "guilty". Mrs. Bywaters testified at the appeal.

sons was also questioned, and it was Mrs. Lester who put the police on the track of the killer. She stated that about 18 months previously Frederick Bywaters had lodged in the house for some weeks. He had left due to a row he had had with Percy Thompson caused by the attentions Bywaters had apparently been paying Edith. The police also learned that Bywaters was a steward with the P. & O. line. In turn this led the officers to find the letters Edith had written to him and which he picked up at the various ports at which his ship called.

Stifled sobbing

Bywaters was eventually traced to the home of Edith Thompson's parents who lived at Manor Park, near Ilford. There he was arrested and taken to Ilford police station where he was formally charged with the murder. Later that day Edith Thompson was picked up and taken to the same police station where she was likewise charged on the basis of the letters with being a principal in the murder; or, alternatively, with being an accessory to it.

At this time neither she nor Freddy Bywaters knew that the other had been arrested. As she was being led past a window of the police station, she looked in and saw her lover sitting there obviously in police custody. The sight shook her extremely. "Oh, God, why did he do it?" she cried, the words coming out involuntarily between stifled sobs. "I didn't want him to do it."

Under police interrogation, Bywaters agreed with what his mistress had said. At the same time he did his best to shield her and insisted that she knew nothing of his intention to waylay Percy Thompson on their homeward journey from the theatre. Both prisoners signed statements confirming what they had told the police when they were arrested, and they were put in evidence by the prosecution in

addition to Edith Thompson's letters.

The story of the fatal encounter which Bywaters told in his statement was as follows:

"I waited for Mrs. Thompson and her husband. I pushed her to one side, also pushing him up the street . . . We struggled. I took my knife from my pocket and we fought and he got the worst of it . . .

"The reason I fought with Thompson was because he never acted like a man to his wife. He always seemed several degrees lower than a snake. I loved her and I could not go on seeing her leading that life. I did not intend to kill him. I only meant to injure him. I gave him an opportunity of standing up to me as a man but he wouldn't."

Bywaters stuck to this story when he went into the witness-box on the third day of the trial, although he did qualify his admission, "I only meant to injure him," by saying that what he really intended was "to stop him from killing me."

Nor could the Solicitor-General shake him in cross-examination about his mistress's compromising letters, for which the witness had a ready explanation.

"As far as you could tell, reading these letters," Sir Thomas Inskip asked, looking sternly at the man on the witness stand, "did you ever believe in your own mind that she herself had given any poison to her husband?"

"No," replied Bywaters with an air of self-confidence, "it never entered my mind at all. She had been reading books. She had a vivid way of declaring herself. She would read a book and imagine herself as the character in the book."

He also stated in reply to the Solicitor-General that it was Percy Thompson who attacked him first. The expression on Sir Thomas Inskip's face clearly showed that he did not believe the witness. "Do you mean to suggest that he made the first assault upon you?" he asked incredulously.

"Yes, he did."

"And that you then drew your knife?"

"I did."

"Is it the fact that you never saw any revolver or any gun at that moment?"

"I never saw it, no," Bywaters had to admit.

Mr. Cecil Whiteley, K.C., did something to repair the damage caused by this admission when he re-examined his client about the possibility of Percy Thompson having a gun. "Although I never saw a revolver," said Bywaters, "I believed that he had one, otherwise I would not have drawn my knife. I was in fear of my life."

"At any time have you had any intention to murder Mr. Thompson?" defence counsel asked in conclusion.

Tension mounted

"I have not," replied Bywaters firmly and unhesitatingly. He added that he had met Mrs. Thompson in a teashop near her place of work on the afternoon of the killing, but he strongly repudiated the prosecution's suggestion that the purpose of the meeting was to plot her husband's death.

The atmosphere of tension mounted when the usher called out "Edith Jessie Thompson", and the prisoner left the dock to follow her lover on to the witness stand. There was no need for her to testify. Had she remained silent, the prosecution could not have commented upon the fact. The only evidence against her consisted of the letters, and Curtis-Bennett would have preferred to have dealt with them himself in his speech to the jury, rather than risk his client being cross-examined by the ruthless Solicitor-General and probably convicting herself out of her own mouth.

However, Edith Thompson brushed aside all her counsel's objections, determined as she was on getting the limelight. She realized the enormous public interest in the case, her counsel said afterwards, and decided to play up to it by entering the witness box.

The story of her relations with Freddy Bywaters, which she told in her examination-in-chief, was a curious one. She and her husband had known the Bywaters family for some years, she said, the acquaintance going back to the days when her brother and Bywaters were school-mates. In June 1921, Bywaters was on extended leave from his ship, and he accompanied her husband and herself on a holiday to the Isle of Wight in the south of England. At that time she and Freddy, she went on, were no more than friends. The friendship continued after Freddy went to live with the Thompsons as a paying guest until his ship was ready to sail.

"How did you become lovers?" her counsel asked her.

"Well," said Edith, "it started on the August Bank Holiday. I had some trouble with my husband on that day — over a pin!"

Kissed on lips

It was a fine sunny afternoon and all three were in the garden at the back of the house. Edith Thompson was sewing. Suddenly she looked up and said, "I want a pin."

"I will go and get you one," said Bywaters.

When he returned with the pin, husband and wife were arguing, Percy Thompson saying she should have got the pin herself. Edith Thompson then went into the house to prepare tea. Her husband followed her and a further argument ensued as she was laying the table in the sitting room. Her sister Avis Graydon was expected, but she was a little late and, unlike his wife, Percy Thompson did not want to wait for her. He went on to make some uncomplimentary remarks about Edith's family and then began to beat her. Finally he threw her across the room and she collided with a chair which overturned. Hearing the noise from the garden, Bywaters rushed in and told Thompson to stop.

"Why don't you come to an amicable agreement?" said Bywaters. "Either you can have a separation or you can get a divorce."

Thompson hesitated before replying. "Yes — No — I don't see it concerns you."

"You are making Edie's life a hell," said Bywaters. "You know she is not happy with you."

"Well, I have got her and I will keep her."

Edith went upstairs and Bywaters returned to his room. After a short while she joined him there, when he comforted her and for the first time kissed her on the lips. When he came back to the sitting room, he extracted a promise from her husband that he would not knock her about or beat her any more. But Thompson flatly refused to take any steps towards obtaining a legal separation or a divorce from his wife. Shortly afterwards, Bywaters left the house and went to stay with his mother.

During the next few weeks — he was due to embark early in September — he and Edith met secretly from time to time. Most of these meetings took place in tea shops or municipal parks such as Wanstead or Epping Forest near Ilford. There

THE DETECTIVES who handled the case. Who made the first assault? Did Percy Thompson have a gun? Was the crime planned over tea that afternoon?

were not many opportunities for more than hand-holding at dance teas and an occasional embrace on a bench. It was the age of the *thé dansant,* and at one of these occasions the orchestra played *One Little Hour,* which became "their tune". However, just before Bywaters' ship sailed on September 9 the two became lovers, apparently going to a small hotel for the purpose and registering under assumed names.

Poison letters

Questioned by her counsel about the letters and the news cuttings, she explained that she had deliberately deceived her lover into thinking that she wished to poison her husband, but that she had no intention of acting upon what she had written. She had sent the letters with their suggestive enclosures, so she said, because she was anxious to keep Freddy's love. Occasionally he would go out with other girls, one of whom was Edith's unmarried sister Avis, and Edith thought that he might be tiring of her.

When the Solicitor-General rose to cross-examine, it was not difficult for him to entrap her as Curtis-Bennett had feared he would. Inskip held up one letter in which she had written to her lover:

"Why aren't you sending me something? I wanted you to . . . If I don't

mind the risk, why should you?"

"What was it?" the Solicitor-General asked sternly.

"I've no idea," Edith replied as non-chalantly as she could.

"Have you no idea?"

"Except what he told me."

"What did he lead you to think it was?"

"That it was something for me to give my husband."

"With a view to poisoning your husband?"

Edith paused before answering, not knowing exactly what to say and looking distinctly uncomfortable. "That was not the idea," she said at last, "that was not what I expected."

"Something to give your husband that would hurt him?" the Solicitor-General went on.

"To make him ill," she blurted out.

Replying to further questions, Edith Thompson admitted that she had urged Bywaters to send the "something to make him ill", instead of bringing it. "I wrote that," she added, "in order to make him think I was willing to do anything he might suggest, to enable me to retain his affections."

Frank explanation

Again the Solicitor-General eyed her severely. "Mrs. Thompson, is that quite a frank explanation of this urging him to send instead of to bring?"

"It is, absolutely," was the unconvincing reply. "I wanted him to think I was eager to help him."

At this point, the judge leaned forward in the direction of the witness. "That does not answer the question, you know," he remarked.

There was little that Curtis-Bennett could do in re-examining his client to repair the damage caused by her replies to the Solicitor-General's questioning. But he did his best. For example, the phrase, "He is still well", which she had used in one letter, he was able to show referred not to her husband but to a bronze monkey that Bywaters had bought in some foreign port and given her as a souvenir. Her defence counsel also made the most of her conduct on the night of the killing.

Extraordinary life

"As far as you could," he asked her, "from the moment you got to your husband, did you do everything you could for him?"

"Everything I possibly could," echoed Edith Thompson.

Curtis-Bennett came back to this point in her favour when he made his closing speech to the jury. "The letters provide the only evidence upon which the charge of murder is framed against Mrs. Thompson," he stressed his words deliberately. "Everything that was done and said by her on that night shows as strongly as it can that not only did she not know the murder was going to be committed, but that she was horrified when she found her husband was killed."

His client was no ordinary woman, he continued. "She reads a book and then imagines herself one of the characters in the book. She is always living an extraordinary life of novels." So far as her relations with Freddy Bywaters went, Sir Henry made it clear that for his part he did not care whether they were described as "an amazing passion" or "an adulterous

intercourse" or whatever. "Thank God, this is not a court of morals," he told the eleven men and one woman in the jury box. "because if everybody immoral was brought here I should never be out of it, nor would you. Whatever name you give it, it was certainly a great love that existed between these two people."

Mr. Justice Shearman began his summing-up of the evidence to the jury with the ominous words: "You should not forget you are trying a vulgar, common crime!" Edith Thompson's letters to her lover the judge proceeded to describe as "full of the outpourings of a silly but at the same time a wicked affection".

"Members of the jury, if that nonsense means anything," he went on to say, "it means that the love of a husband for his wife is something improper because marriage is acknowledged by the law, and that the love of a woman for her lover—illicit and clandestine—is something great and noble. I am certain that you, like any other right-minded persons, will be filled with disgust at such a notion. Let us get rid of all that atmosphere and try this case in an ordinary common sense way."

Strongly hostile

The summing-up was strongly hostile to both prisoners. The red-robed and bewigged figure on the judicial bench left little doubt in the jury's minds that "these two by arrangement between each other agreed to murder this man Thompson, and the murder was effected by the man Bywaters". The impression was heightened by the sense of moral indignation expressed by the judge at the prisoners' sexual morals. In the event it took the jury just over two hours to find both prisoners guilty of murder.

"I say the verdict of the jury is wrong," exclaimed Bywaters when he heard it. "Edith Thompson is not guilty. I am no murderer. I am no assassin." These words were echoed by the woman who stood beside him in the dock. "I am not guilty," she cried. And again, after both had been sentenced to death by hanging, she repeated, "I am not guilty. Oh, God, I am not guilty!"

Both prisoners appealed on the grounds that the verdict was against the weight of the evidence and that the judge had misdirected the jury. Each of the appeals was dismissed by the Court of Criminal Appeal, which saw no grounds for quashing the conviction or ordering a new trial, the President of the Court describing it as a "squalid and rather indecent case of lust and adultery" and one which

MERCY MAIL: Petitions (left) for Edith Thompson's reprieve failed. She was hanged at London's Holloway Prison on January 9, 1923, at 9.00 a.m. (right).

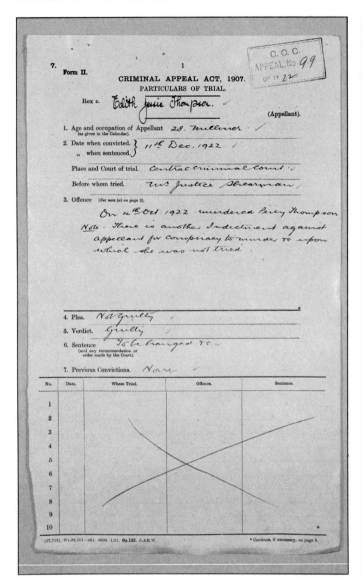

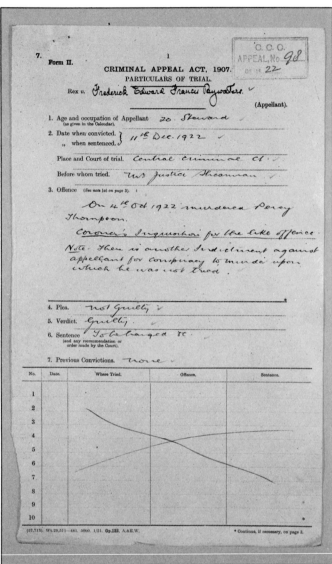

"exhibits from the beginning to the end no redeeming feature".

At the time no woman had been hanged in England for 15 years. Largely for this reason there was considerable public agitation that Edith Thompson should be reprieved, and a petition for reprieve containing many thousands of signatures was sent to the Home Secretary, with whom the final decision rested.

Lawyer's last dash

Three days before the date set for the execution, Bywaters had a meeting with his mother in the condemned cell in Pentonville Prison, where he was being held. He told his mother that he had no grievance against the law so far as he himself was concerned, and that execution had no terrors for him. "I killed him and I must pay for it," he said. "The judge's summing-up was just, if you like, but it was cruel. It never gave me a chance. I did it, though, and I can't complain."

His mistress's case was quite different, he stressed. "I swear she is completely

DEATH DOCUMENTS: They died at the same moment, in places a quarter of a mile apart. Even Bywaters' confession had not swayed the Home Secretary.

innocent. She never knew that I was going to meet them that night . . . For her to be hanged as a criminal is too awful. She didn't commit the murder. I did. She never planned it. She never knew about it. She is innocent, absolutely innocent. I can't believe that they will hang her."

When this was reported to Edith Thompson's solicitor, the lawyer dashed through the night to make a last minute appeal to the Home Secretary who had gone off to spend the weekend at his country house some two hundred miles from London. When he had read Bywater's "confession", the Home Secretary promised to give the solicitor his decision next day, the eve of the execution. He did so, but it was that there could be no reprieve for either prisoner and the law must take its course.

They were both hanged at the same

hour, 9.0 a.m. on January 9, 1923—she at Holloway and he a quarter of a mile away at Pentonville. Freddy Bywaters met his end "like a gentleman", as he told his mother he would, protesting his mistress's innocence to the last. Edith Thompson, however, had to be carried from the condemned cell to the scaffold by two wardresses as she was in a state of complete collapse during her last moments.

Spoiled her chances

Edith Thompson's leading counsel was greatly upset by the verdict and its outcome, which he felt would have been different if she had taken his advice. "She spoiled her chances by her evidence and demeanour," he said afterwards. "I had a perfect answer to everything, which I am sure would have won an acquittal if she had not been a witness. She was a vain woman and an obstinate one. Also her imagination was highly developed, but it failed to show her the mistake she was making . . . In short, Mrs. Thompson was hanged for immorality."

DIAL M FOR MURDER

The ringing telephone shatters the studious evening silence of the club. The captain takes a message for Mr. Wallace from a mysterious Manxman. The call turns out to be historic . . . and deadly.

Popperfoto

Associated Newspapers

THE TELEPHONE call that was to end Julia Wallace's life was made to the Liverpool Central Chess Club at 7.20 on a cold, rainy evening in January 1931. The caller—a man whose voice was later described as "gruff but ordinary"—asked if he could speak to one of the club members—William Herbert Wallace, a quiet, nervous, short-sighted person who worked for the Prudential Assurance Company.

Although Wallace had put his name down to play in the Second Class Championship that night, he hadn't yet reached the club—which met twice a week at the City Café in North John Street. The club captain, Samuel Beattie, spoke to the caller, and so took part in what was to become one of the most controversial conversations in British legal history.

After stating who he was, Beattie told the stranger that Wallace would be arriving shortly. "I suggest you ring back later," he said helpfully. There was a pause, followed by the caller's agitated rejection of the idea.

"Oh, no, I couldn't do that," he protested. "I'm too busy. I have my girl's twenty-first birthday on, and I want to do something for her in the way of business. I want to see Mr. Wallace on a matter of

business. Will you ask him to come round to my place tomorrow evening at 7.30?"

Beattie agreed to pass the message on, and asked for the man's name and address. "The name's Qualtrough," the caller replied, "and I live at 25 Menlove Gardens East, Mossley Hill."

Although an unusual name in other parts of England, Qualtrough was fairly common in Liverpool and the nearby Isle of Man. It was, in fact, a Manx name, but even so Beattie asked the man to spell it out for him. He wrote it on the back of a used envelope, and gave this to Wallace when the insurance agent entered the club half-an-hour later.

"I belong to Liverpool"

At first the 52-year-old Wallace denied knowing anyone called Qualtrough. He also appeared doubtful as to the exact location of Menlove Gardens East—but imagined it must be somewhere in the vicinity of Menlove Avenue. Beattie advised him to look the street up in a directory, but Wallace scoffed at the idea. "I belong to Liverpool," he said airily. "Besides I've a perfectly good tongue in my head. I can make inquiries once I get to the district."

After that the subject of Qualtrough, his daughter's party, and the business he apparently intended putting Wallace's way was forgotten about. Chess ruled the remainder of the evening, and Wallace—who was considered a sound but uninspired player—won his round against a fellow member named McCartney.

He left for his home at 29 Wolverton Street, Anfield in what for him were high spirits. Slow to anger and difficult to please, Wallace was regarded as something of a mystery man. With his steel-rimmed glasses, sparse grey hair, and ragged moustache, he looked like a typical insurance salesman.

But despite his conventional appearance—bowler hat, high white collar, dun-coloured mackintosh—he did not fit in or mingle well with other people. Perhaps his height (he was a slender six feet two inches) had something to do with it; he always seemed anxious, awkward, willing to please yet pathetically failing to do so.

Added to this, he thought himself to be a cut or two above the men and women whom he visited in his job (he earned £260 per annum) and from whom he collected insurance contributions.

As a young man he had spent some years working as a clerk and then an advertising manager in India and Shang-

GRUFF BUT ORDINARY, the voice from the call box leaves a name, Qualtrough—and a non-existent address—with the Liverpool Central Chess Club (facing page). For Julia Wallace, the telephone call signals a violent death.

hai. He was interested in the violin, in chemistry, and was something of an amateur philosopher. He had studied the works of the Roman emperor Marcus Aurelius, and tried to conduct his life on the principles of the Stoics.

Because of this he believed that misfortunes happened only to the wicked. And no one—despite the misfortune that was to strike her the following evening—could have seemed less wicked than Wallace's shy, music-loving wife, Julia.

A childless couple, the Wallaces were noted for their utter devotion to each other. Their neighbours in the terraced cul-de-sac in which they lived had never known them to quarrel or even raise their voices. They played musical duets together, went on weekend rambles in the Cheshire and Lancashire countryside, and shared a deep, but mainly uncreative interest in the arts.

If the Wallaces had a common fault, it was that they were *too* loving, *too* placid, *too* ultra-respectable. At nights when her husband was called out on business, 50-year-old Julia contented herself with daubing one of her somewhat insipid water-colours, or playing nocturnes on the piano.

A not unattractive woman with greying auburn hair, she was not unduly put out when Wallace left the house at a quarter-to-seven on the evening of Tuesday, January 20. He had eaten his usual substantial high tea, and looked as well—or as ill—as he ever did.

A sallow complexion

His years in what he sometimes called the "Mysterious Orient" had left him with a sallow complexion which was not improved by a chronic kidney ailment. He was prone to headaches and severe colds, and Julia told him to wrap up well as the night was wet and chilly.

He did as she counselled, pecked her goodbye on the cheek, and promised to be home as soon as his business with Qualtrough was concluded. Julia returned to her domestic chores—she always kept their two-storey, red-brick house spotless—and Wallace proceeded by tram and foot through the drizzle that blanketed Anfield and Mossley Hill.

Up until that time the worst that could be said about Wallace was that he had been born middle-aged. But before the night was out suspicion of murder was to be raised against him, and within a fortnight he was to be arrested and charged with the brutal slaying of his wife.

Yet to the people he encountered on that rainy night, he was no more than a shabby rather forlorn figure looking for a man and a street which just didn't seem to exist. There was no one called Qualtrough living in the district, and although there was a Menlove Gardens West (and

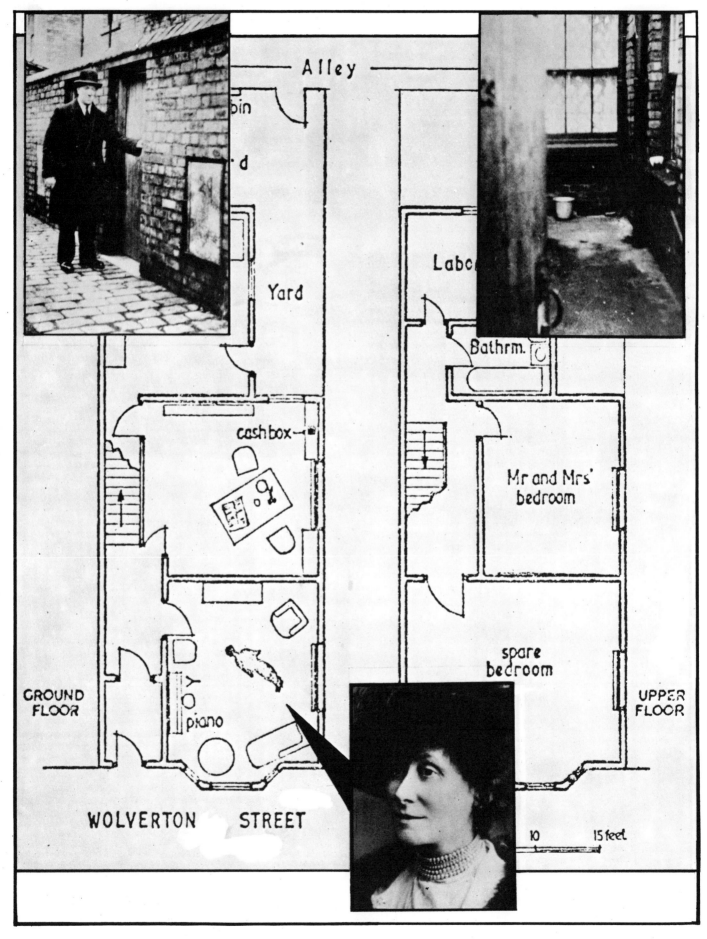

Alley

Yard

cashbox

Labo

Bathrm.

Mr and Mrs' bedroom

spare bedroom

GROUND FLOOR

piano

UPPER FLOOR

WOLVERTON STREET

10   15 feet

a house in it numbered twenty-five) there was no Menlove Gardens East.

In all, Wallace spent nearly two hours roaming through Mossley Hill, asking a tram conductor, a policeman, and the manageress of a newsagent's shop where the "missing" street might be. Those he spoke to—and who later gave evidence at his trial—were impressed by his earnestness, his bewilderment, his persistence.

Finally, frustrated and depressed, he returned to the drab concrete corridor that was Wolverton Street. It was shortly before nine o'clock when, shivering from the cold, he hurried up to his front door. He was eager to be inside, take his damp clothes off, and relax by the fire.

Around to the back lane

He took out his key and fitted it into the maroon-painted front door. He tried to turn the key but the door wouldn't open. Surprised rather than worried, he walked round to the back lane where the door there also refused to budge.

Alarmed now, Wallace began to bang on the kitchen door. The noise he made attracted the attention of his neighbours, John and Florence Johnston, who lived at Number Thirty-One. They were preparing to go out for the evening when they heard the banging and met Wallace as he strode fretfully up to them in the lane.

"I'm locked out," he said excitedly, "and can't get in to see my wife. Have you heard anything unusual tonight?"

The Johnstons shook their heads and told Wallace to try the door again. "Perhaps it's just stuck," said Mr. Johnson bluffly. "Give the handle a good hard twist. We'll wait here while you do it. If it doesn't work this time, we'll have a shot with my back door key."

Muttering his thanks, Wallace did as his friends suggested. This time, to his apparent incredulity, the door did open. He frowned and hurried into the house calling out his wife's name. The dimmed gas-lights in the kitchen and upstairs bedroom were turned up, and a seemingly endless two minutes went by.

Then, just as the Johnstons were becoming uneasy, Wallace rushed out of the kitchen, his yellow face turning white with terror. "Come and see," he shouted. "She has been killed!"

Stifling their own emotions, the Johnstons followed Wallace through the kitchen, down a narrow passage leading to the front door, and turned left into the little-used sitting-room. They halted in the jamb and gazed with horror at the bloody sight that met their eyes.

"THEY'VE FINISHED HER!" cries Wallace. Freed on appeal, he will leave the site of Julia's death (where a detective, left, studies the rear door) and retire to a bungalow in the Wirral (right).

By the flickering light of a gas bracket they saw Julia Wallace lying face downwards on a rug by the burnt-out fire. She was fully dressed with her feet almost touching the fender, her outstretched left arm pointing accusingly to the door. Her head was little more than a battered pulp—with brains and tissue oozing from a three-inch wound on her forehead.

Blood covered everything: the walls, the piano, the music-stand, the violincase, the table, the aspidistra in the bay window. For a long moment no one moved or spoke. Then Wallace—whom the Johnstons later described as "cool, calm and quiet"—shook himself and said dully:

"They've finished her."

Recovering from her initial shock, Mrs. Johnston showed more humanity. She knelt down by the dead woman and took hold of her rigid hand. "Oh, you poor darling," she said softly. "You poor dear."

A few moments later the three of them left the sitting-room, and Johnston went to fetch a doctor and the police. Rather than leave poor dead Julia on her own, Mrs. Johnston and Wallace returned to the parlour where a fresh fire was lit and Wallace discovered that a mackintosh—one of his own—was lying beneath his wife's body.

"Why, whatever was she doing with that?" he wondered aloud. Then, resuming his earlier lament, he intoned: "They've finished her. They've finished her. Look at the brains!"

Within half-an-hour of this, 29 Wolverton Street had more visitors inside its walls than the Wallaces had invited in all the sixteen years they had lived there. Police scoured the building from coalhouse to back bedroom. No evidence was found that directly incriminated Wallace, although an iron bar used for poking the fire was noted to be missing.

Hypnotized by blood

It was obvious that the residence had not been broken into or burgled, and that whoever had slain Julia Wallace that night had been on friendly terms with her. No woman of her temperament and disposition would have allowed a stranger into the house, let alone the hallowed front sitting-room.

Wallace, looking on in stunned dismay, seemed to be hypnotized by the blood and disorder. "Julia would have gone mad if she had seen all this mess," he said weakly. "And all these strangers knocking about the house."

Professor John MacFall, an expert in forensic medicine, examined the body and proclaimed that death had occurred at around six o'clock—almost an hour before Wallace had said he had set out in

All pictures Jonathan Goodman

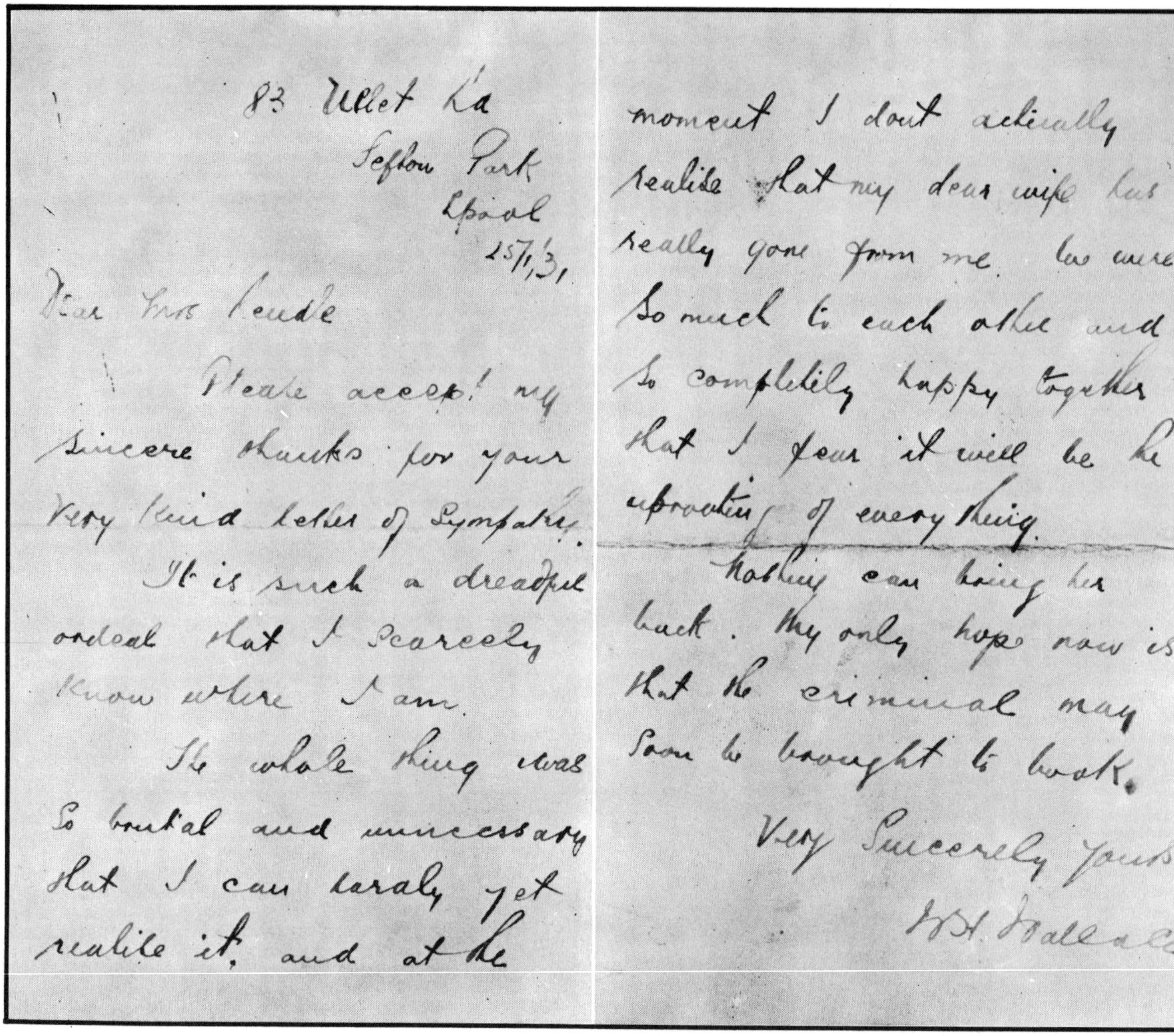

> 83 Ullet La
> Sefton Park
> Lpool
> 25/1/31
>
> Dear Mrs Scudle
>
> Please accept my sincere thanks for your very kind letter of sympathy.
>
> It is such a dreadful ordeal that I scarcely know where I am.
>
> The whole thing was so brutal and unnecessary that I can scarcely yet realise it, and at the moment I dont actually realise that my dear wife has really gone from me. We were so much to each other and so completely happy together that I fear it will be the uprooting of everything.
>
> Nothing can bring her back. My only hope now is that the criminal may soon be brought to book.
>
> Very Sincerely Yours
> W H Wallace

search of Qualtrough. MacFall was also suspicious of the way Wallace behaved while the police ransacked the rooms.

"He was too quiet, too collected, for a person whose wife had been killed in the way described," said the professor later. "He was not nearly so affected as I was myself. . . . He was smoking cigarettes most of the time.

"Whilst I was in the room, examining the body and the blood, he came in smoking a cigarette, and he leant over in front of the sideboard and flipped the ash into a bowl upon the sideboard. It struck me at the time as being unnatural."

For the next few days the police under Detective-Inspector Herbert Gold, of Liverpool City Police, made their way down one blind alley after another. Each time their feet were re-directed towards Wallace — who at least was flesh and blood, and not a mere spectre like the elusive and presumably non-existent Qualtrough.

It came as no surprise to anyone (except, perhaps, Wallace himself) when on February 2 he was arrested by Inspector Gold and charged with the premeditated murder of his wife. "What can I say to this charge," asked the chess-player stoically, "except that I am absolutely innocent?"

Not a single spot of blood

Wallace's trial was held at Liverpool Spring Assizes on April 22, 1931. Witnesses recalled and repeated his now celebrated alibi concerning Qualtrough, and much was made of the fact that Wallace — if indeed he had committed the crime — had done so without getting a single spot of blood on his clothing.

To the defence this seemed a clear sign of his innocence, but the prosecuting attorney, Edward Hemmerde, K.C., took this as proof of Wallace's guilt. "One of the most famous criminal trials," he asserted, "was of a man who committed a crime when he was naked.

"A man might perfectly well commit a crime wearing a raincoat . . . and come down, when he is just going to do this, wearing nothing on which blood could fasten, and . . . he might get away, leaving the raincoat there, and go and perform the necessary thorough washing."

Despite a favourable summing-up by the judge, Mr. Justice Wright, the jury of ten men and two women brought in a verdict of "guilty". Wallace, still protesting his innocence, was condemned to death, and then went on to make startling legal history.

An appeal was lodged before the Court of Criminal Appeal, which, after deliberating from May 18-19, quashed the verdict and made Wallace a free man again. This was the first time since the Court had been established in 1907 that the Appeal Judges had decided that a British jury had made a grave — but not irrevocable — mistake.

SINCERE GRIEF for his wife, as shown in letters to friends (left), may have saved Wallace (above, with brother after the appeal; right, on cover of magazine).

Wallace—who died in February 1933 of his long-standing kidney complaint—returned to Wolverton Street and to an office job with the head Liverpool office of the Prudential. Scandalmongers and his rapidly decreasing health, however, forced him to retire to the Wirral countryside, where he fitted an electric switch and lamp on the porch of his house.

"The position of the switch is known only to myself," he declared, "and before I open my door I touch it, so that the house, outside and inside, and every recess where an assailant may be lurking, is lit up.

"The figure which one day I fully expect to see crouching and ready to strike will be that of Qualtrough, the man who murdered my wife."

THE penalty for changing one's alibi can be more than mere loss of credibility. It cost James Hanratty his life. Hanratty switched alibis in the middle of his trial for murder. Aware that his first alibi was becoming threadbare, he substituted an entirely different explanation for the crucial hours which could have proved his innocence. The price was the destruction of the jury's confidence in a trial that was touch-and-go from the start. The ultimate tragedy was that James Hanratty could have paid the penalty for another man's crime.

Why, people still ask, did James Hanratty alter his story at the worst possible moment? Why undermine his own case with the first alibi and then, when it was gasping for breath, substitute a more convincing one? The question of Hanratty's alibi is only one riddle in the strange and disquieting case of the Murder on Deadman's Hill. British justice is often described as the envy of the world. But as more and more evidence comes to light, many people believe that the trial of James Hanratty ended with the wrong man being sent to the gallows.

The crime itself had been brutal and—on the face of it—both senseless and unmotivated. It started with two people. Michael Gregsten and Valerie Storie were lovers. Although Gregsten was already married, his marriage had been on the rocks for some time. At around 8.30 on the night of August 22, 1961, Gregsten parked his grey Morris Minor car on the edge of a cornfield at Dorney, near the Buckinghamshire town of Slough.

Gregsten and Valerie Storie were together in the front seats when there was a sharp tap on the window. As Gregsten wound down the window, a gun was thrust inside and a voice said: "This is a hold-up. I am a desperate man. I have been on the run for four months. If you do as I tell you, you will be all right."

Drive at gunpoint

What followed was a nightmare. With the gunman sitting in the back, Gregsten was forced to drive round the countryside in search of food. In an attempt to attract attention, Gregsten turned on his rear flashing-light. But nobody took any notice.

They stopped at a milk-machine, a petrol station and a cigarette kiosk. With the gun pointed at Valerie Storie, Gregsten could neither raise an alarm nor make a dash for it. After a pointless drive of 30 miles, they climbed the A6 at Deadman's Hill, where the gunman ordered them into a picnickers' pull-off.

TERROR ON DEAD MAN'S HILL

Gregsten saw his chance. As the gunman started tying Valerie Storie's wrists with cord, Gregsten lunged at him with a duffel bag which was in the front seat. The result was catastrophic. The man fired two shots into Gregsten's head, killing him instantly. "You've shot him, you bastard!" Valerie Storie screamed. The man replied, "He frightened me. He moved too quick."

The man ignored the girl's pleas to get a doctor and snapped, "Be quiet, will you!" Then, in a phrase he had used several times—and with the same mispronunciation—he added, "I am finking." It was a phrase Valerie Storie never forgot.

For a quarter of an hour, they sat in the car with Gregsten's bleeding body. Suddenly and chillingly, the gunman leaned closer to Valerie Storie and ordered: "Kiss me!" At that moment, a passing car lit up his face, which was partly masked. Valerie noticed his eyes. He then forced her into the back seat and raped her.

Valerie Storie's ordeal wasn't over. The gunman told her that he was going to take the car. Together, they dragged Gregsten's body from the driving seat and dumped it in the lay-by. The gunman did not appear to be familiar with the make of car, and made Valerie explain the gears and switches several times.

It was now about 3.30 a.m. As the killer walked to the car for the last time, he turned and without warning fired six shots at the girl. As Valerie Storie collapsed in agony, her legs paralyzed, he calmly reloaded and fired another volley. Leaving her for dead, he drove off in the direction of Luton. But Valerie Storie did not die. Incredibly, she was able to make a statement to the police and within hours every newspaper in Britain carried a "Wanted" description of the killer: "Aged about 30, 5 ft. 6 ins., pale, clean-shaven face, dark brown hair, deep-set brown eyes, talks with an East End of London accent."

While a massive manhunt swept through southern England, the first clues appeared. The grey Morris Minor was found abandoned at Ilford and several passers-by recalled seeing it being driven erratically earlier that morning. Two days later, a cleaner discovered a fully loaded revolver and five boxes of ammunition hidden under the back seat of a 36A London bus. The gun was rushed to Scotland Yard, where it was confirmed as the murder weapon.

The same day, a London newspaper

Keystone

Syndication International

A brutal roadside crime (✗): a married man murdered, his girlfriend raped and left for dead. British justice, so often described as the envy of the world, brings petty crook James Hanratty to trial—and to the gallows. Only then does new evidence emerge . . . too late for the third victim of the tragedy.

Press Association

The murder at Deadman's Hill

ALL DRIVERS TOLD: BEWARE HITCH-HIKING KILLER

Death car abandoned

DEADMAN'S HILL

DEADMAN'S HILL

FOR MORE EXCITING NEWS ABOUT 'DAUGHTER OF JANE'

O.P.S. This was Mum!

AIR HUNT FOR LOST BATHERS

printed this comment: "Police are considering a theory that though Mr. Gregsten and Valerie did not know the killer, he may have known them. The killer may have become attracted to Valerie after seeing her with Gregsten at some time." Throughout the entire case, the theory was never raised again. Yet it was to prove strangely prophetic.

On August 27, the manager of a small hotel in north London telephoned the police to say that one of his guests had been behaving oddly for several days. He had locked himself in his room and refused to come out. Police descended on the hotel and questioned the man about his movements on the night of the murder; the man's claim that he had been visiting his mother was eventually accepted. His name was Peter Louis Alphon.

One feature in common

Meanwhile, the police had been having problems with Valerie Storie's description of the killer. It conflicted sharply with descriptions given by other witnesses—including those who had seen the grey Morris Minor being driven erratically a few hours after the murder. On August 29, the police published *two* Identikit pictures of the wanted man, each one based on a different description. There was one feature in common, however; both pictures showed dark, staring eyes. That night, the pictures were flashed on to TV screens all over Britain.

In a small house in north London, James Hanratty—a small-time house-

breaker and sneakthief—sat watching TV. He was lodging with another small-time criminal, James "Dixie" France, and his wife. As the pictures came up, Mrs. France turned to Hanratty and exclaimed: "Don't they look like you!" It was an illogical remark, for Hanratty's most noticeable feature was his bright blue eyes. There was no reason at all to link him with the crime, and he laughed it off.

But the most bizarre—almost supernatural—coincidence happened two days later, when Hanratty went to take a suit into the cleaner's. On the way, he had to pass an antique shop owned by Mr. William Ewer. Mr. Ewer was the brother-in-law of Janet Gregsten—the murdered man's widow—and he had invited Mrs. Gregsten to stay a few days, to get over the tragedy. When Hanratty walked by, Mrs. Gregsten was standing in the window.

According to newspaper reports, Mrs. Gregsten cried to her brother-in-law: "That's the man. I've got an overpowering feeling. That's him!" Apart from the unnerving coincidence, Mrs. Gregsten's identification of Hanratty as her husband's murderer was way off target; he did not resemble either of the Identikit pictures, and his eyes were blue.

Mrs. Gregsten was so sure, however, that her brother-in-law checked at the cleaner's shop after Hanratty had left. Hanratty had given the name "J. Ryan" and James France's address. Mr. Ewer passed the information on to the police who—clearly reluctant to act on what was no more than a psychic hunch—took

"KISS ME!" said the gunman. Valerie Storie (right, with widow of her murdered lover) remembered his staring eyes as he raped her. Then she and the killer dragged the body of Michael Gregsten (above) from the car to a lay-by (top).

no action. In any case, Hanratty did not fit the description of the killer.

Later, Mr. Ewer denied the "supernatural identification" story. He said he first suspected Hanratty because he fitted the "Wanted" description of "a man with staring eyes".

That was on August 31. Twenty-four hours *later*, the whole picture had—quite literally—changed. Valerie Storie altered one vital detail in her description of the murderer. She told detectives at her bedside, "He had icy-blue, saucer-like eyes." Now it only needed a single, firm clue to link Hanratty with the murder. It came on September 11. William Nudds, an assistant manager at the Vienna Hotel, in London's Maida Vale, was checking one of the rooms when he discovered two .38 cartridge cases, both fired by the murder weapon. On the night before the murder, the room had been occupied by a Mr. J. Ryan.

But the trail did not lead directly to Hanratty. There was one small complication which led the police on to an entirely different track. The Vienna Hotel had had another guest; on the day *after* the murder, another man had booked into the same room: his name was Peter Louis Alphon.

For a moment, the "blue saucer-like eyes" of Gregsten's killer were forgotten, for Alphon bore a striking resemblance to Valerie Storie's original description—right down to the brown, deep-set eyes. A double-check with Alphon's mother destroyed his earlier alibi. "I haven't seen him for two months," she told the police.

Another change of mind

On September 22, Alphon gave himself up to the police, but their satisfaction was short-lived. Valerie Storie failed to recognize Alphon at an identity parade, and they were forced to release him. By now, their attention was already being focussed on James Hanratty, thanks to another "change of mind" on the part of a witness. The hotel manager William Nudds—who was also a police informer—withdrew his earlier statement, which had shed suspicion on Alphon. Instead, he substituted a second version which drastically implicated "J. Ryan".

Now it was Hanratty on the run. As the net closed in, Hanratty made repeated phone calls to the police declaring his innocence, but refusing to give himself up. On October 9, he was spotted in Blackpool and arrested. This time, the police were taking no chances, and at an identification parade Valerie Storie added an extra refinement. She asked all the men to say the words, "Be quiet will you, I am thinking". The mispronunciation "finking" cut through the babble like a knife. It came from James Hanratty, and it was enough to lead him to

the Old Bailey, charged with the murder of Michael Gregsten.

Hanratty's trial lasted 21 days—the longest murder trial against a single defendant in British legal history—and right from the start there was conflict over one fundamental issue, the identification of the killer. Did he look like the Identikit pictures or not? Were his eyes dark and deep-set or blue and icy? Was he medium-built or heavily-built? Was his hair dark or light, swept back or close-cropped? In fact, was it Hanratty at all?

The one person who could answer all these questions seemed oddly unsure; in an earlier identity parade, at which Peter Louis Alphon had been present, Valerie Storie had picked out the wrong man as her attacker. Hanratty's counsel, Mr. Michael Sherrard, reminded her of this—and got an astonishing answer:

Mr. Sherrard: On that first parade you surveyed the men paraded before you for something as long as five minutes before saying something?

Miss Storie: Yes.

Mr. Sherrard: And you then identified a man as being, in your view, the assailant?

Miss Storie: Yes.

Mr. Sherrard: Can you tell us what the man looked like?

Miss Storie: No.

It was an incredible reply. Here was an identity parade, which included a man who fitted the killer's description, yet Miss Storie picked out a completely innocent person; had she picked Peter Louis Alphon, the police would have had enough

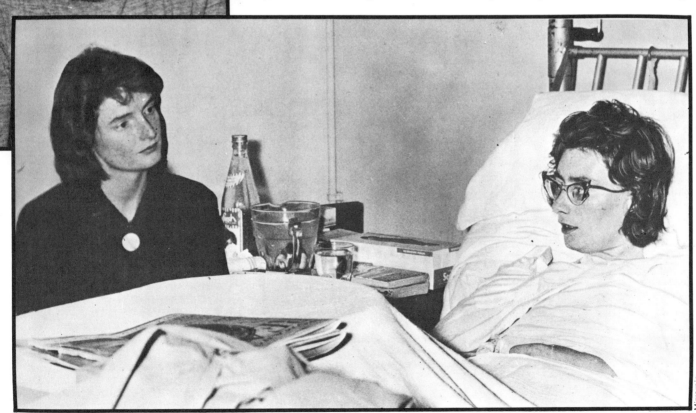

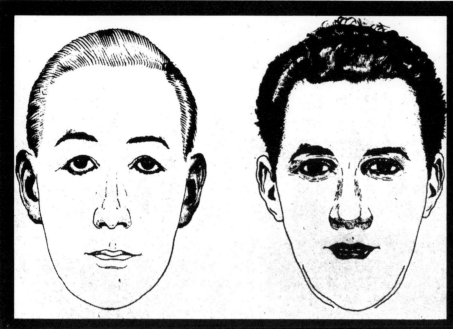

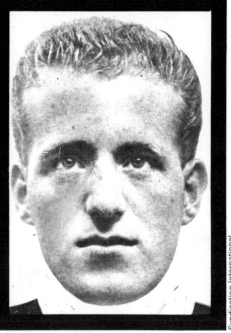

circumstantial evidence against him to charge him with the murder, and he would now be standing in the dock. Yet seven weeks later, at another parade, Miss Storie had settled on Hanratty, although he looked nothing like her original description of the murderer.

There was even more conflict between Valerie Storie's evidence and her statements before the trial. During her testimony, there were significant changes in her description of the murderer's familiarity with the Morris Minor car, his knowledge of the area, his conversation during the car ride—and whether he had been wearing a watch.

At an earlier hearing, Valerie Storie had stated categorically:

There's plenty of time

"We asked him what he wanted. He kept looking at his watch. It was a wrist watch. I can't remember which wrist it was on. I asked him what he wanted. He said, 'There's plenty of time.' We asked what for. He shrugged his shoulders and said again, 'There's plenty of time'."

Hanratty's counsel pounced on this point:

Mr. Sherrard: Had he got a watch on, do you remember?

Miss Storie: He may have. I cannot remember.

One of the most damning statements against Hanratty had been made by—of all people—his own friend in crime, James "Dixie" France. He had told the police that Hanratty had once remarked to him that the best place to "hide something" was under the back seat of a bus. This was where the murder weapon had been found.

In court, Hanratty's version of the conversation was that he had said the back seat of a bus was a good place "to get rid of rubbish", like unwanted loot from a robbery. Hanratty's counsel challenged France:

Mr. Sherrard: One of the things he said about his business was that he had to be very careful what he carried?

France: That is true, and it was a good hiding place in case he needed to drop anything quickly.

Mr. Sherrard: Or if he had his pockets bulging he would sort out what he used to call the rubbish and get rid of that—the paste and so on—and keep the other stuff in his pockets.

France: I do not think he could tell the difference between paste and diamonds.

Mr. Sherrard: But that is what he said he used to do?

France: If that is what he said he used to do, he must have done it.

Mr. Sherrard: Did he say it to you?

France: I cannot recollect.

Mr. Sherrard: He may have done?

France: He may have done.

The many changes in details and shifts in emphasis were significant but inconclusive. What was of vital importance was Hanratty's whereabouts on the night of the murder. Throughout the trial, Hanratty had stuck to one story: on the morning of August 22 he had travelled to Liverpool by train, spent the whole day there and stayed the night with three friends in Scotland Road; it was therefore impossible for him to have committed the murder 4½ hours away.

According to the defence, several witnesses recalled seeing Hanratty in Liverpool. One of them, a sweetshop assistant named Olive Dinwoodie, testified that Hanratty had definitely walked into her

DID HE look like the Identikit picture or not? Were his eyes dark, or blue and icy? Medium or heavy build? What kind of hair? In fact, was it Hanratty at all?

shop during the afternoon. When the prosecution suggested that the day had been the 21st and *not* the 22nd, Hanratty's counsel produced convincing evidence that Hanratty had still been with the Frances in London on the 21st.

However, there was one yawning gap in Hanratty's alibi. He could not produce—or even name—the three men with whom he had stayed the night. The reason was that they were all wanted smalltime criminals, and to identify them would have broken their trust. It was a flimsy excuse and the prosecution hammered the theme day after day: Surely no man in his right mind would risk his own neck rather than name these three men? That is, if they existed—and if they didn't exist, where was Hanratty on the night of the 22nd? The alibi was plainly falling apart at the seams. Hanratty's own legal advisers appealed to him to produce the three men, but Hanratty wouldn't budge.

Changing in mid-trial

The trial had now been running for more than a week, and Hanratty could see his alibi being choked to death. It was then that he performed his disastrous somersault. "The story of the three men is a pack of lies," he told his counsel. "In fact, I travelled to Rhyl on the evening of the 22nd and stayed at a lodging-house there." Hanratty's legal team were aghast. They knew only too well the peril of changing an alibi in mid-trial.

If the defence was mortified, the prosecution was overjoyed. Hanratty had

Syndication International

played right into their hands. "The hallmark of a false alibi is one that is set up at the last moment," said Prosecuting Counsel, Mr. Graham Swanwick, Q.C., with obvious satisfaction. Hanratty's attempt to justify the change in alibi met with scorn from Mr. Swanwick.

Mr. Swanwick: Why did you never go back to Rhyl to find the boarding house?

Hanratty: Because at this stage when I spoke to Detective-Superintendent Robert Acott over the phone I knew I had already told him a lie about Liverpool and it was quite obvious to me inside that I never committed this crime and that I had nothing at all to fear. But as this case eventually went along, I got so frightened with the evidence being brought forward, and the lies in the witness box — well, it is disgraceful to talk about them. But I am just trying to suggest at this stage when I spoke to Mr. Acott I did not fear any danger, because I knew in my heart and soul I did not commit this crime.

Mr. Swanwick: But you had from 7 to 11 October in the Liverpool or Blackpool area, when you could have gone along and tried to find this boarding house, and if you had found it all your troubles would have been over, would they not?

Confused and evasive

Hanratty: Yes, in that sense, yes. But in the state I was in at the time I was very depressed, what with the tension in the papers. It is very hard to say how your mind will react at that stage. I was a wanted man by Mr. Acott. He wanted to interview me. It was in the papers and the police wanted to interview me. I could not go and knock at houses in Rhyl and ask if I stayed there on the 22 and 23 of August. I was a wanted man. I would have had to check and go to those houses.

Rhyl is a Welsh holiday resort, only 40 miles from Liverpool. While the trial continued, Hanratty's legal advisers combed the town to trace anybody who could substantiate his new alibi. The place where Hanratty was supposed to have stayed was identified as the Ingledene Boarding House. Other guests who had stayed there on August 22 were traced but none of them could remember Hanratty; in the witness-box the landlady was confused and evasive and stood up badly to cross-examination and like a hairline crack in the wing of an airplane, Hanratty's change of alibi was the fatal flaw which weakened and finally

THE BEST PLACE to hide something is under the back seat of a bus, quoth Hanratty — according to his accomplice in burglary. But after the hanging, this crucial prosecution witness killed himself. Coincidence . . . or guilty conscience?

destroyed his whole defence.

What on earth made him concoct the feeble story of the "three men" in the first place, knowing that he would eventually have to abandon it?

The clue is in his phrase "I was a wanted man". Hanratty was already on the run for housebreaking and he knew that, if caught, he faced a certain five-year sentence. This fear coloured all his actions. To travel to Rhyl and substantiate his alibi meant taking the risk of being spotted and arrested, and so the easiest way out was to cook up the story of the three men in Liverpool.

Hanratty was also sure of his innocence, and convinced he would be acquitted of murder. Only when he saw his first alibi being torn to shreds did he revert to the truth, thereby creating the worse possible impression. The truth came too late.

But the trial had not turned against Hanratty completely. One of the strongest points in his favour — apart from the jarring inconsistencies in the prosecution's case — was that he had no history of violent or sexual crime. He was an admitted housebreaker, with prison sentences behind him, a smalltime crook, but not a murderer or a sex-maniac. Time and again, he clashed with Mr. Swanwick.

Like a new toy . . .

Mr. Swanwick: I am suggesting it was your ambition to do a stick-up and you had just got this gun. Then you went to the Vienna Hotel to play with it like a new toy, and you went out to use it for the first time on August 22; and that after the murder you abandoned it on the bus. Do you follow?

Hanratty: Sir, are you trying to suggest to the court that I went out on August 22 to do a stick-up with a gun? Is that what you are trying to say?

Mr. Swanwick: Indeed I am.

Hanratty: Well, is it not quite obvious if I did that I would not be looking for a car in a cornfield, as you put it to the court. I will be looking for some cash, a bank, a shop, something to that effect. I would not be looking for a car in a cornfield for some cash for a stick-up.

Hanratty was also quick to spot Mr. Swanwick's ploy in trying to tempt him along a dangerous limb:

Mr. Swanwick: I am right in saying that you have been a professional housebreaker since you were 16?

Hanratty: That is quite correct.

Mr. Swanwick: Breaking regularly into other people's houses, which you describe as your business?

Hanratty: That is quite correct.

Mr. Swanwick: Taking their goods with no conscience and no regrets?

Hanratty: Yes, I agree.

Mr. Swanwick: Is that right?

Hanratty: Yes.

Mr. Swanwick: Selling them for what you can get to your clients?

Hanratty: That is correct, yes.

Mr. Swanwick: No regard, of course, to the sentimental value of anything which you took?

Hanratty: No.

Mr. Swanwick: No feelings towards the house owners who had come back and found their premises broken into and their goods missing?

Hanratty: Sir, I must put this point quite clear. I ain't a man the court approved of as of good character, but I am not a murderer. This is a murder trial, not a housebreaking trial.

Later, the prosecution tried to trap Hanratty again.

Mr. Swanwick: It may be that the predominant motive was that you wanted the girl: it may be that you wanted to practise a stick-up; it may be that you did not mind the money and the car?

Hanratty: I had all the money I wanted. I gave Mrs. France £15 that day. If I wanted a woman I could have gone in the West End and had a woman for a fortnight.

Mr. Swanwick: But is not the difference this, that then you would not have had the thrill of holding them up with a gun?

A maniac and a savage

Hanratty: The man who committed this is a maniac and a savage. I know what you have proved here. I am not a man the court can approve of, but I am not a maniac of any kind. I can prove it with my past girl-friends. I am decent—I cannot say honest—but I try to live a good and respectable life except for my housebreakings.

Maniac and savage . . . or smalltime crook? The jury pondered the verdict for 10 hours. When it came, it was a shock to nearly everyone in the court. Even the judge seemed surprised, for he hesitated a long time before pronouncing sentence. The verdict was guilty, and the sentence was death. Hanratty collapsed in front of the dock, crying, "I am not guilty . . . innocent . . . I am innocent, my Lord."

Early on the morning of April 4, 1962, James Hanratty was hanged at Bedford Jail. The real tragedy of judicial execu-

tion is its finality. No amount of dramatic new evidence, no sensational developments, no important new witnesses can bring a man back from the grave.

Even before Hanratty walked to the scaffold there had been some extraordinary developments. On March 13, Peter Louis Alphon—the original murder suspect—proclaimed Hanratty's innocence and called on the Home Secretary to issue a reprieve. Four days later, James "Dixie" France, the crucial prosecution witness, was found dead in a gas-filled room. He had killed himself.

Exactly one year after the murder—on August 22, 1962—the Hanratty family heard a knock on their door. It was Peter Louis Alphon. After a short discussion, he pulled out a chequebook and asked if he could compensate Mr. Hanratty for what had happened to his son. "I didn't think they would ever get enough evidence to hang him," he said cryptically. The Hanrattys sent him packing.

On the crucial evening

Now—when it was too late—the missing witnesses began to appear who could have supported Hanratty's Rhyl alibi. Several people claimed to have seen Hanratty in Rhyl on the crucial evening. Some remembered his conspicuously dyed hair, which was beginning to revert to its original colour. One man recalled Hanratty trying to sell him a watch.

But the first real hint that a terrible miscarriage of justice might have been committed came on May 15, 1962. The aptly-named Jean Justice, a wealthy and rather eccentric writer, had struck up a friendship with Peter Louis Alphon. He was convinced Alphon had been involved in the killing, and began pumping him for information. On May 15, Alphon handed Justice a sheaf of handwritten notes. To the writer's astonishment they appeared to constitute a detailed confession to the crime, with the implication that Hanratty—under his alias of J. Ryan—had been deliberately framed.

The most important passage read:

"1. Obtaining the gun.

"2. Frame-up in Vienna Hotel. How I knew Nudds. Reasons for this frame. Altering the register. Alibi with my mother. Planting cases in Room 24 when Ryan was out. Asking Nudds if Ryan had left.

"3. Slough. Had gun but hoping not to commit murder at that time but well in mood for it. Couple in car fitted my mood and main plan.

"4. From the moment I went in imitated working-class person with voice and background although I never met Ryan. But a lot of what I said which could be interpreted as Ryan's hatred of ordinary middle-class people stemmed from my heart and was my own hatred of them.

"5. I played with them as cat and mouse—but all the time I was tense and being an extrovert I showed it and exaggerated and a lot of nervousness was communicated to them.

"6. When I killed him and she said 'Oh, you swine, you bastard, you have shot him!', I felt the need to give her some explanation and I said, 'He shouldn't have tried to turn the tables on me.' She said, 'He wasn't, you swine. You are mad.' I said, 'He moved too quickly.' I knew I must kill her but first I might as well rape her. I felt tense and overwrought and that fleeting love would help me."

Justice realized the document could be a hoax, but the confession—with Alphon's name withheld—became the basis for an angry debate in the House of Commons.

It was wound up by the Home Secretary, Mr. Henry Brooke, who declared:

"If I thought there was anything in the memorandum I have received, I would not hesitate to appoint a public inquiry. Indeed, I go further than that. If I thought that on any reasonable view there could be anything in it, I would welcome an independent investigation, but I suggest that we must keep a sense of balance and proportion in these matters. I must tell the House that I have found nothing to cause me to doubt in any way that, after a full trial in which every point in Hanratty's defence was carefully examined, Hanratty was rightly convicted . . . I cannot agree to reopen the case because I believe that it is impossible that Mr. A. could have done it."

Not enough evidence

But it was by no means the last word. Public disquiet mounted. There was a further debate in the House of Lords. The Home Office twice sent a senior police officer to Rhyl to investigate Hanratty's alibi all over again, but on both occasions the conclusion was that there was not enough evidence to alter the original verdict. A succession of Home Secretaries turned down demands for a public inquiry, on the grounds that Hanratty's guilt had been proved beyond doubt.

And then Peter Louis Alphon spoke again. This time there was the suggestion of the one thing that had been missing throughout the whole case: a motive. That wasn't all. For the first time, another man's name was mentioned . . . a mysterious "Mr. X" whose obsession with the relationship between Michael Gregsten and Valerie Storie led to murder on Deadman's Hill.

For weeks, Alphon had been regularly phoning Jean Justice. Unknown to him,

BEYOND A REASONABLE DOUBT?
Perhaps Hanratty's change of alibi doomed him. Or was he, as the mysterious Peter Louis Alphon testified, framed?

SUNDAY PICTORIAL

February 18, 1962   No. 2,444   © Sunday Pictorial Newspapers, Ltd., 1962   5d.

THE A6 MURDER

GUILTY

HANRATTY JURY TAKE 9½ HOURS

By Bill Hamilton and Bill Duncan

THE murder trial of the century ended dramatically at 9.13 last night when James Hanratty was found guilty of the murder of Michael Gregsten. He was senenced to death.

Women at the back of the court at Bedford Assizes creamed when the leven-man jury returned heir verdict in the case f the A6 killing.

Hanratty swayed slightly. efore sentence of death was assed on him he was asked f he had anything to say.

There was a moment of silence nd Hanratty leaned over the ock. Addressing Mr. Justice orman, he said in a stumbling oice: "I am not innocent . . ."

Appeal

He swayed again, licked his ps and corrected himself and aid:

"I'm innocent, my lord, and I give notice of appeal. That's all I have to say at this stage."

The Judge's clerk then called or silence and the black cap was laced above the Judge's wig.

Hanratty's eyes bulged as the entence of death was passed. hen he left the dock and almost ashed down the staircase.

His counsel, Mr. Michael herrard, sat with head bowed, is face pale.

Hanratty had pleaded not guilty o murdering Gregsten and enied raping and shooting Gregsten's friend Valerie Storie.

Hanratty's mother, who was waiting in a room immediately above the court, collapsed when she heard the verdict. A doctor was called. Later, she left in a ar.

When Mrs. Janet Gregsten, idow of the murdered man, was old of the verdict, she said: "I eel relieved.

"The whole tragic business has

'I am innocent' he tells judge

now come to its logical conclusion."

The Hanratty case was the longest murder trial in British history, and lasted twenty-one days.

The jury had spent nine hours forty-eight minutes behind a locked door.

In the early evening they asked for guidance from Mr Justice Gorman.

They wanted to be clear in their minds about the meaning of circumstantial evidence, the legal aspect of identification and other points in the evidence. That was at 6.02 p.m.

But at 8.35 the jury sent a note to a court official.

'Not Called'

It asked that they should not be disturbed under any circumstances by anyone—including His Lordship.

Before he left the court, the judge told the jury: "I shall ask that you be not called for further jury service for ten years."

Ten minutes after he had been sentenced to death Hanratty was whisked away in a small blue police van to Bedford Jail.

More than 1,000 people—many had waited all day—surged around to try to catch a glimpse of him. But they didn't see him. The blinds in the van were drawn.

Their long wait had been in vain.

"Duty of a Jury"—See Page 19

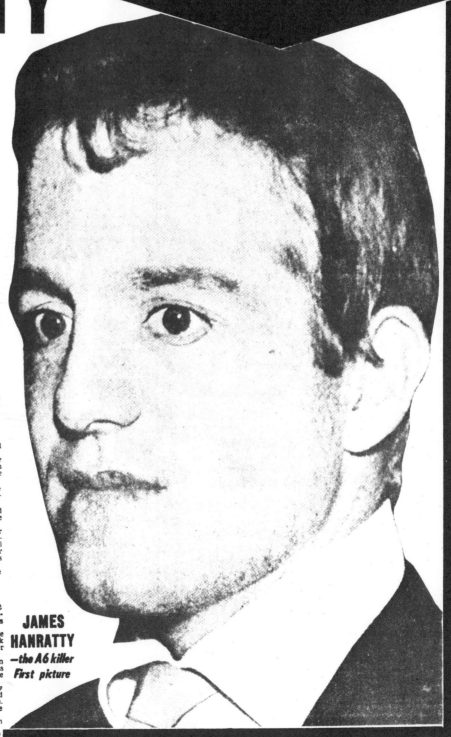

JAMES HANRATTY
—the A6 killer
First picture

129

IN THE BAG. John Lennon and Yoko Ono were among many protesting on behalf of Hanratty. In retrospect it seems likely that he was as much a victim of the crime as Michael Gregsten and Valerie Storie.

all the conversations had been tape-recorded. Justice already knew the identity of "Mr. X", but had no idea of his part in the murder. Now, as they talked on the phone, Alphon dropped the name:

Alphon: Those confession notes . . . what you had was a lot of rubbish. I think you ought to look for a more mundane motive in that murder. You have mentioned someone before, haven't you?

Justice: Who?

Alphon: You have mentioned somebody before. I'm not prepared to mention — well, I will mention him.

Justice: Well, mention him.

Alphon: X! That's who I say.

Justice: Why, is he dangerous?

Alphon: He is going to kill me.

Justice: Why?

Alphon: He is going to try But I don't think he will.

Justice: Well, if he is so dangerous will you tell me why?

Alphon: I want you to give him a message if you are in with him. No, I'm not a copper's nark and I'm not going to go to the police. I've never done that. That is why I was entrusted with the job in the first place because they knew that I wouldn't go. And I was there to separate a couple of people, you understand, in the car. And I gave them five hours to do it . . . If you put a strong man in. Somebody who is willing to go in with a gun and see that justice is done. I gone in and I've given him every chance — five hours — that was the motive.

Later in the conversation, Alphon referred to Gregsten again.

Alphon: Gregsten . . . he had a chance to go. He could have gone and said goodbye for good, there and then. He had five hours' chance to say goodbye and go back to his wife. He didn't take it. And he tried to get funny. He tried to turn the tables and he was shot. Dead. The other one wasn't anything to do with it at all. She just

happened to be there; it could have been her, it could have been anyone else. This is Gregsten at fault, you've got to consider. She was the vital witness after all, so she was shot dead — I thought.

Referring to the conspiracy to break up the affair between Gregsten and Valerie Storie, Alphon said:

"Let's say the mission was to see they were separated. Perhaps the mission was to see that they weren't separated in the way that they were, but the mission was to separate them and they were separated, weren't they? That's the point of it, and that's the only way they could have been separated. I couldn't see any other way myself. He had five hours and he couldn't do it. So there's not much point in giving them any longer, is there? He was determined to be unfaithful. He was going to go. If the man had just walked out with the gun and said goodbye, they would have been in the cornfield the next night. It wouldn't have done any good. The mission was to see that the affair was finished. That was the end of the affair."

Grotesque conversation

The conversation was grotesque. Was the whole thing a figment of Alphon's imagination? Or had there really been a bizarre plot by some puritanical maniac to break up Gregsten's romance? Whatever the confessions and allegations, there was not a shred of proof.

It was not until May 1967 that Alphon — still happily "confessing" to anyone who would listen — filled in the final, startling details in his incredible story. In an interview with author Paul Foot, Alphon alleged that he had been paid

£5000 by "Mr. X" to frighten Gregsten with a gun. He went on:

"Charles 'Dixie' France was a mutual friend of myself, Mr. X and Hanratty. France was broke at the time and he got money to get the gun and he gave me the gun a week before the murder. I wasn't very good with a gun and I had to have some practice, so I shot two bullets into a cushion in a chair at the Cumberland Hotel, Marble Arch. I took the two cartridge cases and gave them to France.

"X had shown me the cornfield where Gregsten and Valerie used to go after work. I'd been there twice before the murder on a reconnaissance. My plan was to persuade Gregsten to get out of the car and run away. And then I would take the girl and rape her, and then she might feel: what sort of man is he to leave me like that.

"But that didn't work. Gregsten had two chances to go, when he got out for cigarettes and milk, but he kept coming back. When I complained to them about their immorality they laughed and told me to mind my bloody business. Gregsten was cocky the whole time, trying to take the micky. I knew that the only way to break up the affair was to kill them."

Then Alphon revealed the diabolical twist in the alleged plot:

"I gave myself up on September 22 after the police had started a nation-wide hunt for me. I was pretty sure I would be all right because Valerie wouldn't recognize me. She didn't recognize me. She never saw my face in the car.

Stupid little crook

"When I was in the clear I began to realize the plot against Hanratty. X had suggested to me that when I was in the car I could pretend I was Hanratty, whom we all knew as a stupid little crook. That's why I said my name was Jim and I was on the run and had done time. What I didn't realize was that they meant to get Hanratty for what I had done. France put the gun on the bus where Hanratty had told him it was a good place to hide loot. And France put the cartridge cases in the Vienna Hotel."

Alphon later retracted the confession, and ever since has blown hot and cold over his alleged part in the murder of Deadman's Hill. Is Peter Louis Alphon a crank? A publicity seeker? Did his interrogation as the original murder suspect make him *imagine* he was the killer?

One thing is certain: with all the new evidence in its possession, no jury could now convict Hanratty "beyond a reasonable doubt". Whether the killer is still at large is irrelevant. The tragedy is that many people believe that James Hanratty was as much a victim of the bullets fired at Deadman's Hill as Michael Gregsten and Valerie Storie.

Syndication International

WHEN THE FAT MAN MADE A KILL...

The pretty young girl with the dark eyes badly wanted
to break into films and the only way seemed to lead through Fatty's bedroom.
It was also the way to a horrible death.

THE party taking place on the twelfth floor of the St. Francis Hotel in San Francisco was unlike any the staff and management had previously known. It began early in the morning of Sunday, September 4, 1921, when the massive, blubber-lipped film comedian, Roscoe "Fatty" Arbuckle, arrived from Hollywood and commandeered a luxury, three-room suite overlooking the city.

Accompanied by two boisterous friends, the silent-cinema star had driven up from Hollywood "to get away from all the pressures there". Taking the hotel floor manager to one side, he said impressively:

"I've just finished making three consecutive movies, and I'm pooped. All I want from you is co-operation and the turning of your blind eye. I'm here for fun — and fun I'm going to have!"

The manager nodded his head understandingly. At the time Arbuckle was America's most loved and laughed-at native comedian, coming second only to the English Charlie Chaplin in the popularity polls. He had recently signed a much-publicized contract which would earn him $3m. during the next three years, and his future seemed as assured and gilt-edged as that of the United States.

"Certainly, sir," the manager complied. "Just let me know what your requirements are, and we'll do our best to fill them."

"You can start by garaging my Rolls-Royce," said Arbuckle brusquely. "After that you can send up the cigars and booze. The girls I'll take care of myself."

Accordingly, for the next couple of hours, a non-stop procession of waiters, deliverymen, messenger-boys and guests made their way up to the "open-house" suite. Porters staggered in with crates of gin, whisky, rum and brandy. There was a constant demand for crushed ice, and lackeys were sent scurrying for cases of Arbuckle's own favourite tipple — French champagne.

By early afternoon it seemed as though the party had been going on forever, and that it was never going to stop. A phonograph blared out the latest gay and bouncy ragtime tunes, and a succession of chorus-girls, models, and small-part actresses arrived to be inspected and possibly sampled by the host himself.

Roadhouse orgy

Separated from his disillusioned wife, the 34-year-old comedian had a sexual appetite that was as great, if not more demanding, than his craving for wine and food. His weight — he had been known to top 280 pounds — and his foolish, tragi-comic appearance did not aid his image as a lover and ladies' man. His romantic technique was crude, and he had acquired the reputation of being something of a "rape artist".

Four years previously he had been involved in a sordid roadhouse orgy near Boston. Two girls hired to entertain the all-male guests complained later to the police that their status as "professional musicians" had been abused and violated. Arbuckle and his Hollywood hangers-on had treated them "just like prostitutes", and, even more insulting, the girls had not received the promised $50 a head (or a body, as had turned out to be the case) for their services.

A frenzied pulling of strings by the West Coast producers who employed Arbuckle succeeded in keeping his name out of the more blatant headlines. The scandal was tactfully played down, and the funny-man was free to continue his off-screen career as a good liver and solid lover.

But although the general public still did not know Arbuckle for the man that he was, there were those in the film industry itself who considered him depraved even by Hollywood's alleycat standards. Director Henry Lehrman, who had been responsible for some of Chaplin's early American films, said of Arbuckle that:

"He often bragged to me that he had ripped the dress off an 'unco-operative' girl and ravaged her. In the end I told him if he didn't keep away from the female dressing-rooms, I'd have him thrown out of Hollywood on his fleshy ear."

Fat octopus

Due to a kink in his psychological make-up, Arbuckle was mainly attracted to girls who played hard to get, and whom he couldn't get. One such "tease" was a petite brunette model and bit-part player called Virginia Rappe — whose face decorated the sheet music of "Let Me Call You Sweetheart".

She had long been pursued and lusted after by the double-chinned comic, and she'd expressed her feelings for him in immoderate terms: "I'd sooner go to bed with a jungle ape, than have that fat octopus groping at me," she told her friends and fellow would-be actresses.

Much as Arbuckle physically repelled her, however, she was prepared to make the scene in his money-making two-reel

131

comedies, if not in the seclusion of his bedroom. More by good management than luck, she also was in San Francisco on that soon to be notorious Sunday — staying at the nearby Palace Hotel with her agent and a friend named Mrs. Delamont. She had given Arbuckle her telephone number, and all day she waited impatiently for him to call.

Admission price

The party had reached and passed its peak when Arbuckle finally tired of the champagne, the chorus-girls, the music, the jokes, the gossip. He wanted Virginia, and he wanted her fast. He rang the Palace and before long the aspiring actress arrived with her personal "bodyguard". She found Arbuckle dressed in pyjamas, carpet slippers and bathrobe — an outfit which did nothing to disguise the extreme grossness of his body.

Refusing an offer of champagne, 25-year-old Virginia settled for a glass of gin and orange-juice — a "screwdriver". She was on her third drink, and still hoping that Arbuckle would agree to star her in one of his farces, when the comedian abruptly tired of business talk.

He jumped to his feet, grabbed Virginia by the arm, hustled her across the drawing-room, and pushed her into an adjacent bedroom. As he closed and locked the door behind them, the half-a-dozen guests present heard him crow: "I've waited for you for five years — and now I've got you!"

Mrs. Delamont and the agent shrugged their shoulders at the incident, and agreed that if Virginia wanted so badly to be in the movies, then she would have to pay the admission price. The couple then freshened their drinks and chatted about everything except what was presumably going on in room 1219.

Suddenly their conversation was punctuated by a series of agonized and blood-freezing screams. They came from the bedroom and Mrs. Delamont ran to the door and unsuccessfully tried to open it. "What's the matter, Virginia?" she cried. "Whatever's happening?"

The screams continued as she wrestled with the knob. Finally she moved over to the telephone and rang down to the reception desk for help. A few moments later the hotel's assistant manager, Mr. H. J. Boyle, burst into the suite. Just as he did so, the bedroom door opened and Arbuckle stood with Virginia's cloche hat perched ludicrously on his head.

Scattered clothes

He gave his innocent, clown's smile and did a little dance on the threshold. For once, however, his audience — captive though it was — was not amused. He dropped his funny-man's mask and said coldly: "Go in and get her dressed. Take her back to where she came from. She makes too much noise."

The horrified Mrs. Delamont slipped past him and entered the room. There she saw Virginia lying white-faced and moaning on the floor. Her flimsy clothes and undergarments were scattered around her, and her black lace garters dangled from

FATTY'S hotel — an artist's impression of the St. Francis in San Francisco where the fast-living fat man's career began to crumble in scandal.

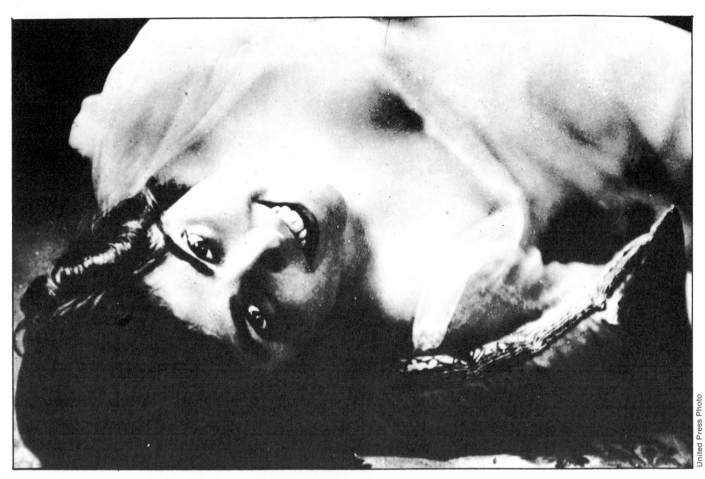

United Press Photo

the chair on which they had been thrown. The cover girl raised her head and looked pathetically at her friend.

"He hurt me. Roscoe hurt me," she whispered. Talking only increased the pain she was in, and she sank back again, sobbing, "I'm dying, I'm dying. Roscoe did it."

Watching the two women from the door, Arbuckle almost spat with disgust. "She's just acting it up," he said contemptuously. "She always was a lousy actress."

At this, Virginia's groans became even more pronounced.

"Shut up, you phoney!" snarled Arbuckle furiously. "Shut your mouth or I'll throw you outa the window!"

Borderline

Before he could carry out his threat, the house doctor was sent for, and Virginia was taken to another room in the hotel—far from the suite in which Roscoe Arbuckle had tried to consummate his passion of five years' standing. For the next three days, Virginia Rappe trod the borderline between life and death. She failed, rallied, and failed again. On the Thursday she was transferred to a private nursing home, where she died shortly after admittance.

The Deputy Coroner of San Francisco, Dr. Michael Brown, was called in to perform an autopsy on the dead actress. He

SHE TEASED the double-chinned comedian but for five years kept her beautiful body out of his reach. When she stepped into Arbuckle's bedroom on the fatal night she was, no doubt, sure of gaining ample reward in exchange for "giving in" to the man she once referred to as an octopus. She got more than she bargained for. Judging by the condition of her clothing, torn and crumpled (below), she walked into a fierce attack.

UPI

examined the body in the morgue—shook his head in horror and disbelief—and then rang the police.

"You'd better get round here straight away," he told them. "This is no natural death. The poor girl's bladder has been ruptured. It looks like murder to me!"

When the police arrived they confirmed the doctor's opinion, and the next morning newspapers across America proclaimed in dramatic headlines that Arbuckle had once again centred in an orgy—one that had climaxed in rape and death.

Bedroom antics

The inquest which followed recorded that Arbuckle was "criminally responsible" for Virginia's death, and the jury recommended that he be charged with manslaughter. The District Attorney went further than this and raised the charge to murder—although there was no evidence that the comedian had intended to kill the over-ambitious model.

At a preliminary hearing before the first of Arbuckle's three trials, the accounts of what had actually occurred in room 1219 were considered so appalling that they were written down on paper and handed round the court.

Outside the courtroom, however, one of the principal witnesses—a friend of Arbuckle's called Al Seminacher—said that on the day after the assault, while

133

Virginia was still fighting for her life, the comedian had "won laughs" by describing his bedroom antics.

"He didn't rape her in the sense that he forced her to have intercourse with him," Seminacher stated. "He simply took a piece of ice from an ice-bucket and thrust it into her genitals."

The public outcry that followed this disclosure ensured that Hollywood's first major scandal would be broadcast and discussed throughout the world. In America itself church groups and the powerful women's clubs demanded that the comic's current films be withdrawn from circulation, and that the $½m.-worth of unreleased Arbuckle movies be kept from the exhibitors.

For the first time in his hitherto triumphant career—which had shot him from obscurity as a $3 a day Keystone Cop to millionaire stardom—Arbuckle found himself branded as a "monster". His boast that he "lived only for women" was turned against him. His grotesque appearance was no longer considered to be a laughing matter. From then on he was "the fat beast", "the fat rapist", "the fat killer".

Great injustice

Arbuckle was released on bail until his first trial in November 1921, when the jury failed to agree and was subsequently discharged. A second trial also ended in dispute, and it was not until April 1922 that a third jury decided that Arbuckle was "not guilty" as indicted. In acquitting him the jurors added a rider saying:

"Acquittal is not enough for Roscoe Arbuckle. We feel a great injustice has been done to him and there was not the slightest proof to connect him in any way with the commission of any crime."

But although he was once again a free man, Arbuckle was professionally as dead as if he had been put in the electric chair. His fortune had been spent on legal fees, his films were on the banned list, and the studios refused to employ him. Indeed such was the indignation levelled against Hollywood that later in 1922 the famous Hays Office—presided over by the ultra-religious William Harrison Hays—was established to stamp out immorality in the film capital. A special "morality clause" was written into the players' contracts, and the man who had unwittingly inspired this lingered in the outer shadows of the spotlight.

For the next ten years Arbuckle toured the sticks in a number of farces that were mostly booed off the stage. He directed a few indifferent films under his mother's maiden name of Goodrich, and it was left to his third and last wife to give him what comfort she could.

In the summer of 1933, however, the former funny-man at last got back into favour with the studio executives. He was hired by Warner Brothers to make a series of short comedies. But before they could be completed and released, he returned to his New York hotel after a celebration party, and died quietly in the early hours of the morning.

The newspaper obituary writers sought fitting epitaphs for the dead clown, but Arbuckle had provided his own, twelve years earlier, shortly after he had interfered with and killed Virginia Rappe.

"Someone tall, dark and handsome could have gotten away with what I did," he lamented. "But I was fat, foolish and moon-faced. I hadn't a chance."

COLLAPSE of stout party . . . Arbuckle
is pictured (left) in three scenes from
his comedy films and (this page) being
booked at the Hall of Justice—now
despised and reviled by press and public.

THE RIVERSIDE RAPIST

Two teenage girls on their way home one evening in May 1953
had been raped, murdered and flung into the
River Thames. Now, the prime suspect stood on trial.
Few accused have succeeded so well in arousing feelings
of revulsion in a court audience . . .

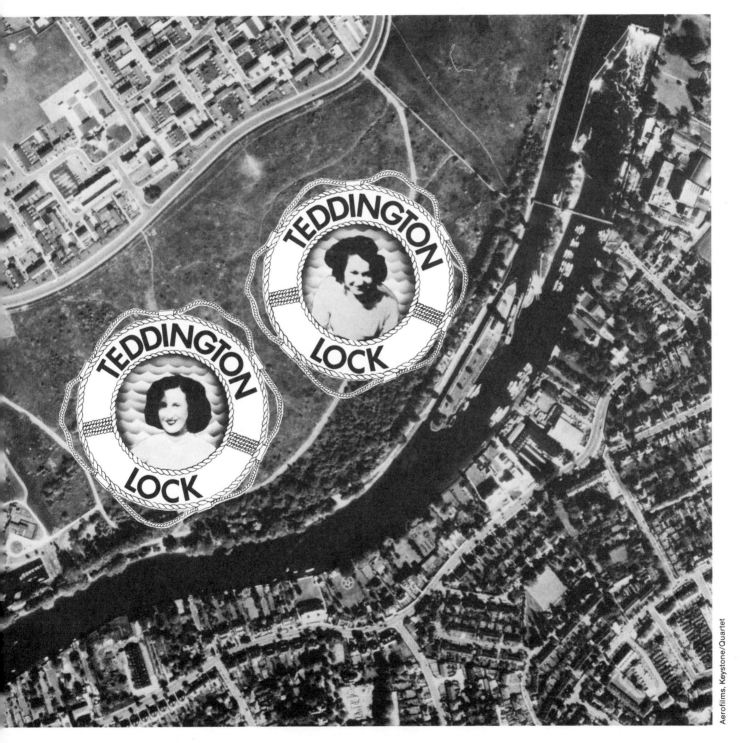

THERE WERE two notable characteristics about the pallid face of 22-year-old Alfred Charles Whiteway as it was gazed upon by the 12 members of London's Old Bailey jury on a chill October morning in 1953. It was badly blotched by acne, and the eyes were tensed and partially closed by trying to overcome defective vision.

It was a face remembered with horror by many women, and even by schoolgirls, who had suffered from attacks by Whiteway, the rapist. Among the last frightful sights seen by two teenaged girls, as they were raped and slain on a quiet towpath by the River Thames, were the ugly contours of that lusting, pitiless face.

Both girls, 16-year-old Barbara Songhurst and 18-year-old Christine Reed, had been assaulted and killed within minutes of each other close to Teddington Lock, where the Thames swings in a broad arc on its way down to Richmond and Kew Gardens. But, in the tradition of the law where more than one victim is involved, Whiteway was charged with the murder of only one girl – Barbara – although the jury would be told of both deaths.

Silent court

As he climbed the steps from the cells and rose into view in the massive prisoner's dock in the famous Number One court, Whiteway, a builder's labourer, looked more like a dull-witted, shambling youth than a brutal killer. He stared vacantly as a side door opened and the judge, Mr. Justice Hilbery, swept through in his grey and scarlet robes and took his seat on the dais beneath Edward VII's coat of arms and the sword of justice.

He twitched just discernibly as the black gowned usher cried out in booming tones: "All persons who have anything to do before my Lady the Queen's Justices of Oyer and Terminer and General Gaol Delivery for the jurisdiction of the Central Criminal Court draw near and give your attention – God Save the Queen!" He seemed startled when, having read the charge, the clerk of the court demanded to know his plea, guilty or not guilty. He paused for a moment and then, at last, in his brittle, near-Cockney tones he muttered, "Not guilty."

There was a distinct sense of revulsion in the silent court as Mr. Christmas Humphreys – one of Britain's most eminent lawyers and a leading member of the followers of Buddhism in the Western world – opened the case on behalf of the Crown. To aid the jury Mr. Humphreys produced a map of the Thames, with its towpath prominently marked, and pointed to one small area marked with a cross. It was there, somewhere between 11 and 11.30 on the night of Sunday, May 31, 1953, that the two friends, Barbara and Christine, had last been seen alive, riding their bicycles towards Kingston Bridge

on their way home to Teddington.

Early the following morning an employee of the Port of London Authority found Barbara's body, floating face downwards, in the river off Richmond. She had been violently battered over the head with some heavy object and stabbed three times in the back – so deeply that each thrust of the knife had penetrated the lungs. Five days later Christine's body was discovered, even further downstream, also with severe head injuries and six stab wounds, into one of which a blade had been plunged four times. Both girls had been virgins before the fatal attacks and Barbara had certainly been raped before death. In Christine's case there was no certainty, from the medical evidence, as to whether she had been raped before or after she died.

Half turning towards Whiteway, as he concluded his description of the victim's wounds, Mr. Humphreys told the jury: "This case does not depend on the details of the injuries to these girls, or how and at what time they died. The issue is that someone brutally assaulted, raped and murdered these girls and you have to satisfy yourselves if this was the man."

On the table in front of the prosecuting counsel as he spoke lay an axe – an axe, said Mr. Humphreys, that had belonged to Whiteway and had been used to bludgeon the two young girls.

Other exhibits were also laid out on the table, exhibits that included a man's clothing and a shoe contained in a transparent box and the members of the jury, and spectators, could see, as they craned forward, that to each was tied a label marked with the one word "Whiteway".

The shoe box was handed to Dr. Lewis Charles Nickolls, of Scotland Yard's Metropolitan Police Laboratory, who testified that he had examined the shoe and found strong traces of blood around the lace tags and the area where the sole was joined to the upper.

Dr. Nickolls went on: "I took the shoe to pieces and in the dust around the stitch-

FORENSIC expert Dr. Lewis Charles Nickolls gave evidence at the trial . . .

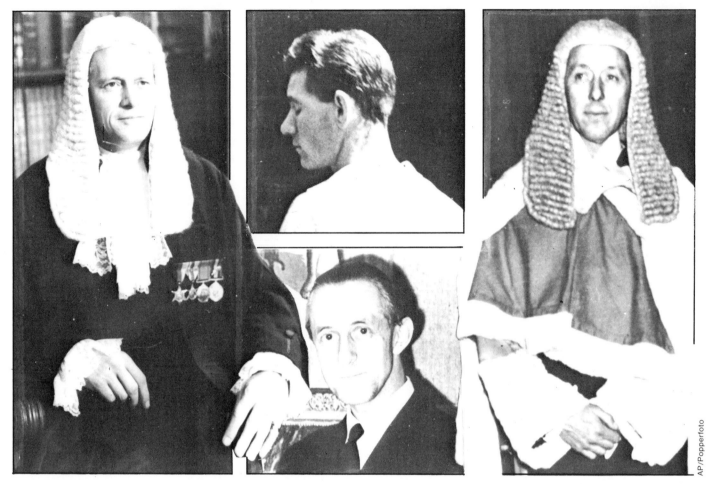

AP/Popperfoto

ing I identified the presence of human blood. This was similar to the reaction when a shoe is extensively bloodstained and either washed or worn in wet grass."

He had found no traces of blood on Whiteway's clothing nor on the axe, he said, and Mr. Peter Rawlinson, Whiteway's energetic and assiduously vigilant defence counsel, leapt in with a key question. "You found so little blood that you were unable to group it?" Fairly and promptly Dr. Nickolls answered "Yes."

Painful task

It was police-constable Arthur Henry Oliver, driver of a police patrol car, who told of the first official encounter with Whiteway after the murders. Acting "upon information received", he went to Oxshott Common, in Surrey, where he saw Whiteway and took him to the police station at Kingston-on-Thames. There he was briefly questioned and then allowed to go but, although detectives were not to learn of it until later, a most important thing had happened while Whiteway was in the car on its way to the interview.

One of the most unhappy policemen ever to step into an Old Bailey witness-box had the painful and upsetting task of explaining that event to the jury. He was police-constable Arthur Cosh, of Kingston, who had inspected the police patrol car the day after Whiteway's interview. As he was about to close the rear off-side door he saw an axe lying on the floor with its head pushed under the driver's seat. PC Cosh, looking increasingly distressed with each word he uttered, described the subsequent series of events:

"I put the axe in a locker in the station garage. I went sick on June 30 and did not return to the police station until July 8. When I returned I went to my locker and the axe was still in it. I took the axe out and put my hammer in the locker as there was not room for both. I took the axe home and put it in a tool box in the shed."

Did he ever use the axe? he was asked. Yes, he had "chopped a few sticks with it" on the concrete floor of his shed, and had noticed that the blade was sharp enough to cut easily through the wood. Mr. Rawlinson demanded to know why he had not immediately reported his discovery to his superiors.

The policeman hesitated for a moment. "The practice among drivers," he said, "is that if anything is found in a car it is claimed by the driver finding it."

The judge pounced upon this answer. "You are not suggesting that if a man leaves a jemmy in the car the officer claims it?" Laughter fluttered through the court. "No, sir," Constable Cosh replied, almost inaudibly.

TWO of Britain's most eminent lawyers took part in this trial — Mr. Peter Rawlinson (far left), who led for the Defence on behalf of Whiteway (above centre), and Mr. Christmas Humphreys, Q.C. (below centre) Counsel for the Prosecution. Mr. Justice Hilbery was the trial judge.

The strain of it all, the severity of the frowns on the faces of judge and barristers, proved too much for Cosh. As the end of the questioning approached his complexion suddenly turned ashen and he slumped forward in the witness-box.

Shakily he rose again, heaved himself from the witness-box and stumbled towards the exit. He did not return to the Old Bailey to hear the judge later refer to the axe incident as "that extraordinary piece of conduct by the officer Cosh".

Next came the one policeman whom the spectators had come especially to see, and whose evidence had been eagerly awaited — the "man from Scotland Yard", Detective Superintendent Herbert Hannam. It was he who had headed the investigation and directed the team of uniformed police and C.I.D. officers who had called on 4,000 homes in the murder area, interviewed 7,000 people, and taken 1,650 written statements.

From the earliest stages Whiteway had

been one of Hannam's prime suspects. For, although the superintendent could not disclose this to the Old Bailey jury, Whiteway had also been arrested, at around the same time, for attacks on a woman of 56 and a girl of 14.

So, without needing to explain what had led to the encounter, Hannam told how he questioned Whiteway on July 1. Whiteway, according to the detective, said: "I guessed this would come before long. It looks like me, I grant you, but I can save you a lot of time by telling you that when the job was done I was with my wife at her home . . ." (Because of housing difficulties Whiteway and his wife lived apart.)

"I am keeping my bloody mouth shut or you will pin it on me. You know what bastards coppers are. I had nothing to do with the girls. You are wasting your time. The bloke that did that job was mad."

Dramatic evidence

More interviews followed, on other days, and then Superintendent Hannam came to a crucial date in the investigation, July 30. The whole court listened intently as Hannam told how Whiteway was once again ushered into the room at Kingston police station used by the Yard man as his murder hunt headquarters.

"I took the axe from my briefcase and placed it on the table in front of us," he said. "I made no comment at all. He said, 'Blimey, that's it. It's been buggered about. It was bloody sharp when I had it. I sharpened it with the file.'"

Hannam paused, watching the judge swiftly scribbling his notes on the evidence. Then, he went on, he took a further object from his briefcase—a kukri knife, a curved knife broadening to a point and a type used in India. "Again," said the superintendent, "I made no comment. He said, 'That's it. You got it out of the water, didn't you?'" It was not Hannam's place to answer questions, and he did not reply to that. But he *did* tell Whiteway that an examination of one of his shoes disclosed heavy bloodstains.

Then the superintendent came to the most dramatic piece of evidence in the case, and the one piece over which the police were to be subjected to severe strictures by the defence. "I noticed then," the superintendent told the jury, "that the accused man turned noticeably pale. He stood up. I saw he was trembling considerably and he then said to me, 'You know bloody well it was me, don't you? I did not mean to kill 'em. I never wanted to hurt anyone.'"

Immediately a suspect seems to be ready to talk he must be cautioned that anything

he says may be used in evidence, and he must be invited to make a formal statement. Superintendent Hannam did just that and wrote down Whiteway's dictated statement. With its meticulously recorded illiterate touches, it was read to the jury by the clerk of the court.

"It's all up," the statement ran. "You know bloody well I done it. That shoe's buggered me. What a bloody mess. I am mental. Me head must be wrong. I cannot stop meself. I am not a bloody murderer. I only see one girl. She came round the tree where I stood and I bashed her and she went down like a log. Then the other screamed out down by the lock. Never saw her till then I didn't.

"I nipped over and shut her up. Two of 'em and then I tumbled the other one knew me. If it had not been for that it would not have happened. Put that bloody chopper away. It haunts me. What more do they want to know? Why don't the doctors do something? It will be mental, won't it? It must be. I can't stop it. Give us it. I will sign it."

Mr. Rawlinson then rose to cross-examine the superintendent. It soon became clear that Whiteway's defence was to hinge on an extremely delicate issue: the suggestion that the alleged confession had been "concocted" by the police.

Defence counsel began with the submission that Whiteway had not had an opportunity to see what had been written

THE HUNT is on . . . Detectives search for clues on the banks of the Thames, using a mine detector to locate a weapon.

Syndication International

down, and that when he signed the statement it was half covered by blotting paper. To this Superintendent Hannam replied sharply: "That is absolutely untrue and the suggestion behind it is a terrible one."

Mr. Justice Hilbery was determined that the jury should not miss the full implications of the line of questioning, and he directly asked Mr. Rawlinson:

"The suggestion is that Exhibit 24 [the "confession" statement] is a complete piece of fiction made by the officer?"

Rawlinson quietly replied: "That is what I am suggesting to the officer."

Turning again to Hannam, he declared: "I repeat the suggestion so that there should be no doubt about it, that that statement was invented by you."

Calmly the superintendent answered: "I repeat it is a shocking suggestion and I am pleased to deny it."

Doggedly, Mr. Rawlinson pursued his point and once more the rows of spectators fluttered with anticipation as he invited the superintendent to give a demonstration, there and then, of how he had written down Whiteway's statement at the accused man's dictation.

At once Superintendent Hannam left the witness-box, walked across the floor of the court and seated himself at the solicitors' table. For the second time the ushers showed their readiness to attend to the mechanics of the law. In an instant, they had placed sheets of paper before the superintendent. Peering over the top of the high dock, Whiteway followed every move with as avid a concentration as everyone else in the court. The judge asked Hannam whether he had the same pen with which he had written down the original statement, and he acknowledged that he had.

Not invented

Rapidly Mr. Rawlinson read one extract from that statement and asked if that was how Whiteway had spoken. Superintendent Hannam looked up from his seat at the table and replied:

"The circumstances there can never be repeated here. The caution was written first in a very quiet atmosphere. I walked round the table for him to sign it. He was still trembling. He was badly shaken and very pale. His knees were moving and his hands."

The demonstration continued, with Mr. Rawlinson briskly speaking Whiteway's words and Superintendent Hannam's pen moving unceasingly back and forth across the paper. At the end Hannam returned to the witness-box and Rawlinson stood for a moment, hitching his lawyer's gown around his shoulders as he gazed first at the alleged confession and then at the detective's newly-written version.

"You will notice that what you have just written is all joined together," he told

the superintendent. "Were you in a greater hurry?" Hannam replied: "I was writing something in my normal way there. The atmosphere here is entirely different."

One of Hannam's assistants, Detective-sergeant Harold Hudson, then entered the witness-box to confirm his chief's evidence that the statement was not invented. When he left, his place was taken by the central figure of the courtroom battle: Whiteway himself. He seemed even less imposing than before as he moved from the dock to the box.

He, too, was brought quickly to the circumstances of his statement. Had it been read to him after he had dictated it? No, it had not. Had he looked at what he was signing? No, he had not. He mumbled his answers and was ordered to speak up.

Gradually, Mr. Humphreys, for the prosecution, pinned him down to separate sections and sentences in his statement. He agreed that he had said "I am keeping my bloody mouth shut or you will pin it on me." He agreed that other parts of the statement were accurate. Then he went even further and told the prosecuting counsel:

"I said most of that statement except the sentence in the middle. They put that in themselves." Of course, Mr. Humphreys insisted, if he had in fact made that statement, "it is a confession of murder, isn't it?" Whiteway nodded. "Yes, sir," he grudgingly agreed.

In essence, Whiteway's evidence and his plea of not guilty thinned down to two single points: not only was the "confession" a police fake but, at the time of the murders, he was at the house in Teddington where he lived with his uncle and nowhere near the towpath. The uncle testified that Whiteway had come home, on the fatal night, at "about 11.30 by the clock", but the clock was 10 or 15 minutes slow. The witness admitted having said in a statement, "I have not got a good memory either for dates or times."

The moment was now approaching when the jury would decide the final issue, and its members listened to a last spirited appeal from Mr. Rawlinson for a not guilty verdict. He repeated his suggestions of police collusion, and laid great stress on the fact that no blood had been found on Whiteway's clothing.

In *his* summing-up, Mr. Humphreys also moved swiftly towards that last point — but with a very different argument. There had been no evidence that the clothing in which Whiteway was dressed when first seen by the police, or the clothing found at his home, was worn by him at the time of the murders. There was no proof there to support an alibi.

Both sides had expended all the legal energy at their command and now, on the last day, lawyers, spectators and newsmen crowded back into court to hear the judge's round-up of the evidence. It took

Mr. Justice Hilbery two hours and fifty-five minutes to deliver his address to the jury and, inevitably, he devoted close attention to the Whiteway statement.

"Whiteway," he said, "denies that there is a word of truth in the statement. If he did say it, it is a confession and he is guilty. There is no escaping from it. If he did not say it, you are faced with one of the most wicked pieces of evidence that has ever been made in this country."

In a single sentence the judge summed up the appalling events that had overtaken young Barbara and her friend, Christine. "One has the tragic thought," he said, "of these girls riding along in good spirits, little knowing that they were to be struck down and that this awful death was waiting for them along that towpath."

The kind of man who had committed the murders must have been a man who possessed such weapons as an axe and a double-edged knife. He would be a man who knew the murder spot well. There, the judge added, was the general picture of events; only the jury could decide whether or not Whiteway fitted into it.

The verdict

For the first time during the trial the tension eased as the jury of 10 men and two women rose and made their way in single file to the juryroom. Pressmen decided not to go far from the courtroom. Instinct and experience suggested that the jury would not be absent long. Forty-five minutes later they were proved right. The jury trooped back in again, the judge was summoned, and the clerk of the court asked for the verdict.

"Guilty," the foreman announced, and Whiteway stared ahead, unmoved. The court chaplain stepped to the judge's side, and carefully laid the small black "cap" on Mr. Justice Hilbery's head. Within seconds Whiteway had been sentenced to death and hustled out of sight to the cells below the prisoner's dock.

Whiteway's defenders took his case to the Appeal Court — but, after a two-hour hearing, it was dismissed in 20 minutes. The Lord Chief Justice of England, Lord Goddard, who heard the appeal with two other judges, described the case as "one of the most brutal and horrifying before this court, or any other, for years". Of Whiteway's plea to Superintendent Hannam, "Put that bloody chopper away. It haunts me", Lord Goddard commented: "If ever there was a case of the phrase of bloody Lady Macbeth being brought into real life, this was it."

On Tuesday, December 22, 1953, Whiteway was hanged in London's Wandsworth Prison. Only when his doom had been finally sealed did the public learn of the other attacks he had made on women — some of which only just escaped ending in murder.

UGLY VIEW . . . Superintendent Hannam peers through a telescopic "water glass" at the muddy Thames bed, looking for some new clue that will pinpoint the killer.

AN ICE-COOL MURDER

IT WAS just after nine on the evening of Easter Sunday, 1955, and business was brisk in the saloon bar of the Magdala public house, at the foot of South Hill Park, a hillside road in the leafy North London suburb of Hampstead. As was usual for a Sunday, the pub's "regulars" were crowded around the bar, a fair cross-section of sports-jacketed young men, who talked mostly of cars and women,

and of girls who laughed just a little too readily and noisily. Mr. Colson, the landlord, occasionally joined in the banter, as any good publican must, but mostly he busied himself setting up his customers' continuous orders.

He did pause once in his routine, however, to attend to a Mr. David Blakely, a 25-year-old, good-looking racing driver whom he knew well. Blakely had come

into the Magdala with his friend, Clive Gunnell, a 30-year-old Mayfair car sales-man, and he was anxious to cash a cheque for £5. Mr. Colson obliged and, after spending some time drinking with his friend at the bar, Blakely bought three

MANAGERESS of a club, but not of her passions, Ruth Ellis (left) gave her boyfriend Blakely (inset) no chance.

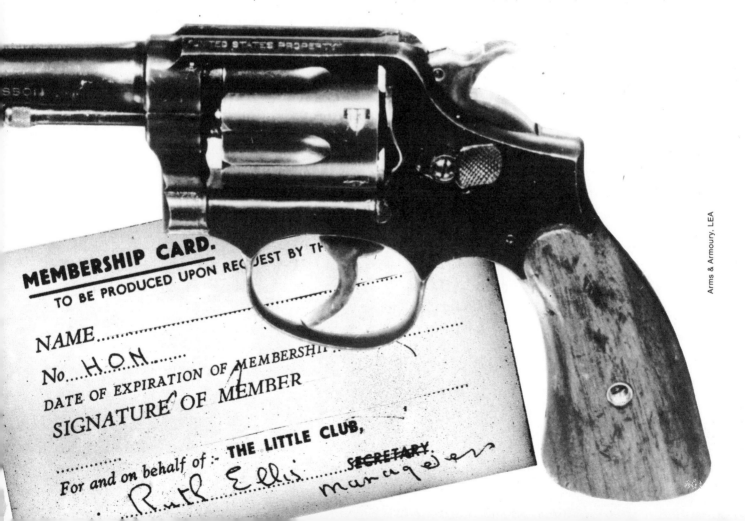

flagons of beer to replenish the stocks of a party to which he and Gunnell were now returning.

Waving goodnight to other regular customers, the two men left the bar and went out to Blakely's grey-green Vanguard van, parked at the kerbside immediately by the pub door. Gunnell waited by the passenger door while Blakely went around to the driver's side and—juggling with the flagon of beer he was carrying—searched in his pockets for his car keys.

Sinister tableau

Neither at that moment had noticed a slight, determined, platinum blonde walking down the hill, past a newsagent's shop, towards the pub. But she was observing Blakely carefully as she walked, and she called his name—"David!" Blakely, still having difficulty in finding his keys, took no notice and showed no sign of being aware that the girl was approaching him.

Finally, she stood beside him and as Blakely looked up he saw her swiftly open

her handbag and take out a heavy Smith and Wesson ·38 revolver. She raised the gun and pointed it straight at Blakely, saying nothing, making no other movement. For a moment the scene was frozen as in some sinister tableau, the blonde appearing to be making an effort to hold the bulky revolver, the man staring mutely at her with the beer flagon still cradled in his arm.

Then, as if at the movement of a switch, the tableau sprang to life. Blakely turned and began to run towards the back of the van but, before he reached it, the woman fired two shots in quick succession. Blakely, who had assumed the stooped posture of a man fleeing for his life, reared up, slammed into the side of the van and stumbled forward again, appearing to reach out towards his friend Gunnell and screaming "Clive!"

Gunnell stood absolutely still, hypnotized by disbelief. But still the woman came on, walking in steady pursuit of Blakely, whose blood was already smeared along the Vanguard's side. "Get out of the way, Clive," she shouted and relentlessly followed Blakely, who had now stumbled around the other side of the van and was trying to stagger away.

Feminine cry

Again the woman fired and Blakely reacted with a sharp half-spin of his body, lurched sideways, and fell full-length on his face with his head parallel to the billboards outside the newsagent's shop. The blonde walked towards the inert form and fired more shots directly into it, until the emptied six-chamber gun clicked uselessly. She seemed totally oblivious of a sharp, feminine cry of pain uttered by a bank official's wife who had walked unawares into the incident on her way to the Magdala, and whose thumb had been struck by a misdirected bullet.

Blakely was dead, the final coursings of his blood covering the pavement and mingling with the frothing beer from the smashed beer flagon which he had carried with him to the last. Magdala customers, who had first dismissed the sound of shots as a car back firing, now poured out into the street and surrounded the body in a gabbling, shocked group.

Someone looked towards the blonde woman and screamed: "What have you done?" But she remained absolutely motionless, standing with her back against the wall of the pub, not a mark or bloodstain on her grey two-piece suit and green sweater. Her right hand still gripped the Smith and Wesson.

Completely unmoved

A tall, purposeful man strode from the Magdala and the woman spoke to him, quite calmly and distinctly. "'Phone the police," she said. The man studied her for a moment. "I *am* a police officer," he replied and, reaching out his hand, he took the revolver from her. She made no attempt to stop him and together she and the officer—Police Constable Alan Thompson, of "L" Division, Metropolitan Police—stood silently waiting while an ambulance arrived and took Blakely's body away.

UNSUCCESSFUL as a racing driver, Blakely had even less fortune as a lover. Clive Gunnell (far left) witnessed his death. Ellis (left) showed no emotion.

Topix

Following quickly behind the ambulance came a police car and, with the plain-clothes P.C. Thompson still at her side, the woman was driven to Hampstead police station, where she was given a cup of tea. She still seemed completely unmoved, drained of all emotion. She sipped the tea, turned her head so that the reflected station lights danced in her platinum hair like heliograph signals, and pronounced suddenly and solemnly: "My name is Mrs. Ruth Ellis. I am a model. I am 28 and I live at 44, Egerton Gardens —that's in Kensington."

Fragments of passion

While Ruth Ellis, born Ruth Neilson in the Welsh seaside town of Rhyl on October 9, 1926, reverted to silence and sat upright and trance-like on her uncomfortable police station chair, three C.I.D. officers had already opened their murder investigation.

At just after two in the morning the three came into the room where she waited, and one, Detective Superintendent Leonard Crawford, said to her: "I have just seen the dead body of David Blakely at Hampstead mortuary. I understand you know something about it. You are not obliged to say anything at all about this unless you wish to do so, but whatever you say will be taken down in writing and may be given in evidence."

HIDEOUT for Blakely was the home (left) of the Findlaters, pictured with the ill-fated couple (below) in happier times. Ellis had known where to find him.

Ruth Ellis looked directly at the be-spectacled detective as though the words of the official "caution" held no fears for her whatsoever. Then, softly but without hesitation, she replied: "I understand what has been said. I am guilty. I am rather confused." She then dictated a lengthy, coherent account of her past relationship with the murdered man, and of the kaleidoscopic fragments of passion, jealousy, and frustration that had culminated in the ultimate image of murder.

Her statement began with a reference to the Little Club, a sleazy upstairs drinking room in Knightsbridge catering daily from three in the afternoon until eleven at night to a regular crowd of boozy businessmen and young, well-born drifters. It was here that the voyage towards murder was launched, over a gin-and-tonic served by Ruth Ellis, the manageress, to the attractive new member, David Blakely.

To many men in the Belgravia-Knightsbridge, second-rank social world, Ruth was the Little Club's main attraction. In the argot of the times she was "that smashing blonde", and this was precisely why the club owner had installed her as manageress on a £15 a week basic salary, plus a £10 a week entertainment allowance. In addition to the money, he gave her a rent-free, two-roomed apartment with kitchen over the club.

Marriage mockery

It was the peak of her achievement for Ruth, the former waitress and machine-minder in a South London factory, who had longed to escape from her humble family background and move among a "better class" people. And she had done much to fulfil her ambition, from the tedium of service as a clip-joint hostess, to a highly versatile career as a prostitute.

In September 1944 she had given birth to an illegitimate son (by a French Canadian Serviceman who had a wife and two children back in Canada), and subsequently she became the wife of George Ellis, a divorced dental surgeon from Surrey.

They were married in November 1950, when Ellis was 41 and she was 24, and she bore a daughter in October 1951. But Ruth's maverick life, and her husband's alcoholism, had made a mockery of the marriage from its very beginning, and the couple parted a month after their daughter's birth.

So it was that, even with two children to care for, Ruth Ellis had embarked upon yet another romance, at the Little Club, that afternoon in 1953 when she took young Mr. Blakely's order for a gin-and-

PUBLIC opinion swayed for and against the execution of the murderess. Her physical attractiveness created sympathy —and the interest of the press.

tonic. It was not an auspicious encounter. She had met him at another West End club a few weeks previously, had objected to some of his derogatory remarks about the hostesses, and called him a "pompous ass". He had displayed an equal antipathy towards her.

David Moffet Drummond Blakely, born the son of a Sheffield doctor on June 17, 1929, compensated with charm for what he lacked in natural ability and the will to find regular and useful employment. Even though he was no Adonis — he was only five feet nine inches tall — there was a certain little-boy-lost look about his deep, brown eyes, with their long, almost feminine eyelashes.

Outward charm

When he was sober he could exhibit a great deal of well-bred charm and easy, confident manners. But when he had drunk too much, which he did fairly regularly, he could be truculent and stupidly offensive.

But Blakely's obsessive interest, which outweighed his taste for drink and casual encounters with women, was in racing cars. He raced, without notable success, at a number of well-known tracks, including Le Mans in France. But he was neither able nor prepared to make the effort to acquire the kind of capital necessary for a serious

motor-racing career. He received a £7,000 legacy from the estate of his father, who died from a coronary thrombosis in 1952, but most of that he quickly frittered away.

However, no problem seemed to diminish his outward charm and, despite her first reaction to him, Ruth Ellis began to show an increasing interest in the young man whose "better class" background she couldn't help but admire. Very soon she was sleeping with him in her apartment above the club. Occasionally, during the afternoons before the club opened, Ruth reverted to her call-girl role and entertained a number of regular "clients". But her sex life with Blakely was governed by affection, not money.

Simmering affair

At the time, Blakely was engaged to the daughter of a wealthy North of England businessman. Ruth afterwards stated:

"In December 1953 I had an abortion by him and he was very concerned about my welfare. Although he was engaged to another girl, he offered to marry me and he said it seemed unnecessary for me to get rid of the child, but I did not want to take advantage of him. I was not really in love with him at the time and it was quite unnecessary to marry me. I thought I could get out of the mess quite easily. In fact, I did so with the abortion."

Since she was "not really in love" with Blakely, Ruth saw no reason to allow him exclusive "privileges". She started to

encourage the attentions of one of his Little Club friends, a 33-year-old bachelor and company director. On the man's part, what began as rather pleasant love-making to an attractive woman rapidly flowered into passionate and sincere love.

Ruth's interest was no more than superficial. She continued to see Blakely and to keep their affair simmering, even if at a slightly lower temperature than before.

Whether or not it was the result which, deep down, Ruth Ellis had hoped for, this new affair heightened Blakely's desire. At her trial she recalled: "David was getting rather jealous. He asked me what I had been doing, and things like that, and, of course, I did not tell him . . .

"Our association began again at his insistence. It was very difficult. I was running a business and he was there all the time. He was entitled to walk in; he was a customer and he was hanging around the bar all the time. He was spending money in my bar. I could not tell him to go."

Emotionally upset

It was unlikely that she really wanted him to avoid her. Even though there was evidence that, despite all her bedroom experience, Ruth got very little satisfaction from sex, she could not be without the flattering attentions of men. Blakely's own capability for sexual fulfilment was of an equally low level — but despite this the unstable couple were now set on a course which drove each to a consuming need for personal possession of the other.

The ultimate tragedy was that the periods of possessiveness did not always coincide. Sometimes one would be in a fever-heat while the other was cool — and then the roles would be reversed. This, inevitably, established an atmosphere of continuing jealousy.

At her trial at London's Old Bailey, Ruth recounted an occasion, after her divorce from George Ellis, when his ardour was at a peak and her's at a low ebb: "He 'phoned from the box just in the entrance to the club to my place upstairs and asked if he could please come up, and I said 'No'. After half an hour he came upstairs and I was fooling around in the flat, doing one thing and another. He was very emotionally upset and he went down on his knees, crying and saying: 'I'm sorry, darling. I do love you. I'll prove it.' He asked me to marry him."

She declined, but in February 1955 she found a one-room apartment at 44 Egerton Gardens, Kensington, and she and Blakely moved in together as "Mr. and Mrs. Ellis". But this was to be no cosy nook of regulated domesticity. Ruth continued to see her second-string lover, the bachelor company director, and he was lending Ruth money to pay the rent. Blakely had put such money as he had into the building of a new racing car — which, despite its name, The Emperor, abdicated on its first race-track outing by falling apart.

At the Egerton Gardens apartment there were continuous rows, during some of which Blakely — who was drinking more than ever — beat Ruth and severely bruised her. These fights were followed by alcoholic reconciliations. Ruth again became pregnant and underwent yet another abortion. She insisted that the father was Blakely — but, in view of the presence in her life of the other lover, there could be no certainty about that.

By this time Ruth had brought her 10-year-old son to the apartment and he slept each night on a camp-bed while, in the same room, Ruth demanded Blakely's sexual attentions, more as a symbol of her possession of him than for physical need.

Lack of money, the strain of life with the constant noise of a boisterous and growing child, and hard, daily drinking began to tell on Blakely's nerves. He was not the first man to discover that a highly extrovert, attractive woman may be ideal as the life-and-soul of a party, but is not necessarily easy to live with.

In the Magdala public house one evening some friends, a young married couple named Carole and Anthony Findlater, found Blakely moody and despondent. "I'm supposed to be calling for Ruth at eight tonight, but I can't stand it any longer," he told them. "I want to get away from her."

He seemed, by then, to have grown afraid of Ruth, and he told the Findlaters he was worried about what she might do if he left her. Mr. and Mrs. Findlater did their best to calm his fears, and invited him to spend the week-end with them at their flat in Tanza Road, just a few minutes away.

Meanwhile, back at Egerton Gardens, Ruth waited for Blakely until 9.30 p.m. — then she rang the Findlaters. Ruth knew them and she knew that Blakely was a close friend of theirs. Anthony Findlater answered the telephone and Ruth asked: "Anthony, is David with you?" Findlater, enacting the protective role that had been agreed with Blakely, replied: "No." "Oh," said Ruth, "I'm very worried because he should have been back to meet me. Do you think he's all right?" With assurance, Findlater answered: "Oh, he's all right." Ruth thought she detected a slightly mocking tone in Findlater's voice and was convinced that Blakely was there.

Domestic tiff

From then onwards that evening she telephoned the Findlaters several times, but as soon as her voice was recognized the receiver was replaced. Later, angry and worried, she went to Tanza Road and saw Blakely's Vanguard van parked outside the Findlaters' flat. She rang the bell but no one answered. "I was absolutely furious with David," she testified at her trial. "I just wanted to see him and ask for the keys back . . . I just wanted him to jump in the lake, or go and lose himself, something silly."

In her fury she turned her attention to the Vanguard. It had been partly converted by having its metal side panels replaced with glass windows, held in place by rubber strips, and she went to the van and thumped each window until it fell in. The noise this caused brought Anthony Findlater to his doorstep in pyjamas and robe, and Ruth demanded: "Where is David? I want to speak to him." Findlater replied that he didn't know where Blakely was, but Ruth persisted. "I know where he is," she shouted. "Ask him to come down!"

At that moment, a police inspector, whom the Findlaters had summoned by 'phone, appeared from the shadows and gently urged Ruth to go home. She declared: "I shall stay here all night until he has the guts to show his face!" After a further attempt at persuasion the inspector, unwilling to interfere in a domestic tiff, drove away.

Woman's giggle

But Ruth did not go home. She spent the whole night, walking around the Vanguard, huddling in nearby doorways — all the time watching the darkened windows of the Findlaters' flat. She was convinced that the Findlaters were deliberately trying to break up her affair with Blakely, and she was equally certain that Blakely must have found another woman. Overwrought and emotional, she decided that her "rival" must be the nanny employed to look after the Findlaters' baby.

At around eight in the morning Findlater and Blakely emerged cautiously from the flat. Seeing no sign of Ruth, who was concealed in a doorway, they inspected the damaged Vanguard and drove it away. Ruth went home to Egerton Gardens, gave her son some money and sent him off, alone, to spend the day at the London Zoo.

She then persuaded her ever patient second lover to drive her to the Magdala pub in search of Blakely. But he was not there and that Saturday night she was back watching the Findlaters' flat — more enraged and embittered than ever by the sound of what seemed to be a high-spirited party. An occasional high-pitched woman's giggle stoked her jealousy. She was certain it came from the nanny, and that Blakely was its inspiration.

The next evening, the evening of Easter Sunday, Clive Gunnell, another of Blakely's friends, brought his record-player to the Findlaters' flat and everyone there settled down to a few noisy hours of music. At about nine o'clock Blakely and Gunnell decided to go around to the Magdala and buy some beer and cigarettes.

Ruth, by now unhinged with jealousy and rage, arrived outside the flat just after the two men had driven away. When she saw that the Vanguard had gone she was sure that Blakely would be at the Magdala, and she set off towards the pub, on foot. In her handbag she carried the Smith and Wesson, given to her, she later claimed, "about three years ago by a man in a club whose name I don't remember".

As she walked she felt herself to be, she said, "somehow outside of myself, in a sort of daze". She saw the Vanguard outside the pub, saw Blakely emerge, and fired at him. Four bullets entered his body, and the subsequent post-mortem showed that one—almost certainly the first—had been fired from less than three inches away.

Brief moments

Murder having been committed, the once talkative, ebullient Ruth Ellis entered into the cocoon of calm detachment in which the Hampstead police found her, and from which she never fully emerged. When she entered the prisoner's dock of the Old Bailey's number one court on Monday, June 20, 1955, her platinum blonde hair was as immaculate as ever, her voice as quiet and controlled as on the night of the murder.

The decisive question in the case took only a few brief moments to ask and be answered. Mr. Christmas Humphreys, Q.C., put it, on behalf of the Crown: "Mrs. Ellis, when you fired that revolver at close range into the body of David Blakely, what did you intend to do?"

Without hesitation, almost tonelessly, she replied: "It was obvious that when I shot him I intended to kill him."

Mr. Justice Havers warned the jury that, bearing that evidence in mind, it was not possible for them to return a verdict of manslaughter. It was as no more than a formality that the jury, of 10 men and two women, retired to their room for 14 minutes before returning a verdict of guilty. The black cap was adjusted on the judge's head, and Ruth Ellis stood, unmoving, as the sentence was pronounced. When it was finished, Ruth turned and smiled faintly towards friends in the spectators' gallery. The last public sight and sound of her was a flash of her silvered hair and the clicking of her high heels on the steps leading down to the cells below the court.

She was taken to Holloway, the London women's prison, and—although her solicitor announced that there would be no appeal—there were strong pleas for a reprieve from leading supporters of the campaign for the abolition of capital punishment. The organizers of one petition collected 50,000 signatures. But others took a different view. The bank official's wife, whose right hand had been partly crippled by the stray shot from Ruth's gun, wrote in a London newspaper: "If Ruth Ellis is reprieved we may have other vindictive and jealous young women shooting their boy friends in public . . ."

OUTSIDE the Magdala public house (below), Ruth Ellis finally caught up with Blakely and riddled him with bullets.

Ruth Ellis said nothing more about the shooting and made no move to solve the mystery of how she had acquired the gun or whether anyone else had helped her with the murder plan. She showed no signs of remorse, although she asked for a photograph of David Blakely's grave, and kept it on her table in the death cell. She wrote to Blakely's mother to say she was sorry to have caused her "unpleasantness" but added: "I shall die loving your son, and you should feel content that his death has been repaid."

After she learnt that there was to be no reprieve, she sent a brief and cheerful note to a friend assuring her that she expected her execution to be no more alarming "than having a tooth out". She shed no tears and the woman who had been a call-girl, a lush, and a neglectful mother attained a death cell dignity that evoked admiration in the women prison officers assigned to watch over her.

Steady hand

On the morning of July 13 the solemn procession of officials came for her. She was given a tot of brandy and drained the glass with a steady hand. Then, after thanking the Holloway staff for their kindness, she walked—almost as if willingly—the few feet from the condemned cell into the execution shed. Ruth Ellis was the last woman to be hanged in Britain. Ten years later, in November 1965, capital punishment was abolished.

In December 1973 details of a statement about the murder gun—alleged to have been made to lawyers by Ruth Ellis just before her execution—were published in Britain. According to the statement, she said that a jealous second lover had given her the loaded ·38 Smith and Wesson and driven her on her final and fatal journey to Hampstead. She had not disclosed the details at her trial, she said, in order not to involve the man.

Had there been evidence during the trial that a second person was knowingly implicated in the murder it is possible—although by no means as certain as some commentators suggested—that Ruth Ellis would not have been hanged.

None of the police officers in the case believed her story that she had been given the gun "about three years ago by a man in a club whose name I don't remember". There can be little doubt that she must have practised with the gun. It was not the sort of weapon that anyone could use without some elementary instruction.

But in the kind of shady club world in which Ruth Ellis moved there were many men who had easy access to weapons. The fact that she either asked for, or accepted the offer of, a gun could well have been taken by the jury as added confirmation of her story that she had intended to kill Blakely.

THE MURDER AT THE VILLA MADEIRA

Popperfoto

Mrs. Alma Rattenbury was outwardly a conventional married woman who lived an apparently impeccable existence with her ageing husband. Within the refined walls of their Bournemouth house, however, the respectability was torn away to reveal a cesspool of lust, licence . . . and—finally—murder.

THE small advertisement lay buried in the dull, grey columns of the *Bournemouth Daily Echo*. A more innocent and innocuous offer it would be hard to imagine:

"Willing lad wanted, aged 14-18, for house-work. Scout training preferred."

The "willing lad" who replied was a dim-witted 17-year-old named George Percy Stoner, a semi-literate who lived with his grandmother and worked part-time at a garage. No Scout training ever devised, however, would have prepared him for what he soon discovered was to be his main duty—sharing the bed of his employer's wife.

Mrs. Alma Victoria Rattenbury was no ordinary woman. She was that most overpowering of female types, the Frustrated Artist. Impulsive, passionate and unbalanced, she saw herself as a creative personality caught in the dreary and soul-destroying labyrinth of married life.

Dull, stodgy husband

Alma Rattenbury's unconventional behaviour made the contrast between her and her husband even more pronounced. Francis Mawson Rattenbury was a retired architect, a dull and stodgy man whose main interest in life was rendering himself unconscious every night with a bottle of whisky. There was little sexual contact between the couple and their rooms were set apart on different floors.

As if all this wasn't enough to create an unbridgeable gulf between them, Mr. Rattenbury was 66, while Mrs. Rattenbury was an attractive and well-preserved 37. The word "incompatible" could have been coined for them.

In this sexually explosive atmosphere,

PASSIONATE and impulsive, pretty Alma Rattenbury became besotted with 17-year-old George Percy Stoner (above).

the arrival of Stoner as chauffeur-handyman acted like a detonator, but even in her most melodramatic moments, Alma Rattenbury could never have foreseen the appalling repercussions of her passion for her loutish and immature employee. For within eight months of Stoner walking through the respectable door of the Villa Madeira, in Britain's archly-refined town of Bournemouth, both he and Alma Rattenbury were on trial for their lives.

And her teenage lover

In court, prosecuting counsel would point at Alma Rattenbury and accuse her of dominating and corrupting her lover. The judge would thunder, "You cannot have any feeling except disgust for her." And Alma Rattenbury, dazed and shocked at the ghastly train of events she had set in motion, would only explain, "I loved him, that's all, I loved him."

The Mr. Rattenbury-Mrs. Rattenbury-George Stoner triangle that had been constructed so satisfyingly in the Villa Madeira had shattered under a strain unusual even in this fragile sexual geometry. It was not the customary case of the "wronged husband" demanding the return of his marital rights. Far from it. Throughout the affair, Mr. Rattenbury, complacent, incurious and uncomplaining, happily confined his embraces to the whisky bottle. Nor did Alma Rattenbury tire of her teenage lover—the flame of her passion burned to the bitter and brutal end. What nobody could have expected was that—inspired by his novel and elevated position—the loutish Stoner would develop airs and graces; that he would start behaving like a jumped-up ladies' man, that he would make demands and throw tantrums, and that he would become insanely jealous of the timorous and undemanding Francis Rattenbury.

In barely six months, the festering jealousy of George Stoner had led to a bloody climax which would have been more in keeping with the stage of the Grand Guignol than the prim backcloth of the Villa Madeira.

At the trial at the Old Bailey in May, 1935, Alma Rattenbury relived the grisly night when Stoner came into her room and, as usual, climbed between the sheets. "At first, I didn't notice anything unusual," she told the court. "But a little later I noticed he was looking a bit odd."

Counsel: What do you mean—odd?

Mrs. Rattenbury: Well, he seemed agitated and I said 'What's the matter, darling?' and he said he was in trouble and could not tell me. I said 'Oh, you must tell me' and we went back and forth like that for two or three minutes. He said no, I would not be able to bear it. I thought he was in some trouble outside. Then I said that I was strong enough to bear anything and then he told me . . . he told me he had hurt Mr. Rattenbury. It didn't penetrate my head what he had just said until I heard my husband groan; and then my brain became alive and I jumped out of bed and went downstairs as fast as I could.

I cannot remember

Counsel: Did you stop to put any clothes or slippers on?

Mrs. Rattenbury: Oh no.

Counsel: Did Stoner say anything about how he had done it?

Mrs. Rattenbury: He said he had hit him over the head with a mallet.

Counsel: Anything more about the mallet?

Mrs. Rattenbury: That he had hidden it outside.

Counsel: What did you find when you got downstairs?

Mrs. Rattenbury: Mr. Rattenbury sitting on the chair and he . . . and he . . .

Counsel: I don't think you need trouble to describe exactly what you saw, but he was sitting in the chair?

Mrs. Rattenbury: I tried to rub his hands, but they were cold. I tried to take his pulse and I shook him to try to make him speak. I tried to speak to him, and then I saw this blood, and I went round the table and trod on his false teeth and that made me hysterical and I screamed. I cannot remember, only vaguely. I. drank some whisky to stop being sick.

Counsel: You say you screamed. Did you scream for anyone?

Mrs. Rattenbury: Yes, for Irene Riggs, my companion.

Counsel: Did she come down?

Mrs. Rattenbury: Yes.

Counsel: Was that the only drink of whisky you had?

Mrs. Rattenbury: No. I took one drink of whisky neat and I was sick and then I remembered pouring out another. I cannot remember drinking the next one. I tried to become insensible, to blot out the picture. I cannot now remember anything, from putting a white towel round Mr. Rattenbury's head and the vomiting and treading on those . . . aagh.

Counsel: You can remember nothing more about the events of that night?

Mrs. Rattenbury: No.

The mallet-blows had shattered Mr. Rattenbury's skull. But what had channelled Stoner's jealousy into such an outburst of ferocious violence? Just a small and insignificant incident . . . only its timing had been disastrous.

By March, 1935 — only 5½ months after answering the advertisement — Stoner's vanity had grown out of all proportion. Day by day, theatrical posturing alternated with sulks and scenes. Mr. Rattenbury kept out of the way, disinterested by day and tipsy by nightfall. Every night, Irene Riggs, Mrs. Rattenbury's companion, watched Stoner swagger into his mistress's bedroom, but although she was scandalized she said nothing. Mrs. Rattenbury was clearly besotted with him.

On March 19 — after asking her husband for £250 — Mrs. Rattenbury took Stoner on a trip to London. They stayed in the Kensington Palace Hotel for four days as man and wife, although listed in the register as "brother and sister". This was to be Stoner's introduction to the life-style of a gentleman-about-town. Mrs. Rattenbury took him to the most expensive shops, where fawning assistants fitted the bumpkin with fashionable suits, shirts, underwear, shoes and gloves.

She bought him expensive silk ties and crêpe-de-Chine pyjamas, and in a humiliating act of self-abasement paid £16 for a diamond ring, which she then accepted as a present. As if "cohabiting above his class" had not already turned Stoner's head, the dazzling experience in London completed his mental picture of himself as an elegant stud, a kept man in crêpe-de-Chine pyjamas. It was with his absurdly inflated ego that Stoner returned to the Villa Madeira.

But instead of entering as master of the house, Stoner returned with a bump to reality. Probably through the effects of alcohol, Mr. Rattenbury was in a depressed mood, and to cheer him up Alma Rattenbury suggested staying overnight with friends at Bridport. "Stoner will drive us," she told him. Stoner, however, had other ideas. He had no intention of reverting to his menial role as chauffeur-handyman.

When Mrs. Rattenbury broke the news, Stoner produced an air-pistol and waved it at her threateningly. "If you go to Bridport, get this straight, I will kill you!" he said. Mrs. Rattenbury tried to placate him, but his eyes narrowed in an expression of half-witted cunning.

Vanity and pride

For some reason, the idea had lodged in his head that Mr. and Mrs. Rattenbury might share the same bed in their friends' house. "Ratz went to your room today —I saw him," he said. "You were both inside there and the door was shut. Think I'm blind? Think I don't know what was going on? It'll be the same at Bridport, won't it?"

For once, Alma Rattenbury ignored his tantrums and stood her ground. It was a fatal psychological mistake. Stoner's vanity and pride—boosted by his extravagant fling in London—had been wounded. Whatever happened, he was not going to sit meekly behind the wheel and drive the Rattenburys to Bridport like some miserable servant. If Alma Rattenbury refused to cancel the arrangement, then he would have to think of some other way of stopping it.

At around eight o'clock on the evening of Sunday, March 24, Stoner appeared at his grandparents' home at nearby Ensbury Park and asked if he could borrow a wooden mallet. "I've got to put up a tent and I need to drive in some pegs," he explained. By 10.30 that night, everyone in the Villa Madeira was asleep —well, almost everyone. Padding along the corridor from her bedroom to the toilet, Miss Riggs was surprised to find Stoner leaning over the banisters in his pyjamas and listening intently.

From below came the muffled snores of Mr. Rattenbury, who had fallen asleep in the drawing-room, cradling his bottle of whisky.

RELEASED but broken . . . Alma leaves London's Old Bailey after being found not guilty of her husband's murder. But without Stoner she had no wish to live.

"What's the matter?" asked Miss Riggs. "Nothing," replied Stoner. "I was just checking to see if all the lights were out, that's all."

Miss Riggs returned to bed and was joined a few minutes later by Alma Rattenbury, who came in for her usual night-time gossip. She could talk of nothing else but the forthcoming visit to Bridport and how much she was looking forward to it. Whispering "Goodnight" excitedly, she left.

It was exactly 15 minutes later that Alma Rattenbury's piercing scream shattered the peace of the Villa Madeira. In the gruesome moment she was to describe so graphically at the Old Bailey, she had just stepped on her husband's false teeth, lying in the pool of blood flowing from his wrecked head.

"Oh look . . ."

Miss Riggs dashed downstairs to the drawing-room. The door had been flung open and Alma Rattenbury was standing in the shaft of light moaning, "Oh look . . . oh look . . . oh look." It was a sickening sight. Francis Rattenbury sat in his armchair, his head a scarlet mop. A rivulet of blood flowed down his clothes and spread across the floor. It was Miss Riggs who took control. She telephoned Dr. O'Donnell nearby and, to make sure he left immediately, sent Stoner to his home with the car.

Dr. O'Donnell took one look at Francis Rattenbury and phoned for a local surgeon, Mr. Rooke. Mr. Rattenbury was still alive . . . but only just. Despite the obvious and grisly evidence that Mr. Rattenbury had been attacked from behind by a blunt instrument, Alma Rattenbury started babbling about suicide. Her voice was hysterical. "Ratz was feeling depressed . . . we were going away . . . tomorrow, I mean, but that was this afternoon . . . he read me something out of a book . . . he said he admired a man who could do that . . . what it said, taking his own life . . . people do live too long, don't they, or at least that's what he thought."

Mrs. Rattenbury jumped to the piano, where a book was lying half-open. "Look, here it is, here it is," she stuttered. "Just where he put it . . . this is the book . . . where the man commits suicide . . . it's in it somewhere . . . he had lived too long."

While Mr. Rattenbury was rushed to hospital by ambulance, the distraught and incoherent Alma Rattenbury stayed at the villa. Emotionally unstable at the best of times and now demented by shock and alcohol, her condition had deteriorated frightfully by the time the police arrived at 2 a.m.

They were confronted with a grotesque scene. Still dressed in her nightclothes, Alma Rattenbury darted restlessly about the room babbling a stream of semi-gibberish. Her eyes were fixed and bulging and her movements were jerky and uncontrolled. She had put on her radiogram and it was whooping away at full blast; as soon as one record finished, she put on another. Even more alarming, Alma Rattenbury had become drunkenly lecherous. She tried to kiss and paw the bewildered policemen, and had to be physically restrained from following one of them out of the house.

In her unhinged state, Alma Rattenbury presented the perfect picture of the drunken nymphomaniac and it was hardly surprising that suspicion first fell upon her rather than the saturnine Stoner. Indeed, she did everything she could to incriminate herself. Unknown to the policemen, the one rational thought that had somehow pierced her fuddled brain was to protect her lover.

Within a few hours, Alma Rattenbury had made four "statements", each one more incriminating than the last. With the radiogram blaring deafeningly, the police took down the first two statements only minutes after arriving. Mrs. Rattenbury described how she had "heard a yell" or "someone groaning" and, running downstairs, had found her husband sitting unconscious in his armchair. There was no mention of Stoner. Indeed, the police were still unaware of his very existence.

Half-an-hour later, while agitatedly pacing round the room, Mrs. Rattenbury suddenly exclaimed, "I did it!" The policemen scrambled for their notebooks. "I did it with a mallet," she continued dramatically. "Ratz has lived too long . . . it is hidden . . . no, my lover did it." At this point, Mrs. Rattenbury lost the thread of the sentence and drifted into what sounded like a feeble attempt at bribery. "I would like to give you £10 . . . no, I won't bribe you." But it was enough, however garbled. Alma Rattenbury had undeniably admitted her guilt.

"I did it"

The last statement under caution—even more halting and confused—came at around 3.40 a.m. "I did it," she repeated. "He gave me the book . . . he has lived too long . . . he said, 'Dear, dear' . . . I will tell you in the morning where the mallet is . . . have you told the coroner yet? . . . I shall make a better job of it next time . . . Irene does not know . . . I made a proper muddle of it . . . I thought I was strong enough."

The words were barely out of her mouth when Dr. O'Donnell returned from the hospital. He was furious. Mrs. Rattenbury was about to make another statement when the doctor intervened. "Have you cautioned this lady?" he asked the inspector in charge, with some asperity.

"No," said the inspector. "Well, look at her condition," snapped the doctor, who had just given her half a grain of morphia as a sedative. "She is full of whisky and I have given her a large dose of morphia. She is not fit to make a statement to you or anybody else."

Alma Rattenbury was carried upstairs to bed. But she was not allowed to rest. At 8.15—still half-drugged from the morphia administered only $4\frac{1}{2}$ hours earlier—she was charged with the attempted murder of her husband. Before she left the house, she made one final, disjointed statement. "I was playing cards with my husband when he dared me to kill him as he wanted to die. I picked up the mallet. He then said 'You have not got enough guts to do it.' I then hit him with the mallet and hid it outside the house. I would have shot him if I had a gun."

Talking too much

On the way out, Mrs. Rattenbury passed her little son John—only now aroused from bed, and white-faced and bewildered—the loyal Miss Riggs and the silent Stoner. "Don't make fools of yourselves," she told them. Only Stoner replied. "You have got yourself into this mess by talking too much," he muttered.

Stoner stayed silent for four days. On March 28, Francis Rattenbury died in hospital without ever regaining consciousness. By now, Stoner had been told about his mistress's incriminating statements. Plagued by conscience—and a genuine concern for Alma Rattenbury—he blurted out to Miss Riggs, "She is in jail and I have put her there. I am going to see her tomorrow and I shall give myself up. I want to be up at half-past six in the morning. Don't let me oversleep, now."

Miss Riggs didn't give Stoner a chance to change his mind. Forestalling the alarm-call, she telephoned the police and reported the conversation. That evening, Stoner was arrested and charged.

Nobody could ever claim that the passionate affair between Mrs. Rattenbury and George Stoner represented love at its most exalted and sublime, but faced with the hangman's noose, their devotion and loyalty to each other transcended the sordid details of their relationship. Each one was prepared to shoulder the blame for Mr. Rattenbury's murder, and vindicate the other.

Right up until the trial, Alma Rattenbury refused to withdraw her confession—until her legal advisers finally persuaded her that her own sacrifice would not make the slightest difference to the case against Stoner. Stoner himself instructed his lawyers not to suggest in any way that he had been incited or influenced by Mrs. Rattenbury, or that she had known anything about his intention to murder her husband. To help her own case, he refused to give evidence.

On the day of his arrest, Stoner had told the police: "Do you know that Mrs. Rattenbury had nothing to do with this affair? Yes, when I did the job I believed he was asleep. I hit him and then came upstairs and told Mrs. Rattenbury. She rushed down then. You see, I watched through the french windows and saw her kiss him good night, then leave the room.

"I waited and crept in through the french window, which was unlocked. I think he must have been asleep when I hit him, still it ain't much use saying anything. I don't suppose they will let her out yet. You know, there should be a doctor with her when they tell her I am arrested, because she will go out of her mind."

On May 27, 1935, George Stoner and Alma Rattenbury stood before one of Britain's sternest judges, Mr. Justice Humphreys, jointly charged with the murder of Francis Rattenbury. Local feeling against the couple had run so high that the hearing had been moved from Winchester Assizes to the Old Bailey in London. Both pleaded not guilty.

Stoner claimed that he was a regular cocaine addict and had been under the influence of the drug at the time. His defence was knocked right out of court by expert medical evidence which proved that he had not shown the faintest signs of drug-withdrawal in the days immediately after his arrest.

But the strangest feature of the trial was Alma Rattenbury's almost total loss of memory. She could recall nothing of the events following the discovery of her husband's body. The combination of morphia, alcohol and shock—probably coupled with a psychosomatic "blackout" —had left her mind a complete blank. Earlier, she had described how she had tried to "blot out the picture" with whisky.

Apparently, she had been completely successful, for no efforts by counsel could make her see again that macabre night when the radiogram blared while she alternately flirted, babbled and wept in a bloodstained room.

"I cannot remember"

Her own counsel, Mr. Terence O'Connor, K.C., tried first.

Counsel: Do you remember the police officers coming?

Mrs. Rattenbury: No.

Counsel: Do you remember sending for Dr. O'Donnell?

Mrs. Rattenbury: I cannot remember anything.

Realizing that the line of questioning was getting them nowhere, Mr. O'Connor turned to a more constructive approach:

Counsel: Mrs. Rattenbury, did you yourself murder your husband?

Mrs. Rattenbury: Oh, no.

Counsel: Or take any part whatsoever in planning it?

Mrs. Rattenbury: Oh, no.

Counsel: Did you know a thing about it till Stoner spoke about it in your bed?

Mrs. Rattenbury: Naturally, I would have prevented it if I had known a half —a quarter of a minute before.

To the court—half-expecting some kind of hideous, drunken degenerate to mount the steps of the witness-box—Mrs. Rattenbury had already emerged as a sympathetic figure. She was attractive and smartly dressed. Her voice was clear and her answers frank. Above all, she had a natural dignity which seemed to be completely out of keeping with the distasteful details of the case. Could such a sensitive woman really have conspired to bludgeon her husband to death?

Prosecuting counsel, Mr. R. P. Croom-Johnson, K.C., was less impressed. Undaunted by Mrs. Rattenbury's plea of amnesia, he decided to break down her mental block with a brisk approach:

CROWDS turned up for the funeral of Mrs. Rattenbury after her desperate suicide. The salacious details of the trial had aroused the usual interest . . .

Counsel: Are you seriously telling members of the jury that, practically from the time you were sick and poured yourself a glass of whisky, your memory does not serve you *at all*?

Mrs. Rattenbury: I can remember a few things, like in an awful nightmare.

Encouraged, Mr. Croom-Johnson asked "Tell me a few things you recollect on that night?" But it was a false start.

Mrs. Rattebury: Oh, nothing . . .

Impatiently, Mr. Croom-Johnson returned to jogging her memory on the night of the murder.

Counsel: Do you recollect Dr. O'Donnell coming?

Mrs. Rattenbury: I cannot.

Counsel: *What?*

Mrs. Rattenbury: I have tried so hard to remember, even with piecing together what I have heard, and I cannot.

Counsel: Dr. O'Donnell was a friend of yours and your medical adviser?

Mrs. Rattenbury: Yes.

Counsel: As a rule, a person calculated to soothe rather than excite you?

Mrs. Rattenbury: Yes.

Counsel: And you recollect *nothing* of Dr. O'Donnell that night?

Mrs. Rattenbury: No.

Counsel: Or a succession of police officers coming in?

Mrs. Rattenbury: No.

Time and opportunity

No amount of hinting or nudging could elicit more than a shake of the head or a firm "No" from the witness. Counsel took a logical detour and suggested to Mrs. Rattenbury that she had been a regular drinker, used to taking large quantities of alcohol—a tactic aimed at making the jury wonder why a couple of whiskies could have produced total amnesia. Mrs. Rattenbury agreed unhesitatingly. After this cunning short cut, Mrs. Rattenbury's brisk admission only brought counsel face to face once again with the brick wall of her loss of memory.

Counsel: About incidents, your mind is completely blank?

Mrs. Rattenbury: It might be somebody else you are talking about.

Counsel: Blank about people too?

Mrs. Rattenbury: Oh, yes.

Counsel: About conversations?

Mrs. Rattenbury: Quite.

With the long-suffering air of someone who knew exactly what answer was coming, Mr. Croom-Johnson held up a policeman's yellow notebook:

Counsel: Is your mind a complete blank about making a statement to the detective-inspector, which he wrote down in this?

Mrs. Rattenbury: I cannot remember that. I've tried and tried. Yesterday, last night, I tried to remember again that—

Counsel: Just look at the book. Do you see the words 'Alma Rattenbury'?

Mrs. Rattenbury: Yes, I see them. It is all absolutely double Dutch to me.

Determined to evoke *some* flicker of recollection, Mr. Croom-Johnson moved on to midday of March 25, after Mrs. Rattenbury had been in the police station some hours. This time she responded.

Counsel: At the police station that morning, somewhere around 12.30, do you recollect writing a cheque for Stoner for £5?

Mrs. Rattenbury: I remember writing two cheques, one for Irene and one for Stoner, but I do not remember who I gave them to.

Counsel: Do you remember how much were they for?

Mrs. Rattenbury: £5 each.

Counsel: And who they were for?

Mrs. Rattenbury: Yes, absolutely.

Counsel: Up to that moment, according to your evidence, your mind is a complete blank for many hours?

Mrs. Rattenbury: I cannot even remember how I got the cheque book.

Counsel: So that from the moment you poured that glass of whisky, do you wish the members of the jury to believe that your mind is a complete blank, with the exception of one or two trifling things which you have told us, until you recollect about the two cheques at the police station at 12.30 on the Monday morning?

"That," replied Mrs. Rattenbury with some finality, "is absolutely true."

Throughout the trial, nothing could shake Alma Rattenbury from her story. But consistency is one thing, truth another. Would the jury believe in her loss

THE SEDATE STYLE of the Villa Madeira (below) gave no inkling of the high passions at play behind the walls . . .

of memory, so selective in its timing? And would there be any sympathy to spare for Stoner, now left with the full burden of guilt?

The night before the verdict, Alma Rattenbury sat late in her cell in Holloway Prison and wrote a number of letters. In one, she said, "I have quite made up my mind here to finish things should Stoner hang; it would only be a matter of time and opportunity." In another, she said, "If I only thought it would help Stoner, I would stay on. But it has been pointed out to me all too vividly that I cannot help him. That is *my* death sentence."

On May 31, 1935, the Old Bailey jury returned to their benches with their verdicts. Alma Rattenbury was found Not Guilty, and acquitted. George Percy Stoner was found Guilty and sentenced to death by hanging.

Three days afterwards, on June 3, Alma Rattenbury took a train to New Milton in Hampshire and sat for a while on the river bank smoking a cigarette. She put her fur coat and handbag on the grass beside her and stared at the sun reflected in the water. The words of her own letter must have drifted through her mind . . . "I have quite made up my mind to finish things should Stoner hang; it would only be a matter of time and opportunity." A man walking along the opposite bank saw something glint in the sun. Alma Rattenbury had stood up.

Before the man could move, she had plunged a knife six times into her breast, with such ferocity that three wounds entered her heart. She sank into the water, which carried her gently away from the bank.

A few weeks later, George Percy Stoner was reprieved and his sentence commuted to life imprisonment.

DOCTOR CRIPPEN

EVERYONE aboard the S.S. *Montrose* considered them to be a most considerate and devoted couple—the father and son who were travelling to start a new life in Canada. Mr. and Master Robinson—to use the names they gave to the purser—were never seen apart, and although they were polite and agreeable they spoke to no one unless they had to.

During the day they sat together on deck, chatting quietly about the sea, the weather, and the marvels of the recently installed Marconi wireless aerial which crackled above their heads sending messages both ways across the Atlantic.

At meal-times their concern for each other was even more marked. Mr. Robinson made an inordinate fuss of the boy—a shy, delicately-built youth who appeared to be in his mid-teens.

Mr. Robinson was quick to crack nuts for his son, to help him cut up his meat, and to give him half of his own helping of salad. Master Robinson thanked his father in a low gentle voice, and ate his food in a fastidious, almost ladylike way.

But as the voyage continued, one person on the ship found the Robinsons a little too loving to be true. Captain Kendall's suspicions were first aroused when he noticed that Master Robinson's trousers were too large for his slender body, and were held in place by means of a large safety-pin.

Long wavy hair

Added to that, there was the slouch hat which sat somewhat incongruously on top of the boy's long brown hair—the locks so soft they could be a girl's.

But what really set the captain thinking was the regularity with which Mr. Robinson kept on fondling his son, squeezing his hand and kissing him tenderly on the cheek.

Captain Kendall was an avid newspaper reader and knew that the *Daily Mail* was offering a reward of £100 for information concerning the whereabouts of the suspected wife-killer, Dr. Hawley Harvey Crippen. Crippen was said to be on the run with his mistress, Ethel Le Neve, and Scotland Yard detectives were on their trail.

According to the press, American-born Dr. Crippen—who stood at only 5 feet 4 inches—could be identified by his sandy moustache, balding hair, gold-rimmed glasses and false teeth.

Except for the teeth—which Captain

Kendall had not been able to examine—this was a perfect description of the man calling himself John Philip Robinson. On the second night out from Antwerp, the captain made a point of inviting the Robinsons to dine at his table.

The ship's master was at his best, cracking jokes, telling humorous naval stories, making Mr. Robinson open his mouth and throw his head back in laughter. Under cover of the merriment, the captain looked closely at his guest's undeniably false teeth.

When the joviality had died down, and the meal was over, Captain Kendall excused himself, hurried to the wireless room, and sent an urgent radio message to the authorities in London:

Criminal history

"Have reason to believe Dr. Crippen and Miss Le Neve are travelling as passengers on my ship. They are posing as father and son and should reach Quebec on July 31. Await instructions. Kendall."

The year was 1910, and it was the first time in criminal history that such a message had been sent by wireless. It was sufficient to make Chief Inspector Walter Dew of Scotland Yard book a passage on the *Laurentic*, a faster vessel than the *Montrose* and one which would reach Canada before her.

For the rest of the voyage, the captain kept the suspect couple under close surveillance. If Crippen knew he was being watched he gave no outward sign of it, and nor did he look the kind of man who was soon to appear at the Old Bailey accused of murdering and mutilating his buxom American wife, Cora.

The marital problems of Hawley Harvey Crippen began some while after he and his wife left New York, where he

practised as a doctor, and came to live at 39 Hilldrop Crescent, Camden Town, in North London.

At the time Crippen was employed as the manager of an American patent medicine company with an office in London's Shaftesbury Avenue. By 1907—seven years after their arrival—the 45-year-old physician found that his boisterous, full-bosomed wife was beginning to irritate him, in two deadly ways.

First of all there were constant and steadily increasing sexual demands, which took more out of him than he was willing to give. Then, and even worse, there was her grandiose ambition to become an opera star.

As a classical singer Cora—or Belle Elmore as she called herself professionally—made a fairly indifferent chorus-girl. Her voice matched that of her personality, and was loud, vulgar, unsubtle and lacking in feminine charm.

This obvious dearth of talent, however, did not prevent her joining and becoming treasurer of the Music Hall Ladies' Guild, and filling her three-storied terrace-house with a collection of so-called artistes—mainly low comedians and third-rate vocalists like herself.

Flamboyant characters

In comparison to these flamboyant but shallow characters, Dr. Crippen seemed even more mild-mannered, self-effacing and meek. His place in Cora's bed was taken by an American entertainer Bruce Miller, and he found himself reduced to the status of unpaid domestic servant.

To pay for her costumes, stage attire, and blonde wigs, Cora took in a succession of theatrical lodgers. Too lazy to look after these boarders herself—and too mean to employ a maid—she forced

THE VICTIM ... Cora Crippen (left) was left mutilated and buried in a cellar while her husband and his mistress, Ethel Le Neve (insets, left) fled to Canada on the S.S. *Montrose* (right). But Captain Kendall (inset right) became suspicious. And, for the first time, radio caught a killer ...

THE HUNTERS . . . Detective Sergeant Mitchell and wardresses Miss Stone (left) and Miss Foster set off for Canada to arrest Crippen and Le Neve.

her husband to rise each morning at dawn.

Outwardly uncomplaining, Crippen went down to the kitchen where he blacked the grate, cleaned-out and set the fire, made the tea and polished the "paying guests' " boots.

These tasks done, he left the house, went to his office, and consoled himself with the modest, undemanding love offered to him by Ethel Le Neve, whom he had recently engaged as a book-keeper and secretary.

Ethel, aged twenty-four and unmarried,

was everything Cora was not – demure, understanding, sympathetic and genteel. She cared for Crippen in a way that made him feel a man again and not a flunkey. Most important of all, she was the one person with whom he could discuss his shameful and humiliating home life.

Three years passed in this way – with Crippen and Ethel meeting and consummating their love in cheap hotel rooms in London. Apace with this, Cora's conceit reached almost manic proportions, and resulted in her being booed off the stage at her one professional appearance at the Bedford Music Hall in Camden Town.

By 1910 it was clear that things could not continue as they were. To satisfy Cora's sexual appetite, Crippen was still

expected to act as a stand-in whenever she was without an admirer, and he took to staying her passion with hyoscine – a poisonous drug used as a nerve-depressant and hypnotic.

On January 17, he bought five grains of the narcotic from a chemist and two weeks later invited two of Cora's music hall friends, Mr. and Mrs. Paul Martinetti to dinner. The meal broke up at 1.30 on the morning of February 1st. The Martinettis bade a genial goodnight to Cora who had been in typical form all evening – flattering her guests and speaking angrily to her husband.

Although they didn't know it, the Martinettis were not to exchange theatrical gossip with Cora again. A month afterwards Crippen pawned some of his wife's jewellery for £80, and wrote to the Ladies' Guild explaining that she could no longer attend their meetings as she had gone to stay with a sick relative in America.

At the time nothing was thought of this, although plucked eyebrows were raised when Ethel Le Neve moved into 39 Hilldrop Crescent and was seen in the district wearing clothes and furs belonging to the absent Cora.

In fact, Mrs. Crippen was not far away. Her fleshly remains were buried in the cellar, wrapped in a man's pyjama jacket containing quicklime, while her bones had been filleted from her body and burnt in the grate which her husband had spent so many hours cleaning on his hands and knees.

The death notice

On March 26, Crippen inserted a notice of his wife's death in the *Era* magazine. "She passed on of pneumonia," he told sympathisers, "up in the high mountains of California."

This story was accepted, and Crippen might well have been left to marry his Ethel and live lovingly ever afterwards. What happened next, however, is beyond rational explanation – unless his actions are viewed as an unconscious Freudian desire to draw attention to his crime and be caught.

He took Ethel to a ball given by the Music Hall Ladies' Guild at which she prominently displayed a diamond clip which had last been seen decorating Cora's ample chest. Reports of this "tastelessness" were passed on to Scotland Yard, and in July Chief Inspector Dew visited Crippen at his home.

The quietly-spoken doctor then confessed that Cora was not lying in a grave on the west coast of America. She had,

THE GUESTS . . . Paul Martinetti and his wife were the last people – apart from Crippen – to see Cora alive. They were guests of the Crippens at Hilldrop Crescent (large picture).

IN DISGUISE . . . Ethel Le Neve (left) dressed as Crippen's son. But she was really his mistress. An eagle-eyed captain spotted her wavy hair and soon police were sailing out to take Crippen to face trial (above).

he claimed, run away with her old flame, Bruce Miller. The couple were living somewhere in America, and only pride had stopped him from publicly admitting this.

This seemed a reasonable explanation, but even so the inspector insisted on searching the house from cellar to attic. Apart from her gaudy clothes no physical trace of Cora was found and the detective went away satisfied.

Crippen was not under any definite suspicion, and could have remained where he was without further interference from the police. He could not, however, believe that the inspector really accepted his story.

He felt he would be arrested at any moment and charged with the crime he had so painstakingly committed. To avoid this possibility, he obtained a boy's outfit for Ethel, and fled with her to Rotterdam. On July 11, while they were still in Holland, Inspector Dew returned to Hill-

drop Crescent to check a date in the account of Cora's alleged desertion.

To his surprise, he found that the house was empty and learnt that Crippen and his "housekeeper" were not expected back. Dew immediately sensed that the building had at least one occupant—Cora, or whatever was discovered to be left of her.

Pieces of flesh

This time Dew's investigation included the digging up of the cellar and the uncovering of a man's pyjama jacket, parts of a human buttock, pieces of skin and bits of muscle, and chest and stomach organs. Although the remains were sexless, old scar tissue showed that the subject had undergone an abdominal operation.

This tallied with what little was known of Cora, and on July 16th, a warrant was issued for the arrest of Crippen and Miss Le Neve. Four days after this—without knowing that the search for them was on—they boarded the *Montrose* at Antwerp and began their extraordinary but unsuccessful deception as father and son.

After Captain Kendall had sent his first radio message, he kept abreast of the

ON TRIAL . . . Crippen and his mistress in the dock (top) facing murder charges. Some of Mrs. Crippen's friends (above) were called as witnesses and the deadly doctor was sentenced to death. But Ethel Le Neve went free . . .

developments as Inspector Dew and his sergeant sailed from Liverpool. Their ship forged ahead of the *Montrose* at the entrance to the St. Lawrence River.

The *Montrose* arrived in Canadian waters early in the morning of July 31. At 8.30 a.m. the pilot boat came alongside, and Dew and Sergeant Mitchell boarded the liner. They were accompanied by a chief inspector of the Canadian police, and posed as river navigators.

They were taken straight to Captain Kendall's cabin, and there brought face to face with the self-styled John Philip Robinson. Dew wasted no time in bothering with questions of identity of disguise.

Wife mutilated

"Good morning, Dr. Crippen," he said briskly. "I am Chief Inspector Dew of Scotland Yard. I believe you know me."

Crippen blanched, but found the voice to say: "Good morning, Mr. Dew."

The detective gazed down at the small, clerkish-looking fugitive and told him: "I am arresting you for the murder and mutilation of your wife Cora Crippen in London on or about February 2 last."

Crippen made no reply, and Dew went out to find and charge Ethel. The run-

Mary Evans

away lovers were then taken on to Quebec and a month later brought back to England, London, and the Old Bailey.

The doctor was the first of the two to be put before a jury, and his five-day trial opened on October 18, 1910. From the start it was clear that he had no chance of being acquitted. He seemed indifferent to his own fate, and his main concern was for Ethel, whom he swore knew nothing of Cora's murder.

After duly being pronounced guilty,

WIFE-KILLER Crippen, his life in ruins, was only too happy to leave a world where he had known only the briefest moments of happiness.

he waited feverishly to hear how Ethel had fared on a charge of being an accessory. As it turned out, he had nothing to fear.

Her trial four days later was almost a formality for her defence counsel, the brilliant and foxy F. E. Smith. He chal-

lenged the prosecution to prove that she was anything other than innocent. The case against her failed, and she was found not guilty and discharged.

For Crippen there was little to live for — even if his neck had been spared. Without Ethel — who disappeared without trace from the public eye — he wished only to die, and to do so quickly.

He was hanged on November 23, and his last request was that a photograph of her be buried with him.

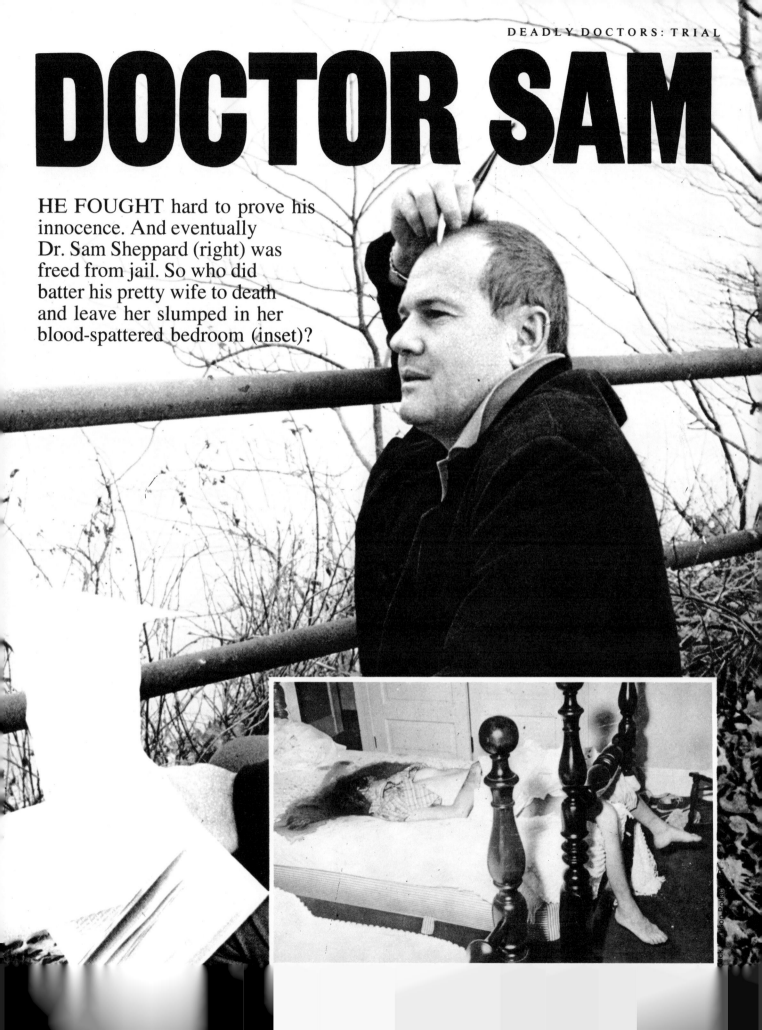

DOCTOR SAM

HE FOUGHT hard to prove his innocence. And eventually Dr. Sam Sheppard (right) was freed from jail. So who did batter his pretty wife to death and leave her slumped in her blood-spattered bedroom (inset)?

WHEN Dr. Samuel Sheppard stepped into the dingy grey building that housed Cuyhoga County criminal court on October 24, 1966, his surroundings must have been only too familiar. He had been there before, 12 years ago, on the same charge: the brutal murder of his own wife, Marilyn, who had been battered to death in the early hours of July 4, 1954.

The first trial had been the longest murder trial in American history. For over 2 months, from October 18, 1954, until December 21, 1954, the jury had been battered with torrents of words. Accusations, pleadings, denials and passionate legal arguments had rattled across the courtroom like machine-gun fire.

Silver-haired Judge Edward Blythin presided over the proceedings like a man suffering from shell shock. Before his eyes he had watched the court transform from a solemn house of justice into what seemed like a circus. Camera bulbs flashed continuously, television crew men hurried back and forth loudly whispering directions to each other and the press gallery was in constant noisy movement as journalists hastened to telephone their editors with news of the latest developments.

Amid the hubbub, the father of the accused, Dr. Richard Allen Sheppard and Sam's two brothers, Stephen and Richard, sat solemnly at the back of the court. As they awaited the jury's verdict on the final day they looked as tense and drawn as Sam himself.

Damaging innuendo

There was a sudden hush as Judge Blythin entered and resumed his seat. William J. Corrigan, Sheppard's tough, veteran attorney followed, looking grim. Then came John J. Mahon, leader of the prosecution, his assistants Saul S. Danaceau and Thomas Parrino — whose verbal skill and gift for damaging innuendo had left Samuel Sheppard bewildered and exhausted.

As they filed in, not one of the jury so much as glanced at Sheppard. Defending counsel Corrigan placed his hand on Sheppard's shoulder and prepared him for what was to come. "I think we've lost," he whispered.

Corrigan was right. Sheppard was found guilty of second-degree murder and sentenced to life imprisonment.

But the nightmare that started on July 4 had only just begun. For the conviction unleashed a chain reaction of tragedies both on the Sheppard family and on others involved in the case. A month after the trial Sheppard's mother committed suicide overcome by grief at the fate of her son whom she believed innocent; shortly afterwards Sam's father died, his health broken by the worry and disgrace. The murdered woman's family suffered

The Cleveland Press

WEDDING DAY . . . Dr. Sam and his wife, Marilyn (above). They moved into the luxurious Ohio house (right) where the bride was to be beaten to death . . .

equally, culminating in a further suicide: that of Marilyn's father. Even a member of the jury, depressed and exhausted by the strain of the ordeal and the sensation surrounding it, had taken his life.

For the case had divided the state of Ohio as it was to divide the nation. Was Sheppard a ruthless wife-killer as the verdict indicated, or the victim of a cruel miscarriage of justice?

The tale unfolded to the jury was a complex one; and reasoned judgement was made infinitely more difficult by the press which had conducted, from the start, a powerful vendetta against Sheppard, his family and the comfortable background from which they came.

Screaming headlines had fomented suspicion and dislike long before Dr. Sam set foot in court. The *Cleveland Press* was one of the worst offenders. WHY ISN'T SAM SHEPPARD IN JAIL? its banner headlines demanded.

In effect, the *Cleveland Press* had pointed to Dr. Sheppard as the murderer, and implied that his family and friends were using their influence to shield him.

When, as a result of the hysterical press campaign against him, Sam Sheppard was finally arrested, his family continued to suffer threats, insults, and anonymous telephone calls at all hours of the day and night from people fired to anger by what they had read in their local newspapers.

The trial itself proved a sort of public entertainment; each instalment was an event eagerly awaited and discussed; newspapers sold by millions and television items were given peak viewing.

At 30, Sam was a brilliant neurosurgeon and the youngest son of Dr. Richard A. Sheppard, a general surgeon and osteopath who had founded Cleveland's Bay View Hospital. Sam worked there with his father and two brothers, Richard and Stephen. He had married pretty Marilyn Reese in 1945 and later bought a pleasant, four-bedroom house for them near the hospital. The house was perched nearly a hundred feet above the winding shore of Lake Erie and included a private beach. It was, like the Sheppards themselves, typically suburban, fashionable and expensively middle-class.

The court heard how, on the evening of July 3, 1954, Samuel Sheppard and his wife had entertained Mr. and Mrs. Ahern to dinner at their house. Afterwards Chip, the Sheppard's young son, was put to bed and the two couples sat down to chat, drink, and watch television.

By 12.30 p.m. everyone was tired and the Aherns were shown out by Marilyn alone because Sam, who had had a tough day at the hospital, had already fallen asleep on the couch. What happened afterwards depended solely upon the evidence of one witness, Samuel Sheppard; and the story he told, though it never varied over the years, was undeniably vague.

Marilyn left Sam lying on the couch downstairs and went up to bed. Some time later, according to his testimony, he was awakened by the sound of her screams, rushed upstairs and was struck down from behind.

"The next thing I knew was coming to, a very vague sensation, in a sitting position right next to Marilyn's bed, facing the hallway, facing south." He looked at his wife, realized she was "in very bad condition" and felt that she was "gone". Fearful for his son he went into Chip's room and "in some way evaluated that he was all right".

Hearing a noise downstairs he dashed down in time to see a shadowy figure fly through the back door and make for the beach. Sam gave chase, and managed to grasp the figure from behind but was again knocked unconscious.

This time when he regained his senses he was lying face down on the edge of the lake with most of his body in the water. He staggered to his feet, frozen and dripping wet, lurched once more towards the house, and went upstairs.

There he saw, in the dawn light, that Marilyn had been "terribly beaten". He thought he determined that she was dead. Then, at 5.45 a.m. he phoned his friend and neighbour J. Spencer Houk, mayor of the town:

"For God's sake, Spen, come quick!" he gasped. "I think they've got Marilyn!"

Missing morphine

But, as the prosecution pointed out, there were some puzzling gaps in the story. The T-shirt he was wearing had disappeared. Why and where? Why had his medical case been found upside down, the contents spilled and a box of morphine ampoules missing? If he had been lying with his head on the shore of the lake, why was there no sand in his hair?

When Mayor Houk arrived, accompanied by his wife, he found Sheppard stripped to the waist, sodden wet, slumped in a chair. Mrs. Houk rushed upstairs. She found the victim lifeless in her blood-soaked bed, pyjama top drawn over her breasts, outspread legs dangling under the crossbar of the fourposter.

The entire room was spattered with blood. Marilyn's skull showed that she had been beaten savagely on the head with a blunt instrument—35 times, the authorities said later.

The police arrived, followed by Sheppard's brother, Dr. Richard Sheppard, and finally the coroner, Dr. Samuel Gerber. From the start Gerber was sceptical. The displaced drawers and ransacked con-

The Plain Dealer

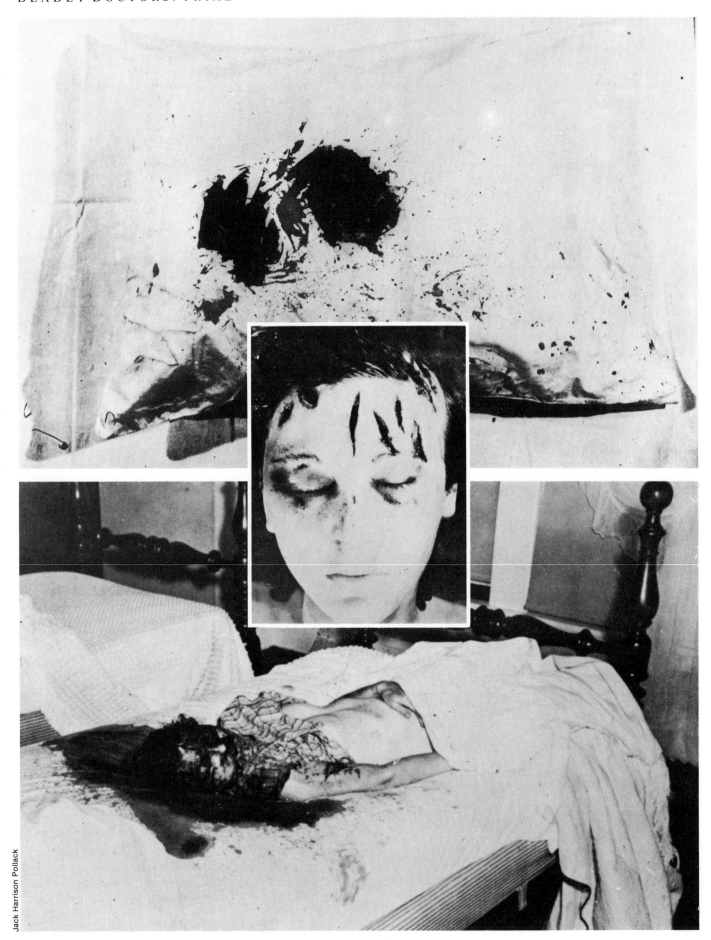

tents seemed like a clumsy attempt to simulate a burglary.

He put Marilyn's death at between 3 a.m. and 4 a.m. – which would have given Samuel Sheppard nearly three hours at least in which to remove evidence and arrange the house to suit his story.

Richard broke the news to his brother that Marilyn was indeed dead. Mayor Houk, however, gave the jury a much more damaging account of their dialogue. According to him Richard had said, "Did you do this, Sam?" – implying that even Sam's own brother thought him capable of such an act.

Bloodstained watch

The jury heard of other oddities. Searchers found, among the shrubs near the house, the canvas bag Sam used on his boat. Inside the bag were his wristwatch, slightly bloodstained, his fraternity ring, and the keys and chain that were normally affixed to his trousers.

How had the bag arrived there with its contents? Had it been left there by the attacker? If so, why? Or had Sam left it there himself in some vague attempt to misguide the police?

These questions were never answered. Others were never asked. Where, for example, had the fragment of torn red leather come from which was found under Marilyn's bed? Fibres found under her fingernails were produced in court. But neither prosecution nor defence sought to explain their origin.

A fragment of tooth was ignored as evidence, although it appeared that it may have broken off as Marilyn bit her attacker who withdrew his hand with force; and Dr. Sam had no scratches or bites on his hands or arms.

In the end three things were responsible for the jury's verdict of guilty. The first of these was the evidence given in court by the coroner, Dr. Samuel R. Gerber. He testified that the bloody "imprint" on the pillow case beneath Marilyn's head was caused by a "surgical instrument". The murder weapon had never been found in spite of intensive searches by the police.

In its absence what could be better than a testimony from the respected coroner that it was a surgical instrument, the kind of instrument, in fact, which only a surgeon such as Dr. Sheppard was likely to possess?

Gerber never explained and was never asked what kind of surgical instrument he

BEATEN TO DEATH . . . How police found the body of Marilyn Sheppard. The bloodstained pillow (top) was produced as evidence when her husband was put on trial. But the murder weapon and "a surgical instrument" that left a bloody imprint on the pillow were never found by police.

UPI

UNDER ARREST . . . Dr. Sam, handcuffed to a detective, is led to his trial. It was the first of many courtroom appearances before he was cleared.

had in mind. Nor was one ever produced; but the jury were greatly impressed.

The second factor was Sheppard's penchant for extramarital affairs – which he had, at first, denied. This was taken up with great enthusiasm by the media and provided the prosecution with a perfect motive. Sheppard had been having an affair with a young colleague, Susan Hayes. Perhaps he wanted his wife out of the way. And if Sheppard could lie about marital infidelity, the prosecution suggested, would he not also lie about killing his wife?

Finally, and perhaps most important of all, there was the influence of the press, not only on the public in general, but also

on the jury – whose members had followed the case with interest as reported in local newspapers before the trial and even during it. And the local press had been particularly vindictive towards Sheppard.

But if the press campaign against him had helped to secure a conviction in 1954, it was the main reason why Sheppard secured a new trial in 1966. For, on June 6 of that year the U.S. Supreme Court overthrew his murder conviction on the grounds that "prejudicial publicity" had deprived him of a fair trial. It was the first decision of its kind in American legal history.

For most of the intervening 12 years, Sheppard had been in jail. But he had remained firmly in the news. Firstly, there were the repeated efforts at every level – local, state, and federal courts – to secure a new trial. Again and again William Corrigan, Sam's fighting lawyer, saw his efforts fail; but Sam was still in jail when Corrigan died in 1961.

Then, in 1963 there was another bizarre development. A wealthy young German divorcée from Düsseldorf, who had been corresponding with Sam Sheppard after reading about his case, decided to come to the United States to see him.

Ariane turned out to be stunningly beautiful, and at their first meeting in Ohio's Marion penitentiary the couple gave each other love tokens in the presence of the prison guards, as a symbol of their engagement.

Once more the press latched on. Wherever she went, cameras flashed and reporters barked their questions. Was this some stunt engineered by Sheppard's new lawyer, Lee Bailey?

Bailey was shrewd, young, dynamic, ambitious for success, hardworking and, above all, a masterly manipulator of publicity. If publicity had put Sheppard in, perhaps it would also help to get him out. In any event, once the flamboyant Boston

second time, in the same place, for the same murder.

Judge Francis Talty entered the courtroom first. Handsome and grey-haired, he was known to be tough but scrupulously fair. It was he who ordered all photographers and movie cameramen to stay outside the court building, and forbade newsmen to seek information from anyone directly involved in the case.

An imposing figure

Next came the prosecutors, John T. Corrigan—no relation to Sheppard's first defence lawyer, William J. Corrigan—and his assistant Leo Spellacy. They were both highly skilled courtroom performers and looked confident right from the start.

But then so did the two who followed: Sheppard's prime defence laywer, the youthful F. Lee Bailey, and his boyish, crew-cut assistant Russ Sherman. Bailey was an imposing figure; his suits were impeccable, almost too impeccable some said, and his tone of voice resonant and sure. Perhaps a little too sure.

Finally Dr. Samuel Sheppard appeared—not to the flashing cameras and buzzing whispers of anger and innuendo, as before, but to a court that seemed eerily silent. Sam looked fit, but his tightly drawn lips were a clear sign of the strain he was undergoing.

This was his last chance to prove his innocence. If the jury found him guilty this time he would be guilty forever; even when finally released from jail he knew that society would never take him back. He would remain an outcast, a convicted murderer, for the rest of his life.

Sergeant Robert Schottke, one of Cleveland's best homicide detectives, was the first important prosecution witness to take the stand. He had been the first to accuse Dr. Sam back in 1954, and this "coup" had helped to make his name as a brilliant officer.

In the cross-examination Bailey fired at him with both barrels. He referred to the canvas bag containing Sam's blood-smeared watch, ring and key.

"Did you realize that Marilyn's killer

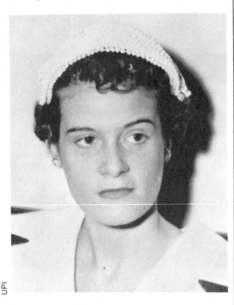

UPI

THE MISTRESS . . . Dr. Sheppard, pictured right with his father during the first trial, made love with pretty Susan Hayes (above), a technician at the osteopath's hospital. At first, he denied having any extramarital affairs. But before he stood trial, his secrets were out . . .

lawyer had taken over the case Sam Sheppard was rarely out of the news for any length of time.

Bailey vowed to secure a retrial. And he did. But after the Supreme Court decision the press were very wary of attacking Dr. Sam, and the coverage was guarded and often sympathetic.

So it was that on October 24, 1966, Dr. Samuel Sheppard—now remarried to the glamorous Ariane—stood trial for the

INP

had probably left prints on those items of jewellery?''

Schottke admitted that this was probably true.

''And did you . . . ascertain just what prints were there before accusing *anyone* of this murder?''

There was a pause; and then a faint but audible, ''No''.

A defence victory

Bailey then asked the witness about the injuries which Sheppard received at the hands of the supposed attacker. Schottke admitted that he had not inquired whether Sam could have inflicted the injuries himself, or whether they *must* have been inflicted by someone else.

The astute lawyer pounced. ''So you accused the doctor without finding out whether it could have been him or not?'' he snapped. Schottke nodded agreement. It was an opening victory for the defence.

Next on the stand was Dr. Samuel Gerber, the coroner. He, too, had become well-known since the 1954 trial, and had

''Tell the jury, Doctor, where you have searched for the instrument during the last 12 years.''

''All over the United States.''

Delighted, Bailey feigned an expression of surprise, ''Please tell us what you found,'' he demanded of the coroner.

Gerber shook his head sadly. ''I didn't find one.''

There was a murmur of astonishment round the court. Even Judge Talty reacted. Corrigan and Spellacy looked as if they were on the point of choking their star witness with the blood-smeared pillow.

''Did you, Coroner Gerber, once say, about a month before Marilyn Sheppard was murdered, that you intended someday to 'get' the Sheppards?''

''Any man who says that is a liar!'' Gerber shouted back. But to the jury he was now a blusterer more interested in convenience than the truth.

The trial was going well for Sheppard, and everyone both inside and outside the courtroom knew it. The odds in Las

Vegas were approaching 20-1 for Dr. Sam's acquittal. But the prosecution had another ace. They called Mary Cowan, Gerber's assistant.

It was she who had examined the contents of the canvas bag, and she came to court with colour transparencies of the objects found inside. She flashed onto the screen the picture of Dr. Sam's watch as it was then, speckled with blood. These speckles, she testified, were caused by ''flying blood''.

It was a tense moment. The speckles must have appeared on the watch while Sheppard was beating his wife to death, argued Corrigan—there was ''no other way'' it could have happened.

The flying blood

It was Bailey's turn to look worried. He questioned Mary Cowan on every aspect of her testimony, but failed to make her change it. The longer the trial proceeded the more it became obvious that the entire case hung on the ''flying blood'' theory. When he was not in court, Bailey spent his whole time, questioning Sam, probing, searching for an answer to the riddle.

How had the blood spots appeared on the watch? Bailey, Sherman, and Sheppard spent hours examining every possibility, casting their minds back to the damning transparency. Typically, it was Bailey who found an answer.

He remembered seeing minute particles of blood on the *inside* of the watch band. So, he concluded, the blood must have got onto the watch after it had been removed from Sam's wrist.

It was a clever argument and the jury accepted it. From then on the defence

UPI

ON TRIAL . . . Medical technologist Mary Cowan and prosecutor Thomas Parrino (above) discuss spots of blood found on Dr. Sheppard's watch. The blood riddle baffled lawyers at the first trial (right), but 12 years later, the doctor's counsel found an answer that convinced a jury.

lectured all over the country on the Sheppard case always ''proving'' that Dr. Sam was guilty. Bailey went straight to the crux of Gerber's argument: the blood-stained pillow which showed, according to the coroner, the imprint of a ''surgical instrument''.

Gerber admitted at once that he had never seen an instrument of the sort he had in mind, though he had certainly looked.

The Cleveland Press

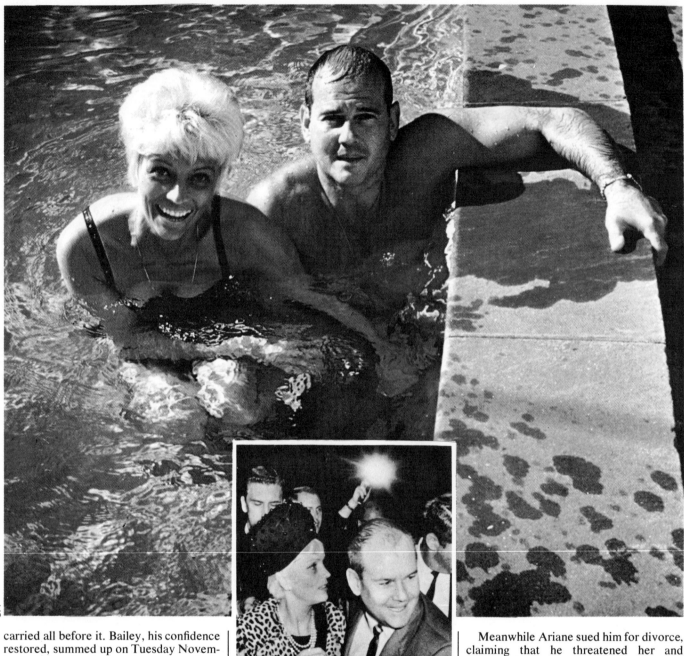

UPI

carried all before it. Bailey, his confidence restored, summed up on Tuesday November 15 by dismissing the prosecution's case as "ten pounds of hogwash in a five-pound bag".

No happiness

On the following day the jury declared Dr. Samuel Sheppard "not guilty".

But life outside prison brought him none of the happiness for which he had fought so long. He made numerous efforts to be reinstated in the medical register; but prejudice against him remained and it was more than a year before he was able to resume his practice. When he did begin medical work again he found that many of his patients distrusted him and were only too eager to sue him for negligence. Finally he was forced out of the profession because no insurance company would continue to cover him.

WIFE No. 2 ... Dr. Sheppard and Ariane (above and top) celebrate after he is eventually cleared. But their happiness did not last ...

Meanwhile Ariane sued him for divorce, claiming that he threatened her and carried a heavy axe and a knife.

Frantic bride

Later, Sheppard met up with an athlete called Strickland and turned to professional wrestling to earn a living. He also got married for the third time—to Strickland's pretty 19-year-old daughter. But his efforts to regain a place in society were all in vain. Six months after his marriage his health began to decline and, ignoring his frantic bride's pleas to see a doctor, he died a sad and inwardly lonely man on April 6, 1970.

The coroner's verdict was death by natural causes. But perhaps he wanted to die, as those near him suggested, worn out by society's rejection of him and the hopelessness of his struggle to re-establish himself.

NIGHTMARE AT THE YWCA

The dark stranger appeared in the girls' hostel, then left.
Months later he was back on his fatal trail.

365 THREE SIX FIVE

handkerchiefs

GUARANTEED FOR 365 DAYS

Sunday Mercury

THE MIDLANDS' OWN SUNDAY NEWSPAPER

PRICE 4ᴰ.

No. 2,131 **

THE GREAT CHRISTMAS MANHUNT FAILS

Mercury Staff Reporter

AS Birmingham's most intensive-ever Christmas manhunt enters its fourth day, the sadistic killer who murdered a young woman at an Edgbaston YWCA hostel is still at large.

And last night Det. Chief Supt. Jim Haughton, head of the City CID, asked: "Where are the 60 bus passengers who travelled with a bloodstained man on Wednesday evening?"

Despite Press, TV and radio appeals none of the passengers on the 7.40 p.m. No. 8 (Inner Circle) bus have come forward.

Yesterday, police announcements were made at Birmingham and West Bromwich Albion football grounds, and in Birmingham cinemas.

Notices appealing for any information were posted on buses and in public houses throughout the city.

The headless body of 29-year-old Miss Sidney Stephanie Baird was found in the YWCA annexe at Wheeleys Road, Edgbaston. She had been brutally murdered with a table knife.

After he had murdered Miss Baird, the killer attacked Miss Margaret Brown, who was also staying at the hostel.

Police believe the man caught a No. 8 bus at Wheeleys Road and travelled towards Five Ways, The Ivy Bush, Hockley Brook and Aston. His hands and clothing were dripping with blood. Other passengers moved away from him.

STEPHANIE BAIRD

DELAYS

THE GIRL WHO ESCAPED

A holiday flash-back to a smiling Margaret Brown.

'My 10 seconds of horror'

THE girl who spent a frightened Christmas, 21-year-old Miss Margaret Brown, yesterday told for the first time of the terrible 10 seconds which she cannot forget.

In those ten seconds a ...er struck at her—a man ...rying to kill...

Woman of 66 and son die in house blaze

A 66-YEAR-OLD woman, and her 36-year-old son died in a Christmas morning fire at West Bromwich despite rescue attempts by five men.

The woman was Mrs. May Jones, of 14 Neal Street. Her son, who was spending the night with her and his step-father, Mr. George Jones (68), was Mr. Jack Hooper, father of a young daughter, of 9 Larchwood Road, Yew Tree Estate, West Bromwich.

Mr. Jones managed to escape from the blazing house, but firemen, wearing breathing apparatus, found the bodies of Mrs. Jones and Mr. Hooper in a smoke-filled bedroom.

It is believed that Mr. Hooper was trying to save his mother's life when he was overcome by smoke.

Mr. Thomas William Parsons, a 36-year-old welder, of 12 Neal Street, said: "We were opening the children's presents when we heard a milkman shouting that No. 14 was on fire. I saw Mr. Jones in the backyard. He was doubled up with coughing.

"Mr. Sidney Taylor and his son from No. 18, joined me and Mr. Bert Barnard, the caretaker of a nearby school. Mr. Barnard brought a ladder and I got to a bedroom window but was driven back by the heat and smoke.

"It was impossible to get in."

Flames rushed out

Mr. Taylor said: "My son and I dashed along in our night clothes and with bare feet. We burst the back door open, but the flames rushed out at us, making it impossible for us to get into the house.

"The milkman was also helping but I don't know his name."

Mr. Jones was detained in hospital with severe shock.

Yesterday police and fire officers were trying to establish the cause of the fire.

A Fire Brigade spokesman said: "So far we have no idea how it started."

IT WAS 11.15 p.m. on a cold evening in March 1959. A beautiful young teacher who occupied a single room in the annexe of the Y.W.C.A. hostel in Birmingham, England was lying in bed. Outside all was quiet. She had heard the comforting sound of the porter as he made his rounds and felt that all was safe. Soon she would be asleep. Suddenly the door opened — the light was switched on and a dark figure stepped into the bedroom. "Hello," he said softly, "I'm looking for Kathleen Ryan."

The girl sat up in bed, her heart pounding with fear. She made a desperate effort to keep calm. "How did you get in?" she asked. "I climbed in through a window," came the reply. The man approached the bed with a purposeful look on his face. He stared fixedly at the girl's breasts outlined beneath her flimsy nightdress, and she realized that only a miracle could save her from assault.

"Please," she pleaded, "I'm engaged to be married. Perhaps you had better be going."

Something in her tone of voice seemed to calm the stranger. For a second he hesitated. Then the miracle happened: he turned and walked towards the door. The girl quickly jumped out of bed and with a bravado which astonished even herself, ordered the man to follow her. She led the way down the corridor, opened the front door, and let him out of the hostel. Seconds later she was on the telephone to the police; but there was no sign of the intruder when they arrived.

Clothes and presents

Nine months later, on December 23, 1959, another girl who occupied the next room in the Y.W.C.A. annexe came face to face with the same man. Her name was Stephanie Baird, a highly attractive but retiring girl who was totally uninterested in men. As before, the intruder climbed in through a small window at the rear of the building, and again, no one saw him. There were very few girls staying at the hostel that night since most of them had gone home to spend Christmas with their families. Stephanie, too, was packing a few clothes and presents with the intention of leaving on the following morning for her mother's house.

She moved confidently round her room in a red pullover and petticoat, little suspecting that she was already being watched. Outside in the corridor, the stranger found a chair, stood on it, and looked through the high glass panel set above Stephanie's door. Soon, however, he began to get bored. He jumped off

HOSTEL OF TERROR: In the annexe (left) Stephanie Baird died horribly. In the ironing-room (right) Margaret Brown's screams saved her from the same fate.

the chair and was about to steal away when the door opened.

"What are you doing?" demanded Stephanie.

"I'm looking for somebody," the intruder replied.

Then, without warning, she was in his arms. He began kissing her frantically and edging her, at the same time, back into her room. Stephanie struggled desperately, and for a brief second managed to tear her face away long enough to scream. It was the last voluntary sound she ever made. To silence her the man closed his powerful fingers round her throat and squeezed. Under his weight she fell backwards, fracturing her skull on the floor. By this time she was already unconscious, but the man kept on squeezing until her body lay limp and lifeless in his arms. What followed led police and doctors to label Stephanie's killer as one of the most monstrous sexual psychopaths in the history of crime.

Panting and moaning with excitement, the man proceeded to make love, in a variety of ways, to the dead body. But this was only a beginning. Having satisfied his first urges, he remembered the chair outside and took the precaution of putting it back where he had found it. Re-entering Stephanie's room, he locked it from the inside and got undressed. Then, as if he were unleashing all the suppressed passions of a lifetime of ugly, frustrated desires, he attacked the girl's body with unprintable bestiality, running through the whole gamut of sexual activities which his warped imagination could invent.

Even this, however, lost its attraction to him. He was about to stop when he spotted a table knife lying on the shelf of an open cupboard. With it, he carved off Stephanie's right breast and flung it onto the bed. Next he tried to cut open her stomach, making deep scores on both the back and front of the body. Finally, when this failed, he attacked the head and succeeded—although he had no knowledge of anatomy—in cutting it off within the space of a few minutes. He then held it up by the hair and stared at it in the mirror.

At that moment a noise interrupted him. Startled for the first time, he dropped the head onto the bed, wiped his hands on Stephanie's underwear, dressed quickly and climbed out through the window. He left a note, scrawled in ballpoint, on the dresser. It said: "This was the thing I thought would never come." It was an extraordinary and horribly pathetic message; so much so, that police were unsure whether it was the remark of a madman or a disgusting joke.

She raised the alarm

Outside once more, the criminal composed himself for a further assault. He was still excited and breathing heavily and, after thoroughly inspecting the annexe for a second victim, made his way over to the main block. There was a light on in the hostel laundry. Twenty-one-year-old Margaret Brown was busy ironing some underwear. She, too, was preparing to go home for Christmas. Once, she put the iron down and walked through the adjoining washroom to close the outside door, which she had noticed had blown open. She returned and was about to continue ironing when she suddenly heard the door click open again. Once more she walked through the washroom to close it and returned. But as soon as she picked up the iron the same thing happened a third time.

The washroom lights went out almost at the same moment. Margaret, suspecting nothing, again turned to close the door. As she entered the washroom, she just glimpsed a shadowy figure before being struck a violent blow on the head. The man lunged forward and Margaret screamed and screamed again at the top of her voice. Unlike Stephanie, she was lucky. This time the intruder took fright and fled, and the terrified girl was able to raise the alarm.

When police arrived they had no inkling that Stephanie Baird had been murdered and mutilated in her room. They interviewed Margaret Brown, who gave them a reasonably accurate description of the attacker. "He was about 28 years old," she told detectives, "five feet eight inches high with a ruddy complexion and a well-defined chin." Some footprints were found outside an open window and plaster casts were taken. Then, as a matter of routine, the police decided to check on the other girls staying in the hostel. They found that Stephanie Baird's door was locked, and an officer was sent outside to look through a chink in the curtains. He could just see a pair of motionless, naked human legs.

"Batter down the door," came the order. Seconds later the police had burst in on the scene of blood and chaos left by the killer. One of the young officers was physically sick. All of them were numbed by the awfulness of the sight before them.

A televised warning

The news of the murder was quickly relayed to Birmingham Police Headquarters, and the entire local police force was placed on the alert. Detective Chief Superintendent James Haughton, head of Birmingham's Criminal Investigation Department, took over the case. Contact was made with every other police department in Great Britain, and also with various European countries through Interpol. In addition, Haughton called in the Press and also made sure that there would be radio and television news flashes on the murder; later he appeared on television programmes to warn the public of the possibility that the killer might strike again, and to ask for help in finding him. It was a nation-wide man hunt.

From the start, however, Haughton was beset by bad luck. A police dog picked up the murderer's scent, and was avidly on the trail when a traffic accident scattered the contents of an overloaded truck over the highway. The scent was lost. The Press was keen to support the police effort, but the date was against them. Late editions of the newspaper carried the

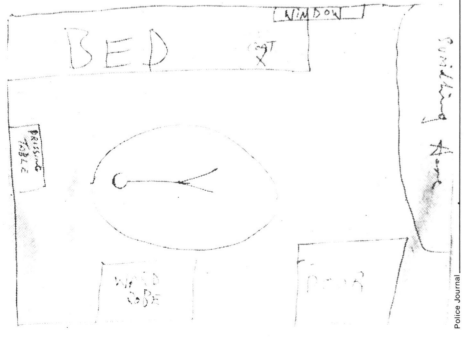

"I WANT TO TELL YOU . . . it's been on my mind." Pathetic psychopath and brutal killer Patrick Byrne even drew a "map" to help ensure his own conviction.

Popperfoto

story on Christmas Eve, but no more editions were due to appear again until Sunday, December 27. Many local people had gone away for the national holiday whilst others had come into the area from elsewhere, thus increasing the difficulty of checking on possible suspects.

Then, just as Haughton was preparing for what looked like a long and arduous inquiry, he seemed to get a break. At a police check point some distance from the scene of the crime an officer had stopped a bus and questioned the conductor. He learned that earlier on the same evening a man whose description coincided with that of the suspect had boarded the bus near the Y.W.C.A. He was heavily soaked in blood—so much so, that it had dripped from his arms onto the seat. Days were spent trying to trace this man and all the other passengers on the bus who might possibly have seen him. Tests on the blood confirmed that it was of the same group as Stephanie's. Detectives drove the conductor round and round the bus route in an effort to help him remember where the man had left the bus. He had to be traced, if only to be eliminated from the inquiry.

Despite the most urgent appeals, however, he never came forward and police were forced to continue their search without ever discovering his identity. Eventually, a reconstruction of the crime satisfied detectives that the blood-stained passenger was not the murderer. He was *too* covered in blood; for it was soon realized that since there was no trace of blood en

THE KNIFE of a madman? And what of the note? Was that some kind of sick and disgusting joke? There were clues by the score, but from the start the police were dogged by bad luck. Even an apparently lucky break set them on the wrong track.

route from the hostel to the bus stop the murderer probably had very little on his clothes. Because of this, Haughton guessed that he had undressed before mutilating the body.

The two who confessed

When this avenue of investigation failed, Haughton realized that he had no choice but to begin a house to house search, radiating outwards from the hostel. A questionnaire was carefully prepared so that every detective would ask exactly the same questions, and this was given out to small teams who visited all the houses in their area to check out the movements of every adult male. The initial investigation resulted in 20,000 completed questionnaires. Gradually, as no new information appeared, the area was extended until it covered a three-quarters of a mile radius round the Y.W.C.A. The number of people interviewed in the death area alone reached the total of 100,000.

Because the intruder had been seen in the hostel on at least one other occasion, Chief Superintendent Haughton was convinced that he was a local man. Nevertheless, thousands of criminals who lived outside the area were interviewed, and everyone in Birmingham and surrounding districts who had a record of conviction for peeping, or indecency, or accosting, or assaulting women, was methodically checked. They were all eliminated. So were two men who actually confessed to the crime.

Then came a further blow. The fingerprint men had been working day and night in an attempt to produce a legible set of prints. They finally admitted defeat. The night had been so cold and wet that insufficient sweat exuded from the killer's fingers to make prints. Even the paper on which he had written the strange message yielded nothing.

There was only one clue left: the footprints left by the killer under the annexe window. The police had been anxious to keep photographs of these from the Press for fear that the criminal would destroy his shoes if he thought that they might

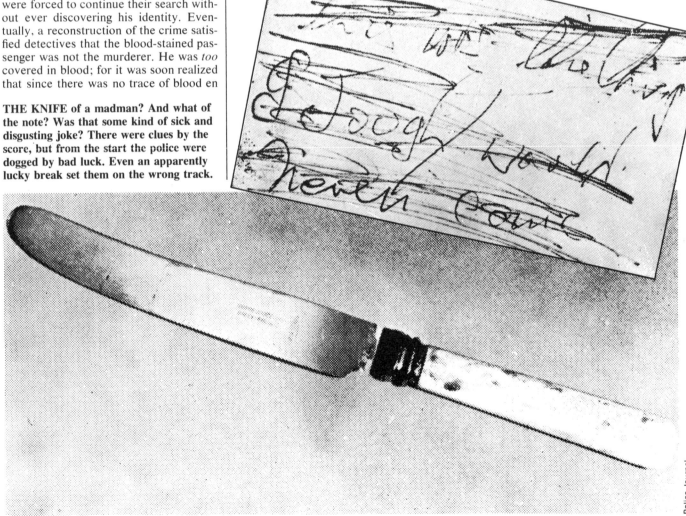

Police Journal

Keystone

trap him. With every other line of investigation drawing a blank, however, Haughton decided that the risk must be taken. The pictures were released along with an appeal to anyone who had seen a man wearing this type of shoe to come forward.

Unknown to the police, the shoes, with their distinctive pattern of transverse bars on both soles and heels, were being driven round in a Birmingham City Corporation garbage truck—the discarded property of an Irish labourer named Patrick Joseph Byrne. Byrne was already known to the police. He had, until Christmas Eve, been living in lodgings quite close to the Y.W.C.A. During the exhaustive house to house inquiries, his name had appeared on the police lists. The fact that he had left his lodgings the day after the murder had not made him a suspect. He had told his landlady well before December 23 that he intended to leave and was going to stay with his mother in Warrington, Lancashire. His previous employers had also been notified.

On the night of the murder his landlady confirmed that she had seen him leave the house at 5.30 p.m., and again at 8 p.m. and 10.30 p.m.—at which time Byrne asked if he could stay an extra night as

he had drunk too much to go to his mother's house. The landlady agreed, and he left early the next morning. A friend of Byrne's testified to police that they had been drinking together during the evening. He seemed to have a sound alibi.

On leaving, Byrne placed the shoes and the suit he had worn on the murder night into a paper carrier bag and gave them to the landlady to throw out. The landlady left the bag beside her garbage can and, as a result, the garbage collector spotted them and decided to rescue them. "They were too good to throw out," he said later.

We mustn't let him go

Byrne, now safely in Warrington, had forgotten all about the discarded shoes. But when the police released the pictures of his footprints—and he saw them splashed over the front page of his newspaper—he remembered them with a shock. Suppose his landlady had forgotten to throw them away? Suppose she had recognized them and was on her way to the police? He began to worry; soon he was on the verge of panic.

Meanwhile, Chief Superintendent Haughton was suffering agonies of frustration. He spent days travelling through-

WITNESSES: The bus conductor (left); the fortunate Margaret Brown (with fiancé, centre); and the landlady. On the London train for a visit to Scotland Yard.

out the City of Birmingham and the surrounding districts showing slides of the murder to groups of policemen. "The majority of the police had not been to the scene," he said later, "and hadn't seen the gruesome nature of it. These slides helped to give them impetus and have them going away saying, 'We must find this person!' and conveying this enthusiasm to everyone in the area: 'We mustn't let him get away. We've got to find him.'"

In this way, an attempt was made to retain police interest through the long, hard weeks of fruitless searching. Finally, Haughton decided that the only answer lay in repeating the house to house search. He felt sure that somewhere, some minute detail had been missed which held the key to the killer's identity. The only way to obtain this was by interviewing the 100,000 people again.

Almost immediately, a flaw in the original search was noticed. It was pointed out that none of the men who had left the area during the Christmas period and

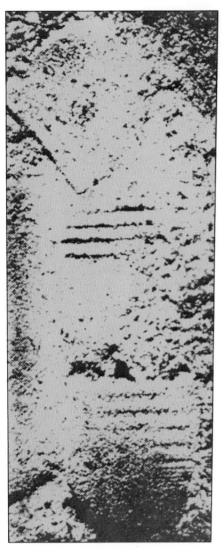

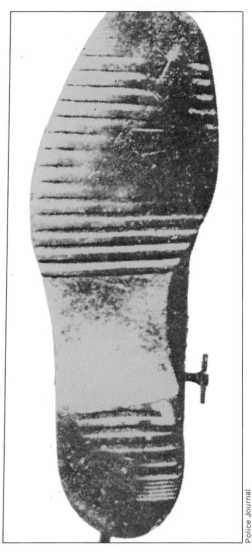

Police Journal

failed to return had been interviewed *personally* by the police. Perhaps the killer was one of these. Accordingly a list of their names was made up and among them was that of Patrick Joseph Byrne. He was quickly traced to Warrington and a message was sent to the local police requesting them to interview him.

On February 10, 1960, Byrne, clearly terrified, called at Warrington Police Station. He was seen by Detective Sergeant George Welborn, who observed Byrne's agitation. Nevertheless, the Irishman made a good attempt to appear unconcerned. He freely answered the sergeant's questions about his movements on the murder night, and everything he said coincided with what the police already knew. Welborn, however, was a highly professional officer. To satisfy his professional conscience, he asked one extra question which didn't appear on the questionnaire: "Would you have any objection to having your fingerprints taken?"

There was a moment of silence. Byrne made an effort to reply, but the words refused to come. In those few seconds his resistance collapsed and panic took over.

He became sure that the police knew more than they said. They probably already had the shoes. It was a trap. Sensing that the silence had been a little too long, the astute policeman asked a further question: "Have you anything you care to mention about your stay in Birmingham?"

Without warning Byrne blurted out, "I want to tell you about the Y.W.C.A. I have something to do with it." The sergeant then pointed out to Byrne the seriousness of what he had said.

"I know," replied the killer, "I cannot sleep. It's been on my mind. I was coming down to see the police. These last seven weeks have been no good to me."

Within hours Chief Superintendent Haughton had driven to Warrington to collect the suspect. He had had two confessions already, but he soon realized that this one was different. The facts tallied. Byrne related details which only the real murderer could know. Later, the tell-tale shoes were picked up and definitely identified as belonging to him. At his trial, Mr. John Hobson, representing the Crown, read out in full the remarkable statement Byrne made to police after his arrest. It

FOOTPRINTS TO FATE: The evidence that the police held back from the public . . . yet these traces were enough to spur the killer's blurted revelations.

told, in graphic and obscene detail, the story of his nightmarish attack on Stephanie Baird and the bestial feelings which prompted it.

"I wanted to get my own back on them for causing my nervous tension through sex," he said at one point. "I felt I only wanted to kill beautiful women. I watched her for a time, and stood close to the window . . . the urge to kill her was tremendously strong."

Byrne was subsequently found guilty of murder and sentenced to life imprisonment. On appeal, the Lord Chief Justice, Lord Parker, substituted for the verdict one of manslaughter on the grounds that Byrne was on the borderline of insanity. The sentence, however, remained the same. As Chief Superintendent Haughton later stated, it was only by "unremitting effort" and police tenacity that the brutal psychopath was put where he belonged — behind bars.

THE CAULDRON OF DEATH

The cauldron held the secret of Emily Kaye's disappearance, but it took the most brilliant of pathologists to sift the abundance of horrifying clues (above) at the Bungalow of Love. Ironically, for Emily and the man of her dreams it was to have been the scene of an idyllic experiment in happiness. But their relationship reached its climax instead at the height of a raging thunderstorm . . . in a flash of lightning, tragedy and terror.

Mirrorpic

Syndication International

GOOD FAMILY MAN . . . so his Richmond neighbours might have described Patrick Mahon (with daughter). But they didn't know about the Eastbourne bungalow.

SIR Henry Curtis Bennett, counsel for the prosecution, held up a sheaf of papers for the jury to see. "These," he said, "are the transcripts of two statements made by the accused to the police. I shall read them to you." There was a short pause. An atmosphere of restless expectancy pervaded the crowded British courtroom. After weeks of sensational stories from the press — accompanied by

even more gruesome rumours—the trial of 33-year-old Patrick Mahon had finally begun.

Hours before the opening proceedings on the morning of July 15, 1924, the doors of the Lewes County Court in Sussex had been closed to hold back the eager throngs of people who had turned up in the hope of obtaining a seat in the public gallery.

Judge Avory, white-haired and thin-lipped, entered first, closely followed by the redoubtable figure of Sir Henry Curtis Bennett. Then came the dour defence counsel J. D. Cassels, looking grim and

very conscious of the uphill fight he would have in attempting to save his client from the death penalty. Finally, the accused man himself, dwarfed by two burly police officers, emerged into the arena with a somewhat sickly smile at the audience.

The feverish interest which the trial aroused had been largely the responsibility of the press, which had not been slow to warn the public that—even by the standards of other murder cases—this one was exceptional for its macabre brutality. Sir Henry's opening speech soon confirmed the news stories. He began by relating the details of Mahon's

arrest two months previously.

The prisoner had been stopped by police at Waterloo Station, London, where he had gone to collect a Gladstone bag from the cloakroom. Inside the bag were a pair of women's panties and several other garments all soaked in blood, a carving knife, ten inches long, and a racket case engraved with the letters E.B.K. These were the initials of the dead woman in the case: Emily Beilby Kaye.

When asked for an explanation, counsel announced, Mahon replied: "I am fond of dogs. I must have carried meat for the

A SUSPICIOUS wife and a cloakroom ticket led arresting officer Superintendent Sinclair (below) to murderer Mahon . . . ironically "headless" at Sussex inquest.

dogs in it." Even the accused man had realized, shortly afterwards, the full absurdity of his explanation, and later he had made—and signed as correct—the two statements which Sir Henry, in his clear, clipped voice, read out to the jury. The chain of events which they revealed was bizarre in the extreme.

According to Mahon, he had first met Emily Kaye about a year previously, and they were soon "on intimate terms" in spite of the fact that Mahon admitted to being married. "I realized very quickly," Mahon had said, "that she was a woman of the world."

Miss Kaye responded by falling in love with the prisoner and becoming increasingly demanding of his time. If, at first, Mahon had enjoyed her attentions, he quickly began to feel that she was forcing him into a corner. Over a period of time she developed a number of schemes whereby Mahon would leave his wife and child and accompany Miss Kaye to a new life far away in Paris, or Cape Town, or "somewhere else".

Mahon became increasingly embarrassed. After a slow start in life—which, it later transpired, included a five-year spell in jail for assault—he had acquired a steady job as sales manager of a soda-fountain company, and was secretary of

the local bowling club at his home in Richmond, Surrey. In short, he was now a respectable member of society and afraid of scandal: "I temporized in the hope of gaining time but . . . I felt more or less at the mercy of a strong-minded woman whom, though I liked her in many ways, I did not tremendously care for."

Then matters came violently to a head. With Miss Kaye constantly demanding that the two should go abroad, and Mahon insisting that the scheme was impossible, an ill-fated compromise was reached. Mahon's version was carefully phrased to foster the impression that he was acting under the intense pressure of a wilful woman: "She suggested I should take a holiday and go away with her for a week or two and take a bungalow where we would be alone together and where she would convince me with her love that I should be perfectly happy with her."

At this point Sir Henry interrupted his reading. He pointed to a scale model of the bungalow set out on a table in full view of the court. "This," he said, "was where the 'love experiment' took place. It lies on a lonely stretch of beach between Eastbourne and Pevensey Bay and is known as Officer's House." Mahon obtained the keys from the owner, Mr. Muir, on April 11, 1924 and on the following day the couple arrived there together. Miss Kaye had with her a great deal of luggage, including a large trunk, in the belief that after the two months' lease on the cottage had expired they would then proceed with their plans to leave the country permanently.

Furious argument

From this moment, the tragedy moved quickly to a climax. The couple quarrelled incessantly about Mahon's failure to obtain a passport. It was obviously of prime symbolic importance for Miss Kaye that he should do so, and he was even persuaded to make a trip to London —on April 14 or 15—with the express purpose of arranging this at the passport office. Again, he failed to comply with her wishes and a furious argument ensued.

Here, the prosecuting counsel warned that the prisoner's version of what happened differed in small but important ways from the evidence which he would present later, and he asked the jury to pay particular attention to the dates involved. Mahon claimed that the trip to London was made on April 15, and that the two of them had travelled together in both directions. Soon after returning to the bungalow Miss Kaye wrote two letters committing both of them to a definite line of action:

"She also asked me to write to the Assistant Secretary of a function of which I am Honorary Secretary, stating that I was giving up work and going overland to Paris for a time and then on to South Africa. I refused to write such a letter and so, fuming and raging, she finally wrote the note herself and begged me to sign it; again I refused. Suddenly, she picked up a weapon—an axe—and threw it at me. It struck me on the shoulder and glanced off the bedroom door, breaking the shaft."

This was the start of a rapid and fatal sequence of events. According to Mahon, the two grappled, "she was a powerful, athletic girl", and in the struggle they fell over an easy chair. Emily Kaye's head smashed against the coal cauldron which lay to one side of the fireplace, and the blood spurted out. She was dead within seconds.

Unpleasant details

Sir Henry Curtis Bennett dramatically dropped the papers he was holding on to the table. The defence, he said, would undoubtedly claim that the death was an accident and that Mahon had no intention of murdering Miss Kaye. However, the most intriguing—and unpleasant—details were yet to come.

Two days before Mahon was due to take possession of the bungalow with Emily Kaye, he met Ethel Duncan, a lonely and passionate young woman, who was immediately charmed by his good looks. He made a date with her, and, in spite of the intervening death of Miss Kaye, appeared at the appointed time. He showed no anxiety, and even invited her to the bungalow. She accepted and went down to spend the following weekend with her new lover.

"Meanwhile," continued Sir Henry, "where was the body?" He turned, for the first time, towards the prisoner. Briefly, their eyes met. Mahon knew what was coming. A grim silence descended on the court; jury and spectators alike held their breath. The body, revealed the lawyer, lay in the second bedroom of the bungalow. Both legs and the head had been severed by means of a saw and a carving knife which the defendant claimed he bought for the specific purpose of disposing of the corpse.

After a "delightful weekend" spent with Miss Duncan, Mahon invented an excuse for cutting short her stay. He sent a telegram to himself stating that he was urgently required at his office. Then, with Miss Duncan safely out of the way, he set to work on April 22 to rid himself of the "unwanted flesh".

A heavy storm was brewing as Mahon stoked up the sitting-room fire and placed the severed head on top. Suddenly, the storm broke with a violent flash of lightning and a crash of thunder. As the head lay upon the coals the dead eyes opened and Mahon, in his shirtsleeves,

fled blindly out to the deserted, rainswept shore. By the time he returned the fire had done its work.

Other portions of the body were burned in a similar way, Sir Henry told the court, but the smell was unbearable, so Mahon tried a different method. He placed some carved up pieces of the body in a large pot, boiled them and then packed them tightly into the Gladstone bag. Back in London with his macabre luggage, he caught a late-night suburban train and threw the pieces, one by one, out of the window. Then he deposited the bag in the cloakroom at Waterloo Station with the intention of collecting it before he returned to the bungalow to continue the work. Subsequent arrest prevented him from doing so.

"It is, at best, a revolting story," remarked Sir Henry, "but in spite of its confessional nature, it could not be relied upon." Evidence would be produced to show that Miss Kaye could not have died from injuries received by falling on the coal cauldron. There was also proof, he claimed, that the saw and carving knife were, in fact, purchased on April 12, *before* Emily Kaye's death, as part of a plan for murdering her.

A further question concerned the dead woman's financial situation. She was not rich. But, by working hard and saving, she had managed to accumulate a little capital. Nearly all of this had passed into Mahon's hands during their year-long affair, and he had cashed a number of money orders she had given him, under false names and addresses. Was it simply a coincidence, Sir Henry asked the jury, that her bank account was empty at the time of her death? The prosecution would prove, beyond reasonable doubt, he stated, that Mahon had cold-bloodedly planned Miss Kaye's death.

It was a mammoth opening speech, and it occupied the entire first day of the trial. At the end of it, the odds looked firmly against the defendant—and the stream of prosecution witnesses who testified on the following two days appeared to confirm that impression. Police described in detail the appalling scene of torn flesh, bloodstains, and half-burnt bones which greeted them at the bungalow. Home Office pathologists confirmed that the blood was human and almost certainly that of Miss Kaye; dozens of other witnesses allowed Sir Henry Curtis Bennett to trace every movement made by the accused man during the days before and after the murder.

Then, one of the most brilliant forensic pathologists of all time was called to the stand: Sir Bernard Spilsbury. Prompted by questions from the prosecution, he gave a description of what he had found and examined at the bungalow.

"There was a large two-gallon sauce-

A GRIM SMILE . . . and Sir Henry Curtis Bennett has completed his case for the prosecution. His scale-model bungalow sets the horror scene in court.

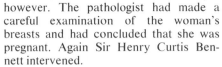

pan half full of a reddish fluid. At the bottom I found a piece of boiled flesh with some skin adhering to it.''

Sir Henry interrupted: "There was also a hat-box and a trunk. Did you examine these?''

"Yes.''

"Please describe what you found in the hat-box.''

"I found articles of clothing, together with a large number of pieces of flesh. Thirty-seven in all.''

There was an audible gasp from the public gallery. Even the judge was startled. "Thirty-seven separate pieces?'' he enquired. Sir Bernard Spilsbury confirmed the number.

"Had they been boiled?''

"Yes.''

"And the trunk?'' pursued the prosecution counsel.

"The trunk contained four large pieces of a human body. Fitted together they would form almost the whole of the trunk of a woman.'' This was not all, however. The pathologist had made a careful examination of the woman's breasts and had concluded that she was pregnant. Again Sir Henry Curtis Bennett intervened.

"Have you been able to find the uterus?''

"No.''

It looked, at first, like an innocent question. But the inference was plain: Mahon had known that Emily Kaye was pregnant and had made sure he disposed of that portion of the body first. It would hardly assist his case, in the event of arrest, if it were discovered that he had callously quartered the body of a woman who bore his child.

Finally, counsel inquired about the head. Had any traces been found of the skull bone? The answer, inevitably, was no. Not only had the defendant burnt the head thoroughly, he had also, as he was later to testify, disposed of the ashes. As a result, it was impossible to determine the cause of death—for there were no marks of any kind of violence prior to death on the rest of the body.

For the first time, the counsel for the defence, J. D. Cassels, fully entered the fray. He went over Sir Bernard Spilsbury's evidence in minute detail in a desperate effort to get a statement from him on the cause of death—all the while suggesting that, technically, it would be possible for Miss Kaye to have died by striking her head on the coal cauldron. Sir Bernard, however, would not be drawn. Miss Kaye, he confirmed, had been a healthy woman. It was virtually impossible for her to die by falling on the cauldron in the way suggested.

Slim chance for defence

Ironically, the defence had completed the prosecution's case. When Cassels' cross-examination had finished, Sir Henry Curtis Bennett stood up and announced, with a grim smile, that the prosecution case was complete. The immediate reaction from the defence was the only one open to them. The evidence which had been presented was so overwhelmingly weighted against the prisoner —and appeared so entirely conclusive— that only a remarkable performance by Mahon himself would be likely to sway the jury. This slim chance rested on the answer to one important question:

Did Mahon plan the murder beforehand, or was Emily Kaye's death really the result of a violent, but unforeseen, fight between the two?

Accompanied still by the obligatory two police officers, Mahon shuffled into the witness-box. There were no women in the jury—Judge Avory had ruled them out on account of the obscene nature of the murder details—but there were plenty in the audience, and Mahon could

189

occasionally be seen trying to catch some female eye as if he needed continually to reaffirm his "way with the ladies".

Then Mr. Cassels skilfully guided Mahon's courtroom account of his activities with Emily Kaye. One crucial error in the defendant's statement read out by Sir Henry Curtis Bennett was in the date he gave for the purchase of the saw and carving knife. Mahon had said this took place on April 17. Other witnesses, including the shop assistant who made the sale, testified that it was on April 12. Proof had been supplied that both instruments were used to cut up the body. If Mahon bought them *before* the murder, it was clear that he knew the purpose for which they would be used.

Could he be insane?

Under questioning, Mahon, in his plain-speaking, unemotional voice, confessed that he *had* bought both instruments on April 12. His explanation was breath-takingly naive; so much so that it caused some speculation in newspaper reports about the defendant's sanity.

"I entered the shop," he told the jury, "in order to buy a new lock for the bungalow." He failed to buy the lock, but emerged with a saw and a carving knife "because they would be useful". He insisted that the mistake he had made about the date of purchase was just that: an innocent error.

Cassels, understandably, hurried on to other points of Mahon's story. The money which the defendant had taken from Miss Kaye was explained away as the proceeds of a business speculation in French francs in which the two had engaged. As for Miss Kaye's untimely death, the whole thing, according to Mahon, was a dreadful accident. He had desecrated the body in fear and panic at the thought of what a police investigation might mean.

There was nothing noticeably dramatic or convincing about Mahon's performance. But, with one or two unexplored gaps, it built up into a coherent story. No one in the courtroom could possibly have imagined that Cassels' final, innocent sounding question would galvanize the atmosphere in the way that it did.

"Did you," he inquired, "desire the death of Miss Kaye?"

"Never at any time," came the reply.

When these words were spoken, a violent thunderstorm was raging outside. Just as Mahon finished speaking, the court was lit up by lightning and echoed with an ear-splitting crack of thunder. It was an extraordinary coincidence. For a few brief seconds, Mahon was transported back to the gruesome scene at the bungalow when he had burnt the head of his victim. He shrank back in terror into a corner of the box.

Radio Times Hulton

No word was spoken about this incident at the trial; but the effect on the prisoner was startling. When Sir Henry Curtis Bennett began his cross-examination, Mahon seemed a different man: subdued and broken almost to the point of indifference.

Sir Henry poured scorn on Mahon's explanation of the purchase of the saw and carving knife. He emphasized the point that both instruments had been used to dismember and carve up the body, despite the fact that — against expert evidence — the defendant insisted he had used a different knife. Piece by piece, the eminent lawyer demolished the fabric of Mahon's defence.

It became obvious, as Sir Henry pursued his cross-examination, that Mahon was lost. Before the end, however, there was one final macabre piece of evidence. Under questioning, Mahon described with words and gestures what he did with the skull bones — most of which had remained intact after burning.

"I picked up the skull and broke the

HIS DISTASTE is reflected in the manner of his summation. Then Mr. Justice Avory sentences a subdued and broken murderer to the gallows.

bones with my hands, like this," he remarked almost casually, "then I threw them over the garden wall."

After this the final speeches were simply a formality. The judge, Mr. Justice Avory, summed up in a manner which reflected his distaste for the accused man, and 40 minutes after retiring the jury brought in their verdict. Mahon was found guilty of murder and was hanged on September 9, 1924.

Throughout the trial the fact that Mahon was married was made little of. It was only later that his wife's role in his arrest and subsequent execution became generally known. It was she — suspicious of her husband's frequent absences from home — who had discovered the vital cloakroom ticket while searching through one of his suits. That ticket took Mahon to the gallows.

AL CAPONE

The flashily-dressed hood who became the prosperous and impeccably-tailored self-made businessman. He had a ready smile and a quick handshake . . . which often turned out to be fatal. For it took 500 gangland murders to make Capone the boss of Chicago . . . they called him Public Enemy Number One.

JOHNNY TORRIO, new boss of the Chicago underworld, was a man of vision. The response to the introduction of Prohibition in the United States had been like a gold rush. Small-time bootleggers were springing up everywhere. Torrio grasped that a fortune of millions of dollars awaited the first man to control this new get-rich-quick industry, and he decided he would be that man—not merely in Chicago but in the 932 square miles of neighbouring Cook County.

It would be a mammoth task, requiring both organizing genius and ruthlessness. He needed help, and in search of it he turned to the Five Points gang in New York City. Torrio, himself an ex-Five Pointer, had had his eye for some time on a 21-year-old Five Points lieutenant, good with guns as well as his fists, who had already twice been questioned by New York City police over murder cases. His name was Alphonse "Scarface" Capone, known to his friends as Al.

Straightforward offer

At the time, 39-year-old Torrio was netting $100,000 a year from gambling, vice, and other rackets. His offer to Capone was simple and straightforward. "Al," he said after outlining his plans, "you can have a quarter—$25,000 a year—of what I'm making now, plus half the profits out of bootlegging." "It's a deal," snapped Capone.

It was the first step up the ladder for the man who, within less than a decade, would earn himself the label Public Enemy Number One . . . who would be known as the wickedest, and one of the richest, men of his time . . . whose name would be synonymous in every corner of the globe with American gangsterism.

Miscellaneous rackets

By 1927, when Torrio's dream of a bootleg monopoly in Chicago and Cook County was a reality, it was estimated that he and Capone were pocketing $105 million a year between them. Sixty million came from beer and liquor, 25 million from gambling saloons and dogtracks, 10 million from dancehalls, roadhouses, and the sale of sex, and a further 10 million from miscellaneous rackets.

Making him rich wasn't the only change the years wrought in Capone—the product of poor Neapolitan parents and the slums of Brooklyn, New York. The loud-mouthed, flashily-dressed hoodlum brought to Chicago by Torrio in 1920 had disappeared. Capone was now impeccably tailored, with a rose in his buttonhole and a diamond solitaire—the badge of the Big Shot—in his tie pin.

He had two fortified headquarters and a home in Chicago, plus a magnificent estate on Palm Island off Miami Beach,

THE INCREDIBLE IRONY of Capone's downfall was the charge brought against him . . . failing to fill in tax forms. His impudent, but realistic, defence . . . that he didn't realize tax was payable on money earned by illegal means.
The man who taught him to be a gangster, Johnny Torrio, was jailed for the same offence (top centre), betrayed by Capone. Pupil Capone laughed at the Federal Grand Jury (right, top picture), but ended up in an undignified position, handcuffed to a lesser criminal (right, bottom picture). It was a wry exit for Chicago's Caesar of Crime . . . though he lived well in jail, and was released after eight years to return to his luxurious Palm Island Estate.

Florida. He had learned the usefulness of the ready smile and the quick handshake.

Capone's life style was, in part, very much that of the prosperous self-made businessman. That, indeed, was how he saw himself—a tough, but honest man of affairs. And if bootlegging, his chief business, happened to be against the law, well, it was legitimate in human terms.

"They call Al Capone a bootlegger," he used to complain. "Yes, it's bootleg while it's on the trucks, but when your host at the club, in the locker room, or on the Gold Coast hands it to you on a silver tray, it's hospitality. What's Al Capone done then? He's supplied a legitimate demand. Some call it boot-

legging. Some call it racketeering. I call it a business. They say I violate the prohibition law. Who doesn't?"

He conveniently overlooked the murders it took to put him on the top of the heap and keep him there, and the corruption of politicians, judges, and police which ensured the law did not interfere with his activities. In 1929, after he called a conference in Atlantic City, at which the major gangs carved up the United States between them, it was said of him admiringly that—like J. P. Morgan, the financial wizard of Wall Street—he was "the first man to exert national influence over his trade".

In fact, Capone was a fat, syphilitic killer, whose sordid empire was founded on the Thomson sub-machine gun, the revolver, the sawn-off shotgun, and the bomb. It took 500 gangland murders to establish him as the boss of Chicago, and rival gangs offered rewards as high as $50,000 for anyone foolhardy enough to take on the task of rubbing him out.

This, too, was reflected in his life style. By day he travelled in a steel limousine which weighed seven tons and cost him $20,000. It was equipped with bullet-proof glass and a special combination lock so that his enemies couldn't break in and plant a bomb under him. Once inside, he was safe from buckshot, shrapnel, or machine gun bullets. Nevertheless, a scout car always preceded his "personal tank", and a gang of handpicked sharp-shooters followed it in a second car.

When he went to the opera, one of his favourite relaxations, he was accompanied by a bodyguard of 18, bigger even than the President's. The trouble-shooters were scattered strategically around the theatre, watching the audience instead of the show. If Capone decided to step outside for a cigarette between acts, they would rise as one man to follow and surround him.

At the peak of his career, in the latter part of the 1920's, Capone had 700 of the toughest hoodlums in America under his command, 30 per cent of them paroled convicts, 20 per cent aliens. It was as vicious a gang as has ever been assembled outside a penitentiary.

In the early days, however, Capone did his own killing at Torrio's behest. One of his victims was Joe Howard, a small-time crook who made the tactical mistake of hi-jacking two loads of Torrio booze in one night. The next evening, about six o'clock, Howard was having a quiet drink in the bar where he usually hung out, when the door opened and two men walked in.

"Hello, Al," he said, sticking out his hand. Capone fired six shots into him and Howard slumped to the floor dead—his smile of welcome still on his face. The police put out a general arrest order for Capone, but by the time they found him all of the eyewitnesses had suffered an attack of lost memory. It was a common ailment in Chicago in the 1920's. Two months later a jury found that Howard had been killed by "one or more persons unknown". The case against Capone, like all the cases except his last two, had been effectively blocked.

By 1924, he had established himself in control of the respectable Chicago suburb of Cicero. By a combination of sluggings, kidnappings, shootings, and intimidation, he had done what the politicians demanded—delivered the vote. Now, in return, he had his own mayor, his own town clerk, and his own town attorney.

Nothing and no one could touch him. Gambling was illegal, but he ran what was reputed to be the biggest roulette game in the country, with as much as $150,000 riding on a single turn of the wheel. Capone also had 161 bars, open night and day. In adjoining Stickney were the brothels, the form of vice in which Torrio specialized. Some of the houses offered a choice from as many as 60 prostitutes of different colour, skills and nationalities.

By this time he and Torrio were each pocketing $100,000 a week. But they were still a long way from controlling the whole of Chicago. The two major impediments

193

to their ambitions were Dion O'Banion —Torrio's only serious contender to become boss of the underworld—and the six Genna brothers from Sicily, who controlled the Unione Sicilione, the chief source of alcohol.

O'Banion was ostensibly a florist, but he always carried three guns and could shoot with either hand. He had an Irish face with a perpetual grin and fathomless blue eyes. Although he had never been brought to trial, he was credited in gangland with 25 killings. His territory was the 42nd and 43rd wards—comprising the Gold Coast, where the houses and apartments of the city's richest and most fashionable residents look out over Lake Michigan.

With the coming of prohibition, the Gennas had had the bright idea of importing poor Sicilian families, setting them up in tenements with a still, and paying the man of the house $15 a day—a fortune by "old world" standards—to smoke his pipe and keep the still stoked up.

Flowers for funeral

Alky-cooking, as it was known, had grown into a $10 million-a-year industry, supplying the basic ingredient for synthetic bourbon, rye, Scotch, brandy, rum, and gin—and controlling the sale of sugar to the affiliated Italian districts of Melrose Park, Cicero, and Chicago Heights.

On 4 November, 1924, O'Banion was in his florist's store awaiting a visit from some friends of Mike Merlo, president of the Unione Sicilione, who had just died a natural death. One former henchman had already been in to place a $750 order for flowers for the funeral.

O'Banion was in the back room, just saying to William Crutchfield, a Negro porter, "Better brush up the leaves on the floor, Bill," when he heard some more customers enter. There were three of them. "Hello, boys. You from Mike Merlo's?" he asked, going forward to meet them. In his left hand, he had his florist's shears. He held out his right.

"Yes," replied the man in the centre, grasping the extended hand. Five shots rang out in quick succession, followed a few seconds later by a sixth, the clincher. The last bullet was fired into O'Banion's left cheek as he lay sprawled among his flowers. The gun was held so close that his skin was burned black with powder.

Police inquiries were met by the inevitable Mafia wall of silence, imported like the alky-cookers from Sicily. Torrio, Capone, and the Gennas were then questioned. "The day before he was killed I gave him an order for $10,000 worth of flowers," stated Torrio. "Our boys wanted to send some floral pieces to Mike Merlo's house and we all chipped in and gave the business to Dion." The coroner,

unable to surmount the wall, finally wrote the killing off.

The era of the lavish big-time gangster's funeral began with the burial of O'Banion. He was laid to rest in a $10,000 coffin, shipped out to Chicago from the East in a special express freight car. A woman columnist described it as "equipped with solid silver and bronze double walls, inner sealed, and airtight, with heavy plate glass above and a couch of white satin below, with tufted cushion extra for his left hand to rest on; at the corners, solid silver posts, carved in wonderful designs."

Another recorded the scene at the undertaker's where O'Banion's corpse was exhibited for three days. "Silver angels stood at the head and feet," she wrote, "with their heads bowed in the light of ten candles that burned in solid

golden candlesticks they held in their hands. Beneath the casket, on the marble slab that supports its glory, is the inscription, 'Suffer little children to come unto me.' And over it all the perfume of flowers."

Mounted police cleared the streets on the day of the funeral—at which there were 26 truckloads of flowers, valued at $50,000. They included a heart of American beauty roses standing eight feet high; a blanket of roses, orchids and lilies, measuring seven feet by ten, sent to cover the grave at Mount Carmel; and a basket of roses labelled simply, "From Al."

Capone and Torrio solemnly attended the funeral. Their show of piety, however, did not fool anyone. The coroner might be forced not to put a name on the assassins, but the O'Banion gang had no doubts about where the responsibility lay. Three of its gunmen, Drucci, Moran, and Weiss, sought out Capone's automobile—an ordinary sedan at that time —and raked it from front to back with machine guns and sawn-off shotguns.

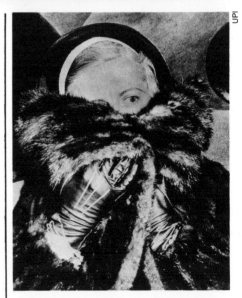

MRS. CAPONE avoided photographers . . . here she ducks cameramen outside Alcatraz. Top: Capone's $20,000 steel "armoured car", with gun-turret.

QUICK ON THE DRAW . . . one of Capone's bodyguards has his gun ready as a popcorn seller accidentally brushes his arm. No chances are taken when Capone makes a rare public appearance at a baseball game, especially when a small disruption is created by the arrival of star Gabby Hartnett to sign for young Al Capone junior.

Capone missed death by minutes. He wasn't in the vehicle, having just stepped into a restaurant in the course of an inspection of his liquor empire.

Torrio, who had left town to give things a chance to cool off, was trailed to Hot Springs, Arkansas, New Orleans, the Bahamas, Cuba, Palm Beach, and finally back to his Chicago home—where he was shot down by two gunmen in full view of his wife, with whom he had been shopping. He survived the attack after 16 days in hospital.

Moran, one of the three men involved in the attempted assassination of Capone, was identified as the man with the revolver in the shooting of Torrio. Neither Torrio nor Capone would help the police, however. They remained true to the Mafia tradition of silence, and put the two attacks down to "unfinished business".

Although they had survived, their experiences had given both men a healthy respect for the opposition. His narrow

escape persuaded Capone that $20,000 for a steel limousine would be a worthwhile investment. For his part, Torrio was so badly scared that, when jailed for nine months shortly afterwards on a charge of operating a brewery, he had the three windows of his cell equipped with steel screens and hired three extra deputy sheriffs for sentry duty.

Uncharacteristically, no reprisals followed the attacks on Capone and Torrio for well over a year. The reason was that Capone had more important matters on his mind. With Mike Merlo dead, there was the question of who would now control the vital Unione Sicilione with its vast network of stills. Capone was eager to put in his own candidate as president, Antonio Lombardo, partner in a firm of commission brokers and cheese merchants.

The six Genna brothers, however, had other ideas. They installed the toughest of them, Angelo, in the post. Throughout the latter part of 1924, and much of 1925, Capone was preoccupied with the task of "persuading" them that they had made the wrong decision.

Angelo was the first to die. On May 25, 1925, he was assassinated in his own automobile by a volley of slugs from sawn-off shotguns. Mike Genna was next, killed by a policeman in a shoot-out while —without knowing it—he was being taken for a ride by Capone's two star gunmen,

Scalise and Anselmi. That was on June 13. Less than a month later, on July 8, Antonio, brains of the Gennas, got his in yet another "handshake murder", when he kept an appointment with "a friend".

The remaining three Gennas acknowledged that they had received an offer they could not refuse. They fled to their home town of Marsala in Sicily, leaving Capone to instal the man of his choice as boss of the Unione Sicilione.

But peace still did not come to Chicago's gangland. The O'Banions made yet another attempt to remove Capone from the scene—an attempt which demonstrated clearly in what contempt the mobs held the forces of law and order. In broad daylight, eight carloads of gunmen made an assault on the mobster's Cicero headquarters, firing a thousand shots into it from machine guns and the familiar sawn-off shotguns in a matter of seconds.

Generous gesture

Once again Capone escaped and, in the kind of generous gesture for which he was well known, paid $10,000 out of his own pocket to save the sight of a woman accidentally injured in the eye during the incident. This time, however, he was not prepared to file the matter away under "unfinished business".

Leadership of the O'Banion gang had

195

World Wide Photos

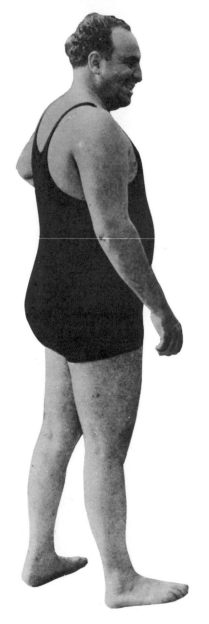

AP

AP

A HOOD'S HAVEN . . . Palm Island, near Miami, Florida. In his heyday, Capone would entertain 100 guests for a weekend. After eight years in jail, the sweeping solitude of his sea-lapped, palm-fringed isolation was a solace for him in his pursuit of more leisurely pastimes. But the sins of his youth caught up with him, as the syphilis of long ago rotted his brain. In his final madness, friends would gather for a game of cards . . . always letting Capone win. When one forgot himself and won by mistake, Capone cried: "Get the boys . . . I want this wise guy taken care of!"
On his death, he was surreptitiously buried . . . in Chicago. His tomb at Mount Olivet was an imposing affair . . . a dynasty had ended.

been taken over by Earl "Little Hymie" Weiss, the only man in the world Capone was said to be afraid of. Weiss was a Pole, unemotional and coldly ferocious, who had brought a new sophistication to gang murders. It was his killer's brain that had originated the ceremony of taking a victim for a ride, using a stolen car and carrying out the "execution" in another county, or even another state. It made the crime virtually impossible to solve.

The removal of Little Hymie, three weeks to a day after the Cicero attack, is looked back on as the most scientific killing in the history of the gang wars of the 1920's. Little Hymie's headquarters was above the flower store of the late Dion O'Banion. A few days after the Cicero raid, a young man using the name of Oscar Lundin took a second-floor room in the boarding house next door. The

window gave a clear shot at the pavement outside O'Banion's store. Meantime, a young woman had taken a room in another nearby boarding house which overlooked the rear exit from the florist's.

The new tenants were not then seen again. Instead, three gunmen moved into each room. They had to wait ten days for a clear shot at Weiss, unimpeded by pedestrians. Then, as he stepped from his car, the guns roared and he collapsed on the sidewalk with ten bullets in his body. He died without regaining consciousness.

One of his companions, a beer pedlar named Patrick Murray, stopped seven bullets and was dead before he hit the sidewalk. The other three—W. W. O'Brien, a criminal attorney; Benjamin Jacobs, a politician and O'Brien's investigator; and Sam Peller, Weiss's chauffeur—were seriously injured but survived.

But they told no tales. They hadn't seen a thing, couldn't identify the killers, didn't know what it was all about. Capone, informed of the death of his hated foe, commented: "I'm sorry, but I didn't have anything to do with it. I telephoned the detective bureau to say I would come in if they wanted me, but they said they didn't. I knew I would be blamed for it, but why should I kill Weiss?" So another coroner's inquest was stymied.

For a time after that, Chicago was comparatively quiet and murder-free. With the main opposition out of the way, Capone got together with what rivals remained and agreed, "We're a bunch of saps to be killing each other." The truce did not last long, however. Three strangers, found dead with a nickel clutched in one hand, turned out to be out-of-town hoodlums. They had come to Chicago because someone had put a price of $50,000 on Capone's head.

Who was that someone? Once again the finger pointed at the O'Banion's and, in particular, George "Bugs" Moran. Moran, who had taken part in the attempts on the lives of Torrio and Capone four years earlier, now led the O'Banions. Settling that old score led to the legendary St. Valentine's Day massacre in which seven members of the Moran mob were gunned down in a garage as they prepared to set out on an expedition to hi-jack some of Capone's rum.

Moran himself escaped, having spotted a telltale sedan with drawn curtains just before he arrived at the garage. But he was left a leader without a gang. Capone was at last without a serious rival.

Throughout the years when Capone's killers roamed the streets, butchering their rivals, shooting up and beating up saloon keepers who showed a reluctance to buy Capone beer and liquor, they had

197

virtually a free hand. With votes and money, Capone bought politicians, judges, and policemen. If necessary, he bribed juries. And, if anything went wrong, there was always a friendly governor to grant an early parole.

Capone outlasted four chiefs of police, two municipal administrations, three U.S. district attorneys, and a regiment of Federal prohibition agents. He survived innumerable crime drives, grand jury investigations, reform crusades, clean-up election campaigns, police shake-ups, and Congressional inquiries and debates.

Now he was sitting pretty. In Chicago he had 10,000 speakeasies buying six barrels of beer a week at $55 a barrel, a total of $3,500,000 a week. They also bought two cases of liquor a week at $90, a total of $1,800,000 a week. Beer cost about $4 a barrel to make, liquor about $20 a case. With vice, gambling and other rackets he was pulling in about $6,500,000 a week.

Then he slipped up for the first time. He was arrested while leaving a cinema in Philadelphia and jailed for a year for having a gun. In prison, he made plenty of friends, including Dr. Herbert M. Goddard, of the Pennsylvania State Board of Prison Inspectors, who removed his tonsils and operated on his nose.

"I can't believe all they say of him," the doctor later declared. "In my seven years' experience I have never seen a prisoner so kind, cheery, and accommodating. He does his work as a file clerk faithfully and with a high degree of intelligence. He has been an ideal prisoner. I cannot estimate the money he has given away.

"Of course, we cannot inquire where he gets it. He admits he's in the rackets. But you can't tell me he's all bad after I have seen him many times a week for ten months, and seen him with his wife and his boy and his mother."

Capone lived well in jail. His cell had a $500 radio, a pair of easy chairs, a table, tufted rugs, and other hotel comforts. He was finally allowed to leave it after ten months, his sentence commuted for good behaviour, but he returned to a changing, hostile world.

The newspapers, which had once made

THE ODD MIX of comfort and starkness which Capone grew accustomed to in jail seemed to be echoed as he whiled away the twilight of his life . . . his violence spent.

him something of a folk hero, were now bent on destroying him. President Hoover had been jolted into starting a personal campaign against him, and a picked band of agents from the Justice Department set out to smash his booze empire by physical force, raiding and wrecking 30 of his breweries and seizing 50 of his heavy trucks in one year. Finally, it was the taxmen who got him, with the aid of informers.

Found guilty of three years' tax evasion and of failing to file tax forms for another two years, Capone—who could think of no defence except that he didn't think he had to pay tax on money made from illegal operations—was fined $50,000 with $30,000 costs and sentenced to 11 years in a federal penitentiary.

He was released after eight years and retired to live quietly at the Palm Island, Florida, estate, where, in his heyday, he often entertained as many as a hundred guests for the weekend. He died in January 1947, aged 52 and a raving lunatic, his brain eaten up by paresis from an early case of syphilis. One of the most remarkable facts about him is that he died in bed, instead of being gunned down in a Chicago gutter.

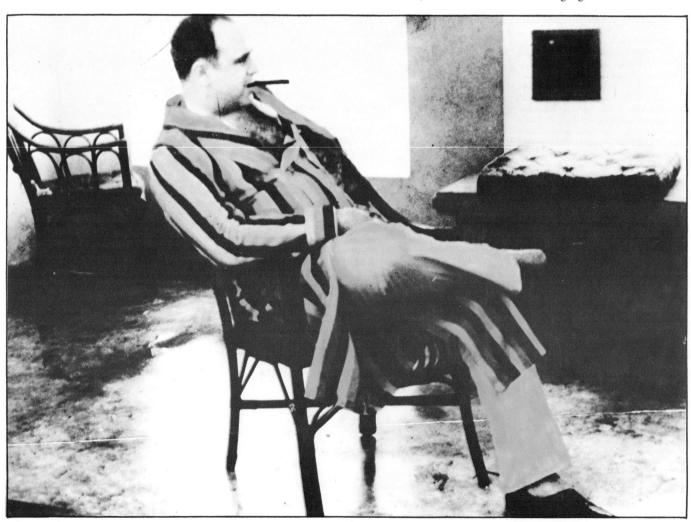

THE DEADLY DELINQUENTS

THIS WAS NO WEST SIDE STORY... IT WAS THE THEATRE OF CRUELTY

It had all the vivid romance that the teenage gangs of New York could muster . . . with their names like the Dragons and the Jesters. But slum life could get too colourful among the Puerto Ricans and Irish Whites around 152nd Street. During a stifling summer in the late 1950's, the Dragons went looking for trouble. It was a swimming pool that caused blood to flow . . . and the night had a dramatically tragic finale.

Antony Cobb

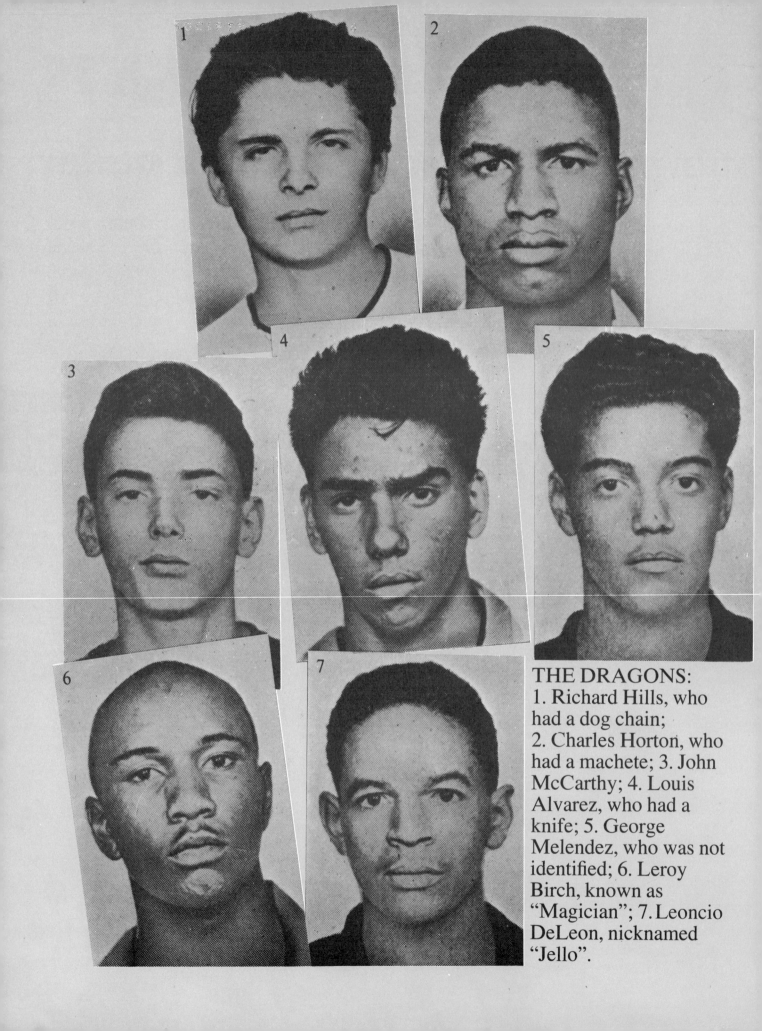

THE DRAGONS:
1. Richard Hills, who had a dog chain;
2. Charles Horton, who had a machete; 3. John McCarthy; 4. Louis Alvarez, who had a knife; 5. George Melendez, who was not identified; 6. Leroy Birch, known as "Magician"; 7. Leoncio DeLeon, nicknamed "Jello".

THE trial, which began on the morning of Monday, January 13, 1958, in the Court of General Sessions on the 11th floor of the Criminal Courts Building in Center Street, New York City, aroused immense interest from coast to coast of the United States. It was a high spot in juvenile delinquency in America's overcrowded cities, and it served to focus public attention upon a major problem of community living—what to do about teenage, kids who roam the streets in gangs, get into fights with rival gangs, and terrorize the neighbourhood generally.

In London there were the Mods and Rockers. In New York there were the Egyptian Dragons and the Jesters. At this trial seven Egyptian Dragons were arraigned before Judge Irwin Davidson on a charge of murdering a boy named Michael Farmer.

Two of the youths were white, John McCarthy, aged 15, and Richard Hills, aged 16. The other five were Negroes or dark-skinned boys of Spanish-American descent. Leoncio DeLeon, for instance, nicknamed Jello, was a Negro from the Dominican Republic, while George Melendez, incidentally the best-looking of the group, was a Puerto Rican—both were 17-year-olds. The most powerfully built was Leroy Birch (18), a Negro of five foot ten in height who was known as "Magician".

The remaining two defendants were 18-year-olds—Charles Horton, a Negro, and Louis Alvarez, the most sinister looking of all, whose face was lined and pock-marked with pimples and boils. The two white boys and Melendez seemed frightened and were less tough-featured than their companions. From their general appearance in court, it was obvious that all seven came from poor families.

Meaningful glance

Robert R. Reynolds, the New York District Attorney, presented the case for the prosecution in a terse and business like manner. The crime he described took place about 11 p.m. on the hot and stifling night of July 30, 1957, at Highbridge Park—a public recreation area that borders Amsterdam Avenue between 155th Street and Dyckman Street not far from Columbia University and which is the site of a fine municipal swimming pool.

According to the best estimates, about 18 boys were involved, all belonging to the Egyptian Dragons. It was the contention of this gang that their members were being prevented from using the facilities of the pool by a number of other gangs in the neighbourhood, mainly by the Jesters, who consisted for the most part of white American-Irish boys.

Earlier in the evening the Egyptian Dragons had gathered at the corner of 152nd Street and Broadway and made

VICTIM: Mrs. Farmer lost her son. He fought polio as a child . . . but did not survive the beating handed out by the Dragons. Whether he was a member of the rival Jesters gang was never established. His father was angered by what he felt was the court's leniency.

their way in twos and threes to Highbridge Park where they lay in wait for members of any rival gang which might appear. Two youngsters did so in the persons of Roger McShane, a slender 16-year-old, and Michael Farmer, a small boy who was a year younger. The Dragons assumed they were Jesters, although it was never established that either of them belonged to this gang. Farmer had been afflicted as a child with infantile paralysis. The newspapers covering the case invariably referred to him as the "polio victim" or the "polio boy", although he had made a satisfactory recovery from the disease.

"The defendants and their associates descended upon Farmer," said the District Attorney with a meaningful glance at the youths in the dock, "and wilfully feloniously and with malice aforethought, hit him with fists and feet, a dog chain, a garrison belt, a club, a metal pipe, and stabbed him with a knife and a machete. These acts were going on simultaneously with each other. In the meantime McShane ran about 240 feet from the swimming pool steps towards Amsterdam Avenue until he too was stopped and assaulted."

Both were left lying on the ground as

the gang scattered. Farmer, discovered by Patrolman John T. Collich of the 34th Precinct, died a few minutes after he arrived at the local hospital. McShane, fearfully battered, took three months to recover from his injuries. He was the prosecution's key witness.

First to take the stand after formal police evidence had been given was the murdered boy's father, Raymond Farmer, a New York City fireman.

"Do you have a son, Michael?" the District Attorney asked him.

"I *did*," the witness replied after a pause.

"Was there anything wrong with Michael's foot?"

Before Raymond Farmer could answer, one of the defence lawyers, James Murray, who appeared for McCarthy, the youngest of the accused, was on his feet, objecting that the question was immaterial and irrelevant. The objection was sustained.

The District Attorney tried again. "Did you ever observe Michael walk?" Again Murray objected.

Dreadful crime

The D.A. had two good reasons for asking these questions. First, he wanted to bring out the newspapers' characterization of Michael Farmer as a polio victim, which would make the jury regard the gang's crime as more dreadful than it would appear if it had been committed against an unhandicapped boy. Secondly, he wanted to show that Farmer could not run very well, and he did not wish the jury to draw the inference that Farmer had chosen to stand and fight, while McShane had run away. However, the judge sustained Murray a second time.

Raymond Farmer was followed on the stand by Roger McShane, who recounted how he and Michael had been walking along the promenade alongside the swimming pool when they were set upon by the Dragons.

"How many boys were there in the group that stepped out from behind the bushes?" Reynolds demanded.

"A large group."

"Well, give us your best guess."

Another defence counsel objected to a guess, but he only succeeded in heightening the suspense in court.

Lives menaced

After the witness said he thought there were about 15, the D.A. asked him whether he could point out any in court at that moment. "Yes, sir," was the reply.

McShane then stepped down from the witness chair and went across to the dock, where he pointed his finger at each boy with the exception of Melendez.

"There is one defendant you have not identified," said the D.A. "Are you able to say whether he was there or not?"

"No, sir."

McShane was being cross-examined when the court recessed for the weekend. During the recess, young Roger received a threatening letter, advising him to watch his step and telling him that "if them guys gets the chair, we'll kill you". As a result he was assigned police protection for the remainder of the trial. The lives of other witnesses and even the judge himself were similarly menaced.

Try as the defence lawyers did, none of them could make McShane admit that either he or the murdered boy had been members of the Jesters—although the youngster did say that he and Farmer were looking round for "our friends" on the night of the affray.

"Were you looking to collect a group?" asked the attorney who appeared for Hills.

"No, sir," McShane persisted.

Murray did particularly well for his client, McCarthy, since he got McShane to agree that he had never spoken to the accused teenager, although he had seen him on a previous occasion.

"You didn't see McCarthy do anything to Farmer, did you?"

"No, sir," was the reply.

The next witness was 14-year-old Ralph Lago, who in spite of his extreme youth was actually the leader, or "War Lord", of the Egyptian Dragons. He had been present on the fatal night, but because he was under 15 had to be dealt with by the Children's Court which sent him to a reformatory school. He had

subsequently agreed to testify for the prosecution. He described how he had gone uptown with Horton and Alvarez and another teenager who was not charged. Horton carried what Lago thought was a broom stick, and Alvarez a knife. "If I catch 'em," Alvarez had said, "I'm going to try to stab 'em."

Horrifying exhibit

The knife which Alvarez used was then produced. It was a vicious looking instrument made in Japan. The blade was razor sharp, so much so that when Reynolds picked it up to display it to the jury it accidentally cut his finger. Another equally horrifying exhibit which Lago identified was the dog chain. This the witness swore he had seen Hills carrying "with a weight on it" at the scene of the crime. The D.A. then wrapped a couple of hitches of the chain around his hand and let a length dangle down to show the jury that it could have the effect of a lethal weapon. Another such weapon, which formed an exhibit in the case, was "an object wrapped with the black handle sticking out", which Lago stated had been passed to him by Horton. It was a machete.

A further teenage witness, too young to be tried in this court, was Patrick O'Kelly, who said he was a member of the Dragons. He, too, saw Horton hit Farmer, who was lying on his face with his right arm extended. Asked how and with what Horton had struck Farmer, O'Kelly stated that it was with the "object" that had been wrapped in paper. "I am not sure if it was with one hand or two," he added, "but he went up and down."

"You saw the object come down?"

"Yes."

"After you saw Horton hit Farmer with the object, where did you go?"

"I went around and I ran down the steps."

Machete, chain

Like all the other prosecution witnesses, young O'Kelly was unshaken under cross-examination. He had no weapon when he went up the steps to the pool, he said, and nobody forced him to go. Horton's defence attorney failed to shake O'Kelly's statement that he had seen Horton strike the boy on the ground.

It was the same with Vincent Pardon, another 14-year-old, who related how Horton had told him to go to Hills' house in West 135th Street off Riverside drive. Pardon did so and was given "a thing wrapped in a bag" which turned out to be a machete. Hills himself, according to the witness, had a dog chain.

The D.A. then interrupted the parade of reformatory inmates to call Martin ("Marty") Sullivan, a tall youth, of

17, with a bland, insolent face, a weak chin, a protruding upper lip and shifty eyes. Sullivan had had nothing to do with the killing. A short time before he had been arrested on a charge of burglary, and while being held in the Brooklyn Prison for Youths he had met Leroy Birch in the "TV playroom", and while there he had a conversation with him.

According to Sullivan, he asked Birch, "You didn't mean to kill Farmer, did you?" To which Birch was said to have replied, "I told you the next time I came up we were going to kill somebody."

This testimony threw the court into an uproar, since it was the first time that premeditation had been alleged in the trial. Hills' attorney Irving Mendelson jumped to his feet and waving his hand in the direction of the jury, exclaimed: "The testimony is so inflammatory it is now impossible for the defendants to get a fair trial."

Torrent of blows

Judge Davidson replied that the testimony only applied to Birch and he would so instruct the jury. "You can tell them from now to doomsday," Mendelson retorted angrily, "but how anyone can eliminate it from his mind is beyond human understanding." Nevertheless, the judge held fast to his ruling and the testimony stayed on the record.

At this point in the proceedings the D.A. called the medical evidence, after producing photostatic copies of the autopsy which had been performed on the body of Michael Farmer. The doctor's testimony indicated that Farmer had raised his hands to defend himself against the torrent of blows inflicted on him, since one incised wound appeared beneath the left armpit.

There were other stab wounds including one four inches deep which went through his back and penetrated his lungs. It was this wound which caused his death, the doctor said. The jury were plainly impressed by the doctor's matter-of-fact but none the less horrifying description.

Perhaps the most graphic description of the attack came from another of the prosecution witnesses, pale little Victor Carasquillo, who was visibly shaking throughout his testimony and spoke with a thick Puerto Rican accent. Horton, whom Carasquillo called "Big Man"—he was over six feet in height—was close to Farmer. "He picked up his hand and he had the blade (of the machete) and he hit him once and he put it back in the paper thing and he hit him again and ran."

Carasquillo added that he then came over next to Farmer and he saw "Jello" DeLeon hit the polio victim twice with his stick and the third time the stick broke.

"Can you tell us what part of the boy's

HOMICIDE is the charge . . . and a bunch of kids, aged from 15 to 18, are ordered to be held without bail for more than two weeks pending the hearing of their case. Sixteen-year-old Roger McShane, who came to court with his mother, was one of the gang's victims. Fearfully battered, he took three months to recover, but his friend Michael Farmer died within minutes of the attack. The spectre of brutal death stayed with McShane . . . he received a murder threat during a court recess, and was given police protection. He is pictured below under guard with Ralph Lago, a member of the murder gang who was dealt with in a children's court, and who later gave evidence against his associates. One of the main attackers was the smiling Louis Alvarez (bottom left).

body Jello hit with the stick?"

"The back."

"Across the back of the head and the back of the neck, right?"

Carasquillo nodded.

"Did Jello say anything to you?" the D.A. went on.

"He said 'Kick him!' I swung with my leg, but I didn't touch the boy." He was so scared, he continued that he "swung out" and missed. He then started running and did not stop until he got home.

An unexpected witness was a pretty 14-year-old girl, Mary Jean Rivera, who appeared neatly dressed in a grey cotton dress over a stiff petticoat, with a crimson cardigan and matching crimson knee socks. She turned out to be Louis Alvarez's girlfriend ånd she described how Alvarez gave her his knife, as also had another member of the gang named José Garcia. The newspapers called her the "knife moll".

"What did you do with the knives?" Reynolds asked her.

"I brought them home."

"What did you do with them at home?"

"I put them in my bureau," the child answered without a trace of emotion. "Then I took them out and looked at them. Then I put them in my bureau in a bag."

After Alvarez had been picked up by the police, he guided them to the girl's house where the police recovered the knives, and this was confirmed by Mary Jean. There must have been some in court like the judge who looked at Alvarez, pock-marked, sullen and greasy-haired, and wondered what this fragile child could have seen that attracted her to him.

The defence attorneys were faced with a difficult task, since it was impossible to deny that all their clients had been present when Farmer was killed. It was particularly difficult for Hills' attorney Irving Mendelson, since Hills was the defendant with the dog chain. However, he was able to convince the jury that Hills had a dog, and that he was in the habit of walking about with the unattached chain. He was also able to show that Hills' actions were largely the result of fear that if he refused to cooperate with the other gang members he would be beaten up—which indeed he had been on one occasion.

PROSECUTION WITNESS . . .
Michael "Pee Wee" Ramos (ringed) was said to have been invited to the killing . . . and told to bring some guns. Shortly after the trial, he himself was killed in a gang shooting at a Bronx candy store. The killer, who fired a shotgun blast into his face, was Ramon Serra (inset). He nonchalantly admitted his guilt, according to police.

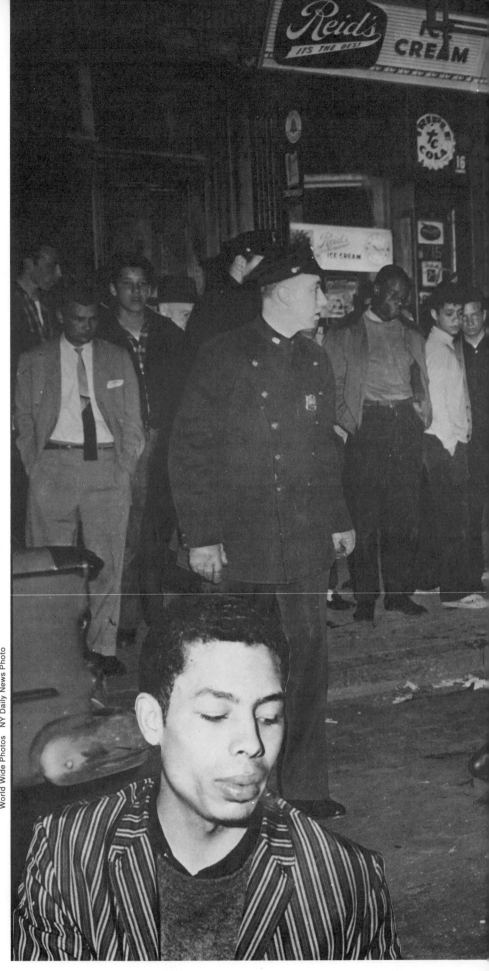

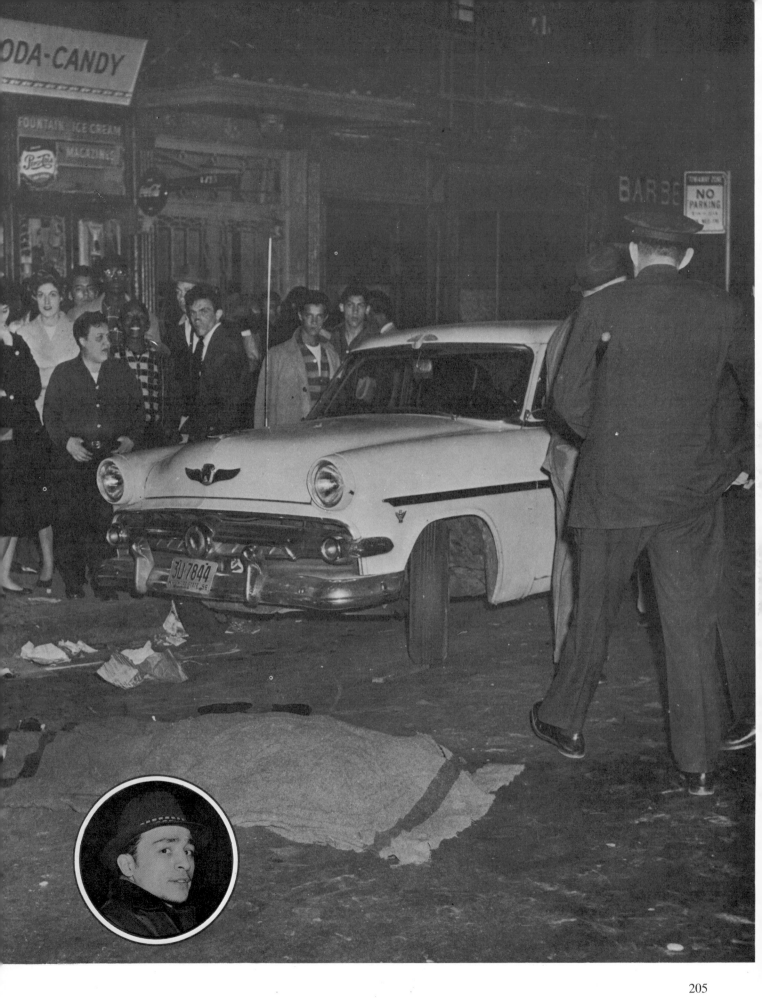

The case against Alvarez was particularly strong since he was shown to have boasted that he was "not chicken" and had blood on his knife after the attack. Indeed his attorney, seeing that there was a strong likelihood of his client going to the electric chair for murder in the first degree, tried to persuade the prosecution to accept a plea of manslaughter. But the D.A. refused.

The other tactics employed by the defence consisted of trying to show that the statements made by the defendants after their arrest were made under pressure and the result of rough treatment in the police station. In several instances the defendants had gone back on their statements and said they had lied to avoid being assaulted by the police.

As a rebuttal witness, the D.A. called another gang leader, Michael Ramos, known as Pee Wee, a sinister looking youth, with previous convictions for assault and burglary, who stated that Alvarez had telephoned him twice on the night of the killing asking him to come up to the swimming pool and bring some guns with him. But Pee Wee had his own troubles and did not show up. Shortly after the trial these troubles culminated in Pee Wee being shot to death by a member of a rival gang outside a Bronx candy store.

In his summing up to the jury, Judge Davidson explained the different kinds of homicide. Under United States' law, he said, murder in the first degree involved proof, beyond all reasonable doubt, of premeditation and deliberation and intent to kill. Murder in the second degree required proof of intent to kill, without proof of premeditation or deliberation.

Manslaughter in the first degree is homicide without design to effect death. It may be committed in the heat of passion, in a cruel or unusual manner or with a dangerous weapon, while manslaughter in the second degree is killing in the heat of passion but without the use of a dangerous weapon or other cruel or unusual means.

The judge made it clear that murder in the first degree could only apply to those who went up to Highbridge Park with lethal weapons in their hands — namely Alvarez with his knife and Horton with his machete.

The jury deliberated for a total of nine hours and 35 minutes, this being divided by the court adjourning for the night. The verdict they eventually brought in found Horton and Alvarez guilty of murder in the second degree, while Birch and DeLeon were found to be guilty of manslaughter in the second degree. The remaining defendants, McCarthy, Hills and Melendez were acquitted.

"a farce"

The judge sentenced Horton and Alvarez to 20 years to life imprisonment, while DeLeon got 5 to 15 years and Birch 7½ to 15 years. "I am not happy about sending them to jail," said Judge Davidson afterwards, "but under the law this is what I am compelled to do."

Asked to comment on the verdict, the murdered boy's father thought it had "made a farce of our society". He said: "It's a sign to juvenile delinquents that they can get away with murder — a green light for them to get away with anything."

CANDY STORE ARREST . . . in striped jacket, Ramon Serra is held by police. The scene of the murder is marked out in the blood of his victim.

THE STRONG-ARM MAN AND THE SONGBIRD

NEW YORK rode into the twenties on a tidal wave of gambling, corruption and murder. More than ever, the city looked to its law officers to make a drive against gangsterism and violence. But when Herman Rosenthal was shot dead on the steps of the Metropole Hotel, questions began to be asked even about the police. Was this the open highway to anarchy . . .?

R. Hammond/UPI

ALL OVER New York City in the early hours of July 16, 1912, people lay awake, cursing the oppressive heatwave that defeated all chance of tranquil sleep. Many had given up the hopeless struggle for rest and sat out on front steps, sharing their irritation at the humidity with neighbours, or wandering aimlessly up and down. Others had gone to join the throng of seedy nightlifers who ebbed and flowed along Broadway, around Times Square and, especially, near the run-down Hotel Metropole on 43rd Street.

It was there that a motley collection of gamblers, con-men, pimps, prostitutes, and gangsters gathered regularly with names like Gyp the Blood, Lefty Louie, Itch and Moe—the kind of Broadway denizens whom Damon Runyon would recreate, only with romanticized amendments which turned them into golden-hearted "characters".

That morning around the Metropole some of them were to witness an event which had been whispered along the grapevine of the Tenderloin. They had not long to wait. Shortly before two o'clock, a dumpy, bespectacled, small-time gambler named Herman Rosenthal appeared at the top of the steps leading to the hotel's café entrance in answer to a message that he was wanted outside. In his right hand he carried a cigar; under his left arm was a bundle of early morning editions of the New York *World*.

For a moment 38-year-old Rosenthal hesitated and searched around, scowling, for the person who had summoned him. Then, unable to pinpoint anyone, he started to descend the steps. As he did so, five pistol shots barked in rapid succession from the direction of an open, seven-seater Packard car parked by the sidewalk and occupied by four or five men. Four of the shots struck him in the face and head and, staggering backwards and then spinning over, he toppled down the rest of the steps and was dead almost as soon as he reached the last.

Dramatic exposés

The newspapers cascaded from under his arm and settled over his body like a shroud. An appropriate one, it seemed, for all over the front pages appeared his name—as though some soothsayer had predicted his death and prepared the obituary in advance. As it turned out, it was because of the newspapers that Rosenthal had met his sudden end.

Rosenthal had been a "songbird" in the Tenderloin, launching a series of complaints against the New York Police Department in revenge for the shutting down of his gambling house on West 45th Street. As his enthusiasm for his campaign accelerated he enlisted the aid of a young New York *World* reporter, Herbert Bayard Swope, who wrote increas-

REPORTER Swope (above) was a young man when he set out to expose police corruption in the Rosenthal case. Rosenthal (inset opposite) was emerging gingerly from the Metropole Hotel (opposite) when a hail of bullets ended his life.

ingly dramatic exposés of the police and their supposed double-dealing.

In particular the two men concentrated on Lieutenant Charles Becker, head of one of the so-called "strong arm squads" charged with halting the tidal wave of graft, gambling, and corruption that was washing its way over the city.

According to Rosenthal, Becker had been his partner in gambling and, until they fell out, had been lining his own pockets through graft. On one occasion Becker, embracing the gambler, had cried out: "Anything in the world for you, Herman. I'll get up at three o'clock in the morning to do you a favour. You can have anything I've got."

But it was Becker, Rosenthal asserted, who had been receiving the favours. The latest instalment of this circulation-building saga was in the editions that now covered Herman's body. Only six hours after they appeared the gambler had been due to have a second, and crucial, interview on the matter with Charles Whitman, the New York District Attorney.

The clear inference of the murder, to the criminal know-alls along Broadway, was that the talkative Herman had been silenced before he could produce more embarrassing evidence. The important question, however, was: Had he been disposed of by fellow hoodlums, anxious not to attract unnecessary public attention

to their private world, or had Becker himself had Herman Rosenthal "removed"?

Many people—especially readers of the *World*—immediately assumed that Becker was involved. They were further shaken when, the day after the killing, District Attorney Whitman announced that "a great and powerful secret organization" existed to provide payoffs; and that someone in the Police Department had been responsible for this intended "blockage of justice".

Innuendoes

Certainly there seemed to be something suspicious about Becker's movements on the night of the murder. Not long before Rosenthal was removed, the lieutenant had been near the Metropole and—although he had afterwards returned to his apartment on West 165th Street—he was back at the 47th Street police station by about 3 a.m. He was in plain clothes, this was not his precinct, and the District Attorney—who had called into the station to examine the murder reports—regarded Becker's appearance with suspicion.

It looked very much as though Becker was anxious to keep an eye on the investigation—even though it did not concern him officially. Others thought so, too, despite the fact that the lieutenant had actually been called out by *World* reporter Swope, the dead Herman's public "voice".

As Whitman continued to throw out innuendoes about the police, Becker decided to hold an impromptu press conference. "It ought to be needless for me to say," he told the avid reporters, "that I know absolutely nothing about the crime, who perpetrated it, what the motive was, or what was to be gained by it.

"It was to my best and only advantage that Rosenthal should have been permitted to live for many years. I bear this man no malice, even though he set himself up as my enemy."

At 42, Lieutenant Becker, a strapping, ox-like man, appeared to be the ideal protector of law and order. He was highly articulate, happily married to an ex-school teacher, and had spent 19 years in the force. However, his personal police record was far from impeccable. In his earliest days he had come under the influence of an Inspector Alexander Williams who made no secret—even to newspapermen—of the fact that he regarded payoffs as part of his "emoluments". Williams owned a $17,000 yacht and was alleged, at one time, to have been worth $500,000.

During his own career, Becker had played the tough and brutal cop when it came to prostitutes and other minor-league lawbreakers. But, right up to the day of the murder, he had been taking handsome bribes in return for "protecting"

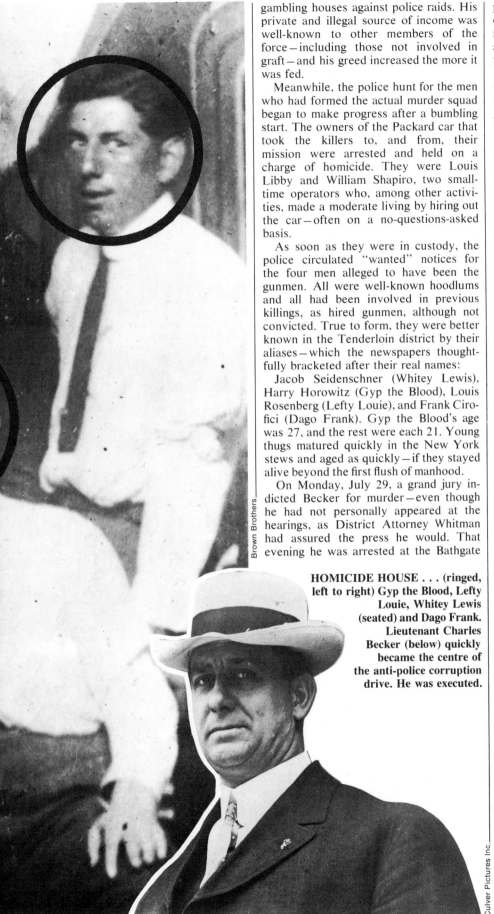

HOMICIDE HOUSE . . . (ringed, left to right) Gyp the Blood, Lefty Louie, Whitey Lewis (seated) and Dago Frank. Lieutenant Charles Becker (below) quickly became the centre of the anti-police corruption drive. He was executed.

gambling houses against police raids. His private and illegal source of income was well-known to other members of the force – including those not involved in graft – and his greed increased the more it was fed.

Meanwhile, the police hunt for the men who had formed the actual murder squad began to make progress after a bumbling start. The owners of the Packard car that took the killers to, and from, their mission were arrested and held on a charge of homicide. They were Louis Libby and William Shapiro, two small-time operators who, among other activities, made a moderate living by hiring out the car – often on a no-questions-asked basis.

As soon as they were in custody, the police circulated "wanted" notices for the four men alleged to have been the gunmen. All were well-known hoodlums and all had been involved in previous killings, as hired gunmen, although not convicted. True to form, they were better known in the Tenderloin district by their aliases – which the newspapers thoughtfully bracketed after their real names:

Jacob Seidenschner (Whitey Lewis), Harry Horowitz (Gyp the Blood), Louis Rosenberg (Lefty Louie), and Frank Cirofici (Dago Frank). Gyp the Blood's age was 27, and the rest were each 21. Young thugs matured quickly in the New York stews and aged as quickly – if they stayed alive beyond the first flush of manhood.

On Monday, July 29, a grand jury indicted Becker for murder – even though he had not personally appeared at the hearings, as District Attorney Whitman had assured the press he would. That evening he was arrested at the Bathgate

police station in the Bronx. True to the energetic and publicity-gaining manner in which Whitman had taken control of the affair, the arrest was made by detectives from his own office.

The police knew nothing of the arrest until it was accomplished, and the Police Commissioner, Rhinelander Waldo, was given the news while out dining. His informant was newspaperman Swope – who spent almost as much time and energy "wising up" the authorities as he did in writing it all up for his excited readers.

The evidence on which the grand jury based their indictment was taken from three gamblers, who had at first been implicated and then turned state's witnesses. They swore that they had arranged with an East Side mobster, "Big Jack" Zelig, to hire the four gunmen. The "client" who footed the bill, they claimed, was Lieutenant Becker. They added that he had "terrorized" them into acting on his behalf with the threat that he would have guns planted on them and "send us up" for seven years.

Punctured body

(It was ironic that the law prohibiting the carrying of a concealed weapon – the Sullivan Law – had been introduced by Big Jim Sullivan, the then Tammany Hall political boss, who had no qualms about shady dealings and was desperately trying to avoid becoming embroiled in the Becker case.)

Most talkative of the trio of gamblers was "Bald Jack" Rose, so-called because a childhood illness had stripped every vestige of hair from head and face. Over the years, he said, he and his "agents" had collected something like $640,000 in payoffs for Becker – although he admitted that some of this had eventually been shared among other senior policemen, including the Deputy Commissioner.

Bald Jack, who stated he lived in fear of Becker, explained his acquiescence to the murder plan in the way of any browbeaten employee:

"Well, I gotta live, don't I?"

According to Bald Jack, Becker had told him: "I want Rosenthal murdered, shot, his throat cut, any way that will take him off the earth. All that's necessary is to walk right up to where he is and blaze away at him and leave the rest to me. Nothing will happen to anybody that does it. Walk up and shoot him before a policeman if you want to."

On the night of the shooting, Bald Jack continued, Becker told him: "If only that s.o.b. would get croaked tonight how lovely that would be." When the killing had been done, and Becker had been to view the punctured body at the 47th Street police station, he told Bald Jack:

"It was a pleasing sight to me to see that squealing Jew lying there and, if it

West Side Prison on 53rd Street. Restaurant meals were sent in to them, tailors came to care for their clothes, and wives and friends drifted in and out whenever they chose. Reporters dubbed the prison "Whitman's Ritz", being there was clearly no hardship to the men on whom the District Attorney was pinning such faith and hope, and expending such charity.

By September 14 all four "wanted" gunmen had finally been captured—after a good deal of frantic and expensive police activity, including a hunt for Gyp the Blood and Lefty Louie in Panama City while they were, in fact, hiding out in Brooklyn. Whitman, still passing up no opportunity of lambasting the police, hinted that the delay was part of the Department's incompetence—if not corruption.

To ensure that all his careful prepara-

GOVERNOR Whitman (left) used the Becker case as a stepping stone to political success. As District Attorney he was forced to allow Becker a second trial. But the new jury (below) was unconvinced by new evidence and found him guilty.

had not been for the presence of Whitman, I would have cut out his tongue and hung it on the Times Building as a warning to future squealers."

In return for their evidence as state's witnesses, Bald Jack Rose and his two gambler-associates were granted immunity from criminal prosecution. What the District Attorney failed to make public, however, was that the immunity depended solely upon their testifying that Becker was a principal figure in the murder. From that moment on the witnesses realized that their freedom would certainly be lost if they went into court and told any other story than the one which Whitman required—the story of Becker's guilt.

To assist in preparing them to do their "duty", Bald Jack and his friends were held not in The Tombs—the dark and forbidding jail opposite the Criminal Courts Building—but in the more comfortable

tions should not be in vain, Whitman saw to it that Becker would be tried before Justice John W. Goff — who, some years before, had been counsel to a Senate committee investigating New York police graft, and who was known to bear little goodwill towards the Police Department. Moreover, Goff was not averse to personal publicity — and the Becker affair was gripping the attention of every newspaper reader in the United States.

Mass rally

As the case itself began to build up, Whitman took advantage of the upsurge of angry public opinion in New York. A group of prominent private citizens, including the banker John Pierpont Morgan, staged a mass rally on behalf of "municipal righteousness". When the District Attorney appeared at this he was given a roof-lifting ovation, with cries of, "Three cheers for our next Governor!" The murder, he told the tightly-packed ranks of the righteous, "was a challenge to our very civilization itself". There were few present who doubted that Becker was already as good as strapped in the electric

chair — with the forthcoming trial no more than a tedious formality.

Indeed, it seemed that way to most New Yorkers. Becker was already being tried repeatedly and found guilty by almost every newspaper edition that appeared on the streets. Reporters were mesmerized by his "low forehead", "shifty eyes", and "wolf-like appearance". The general implication was that any jury had better return their verdict swiftly before they were gunned down in the very courtroom by more of the lieutenant's hired guns. Added to this, there were the Becker "confessions" allegedly overheard by other villains, sweating out the hours in The Tombs with him.

One had "heard" him saying: "After this is passed over the public will give me a pension for killing that dirty crook!"

But the grime was beginning to settle on too many people in high places. Some of it flaked off upon Mayor William Jay Gaynor, who regarded the whole outcry against crime and graft as a reprehensible example of public hysteria. Accused of ineptitude and sloth in dealing with the situation in the Police Department, he croaked out a feeble defence — he had been wounded in the throat by a would-be assassin's bullet two years before the Rosenthal murder, and that had not helped to make him any more articulate.

So it was, against a background of political upheaval, that Lieutenant Charles Becker was brought to trial on October 7. He was convicted on the evidence of the carefully rehearsed gamblers, and a loaded charge to the jury by Justice Goff. The verdict was greeted throughout the nation with purple-prose enthusiasm. Attorney General Whitman seemed set upon the road to political advancement, while Becker was taken on another road — to Sing Sing.

Conscience at ease

But Becker had not given up hope. On the grounds of perjured witnesses, and important evidence that had not been heard, his lawyers sought, and gained, a new trial from the Court of Appeals. The Court, strongly adhering to its impartiality in the face of popular clamour, ruled that Becker had been entitled to a fair trial and "we do not think the defendant had such a trial". Whitman then swallowed his pride and offered the newspapers the bromide quote:

"The District Attorney is the last man in the world who should want a conviction to stand that is not justified in law."

But Becker fared no better at his second trial, which opened on May 5, 1914. He was again found guilty and his execution fixed for the week beginning July 6. This was postponed while further attempts were made to save his life. In a second judgment, nearly a year after its first,

BLOOD SPATTERED Mayor Gaynor of New York City reels unsteadily as would-be assassin's bullet rips into his throat. He never again spoke out against city crime.

the Court of Appeals ruled against Becker who, as prisoner number 62,499, waited hopefully in Sing Sing's death house. The four gunmen, Gyp the Blood and the rest, had already been electrocuted.

Only Charles Whitman had prospered by it all. He had been elected Republican Governor of New York — "a political career built upon the stake of a human life", one critic remarked — and was already being tipped as a possible opponent to President Woodrow Wilson in the presidential election to come in 1916.

Now Becker was faced with the unpalatable task of having to appeal to the new Governor — "Your Excellency" — for clemency. He did so with dignity, forwarding with his papers a note that read: "In these days when we read of men dying by tens of thousands every day in battle, the disposition that may be made of one poor human life seems scarcely worth the trouble . . .

"But I do not feel I should withhold a single word that might by chance aid you in reaching a conclusion which will win approval of your own conscience and of the people who have entrusted you with the sovereign power to take my life or spare it."

Whitman's conscience, however, was totally at ease. Not only did he reject Becker's appeal, but took the extra-

ordinary step of holding a press conference in which he once again condemned Becker for the murder, and made the additional and wholly unsubstantiated statement that the lieutenant had killed his first wife—"she died suddenly in a bathtub".

So, in the early hours of July 30, 1915, Becker went to his death in the electric chair—and even the final act against him was bungled. The first flood of 1850 volts burned his flesh, sent a haze of grey smoke rising over his body, but failed to kill him. It took two more surges of current to stop

DEATH DEALERS . . . Sing Sing prison's death house (A) and (inset) Charles Becker who was electrocuted on July 30, 1915. His wife (left) blamed the ambitious governor Whitman for her husband's death.

his heart. Two days later his widow attached his epitaph to his coffin, engraved on a silver plate: "Charles Becker, murdered July 30, 1915, by Governor Whitman."

True to his style, Whitman had the last word. He ordered the plate to be removed on the grounds of criminal libel.

THE BUCKET OF BLOOD

Three policemen stood in the dock on charges of running a protection racket. Their accuser was a crooked "company director" in a pin-stripe suit . . .

MR. JUSTICE DONOVAN, the Old Bailey judge, described the case as "one of the most serious tried in this or any other criminal court for a long time". The majority of people in Britain agreed with him, for there, in the internationally-famous Central Criminal Court, surmounted by its figure clasping the scales of justice, roles had been reversed in an alarming fashion. Three policemen, one of them a Chief Constable, stood where, by the very nature of society, no police officer is ever expected to stand without bringing the very foundations of law and order into disrepute: in the prisoners' dock.

They had been brought there, after months of meticulous investigation by their Scotland Yard colleagues, from the flourishing and wealthy south coast resort of Brighton. A place of piers and Regency architecture, and now, it was alleged, of that most dangerous of crimes, police corruption.

Popular quip

The crowds who lined the pavements and packed into the court on that first day of the trial, February 3, 1958, had already been filled with wonder and anticipation by the magistrates' hearings. The hearings, held before the Old Bailey arraignment, highlighted the accusations that policemen were lining their own pockets through favours to crooks, or promises to "help" those who offended against the law.

Most of the onlookers knew at least some of the cynical wisecracks that dogged the lives of those other Brighton police officers, loyally and incorruptibly pursuing their daily duties. "Brighton," one of the most popular quips declared, "has the finest police force money can buy!"

Such was the background at 10.30 that morning when the bewigged and scarlet-robed Mr. Justice Donovan took his seat on the dais above the rows of barristers, newspapermen, and spectators—and the black-gowned usher bellowed forth the archaic cry which traditionally sets the Old Bailey machinery in motion:

"All persons who have anything to do before my Lady the Queen's Justices of Oyer and Terminer and General Gaol Delivery for the Jurisdiction of the Central Criminal Court draw near and give your attention. God save the Queen!"

Endless names

The Clerk of the Court read the names of the prisoners to be "put up" and, from rooms beneath, came five men. It was immediately apparent from their bearing, and the manner in which they came to attention, who were the three Brighton policemen: Charles Feild Williams Ridge, 58, Chief Constable; Detective-Inspector John Richard Hammersley, 40, second-

Keystone

in-command Criminal Investigation Department; and Detective-Sergeant Trevor Ernest Heath, 36.

The other two were more obviously civilians: Anthony John Lyons, 59, licensee of Marine Gate, Brighton; and Samuel Bellson, 42, bookmaker, of The Drive, Hove—Brighton's neighbouring and more select borough.

The Clerk again rose and the spectators, who had stirred and craned forward as the defendants appeared, fell silent as the formal charge was read:

"You are charged that between January 1, 1949, and October 18, 1957, you conspired together, and with other persons unknown, to obstruct the course of public justice in that you, Heath, Hammersley and Ridge, did act contrary to your public duty as police officers in relation to the administration of the law. Are you guilty or not guilty?" In each

enemies, the police officers.

The jury were told, for example, that they would hear from a 41-year-old whole-sale fish merchant who claimed that Detective-Inspector Hammersley and Detective-Sergeant Heath had asked him for £250 to drop a charge against him of receiving stolen property. They would hear that Bellson, the bookmaker, and Lyons, the licensee, had acted as go-betweens in the collection of "fees" for the police.

Star witness

All this was merely curtain-raising material, and it lasted until the trial's third day — when the Crown decided that the time had come to produce its star witness. There was silence as the usher called "Alan Roy Bennett", and in walked a 40-year-old tall, slim man, his upper lip shadowed by a thin moustache, and dressed in an impeccably cut dark suit with barely discernible stripes.

He wore a black woollen knitted tie, a crisply white handkerchief peeped from his breast pocket, and in his right hand he carried a large, unlit cigar. He was described on the witness list as a "company director", and he looked just that.

Those whose job it was to know the background knew that this was the man who had set the wheels of the case turning. It was he who had gone to Scotland Yard with information that prompted a small team of investigators, led by Detective-Superintendent Ian Forbes-Leith, to probe into the state of affairs in the Brighton police force. It was he who had once accepted police demands for bribes — and then grown apprehensive of the net into which he had been drawn.

Coolly and in a clear, clipped voice, Bennett outlined his story. Nine months previously he had changed his name by deed poll from Brown, and until 1949 he had been in "quite a lot" of criminal trouble. In Brighton he had opened a club called the Astor, better known as the "Bucket of Blood" — since "some customers did not behave", and often left in a battered state as the result of differences of opinion with fellow-members. For all its problems, however, the club had never attracted adverse police attention — and the reason for that had everything to do with the basis of the Crown's case.

Back pocket

According to Bennett, John Lyons, one of the civilian defendants, had brought Chief Constable Ridge to meet him at the Astor — and from that day he had paid Ridge a "retainer" of £20 a week. The money was at first personally collected by Ridge, and then by Sergeant Heath who also occasionally received a £5 "present" from Bennett. In return for

---

IMPECCABLE and flashy, Alan Roy Bennett is driven away from the court by his chauffeur (above left) and (right) is seen arriving to give evidence in the company of a plain clothes C.I.D. man. His crude display of wealth made an unfavourable impression in court, but his testimony was, nevertheless, clearly important — and the jury accepted it. There was a certain irony in the fact that this ex-criminal remained both rich and free whilst two police officers who had excellent records as crime fighters had, for years, been forced to eke out a miserable existence on pitiful and unjust salaries only to fall prey, at last, to the desperate temptation to earn a little extra money. Is there something wrong with a society which rewards so badly the efforts of its lawmen? It was one question which the solicitor-general (left) apparently thought unimportant.

case came the firm reply, "Not guilty."

Mr. Justice Donovan warned the jury, of 10 men and two women, that "you are likely to be here for some weeks". A moment later, Sir Harry Hylton-Foster, Q.C., Solicitor-General and the nation's number two Crown law officer, was on his feet with a "May it please your Lordship" and launching into an outline of the prosecution's case.

From the mass of documents on the table before him he plucked an endless harvest of names. It was soon clear that the Crown would be relying for much of its case on persons who, at one time or another, had flouted the law and paid the penalty.

Veteran Old Bailey reporters immediately grasped what was to be the focal point of the lengthy trial: the evidence of admittedly shady characters pitted against the evidence of those supposedly their

SEASIDE SCANDAL . . . the elegant and justly famous resort in the South of England was the scene of one of the first British cases of police corruption. The accused men are (left to right) Heath; Chief Constable Ridge; Insp. Hammersley.

the payments Bennett was free to keep the club open until any hour he chose, without interference.

Bennett "shot" his whiter-than-white shirt cuffs, gently stroked his unlit cigar —two frequent gestures that seemed to fascinate the jury—and declared: "I had the freedom of the city. I opened the club and closed it when I wanted to." Where had he got the money from for all this help? Mr. Maxwell Turner, one of the Crown barristers, asked.

To an audible gasp from the spectators, and a visible but silent "tut-tut" from the judge, Bennett, like a conjurer, produced a bulky wad of notes. "Here, where I always carry them. In my back trouser pocket. There's £500 here!" Mr. Justice Donovan looked askance. "Put it away," he demanded sharply, and the wad of notes disappeared as swiftly as it had been produced.

Mr. Edward Clarke, for Sergeant Heath, rose to cross-examine and recited a litany of Bennett's pseudonyms. Had he, at various times, been Brown, Ferguson, Poyner, Holt, Austen-Montgomery? Bennett agreed—although he was doubtful about Holt and Austen-Montgomery.

Verbal battle

However, he did clearly recall that during the previous 25 years he had been before the courts on 14 occasions, and had served 10 terms of imprisonment for offences including housebreaking. Soon after his last release from prison he went to Brighton as a chef, and opened the Astor Club in 1954.

"Before you saw Lyons did you know anything about the Brighton police, Ridge, Heath or Hammersley?" Mr. Clarke asked. "I never met them." Well, then, "Did it surprise you very much when it was first suggested by anybody that by paying the police money you could . . ." But Mr. Clarke did not finish his question. His cuffs flashing, Bennett interjected loudly: "It didn't surprise me. It was known that the Brighton police had been crooked all their lives!"

Mr. Clarke adjusted his gown like a man settling down to an important verbal battle. "You knew that from the start, did you?"—"I did. I had been told by many people." All the Brighton police, all crooked, all their lives? "Well, some of them, not all." Mr. Clarke passed to the question of the neckties that Bennett claimed he had bought for Sergeant Heath in the fashionable Burlington Arcade, off London's Piccadilly.

"Did you go to the Burlington Arcade with Heath?"—We might have walked through it. "Is the answer this, that you selected several ties that day and Heath selected two, if not three, intending to pay for them himself; and that he put the money down, although you offered to

Popperfoto

pay for the lot?"—That is not true. I did buy those ties there for Heath.

According to Bennett, Sergeant Heath had been the recipient not only of ties but of cast-off clothing. Bennett had given him a discarded sports jacket and a pair of flannel trousers because, he explained, "I don't wear my clothes when they are falling to pieces and Heath has the same figure as myself."

Housebreaking

The sergeant had also mentioned that he would be "grateful" for any old shirts. "I should say I have got 50 shirts at any one time," added Bennett in a throw-away line.

Mr. Clarke returned to the attack. "Once the police knew you were of bad character you realised you were not very welcome in Brighton, didn't you?" Bennett seemed astonished at the question. "I was more than welcome—more than welcome," he replied. "I was providing them with money. I did what I wanted. I kept the club open all night."

Did what he wanted? Mr. Clarke wondered. What, anything? Housebreaking, his old profession, for example? There were smiles in court at Mr. Clarke's touch of irony. But they were quickly swept away as Bennett answered, evenly: "Yes, it was suggested by Heath that I did do housebreaking."

Perceptibly, the whole courtroom stirred. Frantically, the evening newspapermen scribbled away, already visualizing the banner headlines for the late-extra edition. Mr. Clarke sought more details and Bennett rattled them off.

Sport & General Press

GUILTY JOKE? Hammersley and partner in crime Heath (above) appear happy and unconcerned on their way to court as if the whole scandal were simply a source of amusement. They were found guilty and sentenced to a fairly mild term of 5 years' imprisonment. Ridge (facing page) looked less happy, but was acquitted.

"Heath," he said, "knew a manager of Woolworth's and it was suggested I take the keys and open the safe and Heath would share in the proceeds. He suggested I should open it at Christmas when there was plenty of money in it. I told him I had enough money of my own."

Bennett was followed into the witness-box by his slight, attractive, Norwegian-born wife, Winche. Standing there, in a black coat trimmed with black Persian lamb and a small black hat perched on her head, she brought a refreshing air of femininity into the austere surroundings. She did not look the kind of woman likely to be associated with a "Bucket of Blood" club, and the jury's normally tight-muscled expressions softened as she heaped retrospective curses upon the Astor.

Almost every week, she said, people were carried out of the club with bleeding noses and drunk. "It was the unhappiest time of my life. I would have loved my husband to have given it up. I told him not to give any money to policemen." Chief Constable Ridge, she testified, had come to the club with John Lyons about three weeks after opening day. She could not remember the conversation "word for word", but "the general idea was to pay the police some money and then we could stay open as long as we liked".

From that day onwards the Astor was never raided by the police, and Ridge came to collect money which "I saw my husband give him in a newspaper. It was in £5 notes". Later Sergeant Heath was the collector; if her husband was absent the notes were left in an envelope on a shelf below the bar. "I gave it to him on several occasions and I think other people gave it to him."

Criminal lingo

But there were times, it appeared, when other Brighton policemen, not implicated in the corruption racket, decided that the Astor was due for a raid. On such occasions, Mrs. Bennett recalled, Sergeant Heath would telephone the warning: "Don't open tonight."

In the trial's second week there came to the Old Bailey a Mrs. Alice Brabiner who said she had been involved in an illegal abortion, and that Sergeant Heath had taken a total of £68 from her to "do what he could to help me". A Mrs. Mabel Lawrence—who had also been questioned by Heath—said she had expressed fears that her husband would discover the operation had taken place in their flat.

Heath advised her to "see Mr. Lyons at Sherry's Bar". She did so and found Lyons there with two other men. Someone said something about a "ton"—it was hastily explained to the jury that "ton" was criminal lingo for £100—and, Mrs. Lawrence recalled ruefully, "they all laughed".

Stolen goods

When she telephoned Heath to tell him she could not raise £100 "he said 'Try to get £50'". At first she could manage only £25 and Heath told her to "get the rest as soon as possible because the governor will be annoyed". She gave him the second £25 on the day Mrs. Brabiner's trial for the illegal operation opened. To those sitting through the trial it seemed that every day was opening up some new area of police "co-operation" with sinners.

From buckets of blood and illegal operations, the scene switched to stolen goods. Ernest Waite, a Brighton greengrocer, who admitted dealing in stolen property, claimed he had a "gentleman's agreement" with Inspector Hammersley. The agreement laid down that Waite would not receive goods in Brighton, "but I was given a sort of freedom of the town with regards to things outside Brighton. If any goods came to the town and I was suspect, Hammersley would give me the tip-off to get rid of them."

As a result Mr. Waite's "business" flourished, and Hammersley benefited

Popperfoto

to the extent of £200 for his "help" — in addition to regular supplies of produce from Waite's shop. The procedure there, Waite explained, was that Hammersley would "pay" for the produce with a £1 note and be given several pounds in "change".

Witness followed witness, most of them with convictions to their names, to tell how the police had made their lives bearable by what some of them described, euphemistically, as "a consideration". One man said he carried two £5 notes wrapped around a pen which was then concealed in the hem of his raincoat.

Complete denial

Mr. Justice Donovan ordered the coat to be produced and the witness, apparently looking to the judge for assistance, suggested, "My Lord, if I could demonstrate . . ." My Lord quickly realized his expected role in the "demonstration". Blandly he declared: "I have not got two £5 notes."

It was not until the twelfth day that the procession of prosecution civilian witnesses ended and the police at last moved into the centre of the stage: both the police officers on trial and those who had conducted the investigation that brought them to that trial.

Sergeant Heath was the first, stepping briskly from the dock into the witness-box in a dark blue suit and the blue and white tie of Hendon Police College — the training establishment in North London. So far little had been heard about his personal career, except that, up to the moment of his suspension from duty, he had been earning £18 2s. 7d. a week — of which £14 8s. 7d. remained after deductions.

Now, in a clear, resonant voice, he reeled off the details of his professional

SUPERINTENDENT in charge of the police corruption investigation was Ian Forbes-Leith (above) who later turned to business himself — but strictly legally.

life: married 11 years, joined the Criminal Investigation Department in February 1948, made more arrests in 1955 than any other detective constable on the Brighton force, and had received 11 commendations. He had first teamed up with Hammersley in C.I.D. work in August 1949.

Heath's defence was a complete denial of all the charges. "Certainly not," he replied, unhesitatingly, as each of the main Crown points of testimony were repeated to him. At the end of his five-and-a-half hours of evidence Mr. Edward Clarke asked him the decisive question:

"At any stage during your period of duty as a detective-constable or detective-sergeant had you had any fiddles to the extent of any corruption or receiving any bribes?" Heath looked towards the jury. "No, sir," he replied. "Certainly not."

Inspector Hammersley, too, was able to boast of a good past record: joined Brighton police in 1937, served during the war in the Far East as a Royal Armoured Corps officer, mentioned in despatches. "Not the slightest," he snapped when asked if there was any truth in his involvement in any "disgraceful crime". Finally, bothered by a persistent cough which he attempted to suppress with the aid of throat pastilles, came the tall Chief Constable, Charles Ridge.

He had always been careful of the honour of the force, he declared; always took steps to warn young officers of the perils of accepting bribes. Moreover, Mr. Ridge had come armed with charts and graphs to show just how well the war against crime had gone in Brighton since

he took command. He produced them and read from them, swiftly flooding the court with total figures and percentages. Crimes substantially down; arrests steeply risen.

On February 27, more than three weeks after the trial started, the courtroom exchanges were at last over, and the jury retired to consider their verdicts. For four-and-a-half hours they were locked in their room. Then, at 7.30 p.m., they returned to confess they had run into problems. The judge looked worried, and the thoughts of the trouble and expense of a re-trial were reflected in his expression.

However, the jury foreman explained that they were agreed on verdicts in four of the defendants' cases, but disagreed about Chief Constable Ridge. The judge advised them to deliver the verdicts they had reached and return to consider Mr. Ridge further.

The defendants' names were called over and the foreman answered: Inspector Hammersley, Sergeant Heath and Samuel Bellson: guilty. Anthony John Lyons: not guilty. The guilty men were ordered to be held for sentencing and John Lyons hurried from the court to greet well-wishers and reporters with the comment: "Justice has been done."

For Chief Constable Ridge the ordeal was to last a further 72 minutes — which he spent, sitting alone, in a room below the dock. Then sounds of movement brought him back up the stairs. As he waited for the jury foreman to speak he fixed his eyes, unmovingly, on the judge. "How say you?" the Clerk demanded. The foreman answered rapidly, as though relieved to have done with the whole business: "Not guilty."

White-faced

For a moment the Chief Constable hesitated, and then strode towards the courtroom door. There a hand grasped his in congratulation. It was the hand of Detective-Superintendent Forbes-Leith, who had led the Scotland Yard investigation.

Next morning, white-faced but still sprucely upright, Hammersley and Heath re-appeared in court to receive their sentences. Bellson had already been sent away for three years, and the judge gave his own dramatic footnote to the case. "Neither of you," he told them, "had the professional and moral leadership which both of you were entitled to expect, and should have had, from the Chief Constable of Brighton, now acquitted."

In view of that he was reducing the sentence he would otherwise have imposed. Each of them would go to prison for five years. No longer police officers, and about to join the kind of men they had once been appointed to hunt, Hammersley and Heath were driven off in a prison van. Brighton's season of corruption was over.

WHO WAS JACK THE RIPPER?

The twisted sexual savagery of the Ripper murders terrorized the women of London's East End in the autumn of 1888. But who, exactly, was the killer . . . ?

JACK THE RIPPER left his women victims gutted like a fish. What has kept his name alive for the better part of a century, however, is not the gruesome nature of his crimes but the mystery of his identity. No killer has inspired more amateur criminologists, fiction writers, and playwrights. Yet the name of the creator of London's autumn of terror in 1888 remains as shrouded as the fog which nightly blanketed the city's East End.

Candidates range from a distinguished surgeon, seeking to revenge himself on the prostitute who had given his son VD, to Prince Albert Victor Christian Edward of Wales, Duke of Clarence and elder son of King Edward VII; from an unknown *kosher* slaughterhouse worker to Dr. Alexander Pedachenko, named by Rasputin, the monk at the Tsar of Russia's court, as a secret agent sent to London to foment ill-feeling against the Russian revolutionaries who had settled in the East End.

Leonard Matters, a journalist, put forward the surgeon as a suspect in *The Mystery of Jack the Ripper,* published in 1929, giving him the fictitious name of Dr. Stanley. According to Matters, Stanley's son Herbert caught syphilis from Mary Kelly, generally believed to be the last of the Ripper's six victims, and died within two years.

Standing by the deathbed of the son he had dreamed would follow him into the medical profession, Stanley vowed: "I will find the woman. When I find her I will kill her; by God, I will. I will cut her to pieces, the devil."

Dr. Stanley, so the story goes, used to leave his practice in exclusive Harley Street each night and, armed with a dagger and long surgical knife, scour the shabby streets of the East End for Mary Kelly. After questioning his first five victims, he killed them to avoid any possibility of future identification.

Then, when he had found and "executed" Kelly, he closed his practice and emigrated to South America. There, on his own deathbed, he confessed to a doctor who had once studied under him: "I am Jack the Ripper. My son, he died an idiot, and all my hopes died with him. I swore to avenge him. I murdered all those women."

Royal scandal

It is a fine, dramatic tale to which, unfortunately, there are some serious objections. It takes 20 or 30 years, not two, for syphilis to cause insanity and death; Mary Kelly did not suffer from VD; and there is no record of a British surgeon dying in a Buenos Aires hospital at the time Matters alleges Dr. Stanley

made his confession.

The Duke of Clarence, heir to the throne of England, was floated as the bloodthirsty culprit as recently as 1970 in an article in the specialist magazine *The Criminologist.* The author was Thomas Stowell, another distinguished surgeon, who was in his eighties and who died a few days after the article appeared.

According to Stowell, the Duke caught syphilis from a sailor at the age of 16 when he was on a world cruise with his brother, later King George V, aboard *H.M.S. Bacchante.* Subsequently, at the age of 24, the Duke resigned his Army commission after being caught in a police raid on a male brothel in the West End frequented by homosexual aristocrats.

To hush up this scandal he was despatched on another cruise. On his return his brain gave way under the advancing syphilis. He committed five murders, was caught and locked up in an asylum, and then escaped to murder Mary Kelly. He was put away again, wrote Stowell, and "relapsed and died of broncho-pneumonia a few years later—the usual cause of death in such cases". The Royal Family connived at the cover-up by putting out the story that the Duke was a victim, at the age of 28, of the great 'flu epidemic of January 1892.

Stowell claimed that the source of his

information was the private papers of the late Sir William Gull, Physician in Ordinary to the Royal Family, who had attended the Duke. Gull's daughter asked him to examine the papers after her father's death because she believed they contained "highly confidential" information.

Once again there are several objections. As in the case of the mysterious Dr. Stanley's son, syphilis does not cause softening of the brain so quickly. The Duke was at Sandringham on November 9, his father's birthday and the night Mary Kelly was murdered. Later—when he had already been certified as insane—he went to Copenhagen to represent his father on a State occasion.

Naming the Duke, therefore, seems to be just the aberration of an old man. In his book *Clarence,* published in 1972, author Michael Harrison dismisses the theory entirely and names a friend of the Duke's as the Ripper—James Stephen, son of Sir James Fitzjames Stephen, a High Court judge from 1879 to 1891; and Virginia Woolf's cousin.

Stephen, he claims, was started on the road to insanity when "watching an engine employed in pumping water . . . he received a terrible blow on the head". Later, when the Duke "jilted" him in favour of a new lover, the emotional shock proved great enough to turn a brain ripe for post-traumatic mania.

Harrison makes a variety of claims. He alleges, for instance, that there were 10 Ripper murders, not six and—like the murder of Mary Kelly on the birthday of the Duke's father—the killings were timed as a kind of "blood sacrifice" to mark Royal occasions. He also quotes several poems, such as *A Thought,* written in 1891, to illustrate Stephen's innate dislike of women. *A Thought* said:

If all the harm that women have done
Were put in a bundle and rolled into one,
Earth would not hold it.

An East End *shochet*?

Harrison does not explain, however, how a manic murderer was able to address the Cambridge Union and publish two volumes of verse in 1890 and 1891. Nor has he any explanation for the fact that Stephen's name does not appear to have reached the ears of Sir Melville Macnaghten, who joined Scotland Yard after the last of the Ripper murders and was given the job of compiling the final report on the killings.

We are on more prosaic ground with Robin Odell's *Jack the Ripper in Fact and Fiction.* He claims that the murderer was just a run-of-the-mill sexual psychopath who was also an East End *shochet,* or ritual Jewish slaughterman. *Shochets*

are trained in anatomy and pathology for their task of killing beasts and draining the blood from them to provide the only kind of meat orthodox Jews are allowed to eat. This, claims Odell, is how the Ripper acquired the "surgical" skill which enabled him to dismember his victims and remove an elusive kidney. He writes:

"One of the most significant aspects of the murders was the killer's ability to inspire trust in his victims. The *shochet's* background and social standing among his own people, together with his education and official position, would have made him a cut above the ordinary East Ender. He would have been an easily recognized figure on account of his sober clerical appearance in dark clothes and black frockcoat. . . . The *shochet's* appearance, clean and tidy, but probably a little threadbare, would have earned him the title of 'respectable'."

Nor is this without significance, for it was a description of this sort that most frequently appeared in statements made by witnesses who claimed to have seen Jack the Ripper. "Shabby-respectable" was the term used; not a real East Ender,

MYSTERIOUS MONSTER . . . As soon as the killings began so did speculation on the Ripper's identity. Fact and fantasy mingled and the great legend began . . .

but not out of the top drawer either. In broad terms this described the appearance of the *shochet*.

"The respectable figure of the *shochet* was an accepted sight in Whitechapel: he lived and worked in the neighbourhood and would have been known, at least by sight, to a great many people. In all reason it was only the familiar-looking person who could have captured the trust of women in the East End when the area was paralyzed with terror.

"A well-dressed stranger might conceivably have worked his charm on one or two occasions, but it is contrary to common sense to believe that this could have happened after Annie Chapman's murder, when the papers were full of well-dressed doctors and their like being the Ripper. So great, in fact, was the terror in this respect that innocent people only slightly resembling this popular conception of the killer were hounded in the streets by screaming mobs."

Odell also claims that the *shochet's* professional expertise would have enabled him to avoid getting his clothes soaked with blood, or, if he had just slipped away from the slaughterhouse for a few minutes to commit his crimes, bloodstains would not have been considered unusual on his working "uniform". He would, too, have been sufficiently well-educated to write the Ripper letters. Well, maybe. Most authors, however, prefer more exotic theories.

Donald McCormick, in his book boldly called *The Identity of Jack the Ripper*, plumps for a Dr. Alexander Pedachenko. Dr. Pedachenko had been a *feldscher*, an unqualified doctor's assistant, in the Russian army. At the time he lived in London so did another Russian army *feldscher*, a Pole named Severin Klosowski. By one of those curious coincidences with which the tale of Jack the Ripper abounds, Pedachenko and Klosowski were physical doubles and, for reasons unexplained, sometimes swopped identities from time to time.

A Russian scoundrel?

Inspector Abberline, who led the CID hunt for Jack the Ripper, considered Klosowski one of his leading suspects (five years later, Klosowski, using the name George Chapman, was arrested, convicted and hanged for poisoning three bigamous wives). It was William Le Queux, writer and secret agent in World War I, who first suggested Pedachenko.

He revealed in his book *Things I Know About Kings, Celebrities and Crooks* that the post-Revolution Soviet government "handed to me, in confidence, a great quantity of documents which had been found in the safe of Rasputin's house in order that I might write an account of the scoundrel's amazing career". One of

them, in French, identified Pedachenko as the Ripper and went on to say:

"Eventually, at the orders of the Ministry of the Interior, the Secret Police smuggled the assassin out of London, and, as Count Luiskovo, he landed at Ostend and was conducted by a secret agent to Moscow. While there he was, a few months later, caught red-handed attempting to murder and mutilate a woman named Vogak and was eventually sent to an asylum, where he died in 1908."

Other suspects

There is no doubt that counter-espionage agents employed by Russia's Royal Family, the Romanoffs, tried to stir up ill-will against Russian revolutionaries in the East End, and, on the pretext that they were working against the Tsar, even involved them in active crime so that they would be deported.

A classic example was the Siege of Sidney Street. A police sergeant investigating a report of "strange noises" coming from a house in Sidney Street, Houndsditch, was shot dead. Police who surrounded the house were met by a barrage of fire, and, eventually, Winston Churchill, then Home Secretary, called out the Scots Guards to break the siege.

The Sidney Street gang, who had been planning the robbery of a Houndsditch jeweller's shop when the sergeant interrupted them, proved to be refugees from Baltic Russia. The identity of their leader, a mysterious figure known as Peter the Painter, has never been revealed officially. It is believed, however, that he was a Tsarist *agent provocateur* who inveigled the Russians into the crime with the false story that the jeweller was storing treasure belonging to the Romanoffs.

Robin Odell makes the point, however, that Rasputin had no interest in Russian criminals and was therefore unlikely to have penned the document Le Queux claimed was handed to him. He also quotes the Tsarist police chief A. T. Vassilyev as saying that no compromising documents were found during the search of Rasputin's apartment.

Equally telling is the question: Why did Pedachenko restrict himself to prostitutes if his purpose was to direct ill-feeling towards the Russian revolutionaries? Odell asks: "Surely . . . his activities would have had far greater impact if he had chosen his victims from ladies, or for that matter gentlemen, of greater eminence. Then again, why did the killer, if he was thus motivated, endanger his escape by stopping to remove organs from the bodies of some of his victims?"

The list of possible suspects does not stop there. It includes Jill the Ripper, a midwife-abortionist exposed by a prostitute to the police and now taking her revenge; Glasgow-born Dr. Neil Cream,

WINDOW FROM WHICH BURGLARS FIRED.

ARMED POLICE

SIDNEY STREET . . . Was the East End killer involved with the Russian émigrés whose activities included the famous gun battle in the heart of the city . . .? This is one of the less likely theories.

227

poisoner of women, who confessed several times in prison to being the killer and cried out as they hanged him: "I am Jack . . ."; and, as American author Tom Cullen mentions in his book *Autumn of Terror*, an anonymous social reformer who had chosen this bizarre way of calling attention to the squalor of the East End.

In his fairly recent book, *Jack The Ripper*, author Daniel Farson puts forward yet another candidate, Montague John Druitt. Druitt, says Farson, was the chief suspect of Sir Melville Nacnaghten, who joined Scotland Yard in 1889 and later became head of the CID.

Through a casual meeting with Sir Melville's daughter, the Dowager Lady Aberconway, he was allowed to look at her father's private notes. "Because the official Scotland Yard files will not be open to the public until 1992," he writes, "no one has known the name of the man whom the police suspected. Now, for the first time, this name lay in my hands."

A doctor?

Sir Melville's notes said: "Mr. M. J. Druitt, a doctor of about 41 years of age and of fairly good family, who disappeared at the time of the Miller's Court (Marie Kelly) murder, and whose body was found floating in the Thames on December 31, i.e. seven weeks after the said murder. The body was said to have been in the water for a month, or more—on it was found a season ticket between Blackheath and London. From private information I have little doubt but that his own family suspected this man of being the Whitechapel murderer; it was alleged that he was sexually insane."

In a foreword to Farson's book the pathologist Professor Francis Camps writes: "If the culprit he suggests satisfies three criteria—have been associated with the medical profession, have had access to somewhere in the neighbourhood where he could disappear at short notice, and finally have died within a reasonably short time of the last murder—I feel we are getting near the truth."

Initially, Farson had some difficulty in tracking down Druitt because Sir Melville had made two mistakes in his notes, written from memory after the events. Druitt was a failed barrister turned teacher, not a doctor, and was aged 31, not 41. Once these mistakes had been picked up, Farson was able to set about satisfying the three criteria.

Druitt, who had been educated at Winchester College and New College, Oxford, came from a family with strong medical connections. His father, William, his uncle, Robert, and his cousin, Lionel, were all doctors. Farson writes:

"Though it's virtually certain that the Ripper was not a doctor, I believe he did have some basic medical or surgical knowledge. Druitt . . . was brought up in a medical atmosphere and may well have attended post-mortems. He would have had easy access to surgical instruments. One weapon which the police suspected the Ripper used is a post-mortem knife."

On the question of a hide-out near the scene of his crimes, Druitt had chambers at 9 King's Bench Walk in the Temple, some 30 minutes' walk away. It is even possible that his lair was in The Minories, which is even closer. Farson discovered that Druitt's cousin Lionel had a surgery in The Minories in 1879. Says Farson:

"I am certain that the Ripper had access to some private room near the scene of the murders. A doss-house, or any communal lodging house, would have been far too dangerous . . . If Druitt kept in touch with the surgery in The Minories, even passing himself off as a doctor, we would have a simple explanation. The Minories is only 10 or 15 minutes' walk from all the murders."

Lastly, on the subject of why the murders stopped as suddenly as they had begun, Druitt was last seen alive on December 3, 1888, less than a month after the Mary Kelly murder.

The Ripper was believed to be ambidextrous: Druitt was his school champion at fives, a wall tennis game played with both hands. Farson was also sent a letter telling him about a pamphlet entitled *The East End Murderer—I Knew Him,* written by a Lionel Druitt and published privately at Dandenong, in Australia, in 1890. Druitt's cousin Lionel emigrated to Australia and practised in Dandenong.

Finally, Farson quotes a number of officials who stated at the time, without revealing his identity, that the Ripper had been found drowned in the Thames. He says: "I gather that the official files in Scotland Yard, which are not open to the public until 1992, confirm my conclusions and have little else to add."

The latest, most comprehensive, and easily the best Ripper book is *The Complete Jack the Ripper,* by Donald Rumbelow, a City of London policeman. While vividly listing and commenting on the various identity theories, he wisely does not offer a positive solution of his own. Instead he says that on Judgement Day, when the Ripper is asked to step forward, we will gaze at him in disappointment and gasp—*"Who?"*

One thing is certain, if this is *not* allowed to happen, the revelation of the Ripper's identity will take all the fascination out of a criminal who, in his twisted way, was a genius.

BAFFLED POLICE had to endure the taunts and jibes of magazine cartoonists (right). But perhaps they did know who the Ripper was, after all. The chief suspect was M. J. Druitt (above).

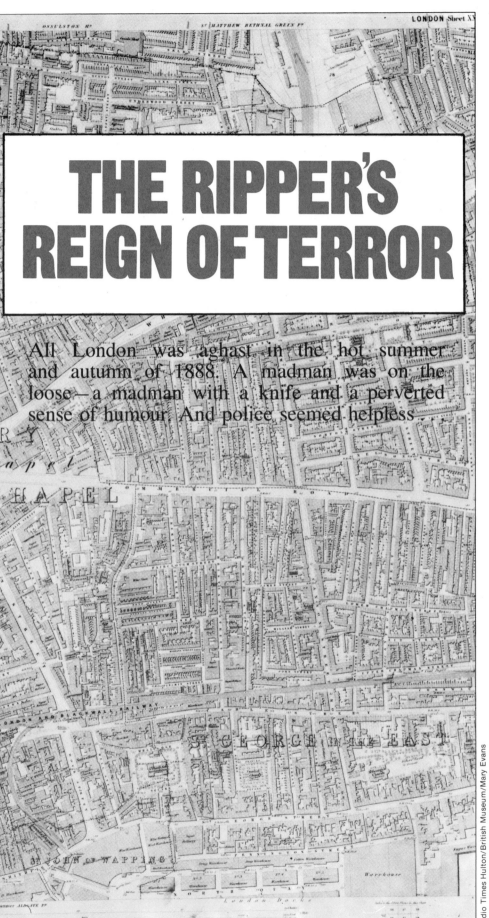

THE RIPPER'S REIGN OF TERROR

All London was aghast in the hot summer and autumn of 1888. A madman was on the loose—a madman with a knife and a perverted sense of humour. And police seemed helpless...

IT WAS lunchtime when the police—Inspector Beck and a young detective named Walter Dew—arrived at the scene of the crime. A light but steady rain was falling, and an inquisitive band of onlookers had gathered outside the entrance of No. 13 Miller's Court, in London's East End. On the inside, in a cramped and squalid room, lay the butchered remains of prostitute Mary Kelly—the sixth and final victim of Jack the Ripper.

The spectators knew of her death, but they didn't yet know the extent and nature of her injuries . . . how she had been cut up as though she were a specimen for dissection . . . how bits of her flesh were hung on picture-nails on the walls . . . how she had been ritually disembowelled . . . how her heart and kidneys had been placed on a table beside her severed breasts . . . how her face had been slashed beyond recognition . . . how her nose and ears had been sliced off and her throat slit.

Bloodbath

As he gazed through a broken window at the bloodbath—"It was more like a slaughterhouse than a room"—Inspector Beck paled, retched, and staggered backwards. "For God's sake, Dew, don't look!" he gasped. But Dew (later to win fame as the officer who arrested Crippen) ignored his superior's warning and took the other's place at the opening. He looked beyond the bread and soft drinks bottles, past the print of "The Fisherman's Widow", and at the naked body.

"What I saw when I pushed back an old coat and peeped through a broken pane of glass into the sordid little room which Kelly called her home," he wrote afterwards, "was too harrowing to be described. It remains with me—and always will remain—as the most gruesome memory of the whole of my police career."

The date was Friday, November 9, 1888, the day of the Lord Mayor's Show, which passed not far away from the building in which Mary was found. While the news of the killing of the 25-year-old whore—who a few hours earlier had still been attractive, her features not yet riddled by disease or drink—spread throughout the crowds, the police decided to break into the room. The door had been bolted from the inside and blocked by some furniture, and the officers used a pickaxe to gain entrance.

The policemen deduced that the Ripper had spent some two hours cutting the girl up. He had escaped by the window, leaving Mary Kelly—who was pregnant—to be discovered by the first interested person (a rent collector, as it happened). As soon as the detectives had finished their preliminary examination it was the turn of the doctors to make what they could of the corpse.

It took a team of surgeons six hours to

piece the organs and shreds of flesh together. When the body bore some resemblance to that of a dead human being, the photographers moved in – and took pictures of the remains from every side and angle. They even – following a theory popular at the time – photographed Mary Kelly's eyes thinking the image of her murderer would be recorded on them.

Meanwhile, as the dead woman was placed on the public death-cart and taken to Shoreditch Mortuary, news came that the Commissioner of the Metropolitan Police, Sir Charles Warren, had resigned – and that Sir Robert Anderson had taken his place. This was learnt too late to stop Sir Charles's bloodhounds from nosing into the court, baying wildly, excited by the smell of blood.

Four days later, when an inquiry into the killing was held by the Shoreditch coroner, *The Times* put into black and white what many people in the capital were thinking – and some were saying. "When evidence is not to be had, theories abound. Even the most plausible of them do not carry conviction; but enough is not known to justify search being made in certain specific directions. In this, as in the other crimes of the same character, ordinary motives are out of the question.

Bank Holiday Monday

"No hope of plunder could have induced the murderer to kill one who, it is clear, was reduced to such extremity of want that she thought of destroying herself. The body bore the marks of the frenzy and fury which characterized the previous murders. An appetite for blood, a love of carnage for itself, could only explain what has been done. And there are the same indications of dexterity, if not anatomical skill, such as would be possessed only by one accustomed to handling the knife."

The cry for the Ripper's blood was taken up by Queen Victoria, dwelling in gloomy widowhood in Scotland's Balmoral Castle. In a sharp note to the British Prime Minister, the Marquis of Salisbury, she stated: "This new most ghastly murder shows the absolute necessity for some very decided action. All these courts must be lit, and our detectives improved."

Earlier, after receiving a catch-the-Ripper petition signed by some 5000 women of the East End – "we would also beg that Your Majesty will . . . close bad houses within whose walls such wickedness is done and men and women ruined in body and soul" – the Queen had turned her displeasure on the Home Secretary.

"Have the cattleboats and passenger boats been examined?" she demanded. "Has any investigation been made as to the number of single men occupying rooms to themselves? The murderer's

clothes must be saturated with blood and must be kept somewhere. Is there sufficient surveillance at night?"

Although she got no immediate satisfaction from her ministers, she did attract the attention of the Ripper himself. On November 21, in a letter sent to the magistrates at Thames Police Court, the killer – who, according to the postmark, was in Portsmouth – wrote chirpily:

"Dear Boss, It is no use for you to look for me in London because I'm not there. Don't trouble yourself about me until I return, which will not be very long. I like the work too well to leave it alone. Oh, it was a jolly job the last one. I had plenty of time to do it properly in. Ha, ha, ha! The next lot I mean to do with

WINDPIPE SEVERED, Elizabeth Stride, a 45-year-old prostitute, died in Berner Street. Police posters (right), showing letters from the Ripper, had no effect.

vengeance, cut off their head and arms. You think it is a man with a black moustache. Ha, ha, ha! When I have done another one you can try and catch me again. So goodbye, dear Boss, till I return. Yours, Jack the Ripper."

The man who terrorized the East End of London for three months in the autumn of 1888 made his debut on the night of August 6, the Bank Holiday Monday. At the time the area – a sprawling slum described by the American novelist Jack London as a "Social Abyss . . . [where men] live worse than the beasts, and have less to eat and wear and protect them from the elements than [savages]" – contained the "flotsam of humanity".

Some 15,000 men, women and children were homeless, another 130,000 were in workhouses, and the foggy streets, alleyways, courts and yards were prowled by more than 80,000 prostitutes. These

women – who usually looked some 15 to 20 years older than they were – would go to bed with a man for sixpence, and would accept a penny if it was nearing 3 a.m. and that was all he had.

Such a person was 35-year-old Martha Turner, who on the Monday evening had been drinking with some soldiers in pubs along the riverside in Limehouse. She needed money for a bed for the night, but it is not known whether or not she got it from one of the young men – who belonged to the regiment guarding the Tower of London. What *is* known, however, is that Martha's slashed body (there were 39 knife wounds on it) was found lying on the first landing of George Yard Buildings in Commercial Street early on the Tuesday morning. "Whoever it was," said the examining doctor, "he knew how and where to cut."

Carved to death

The Ripper had struck, and it took him 24 days (a long time by his standards) to strike again. This time the prostitute he chose to carve to death was even less prepossessing than Martha Turner. Mary Ann Nicholls, 42, with five of her front teeth missing, badly needed fourpence for a doss-house bed on the night of August 31. Drunk and wearing what she called a "jolly, new bonnet", she was last seen alive staggering around the vicinity of Bucks Row. She was next seen dead, disembowelled and with her throat hacked across, at 3.45 a.m.

In a report in the *Star* newspaper it was stated that, "No murder was ever more ferociously and more brutally done. The knife, which must have been a large and sharp one, was jabbed into the deceased at the lower part of the abdomen, and then drawn upwards, not once but twice. The first cut veered to the right, slitting up the groin, and passing over the left hip, but the second cut went straight upward, along the centre of the body, and reaching to the breast-bone. Such horrible work could only be the deed of a maniac."

At the inquest on Mrs. Nicholls it was suggested by a medical witness that the murderer was left-handed, and that the wounds were "deftly and . . . skilfully performed". Those who knew the dead woman betrayed no surprise at her savage end. "She was a dissolute character and a drunkard," said her father. But her estranged husband, William Nicholls, a labourer, showed more sympathy when he identified the body. Looking down on the corpse, he said brokenly, "I forgive you for what you did to me, now that I find you like this."

For his third scarlet woman victim the Ripper settled upon 47-year-old Annie Chapman, known to her friends as "Dark Annie". This time there was a gap of

METROPOLITAN POLICE.

Fac-simile of Letter and Post Card received by Central News Agency.

25. Sept. 1888.

Dear Boss

I keep on hearing the police have caught me but they wont fix me just yet. I have laughed when they look so clever and talk about being on the right track. That joke about Leather Apron gave me real fits. I am down on whores and I shant quit ripping them till I do get buckled. Grand work the last job was. I gave the lady no time to squeal. How can they catch me now. I love my work and want to start again. You will soon hear of me with my funny little games. I saved some of the proper red stuff in a ginger beer bottle over the last job to write with but it went thick like glue and I cant use it. Red ink is fit enough I hope ha. ha. The next job I do I shall clip the ladys ears off and send to the police officers just for jolly wouldnt you. Keep this letter back till I do a bit more work. then give it out straight. My knife's so nice and sharp I want to get to work right away if I get a chance. Good luck.

yours truly

Jack the Ripper

Dont mind me giving the trade name

wasnt good enough to post this before I got all the red ink off my hands curse it No luck yet. They say I'm a doctor now ha ha

The Boss
Central News
Office
London City.

POST CARD
THE ADDRESS ONLY TO BE WRITTEN ON THIS SIDE

Central News Office
London E.C.

Any person recognising the handwriting is requested to communicate with the nearest Police Station.

Metropolitan Police Office,
3rd October, 1888.

Printed by M'Corquodale & Co. Limited, "The Armoury," Southwark.

only eight days between killings, and it was late on September 7 when Annie found herself without a client and with nowhere to sleep. Midnight came and went, and at two in the morning she was turned away from her usual doss-house in Dorset Street. The keeper dismissed her with an abrupt, "No money, no bed", and scoffed at her reply: "I haven't got it. I am weak and ill and have been in the infirmary."

She stumbled wearily off to No. 29 Hanbury Street, and passed through a passage leading to the backyard – where fellow prostitutes sometimes conducted their business, and where drunks went to be sick or to sleep it off. It was there – after a dawn cry of "Murder!" – that she was discovered, with her entrails hanging out, near the ground-floor room of a woman who sold cat's meat. The murder had been carried out as viciously and diabolically as before, but this time there was a macabre difference: two new farthings, various other coins, and two brass rings were laid around her feet in the form of a sacrifice.

The wife of a veterinary surgeon who had left her because of her drinking, Mrs. Chapman was regarded as being a rung or two above the other East Enders. The details of her death – "the abdomen had been entirely laid open; the intestines . . . had been lifted out of the body, and placed on the shoulder of the corpse"

EIGHTY-FOUR YEARS ON. The last picture of 29 Hanbury Street before it was demolished in 1972. Here Annie Chapman, victim number three, was murdered.

– were fully given in the medical journal, *The Lancet*. The knife used, it was stated, must have been "at least five inches long", and the Coroner declared: "An unskilled person could not have done this, only someone used to the post-mortem room."

The head, it was revealed, had been almost severed, and a handkerchief tied round the neck to stop it from being "sucked into her throat". The blood must have cascaded like a fountain, and this led *The Times* to ask how the murderer could have made his getaway – going back along the passage through the house – "reeking with blood, and yet . . . he must have walked in broad daylight along streets comparatively well frequented, even at that early hour, without his startling appearance attracting attention".

Public outcry

The newspaper answered its own question by concluding: "He is a man lodging in a comparatively decent house in the district, to which he would be able to retire quickly, and in which, once it was reached, he would be able at his leisure to remove from his person all traces of his hideous crime." Other, less reputable, journals took up the call, and the walls

of the East End suddenly bloomed with vividly coloured hoardings about the incomparable and elusive killer.

The satirical magazine *Punch* took serious exception to this, and blustered: "Imagine the effect of these gigantic pictures of violence and assassination by knife . . . on the morbid imaginations of imbalanced minds. These hideous picture-posters are a blot on our civilization, and a disgrace to the drama"; while *The Times* became even more socially conscious and announced that: "London at large is responsible for Whitechapel and its dens of crime. If the luxury and wealth of the west cannot find some means of mitigating the squalor and crime of the east, we shall have to abate our faith in the resources of civilization."

George Bernard Shaw, then a novelist and music critic, joined in the denunciations in a letter to the *Star*. "Less than a year ago the West End Press were literally clamouring for the blood of the people – hounding on Sir Charles Warren to thrash and muzzle the scum who dared to complain they were starving – heaping insult and reckless calumny upon those who interceded for the victims – applauding to the skies the open class bias of the magistrates and judges . . . behaving, in short, as the propertied class always does when the workers . . . show their teeth."

Sir Charles Warren, however, was

more generally regarded as being, morally, as villainous as the Ripper. A former military man with experience of handling troops in Egypt, he treated his policemen as if they were perpetually on parade. He had more faith in bloodhounds than detectives, and had two champion dogs — Burgho and Barnaby — specially trained for their duties in Hyde Park. After tracking down innocent strangers and, on one occasion, a plain-clothes officer, the hounds proved their ultimate futility when brought panting to Miller's Court.

"Double Event"

Before that, Sir Charles' deputy, Assistant Commissioner Sir Robert Anderson, displayed his indifference to the murders by taking a month's holiday in Switzerland, and later wrote in his memoirs that: "When the stolid English go in for a scare they take leave of all moderation and common sense. If nonsense were solid, the nonsense that was talked and written about these murders would sink a Dreadnought." And, in a magazine article, he blamed the extreme public interest in the Ripper on the Press.

"At the time," he pontificated, "the sensation-mongers of the newspaper press fostered the belief that life in London was no longer safe, and that no woman ought to venture abroad in the streets after nightfall, and one enterprising journalist went so far as to impersonate the cause of all this terror as 'Jack the Ripper', the name by which he will probably go down in history. But no amount of silly hysteria would alter the fact that these crimes were a cause of danger only to a particular section of a small and definite class of women in a limited district of the East End."

This complacency was soon shattered by the Ripper when he performed his famous "Double Event", which accentuated the words of the Whitechapel Vigilance Committee (formed after the death of Annie Chapman) that: "Finding that, in spite of murders being committed in our midst, the police force is inadequate to discover the author or authors of the late atrocities, we . . . intend offering a substantial reward to anyone, citizen or otherwise, who shall give such information as will be the means of bringing the murderer or murderers to justice."

The Double Event took place within an hour on Sunday morning, September 30.

"I SEND YOU HALF THE KIDNE". Jack sent a piece of the organ to the Chairman of Whitechapel Vigilance Committee. He claimed to have eaten the other half.

The first prostitute to go under the Ripper's knife was 45-year-old Elizabeth Stride a carpenter's wife, nicknamed "Long Liz", who was found by a hawker in an alley off Berner Street with her windpipe cut and her throat still bleeding. The time was shortly after one o'clock, and 45 minutes later the second body was discovered in nearby Mitre Square by Police Constable Watkins — whose beat took him through the area, and who, like every other officer on duty in the East End that autumn, heard and saw nothing suspicious.

Pig-headed dolt

Like Mrs. Stride, 43-year-old Catherine Eddowes had joked at the thought of meeting the Ripper. "He's got other girls to bother about instead of me," she told her friends drunkenly. "'Sides, the minute I see any man carrying a shiny black bag I'll throw me head back and scream it off!" She was so drunk at eight o'clock on the evening of September 29 that she reeled about, imitating a fire-engine. For this she was arrested and kept in Bishopsgate Police Station until 1 a.m. the next morning. As she was released, she flounced past the duty sergeant, calling out: "Ta-ta, old cock. I'll see you again soon!" The irony of which was lost on the sergeant.

Donald Rumbelow

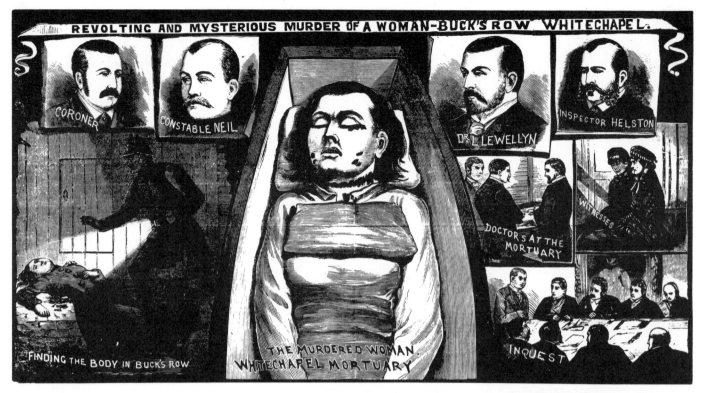

REVOLTING AND MYSTERIOUS MURDER OF A WOMAN-BUCK'S ROW WHITECHAPEL

CORONER

CONSTABLE NEIL

Dr. LLEWELLYN

INSPECTOR HELSTON

WITNESSES

DOCTORS AT THE MORTUARY

FINDING THE BODY IN BUCK'S ROW

THE MURDERED WOMAN. WHITECHAPEL MORTUARY

INQUEST

AN ARTIST'S grisly impression of Mary Ann Nicholls in the mortuary (above). Broadsheets kept the East Enders informed. But in fact there was no capture.

She spent the next 30 minutes walking from the police station to Mitre Square—where presumably she met the murderer, and where he ripped her open "like a pig for the market" according to P.C. Watkins. "I have been in the force a long while," he told newsmen later, "but I never saw such a sight." For once the excess of blood proved too much—or too embarrassing—for the killer. He stopped to wash his hands in a public sink, and then (so the police reasoned) chalked on a doorway the ambiguous message that: "The Juwes are the men who will not be blamed for nothing."

The writing of the "Juwes" slogan (Jews?—or some masonic reference?) could have provided the most fruitful clue yet—but for the intervention of Sir Charles Warren. He descended on the scene (without dogs, for once) and ordered the words to be rubbed out before they could be photographed. His explanation for this was the lame one that the sentence could have caused "religious trouble", and that there were not the men available to deal with a "racial riot".

Sir Charles's action was even more extraordinary as the crime had taken place in the City of London, over which he had no jurisdiction. This brought him into conflict with the Commissioner of City Police, Major Henry Smith, who privately recorded that Warren was "a dolt, a sheer, pig-headed dolt". In an attempt

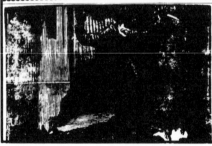

TWO MORE HORRIBLE MURDERS IN THE EAST-END.

to bring the Ripper, or those sheltering him, out into the open, the police next released a letter which the murderer had sent to the Central News Agency two days before the Double Event. It read:

Ghoulish missive

"I am down on whores and I shan't quit ripping them till I do get buckled. Grand work, the last job was. I gave the lady [Annie Chapman] no time to squeal. How can they catch me now? I love my work and want to start again. You will soon hear of me and my funny little games . . . The next job I do I shall clip the lady's ears off and send to the police officers just for jolly . . . Keep this letter back till I do a bit more work, then give it out straight. My knife is nice and sharp. I want to get to work right away if I get

GHASTLY MURDER IN THE EAST-END. DREADFUL MUTILATION OF A WOMAN.

Capture : Leather Apron

Another murder of a character even more diabolical than that perpetrated in Buck's Row, on Friday week, was discovered in the same neighbourhood, on Saturday morning. At about six o'clock a woman was found lying, in a back yard at the foot of a passage leading to a lodging-house in Old Brown's Lane, Spitalfields. The house is occupied by a Mrs. Richardson, who lets it out to lodgers, and the door which admits to this passage, at the foot of which live the yard where the body was found, is always open for the convenience of lodgers. A lodger named Davis was going down to work at the time mentioned and found the woman lying, on her back close to the flight of steps leading into the yard. Her throat was cut in a fearful manner. The woman's body had been completely ripped open, and the heart and other organs laying about the place, and portions of the entrails round the victim's neck. An excited crowd gathered in front of Mrs. Richardson's board ...

a chance. Good luck. Yours truly, Jack the Ripper."

The letter was considered to be genuine, as on Sunday, September 30, just a few hours after the double murder, the police received a postcard referring to the killings. They had not yet been officially announced, yet the writer of the card said:

"I was not codding, dear old Boss, when I gave you the tip. You'll hear about Saucy Jack's work tomorrow. Double event this time. Number one squealed a bit. Couldn't finish straight off. Had not time to get ears for police. Thanks for keeping last letter back till I got to work again. Jack the Ripper."

A few days later he followed this with a typically ghoulish missive. It was a cardboard box sent to George Lusk, Chairman of the Whitechapel Vigilance

authenticity of the letters was Sir Melville Macnaghten (later Chief of the Criminal Investigation Department at Scotland Yard, and then a young man about to join the Force). "I have always thought I could discern the stained forefinger of the journalist," he wrote in his autobiography, *Days Of My Years*. "... Whoever did pen the gruesome stuff, I am certain that it was not the mad miscreant who had committed the murders."

Suicide?

Even so, Sir Melville did not decry the fear that pervaded the entire city. "No one who was living in London that autumn will forget the terror created by these murders," he stated. "... I can recall the foggy evenings, and hear again the raucous cries of the newspaper boys: 'Another horrible murder, murder, mutilation, Whitechapel.' Such was the burden of their ghastly song ... no servant-maid

BUCKS ROW just prior to demolition in 1972. Renamed Durward Street, the site of Mary Nicholls's killing was a tourist spot for over 80 years.

VICTORIA AND DISRAELI. The Queen took a keen interest in the murders. Later her son, the Duke of Clarence, was suspected. Right, another splash on Jack.

Committee, and it contained a kidney taken from the body of Catherine Eddowes. Also enclosed was a note headed, "From Hell". It said, "Mr. Lusk. Sir I send you half the Kidne I took from one woman prasarved it for you, tother piece I fried and ate it was very nice. I may send you the bloody knif that took it out if you only wate a whil longer. Signed Catch me when you can Mister Lusk."

It was followed by two more letters from another port—Liverpool, this time—suggesting that the maniac was a sailor, or was planning to leave the country by ship. One person who doubted the

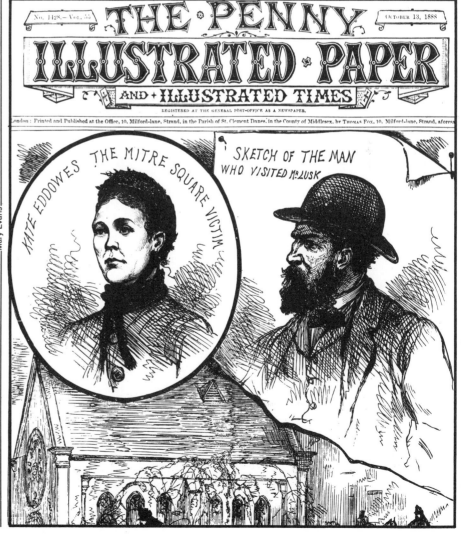

237

deemed her life safe if she ventured out to post a letter after ten o'clock at night."

The terror—and the killings—came to an end with the cutting up of Mary Kelly in Miller's Court on November 9. By then various theories had been put forward as to the Ripper's identity—he was a mad surgeon, a mad policeman, a mad lodging-house keeper, even a mad midwife, Jill the Ripper.

He had been variously described as "a man aged 28, height five feet eight inches, complexion dark, small dark moustache; dress: black diagonal coat, hard felt hat, collar and tie, respectable appearance";

WAS THIS JACK THE RIPPER?
Montague John Druitt committed suicide. After his death the murders stopped. Many experts believe he was responsible.

and, "a man aged 30, height five feet seven or eight inches; complexion fair, moustache fair, medium build; dress: pepper and salt colour loose jacket, grey cloth cap with peak of same material, knotted reddish neckerchief like a sailor."

Whoever he was, whatever he looked like, Sir Melville was convinced that he was not a religious maniac, nor an asylum lunatic. "I incline to the belief," he wrote,

"that the individual who held up London in terror resided with his own people; that he absented himself from home at certain times, and that he committed suicide on or about November 10, 1888."

But even in that the "fiend" had his own final say. One of the first documents Sir Melville read when he took office at Scotland Yard was a verse supposedly written by the killer. It went:

I'm not a butcher.
I'm not a Yid,
Nor yet a foreign skipper,
But I'm your own light-hearted friend,
Yours truly, Jack the Ripper.

THE UNLAMENTED DEATH OF MAX THE RED

He was just another one of Soho's has-beens, a second-rate pimp who had seen better days. But even Max Kassel should have known better than to borrow from killer George Lacroix (below).

Popperfoto

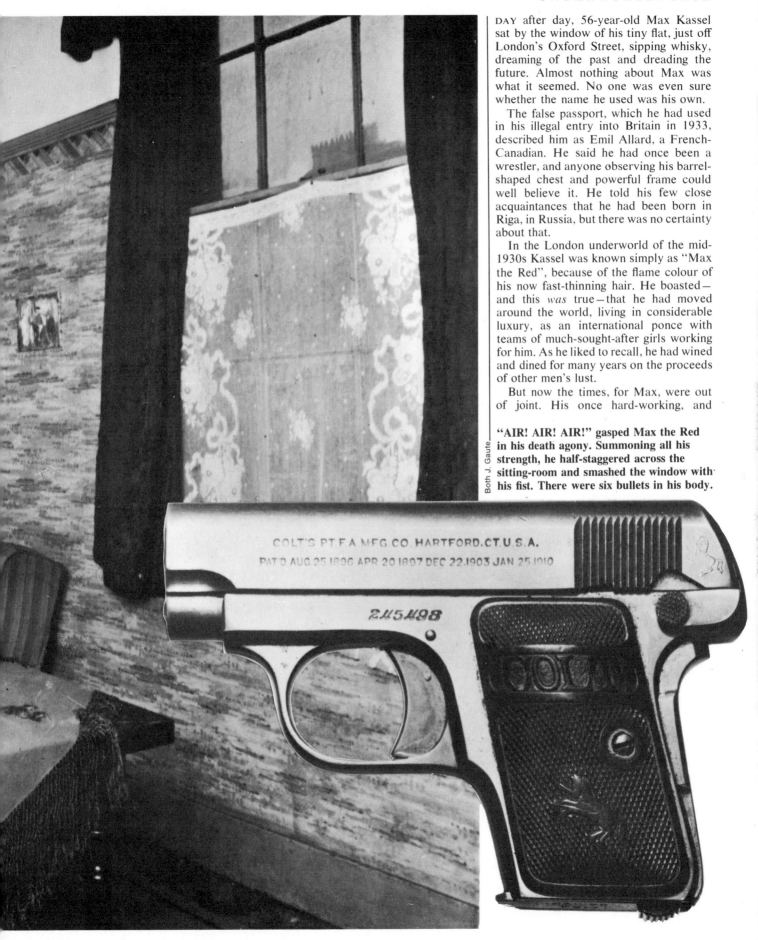

DAY after day, 56-year-old Max Kassel sat by the window of his tiny flat, just off London's Oxford Street, sipping whisky, dreaming of the past and dreading the future. Almost nothing about Max was what it seemed. No one was even sure whether the name he used was his own.

The false passport, which he had used in his illegal entry into Britain in 1933, described him as Emil Allard, a French-Canadian. He said he had once been a wrestler, and anyone observing his barrel-shaped chest and powerful frame could well believe it. He told his few close acquaintances that he had been born in Riga, in Russia, but there was no certainty about that.

In the London underworld of the mid-1930s Kassel was known simply as "Max the Red", because of the flame colour of his now fast-thinning hair. He boasted — and this *was* true — that he had moved around the world, living in considerable luxury, as an international ponce with teams of much-sought-after girls working for him. As he liked to recall, he had wined and dined for many years on the proceeds of other men's lust.

But now the times, for Max, were out of joint. His once hard-working, and

"AIR! AIR! AIR!" gasped Max the Red in his death agony. Summoning all his strength, he half-staggered across the sitting-room and smashed the window with his fist. There were six bullets in his body.

Both J. Gaute

COLT'S PT.F.A.M·F·G·CO.HARTFORD.CT.U.S.A.
PAT·D·AUG.25.1896·APR·20.1897·DEC·22.1903·JAN·25.1910

2M5M98

241

fast-earning teams of whores had long ago been taken over by other "protectors". His one minor source of income was a tired, middle-aged prostitute clinging to the residue of a clientele in Mayfair. Moreover, Max was so hard up that he couldn't raise £25 to repay an overdue debt.

Lack of money was not the only thing that worried him, as he sat in his stuffy room. He had a nagging but indefinable fear that he was destined to be a victim; that an enemy would arise from somewhere and strike him down.

Just the year before, in 1935, a Soho prostitute, known as French Fifi, had been murdered in her room, and her killer was still at large. Max, in his muddled, anxious way, was certain that she had been dispatched by a "gang over from France" and that he would be next on the murder list.

In reality his more immediate problems centred on the £25 which he had borrowed from a Frenchman calling himself Roger Vernon, who, like Max, was living illegally in Britain on a false passport.

Vernon was a criminal and murderer, who had escaped from Devil's Island. Now, apparently safe from detection in Britain, he lived on the earnings of an attractive young French prostitute known as Suzanne.

Foreign-born harlots

Like many foreign-born harlots of the time, she had contracted a "marriage of convenience" with a British subject so that she could gain the citizenship and earn her living in London. In her case contacts had chosen for her a sailor named Naylor, who had been paid £10 for his services. Officially, Suzanne was Mrs. Marguerite Simone Naylor. Unofficially she owed her livelihood and "protection" to Vernon—or George Lacroix to give him his real name.

At the beginning of January 1936 Lacroix invited Max to the apartment in Soho's Little Newport Street from which Suzanne operated. Instead of a pleasant social gathering between fellow businessmen, the two criminals engaged in sharp words over the £25 debt. Firmly and truculently, Max told his younger colleague that he had no money to spare, no prospect of acquiring any beyond his immediate needs, and that Lacroix had no choice but to wait.

Lacroix seethed with rage. It was bad enough to be treated in such a high-handed fashion, but to be treated that way in front of his "girl" was too humiliating. The time for action had come, Lacroix

GEORGE LACROIX, alias Roger Vernon, was a vicious criminal and murderer, a fugitive from Devil's Island. A young French prostitute supported him.

decided, and after Max left he began to lay his plans for vengeance.

On January 22 Max went to the West End address that he used as a "post office" and there found a number of letters waiting for him. One, written in French, read: "Monsieur, Will you call at the flat to-morrow, Thursday, between 6.30 and 7 p.m., as I have a letter to hand to you personally—Suzanne."

What Kassel made of the mysterious invitation was never known. But the next evening he dressed smartly in a grey, herring-bone suit, a mauve silk shirt, a dark grey overcoat and brown shoes. He walked swiftly—his eyes ever alert—along Oxford Street towards Leicester Square and so into Little Newport Street.

Argument under way

At 6.45 he rang Suzanne's door-bell and the door was immediately opened by Marcelle Aubin, Suzanne's maid. The flat occupied the second and third stories of the building, and Miss Aubin led Max up to the third floor, where Suzanne Naylor had her sitting-room. As he reached the stairhead Kassel suddenly paused. From behind the closed sitting-room door he heard Lacroix shout, in French, "Come on in, come in!"

Max entered the room and closed the door behind him. Miss Aubin went back down the stairs, where she joined Suzanne in her bedroom—and they listened, tensely, to the sounds from above. In the sitting-room the radio was blaring away, and it was difficult to distinguish actual words being spoken. But, after a few moments, Miss Aubin and Suzanne were aware that an argument was under way, and getting louder every minute.

Soon the shouting was accompanied by banging noises, back and forth across the floor, as though a scuffle was taking place. Then, heard distinctly above the jangling of music from the radio, came a series of sharp cracks.

Immediately afterwards Miss Aubin heard Lacroix shout "Marcelle!" She bounded up the stairs, and as she neared the sitting-room the door was flung open and Lacroix and Max staggered out. Their feet were shuffling and kicking, their arms about one another. They looked like a pair of drunks—except that Max appeared to be the more intoxicated, and was leaning on Lacroix for support.

With a deft twist of his arms Lacroix pushed Max from him. As he did so Marcelle and Suzanne saw that Max the Red was not drunk, but staggering as though wounded. "Oh, Mademoiselle," he cried, tottering towards Marcelle, "he's shot me!" Marcelle almost unable to think gently tried to propel him back into the sitting-room.

He broke from her, staggered across the room and, summoning all

his available strength, smashed two panes of the window with his fist, gasping, "Air! Air! Air!"

Marcelle and Suzanne hurried over to Max and pulled him away from the shattered glass. He was bleeding profusely, and, although they didn't yet know it, there were six bullets in his body.

"Take me to the hospital!" he begged them. Then, as Lacroix pinioned his arms and began to push him towards the bathroom, he begged again: "Take me to the hospital! I won't say anything. I'll say I did it myself. Please, take me . . ."

Unheeding, Lacroix heaved and chivvied him until finally he got him into the bathroom and let him flop on to a small bathside chair. By this time a greyness was settling over Max's face, and his voice was weakening. "I'm going to die," he panted. "Give me some water." Marcelle filled a glass and handed it to Max. His hands trembled so much that she had to help him to drink.

"Give me air!" Max pleaded, and when Lacroix ordered him, in French, to "shut up" he gave a terrifying, bull-like roar. He rose to his feet as if life had suddenly rushed back into his body. He threw open the bathroom window and swallowed air with a heavy wheezing. Lacroix then leapt forward, hurled Max to the floor, and slammed the window shut.

No more groaning

Max the Red had made his last, exhausting effort to stay alive. Feebly he raised himself into a kneeling position and slumped against the bath, his head and arms hanging over the edge. In the sitting-room the two women and Lacroix sat mutely staring at each other, listening to the eerie groans coming from the bathroom. Finally Lacroix went in to observe his victim. When he returned, Marcelle protested: "I don't want to hear that groaning any more!" Unemotionally Lacroix replied: "It's all right. You won't hear him any more—he's gone."

The front-door bell rang, and a few minutes later the telephone rang. But no one in the apartment made a move. The agitated Marcelle had now one object in mind: to get away as quickly as possible. "Marcelle wants to go home," Suzanne told Lacroix. The killer studied the maid thoughtfully for a few moments. "Yes, that's all right, Marcelle, I trust you," he said. Then he leaned over and kissed her on both cheeks.

With Marcelle gone, Lacroix began to plan for the disposal of the body. He telephoned an old friend, another Frenchman, Pierre Henri Alexandre. A Soho garage proprietor, Alexandre also let the apartment in Little Newport Street—among other apartments in the area occupied by Frenchwomen. What interested Lacroix was the large Chrysler car that

Alexandre owned. Would Alexandre come round with his car? Yes, he would.

Alexandre arrived shortly before midnight, and Lacroix's first move was to take him up to the sitting-room and pour him a large whisky. Next Lacroix rattled out his story: "You know Max the Red owes me some money. He has kept on insulting me, so I got him to call here. He came and we had an argument about the money, and about him insulting my girl and threatening to break my neck. He jumped on me, and I shot him."

Alexandre put his whisky down, his mouth dropped open in alarm. Lacroix hurried on: "In the fight I shot once or twice, and then the window got broken and I shot again. That's the situation. Will you help me?" Alexandre thought briefly. Then, appreciating Lacroix's reputation as a muscle-man, he said: "I suppose I've

"I TRUST YOU," Lacroix (above, in the dock with prostitute Suzanne) when Marcelle (right) asked to go home. Then Pierre Alexandre (far right) and his large Chrysler helped dispose of the body. . . .

got to help you. Where is Max now?"

Lacroix took him into the bathroom and showed him the corpse, still hanging over the edge of the bath. "We'll wrap him up and get him out of here," he said. "What time can you come back when it's safer to move him?" Alexandre suggested four in the morning and Lacroix agreed, adding: "Ring three times and I'll know it's you."

Sharp at four Alexandre was back at the apartment. The two men wrapped the body in a blanket, and half-carried, half-slid it down the stairs and into the street. Even at that hour Little Newport Street

was bustling with activity, with street-walkers still soliciting potential customers. But, surprisingly, no one noticed the two men from the apartment, heaving and shoving their heavy burden on to the back seat of Alexandre's Chrysler.

Take him anywhere

"Where shall we take him?" Alexandre asked. "Anywhere—north, east, south or west," Lacroix snapped. Since he knew the northern fringes of London best, Alexandre decided to head north. He eased himself into the driving seat, Lacroix got in beside him. Slowly the car drew away and disappeared among the late-night taxis in Shaftesbury Avenue. Back in the apartment lights still burned. Suzanne was not receiving "clients". Instead, she was busy packing.

In order not to attract police attention,

Alexandre drove cautiously. Forty minutes later he and Lacroix found themselves in deserted country near the town of St. Albans. Helpfully, fog was settling in, and Lacroix, who was peering through the gloom at the roadside, spotted a hedge with a gap in it. "This is a good place," he said, and Alexandre stopped the car.

Death seemed to have added to Max the Red's 16 stone, and the two men were soon panting for breath as they dragged his corpse across the grass and through the hedge. There they left it, unconcealed, and made their way back to London. Lacroix, at least, had much to do to cover his tracks.

Some five hours afterwards, at 10 a.m., Henry Sayer, a St. Albans carpenter, walking along the road, noticed a "bundle" behind the hedge. Inspecting it, he found it to be a body, and he informed the police.

The local force asked for Scotland Yard's help and Chief Inspector Frederick Dew Sharpe, Head of the Flying Squad was put onto the case.

Stains on the floor

Once the body had been identified, Sharpe and his men moved fast. They found Alexandre, who told them of his part in the disposal of the body, and they traced Marcelle Aubin, who gave her version of the underworld murder.

When the police raided the Soho apartment there was no sign of Lacroix or Suzanne. However, there were stains on the floor which proved, under forensic tests, to be blood; the bottom of the sitting-room curtains had been snipped off with scissors, presumably to remove more traces of blood.

Sharpe quickly learned that Lacroix and Suzanne had fled to Paris. There, with the co-operation of the French police, they were held for questioning. In London warrants were issued charging Lacroix with Max the Red's murder and

All Popperfoto

Suzanne Naylor with "receiving, comforting, harbouring, assisting and maintaining George Lacroix, knowing that he had murdered one Max Kassel".

The warrants were handed to Foreign Office officials in Whitehall and, through them, to the British Ambassador in Paris.

In France there began a long legal wrangle over the British claim to have the couple extradited. Scotland Yard still believed that Lacroix was a British subject, born in Canada — but the French police proved that he was French and an escaped convict from Devil's Island. Suzanne was technically British since her arranged marriage. But, again, the Yard was thwarted. A search of Paris records showed that, all along, she had been the lawful wife of a French citizen named Bertrand, and that her second "marriage" was bigamous.

Please have mercy!

On these grounds the Paris authorities refused extradition; however, they decided to bring Lacroix and Suzanne to trial under French law. The court was deprived of the important evidence of Marcelle Aubin, for — although she, too, had travelled to France — she had died before the case came on.

Chief Inspector Sharpe was present at the trial and was startled to discover that much of the hearing was given over to Lacroix's aged father — who, gesticulating with his walking stick, appealed to the jury to "please have mercy on my son". Sharpe was even more disconcerted when the court asked for his opinion of the case. In line with British procedure that police officers offered only facts and not opinion, he refused to answer the question.

No great loss

Finally, Lacroix was found guilty and sentenced to 10 years' imprisonment with hard labour, to be followed by 20 years' exile from France. Suzanne Naylor/Bertrand was acquitted. Although she had been present at the events in Little Newport Street, there was no evidence to show that she had willingly participated in the murder or its sequel — except to stay with her "protector", Lacroix.

For the British police it was something of an anti-climax. There was little doubt that if Lacroix had been tried in England, and found guilty, he would have been hanged. On the other hand — despite Press attempts to present him as a Czar of European prostitution — Max the Red was no great loss to anyone in or outside the underworld.

THE ATTRACTIVE young French prostitute (embracing her mother after the trial) was acquitted. There was no evidence that she had participated in the murder. But Lacroix got 10 years' imprisonment.

Popperfoto

They called it "Bloody Williamson" County. Charlie Birger (above) called it his. The Shelton brothers begged to differ. . . .

GANGLAND COUNTY

Chicago Historical Society

FEW men have been carried to justice on such a local whirlwind of violence as that which bore Charlie Birger, underworld gang leader, to the courthouse in Benton, Illinois, in July, 1927, Birger had been brought by the authorities from Williamson County—less than 20 miles south of Benton—where death and destruction had been so rife for the previous five years that throughout the United States the district had earned itself the title of "Bloody Williamson".

There had been labour disputes in the coalmines that culminated in massacre—19 strike-breakers brutally done to death in one day alone—a local war involving the Ku Klux Klan, and endless blood-letting feuds between rival bootlegging gangs. Altogether the total violent death roll was around the 200 mark.

Of all the gang warfare none was more bitter or pitiless than that between two groups of thugs: one led by three brothers named Shelton—Carl, Earl, and Bernie—and the other by Charlie Birger. Under their leaders' directions the two gangs murdered each others' members, fired

their homes, and bombed their hideouts. In five short months the Shelton-Birger shoot-outs accounted for 13 lives.

"When men meet on the street corner the talk is of the gang war," commented the *St. Louis Post-Despatch*. "What is Charlie Birger going to do? Will he stand for the killing of his men? Is his reply to be a pitched battle with the Shelton crowd, perhaps along the Williamson County roads, or are his men to make reprisals only where they can find single Shelton gangsters by themselves?"

The jungle code

But now it was, as a result of that gang warfare, that Charlie Birger found himself on trial, accused of the murder of Joe Adams, roadhouse owner and mayor of the small community of West City, just across the border from Williamson in Franklin County. Adams's "offence", under the jungle code of the underworld, was that he had provided shelter for the armoured truck in which the Shelton brothers travelled the countryside and which they used like a tank in their battles.

OF ALL GANG WARFARE none was more bitter or pitiless than that between two rival groups of thugs: the Sheltons (above) and the Birger mob (right). They murdered each other's members, fired their homes and bombed their hideouts. . . .

Jointly charged with Birger were two of his henchmen: Art Newman, small-time gambler and former Shelton associate, who had switched his gangland allegiance, and Ray Hyland, a Birger gang 'chauffeur'. But it was upon Birger that the main attention focused, for there were few in that part of Illinois who had ever expected to see him before a jury.

As he was led from the jail to the little courtroom, Birger walked with ease and confidence. He was an impressive and, on first sight, deceptively attractive figure, nearly six feet tall, dark and swarthy. He was smartly dressed in well-cut riding-breeches and leather jacket and looked much younger than 44.

Before taking his seat at the front of the courtroom, he turned to smile at his pretty young wife who had brought their

Chicago Historical Society

two small daughters to the hearing. Look at me, Birger seemed to be suggesting to the jury, I'm really just a decent family man, trapped in this place by some mischance and on false information.

But as the State's Attorney, Roy C. Martin, called on his witnesses to unfold their evidence, the true nature of Birger, the ruthless and violent gangster, began to emerge. And it was the widow of Joe Adams who, quietly and unemotionally, sketched in the background of the events which led up to the death of her husband at her side on the afternoon of December 12, 1926.

"Two young men knocked on our door, and when I opened it they asked if Joe Adams lived here," she testified. "I said he did, and they asked me if he was home. I said yes, but he was asleep. I asked them if I would do. They said they wanted to see Joe personally. They said they had a letter from Carl Shelton."

Mrs. Adams went back into the house and roused her heavily built, giant of a husband who lumbered, hardly fully awake, to the door. Mrs. Adams stood

with him, and, as she now recalled, one of the young men handed Joe Adams a note. It was brief and was, of course, a fake — supposedly signed by Carl Shelton, but drafted by Birger in order, stated the prosecution, to distract Adams while the two young men at the door prepared to carry out their orders.

The note read: "Friend Joe: If you can use these boys, please do so. They are broke and need work. I knew their father. C.S."

As he fell dying

What did those two young men do as Joe Adams read the note? the State's Attorney asked Mrs. Adams. Softly, without a tremor in her voice, she replied: "They shot him."

As he fell dying in his own doorway Joe Adams gasped to his wife that he couldn't identify the two killers — who were then fleeing from the scene. But Mrs. Adams had not been in doubt for one moment as to who was the real instigator of the murder. She told the court that on previous days Birger had

telephoned her regularly with threats and, on one occasion, asked:

"Have you got much insurance on Joe's life?" When she had replied, "No, not very much," Birger added, darkly, "Well, you'd better get a lot more, because we're going to kill him and you'll need it."

The murder "contract" had been carried out by the brothers Thomasson — Harry, 19, and Elmo, 21. They were orphans who had drifted into Birger's gang, and since the Adams killing, Elmo had mysteriously disappeared. Harry Thomasson, however, had confessed to his part in the affair — driven by the suspicion that Birger had killed his brother and should not escape the law. Now he was ready to tell everything he knew about how the Adams murder had been planned, and who had masterminded it.

On the night of December 11, 1926, he told the jury, he and his brother had been called to Shady Rest, the log cabin, near the Williamson County town of Marion, which Birger used as a headquarters and which was stocked with machine-guns, rifles and ammunition. As the boys approached it, the cabin was bathed in the glare of floodlights—a routine precaution by the Birger gang to guard against night surprise attack.

Birger was waiting inside the cabin with Newman and another gang member. "Birger," Thomasson recalled, "said, 'We've got a job for you two boys and it's got to be done tomorrow.' Art Newman asked me if I had ever killed anyone, and I said, no, I had never had enough against anyone to kill them.

"Birger said, 'You are the boys to kill Joe Adams. He don't know you, and the law won't suspect you. What I want you to do is this: Go to West City and leave your car about a block from Joe Adams's house. Then go up to the front door and knock. If Carl Shelton, Joe Adams or

Ray Walker [another Shelton mobster] comes to the door, shoot, and don't stop to ask questions. If anybody else comes to the door, ask for Joe. If they say he's not there, stick around the neighbourhood and watch the house.'"

Poisoned bullets

It was arranged that Ray Hyland, the "chauffeur", should drive the murder car, and, said Thomasson, the next morning the two young "contract" men were presented with bullets which had been dipped in poison and Birger's decoy note to Adams, signed "C.S."

"Birger, Newman, Hyland and the others gave Elmo a .38 and me a .45," young Thomasson testified. "Hyland drove us, and when we reached West City, Elmo and I went to Adams's house,

leaving Hyland sitting in the car. We knocked on the door and then Adams came. Elmo handed him the note, and while he was reading it I shot him twice with the revolver which I had hidden up my sleeve.

"Elmo then shot him once. We then ran back to the car where Hyland was waiting, and drove away. That night Elmo went back to Shady Rest and stayed there all night, but I stayed in an hotel in Harrisburg [in Saline County, Illinois]. The next day I went back to Shady Rest, and they paid us $150—50 dollars for each shot fired."

Already, in a previous trial, Harry Thomasson had been convicted for his part in the Adams murder. But following a mercy plea by his defence counsel—which was supported by State's Attorney

A VICTIM and his widow (above) . . . the testimony of Mrs. Joe Adams was crucial in sending Birger to the gallows. The killer tried to pass himself off in court as just a decent family man (near left). But his conviction, with henchmen Ray Hyland (far left) and Art Newman (left), was inevitable, as was the end of unbridled gangsterism in the county.

Martin—he had been sentenced not to death but to life imprisonment. He had come from prison to give evidence at this Birger trial, and there seemed little doubt that what he had told the court would put the final seal on the gang leader.

Birger's lawyers took the only line that seemed open to them. They presented a blanket denial of Birger's involvement in the murder, protested that their client had been nowhere near Shady Rest on the night of December 11 and knew absolutely nothing of who had planned and carried out the killing. Similar pleas of innocence were submitted on behalf of the other two defendants. Then, without warning, the trial took a sudden and dramatic turn.

Art Newman's lawyer announced that his client wished to go on to the witness stand and make a full confession about his part, and Birger's part, in the crime. Thoroughly alarmed, and realizing that fellow-gangsters were about to conduct a vendetta against each other in front of the jury, Birger's lawyers appealed for an adjournment. The judge refused the plea and called on the defence lawyers for Birger and Hyland to produce the witnesses speaking for their clients.

In turn, each declined on the grounds that they wanted to hear what Newman had to say first, and then they would be prepared to call evidence to rebut his statement. This got them nowhere since the judge ruled that, in view of the deadlock, the case would go straight to the jury, after final speeches, and Newman's confession would not be heard.

Each of the defence lawyers laced his appeal to the jury with as much dramatic intensity as he could muster. First, H. R. Dial, for Hyland, thundered: "Is it blood you want? I know that back under the old Mosaic law it was a tooth for a tooth and an eye for an eye, but even in those days you didn't take three lives for one.

"If you find these men guilty of crime, why do you have to hang them? Won't confinement in the penitentiary satisfy you? Do you have to have blood? I thought we were trying to stop the shedding of blood in Franklin County and Williamson County."

W. F. Dillon, Newman's counsel, then cried: "He [Harry Thomasson] is going to dope you, gentlemen, into signing a death warrant for these men to hang until they are dead, dead, dead; until their tongues stick out of their mouths and they hang suspended in the air.

Humane punishment

"If you have to find these men guilty, give them some humane punishment, so that when the end of time comes, and the lightning strikes, the hills crumble, and the fire rages, as the pearly gates open we may meet these men, take them by the hand, and say that we have forgiven them!"

On Birger's behalf, his counsel, R. E. Smith, was somewhat more restrained, but used much of his time to contest Thomasson's evidence and brand him as a perjurer. "Thomasson did not hang," he reminded the jury, "and yet he is the confessed murderer!" Striding across to the jury box, he demanded:

"If I hand you a pistol would you kill Birger as he sits there? If you wouldn't, would you ask the sheriff to do it? In the county to the south of us [Williamson] they hang men, and hang men, and more and more murders are committed." He turned away and walked towards Birger. Quietly, he concluded: "Charlie, in a few minutes your life is going to be taken from my hands and given to these 12 men."

But it was State's Attorney Martin who had the last words, and he concentrated them upon pressing for the death sentence. Death it should be, for all three men, he declared, and added: "I see in your verdict the passing of the rule of the machine-gun gang and the establishment of the rule of the law. I know you men will say that the gang war has no place in this part of the state of Illinois,

251

and that the gunman and gangster has no place in Franklin County."

In the early afternoon of Saturday, July 26 the jury retired to consider their verdict, argued over the evidence for a whole night and morning, and finally returned into court on the Sunday afternoon. As they trooped in, the courtroom was filled to bursting with excited onlookers – many of them in black, not as a sign of prospective mourning but because they wore their Sunday clothes.

Clearly exhausted

The verdicts were delivered rapidly and by a nervous and clearly exhausted foreman: death for Birger, life imprisonment for Newman and Hyland. Birger at first gave no sign of response, and made no move to look around the courtroom: his wife was not present. But as Judge Miller announced that he would go to the gallows between 10 a.m. and 2 p.m. on October 15, 1927, Birger turned pale and his hands shook uncontrollably.

On October 7, however, the Supreme Court granted Birger a stay of execution – which was subsequently set for April 13, 1928. But on April 12, even while the gallows were being given their final testing, Birger's lawyers filed a petition for a sanity hearing, and a further stay of execution was ordered until the hearing had been held. On April 16 a jury spent just 12 minutes in deciding that Birger was sane, and the final execution date was set for April 19.

On the morning of that day, still protesting his involvement in the Adams murder, Charlie Birger – the scourge of Williamson County – went to his death in the yard of Benton jail. His last reported words contained an element of truth. "They've accused me of a lot of things I was never guilty of, but I was guilty of a lot of things which they never accused me of, so I guess we're about even."

But, in its own curious way, the execution of Charlie Birger was not quite the end of Birger and his sinister influence. Even in an area which had almost come to accept violent death as part of the normal course of events there was shock and horror over the terrible end of a state highway patrolman named Lory Price, and his wife, Ethel. Once again, Birger had been the guiding hand.

The murders had been committed in February 1927, but it was not until January 1929 that Art Newman – serving his life sentence for the Adams killing – and three other Birger hoodlums were put on trial. All pleaded guilty, but it was Newman who told the gruesome story of what had happened to Price and his wife.

According to Newman, Patrolman Price worked closely with Birger in a car-stealing racket. Birger's men would steal the cars, tip off Price as to their location, and then he would "find" them and share the reward money from the insurers. But, said Newman, Birger became suspicious that Price was two-timing him and believed he was responsible for a fire that eventually burned down his hideaway, Shady Rest.

On the day of the killings, Newman said that he and his fellow-defendants now on trial, plus Birger and two others, went to the Price home and put Price and his wife into separate cars. Newman recalled: "Price said, 'Are you going to hurt me, Charlie?' and Birger said, 'No, I just want to talk things over with you.' He said, 'Take that woman out and do away with her,' and Price said, 'Please don't hurt Ethel.'"

Double-crossed

Newman was at the wheel of the car into which Lory Price had been flung, and as he drove away, he said, he heard Birger accusing Price of probing the Adams killing and playing a part in the destruction of Shady Rest. After they had gone a few miles Birger ordered Newman to drive to the site of the burned-out Shady Rest, and there Price was bundled out of the car. Once more Price protested that he had not double-crossed the gang. But, screaming obscenities at him, Birger drew his gun and wounded Price with three shots.

Soon afterwards the second car, in which Ethel Price had been taken away, arrived at the Birger hideout. "I asked what they had done with her," Newman told the court, "and one of them said, 'We shot her and threw her in a mineshaft.' Birger said, 'All right, we'll put him with her,' but he was told, 'We can't – we filled up the place with tin and timber.'"

Birger ordered Lory Price to be taken to another mineshaft. But Newman, so he testified, protested against using his own car – until Birger told him and the rest of the gang, "Everybody will go through this with me or I'll wipe you all out."

So, Newman continued, they drove off, with Birger nursing a machine-gun and sitting on Price's blood-soaked, groaning body. They scouted around an old mineshaft, but, because of the presence of a workman, drove on into open country. There Birger ordered Newman to stop the car, and, with some of his gangsters who had followed in another car, he carried Price into a nearby field. Newman heard the sound of shots; then Birger and

BIRGER'S EXECUTION was not quite the end of his influence. Later, details emerged of a patrolman's brutal murder, vengeance for the Shady Rest fire (left).

Chicago Historical Society

THE SHELTON BROTHERS (from left: Carl, Earl and Bernie) later moved to East St. Louis, taking their battle-scarred armoured car with them. Before long Carl and Ernie met fitting ends, dying as they had lived . . . amid gang warfare.

his henchmen returned to the cars — without Price.

Although, like Newman, the other three defendants at the trial had pleaded guilty, they denied knowing what was to happen when they set off with Birger for the Price home. Their denials caused the judge to inquire, with irony: "Do you mean to tell me that you fellows took two cars down to Price's house with pistols strapped on you without knowing anything was going to happen? Were those pistols for some kind of ornament? Was there some kind of social gathering out there by that mine with only one woman and all you men with pistols and guns?"

The prosecution asked that the court should sentence the defendants to life imprisonment for murdering Ethel Price, 57 years for conspiring to kill Ethel Price, and 57 years for conspiring to murder Lory Price. The judge approved the suggestion and duly delivered the sentences, adding that on each anniversary of the Price murders all four men should spend five days in solitary confinement "for the good of your consciences".

There were yet other trials for other crimes to come — all the direct result of the unbridled gangsterism in that part of Illinois. As long after the event as May 1930 one more man was tried and found guilty for his part in the Birger-directed killing of Joe Adams.

Charlie Birger was by no means a greater menace than the Shelton brothers — who played their own discreditable part in bringing an era of almost medieval lawlessness to one small area of Illinois. After a period of continued operations around Williamson the Sheltons moved to East St. Louis. There fate overtook Carl and Bernie Shelton — who died at the hands of gangster rivals.

THE BEDROOM KILLER

He slaughtered whole families while they slept. Sometimes he even lingered at the scene of the crime . . . to gloat. What was it that stimulated Peter Manuel's loathsome appetite for human suffering?

WILLIAM WATT, master-baker, of Burnside, a comfortable suburb of the Scottish city of Glasgow, was looking forward to forgetting about the cares of his chain of bakery shops for a couple of weeks and taking a holiday around Loch Lomond and on to Lochgilphead, 90 miles away, near Argyll. There he proposed to indulge in nothing more taxing than some quiet, contemplative fishing.

On the afternoon of September 9, 1956, he packed his suitcase, fishing gear and black Labrador bitch, Queenie, into his car and gave his 45-year-old wife, Marion, a goodbye kiss. He was a little concerned about Marion. She had suffered for some time from a heart condition, and although a recent operation had brought an improvement in her health, she was still very frail. However, she had agreed that her husband deserved a short break from his business.

During his absence her sister Margaret — Mrs. George Brown — would be staying with her, and the Watts' 16-year-old daughter, Vivienne, would also be at home. There was therefore no question of Mrs. Watt being lonely.

Later that crisp, fall evening Mr. Watt arrived at Lochgilphead's Cairnbaan Hotel and immediately put through a telephone call to his wife to report on his safe journey and inquire if all was well at home. All was indeed well, Mrs. Watt confirmed, and told her husband not to worry about her but to be sure to enjoy his fishing. He promised to do so but said he would still keep in contact by phone.

"COVERED WITH BLOOD!" gasped the daily help, at the horror scene in William Watt's suburban Glasgow home. Dead were (from left) Watt's sister-in-law Margaret, daughter Vivienne, and wife Marion . . . shot in the head at close range.

Life settled down smoothly and peacefully for the next week in the Watts' bungalow home in Burnside's Fennsbank Avenue, and the evening of September 16 was particularly convivial. Marion Watt and her sister were deeply engaged in women's chatter and there was much noisy giggling from the kitchen, where Vivienne and her girl friend were exchanging teenage gossip.

By midnight the household of three was in bed. Some 20 minutes before that Vivienne had seen her friend off from the front door and called out the parting comment, "I'll see you in the morning." Tragically, she was wrong. She would not see her friend again; she would see no one ever again; and when next she, and her mother and her aunt were seen by others all three would be dead.

At 8.45 the following morning Mrs. Helen Collison, the Watts' daily help, arrived at the bungalow and was surprised to find it still locked and the window curtains closed. Mrs. Collison wandered around the house, rapping on window panes and calling Mrs. Watt's name, but there was no reply. Then, when she came to the front door—it was her last point of call since she normally entered through the kitchen door—she began to grow distinctly uneasy.

Struggling for breath

The door had glass panels and one, set just above the lock, had been smashed. Mrs. Collison's natural and immediate instinct was to fear that the house had been burgled. Anxious for help, she went next door to the home of Vivienne's friend, Deanne Valente. With Deanne and her mother, Mrs. Collison returned to the bungalow, and as the three stood around debating what to do, Mr. Peter Collier, the postman, arrived on the scene.

After listening to the women's story, Mr. Collier suggested that they had better explore further. Slipping his hand through the broken glass panel, he opened the door. Mrs. Collison pushed past him and went at once into the first room on the left. In only a second or two she appeared again at the front door, ashen-faced, clutching at the door jamb for support. She was struggling for breath and for speech. Then, as the alarmed little group gaped at her, she gasped: "They are—they are covered with blood!"

Without waiting to question her, the postman hurried into the room. In the half-light, he saw a bed, dark with blood, and in it Mrs. Watt and her sister, Margaret, dead from bullet wounds in the head. Even at a quick glance it was clear to a layman that they had been shot at close range.

Meanwhile, Mrs. Collison, bravely overcoming her own sense of shock, thought at once of Vivienne and went into her room. From the doorway she could see blood on the bedclothes and a covered form lying in the bed. As she made to move towards it, the form gave out a most terrifying noise, clearly heard by the postman out in the hall. It sounded, he said afterwards, like the growling of a large dog, the sort of sound he would have expected from the Watts' Labrador, Queenie. It was, in fact, the final and dreadful death agony of Vivienne Watt.

By soon after 11 a.m. the murder bungalow was swarming with police, who quickly established that the two women and the girl had been killed by bullets from a .38 revolver. In the circumstances it was understandable that senior officers, puzzling over the fact that robbery was apparently not the motive for the killings, since the rest of the house was in good order, should have paid little attention to the fact that there had been a break-in at another bungalow in the same street during the past night.

Dark eyes and oily hair

But an officer sent to investigate, returned with some important information. There were certain characteristics about the newly discovered burglary, he said, that clearly pointed to the handiwork of a local villain who was, by that time, well known to the police. The suspect's name was New York-born Peter Thomas Anthony Manuel, aged 30, whose family had returned from America to Britain in 1932. He was currently on bail awaiting a court hearing on charges of an attempted break-in at a colliery canteen.

He was already "known" for a series of offences that had first begun when he was 12 years old, and which included shop-breaking, housebreaking, various forms of larceny, unlawful wounding, robbery with violence and indecent assault. The police at once hurried around to Manuel's home—where he lived with his parents, and which was only a short distance from Fennsbank Avenue—and searched it. The search was totally unrewarding.

While the policemen went about their work at his home, Manuel, a strongly built man, with dark eyes and oily hair, slicked down, sat and watched them with a faint smirk on his face. His hatred for the police ran deep, and he fancied himself as something of an amateur lawyer who could outwit authority with his cunning mind. He refused completely to account for his movements on the night of the murders or to answer any questions. Frustrated, the police went away.

Questionable beginnings

A few weeks later Peter Manuel was in jail, serving an 18 months' sentence for the colliery break-in, but by that time the Watt murder inquiries had taken a new and dramatic turn. Suspicion had centred on Mr. Watt, the master-baker, and it had done so for a number of curious reasons. One of these reasons was that the police had been in touch with a river Clyde ferry-master who thought he had ferried Mr. Watt, his car and his dog across the river in the early hours of the murder day.

From such questionable beginnings the police had convinced themselves that Mr. Watt had slipped out of his Lochgilphead hotel soon after midnight on September 16, driven the 90 miles back to his home in Burnside, broken in and murdered his wife, daughter and sister-in-law. Then, they suspected, he had raced in his car back to Lochgilphead, had arrived at the hotel in time to eat a large breakfast, and given the impression that he had spent an undisturbed night. On that theory he was held in Glasgow's Barlinnie Prison, where a fellow inmate was Peter Manuel.

On October 8, Mr. Lawrence Dowdall, the lawyer acting for Mr. Watt, received a very odd letter, from Barlinnie Prison:

"Dear Sir," it said, "Last Tuesday, October 2, I was sentenced to 18 months' imprisonment in Hamilton Sheriff Court. To-day I lodged an appeal and decided I should like you to represent me. I wish to obtain bail during the period as an appellant and desire to have this accomplished with all urgency. I would like you to come and see me on Wednesday. The proposals I have outlined are to our mutual advantage, mainly due to the fact that I have some information for you concerning a recently acquired client of yours who has been described as 'an all-round athlete'." The letter was signed "P. Manuel".

A rambling story

Mr. Dowdall kept the appointment, and Manuel told him a lengthy and rambling story—the main points of which were that he knew the man who had committed the Watt murders, and, as confirmation of that, the man had described the inside of the Watts' home in considerable and specific detail. Manuel refused to name the man.

His suspicions aroused, Mr. Dowdall asked why Manuel did not tell his story to the police, but Manuel insisted that he had no intention of co-operating with any policeman. Then, pointedly, Dowdall declared: "Look, Manuel, information such as you have and the suggestion that the man who committed these murders would start and tell you piffling information about the furniture leads me to one conclusion: that you were there." But, instantly, Manuel protested. "Oh, no!" he said. "No, I wasn't there."

On December 3, Mr. William Watt, who had spent 67 gruelling days in prison was freed. The police action had saddled him, as an innocent man, with the lifelong burden of having been accused of killing those closest to him. He had not even had the extra benefit of a trial and a positive acquittal. His innocence would, in due course, be proved beyond all question. For the moment, however, he had to resume his life and bear such gossip as inevitably must circulate.

Precisely a year later to the day of his release, Mr. Watt met Peter Manuel. Having served his own sentence, Manuel had asked Mr. Dowdall to arrange the meeting, and, at whatever painful cost to Mr. Watt, he repeated his tortuous story.

ALL THE MORE NAUSEATING was the matter-of-fact style in which Manuel told the story of his nocturnal prowling, like a man anxious to boast of great feats. A number of young girls out alone at night ended up buried in remote country spots . . .

GLASGOW

MOUNT VERNON
X
ISABELLE COOKE, 16,
MISSING SINCE DEC. 31st.

BAILLIESTON

COATBRIDGE

MOIRA ANDERSON, 11,
VANISHED FEB. 1957.

RUTHERGLEN

CAMBUSLANG

UDDINGSTON

BELLSHILL

FRANCES CASSIDY, 16,
ATTACKED HERE, DEC. 31st.

BLANTYRE

X BURNBANK

ANNE KNEILANDS, 17,
KILLED JAN. 4th. 1956.

EAST KILBRIDE

HAMILTON

Topix, Syndication International

Once again he described the details of the Watt household, as told to him by "the man", and finally Mr. Watt was moved to shout: "Now look, you know far too much about the house not to have been there!" Manuel vehemently denied this.

Immediately after his interview with Mr. Watt, Manuel made a brief excursion out of Scotland and travelled to Newcastle-upon-Tyne, the English industrial city to which he had previously paid an occasional visit in the course of his criminal career. At 4.30 on the morning of December 7, 1957, he appeared at the city's railway station and hired a taxi, owned and driven by 36-year-old Sydney Dunn. It was a dark night of lashing rain and a gale-force wind screaming through the deserted streets.

The following day, a police constable, cycling along a lonely moorland road near Edmundbyers, 20 miles from Newcastle, saw an abandoned car in a roadside gully. There was what appeared to the con-

stable to be blood on the steering wheel, but no sign of any driver or passengers.

Accordingly the policeman cycled to summon assistance. He returned with colleagues, and 140 yards from the car they found the body of the owner, taximan Sydney Dunn. He had been shot and killed with a .38 bullet, and his throat had been gashed. Nearby was Dunn's wallet containing £5 in notes.

The story of mysterious deaths and disappearances continued. On December 28, 17-year-old Isabelle Cooke set off from her home in the Glasgow suburb of North Mount Vernon to meet her boy friend and go with him to a dance at nearby Uddingston. The boy friend waited at the bus stop where they had arranged to meet, but she did not turn up; and when, by nine o'clock the following morning, she had not returned home her father reported to the police that he feared she was missing.

That day, and the next, various possessions, including panties, an underslip,

a cosmetics bag and a raincoat, were found by police scattered around the area. One by one these pathetically mute witnesses to disaster were shown to Mr. and Mrs. Cooke, who identified them as belonging to their daughter. But of Isabelle herself there was no trace.

In a bungalow in Uddingston, the venue of the dance to which Isabelle should have gone, lived 45-year-old Peter Smart, Glasgow manager of a firm of civil engineering contractors, with his wife, Doris, and their 10-year-old son, Michael. On New Year's Eve, 1957, they had avoided the usually boisterous celebrations of the famous festival that Scots call Hogmanay, not because they were unsociable, but simply because they had planned to drive the 70 miles to Ancrum, near Jedburgh, the home of Mrs. Smart's parents.

At 1.30 a.m., neighbours completing the rounds of first-footing, that Scottish custom of friends and relatives calling upon each other to wish good luck for the newly arrived year, noticed that the Smarts' lights had been extinguished and the family had obviously retired to bed, ready for their early New Year's morning start.

Everyone might have assumed that the Smarts had left for their visiting. However, in the days immediately following their neighbours began to notice strange things about the family's bungalow. It seemed that, at one moment, window curtains were closed and, at the next, were open again. Gradually a sense of unease spread among the adjoining homes. It was intensified at around 5.45 on the morning of January 4, when two local residents, a Mr. and Mrs. John McMunn, awoke in time to see a leering face peering around their bedroom door.

With great presence of mind Mr. McMunn cried out: "Who is it? Where's the gun?" Mrs. McMunn, astutely accepting her cue, answered, "Here it is", at which the intruder fled. When the McMunn story was heard, thoughts turned again to the mysterious movements of the window curtains at the Smart home.

When Mr. Smart failed to return to his work on January 6, and his car was found abandoned in a Glasgow street, the police were alerted and a sergeant and a constable were sent to the bungalow. The sergeant forced open the back door and began a cautious exploration of the house.

The sergeant went first to the main bedroom and, since the curtains there were drawn, even though it was eleven in the morning, he switched on the light. The scene that met his eyes was barbarous and sickening. Beneath their heavily blood-soaked bedclothes Mr. and Mrs. Smart lay dead from gunshot wounds. The officer turned at once to the smaller bedroom, fearful of what he would find there and shaken when his fears were justified. Young Michael lay between his covers, the tell-tale gore around him, also destroyed by shooting.

By this time fear was spreading through the suburban fringes of Glasgow. It seemed that anyone might fall victim to the rash of apparently senseless killings, and the police were baffled by the absence of any clearly discernible motives. But then events began to assume their final, decisive shape.

Information reached senior officers that the usually hard-up Peter Manuel had been seen in bars spending money with surprising abandon. Fortunately, some of the notes he had used were recovered and proved to be part of a newly printed batch. The bank had the serial numbers and reported that one group of notes, in number sequence, had been paid over to Mr. Smart when he cashed a cheque for holiday spending money.

Moving swiftly now, the police swooped upon Manuel and put him into an identification parade. Witnesses from the bar, where he had placed lavish orders, were able to testify that he had tendered crisp new blue Commercial Bank of Scotland notes. Some of these notes had not yet been passed on from the bar, and their serial numbers tallied with the sequence handed over by the bank to Mr. Smart.

Peter Manuel was cornered. On January 13, 1958, he was arrested and, for his own dark reasons, was ready to let his tongue wag. From that tongue came not merely an admission of the Smart family murders, but a confession of the killing of the Watts and Isabelle Cooke, and also of a 17-year-old girl named Anne Knielands – whose body with its brutally smashed skull had been found near the fifth fairway of the golf course at East Kilbride, another Glasgow suburb. The area in which all these people had died was within Manuel's home territory.

There was still the case of the Newcastle taximan, Sydney Dunn, and although Manuel did not include his murder in the confession, there was no doubt in the minds of the authorities that he was the killer. A jury, concluding its hearings after his arrest, cited him as responsible.

All the vicious details

Like a man anxious to boast of great feats which had satisfactorily baffled authority, Manuel poured out the details of his vicious crimes. Much of his narrative was made all the more nauseating by the matter-of-fact style in which he dictated it to the police. Of the heart-rending end of the Watt family, he said:

"There were two people in the bed. I went into the other room and there was a girl in the bed. She woke up and sat up. I hit her on the chin and knocked her out. I tied her hands and went back into the other room. I shot the two people in this room and then heard someone making a noise in the other room. I went back in and the girl had got loose. We struggled around for a while and then I flung her on the bed and shot her, too."

He recounted the end of poor, young Isabelle Cooke, who had left her home with such happy expectations of a pleasant evening at a local dance:

"I met the girl walking . . . When we got near the dog track she started to scream. I tore off her clothes and tied something round her neck and choked her. I then carried her up a lane into a field and dug a hole with a shovel. While I was digging a man passed along the lane on a bike. So I carried her again over a path beside a brick works into another field. I dug a hole next to a part of a field that was ploughed and put her into it."

Even though that murder, like the others, had taken place under the shroud of night, Manuel took the police unerringly to the burial spot. The officers were astonished at his total lack of sensitivity as, leading them across the ploughed field, he stopped suddenly and said, with the air of a craftsman who knows what he is about: "This is it! This is the place. In fact, I think I'm standing on her now." The police dug and, indeed, he was right.

Peter Manuel had confessed to killing eight people. At his trial he was found guilty of killing seven since, on the judge's direction, he was acquitted of Anne Knielands' murder for lack of the corroboration

A SICKENING SCENE met the eyes of police at the Uddingston bungalow (below) where the Smart family died at the hands of Peter Manuel (leaving trial, right).

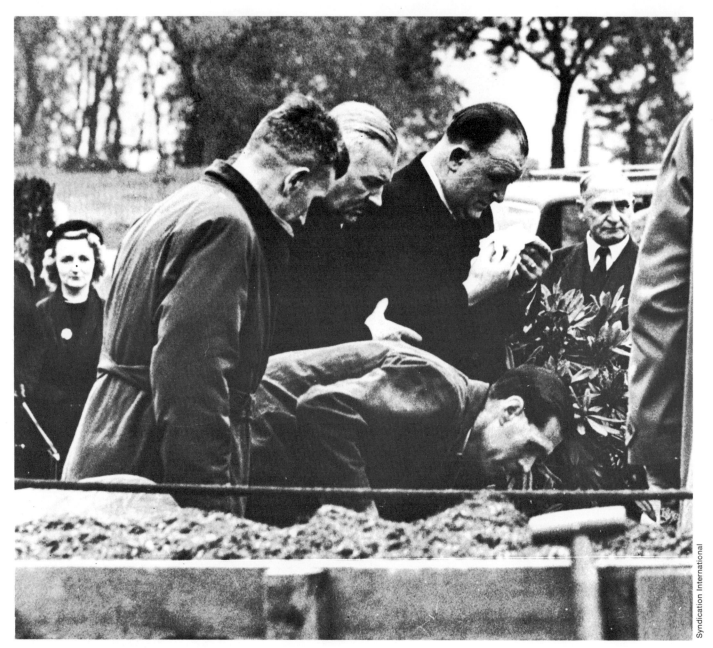

of his confession required by Scottish law. He was not tried for the murder of Sydney Dunn, the taximan, for that had been committed outside the jurisdiction of Scotland. But there is no possible doubt at all that this mass murderer took the lives of nine people.

No one could positively decide what stimulated his loathsome appetite for inflicting so much human suffering. But it seemed likely that, somehow, he gained some dark, partly sexual satisfaction from selecting innocent victims at random and destroying them in their moment of most complete defencelessness.

The mysterious movements of the window curtains at the Smart home quite certainly indicated that Manuel had returned to the house several times after the killings, no doubt to gloat over the gratifying sight of the slaughtered family.

Undoubtedly the two luckiest people were Mr. and Mrs. McMunn, who had awoken to find an intruder in their bedroom and scared him away by their quick thinking—for that intruder was Manuel.

Afterwards it was seen that there had been many earlier, ominously portending moments in Manuel's criminal life, including a night when he had struck down and raped a young housewife while her three-year-old daughter looked on.

If he was mad, it was not a form of madness such as would spare him in the eyes of the law. His trial judge, Lord Cameron, commented: "A man may be very bad without being mad." And since Manuel conducted his own defence with remarkable wiliness, there was evidence of a mind that could be coldly rational when its possessor's survival was in danger.

On July 11, 1958, Peter Thomas

A TRAGIC OCCASION—William Watt (pictured holding handkerchief) at the funeral of his wife, daughter and sister-in-law. He was held for 67 gruelling days in prison on a mere shred of evidence.

Anthony Manuel—named after some of the great saints—met the end to which he had so mercilessly brought others. However, he was shown greater compassion than his victims had received, for he was allowed to hear Mass and take Holy Communion.

When the hangman entered his cell in Barlinnie Prison, he asked simply if the time had come. Told that it had, he muttered that he was ready. In the areas around Burnside, where the mass murderer had stalked, there was overwhelming relief that he had "talked" his way to the gallows.

THE SOFT-SOAP SLAYER

When Mary Ann Cotton was arrested on a
charge of poisoning her stepson, it looked like an ordinary
cut-and-dried case of murder—until the true facts began to emerge . . .

so many people wanted to be at the trial that admission was by ticket only. Even then the demand was so great that special arrangements were made for the gentry of the county and their womenfolk to sit on the bench alongside the judge. On the surface, the case did not seem to warrant so much excitement.

Mary Ann Cotton, a 40-year-old widow, had been committed for trial on a charge of murdering her seven-year-old stepson, Charles Edward Cotton, with arsenic. She had acted, it was alleged, from two motives. There was about £8 to come from the Prudential Insurance Company on the boy's death. Charles Edward was also an impediment to her marriage to an Excise Officer named Quick-Manning, by whom she was already pregnant.

But everyone in the packed Durham Assizes courtroom in the north of England knew that the charge was just the tip of the iceberg. They had read the black headlines in the local newspaper, THE GREAT POISONING CASE AT WEST AUCKLAND — HORRIBLE REVELATIONS, and the story that went with them.

The story, written at a time, the 1870s, when British newspapers were not inhibited by the strict modern libel and contempt of court laws, alleged that Mary Ann might be the greatest mass murderer in the history of British crime.

Soap mixture

Nobody could be certain then, and nobody is certain now, exactly how many people died at her hand. But the candidates include her own mother; two of her three husbands; one bigamous husband; 10 of her 12 children; five other children; one lover; and one of her best friends.

The entire courtroom craned forward for a closer look as the warders escorted her into the dock a few minutes before ten o'clock on the morning of Wednesday, March 5, 1873. She had fine eyes, but she looked pale under her black bonnet, worn with a long black dress and black-and-white shawl.

Despite the setting up of a defence fund, she had not had enough money to pay the full fees of an advocate to represent her. Two days earlier the judge had asked Thomas Campbell Foster, a Leeds lawyer, to act on her behalf. Now she chatted with him for a moment before taking the seat provided for her in the dock. When the charge was read, she rose to plead in a firm, but quiet, voice: "Not guilty."

Charles Russell, Q.C. — later to be known as the greatest advocate of his time, to be appointed Lord Chief Justice and raised to the peerage — opened the case for the prosecution. The basis of his argument was that Mary Ann — who had once been a nurse at nearby Sunderland

Mary Evans

PROSECUTION COUNSEL was Sir Charles Russell (above), one of the great British advocates. Opposite: Mary Ann Cotton's last house in West Auckland.

Infirmary and was therefore familiar with poisons — had murdered her stepson with arsenic because "she was badly off and Charles Edward was a tie and burden to her". Then came the witnesses to relate the events which preceded the child's death on July 12, 1872, and Mary Ann's arrest six days later.

Mary Ann Dodds, a former neighbour, told the court how she had gone to a chemist's in West Auckland — the village where the prisoner lived — the previous May to buy a mixture of soft soap and arsenic. "The mixture," said Mrs. Dodds, "was needed to remove bugs from a bed in Mary Ann's home. I rubbed most of it into the joints of the bed and the iron crosspieces underneath." John Townend, the chemist who sold the mixture, explained that it would contain somewhere between half-an-ounce to an ounce (240-480 grains) of arsenic. Three grains,

according to medical evidence, would be enough to kill an adult. Townend also made the point that his was not the nearest chemist's shop to Mary Ann's three-roomed stone cottage at 13 Front Street.

One of the key witnesses was Thomas Riley, a public relief official. He described how, on July 6 — six days before he was to die — Mary Ann had asked if a place could be found for her stepson in a workhouse. "It is hard to keep him when he is not my own," she explained, "and he is stopping me from taking in a respectable lodger." Riley had asked jokingly if the lodger might be the Excise Officer the village gossips said she was going to marry.

Pauper's grave

"It might be so," said Mary Ann, "but the boy is in the way." The following Friday, about 6 a.m., he was passing Mary Ann's house when he saw her standing at the door, looking upset. He went over to her. "My boy's dead," she told him.

"I was immediately suspicious," said

265

Riley. "The boy had seemed a perfectly healthy little chap when I saw him only six days earlier. I went straight to see the police and Dr. Kilburn, the village doctor." Dr. Kilburn, too, was surprised to hear of Charles Edward's death, although the boy had been ill—with gastro-enteritis, he thought—since the previous Sunday. His assistant, Dr. Chalmers, had called three times during the week, and Dr. Kilburn himself had seen the child twice only the previous day.

"In the circumstances," he said, "I decided to withhold a death certificate and asked for permission to carry out a post-mortem examination." The coroner, on hearing that the doctor had refused to issue a death certificate, ordered an inquest to be held the following afternoon in the Rose and Crown public house, next door to Mary Ann's home.

The pressures of caring for the living prevented the two doctors from starting their post-mortem—on Mary Ann's kitchen table—until an hour before the time fixed for the start of the inquest. As a result, Dr. Kilburn, the chief witness, was ill-prepared when the time came for him to give evidence. He was forced to admit: "I have found nothing to suggest poisoning. Death could have been from natural causes, possibly gastro-enteritis." His words left the jury with no choice but to return a verdict of natural death.

Charles Edward was buried in a pauper's grave. But Dr. Kilburn was not yet finished with his tests. He had bottled

PHYSICALLY she was attractive enough to acquire a new husband whenever she needed one . . . Right: the pharmacy where Mrs. Dodds bought the arsenic and soap.

George Backhouse

contents of the boy's stomach, and the following Wednesday he subjected them for the first time to a proper chemical examination. "I found distinct traces of arsenic," he told the court, "and went to the police at once." The next day Mary Ann was arrested and charged with her stepson's murder. The boy's coffin was dug up, and examination by Dr. Thomas Scattergood, lecturer in forensic medicine and toxicology at Leeds School of Medicine, disclosed arsenic in the stomach, bowels, liver, lungs, heart and kidneys.

It was not merely the suddenness of the little boy's death that had aroused Riley's suspicions. Four other people close to Mary Ann had died in similar circumstances in the two years since she had come to Johnson Terrace, West Auckland.

The Cotton household consisted of Mary Ann; her bigamous husband, coal miner Frederick Cotton (her third husband, a Sunderland shipwright named James Robinson, was still alive); Cotton's two children by a previous marriage, Frederick and Charles Edward; and Robert, her baby by Cotton. Her "husband" was the first to die, on September 19, 1871, two days after their first "wedding" anniversary. He was 39 and had

been suffering from severe stomach pains. The doctor certified the cause of death as gastric fever.

Mary Ann spent a quiet winter, but after becoming the mistress of Quick-Manning—the Excise Officer who lived nearby and called her in to nurse him through a bout of smallpox—she wasted no time when she resumed her murderous career in the spring.

Her next three killings, designed to clear the way for marriage, took place in the space of three weeks. Cotton's son Frederick, aged 10, died on March 10, 1872; her son Robert, aged 14 months, died on March 27; and an old lover, Joseph Nattrass, who had moved in with her again, died on April 1. Gastric fever and, in the case of the baby, teething convulsions were given as the causes of death.

Green wallpaper
One of the most contentious aspects of the trial—long to be argued about in legal circles afterwards—was whether evidence should be allowed about these earlier deaths when, at this particular time, Mary Ann was merely being tried for the murder of Charles Edward.

In the weeks after Mary Ann's arrest,

the bodies of three more of her victims—Joseph Nattrass, 10-year-old Frederick Cotton, and her baby Robert—had been dug up and examined by Dr. Scattergood. In each case he had found evidence of arsenic poisoning. In a letter to the Home Office about Nattrass he wrote:

"There is no doubt that Nattrass was poisoned by arsenic. I find there is a considerable quantity in the stomach and bowels, between four and five grains of it being still in the state of undissolved powder. Arsenic is in all the viscera."

Campbell Foster—whose main line of defence had been that some green floral wallpaper, heavily impregnated with arsenic, was the accidental source of the poison which killed Charles Edward—argued that to allow evidence about the earlier deaths would prejudice a fair trial. The judge, Sir Thomas Archibald, ruled against him, however, relying chiefly on the case of the Queen v Geering.

That case had been heard at Lewes, Sussex, in 1849. Mary Ann Geering was charged with poisoning her husband with arsenic, and in order to prove that death was not accidental, evidence was admitted that she had subsequently poisoned her three sons, two of whom died.

From that point the outcome of the case was virtually a foregone conclusion. Campbell Foster did not call any witnesses on her behalf, and, after retiring at 5.50 p.m. on the third day of the trial, the jury took only an hour to bring in a verdict of guilty. Said the judge, donning his black cap: "Mary Ann Cotton, you have been convicted, after a careful and patient trial, of the awful crime of murder . . .

Indelible record
"You seem to have given way to that most awful of all delusions, which sometimes takes possession of persons wanting in proper moral and religious sense, that you could carry out your wicked designs without detection. But, while murder by poison is the most detestable of all crimes, and one at which human nature shudders, it is one the nature of which, in the order of God's providence, always leaves behind it complete and incontestable traces of guilt. Poisoning, as it were, in the very act of crime writes an indelible record of guilt.

"In these last words I shall address to you, I would earnestly urge you to seek for your soul that only refuge which is left for you, in the mercy of God through the atonement of our Lord, Jesus Christ. It only remains for me to pass upon you the sentence of the law . . ."

A MERE FORMALITY . . . The Home Secretary is duly informed of the impending execution (right). Mary was arrested by the local sergeant (left).

14514

To County Gaol. Durham
7th March 1873

Sir,

I beg to inform you that at
the Assizes holden in Durham
on Friday the 7th day of March
1873. Mary Ann Cotton was
Convicted of Wilful Murder and
sentenced to be hanged. Consequently
in accordance with the Rules laid
down in your Order dated 13th
August 1868. Mary Ann Cotton
will be executed on Monday the
24th Inst. at 8 o'clock Am.

I have the honor to be,
Sir.

The Right Hon. H. A. Bruce   Your Most Obedt Servant
Secretary of State   Armstrong
Home Department   Lt Colonel
Whitehall   Governor
London

Mary Ann paled as she heard the words of the death sentence. Then, semi-conscious, she was half-carried out of the dock and taken to Durham County Gaol to await her execution 17 days later. Meantime, the newspapers had pieced together the bizarre story of a woman — supposedly kindly and good-natured — who spread death wherever she went.

She was born Mary Ann Robson in the Durham, pit village of Low Moorsley in 1832, daughter of a pitman still in his teens, and brought up as a devout Methodist. At the age of 20 she married a labourer named William Mowbray, and, shortly afterwards, they moved to Devon. There four of the five children born to them died. They returned to the north-east, where she constantly changed addresses — South Hetton, Hendon, Sunderland, Pallion, Seaham, Monkwearmouth, North Walbottle and, finally, West Auckland. She and Mowbray had three more children. They died. Mowbray himself died.

Mary Ann married again. Her new husband was George Ward, a Sunderland engineer. In October, 1866, 14 months after the wedding, he died. A month later, Mary Ann moved in as housekeeper to James Robinson, a widower and shipwright, and quickly found herself pregnant by him. He was to become her third husband.

Meantime, within weeks of Mary Ann moving in as housekeeper, Robinson's 10-month-old son John had died. Worse was yet to come. Within the space of 12 days in the spring of 1867, three more children in the Robinson household died — Robinson's son James, aged six, on April 21; Robinson's daughter Elizabeth, aged eight, on April 26; and, on May 2, Mary Ann's daughter Isabella, aged nine, the only survivor of her marriage to Mowbray.

Conventional dosage

Incredibly enough, the catalogue of death did not stop there. Mary Ann went to visit her 54-year-old mother, fearing, she said, that this apparently healthy woman "might be about to die". Nine days later she did — and Mary Ann promptly departed with clothing and bed linen. Mary Ann then made a friend, Margaret Cotton, who introduced her to her brother, Frederick, later to be one of the West Auckland victims. When Mary Ann, finding herself pregnant yet again, decided to become Frederick's bigamous wife, she saw Margaret as an impediment. Margaret also had £60, a sizeable sum in those days, in the bank. She died.

Altogether, Mary Ann bore 12 children of her own. Only two survived her. One was a second daughter — the first died within days of birth — born of her marriage to Robinson: Mary Ann had given her to

AN UNREMARKABLE WOMAN . . . and yet she has gone down in history as Britain's greatest mass murderer. Her motives remain a mystery to all.

a friend to care for when the marriage broke up. The second child to live was Quick-Manning's daughter, born in Durham Gaol and named Margaret Edith Quick-Manning Cotton. Robinson himself is believed to have escaped the conventional dosage of arsenic in his soup and tea because, despite Mary Ann's entreaties, he refused to have his life insured.

In all, 21 people close to Mary Ann met their death in less than 20 years. How many of them did she actually murder? The number is usually put at 14 or 15. Records don't show, for instance, exactly how the children who died in Devon met their end. In nearly all the other cases the death certificate gave the cause as "gastric fever". It was a common ailment in an unsanitary age, with symptoms similar to those caused by arsenic poisoning.

Her motive was to collect insurance or burial money, or to clear the way for marriage with someone new who did not want to be burdened with other men's children, or sometimes a combination of both. A number of factors helped her to escape detection for so long — the state of medical knowledge, the ease with which arsenic could be bought, the trust she created by once having been a nurse, the fact that she always called in a doctor to care for her victims, the regularity with which she moved homes.

The medical profession of the time should not be blamed too harshly for the fact it was only when she over-reached herself in West Auckland that the truth was finally suspected. Even as late as 1939 a survey in the neighbouring city of

Newcastle-upon-Tyne showed that a third of the certified causes of death were wrong, and faulty diagnoses are still far from unknown today.

The morning after the sentence, the *Newcastle Journal* described Mary Ann, somewhat predictably, as "a monster in human shape" and commented: "Murder grew with her. Perhaps the most astounding thought of all is that a woman could act thus without becoming horrible and repulsive. Mary Ann Cotton, on the contrary, seems to have possessed the faculty of getting a new husband whenever she wanted one. To her other children and her lodger, even when she was deliberately poisoning them, she is said to have maintained a rather kindly manner. We feel instinctively that the earth ought to be rid of her. Pity cannot be withheld, but it must be mingled with horror . . ."

Nevertheless, there were feelings of unrest about her death sentence on several grounds — the hanging of a woman, the haphazard way counsel for the defence had been appointed, the admission of evidence of deaths other than the one she was being tried for, the fact that no witnesses for the defence had been called. In prison, Mary Ann busied herself trying to obtain support for a petition for her reprieve. She also arranged for Margaret, her new baby daughter, to be cared for by a married couple who had been unable to have children of their own.

Variety tour

The Home Secretary refused all pleas that her sentence should be commuted to life imprisonment. Five days before her execution, Mary Ann's baby was forcibly taken from her. Then, on Monday, March 24, 1873, maintaining her innocence to the end, she finally went to the scaffold. She was a long time — three minutes — in dying.

She was by then already a legend. What was described as "a great moral drama", *The Life And Death Of Mary Ann Cotton*, was in rehearsal for a variety tour which started eight days later. Mothers of children who would not go to sleep or eat their cabbage threatened them with the spectre of "the monster in human shape".

In the streets the children themselves chanted a rhyme which began:
Mary Ann Cotton,
She's dead and she's rotten.
She lies in her bed
With her eyes wide open.
Sing, sing, oh, what can I sing?
Mary Ann Cotton is tied up with string.

The memories of her dark deeds faded with the years, however. It was not until 1973, a century after they hanged her, that she became the subject of a full-length book, *Mary Ann Cotton: Her Story And Trial*, by the north-country writer Arthur Appleton.

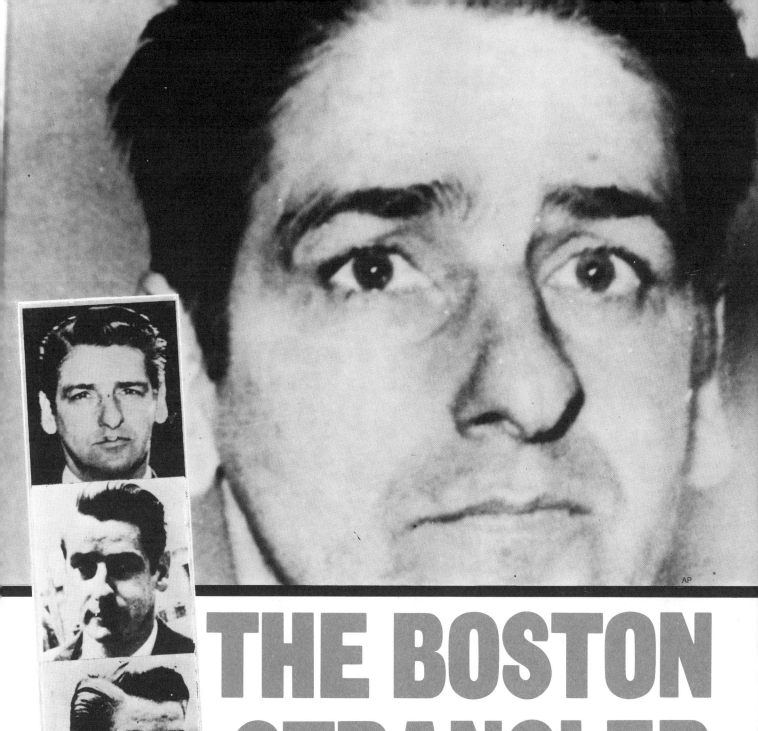

AP

THE BOSTON STRANGLER

The women of the city—and their men—wallowed in fear as police sought a sadistic, perverted killer. What drove this mild-mannered, happily married man to perpetrate one sexual atrocity after another? Unfortunately the answer was to die with him. . . .

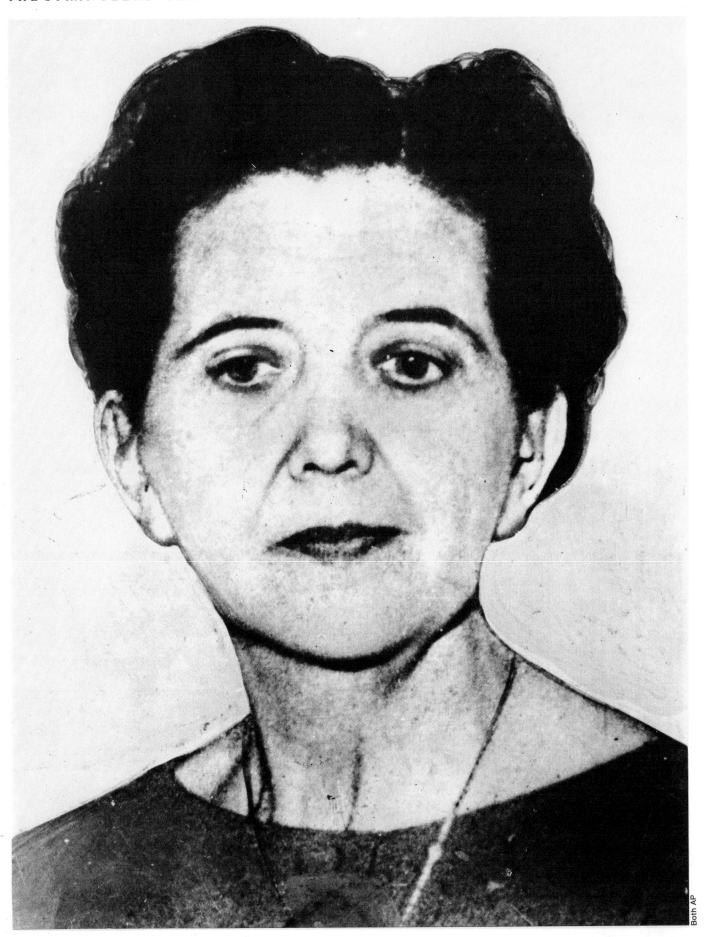

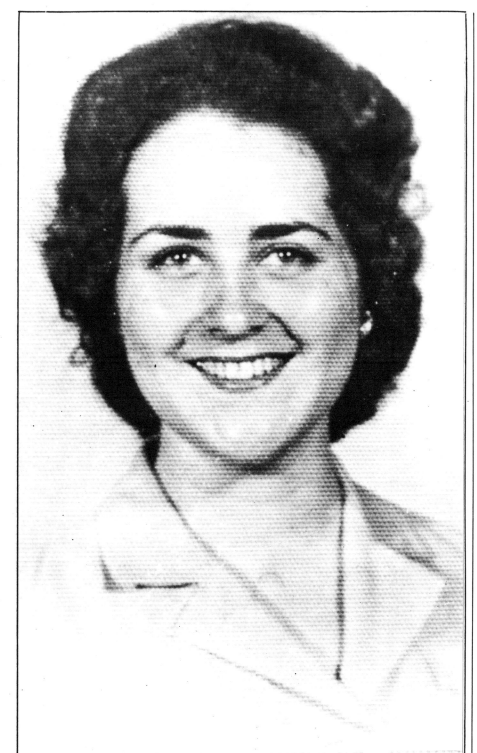

JUST before eight o'clock on the evening of June 14, 1962, 25-year-old Juris Slesers, a bespectacled research engineer with the Massachusetts Institute of Technology, climbed the three flights of stairs to his mother's apartment at 77, Gainsborough Street, in the Back Bay district of Boston.

He was anxious to be on time to drive his 55-year-old mother, Mrs. Anna Slesers, to a service at the nearby Latvian Church. Mrs. Slesers, divorced 20 years earlier, was herself a Latvian who had fled from the Soviet occupation of her country.

Juris knocked at the door and waited. From inside the small apartment there was no sound of movement. He knocked again, and when there was still no response, he hammered on the door. He was rapidly becoming anxious.

It seemed strange that she should either be sleeping or have gone out when she was expecting him to call. In the end Juris decided that he could wait no longer. Summoning his full strength, he took a short run at the door and burst it open.

All was dark inside the apartment, and Juris walked into a chair which—in a manner alien to his mother's usual tidiness—had been left in the middle of the narrow hallway. He looked first into the living-room and then the bedroom. Finding no sign of his mother, he returned to the hallway and strode through it towards the kitchen and bathroom.

Clumsily shaped bow

His mother was there, between those two rooms, lying on her back, her blue housecoat flung open and revealing her total nakedness and her legs spread wide. A blue cord, belonging to the housecoat, was knotted tightly around her neck and fastened beneath her chin in a clumsily shaped bow. Juris could see at a glance that she was dead. He stared around wildly for a moment, taking in the fact that the bath was half full of water, and that rubbish from a wastebin had been spread on the kitchen floor. Then he called the police.

Within minutes detectives and a doctor were at the apartment—but there was not much for them to go on. Apart from the strewing of the contents of the wastebin there were a few other signs of disturbance—drawers had been opened and rummaged through. But there was no evidence of a serious attempt at robbery. Mrs. Slesers had been sexually assaulted, and the officers' initial conclusion was that an intruder had somehow entered the apartment intent upon committing a

A DIVORCEE, Anna Slesers (far left), was his first victim; only six months later the wire services were reporting the Strangler's eighth.

robbery. However, finding a scantily dressed woman who looked much younger than her years, he had been overcome by sexual desire. The intruder had then strangled the woman merely, perhaps, to ensure her silence.

No other leads presented themselves, and the death of Mrs. Slesers was listed, for the time being, as another unsolved murder. But then, on Saturday, June 30, there occurred another series of events that started a new line of police action. Mrs. Nina Nichols, a 68-year-old widow, returned to her apartment on Boston's Commonwealth Avenue after a three-day visit to out-of-town friends. She immediately telephoned her sister, Mrs. Marguerite Steadman, at whose house she was due for dinner within an hour.

The two women chatted for a few minutes, Mrs. Nichols assuring her sister that she would be on time for the meal. Suddenly she broke off the conversation, saying: "Excuse me, Marguerite, there's my door buzzer. I'll call you right back." She did not do so, the dinner hour of six o'clock passed, and Mrs. Nichols failed to arrive at the Steadmans' home.

Two nylon stockings

By 7.30 Mr. Steadman, concerned at his wife's anxiety, rang the janitor at the Commonwealth Avenue apartment building and asked him if Mrs. Nichols had left. No, the janitor said, her car was still parked by the building. At Mr. Steadman's request, he agreed to go up to the apartment and investigate.

Receiving no answer to his knock, the janitor let himself in with his pass-key. He saw at once, from the clothes and other items strewn around the floor, that the apartment had been ransacked. Then, as he looked towards the open bedroom door, he saw the naked body of Mrs. Nichols lying near the bed. Her housecoat had been pulled up above her waist and two nylon stockings had been tied very tightly around her neck.

Even in the few fearful moments in which he stared at the horrifying sight the janitor could see that the end of the stockings had been drawn together in the shape of a crude bow.

It was this strangely brutal "trademark" that immediately made the police associate this killing with that of Mrs. Slesers—and there were other similarities. Like Mrs. Slesers, Mrs. Nichols had been sexually assaulted; when detectives carefully searched the apartment they found that, although its contents had been disturbed, nothing of value had been taken.

Among several easily-disposable items

BOASTFULNESS and contrition mingled in DeSalvo's attitude. The psychiatrists would call him a "completely uncontrolled" schizophrenic.

of value left untouched was a $300 camera. The inference appeared to be that the killer had wanted only to give the *impression* that the motive was robbery —while his real intention was murder-with-sex. The man whom they must seek, the police concluded, was not a thief but someone distinctly more frightening—a sex maniac.

But the pattern was arranging itself even more swiftly and alarmingly than the police yet realized. Two days later, on Monday, July 2, two elderly women living in an apartment house in Lynn, Massachusetts, north of Boston, reported that their neighbour, 65-year-old Helen Blake, had not been seen since the previous Saturday. They had opened Miss Blake's apartment door with a pass-key, they told the police, but on noticing signs of disorder they had been too afraid to look further.

Detectives went at once to the apartment and found Helen Blake lying face downwards on her bed, dead. Her pajama top had been pushed up to her shoulders, leaving her, otherwise, completely naked. She had been sexually attacked and strangled with a nylon stocking. Apparently after death, her brassiere had been bound around her neck. The brassiere straps had been knotted under her chin in the form of a large bow.

There was now no doubt in detectives' minds that they were facing a crisis. Boston Police Commissioner McNamara ordered the cancellation of all police leave, and circulated a warning to women —especially those living alone—to lock their doors, admit no strangers, and report any prowlers. All listed sex offenders in and around Boston were picked up for questioning. Discreet inquiries were made about patients who had been discharged from nearby mental institutions.

Revoltingly obscene

But, as hard as they worked, the police could find no direct clue to the killer. More than a month passed without a report of another similar murder. There were some in Boston who began to hope that the death plague had passed. Then, on August 21, a widow of 75, named Ida Irga, was found strangled in her apartment in Boston's West End. A pillow case was tied bitingly deep around her neck, and she, too, had been the victim of sexual assault.

In her case, however, the murderer had added some appalling touches to his handiwork. He had placed two chairs widely apart and tied a leg of the body to each chair. The result was that the first person to open the apartment door—and that happened to be the 13-year-old son of the building's caretaker—would be confronted with a revoltingly obscene sight.

What baffled the police more than

anything else was that in all these cases the murderer seemed to have been willingly admitted to the victims' homes. There was no evidence of break-ins, therefore the murderer must have adopted a plausible play-acting role that would secure him entrance.

Perhaps he passed himself off as a gas or electricity employee? Perhaps, indeed, he *was* such an employee whose mind had given way? The questions were endless, the answers few. And the shadowy figure—who had by now become known as The Boston Strangler—continued to be received into women's homes and to kill them.

More women were to die at the Strangler's hands between August 1962 and January 1964—until the final total was 13. Four of the prey were in their twenties; the youngest was 19 and the eldest 85. One victim, 23-year-old Joann Graff, was strangled on November 23, 1963, with her nylon stockings left knotted in a bow. This at a time when she, like the rest of America, was stunned by the shock of the previous day's assassination of President John F. Kennedy.

There were suspects who were interrogated, and there were men who, for a variety of reasons, "confessed" to being the Strangler. But when the murders ceased in January 1964 it seemed that

the real killer might never be traced. Then, on October 27, 1964, a report to the police from a young housewife in Cambridge, Massachusetts, dramatically changed the situation.

She said that at 9.30 a.m. she was dozing in bed, after seeing her teacher-husband off to work, when a man suddenly appeared at the door. He was of medium build, dressed in green slacks, and with his eyes shrouded by large green sunglasses. As the young wife gave a startled gasp he said: "Don't worry, I'm a detective," and came slowly towards her. "You leave this room at once!" the girl shouted. But the man leapt forward, pinned her to the bed and waved a knife in front of her eyes. "Not a sound or I'll kill you," he commanded.

Kissed and fondled

Swiftly, he gagged her with her underwear. He tied her to the bed, spread-eagled, with her ankles to the foot of the bedstead, her wrists to its head, and then kissed and fondled her body. She lay writhing and petrified until, to her unbelieving relief, he abruptly ceased and loosened her bonds sufficiently for her to slip from them.

Rising from the bed, he ordered: "You be quiet for ten minutes." Then, in what seemed like an embarrassed after-

Death to

John Harrison

NEW YORK Monday

ALBERT De Salvo, the self - confessed Boston Strangler, was found murdered in his locked prison cell today.

The mystery killing set police quizzing prisoners.

For guards discovered "16 surgical-type punctures" in ⁻nd around his heart, made a weapon like

PRISON RIDDLE A[
BOSTON LADY-KIL[
IS STABBED IN CE[

claimed to have killed 13 women in an 18-month wave of terror was found in a routine morning roll call.

At 10 p.m. last night, a guard locked the self-styled Beast of Boston in his cell after looking in to see De Salvo lying face up on his bed.

Today his body wa⁻ lying face ⁻⁻⁻⁻

stabbed over an blanket.'

De Sa[twice a[with se police sa One

the Strangler

began making because he had so much time on his hands.

They sold in the prison gift shop for £3 to £8. Immediately after his death, visitors to the jail rushed to snap them up.

De Salvo was once involved in drug trafficking in the prison, but there was no information yet to link this with his death.

Walpole State Jail in Massachusetts is one of the toughest in the U.S. There have been riots and a dozen murders in the past year.

Geoage Nasser, De Salvo's friend and former cellmate, was jailed for two vicious killings.

But the Strangler himself was serving a life sentence for armed robbery and sex offences.
... he confessed to ... men in the early ... tried for ... nce.

ER
ER

a then turned him vered him with the

had been beaten up he recently argued al other inmates,

ory is that the lied because other trying to cut his lucrative

THE BEST EPITAPH for DeSalvo came from F. Lee Bailey, his attorney: a "vegetable walking around in a human body".

thought, he added: "I'm sorry." The next instant he fled from the bedroom and the apartment.

The moment she was free, the girl frantically rang the police. When the detectives arrived she gave them so detailed a description of the intruder that, from it, a police artist made a meticulously accurate sketch. One detective recognized the sketched face immediately. "This," he said, "looks like the Measuring Man", and went straight to offenders' records.

In the records was a full account of the Measuring Man—who, in 1960, had assaulted women by calling upon them, posing as an artist's agent, and taking their personal measurements as a prelude to supposed employment as models. The intimacies he sought in using his tape measure led to his arrest and 11 months in jail. He had been released in April 1962; his name was Albert H. DeSalvo.

The police telephoned maintenance man DeSalvo, invited him to talk to them, and on November 3 he presented himself at police headquarters in Cambridge. He vehemently denied attacking the young housewife. But she, watching

Picture by Mark Sennet

De Salvo—13 women died at his hands

through a window of the interrogation room, identified him instantly. To the police it appeared to be no more than a routine matter—although, as a precaution, DeSalvo's photograph was teletyped to neighbouring states. The response was astonishing.

From surrounding police forces there poured in messages saying that the photograph had been identified by scores of women as that of a man who had sexually assaulted them. To many detectives he was known as the "Green Man" because so many women had described

their assailant as wearing green slacks.

When DeSalvo's 30-year-old wife later visited her husband at police headquarters, detectives felt that she suspected him of extreme forms of sexual indulgence. She urged him: "Al, tell them everything; don't hold anything back."

"I've committed more than four hundred breaks, all in this area, and there's a couple of rapes you don't know about," he said, in tones that suggested a mixture of contrition and boastfulness. He pointed out Cambridge apartments to police which he had entered by using a small strip of polyethylene to slip the locks.

277

DeSalvo, held and awaiting trial on "Green Man" rape charges, was sent to the Boston State Hospital at Bridgewater for observation. There he was found to be "potentially suicidal and quite clearly overtly schizophrenic", and not competent to stand trial. In Cambridge on February 4, 1965, Judge Edward A. Pecce accepted that recommendation and ordered DeSalvo to be committed to Bridgewater, because of mental illness, "until further orders of the court".

So, at 34, Albert DeSalvo, broad-shouldered and husky, disappeared for a time from public view. There was still no evidence that he was the Boston Strangler. Finally, however, he began to talk to those he trusted – such as Assistant Attorney General John S. Bottomley.

He recalled his fateful meeting with Anna Slesers, his first murder victim. It was pure chance, he said, that led him to her apartment building. He climbed the stairs, knocked at the door, and, fatally for her, Mrs. Slesers opened it. "I was sent to do some work in your apartment," he said. She, all trusting, let him in. He described how he killed her, but gave no reason for doing so.

Two bottles of milk

He recounted his visit to 65-year-old Helen Blake. Once again he gained admittance by telling his potential victim that he had to do some work in her apartment. Miss Blake was puzzled. "This is the first I've heard about it," she said – but she accepted his further explanation that, "I'm supposed to check all the windows for leaks and I'm going to do some interior painting." Helpfully, he carried in two bottles of milk standing outside her door.

As she got on with her housework, they chatted casually. Then, without warning, he clutched hold of her. "I grabbed my hand right behind her neck," he said. "She was a heavy-set, big-breasted woman. We were standing near the bed. She went down right away, passed right out." Under her housecoat she had been wearing pyjamas and he pulled those off. "She was unconscious," he went on. "I got on top. I had intercourse . . . I think I put a bra around her neck, and a nylon stocking, too."

His encounter with Nina Nichols was equally haphazard, he declared. He wandered around her apartment building, ringing door bells but receiving no answer until he rang one, "and I see the name Nina Nichols over it". Mrs. Nichols answered and was given the inevitable story about checking the apartment. However, she was hesitant. Who had sent him? she wanted to know. The building superintendent, he replied. Still she was uncertain. Boldly, De Salvo took a chance and told her: "Look, you can call him

up." This offer satisfied Mrs. Nichols, and she let him in.

As in the previous killings, he suddenly grabbed at his victim and "she fell back with me on the bed, on top of me". Mrs. Nichols fainted, so he rolled her on to the floor and had intercourse with her before trying to strangle her with a belt he found lying nearby. When the belt broke he took a stocking and knotted it tightly three times around her neck.

He was asked to demonstrate the type of knot he tied. He did so, using his own shoelaces. The listening and watching investigators exchanged glances: the knot DeSalvo tied was in the form of a crude bow – the Strangler's bow.

Between two chairs

Mrs. Ida Irga died in much the same way – but DeSalvo could give no reason for leaving her bound, with her legs yawning between two chairs. "I just did it," was the only explanation he could offer. It was pointed out to him that Mrs. Irga was 75, and could not fairly be counted as a sexually attractive woman. DeSalvo reacted with impatience.

"Attractiveness had nothing to do with it," he snapped. "When this certain time comes on me, it's a very immediate thing. When I get this feeling, instead of going to work I make an excuse to my boss. I start driving and I start building this image up, and that's why I find myself not knowing where I'm going.

Sophie Clark, however, was a desirable, Negro student of 20, found murdered by the Strangler on December 5, 1962. She had been gagged, three stockings had been twisted with enormous force around her neck, and she had been raped and left with her legs forced widely apart. But Sophie had not been such an easy victim as the elder women dispatched by the Strangler – for there were signs in the room of a struggle.

DeSalvo recalled that she had not wanted to let him in because her room-mates were out. Once more, his glib tongue proved persuasive. He pretended to know her room-mates and talked fast about modelling and how Sophie Clark could earn $20-$30 an hour. He asked her to turn around – "to let me see how you're built" – and as she did so he threw her on to the settee. She fainted and he had intercourse. Later, as she revived, she began to fight back, and it was then that he killed her.

Yes, said DeSalvo, almost dreamily, he remembered the date of that adventure very well indeed. It was his wedding anniversary.

One victim, Patricia Bissette – who was 23 and who died among her Christmas decorations in her apartment on Boston's Park Drive on December 31, 1962 – won a kind of post-mortem sympathy

from DeSalvo. She was so trustful that she made him coffee and chatted as if they were old friends. "She talked to me like a man, treated me like a man," he said, sadly. All the same he forced his lust on her, and she died like the others. He made one special concession to the corpse of this girl: he covered it, respectfully, with a bathrobe.

He worried aloud about his reason for killing a girl who had evoked in him a spark of decent, human feeling. "I don't know," he mused, "whether I did this for the sex act or out of hate for her – not her in particular, but a woman. After seeing her body, naturally the sex act came in. But I did not enjoy it. There was no thrill at all. . . . She did me no harm, and yet I did it. Why to her?"

The Strangler's last victim, Mary Sullivan, 19, who died on January 4, 1964, suffered the most savagely at his hands. Her body was found not only strangled, but mutilated by the use of a broomstick handle and with other atrocities committed upon it. DeSalvo acknowledged the sickening handiwork as his – but protested that it seemed, somehow, to have been done by someone who was himself and yet, at the same time, was someone else.

"I'm realizing that these things are true, and that these things that I did do, that I have read about in books, that other people do, that I didn't think or realize I would ever do these things," he pleaded.

Lack of evidence

The stories that he told, the confessions he dictated, the sketches he made of some of the victims' homes, pointed to the fact that Albert DeSalvo was, indeed, the Boston Strangler. That somewhere, in the darkness of his mind, were unknown forces that had driven him to kill so mercilessly and so pointlessly. But, because of lack of supporting evidence, the law felt unable to accept his word. Accordingly, he was not charged with being the Strangler or with committing the Strangler's crimes.

Instead, he was eventually tried for other crimes, pre-dating the Strangler period: crimes of armed robbery, assault and sex offences against four women fortunate enough to have lived to identify him. In 1967 he was sentenced to life imprisonment. However, as it happened, he had only six more years to live.

On November 26, 1973, the 42-year-old criminal was found in his prison cell in Walpole State Prison, Massachusetts, dead from 16 stab wounds. The best epitaph on Albert DeSalvo came from his attorney, F. Lee Bailey, who stated that his client was insane, a schizophrenic, "a completely uncontrolled vegetable walking around in a human body".

THE HONEYMOON MURDER

They found her tiny body sprawled by a remote mountain pool. But who had strangled her, and why? The inscrutable Mr. Miao wasn't talking. . . .

CUMBERLAND had not had a murder for 40 years. But when violent death came at last to the remote and beautiful county, it took the form of a bizarre crime, bizarre because of the nationality of victim and killer, because of the inept way it was carried out, and bizarre—above all—because it was committed in England.

HONEYMOON MURDER: STRANGLED CHINESE BRIDE shrieked the headlines. The bride who died was Wai-Sheung Siu, daughter of a rich Chinese merchant. She was tiny (4 ft. 11 in.), 29, a shrewd and intelligent businesswoman who travelled the world marketing Chinese art treasures. On May 12, 1928, after a whirlwind courtship, she had been married in New York to Chung Yi Miao, 28—who claimed to be the son of a rich Shanghai family, and to have taken law degrees both in China and at Loyola University in Chicago.

A month later the couple sailed for Scotland. Then, on Monday, June 18, they travelled to the picturesque Lake District to continue their honeymoon. They took a room in the Borrowdale Gates Hotel at the foot of Derwentwater. Next morning, like so many honeymooners before them, they set out on a walk to enjoy the fresh Cumberland air and some of England's most striking scenery. At two o'clock, after lunch, they went out again. But when Miao was seen returning two hours later, he was alone.

At 7.30 that evening, a farmer named Tom Wilson found the bride's body, half hidden under a brown umbrella, lying beside a natural pool called Kidham Dub, which was sometimes used for bathing. She had been strangled with three pieces of string and blind cord. She lay on her back with her knees slightly drawn up and opened. Her skirt and underskirt were around her hips, and her knickers slightly torn. The rings she had been wearing were missing from her bare left hand, beside which lay a white kid glove, partly inside out as if it had been peeled from her.

Sexually assaulted

The impression was that she had been sexually assaulted, murdered and robbed. But, by midnight, her husband had been taken, under suspicion, to the police station at Keswick, the town at the opposite end of the lake, for the start of the questioning that would lead to his arrest.

Then—at Carlisle Assizes on November 22, 1928, five months after the killing—began the trial to decide whether Miao was a strangler. There had been big queues, and the public galleries were packed as the sallow, sleek-haired Chinese, looking alert and unperturbed, was escorted into the dock. In a firm voice, he pleaded: "Not guilty." The hearing, which would prove a classic case of conviction by circumstantial evidence, was to last three days.

After returning to the hotel around four o'clock, Miao had gone to his room. At 7 p.m., he dined alone. A woman guest at a nearby table told the court how she had asked: "What has happened to your wife?" He replied, she said: "She has gone to Keswick to buy warm underclothes." After dinner she felt Miao was worried about his wife's failure to return and reassured him: "You need not be nervous. Your wife is a woman of the world who has travelled a good deal."

Miao added that he had not accompanied his wife because he had a slight cold and she had suggested he would be better off in bed. At 8.15, Miss Crossley, owner of the hotel, also asked what had happened to Mrs. Miao. Miao repeated his earlier explanation: "She has gone to Keswick to buy warmer underclothing."

A little later, Miss Crossley mentioned that there was a bus due from Keswick at 9 p.m. and offered to meet it. Miao made the odd reply: "It's no use. She won't come by the bus. She doesn't like the bus. She will come by private car."

Nevertheless, Miss Crossley had gone to the terminus, which was near the Post Office, to see if there was any sign of Mrs. Miao off the nine o'clock bus. During her absence, Miao wandered into the kitchen looking for the proprietress. "She has gone to see if your wife is coming back," a maid named Holliday told him. According to her evidence, Miao asked: "Where would she go to?"

Noose around the neck

Then occurred a curious exchange which, with other circumstantial evidence, went a long way towards tying a noose around Miao's neck. The maid went on: "I said: 'To the Post Office.' He said: 'Would she go to the place where they bathe?' I said: 'No, to the Post Office.'"

The significance of the maid's evidence was not lost on Mr. John Jackson, K.C., appearing for Miao. She agreed with the lawyer that Miao did not speak English well. But she would not accept counsel's suggestion that what Miao had actually said was: "Has she gone to where people take the bus?" Mr. Jackson tried pronouncing "bus" with a slight lisp and "bath" with a short "a" to make the words sound alike. The maid refused to agree she might have misheard.

At 11 p.m. that night, Inspector Graham of Keswick police called at the hotel.

THE BRIDE who died was Wai-Sheung Siu, a shrewd dealer in Chinese antiques. Her husband, Chung Yi Miao, said he was the son of a rich Shanghai family. They were last seen together leaving the Borrowdale Gates Hotel (left).

"Miao was in bed," he said. "I explained I was a police inspector and told him to get up and dress. 'What do you want me for?' he asked. I cautioned him, told him that his wife had been found dead and that he would be detained on suspicion of having caused her death by strangling. 'What do you say?' he asked. 'My wife dead? Suspicion? What do you mean by that?' He appeared very emotional," the inspector went on, "but I had the impression he was acting a part."

While Inspector Graham stayed behind to search the hotel room, Miao was driven to Keswick police station where, in the charge room, he had another curious conversation – which Mr. Jackson tried to explain away by saying Miao had been misunderstood because of his poor English pronunciation.

Had she knickers on?

P.C. Scott then stated that, shortly after arriving, Miao suddenly said: "May I ask you a question, sir?" He replied: "You may." "Did you see my wife?" asked Miao. "I did," said Scott. Then, according to the constable, Miao inquired: "Had she knickers on?" Scott had refused to answer. Mr. Jackson tried to establish that what Miao had actually said was: "Had she a necklace on?" Scott, however, insisted that there had been no misunderstanding.

An hour later, while being searched, Miao had suddenly begun to speak in his halting English. "She had one necklace on," he said. "She had one white one on yesterday afternoon. She had pocket book with her. She had diamond ring on. Had she these with her now?" Inspector Graham, who had arrived after searching the hotel room, did not answer.

The following morning, at 6.45, Superintendent Barron, the Deputy Chief Constable, had arrived to interview Miao. Once again the prisoner had something unusual to say. "It is terrible – my wife assaulted, robbed and murdered," he told the Superintendent. Up to that time nothing had been said to him about the position in which his wife's body had been found and the rings missing from her left hand. Again, that afternoon, Miao asked about his suit and overcoat, which had been taken from him earlier. Superintendent Barron explained that they had been sent away to be examined for bloodstains.

"The bloodstains on my overcoat were got in New York," said Miao – another odd reply in the light of subsequent medical evidence that, in fact, no bloodstains had been found on his clothing.

That was by no means the end of the circumstantial evidence. String and blind cord – although the cord was of a different colour from that found around the dead bride's neck – were discovered in a cupboard in the Miaos' bedroom and an easily-accessible drawer in the hotel kitchen. A week after the murder, Inspector Graham gave two used films, found in Mrs. Miao's unlocked suitcase, to a local photographer to develop. Wrapped up in silver paper with one of the films were two rings. They had quickly been identified as the wedding ring and diamond solitaire Mrs. Miao had been wearing the night before her death.

Then came the medical testimony. Dr. Crawford, who had examined the body at 9.30 p.m. on the night it was found, put the time of death at 3.30 to 4.30 in the afternoon. Professor John McFall of Liverpool, an expert in forensic medicine, said the bride's knickers were slightly stained in front, but there was nothing to suggest "discharge from a man". The tear, exactly at the seam, suggested "a certain amount of force having been used". "I have seen many of these cases," he said, "and it seems to me a very good imitation of an assault."

Mrs. Miao had bled from the nose, mouth and left ear. Professor McFall was able to show from the nature of bloodstains on her left glove that it had been removed – almost certainly after death – by pulling the body of it over the fingers, which is not the way a woman normally removes a glove. On the skirt there were ten horizontal stains of blood. They suggested "a crumpling of the cloth, the ten smudges being the result of one large smear, as if the material had been gathered up by a bloody hand.

"When it is opened out, you see the smudges. They were therefore made by someone tampering with the body after the injuries had been inflicted."

Mr. Justice Humphreys, the judge: Does this all mean that, in your opinion, it is more probable that the clothes of the woman, her skirt and underskirt, were pulled up after bleeding had begun?

Professor McFall: Yes.

Showing off her jewels

It took the prosecution a day-and-a-half to present this formidable mass of circumstantial evidence. Mr. Jackson began his assault on it after lunch on the second day by an address to the jury. His main points were:

1) Miao had been arrested solely on the evidence of witnesses that he had been seen with his wife at 2.30 and alone at 4 on the afternoon she died.
2) Mrs. Miao was fond of showing off her jewellery, even to comparative strangers. This, together with the publicity given to her New York wedding, had made her the target of international jewel thieves. Miao had noticed two Orientals following them in Glasgow, Edinburgh and in Grange, the Derwentwater village where their hotel was situated.
3) Mrs. Miao had sent her husband home at 3 p.m. – 30-90 minutes before the time of her death – because he had a cold. She had gone shopping in Keswick, saying she would get a lift from a passing car because she did not like buses. The jewel thieves, who had been waiting to catch her alone, took the opportunity to kill her and rob her. Although a pearl necklace had been found among the £3500-worth of jewels in her room, another necklace was missing.
4) Miao had gone home as his wife suggested. Finding the fire out in their room, he had gone out again with his camera. He returned again at four o'clock when there was a rain shower.
5) Because of Miao's poor accent, witnesses had confused "bathe" with "bus" and "necklace" with "knickers". To Superintendent Barron he had said "rudely murdered", not "robbed and murdered".

That was the melodramatic story Miao told confidently. How had the two rings got into the Kodak film spool wrapper where the photographer accidentally discovered them a week after the murder? "My wife put them there after lunch," he said. "I was not surprised. I had seen her hide them for safety on top of the wardrobe and in other odd places before." He added that he had never heard the word "knickers". Nor did he know that there was a pool in the vicinity used for bathing.

Impossible to have sex

Mr. John Singleton, the prosecutor, began his cross-examination by trying to establish two possible motives for the murder. First he questioned Miao about his financial affairs, seeking to show that, despite his claims, he was not a man of substance but had married for money. Secondly, there was the matter of an operation performed on the bride on May 25, before they sailed for Scotland, because she had found it impossible to have sexual intercourse. Miao agreed the operation had taken place, but he denied that either his wife or her doctor had told him it would be impossible for her to have children.

The defence then called several witnesses who had seen other "Orientals" in the area on or about the day of the murder. That was the end of the evidence. Mr. Jackson's speech for the defence on the third day of the trial lasted 45 minutes. "What motive was there behind the murder?" he asked. "Both these young people were well-furnished with this world's goods and both were happy. If

THE FIRST MURDER in 40 years in Cumberland was so bizarre and inept that it created a furor out of all proportion to its importance. Most amazing was that it was committed in England at all.

The HONEYMOON TRAGEDY

Chinese Bridegroom on Trial for his Life ~~at Ca~~rlisle Assizes.

PROSECUTION

CHINAMAN'S APPEAL ~~CA~~ DISMISSED.

CHINAMAN FOUND GUILTY

Close of the Wife Murder Trial ~~at~~ Carlisle Assizes.

~~"~~ VERDICT"—THE JUDGE

~~Sentence~~ of Death Received with ~~Pro~~testations of Innocence.

..., Chung Yu Miao, at Carlisle Assizes on a charge of murdering ... in a verdict of Guilty. The Judge passed sentence of death, ... verdict to be a true one. Prisoner, who had excitedly affirmed ... the Judge's summing up, received the death ... ce calmly ... was not guilty.

THE VALUE OF THE JEWELLERY.
Norman Grant, jeweller, Carlisle, who had examined the contents of the jewel case,

stated that he est...

CHINAMAN TO DIE.

"A TRULY DIABOLICAL AND CALCULATED MURDER."

APPEAL DISMISSED.

LORD CHIEF JUSTICE FINDS AMPLE ~~EVIDE~~NCE FOR CONVICTION.

RAIL

MANSLA

TRI

Ernest
Frances
driver of
mail trai
field on C
trates at
day, cha
Dorothy
Mrs Bu

the prisoner had wanted to murder his wife," he went on, "why did he come to England to do so? Why did he not take the opportunity in the liner on the voyage from America and simply push her into the sea?

"The jury's verdict," he pointed out, "must be based on evidence and not on theory. It has been shown that the dead woman was rather vain about her jewellery. There are crooks at almost every port who never miss such opportunities as were offered here. What were those Oriental men doing in Keswick?

"The police arrested Miao when the only evidence against him was that he had been seen with his wife in the afternoon. Since then they have simply tried to build up theories. There is no proof that the girl was even murdered where she was found. She might well have been murdered in a car in which she had asked for a lift to Keswick. The prosecution is relying upon a chain of circumstantial evidence,

each link of which can be explained, and on the prisoner's ignorance of English pronunciation."

The summing-up

With the defence case concluded, some of the main points referred to by Mr. Justice Humphreys in his summing-up were:

Miao's command of English in the witness-box.
You may have noticed that, when he was answering questions put by his learned counsel, he seemed as clear and quick, almost, as an Englishman. But when he was cross-examined you may have noticed that his hesitation was very much greater and more marked. When you come to consider his evidence, you will have to make up your minds whether in the answers he gave to counsel for the prosecution [in cross-examination] he was acting the part of a person who did not understand, or whether he honestly did

want time to be quite sure that he followed what the questions were.

The departure of Mrs. Miao at 3 p.m. (according to her husband) to buy warm underclothes in Keswick.
Do you believe the story that this woman suddenly decided, about three o'clock, to go to Keswick, and if so how did she get there? She certainly did not go by omnibus . . . Do you think it possible that that woman could have gone off to Keswick without being seen by any human being? The police have not been able to find anybody who saw her, and the defence have not been able to trace anybody who saw her.

The removal of Mrs. Miao's left glove and the finding of her rings wrapped up with the spool of film.
If it was done by the person who killed her, why did he do it? Can you entertain any doubt that he had done it for the purpose of taking off the rings? Does the evidence satisfy you that the murderer had taken off the rings? If it does, the significance of that evidence is quite important. If they *were* taken off by the murderer, how did the prisoner get hold of them?

Could the murder have been committed by robbers?
She was found to have been killed by the application very tightly round her throat of a piece of string which had been twisted so as to make it double. Who did it? Can you imagine a robber killing a woman in that way? This was a little woman, only five feet high. Do you think a person who wanted to take her jewellery would have got so near to her without her knowing it as to be able to put round her neck that piece of string and strangle her? Of course, if the person who did it was a person in whom she had every confidence, you may think she would have no objection at all to his putting his hands round her throat or doing anything else he liked . . .

Miao's apparent knowledge, before anyone told him, of his wife's exact fate.
The prisoner made this observation [to Superintendent Barron]: "It is terrible. My wife assaulted, robbed and murdered." The prosecution draws your attention to the word "robbed". How did this man know that his wife had been robbed? All that had been told him was that her body had been found strangled in a wood. The prisoner says what he really said was: "This is terrible. My wife has been *rudely* murdered." There it is . . .

Of Miao's evidence that, before going out, his wife had herself hidden the two

---

THE KING WITH A BUTTONHOLE.

—AND A WALKING-STICK.

The King, taking advantage of the warm sunshine yesterday, walked with the Queen for about 100 yards to the sea wall in front of Craigweil House.

He left his bath chair in the grounds and sat for half an hour in a wicker chair on the sea wall reading newspapers. He had a large pink flower in his buttonhole and carried a walking-stick.

Six women who arrived at the Princess Mary Home of Rest, Bognor, yesterday, learned that the Queen had left Easter presents for them during her visit the previous day. The nature of the gifts, however, is being kept secret from them until Easter Monday.

CLEANER FOOTBALL.

MORE PUNISHMENT FOR FOUL PLAY.

An important move to "clean-up" football will be made when the Council of the Football Association meets in London to-morrow.

Recommendations will be considered which aim at giving 'more effective punishment for foul play. All the rules regarding free-kicks and penalties will be reviewed.

"The Man in the Corner" deals with this problem on Page Twenty-three.

COUPLE WOUNDED.

MAN IN HOSPITAL WITH THROAT INJURY.

Philip Phillips, of Humberstone-road, Commercial-road, Aldgate, is lying in Ilford Emergency Hospital, with a wound in the throat.

Bessie Phillips, of Roman-road, Ilford, is suffering from slight cuts. She was not taken to hospital.

It is not known if the couple are related

A CHINESE BRIDE'S DEATH SECRET.

KILLED TO SAVE HER HUSBAND'S SOUL.

"SHE COULD NOT GIVE ME A SON."

BEHIND the mysterious murder of a Chinese bride by her husband in the Lake District on June 19, 1928, lies a strange secret of the inscrutable Orient.

Chung Yi Miao, the young husband, was executed at Strangeways Gaol, Manchester, on December 6 last year.

Throughout his trial he denied that

THE MURDERED GIRL.

he murdered his rich bride, Cheung Miao.

Before he died, however, he revealed the secret. And this is the strange story he told :—

"I killed my wife, but it was not murder according to my faith and the faith of my forefathers.

stormy sea.

This was the epic story, told day lightheartedly, unemotion Mr. H. M. Morris, then an year-old lieutenant in the Ro Force, who, with Air Mechan Wright, also aged eighteen, hero of this amazing war d 1917.

I found Mr. Morris, who is tain the Essex County cricket t season, about to start out on a golf. He was playing for school, Repton, in the Halford cup—and he told me frankly was much more interested in the story about which I wanted talk to me.

DAWN SEARCH.

Finally, after a lot of persua said :—

"It was early in the morning 23, 1917, that I was roused f sofa in the mess at Westgat where I was on night duty in emergency.

"I was sleeping in my unifo I was told that a 'hornet' w gone in chase of a raiding Zepp not returned, and they wante look for it.

"Air Mechanic Wright was same duty, and when we ha him we set off, without ou clothes, in a Short seaplane.

"I should like to make it c we went without our flying because the picture in the War Museum, South Kensingt ing with our rescue, shows us overcoats.

"We had lots of time late regret that we did not equipped !

"We searched the sea f hours, without observing anyth at last I decided to turn back running short of petrol, and more than forty miles from l

THIRST TORTURE

"Almost as soon as I turned of the machine homewards, th stopped, and I was obliged down into a sea infested wit

"We had then travelled a miles towards the coast. We e the engine, and found that it w neto trouble, and as we did a spare, there was nothing f to wait for rescue.

"It was then about midday sea was calm, but during the a squall blew up, and a gr caught our craft a terrific l sank her, tail first.

"We swam about for a litt and Wright was suddenly bu the float, which had broken a the machine.

"As it was our only hope to it, and it became our 'he nearly a week.

THE HEARING, which was to prove a classic case of conviction by circumstantial evidence, took three days, almost half of which was needed by the prosecution to present all its evidence.

THE ILLUSTRATED POLICE NEWS—JUNE 28, 1928.

LABOUR'S STORMY PETREL.

THE ILLUSTRATED
POLICE NEWS

LAW COURTS
AND WEEKLY RECORD
THE OLDEST AND BEST POLICE JOURNAL IN THE WORLD.
WITH WHICH IS INCORPORATED
GREAT GLOVE FIGHTS.
ESTABLISHED 1864

No. 3357. [REGISTERED AT THE G.P.O. AS A NEWSPAPER.]   THURSDAY, JUNE 28, 1928.   TWOPENCE

SCENE OF THE TRAGEDY

THE BORROWDALE VALLEY.

THE CHINESE BRIDE AND HER HUSBAND WERE SEEN WALKING.

FOUND STRANGLED.

ARREST OF THE HUSBAND.

PRETTY NEWLY MARRIED CHINESE GIRL STRANGLED IN LAKELAND

SCENE OF THE MURDER

CHUNG MIAO

THE MURDERED BRIDE.

EXECUTION OF CHUNG MIAO

rings in the Kodak film spool.
He says: "I asked her why she put the rings there." She said: "I do not want to open the jewel case. We are in a hurry." If you think you can accept that story, I should think you would be able to accept everything else the prisoner tells you. If you think you cannot accept that story, you are in a position that you have a man whose evidence you are asked to accept with regard to whom in one important matter you say: "That man is lying" . . .

Of the other "Orientals" in the neighbourhood.
There is no witness called to say that those persons were seen just at the critical time at Grange Bridge with a motor car, hanging about . . .

It took the jury only an hour on the afternoon of the third day of the trial to find Miao guilty. He responded, when

"ACCURSED is the man who has no son to revere his memory" . . . according to a statement published posthumously, this may have been the reason Miao decided to murder his young bride.

asked if he had anything to say, with a truculent attack in which he complained that his point of view had never been put properly to the jury. He also made the observation: "The last word I say is this. You say: 'How clever he is.' Now you have tried my life and the verdict is I am guilty. If I did that, I must be very nervous. Now you see I am not nervous . . ."

Mr. Justice Humphreys sentenced him to death. Miao appealed immediately. His appeal was heard—by the Lord Chief Justice, Mr. Justice Avory, and Mr. Justice Acton—on November 19 and 20. It was an unusual appeal. Miao decided

to dismiss Mr. Jackson and conduct it himself. He was allowed—probably as a concession to the fact that he was a foreigner—the abnormal privilege of calling new witnesses, who testified to seeing two "Orientals" near the scene of the crime at about the time it was committed.

His basic case, apart from a reiteration of the story that he had told at his trial, was that prosecuting counsel and the judge were so prejudiced that he had not been given a fair hearing.

The Lord Chief Justice, reviewing the evidence, laid great stress on the hiding of the rings with the film spool. "It may well be," he said, "that in this case the jury thought that his cupidity had got the better of his cunning." Of the question of possible misunderstanding of the words "knickers" for "necklace" and "bath" for "bus", he remarked: "Miao complained he was misunderstood. His difficulty is not that. His difficulty is that he *was* understood."

Manacled and in tears

There was no evidence that the "Orientals" in Grange had ever been seen with Mrs. Miao. The summing-up at the trial had been "extremely careful and impartial". No point of law had been raised. Therefore the appeal was dismissed. Manacled and in tears, Miao was driven off from the Law Courts in London on the first stage of his journey back to Strangeways Prison, Manchester—where he was executed on December 6.

All that remains is to try to fathom not only why he killed his bride, but also why he chose to kill her in England when there would have been so many advantages in a simple shipboard accident, or even in waiting until their return to China.

A variety of reasons have been put forward—that he was insane; that he wanted to get his hands on his wife's money and property; sexual desire, thwarted by the fact that, even after her operation, she was still unable to have intercourse; dismay, born of the Chinese tradition of ancestor worship, that his wife could not bear him children; that he was a crypto-member of a Chinese *tong* (secret society) dedicated to duping, or even murdering, rich women to raise money.

There are objections to all these theories. More than three months after Miao went to the scaffold, the London *Sunday Express* did publish an article which claimed to give, in his own words, the reason for the murder. It said:

"We were told we could never have a son to grace our union and to perpetuate my name. The strongest of all religious feelings in China, especially in the south where I come from, is reverence for our ancestors. Thus a man who has no son to revere his memory is accursed."

THE HOUSE OF THE RISING SUN

It was a disreputable pub in a dingy North London Street, but the Rising Sun was a maddening clue in a tale of double-identity and secret sex, ending in the murder of Phyllis Dimmock (left). Robert Wood (below), was finally acquitted, a most popular decision.

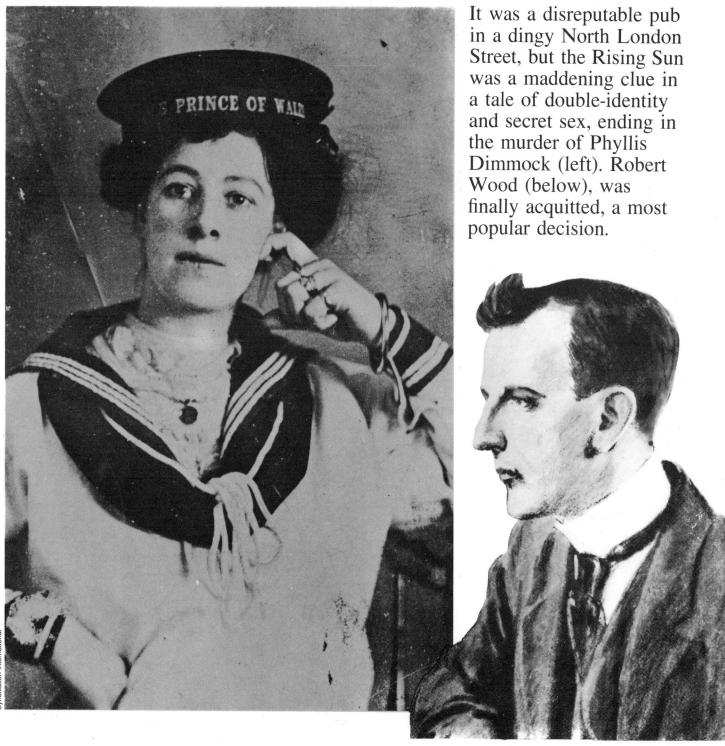

Syndication International

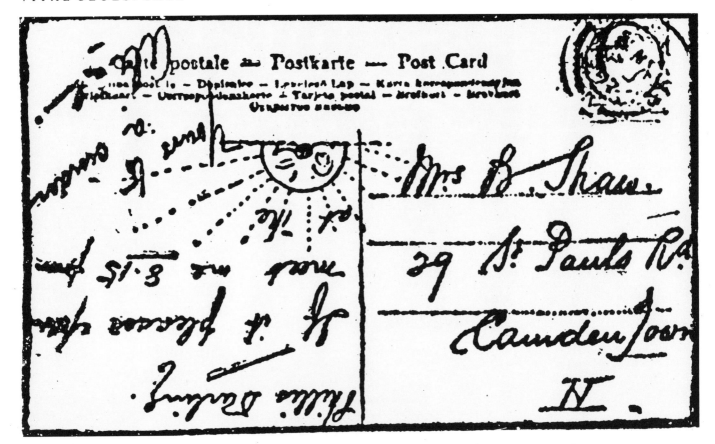

BERT SHAW, a Midland Railway dining car cook, was delighted when the 7.20 a.m. train from Sheffield, on which he had been preparing breakfasts and mid-morning coffee, arrived on time at London's St. Pancras Station at 11.30.

Having been away working since the previous afternoon, he was anxious to get back for a few off-duty hours to his home at 29, St. Paul's Road, Camden Town, half a mile from St. Pancras.

Most of all he was looking forward to seeing Phyllis Dimmock, the attractive 23-year-old girl with whom he had lived for the past eight months and whom, understandably in those narrow-minded days of 1907, he found it necessary to refer to as his "wife".

Number 29 was a small rundown terrace house in a shabby street bordered by a railway goods depot. For eight shillings a week Shaw and Phyllis rented two first-floor front rooms divided by a pair of folding doors.

Phyllis herself paid the rent to the landlady, Mrs. Sarah Stocks, out of the £1 a week Shaw gave her for household expenses. In addition to that, her part of the "marriage" bargain was to cook for Shaw, in between his regular overnight train duties, and take care of the general domestic chores.

On the face of it, it looked like a happy liaison. Shaw and Phyllis got on well together and Shaw was pleased because all the signs were that his "wife" had

THE MURDERER had ransacked the prostitute's apartment not in search of valuables, but in a frantic attempt to find this postcard . . . or so it seemed.

totally abandoned the life she had been leading when he met her.

That life had not been a pretty one. Phyllis Dimmock had been a prostitute, and a low-grade one at that—a cheaply priced street-walker who patrolled the pavements and pubs of the King's Cross area, casually picking up any man encouraged by drink to part with a few shillings.

What Shaw did not guess at was that Phyllis had not changed her way of life. While he was away, working in his railway kitchen car, she was secretly smuggling her clients into their rooms at St. Paul's Road for all-night visits.

The usual routine

But on that Thursday morning, September 12, 1907, Shaw, unaware of Phyllis's return to the streets, hurried expectantly towards the usual routine of her bounding down the stairs to greet him as soon as he opened the front door.

He was surprised to see no sign of her. And even more surprised when Mrs. Stocks, the landlady, appeared in the hallway and announced: "Oh, Mr. Shaw, your mother's here."

This was unexpected and embarrassing. His elderly mother, who lived in Northampton, had given no notice of her

intended arrival, and she had not yet met the new "Mrs." Shaw.

"I haven't taken your mother upstairs because your rooms are locked and I can't get in," Mrs. Stocks explained. She seemed puzzled and so was Bert Shaw—because although there were keys in the doors of the Shaws' rooms they were never turned.

Shaw borrowed a duplicate key to his sitting-room from Mrs. Stocks and ran upstairs. He unlocked the door and looked in at a scene of apparent vandalism. Furniture had been moved, drawers taken out and their contents strewn about.

By now thoroughly alarmed, Shaw could not wait to unlock the folding doors into the bedroom. Instead he burst them open with a heave of his shoulders.

The bedroom was in twilight with the venetian blinds down and only thin shafts of sunlight filtering through between the slats. On the bed lay a rumpled heap of bedclothes. Shaw swept them aside and leapt back with a cry of horror. Face down, completely naked, lay the mutilated body of Phyllis.

Her throat had been slashed from ear to ear with such force and depth that the head remained attached to the neck only by a few muscle fibres. There was blood everywhere. It had soaked the bed and the floorboards beneath and coursed across the room into the fireplace.

Half crazed with fear and grief, Shaw raced down the stairs, out into the traffic whirl of Camden Town and hysterically shrieked the news of his discovery to a beat-duty constable.

The divisional police surgeon concluded that Phyllis had been murdered at between three and six in the morning of September 12. From the position of the body—"a naturally comfortable one," he said—he thought she had been killed as she slept. So deliberate and powerful was the knifing that she had died instantaneously.

It took the police very little time to establish what Bert Shaw had not realized, that Phyllis Dimmock had been pursuing her street-walking career without interruption. Among her favourite pick-up venues were two local pubs, the Eagle and the Rising Sun.

Quickly, too, they discovered a ship's cook who had been seeing a great deal of Phyllis and who freely admitted that, in the week of the murder, he had spent three nights with her at St. Paul's Road.

The cook insisted that the last time he saw her was on the day before the murder, and he produced witnesses to prove that he spent the murder night in his lodgings.

He was, however, able to give the police the lead to an important clue. On his last visit to St. Paul's Road, he said, Phyllis had shown him an unusual postcard.

On one side was a reproduction of a painting showing a woman holding a child. The other side was addressed to: "Mrs. B. Shaw, 29 St. Paul's Road, Camden Town, N." and, with the name Phyllis spelt with an "i" instead of a "y", was the message:

Yours to a cinder

Phillis Darling —If it pleases you meet me at 8.15 p.m. at the—" and then followed a sketch of a rising sun. It was signed: "Yours to a cinder, Alice."

Phyllis had also shown him a letter and, said the ship's cook, he well remembered reading the words "Dear Phyllis, Will you meet me at the bar of the Eagle at Camden Town 8.30 tonight, Wednesday—Bert."

The cook declared that Phyllis had put the postcard in a drawer, but burned the letter in the empty grate by setting light to it with a match.

In the grate the police found the charred remains of the letter, and under a powerful magnifying glass they could just make out parts of words ". . . ill . . . you . . . ar . . . of . . . the . . . e . . . Town . . . Wednes . . ." They indeed seemed to fit the message the ship's cook said he remembered reading.

Of the postcard there was no trace. But one factor interested the police. Shaw reported that Phyllis was an avid collector

ONE OF THE BEST defence lawyers in the history of English law, Marshall Hall's stature was assured by his handling of this perplexing case.

of picture postcards, and that she kept most of them in an album.

Looking around the bedroom after the body had been removed, Shaw was surprised to see the album lying open with some of the cards scattered on the floor. He was surprised because Phyllis had always kept the album in a drawer in the adjoining sitting-room.

This suggested a possible line of inquiry to the police: the murderer was the person who had written the postcard and sketched the rising sun. And the disorder in the apartment was not the result of robbery—since nothing of value was missing—but of the murderer's frantic efforts to find and destroy the postcard which might lead to his doom.

On September 25 Bert Shaw himself found the card that had eluded several police searches. Gathering his belongings to move into other rooms in the house, he pulled out a sheet of newspaper used as lining in a drawer. There, under the paper,

he saw the much-sought pencilled image of the winking, rising sun. The card was postmarked 4 a.m., September 9.

Scotland Yard circulated facsimiles of the postcard to the newspapers, and one appeared in the *News of the World* for Sunday, September 29, under the heading: "Can You Recognize This Writing?"

A freak of chance

A young woman named Ruby Young did recognize it. She knew at once that it was identical to the handwriting of her boy friend, a 28-year-old artist-engraver called Robert William Thomas George Cavers Wood.

By a freak of chance, Robert Wood and Ruby Young, like other characters in this real-life melodrama, also lived double lives.

Wood, who worked as a pattern designer for a Gray's Inn Road glass company, was an artist of some talent from a good, hard-working family. Unknown to

them, he was also a picker-up of minor-league prostitutes.

Ruby Young described herself as an "artist's model". But in her case it had a choicer meaning, and Wood had first met her walking her "territory" in Leicester Square.

Although Wood referred to Ruby as "my sweetheart", there had recently been a noticeable cooling off on his part. She was therefore intrigued when, on September 13, she received a note urging her to meet him that evening.

He took her to a café near Holborn and without any preliminaries asked: "Ruby, if any questions are put to you, you say you always saw me on Mondays and Wednesdays."

Then came the publication of the rising sun postcard. Within hours of Ruby seeing it an agitated Robert Wood called at her digs in Earls Court.

His opening words were: "Ruby, I'm in trouble!"

"Yes, I know," replied the girl, picking up the *News of the World*, "this is your handwriting."

Wood then pleaded: "Have patience and I'll tell you everything."

His story was that in the Rising Sun in Camden Town he got into conversation with Phyllis Dimmock whom he had never met before. A boy came into the pub selling picture postcards, and when Phyllis wanted to buy one, Wood said:

A pretty one

"Don't buy those, they're common. I have some from Bruges, in Belgium," and he showed her the card with the woman holding the child.

According to Wood, Phyllis said: "That's a pretty one. Send it to me. Write something nice on it."

He, to join in the harmless fun, turned the card over and wrote and drew the rising sun "message" that was to become so notorious.

He was about to sign his name (so his story went) when Phyllis pleaded: "Don't do that, the governor might cut up rough. Put my friend's name, 'Alice'."

Wood was so sure the "joke" about the postcard might now land him in dire difficulty that he rehearsed Ruby in a story that he had spent the evening of September 11 with her and not left her until 10.30.

It was, at best, a frail alibi, since he would still have had time after leaving Ruby to meet Phyllis and go with her to St. Paul's Road.

But, frail or not, Ruby could not keep the story to herself. She confided in one

IN THE DOCK, Wood (far left, with guard) did not exactly enhance his chances for acquittal with his phoney alibi. But defence counsel persevered.

of her other "gentlemen friends", who promptly told the police.

On October 4 Wood was arrested, and the following day he was picked out at an identification parade by people who said they had seen him several times with Phyllis in the Rising Sun and other public houses.

A coroner's inquest returned a verdict of wilful murder against Wood, and on December 4 his trial opened at the Old Bailey with Mr. (later Sir Edward) Marshall Hall, K.C., leading his defence.

Wood's attempt to concoct his phoney alibi with Ruby Young and other lies he had told about himself did not enhance his chances of acquittal.

But Marshall Hall was at the top of his defending form and explored every loophole in the Crown's case. Before long the loopholes began to look like yawning chasms.

There was absolutely nothing, he said, to link Wood with the murder. Whoever killed Phyllis must have been covered in blood, but "not a particle of blood has ever been found upon either the accused or upon his razors".

Trace of madness

Only a madman could have slain with such frenzy, and Marshall Hall asked the jury: "Is this man in the dock mad? Does he look mad? There is not a trace of madness in his past history."

Then there was the evidence of Wood's father, a printer with an impeccable character, that his son was at home on the murder night.

There was further evidence that Wood was at work, perfectly normal and displaying his usual, "amiable disposition", at eight o'clock on September 12, only a few hours after the killing.

But the eminent lawyer charged with maximum relish into the evidence of one of the Crown's key witnesses, a man named MacCowan, who said he was walking through St. Paul's Road at five minutes to five on the murder morning and saw a man leaving number 29.

THE JURY took only 17 minutes to find Wood (right), innocent. Public sympathy had reached such fervour that an actress, Mrs. Beerbohm Tree (right), ran on to a West End stage to announce the verdict amid thunderous ovations.

MacCowan had identified the man as Wood because of the "peculiarity of his walk". And he had observed him, he said, by the light of the electric street lamps.

Marshall Hall, however, demolished his evidence with a series of devastatingly phrased questions. MacCowan, it turned out, had not actually seen the man come out of number 29 – he had seen him walking along the street.

As for the help given him by the street lamps, counsel was able to prove that they were switched off at the latest by 20 minutes to five.

Hall was also able to point to gross inaccuracies in a police-drawn plan which attempted to show that St. Paul's Road would have been brightly illuminated from railway lights 40 feet below the road level. Mr. Justice Grantham summed up heavily in favour of Wood, and it took the jury only 17 minutes to find the young artist not guilty.

The demonstration of public sympathy for Wood that followed the verdict reached a fervour that astonished the authorities. Outside the court cheering crowds brought traffic to a standstill, and Ruby Young, whom the public had come to see as Wood's "betrayer", had to be smuggled out of a side entrance disguised as a charwoman.

The actress Mrs. Beerbohm (later Lady) Tree ran on to the stage of a West End theatre and exclaimed:

"I have just come from the court where young Robert Wood stood in peril of his life and I am glad to be able to tell you that the jury found him not guilty . . . I was one of those who burst into tears."

From gallery to orchestra stalls the audience roared out a thunderous ovation. But as the curtain fell on the drama of the Camden Town Murder itself, the star

"villain", the killer, was not to be seen. Neither he nor the murder weapon was ever found.

Lawyers keep the memory of the case alive, for Wood was the first person accused of murder to be acquitted after taking advantage of a new law (the Criminal Evidence Act of 1898), which allowed him to give evidence on his own behalf. And it helped to put the seal on Marshall Hall's stature as one of the best defence lawyers the English Bar has ever known.

For the other principals in the case obscurity was their desired haven. Robert Wood and Ruby Young found it, separately, under changed names. Even St. Paul's Road eventually discouraged morbid sightseers by changing its name too.

"Tourists" ended up footsore and frustrated after walking miles to dingy streets that quick-witted Camden Town folk told them "used to be St. Paul's Road".

DEATH WORE A GOLD CHAIN

The attractive young mother had died horribly, her terminal agony mocked by the idyllic seaside setting. Even those who heard her groan in terror thought she was making love. Could an innocent piece of jewellery hold the key to this mystery . . .?

IT IS an ordinary enough little photo; one of the thousands of tintypes churned out for the tourists who used to flock to the English east coast resort of Yarmouth. A smartly dressed and attractive young mother sits on the sandy beach, steadying a baby with her right hand.

You can see the chain round her neck quite plainly fashioned from gold links and supporting a silver watch. It doesn't look strong enough to take any strain. Yet it hanged John Herbert Bennett as surely as any hempen noose.

Within three days of the picture being taken, the young mother was brutally murdered on the same beach where she had posed with her little girl. It was about 10.30 on the night of Saturday, September 22, 1900, when Alfred Mason and his girl-friend, Blanche Smith, found a secluded hollow on Yarmouth beach and lay down for a cuddle.

Around 30 minutes later, the lovers were disturbed by another couple who walked past them and sat down on a sandy slope some 60 feet away. Blanche first heard the woman crying "Mercy". She and Alfred listened and heard the word repeated several times, followed by the sound of a woman moaning.

When they got up, Alfred and Blanche walked past the couple. The woman was lying on her back, with the man crouching over her. The beach was a favourite spot for courting couples, and what Alfred and Blanche had heard could easily have been the sounds of ardent lovemaking. They hurried on.

The body was found the next morning.

The woman was lying on her back, knees bent and legs splayed. Her bloomers were round her ankles, and the sand under her hands was churned up as if she had struggled violently. She had been strangled with a bootlace, which had cut deep into her neck, and then tied in a reef-knot topped by a granny-knot.

Who was she? She was apparently married—she wore a wedding ring and two other rings on her left hand—but there were no other means of identification. In a pokey bedroom in a third-rate lodging house a short distance across the sands, in one of the labyrinthine alleyways, called "The Rows", a baby awoke and started crying.

Drunk at midnight

The landlady, a formidable woman named Mrs. Rudrum, frowned in disapproval. Her new lodger, Mrs. Hood, the baby's mother, had not returned to her room overnight. "Shocking," she thought. There was something odd about Mrs. Hood. She had arrived around 9 p.m. on the previous Saturday, September 15, with her two-year-old daughter, whom she called Rose. Mrs. Rudrum, her husband John and daughter Alice were impressed with Mrs. Hood's apparent respectability. But their attitude froze a little when their new lodger arrived back drunk at midnight, after being seen to the door by a man.

Mrs. Hood explained that she had met her brother-in-law, who had bought her "a fish supper followed by three drops of brandy". The Rudrums softened when

Mrs. Hood said she had been widowed for two years. But when Mrs. Rudrum asked sympathetically if little Rose had ever known her father, Mrs. Hood looked blank for a moment, as if she had never heard the baby's name before.

From then on, the new lodger behaved perfectly. Still Mrs. Rudrum was not satisfied. Mrs. Hood's somewhat romanticized account of her life—her widowhood, her trip to South Africa, her ability to play the violin and piano—struck the landlady as too good to be true.

On Friday, September 21, after Mrs. Hood had left the house, a letter arrived for her. Mrs. Rudrum noticed that the bluish-grey envelope bore a Woolwich, south London, postmark. It was not until about 10.45 that night that Mrs. Hood returned. Again she had a man with her. Opening an upstairs window, Alice Rudrum overheard him talking at the corner of the Row. She heard him say, "You understand, don't you? I am placed in an awkward position just now." Then there was the sound of a kiss.

When Mrs. Hood came in, Mrs. Rudrum handed her the letter. "Meet me under the big clock at 9 o'clock tomorrow, but be sure you put the baby to bed before you come," Mrs. Hood read out aloud to the landlady. It was clearly a date with a man.

Six hours to live

On the Saturday evening, Mrs. Hood appeared from her room dressed smartly in a dove-coloured blouse, blue brocade bodice, and a dark skirt. She had on her sailor hat and veil and—according to Mrs. Rudrum later—wore a gold chain round her neck. It was the same chain in which she had posed for the beach photographer on Wednesday. It was also one of the two vital clues that were to lead to the Old Bailey's first murder trial of the twentieth century. For Mrs. Hood had only six hours to live.

Now it was morning and she had not reappeared. Several hours elapsed before the slow-witted John Rudrum got round to telling the police. By then, Mrs. Hood's body had been examined in the mortuary. There were signs that she had been sexually assaulted as well as strangled. The only clue to her identity—apart from John Rudrum's inadequate identification of her as their missing lodger—was a laundry-mark on her clothing. It was the number 599, written in heavy marking ink.

It was the second vital clue, and the one that would take the police halfway to the solution of the murder. The chain would do the rest. The same number 599 was found imprinted on some of Rose's baby-linen when, a few hours later, Inspector Robert Lingwood searched Mrs. Hood's room at the Rudrums' house.

The 599 mark was a positive and

unmistakable lead. Yet, incredibly, the local police failed to spot its significance. Three weeks drifted by before the bumbling and complacent Chief Constable of Yarmouth, William Parker, realized he was getting nowhere and handed the case over to Chief-Inspector Alfred Leach, of Scotland Yard's Criminal Investigation Department. Praying that the trail had not gone cold, Inspector Leach immediately circulated the number to every laundry in all the areas Mrs. Hood had mentioned in her conversations with Mrs. Rudrum.

Inspector Leach had also picked up the dead woman's reference to South Africa. Passenger lists were checked, and a Mr. and Mrs. Hood were found to have sailed for Cape Town aboard the *Gaika* on April 10, only to return on the *Avondale Castle* four days after setting foot on South African soil.

One strange thing

There was one strange thing about the Hoods. A shipping clerk who dealt with them remembered that on Mr. Hood's suitcase was a label bearing the name Bennett. And the man who had paid for their passage from England had drawn the money from a bank account also in the name of Bennett. Could the Bennetts be the same people as the Hoods?

The answer to the riddle came in a routine report from Detective-Sergeant Bartle of Bexleyheath, on the south-east borders of London and Kent. He had been plodding round the local laundries with a photograph of the 599 laundry-mark. Only one laundry, Kingdom's of Bexleyheath Broadway, thought it seemed familiar, but they had assured him that they were still receiving washing from the owner. Her name was Mrs. Bennett.

Detective-Sergeant Bartle was back at Kingdom's like a shot out of a gun. This time, he spoke to the proprietor, who confirmed that Mrs. Bennett had been away since the middle of September. Detective-Sergeant Bartle showed him the picture of "Mrs. Hood" on the beach. The man was mystified. "But that's Mrs. Bennett," he said. The 599 laundry-mark had identified the dead woman, linked her to Mrs. Bennett, and now led unerringly to Mrs. Bennett's 21-year-old husband, John Herbert Bennett.

That clue had done its work. Now it was time for the chain to take over. The gold chain, a family heirloom, had been bequeathed to Mary Bennett by her grandmother not long after she had married John Herbert Bennett, a weedy and inconspicuous-looking shop assistant with big ideas. Most of his big ideas, Mary soon discovered, involved breaking the law. Luckily for him, Mary was not above bending it a little herself.

Their first money-making venture was,

THE LANDLADY, a formidable woman named Mrs. Rudrum, thought there was something odd about her new lodger, despite her apparent respectability.

quite literally, a fiddle. An accomplished music-teacher, it dawned on Mary that she could make more money from selling a new violin to a pupil than by giving a dozen lessons. The result was one of the oldest confidence-tricks in the world. During 1898 and 1899 a touching advertisement appeared in several newspapers and bargain-magazines:

"Widow lady offers fine old violin, bow, case, strings, tuning fork, chin-rest, etc. Property deceased professor. Worth £10. Accept 19s. 6d. if immediate."

Although the advertisement appeared repeatedly, above a variety of initials and addresses, there were still plenty of suckers who thought they might be on to a Stradivarius for less than £1. What they actually received for their money from the "professor's widow" was a rubbishy instrument which almost fell apart at the first stroke of the bow. Not surprising, as they cost Mary Bennett all of £1 2s. 6d. for half-a-dozen.

Equally understandably, the Bennett's were constantly on the move. In September, 1899, they went to lodge with a Mrs. Susan Cato in the south London suburb of Balham. Mrs. Cato was a garrulous old busybody who thought Mary was

a "poor wife" to John. But it was Mrs. Cato who noticed something which was to become of paramount importance at John Herbert Bennett's trial—Mary had *two* chains, one the heirloom and one an imitation; also she possessed two silver watches, both of which she allowed her baby to use as teething rings.

By January, 1899, John and Mary had had enough of Mrs. Cato's prying. With the money they had made from soapbox violins they bought a grocery shop at Westgate-on-Sea, in Essex, which promptly caught fire. After claiming on the insurance, John Bennett opened a shop next door and stuffed it with cut-price goods obtained on credit from wholesalers. The shop did booming business. So much so that John and Mary were able to book a passage—as "Mr. and Mrs. Hood"—aboard the *Gaika*, bound for Cape Town. The wholesalers never saw their money; nor did the man who sold them the shop, Theodore Murton, who was left with a useless IOU for £160.

The Bennetts were back almost before they had arrived. For some mystifying reason, never fully explained by the authorities, the South African government suspected John Bennett of spying for the Boers, and they were there for only four days before being deported.

For some time Mary had known that John Bennett had been involved in some shady and dangerous deal, something far more serious than arson or defrauding his creditors. It came out in May, 1899, when they were lodging with Mrs. Emma Elliston at Plumstead. Their marriage had begun to fall apart at the seams and there were frequent rows. Unluckily for them, their new landlady was even more nosey than Mrs. Cato—a reputation she confirmed triumphantly at the Old Bailey.

Horror-struck tones

Mrs. Elliston overheard an argument between them, in which John—who was no longer sleeping with his wife—spat out, "Damn you—you and the baby too! You're nothing to me!" Mary's retort was chilling. "Herbert, I will follow you for the sake of the baby—but remember, if you aren't careful I can get you 15 years." Bennett had the last word. "I wish you were dead!" he shouted. "And if you're not careful you soon will be!" In horror-struck tones, as recounted by Mrs. Elliston, the all-too-ominous line was to be one of the most conclusive of the trial.

On June 10, 1900, the Bennetts finally split up, John moving into Mrs. Comfort Pankhurt's lodging-house at Woolwich, south London, and Mary ending up at a flat in Glencoe Villas, Bexleyheath, in Kent. It was the beginning of the end in more ways than one. For John Bennett had found a new girl-friend, a pretty

22-year-old maidservant named Alice Meadows. Alice had no idea John was married, and every day it became more difficult for him to keep up the pretence. What made it worse was that he was genuinely in love and wanted to marry her.

In July, they decided to go on holiday for a week to Yarmouth. One of Alice's friends had recommended a lodging-house, and she urged Bennett to write to the landlady for rooms. It was none other than Mrs. Rudrum. Unfortunately, Mrs. Rudrum was full up, and they had to make do with rooms 1 and 18 — Alice would not allow sex before the wedding-night — at the Crown and Anchor Hotel.

Three days after they returned, two telegrams arrived for Bennett at his lodgings. One was from Alice wishing him a happy 21st birthday. The other was an alarming message from Mary Bennett's neighbour: "TRY COME HOME M. VERY ILL BEXLEY." Making the excuse to his landlady that his "cousin" had been taken ill, Bennett grumpily cycled to Bexleyheath to console his wife.

The situation clearly couldn't continue, and it was in a determined mood that John Bennett went on holiday for a second time with Alice Meadows. This time they went to Ireland, and on the way there he

proposed and was accepted. He gave her a diamond-and-ruby ring, and fixed the wedding-day for June the following year.

By now, John's friends were beginning to talk about his double relationship, and he was forced into one subterfuge after another. Although he had lied all his life, he had not mastered even the fundamental principles of deceit. He told a different story to every one of his friends. In the end, he was forced into a corner and blurted out one evening that his wife had died "from a fever" in South Africa. It was September 12, 1900, and only a short step from the wish to the deed.

One-way to Yarmouth

It was now Mary Bennett's turn to have a holiday in Yarmouth . . . a holiday from which she would not return. John Bennett passed on Mrs. Rudrum's address to his wife and promised to join her at Yarmouth as soon as he could get away.

On Thursday, September 20 — five days after Mary had arrived at Mrs. Rudrum's — Bennett told Alice Meadows that he would be unable to see her the following Saturday as he had to go to Gravesend to visit his "sick grandfather". Then he sat down and wrote the letter to his wife, making the date for 9 o'clock "under the

clock" at Yarmouth Town Hall on Saturday, September 22.

Bennett was not at his lodgings on the Saturday night. Several witnesses testified to this in court. But he was undeniably back in London by 12.45 midday on the Sunday. For Alice Meadows bumped into him in Hyde Park, where he spun her an unconvincing story about having left his grandfather's house early because he felt "in the way". Bennett had obviously engineered the meeting, probably to substantiate some rough-and-ready alibi. Not that it would have been any more convincing than his tale to Alice. He could easily have caught the 7.20 a.m. from Yarmouth, arriving in London at 11.31 and leaving plenty of time to get to the Park. At his trial, that is precisely what the prosecution claimed.

By Tuesday, all the papers were full of the "Yarmouth Bootlace Murder", though the victim was still being referred to as "Mrs. Hood". Only Bennett knew her real identity, but he still felt vulnerable. So he decided to destroy systematically all evidence of Mary Bennett's life in Bexleyheath. He couldn't have drawn more attention to himself if he had walked through the Law Courts dangling Mary's golden chain and tying reef-knots in an old bootlace.

His attempt to cover up Mary's existence turned into a panic-stricken shambles. He broke into her flat at Glencoe Villas and started distributing the incriminating contents quite indiscriminately.

"Don't tell Alice"

He gave a gold brooch, a coat, and a cape to Alice Meadows, explaining that they had been left behind by his cousin who had "emigrated to South Africa". He sold Mary's piano and bicycle to a workmate, Robert Allen, for £23, after letting him into the flat. He gave a photograph of Mary to an old admirer, after allowing his landlady to catch a glimpse of it. "It's my sister," he said nervously, "only don't tell Alice about it."

He collected his wife's dog from a neighbour who had been looking after it — "She's moved to Yorkshire and I'll send it to her", he said — and gave notice to the flat landlords in Mary's name. Apparently satisfied with his lunatic bungling, he then rented some rooms as an extra "hideout" — right opposite Woolwich police station and next door to the house of a detective-sergeant.

As if all this wasn't conspicuous enough, he moved into his new address just one item of luggage. It was an old trunk. In it were two wigs, a false moustache, a

"I AM CHIEF-INSPECTOR Leach," he cried breathlessly. **"And I arrest you for the murder of Mrs. Hood on Yarmouth Beach. . . ."**

revolver, several collars with the telltale 599 laundry-mark, a receipt from the Crown and Anchor Hotel at Yarmouth . . . and Mary Bennett's gold chain and silver watch, the ones Mrs. Rudrum claimed she had been wearing on the night she was murdered. The police didn't realize it yet, but they had been virtually presented with a do-it-yourself conviction kit. And their hands were almost on Bennett's shoulder.

It was Robert Allen who steered the police towards Bennett, or rather, Bennett towards the police. Allen had been dissatisfied with the price he had paid for Mary's piano and bicycle—"You've been done", said his workmates—and when the police called at his house, following the obvious trail of the removals-van, his worst suspicions seemed justified. The piano had been stolen! He was flabbergasted when the police told him Bennett

THE BEGINNING of the end came when John Bennett (below) split up with his wife and found a new girlfriend. She was a pretty, 22-year-old maidservant named Alice Meadows—and he loved her.

was wanted for murder. Allen told them all he knew, and more . . .

On the evening of November 6, Allen was hanging about outside the gates of Woolwich Arsenal as Bennett finished work. As soon as Bennett appeared, Allen fell in beside him and started complaining about the piano and bicycle. Suddenly, he veered to one side, gestured to two heavily built men coming towards them and pointed dramatically at Bennett. "Mr. Bennett!" he exclaimed. Bennett was still wondering what all the pantomime was about when the taller of the two men hurled himself at him, pinioned his arms to his sides and said breathlessly, "I am Chief-Inspector Leach and I arrest you for the murder of Mrs. Hood on Yarmouth Beach."

February 24, 1901, was a foggy, dirty day, and inside the dismal Old Bailey courtroom—unchanged since 1774 but awaiting reconstruction—the gaslamps cast a hissing and fitful light on the opening of John Herbert Bennett's trial for murder. Bennett's defence counsel was the most flamboyant and theatrical figure at the British Bar—the redoubtable Edward Marshall Hall, then at the beginning of his explosive career.

Marshall Hall's speciality was prising reluctant admissions from hostile witnesses, and he started in superb style. The first to be squeezed was Police-Constable Manship, the man who had first examined the body on the sands. Yes, he admitted, reef-knots and granny-knots suggested a seafaring man rather than a callow young shop-assistant. Dr. Thomas Lettis, the police surgeon, was pressed to say that

sand found on the dead woman's tongue could have resulted from someone placing their hand over her mouth. If the assailant had been the dead woman's husband, and she trusted him, why would there have been any need to gag her? asked Marshall Hall rhetorically. It was a question which required no answer.

But even on the first day everything was drawn like a magnet to the crucial point of the gold chain Mary had been wearing on the night she died. The question was: could there have been *two* chains, so similar in appearance that witnesses could have confused them? For four days everything was to hang on Mary Bennett's chain, including the life of her husband.

Marshall Hall thought he had solved the riddle conclusively when he cornered James Richard Conyers—the man who had taken the beach photograph—in the witness-box. He suggested to Conyers that the chain in the photograph was heavier and more intricate, with the links fashioned to give a rope-like effect. To his delight, Conyers agreed. Triumphantly, Marshall Hall produced the chain found in Bennett's trunk and indicated for all to see that it was formed of simple gold links.

Conyers buried his head in an enlargement of his original photograph and muttered that he couldn't exactly remember what the chain had looked like. "It has a thickish look in the picture," he said, at which the Judge commented that perhaps the photo had been out of focus.

Unfortunate gaffe

"Quite right!" exclaimed Conyers, destroying Marshall Hall's carefully built-up effect in the click of a camera-shutter.

As if to erase the hapless Conyers, Marshall Hall turned on Mrs. Elliston, whose account of the "I wish you were dead" argument between the Bennetts had stirred the court. Mrs. Elliston, the wife of a local policeman involved in the case, had made an unfortunate gaffe by blabbing a highly inaccurate account of her lodgers' lives to the London *Evening News*.

In it, she had poured scorn on the Bennetts' claim to have visited South Africa—although it had been a vital factor in the prosecution case linking "Mrs. Hood" with Mrs. Bennett. Her husband, seeing his promotion vanishing "before his very eyes", had been furious. Marshall Hall was determined to brand her in one swift sortie as a liar, busybody, and eavesdropper.

Mrs. Elliston tied herself in a knot with the very first exchange. First, she admitted that she had "instantly" recognized Mary and her baby in the beach photograph; then she allowed herself to be pushed into conceding that the photograph "had not been very good".

Counsel: Did you tell the newspaper

IN THE CLICK of a camera shutter, beach photographer James Richard Conyers destroyed the theory that there might have been two gold chains.

reporters that when Mrs. Bennett arrived at your house she was richly dressed and wearing a quantity of jewellery?

Mrs. Elliston: I did not say she was wearing a quantity of jewellery. I said she was dressed well, but not richly dressed. I said her bodice was lined with silk, but not her dresses. I said she had a lot of jewellery. She had gold spectacles, ornaments in her hair, a gold bracelet and rings.

Counsel: Did you say her underwear was covered with lace?

Mrs. Elliston: I saw that her underclothes were good and had lace on them.

Counsel: Did you say to the reporters that you observed her purse to be well filled with gold?

Mrs. Elliston: Yes, she had plenty of money.

Counsel: So it seemed that Mr. Bennett had not been such a bad husband after all, certainly not ungenerous?

With Mrs. Elliston on the run, Marshall Hall angled his questions to infer that she had tailored her evidence in hindsight to fit the prosecution case.

Counsel: Did you tell the Press that you didn't believe the story that the Bennetts had come from South Africa?

Mrs. Elliston: I didn't say I didn't believe it.

Counsel: Did you say that they didn't look like people who had come off a sea voyage?

Mrs. Elliston: I don't remember.

Counsel: That must have been an invention of the Press?

Mrs. Elliston: I suppose so.

Counsel: Did you say anything about a fire at a shop in Westgate to the Press?

Mrs. Elliston: No.

Counsel: Did you know what the threat about 15 years meant?

Mrs. Elliston: No.

Counsel: Is your husband a police constable at Plumstead?

Mrs. Elliston: Yes.

Counsel: Has he spoken to you about these matters several times?

Mrs. Elliston: Yes.

Counsel: Was there great excitement at Woolwich about the murder?

Mrs. Elliston: I don't know.

Counsel. How far is it from Plumstead to Woolwich?

Mrs. Elliston: I don't know.

Counsel: Come! You live at Plumstead, and you don't know how far it is to Woolwich?

Mrs. Elliston: I rarely go there, as I have five children.

Counsel: I don't want to know about your children! How many miles is it?

Mrs. Elliston: About two.

It was all too much for the witness. She burst into tears. But Marshall Hall was not in a sympathetic mood. Commenting that "Tears are the common refuge of your sex", he returned to the attack.

Counsel: Did your husband go to the police station to see Bennett the night he was arrested?

Mrs. Elliston: He went there to identify him.

Counsel: Knowing that on November 6 this man had been arrested on a charge of murder, on November 11 you were gossiping about this case to a newspaperman?

Mrs. Elliston: I didn't think it would do Bennett any harm.

Prying troublemaker

Having exposed Mrs. Elliston as a prying troublemaker, Marshall Hall sought to undermine her account of the vital gold chain by making it sound too dogmatic.

Counsel: How many chains and watches did Mrs. Bennett have?

Mrs. Elliston: Only one watch and chain.

Counsel: I suggest she had a sham gold chain?

Mrs. Elliston: No. She didn't have one.

One of Mary Bennett's former landladies, Mrs. McDonald, was more useful —in a negative way—on the question of the chain. She said she had never seen the silver watch, and although she recognized the chain, she did not know if it was the only one. Marshall Hall knocked down John Rudrum like another ninepin, not even bothering to correct the two obvious mistakes in his first answer.

Counsel: When did you first see the deceased woman?

Mr. Rudrum: At about midnight on

it was the same one as in the beach photograph.

Far more damaging was the evidence of Robert Goodrum, a "buttons" from the Crown and Anchor Hotel at Yarmouth, who remembered a man corresponding to Bennett's description "running breathless into the hotel" at around 11.45 on the night of the murder. But he failed to recognize the prisoner as the man who had stayed at the same hotel during August with Alice Meadows. Marshall Hall's parting shot to the lad was typically contemptuous: "When did the police assist you with your memory?"

Identity parade

A waiter at the Crown and Anchor, William Reade, also claimed that Bennett had stayed at the hotel on the night of September 22. Earlier, he had picked Bennett out at an identity parade. But there was no official record of Bennett having been at the hotel. The manager confirmed that the bill counterfoils for that period had mysteriously vanished. Marshall Hall gave Robert Allen a rough ride over the bicycle he had bought from

September 15. When she arrived.

Counsel: Your picture has appeared in certain papers as an important witness in this case?

Mr. Rudrum: It was not my wish.

Counsel: How dare you pose as an important witness?

Mr. Rudrum: It was not my wish. I haven't taken much interest so far as the papers are concerned.

Counsel: Hasn't this been the event of your life?

Mr. Rudrum: Yes, it has. It has been the great topic of Yarmouth.

Counsel: You have talked the matter over with other people?

Mr. Rudrum: Yes.

Mrs. Rudrum was not so easy to terrorize. In fact, the more she was harassed, the more intractable she became.

When first shown the chain by prosecuting counsel, she failed to identify it as the one worn by Mary Bennett. She thought her lodger's chain had "longer links". But when Marshall Hall rose to take advantage of her indecision, her attitude hardened. She was now "positive" that the chain produced was the one the dead girl had worn. "What made you doubt when you first went into the box?" asked Marshall Hall sarcastically. "It was the light," said Mrs. Rudrum.

Her daughter, Alice, was equally vague but less antagonistic. She was sure the chain was Mary Bennett's, but, under cross-examination, said she did not think

STATELY as a galleon, defence witness Sholto Douglas (above) said his piece . . . and the faces of the jury showed every shade of disbelief. This failure blunted the impact of Mrs. Cato (right) and all but sealed the fate of Bennett (top).

Bennett before he had betrayed him to the police. Defence counsel was icy.

Counsel: Did you want to have your revenge on this man who swindled you over the bicycle by having him arrested in the street?

Mr. Allen: I had no idea of revenge.

Counsel: You've got the piano and bicycle, and you propose to keep them?

Mr. Allen: I have them still, and I don't know what I'll do with them. I had an expert examine the piano, and he said it was not worth the price.

Counsel: And yet you agreed to buy it?

Mr. Allen: I took it.

Mr. Charles Gill, prosecuting counsel, tried to save the situation, but only ended up by making his witness look like a treacherous liar. "Did you know that Bennett was wanted by the police on a charge of murder?" he asked Mr. Allen. "No," replied the witness, in what was probably the most unconvincing single-word answer in the trial.

Inevitably, the evidence reverted once again to the all-important chain—so maddeningly out of focus in the beach photograph. Even Chief Constable Parker of Yarmouth had to admit that "I can't say whether the chain in the picture is the same as the chain produced". At the beginning of the trial, things seemed to be going Bennett's way, but gradually the balance was shifting in favour of the prosecution—helped by three witnesses who swore that he had not been in his lodgings on the night of the murder.

Calamitous step

It would have been safer for defence counsel to have kept hammering away at the many inconsistencies in the prosecution case. But at this point, Marshall Hall—urged on by his client—decided to take one new and calamitous step. Hiding in the wings was a secret witness, a fancy-goods manufacturer named Douglas Sholto Douglas. He was imposing and authoritative-looking. And he had an astonishing story to tell.

On the evening of the murder, he had been walking near Lee Green—not far from Woolwich—when a talkative man answering to Bennett's description had forced his company upon him.

During conversation, the man mentioned he lived near Bexleyheath, and on the way from the New Tiger's Head pub—where they stopped for a drink—he pointed to a signboard above a barber's shop and said, "It seems like a namesake of mine lives there!" The name above the door was "F. K. Bennett".

The two men parted company at around

ALL AGREED that Bennett was an utter scoundrel—but did he deserve to die for the murder of his wife? Subsequent events suggest not. . . .

7 p.m.—Sholto Douglas had "overheard a bus conductor telling his driver the time"—far too late for Bennett to have kept his appointment with Mary under the Yarmouth Town Hall clock.

There were two slight snags to the story. One was that it was just *too* perfect and fortuitous. The other was that Bennett couldn't remember a thing about the incident. The jury would have to accept the fancy-goods manufacturer's story completely, or reject it out of hand as something hurriedly stitched up by the defence to support a threadbare case. The situation was not helped by Bennett's refusal to testify on his own behalf, or indeed, to give any evidence at all.

Marshall Hall was against calling the witness, but he left the final decision to Bennett. Torn by indecision, he wrote two sentences on a piece of paper, "I wish Douglas to be called" and "I do not wish Douglas to be called". The paper was handed to Bennett with instructions to make his choice within two hours. The paper was returned on time. The words "I do not wish Douglas to be called" had been crossed out.

Marshall Hall did his theatrical best in introducing Sholto Douglas to the witness-box. "The Press has tried, condemned and everything short of executed the man Bennett within 24 hours of his arrest," he thundered. "However, if the Press has done irreparable harm, it has also done good by bringing to light a witness who might not otherwise have come forward!"

Acrid hiss of gas

The only sound in court was the acrid hiss of the gas jets. Marshall Hall pointed dramatically at the prisoner and bellowed: "On the evening of September 22 this man was in London and in the company of a man I shall now call!"

After the pandemonium had died down, Sholto Douglas swept up, as stately as a galleon, to say his piece. The response was exactly what Marshall Hall had feared. The faces of the jury registered every shade of disbelief. The word "fraud" could almost have been written in lights over Sholto Douglas's head.

After this dubious display, Mrs. Cato's useful evidence failed to achieve its proper

MRS. ELLISTON. MRS. PANKHURST. MRS. MACDONALD. MR. MARSHALL HALL, K.C. MR. SAVAGE. THE PRISONER. THE EARL OF DESART, K.C.B. MR. GILL, K.C. MISS ELIZABETH LANGMAN.

The People.
A Weekly Newspaper for All Classes.

LONDON, SUNDAY, MARCH 3, 1901.

No. 1,012. ONE PENNY. [o.p.o. as a Newspaper.]

KITCHENER'S SEVEN-LEAGUED BOOTS.
A PROPHETIC FAIRY TALE.

Special SUNDAY Edition.

THE WAR.

OTHA MYSTERY.
THE SURRENDER RUMOUR.

THE YARMOUTH MURDER.

YESTERDAY'S PROCEEDINGS.

MORE WITNESSES FOR THE DEFENCE.

A MYSTERIOUS STRANGER.

STRANGE STORY OF A MISSING BOOTLACE.

ELOQUENT APPEAL BY MR. MARSHALL HALL.

MR. GILL'S REPLY.

THE LORD CHIEF JUSTICE SUMS UP.

PRISONER FOUND GUILTY.

SENTENCED TO DEATH.

"So he donned the Magician's Seven-leagued Boots that covered leagues at a stride, and the Bandits could not escape him."—Classic Fairy Tale Modernised.

[Drawn Specially for "The People" by HARRY FURNISS]

REPLY FOR THE CROWN

---

impact. She recalled that Mary Bennett had once pawned her gold chain, and bought an imitation to take its place. She had seen both chains, and there was little difference between the two, "except that in the newer chain the links were closer together". Mrs. Bennett had also possessed two silver watches, and on one occasion she had commented, "No sooner do I get one mended than the other one gets broken!"

In his closing speech, Marshall Hall hit out in all directions before coming to the question of the chain. "I am astounded that the prosecution has endeavoured to prove that the lady's watch and chain that the prisoner had were the property of the deceased woman," he said. "Because not even a madman would have treasured so damning a piece of evidence that could send him to his doom." With more hope than conviction, he added, "However, the sheet anchor of my case is the evidence of Mr. Sholto Douglas, who in the witness-box told the plain truth."

Adopting a more conversational tone, prosecuting counsel, Mr. Charles Gill, reminded the jury that Bennett had had

FOR THE SUPERSTITIOUS, there was no shortage of omens that Bennett had been wrongly executed: from a broken flagstaff . . . to an identical killing at Yarmouth years later.

an overwhelming motive for the murder. His wife had been in the way of his affair with Alice Meadows. As for the chain, "Did the person who murdered Mrs. Bennett take away her watch and chain? The identity of the watch and chain as the property of the dead woman, and their possession by the prisoner, are matters proved beyond the possibility of doubt."

Bennett was as cocksure as ever as the jury filed out to consider their verdict. "I'm pleased with both of you," he told his counsel. "Up to now!" Thirty-five minutes later, the jury returned. The verdict was Guilty. The Lord Chief Justice seemed far more distressed than the prisoner as he pronounced the death sentence. At one point, he almost broke down. "I am not guilty, sir," said Bennett firmly.

There were other people who thought the same. Although everyone agreed that

Bennett was an utter scoundrel, there were serious doubts about the prosecution case. According to medical evidence, Mary Bennett had actually died at about 1.30 a.m.—which made nonsense of the story of John Bennett running breathless into the Yarmouth hotel at 11.45. Who was the mysterious man who had bought Mary the "fish and brandy supper" and kissed her goodnight? Even the uniqueness of Mary's gold chain had not been fully substantiated.

For the superstitious, there was one final indication of Bennett's innocence. On March 21, 1901, Bennett was hanged at Norwich Jail. As the traditional black flag was run up above the roof, a sudden and fierce gust of wind snapped the flagstaff in two. Both mast and flag came clattering down the roof.

Eleven years after Bennett's execution, on July 14, 1912, the body of 18-year-old Dora May Gray was found on the south beach at Yarmouth. She was lying on her back, knees bent and legs splayed, with her skirt above her knees. She had been strangled with a bootlace, which had been tied in a reef-knot.

MURDER MOST FOUL

SHOT
27·9·1927

Was it simply an excess of viciousness, or was there something more that drove the killer of Police-Constable Gutteridge to shoot out the dying man's eyes? A dark streak of superstition, perhaps, deep inside a brutal soul . . .

IT WAS just before six o'clock on the morning of September 27, 1927. The English country lanes of Essex, between Ongar and Romford, were still damp from the patchy, overnight fog.

Along one of those lanes a Mr. William Ward, a motor engineer, was driving from the village of Stapleford Abbotts towards Stapleford Torney.

As he turned a bend in the lane near the hamlet of Howe Green he saw, on his right-hand side, "a huddled-up form" of a man. The man seemed to be lying in a half-resting position, as though resting against the earthen bank skirting the lane. His legs stretched into the road.

Mr. Ward stopped and went across to the man. As a local resident he immediately recognized who it was: Police-Constable George William Gutteridge, of Stapleford Abbotts. He spoke to the policeman but there was no reply. He took hold of his left hand and found that it was cold. P.C. Gutteridge was dead.

He had been shot four times and two of the shots had been fired, at close range, into each of his eyes. Clutched in his right hand was a pencil; nearby lay his note-book and helmet. There was blood all around the body and a trail which stretched to a larger, bloody pool in the middle of the lane.

Torch in his pocket

When Gutteridge's colleagues from the Essex Constabulary arrived at the scene they noticed three other significant facts. The dead policeman's whistle was hanging from its chain outside his uniform jacket, but his torch was still in his pocket and his truncheon in its pouch.

Moreover, a doctor who made an on-the-spot examination estimated that Gutteridge had been killed at around four in the morning. It was obvious, of course, that it would have been dark at the time of his death.

Apparently he had taken out his whistle to signal to someone and clearly he had been about to write something in his note-book. Equally clearly, he had not needed the light of his torch to see by.

So what had he been doing in the moments before he was shot? The circumstances suggested an almost certain possibility to the investigating officers. Gutteridge must have been about to write by the light of a car's headlamps. He must have been killed when, in the glare, he could not see what his murderer or murderers were about to do.

The bullets collected from in and

SHOT FOUR TIMES at close range, the corpse of P.C. Gutteridge was already cold as the overnight fog dispersed along the remote country lane. He seemed to have died in the glare of headlamps, blind to the movements of the murderers.

around the body were of great importance. They were of an obsolete Service type, withdrawn from army issue as far back as 1914. One had been propelled by black powder not in normal use since 1894.

If the police could find a revolver capable of firing the shots and a cartridge case they would be close to the killer.

The first two direct clues in the murder hunt appeared swiftly. Soon after the discovery of Gutteridge's body a Dr. Edward Lovell, of Billericay, some 14 miles from the murder site, reported that during the night his blue Morris Cowley car, TW6120, had been stolen from the garage at his home.

At 6.45 on the evening of September 27 the car was found abandoned in Brixton, S.W. The nearside mudguard was damaged and around it were scrapings of a substance that looked like the bark of a tree. Dr. Lovell's cases of medical instruments, which he had left in the car, were missing.

There were splashes of blood on the car's running board and, under the front passenger seat, an empty cartridge case was found. It was a rare and obsolete type and matched one of the bullets fired at the policeman. Mr. Robert Churchill, the famous London gunmaker, was able to tell the police that this and other bullets used in the crime had been fired from a Webley revolver.

A quiet little business

But after those early clues the police investigations, led by Chief Inspector James Berrett, of Scotland Yard, seemed to have reached a dead-end. Then, nearly three months after the murder, missing pieces from the detectives' jigsaw suddenly began to fall into place.

At 7.50 p.m. on January 20, 1928, a grey Angus-Sanderson car, driven by a man named Frederick Guy Browne, rolled into the Globe garage in Northcote Road, Battersea, S.W. Its arrival was watched by detectives who had been keeping the garage under observation for several days. They suspected that Browne, the owner, was running a quiet little business in stolen vehicles.

The police waited until Browne, dressed as a chauffeur in blue uniform and peaked cap, had got out of the car. Then they moved in and arrested him on a charge of stealing a Vauxhall car from Tooting, S.W., the previous November.

About 10 officers took part in the arrest—at first sight a formidable number to tackle one suspected car thief. But Browne was well known to the police as a tough, professional "villain" who had devoted his life to crime, and whose record included the unlicensed possession of firearms.

Browne, who was 47, had served sentences of more than seven years since the

THE BULLETS were an important clue: all were long obsolete, one even propelled by black powder not in use for more than 30 years. The trail led straight to a Webley revolver—and to Frederick Browne (right) and William Kennedy.

age of 30. During one four-year "stretch" at Parkhurst he earned a reputation as a vicious convict who attacked prison officers and smashed-up his cell.

Now, while he was held at Tooting police station, one group of detectives searched the Battersea bed-sitter where he lived with his wife and young daughter. Another group searched his garage, and a third group searched Browne himself.

Each search provided a valuable haul of evidence. At Browne's home the police found a small nickel-plated gun loaded with six cartridges. From the pocket by the driver's seat in the car they took

a fully-loaded Webley and, from the garage, 16 cartridges and various doctor's instruments including a pair of forceps.

The search of Browne himself yielded a pair of artery forceps, a dozen ·45 cartridges which fitted the Webley, and a stocking mask with apertures cut for eyes, ears and mouth.

Up to the point at which all these "finds" were laid out at Tooting police station (on the billiard table in the recreation room), the detectives still thought they were dealing only with a dangerous car thief. But the facts about the murder of a colleague are fairly

Syndication International

understandably printed clearly in every policeman's mind. The moment that the officers examined the Webley and the doctor's instruments they began to suspect a link between Browne and P.C. Gutteridge's murder.

Browne himself, an over-talkative, snarling-tempered hoodlum, helped to underline those suspicions by his reckless outburst when the various articles were shown to him.

"Ah, you've found that, have you?" he sneered, looking at the Webley. "I'm done for now . . . What I can see of it, I shall have to have a machine gun for you bastards next time!"

The next day another loaded Webley was found at the garage. Chief Inspector Berrett then went to Tooting, told Browne he was investigating the murder and asked him to account for his movements on the night of September 26, and to explain his possession of arms and ammunition.

Browne insisted that he was at home on the night of the killing. "I have no connection with the murder of P.C. Gutteridge," he said, "and it doesn't interest me."

As for the revolvers: the one found in the driver's seat pocket he "gave £3 for down at Tilbury Docks from a sailorman whose name I don't know, neither can I describe him"; the second Webley and its ammunition were also his, he admitted, "but I decline to give any explanation of where I got them".

Meanwhile, still pursuing their inquiries into the Vauxhall car theft, the police began to centre their attention on 36-year-old William Henry Kennedy, an associate of Browne and a criminal with an equally black record.

More serious matters

On January 25 Kennedy was arrested in Liverpool on suspicion of being concerned in the theft. The following day he was brought to London and taken to Scotland Yard, where Chief Inspector Berrett had far more serious matters to discuss with him.

"I have been making inquiries for some time past respecting the murder of P.C. Gutteridge in Essex. Can you give me any information about the occurrence?" the bearded investigator asked.

In his faintly Irish accent—he had been born in Scotland of Irish parents— Kennedy replied: "I may be able to tell you something, but let me consider awhile. . . . Can I see my wife?"

Mrs. Kennedy, who had travelled down on the same train from Liverpool as her arrested husband, and was already at the Yard, was called into the room. She stared anxiously at the red-faced, balding man she had married only eight days before—and whose miserable "career"

ranged from army desertion to stealing a bicycle while armed with a loaded revolver.

The dialogue that followed between husband and wife was one of the oddest ever heard and recorded by police in a murder investigation.

"Well, my dear," said Kennedy, "you know when I was arrested at Liverpool yesterday I told you I thought there was something more serious at the back of it. Well, there is. These officers are making inquiries about that policeman murdered in Essex."

No, Kennedy said in answer to his wife's urgent first question, he hadn't murdered him. But he was there and he knew who had. If he were found guilty he might hang or, if not, he might go to prison for a long time as an accessory. Would she wait for him?

"Yes, love," Mrs. Kennedy assured him. "I will wait for you any time. . . . Tell them the truth of what happened."

A classic account

The story Kennedy then proceeded to dictate to Berrett is a classic among first-hand accounts of what the law used to call "murder most foul".

On the evening of September 26, he and Browne (Kennedy said) went by train to Billericay where Browne had previously earmarked a Raleigh car ripe for stealing.

A persistently barking dog scared them off and, since it was then after 11 p.m., Browne said: "We can't get back by train now, so we'll try somewhere else."

They then "cased" Dr. Lovell's house and garage, and waited in a nearby field until all the house lights were switched off soon after midnight. Then they crept up to the garage, which was at the top of a sloping driveway, and Browne forced the doors with a tyre lever.

For secrecy's sake they let the doctor's car run down the driveway under its own weight, and pushed it about a hundred yards along the road before starting the engine. Browne took the wheel and "drove off around country lanes at a great pace".

After several misdirections they found themselves on a road to Ongar and were speeding along when "we saw someone who stood on the bank and flashed his lamp as a signal to stop".

They drove on but heard the blast of a police whistle and Kennedy (so his story went) told Browne to stop, "which he did quite willingly".

The policeman, P.C. Gutteridge, came up to the car on Browne's side and asked them a series of questions. Where were they going? "Lea Bridge Road garage," said Browne. "We've been out doing repairs." Did Browne have a driving licence? He did not. Was this his

car? "No," Kennedy chipped in quickly, "it's mine."

A beam from the policeman's torch flashed in their faces as Gutteridge asked: "Do you know the number of this car?" Too cocky, as always, Browne replied: "You'll see it on the front of the car."

"Yes," said Gutteridge, "I know the number, but do you?" Kennedy answered: "It's TW6120."

Gutteridge put his torch back in his pocket, took out his notebook and pencil and was about to write in the light of the headlamps when, said Kennedy, "I heard a report, quickly followed by another one.

"I saw the policeman stagger and fall over by the bank at the hedge. I said to Browne 'What have you done?' and then saw he had a large Webley revolver in his hand.

"He said, 'Get out, quick.' I immediately got out and went round to the policeman who was lying on his back. Browne came over and said, 'I'll finish the bugger.' I said, 'For God's sake, don't shoot any more, the man's dying,' as he was groaning.

"The policeman's eyes were open and Browne, addressing him, said, 'What are you looking at me like that for?' and, stooping down, shot him at close range through both eyes."

After the murder they drove off even more wildly, blundering around country roads in the mist that had begun to settle. At one point Browne drove off the road and grazed the car against a tree.

Unimpressed

On the way, said Kennedy, Browne told him to re-load the Webley. He did so nervously, dropping an empty cartridge case on the car floor. At 5.30 a.m. they abandoned the car in Brixton and journeyed to Browne's garage by tram.

On Monday, April 23, 1928, Browne and Kennedy went on trial at the Old Bailey before Mr. Justice Avory, jointly charged with the murder.

Browne, arrogant and argumentative to the end, simply denied the charge as "absurd", and dismissed Kennedy's story as "a concoction". Kennedy's plea that he was "terrified" of Browne made no impression on the jury—especially after it came out in evidence that he had tried to shoot a detective when he was being arrested in Liverpool.

At the end of four days both men were found guilty and sentenced to death. From the death cell Kennedy wrote a final, highly emotional letter to his wife expressing the hope, because of his need for her, that she would soon be joining him in the hereafter.

On May 31 Browne was hanged at Pentonville and Kennedy at Wandsworth.

It is certain that Kennedy's story of

Both Popperfoto

the murder was fairly accurate except for his professed horror at the events. Certainly Browne fired the fatal shots but Kennedy was his willing accomplice.

But one mystery will always remain: why, when P.C. Gutteridge was already dead, or on the very point of death, did Browne add unnecessarily to the night's brutality by shooting into the policeman's eyes?

Maybe it was merely a further manifestation of his viciousness. Or perhaps it was, as some people have suggested, that Browne, the tough, small-time "hood", had a dark streak of superstition in his soul.

Perhaps he believed the old wives' tale that the last thing a dying man sees is "fixed" like a photograph in his eyes.

ACE GUNSMITH Robert Churchill (right) identified a rare cartridge case and the bullets as having been fired from Browne's Webley. The killer (shown with wife) was arrogant and argumentative to the end, dismissing as a "concoction" the testimony of his "terrified" accomplice William Kennedy.

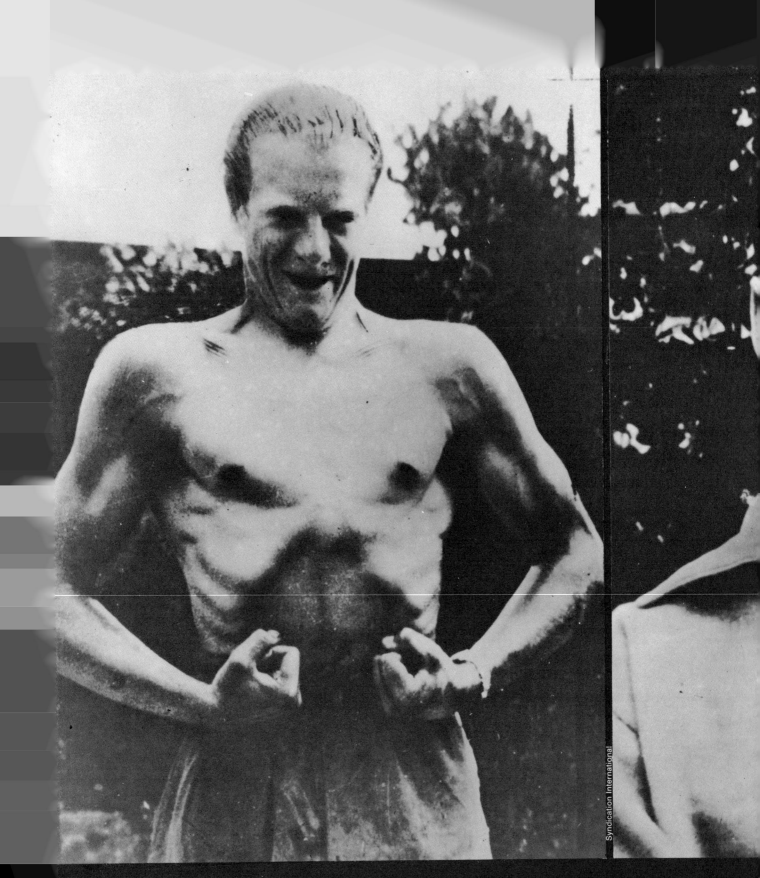

MURDER....BY BRITISH

Syndication International

AN OUTRAGED PUBLIC saw
young Derek Bentley (far left)
and his accomplice Christopher
Craig as symbols of England's
post-war wave of violence.
But were they scapegoats?
The charge was the most serious
under British law,
the murder of a policeman.
Their case would have
historic repercussions . . .

Keystone

JUSTICE

THE two young men in the dock looked uncomfortable in their conservative clothes. They were more used to the flashiness of England's early 1950's: long jackets, bright coloured pants and thick crepe-soled shoes. But both their lawyers had insisted that everything, even details of dress, could play a small but vital role in the courtroom battle that was about to take place. For 19-year-old Derek Bentley, the jury's attitude towards him could mean the difference between life in the bosom of his family and death at the end of a hangman's noose. At 16, co-defendant Christopher Craig was too young to hang, but a conviction would signify detention for an indefinite period.

The charge against these innocent looking teenagers was the most serious offence in English law: the murder, in cold blood, of a police officer in the course of his duty. Yet, as they waited in No. 2 Court of London's Old Bailey for the trial to begin, they looked curiously unconcerned, as if unaware of the implications of what was happening.

If this was so, they were the only ones. John Parris, Craig's brilliant young defence counsel, wore a worried expression as he sifted through the mass of papers on the case. He had accepted the brief at a mere week's notice, and soon became

aware that the complexities of evidence that would be given were going to test his powers of cross-examination severely. Bentley's lawyer, Frank Cassels, was also fully aware of the task which lay before him and, like his colleague, busily engaged in last-minute preparation.

The date was Tuesday, December 9, 1952. At precisely 10.30 a.m., Christmas Humphreys, Prosecuting Counsel for the Crown, entered, closely followed by the Lord Chief Justice, 75-year-old Lord Goddard, the most eminent judge of the time. His presence may well have been a misfortune for the defendants, for he had publicly expressed his views that the wave of violence which hit post-war England should be dealt with harshly, and there was a danger that he would consider Craig and Bentley as typical examples of a general malaise. If he did, then their chances of acquittal might, perhaps, be substantially reduced. Fears had even been voiced that the two youths could become scapegoats, and that the authorities would deal with them severely as an object lesson to other would-be offenders.

The judge's first action did nothing to ease those fears. Having listened to their pleas of Not Guilty, he turned and eyed them steadily. Bentley stood up straight and, it seemed, a little uncomprehend-

ingly in the dock. Craig, however, was clearly in great pain. He had been badly injured just before his arrest and was scarcely able to stand at all. "Craig," intoned the judge, "may sit down."

The 12-man jury was quickly sworn in and Prosecuting Counsel Christmas Humphreys was soon on his feet to make the opening speech. His first words provided one of the most remarkable understatements of the trial: "You may have read something of this case," he told the court. In reality, every detail press reporters had been able to discover—whether true or not—had been splashed across newspapers throughout the country from the moment of Craig's and Bentley's arrest. CHICAGO GUN BATTLE IN LONDON ran one headline over a story which bore almost no relation to the dramatic death of the police officer. But if facts were lacking, public interest certainly was not.

Black marketeers

There was an immediate outcry against the two accused young men, and it continued unabated until the trial began. On the first morning, a huge mass of people gathered outside the doors of the Old Bailey in the hope of securing a seat in the public gallery. Some of them had queued throughout the bitterly cold December night. Others who arrived later found their way barred less by court officials than by black marketeers who demanded up to £30 (75 dollars) for an entrance ticket to the trial—and got the price they asked. It was a new and extravagant form of theatrical entertainment, and already the subject of anger, fierce argument, and sensation.

Against this background of publicity, Humphreys outlined the case for the prosecution. He told how, on the night of November 2, 1952, Christopher Craig and Derek Bentley had travelled the short bus journey from their homes in South London to Croydon with the intention of breaking into a warehouse and stealing "whatever they could find". Both were armed: Bentley with a sheath knife and a vicious knuckle-duster, and Craig with a loaded ·455 Eley Service revolver (commonly known as a ·45 Colt). He also had a spare clip of ammunition in his top pocket.

Entry to the warehouse was more difficult than they had first imagined and, having failed to force the locks, they decided to climb onto the roof to see if they could gain entrance from there. They quickly found a door leading down into the building, but this was also locked

Popperfoto

"LET HIM HAVE IT, CHRIS!" and a policeman was shot dead. But events at the warehouse moved with dramatic speed . . . quicker than the eye of a witness?

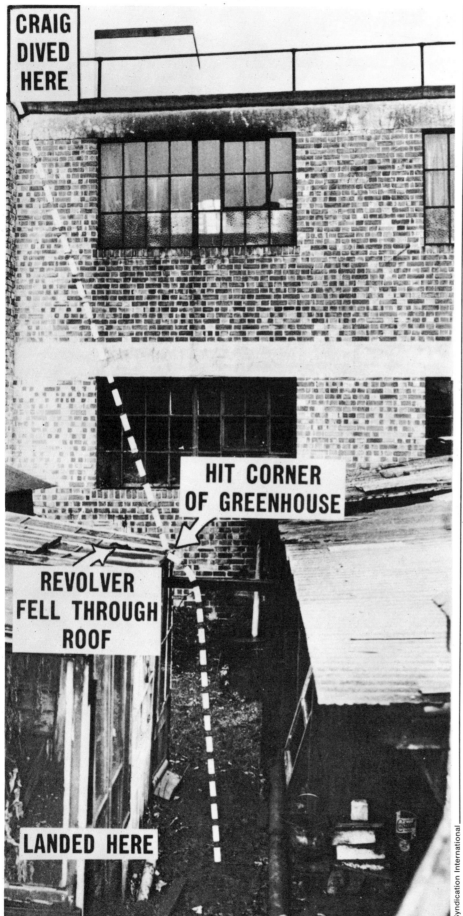

CRAIG DIVED HERE

HIT CORNER OF GREENHOUSE

REVOLVER FELL THROUGH ROOF

LANDED HERE

and barred from the inside. Unknown to them, their luck had already run out at least ten minutes before. They had been spotted from a house across the street, and the police were in the process of surrounding the warehouse at the very moment when the two reached the top.

It was not long before Craig and Bentley spotted the police movements. They looked around desperately for somewhere to take cover. The roof was flat with four low glass rooflights in the middle—totally inadequate for concealment. The only other structure was the lift-shaft situated at one end. It was small, but there was no choice. Almost as they settled behind it, however, the voice of Detective Constable Fairfax hailed them through the darkness:

"Come and get us"

"I'm a police officer. Come out from behind that stack." Craig was unimpressed. "If you want us, f . . . . . well come and get us," he replied. It was the moment of confrontation. From then on events moved at dramatic speed.

Bentley had no heart for a direct battle with the police and immediately walked out and surrendered. Fairfax grabbed him. In his narration, Christmas Humphreys was well aware of the vital importance of the next few minutes.

Bentley, he said, suddenly pulled free from the policeman's grasp and shouted: "Let him have it, Chris!" whereupon Craig drew his ·45 "Colt" and fired, hitting Fairfax on the shoulder. Fairfax fell, but was soon on his feet again, apparently uninjured. It was later discovered that the bullet had merely grazed the skin. By this time two other officers, McDonald and Harrison, had scrambled onto the roof, but found themselves powerless to deal with Craig who fired at every sound of movement.

Between the eyes

Meanwhile, other officers had located the warehouse manager, obtained the keys and were hurrying to the door which led onto the roof. Harrison had retreated and descended to the ground in order to join his colleagues inside the building. He was the second man to appear from the rooftop doorway. The first was Police Constable Miles who was forced to struggle with the lock, before managing to fling open the door. As he emerged a shot rang out and he fell with a bullet wound between the eyes. Within minutes he was dead.

Harrison was next out, but by moving quickly he succeeded in joining his two colleagues on the roof. All three then attempted to shelter behind Bentley's body by positioning him firmly in front of them. At this point, Humphreys deliberately paused to allow time for his words to take effect. The whole court-room had listened in spellbound silence as he built up the scene of tension and danger faced by the police on that December evening. Now he wanted to underline the aspect of deliberation which lay behind Craig's actions. Purposefully, he read out the challenge which the young criminal had hurled at the police.

"Come on, you coppers, I'm only sixteen. Come on, you brave coppers, think of your wives."

Too young to die

The implication of these remarks was clear at least to Humphreys: Craig knew that he was too young to suffer the death penalty, and was reminding the police that their lives were in greater danger than his own.

At once, the officers on the roof held a hurried conference and decided to retreat once more through the open door, taking Bentley with them. Bentley was now terrified. "Look out, Chris," he shouted, "they're taking me down!"

This, it was suggested, was a warning to Craig not to fire, in case he hit Bentley by mistake.

Alone on the roof with the dead man, Craig's nerve began to crack. He continued hurling challenges at the vanished police officers until Fairfax reappeared armed with a gun, which he fired in Craig's direction. This time no reply was forthcoming. Craig had run out of ammunition. In desperation he called out, "It's empty!" Then, without warning, he ran to the edge of the roof and dived off the 30-foot-high building. His body bounced off the corner of a greenhouse before crashing to the ground. He had broken his back, his left forearm and a bone in his chest.

"I wish I was f . . . . . . dead," he gasped as police lifted him from the ground. "I hope I've killed the f . . . . . . lot."

There was no doubt, said the prosecution, that the most crucial piece of evidence was Bentley's remark, "Let him have it, Chris." No one disputed that

Craig had shot Miles. But the case for the prosecution was not only that this tragedy had taken place as a result of Craig's actions, but that Bentley's remark was an incitement to Craig to murder Fairfax. Thus, in spite of the fact that Bentley was under arrest at the time, he was, nevertheless, equally responsible in law for the murder.

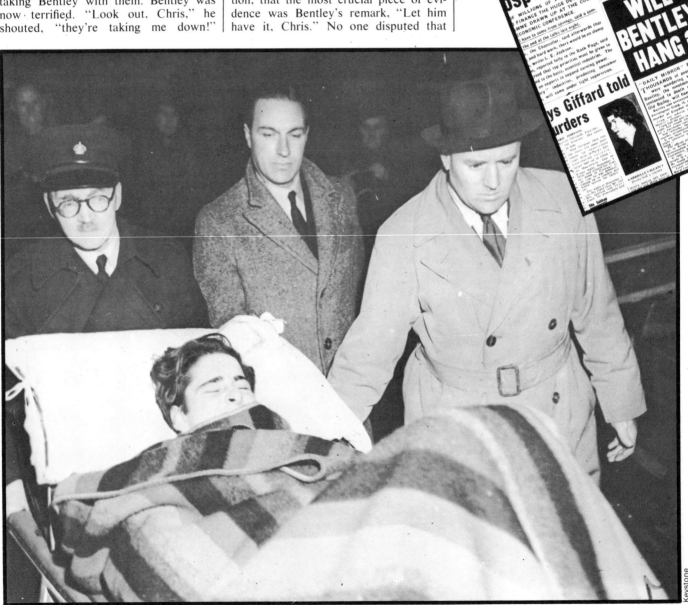

SPLASHED across front pages,
the facts wore a bit thin. But
a few things were certain:
that Craig (far left) had dived
off the 30-foot-high building,
that Sidney Miles (above) was
dead and a courageous colleague,
Frederick Fairfax (right), wounded.

"As for Craig," continued Humphreys, "I suggest that he not only gloried in the murder, but openly regretted that he had not killed more."

It was an impressive finale to his opening speech, and, whether by luck or judgment, it provided reporters with a perfect piece of headline copy. The following morning CRAIG GLORIED IN MURDER was splashed across the front pages of the newspapers. A string of police witnesses followed who testified to having been present at the battle scene. Others submitted plans and photographs of the warehouse roof so that the jury could visualize the positioning of the entrance door and the lift stack. Then Constable Fairfax was called. Under questioning he repeated more or less exactly the story which Humphreys had outlined in his opening speech. He confirmed that Craig had shot Constable Miles, and that Bentley had spoken the fatal words of incitement.

The case against the two youths seemed, at this stage, so watertight that to the press and spectators alike there appeared no line of defence available. Lord Goddard sat tight-lipped and silent on the bench. The facts seemed so far to indicate that the case for the Crown was going well.

In his cross-examination, Frank Cassels tried in vain to cast doubt on Fairfax's evidence. Parris, however, was luckier. He questioned Fairfax about the number of shots fired on the murder night. Evidence so far had indicated that Miles was killed by the third shot from Craig's gun. Was this true?

"Oh no; to my recollection there were several other shots."

"What other shots were there?"

"I should say there were six or seven other shots."

"Before the fatal shot?"

"Before the fatal shot, yes."

The significance of this evidence was enormous. All previous witnesses had testified that Craig had fired a maximum of four shots before Miles' death. Who then had fired the others? It was known that a number of police officers had been armed. Was it possible that one of these had fired the fatal bullet? It was a question which Parris was not to raise when he came to examine the ballistics evidence.

Constable McDonald was next on the stand, and his evidence, though it appeared to corroborate what Fairfax had said, contained some unusual curiosities. It was Cassels, this time, who probed deeper. McDonald admitted that he had heard the fatal sentence spoken by Bentley but stated that, owing to his position, he could not make out any other piece of conversation which had taken place on the rooftop. Immediately Cassels pounced:

"I am suggesting you never heard that remark used by Bentley . . ."

"I could not say whether it was Bentley who used it or not, sir."

Police collusion

It was a cunning line of argument. If doubt could be cast on the truth of one policeman's evidence, then the way would be open for the defence to imply that the police planned their evidence beforehand in order to present a united front against the "killers" of their colleague. The implication was spotted at once by Lord Goddard. Quickly, he intervened.

"Did you hear the word 'Chris' used?"

"I did, my Lord."

"So far as you know there were three people on the roof?"

"Yes, my Lord."

"There was Sergeant Fairfax and the two men?"

"Yes, my Lord."

"And you heard 'Let him have it, Chris'; is that right?"

"Yes, my Lord."

"Very good."

With this, the question was brought to an end. Never once was it suggested that evidence given by the police was anything other than wholly accurate. It seems not to have occurred either to the judge or to the defence that if Bentley did make the remark, he might have been urging Craig to hand over the gun—and *not* inciting him to use it.

As the trial continued, other disturbing points began to emerge. The last police officer to reach the roof, Constable Harrison, claimed to have witnessed the death of Constable Miles from his position within the doorway of the rooftop entrance. Miles, he claimed, "kicked the door open and as he stepped out a shot was fired from the direction of the lift stack". No one asked how Harrison could tell, from inside the warehouse, where the shot had come from.

Worse, however, was to follow. Various police witnesses revealed, under cross-examination, that Craig—although of average intelligence—was unable to read; while Bentley was not merely illiterate, but thought to be feeble-minded and educationally sub-normal. Here, however, the defence found itself faced with the insuperable problem of English law as it stood then. The whole question of the mental condition of the accused youths should have been examined in open court. But, in order to do this, both defence counsels would have been forced to call witnesses to testify on their behalf, and in so doing would forfeit the right to have the last word to the jury—the final speech before the judge summed up.

Thus, a crucial defence factor—particularly for Bentley, whose mental age had been rated as nine—was glossed over. Neither Cassels nor Parris felt that they could take the risk of allowing the prosecution the privilege of speaking last in a case which had been given such sensational and emotional overtones by the press.

The final witness for the prosecution was ballistics expert, Lewis Nickolls, who revealed, under an incisive cross-examination from Parris, that there was, in fact, no reliable ballistics evidence at all which pointed to Craig's gun as the murder weapon. Parris held up, in court, the supposed murder bullet which had been discovered near the body of Constable Miles, and then handed it to Nickolls.

"This is the fatal bullet, is it not?"

"No," came the astonishing reply, "I could find no evidence whatsoever of blood on it. Therefore, in all probability, it is not the fatal bullet."

There was an audible murmur in court. It seemed, for the first time, that the prosecution had made a mistake; and this minor triumph was quickly followed

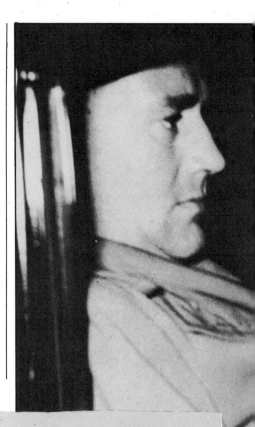

To Sir David Patrick Maxwell Fyffe

I plead with you as Derek Bentley sister to reconsider your decision if you could have been able to see Derek yesterday I am sure to those words. he said to my Mother

"I am not afraid to die because I am innocent—Mum, would have moved you as they did us. I ask are these the words of a boy who has a life on his conscience

Please I beseech you save my Brother's life time is short but we are hopeful

Miss Iris Bentley

316

Popperfoto

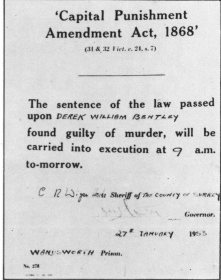

HOW MANY MORE LIVES would society take under this 85-year-old law? Change would come too late to save Bentley (left) from a judge described as "vengeful and biased", despite a pathetic hand-written appeal from the boy's sister.

by another. The gun used by Craig had a sawn-off barrel. This meant, said Nickolls, that as a weapon it was extremely inaccurate. Constable Miles had been 40 feet from Craig when he died, and at that distance, even in the hands of an expert marksman, the gun would fire six feet wide at least.

For some reason, Parris did not pursue this line of inquiry. His intention was to show that the death of Miles was an accident since, if Craig had tried to kill him, the shot would have missed. At no time did he suggest that the shot might have been fired from a police weapon. Nevertheless, even the "accident theory" might have been crucial, and Humphreys decided to re-examine the witness. Dramatically, Lord Goddard again intervened.

"I was following up a possible line of defence, my Lord," Humphreys stated.

"Well, if that defence is run," Goddard retorted, "I shall tell the jury that it is no defence at all."

It now remained for the two protagonists to take the stand. Christopher Craig

was called first and as he shuffled forward spectators craned their necks to get a better view of the 16-year-old boy whom the newspapers had depicted as the embodiment of evil. What they saw was strangely at odds with the publicity. He looked shy, gentle and frightened; and he spoke in a voice which was seldom raised above the level of a whisper.

Vicious hatred of police

Closely examined first by his counsel Parris, and then by Humphreys and the judge, he gave his own version of the events leading up to his spectacular dive from the roof of the warehouse.

In essence, he admitted his own guilt — although he denied firing directly at Constable Miles and, more important, refused to admit that Bentley had shouted "Let him have it, Chris". His very honesty may have made Parris' task more difficult. Parris had been arguing desperately for a verdict of manslaughter on the grounds that Miles' death was an accident. But Craig, though he denied intention to kill Miles, admitted to his vicious hatred

of the police — so allowing the jury to read into this hatred a cold-blooded desire to murder any police officer who happened to provide a target? It was a disturbing possibility.

The arrival of Bentley in the witness-box was somewhat different. Craig's evidence had shown him to be clear-minded and intelligent. Bentley, on the other hand, seemed tragically unable to defend himself in any way. From the start his pathetically low intelligence manifested itself in his inability to read the words of the oath.

The scene in the courtroom was reminiscent of a group of onlookers at a zoo baiting a trapped and helpless animal. One commentator wrote afterwards: "It would not be correct to say that Bentley made a fool of himself in the witness-box — God had already done that for Bentley."

Under a withering cross-examination from Christmas Humphreys the helpless defendant stumbled from denial to contradiction like a blind man on a sinking ship. Some of the dialogue between counsel and witness, in view of Bentley's low I.Q., was tragically ironic. It was part of the case against him that he knew all along that Craig carried a gun — though both defendants denied this — and that he incited Craig to violence in order that the two might escape.

"You were still on the roof when the shooting was going on?" asked Humphreys.

"Yes, sir."

"Your mind was still with Craig?"

"My mind, sir?"

"Yes, your mind."

"No, sir."

The emotional tone which Christmas Humphreys adopted in his cross-examination of Bentley was continued in his final speech. He scornfully dismissed the argument that Bentley could not have been involved in the death of Miles since he was already under arrest, and virtually instructed the jury that various contradictions in police evidence were irrelevant to the main facts of the case. There was no other verdict, he asserted, but Guilty for both defendants.

Parris and Cassels made brave attempts, in their final speeches, to isolate the truth from the strong emotional atmosphere which Humphreys had injected into the trial. Parris argued convincingly that Craig had never intended to kill Miles, and that even if he had the shot he fired would have missed. Cassels wanted to know why, if Bentley was still inciting Craig to violence after his arrest, he had made no attempt to escape or offered any personal violence to any of

the police. He also reminded the jury that Bentley was on trial for murder—even though he had no weapon and fired no shot. In addition he had been under arrest for at least 15 minutes before Miles died.

All these arguments, however, were in vain. Lord Goddard's summing-up was overwhelmingly weighted against the two defendants, and couched in language very similar to that used by the prosecution. At one point he picked up Bentley's knife and knuckle-duster and brandished them in front of the jury. There was an audible gasp from the court. It appeared to onlookers almost as if the judge was performing like a vengeful and biased prosecutor.

After this the verdict was almost a formality. It took the jury seventy-five minutes to find both Craig and Bentley guilty of murder. Craig was sentenced to be "detained at Her Majesty's pleasure"—the only sentence possible for a 16-year-old boy convicted of murder. Bentley, still uncomprehending and seemingly

BENTLEY'S DEATH was not in vain: the public outcry at this "blatant judicial murder" was to result in the abolition of the death penalty in Britain.

unable to grasp the significance of what had happened, was sentenced to death.

At 9 a.m. on the morning of January 28, 1953, Derek Bentley was led, for the last time, from the condemned cell at Wandsworth prison. He was crying silently as the hangman positioned him on the scaffold. "I didn't tell Chris to shoot that policeman," he said pathetically—seconds later he was dead.

Outside the prison gates a large crowd had gathered. This time, however, they did not howl for Bentley's blood—but protested at what has since been called the most blatant judicial murder in British legal history. But Bentley did not die entirely in vain. The outcry provoked by his execution became part of a movement which was to end, shortly afterwards, in the abolition of the death penalty in Great Britain.

THE BLAZING CAR MURDER

The burnt-out Morris Minor yielded a pitiful pile of charred bones. For bigamist A. A. Rouse it must have been a painful death, but so convenient. . . .

Syndication International, Popperfoto

THANKFUL at last to be almost home, the two young cousins, Alfred Brown and William Bailey, stepped out along the moonlit country lane. They had been to a Guy Fawkes' Night dance in Northampton, England, and now they were on the final half-mile lap of their three-mile walk from the town to their village of Hardingstone.

It was lonely in Hardingstone Lane, the air crisp and still, the moonlight so strong that the details of the surrounding countryside were silver-bright. At that hour—it was 1.45 a.m. on November 6, 1930—Brown and Bailey felt sure they must be the only people about.

But, suddenly and astonishingly, they discovered they were not alone. Just ahead of them and out of the ditch on the south side of the lane emerged the figure of a stocky, hatless man wearing a light raincoat and carrying a small overnight case. What impressed Brown, as he later explained, was that such a "respectably dressed" man should be seen in such curious circumstances.

But that was not the only odd thing about the stranger so clearly observed in the moonlight. For, first, he hurried past the two young men without a word, towards the cross-roads where Hardingstone Lane met the main London-Northampton road. Then, having gone some little way beyond them, he half turned and shouted: "It looks as though someone is having a bonfire up there!"

Almost at that very same moment Brown and Bailey had themselves noticed a fire-like glow farther along the lane and closer to the village. Seconds later stalks of flame sprouted from the glow and the two cousins, forgetting the mysterious stranger momentarily, hurried towards the blaze.

It was a frightening sight they came upon. A Morris Minor, a type of car then known as a "baby saloon", was parked close to the grass verge of the lane facing towards the cross-roads. It was totally bathed in flames that leapt as high as 15 feet. The heat was so intense that Brown and Bailey were forced to the opposite side of the lane, 20 feet away.

In the dazzling glare it was impossible for them to see whether anyone was in the

A BONFIRE, thought the two cousins (inset) when they saw the glow late on Guy Fawkes' night. But they found a frightening sight: a car bathed in flames.

car. They raced on to the village and returned with two local constables and buckets of water. It took them 12 minutes to quell the fire.

As the smoke cleared they saw that the car was almost completely destroyed. But in the midst of the ashes and the heat-twisted frame there remained a strange thing, a charred shape that at first puzzled the sweating fire-fighters. Then a closer look disclosed what it had been—a human being, now incinerated; whether man or woman none of the horrified on-lookers could guess.

Carefully the policemen went about the grisly task of gathering together what they could of the remains. Here they found a brittle, twisted stick that had been an arm, there a blackened leg burned off at the knee. A half-broken, rounded object

retained just enough detail to show that it had been a human head.

By dawn the local policemen and senior officers from the Northamptonshire force had wrapped the pathetic remains in sacking and carried them to Hardingstone's Crown Inn. They had also begun positive moves to unravel the secrets of the blazing car. For, luckily, one decisive clue had survived the fire—the car's rear licence plate was intact and perfectly clear: MU 1468.

Life of the party

A check of registrations quickly disclosed the identity of the owner, a Mr. Alfred Arthur Rouse, of Buxted Road, Finchley, north London. But where, now, was this Mr. Rouse—so popular at local clubs and parties when he would sing

the "Cobbler's Song" from *Chu Chin Chow*? His wife had no idea.

"I don't know whether it is my husband who is dead in the car or not," she told one reporter.

Perhaps that oddly fleeting figure, the hatless man seen by Brown and Bailey, could help? The police circulated a description ". . . aged between 30 and 35, height 5 ft. 10 ins., with a small round face and curly black hair." It might be that the small round face belonged to that same missing Mr. Rouse.

The next day, photographs of the burned-out car, under headlines like "Body found in a blazing car", and "Blazing car mystery", were given large-scale display in the national newspapers. A copy of one, the *Daily Sketch* for November 7, was bought in Gellygaer,

Glamorganshire, by Miss Phyllis Jenkins, a miner's daughter.

She showed it at once to a visitor to the household. This man had arrived at eight the previous evening with a tale of great misfortune. "I have been 18 hours on the road," he complained. "I lost my car round Northampton. I went in to have a cup of tea and when I came out my car was gone." He was told of a report, in that evening's local paper, of a burned-out car at Northampton. But, "Oh, no," he said, "that is not my car."

Next morning, here was Miss Jenkins with the *Daily Sketch* and some rather more specific information. "There is a photograph of your car," she told him. "How do you know it's mine?" he asked. "Your name, 'A. A. Rouse', is underneath."

For Alfred Arthur Rouse — smooth-tongued womanizer, bigamist, sex-hungry commercial traveller who later declared "my harem takes me to several places and I am not at home a great deal" — it was almost the end of the road.

Rouse had certainly travelled a long, confused and dangerous road since he was born to a genteel shopkeeping couple in London's Herne Hill on April 6, 1894.

It looked, in his early manhood, as though he might also follow a solid-citizen life. In November, 1914, he married Lily May Watkins, a quiet, domesticated woman. Before they could settle down he was with the army in France and, in May, 1915, suffered a head wound which had lasting effects.

Voracious sexual appetite

For a time his memory was defective and he was prone to frequent headaches. The slightest pressure on the scar of his wound caused severe irritation and for that reason he seldom wore a hat.

Psychiatrists later suggested that his injuries may have contributed to his voracious sexual appetite, and his almost total incapacity to tell the truth about any matter, however trivial. In the fantasies with which he regaled his women he had been educated at Eton College and Cambridge University, and had been a major in the army.

But his phoney charm worked with an endless succession of women — to their cost in many cases. His job as a salesman, covering a wide territory, served him well in his search for recruits to his "harem". By 1930 he almost certainly had at least 80 women on his visiting list — shop assistants, nurses, domestic servants, and married women who "entertained" while their husbands were out.

Several had his children. One girl was delivered of a son at the age of 15 — the child lived for only five weeks — and three years later bore him a second son. He went through a bigamous marriage with her and eventually, when the girl had

Topix

Popperfoto

learned the truth about him, his real and childless wife took the boy into their home and brought him up as her own.

Four days before the destruction of his car another girl was in a London maternity hospital expecting her second child by Rouse. Down in Gellygaer a third girl, Phyllis Jenkins's sister, Ivy, was about to give birth. Rouse had promised her "marriage" and bragged to her family of the beautifully furnished—but needless to say non-existent—house he had bought at Kingston-on-Thames, near the capital.

But Rouse knew that in the great game of catch-a-woman it was he who was about to be caught. Payments on maintenance orders were piling up; his wife's tolerance of his extra-marital exploits was wearing thin. And, unlike many of the girls he cultivated, Ivy Jenkins was surrounded by fair-minded relatives determined to hold her "fiancé" to his promises.

Escape from the vortex into which his amorous adventures had dragged him was becoming urgent. He had somehow to "disappear" and, in doing so, collect enough money to keep himself going while he started a new life. That at least seems to have been the way his mind was working to judge from his subsequent confessions. But, as with so many other things, he was incapable of carrying out any project successfully.

His plan to solve all problems was, he said, suggested by a chance meeting with a down-and-out who "told me the usual hard luck story". He discovered the man had no relatives and no permanent home.

He seemed the ideal victim. He could die, burned in the Morris Minor and mistaken for Rouse, while the real A. A. Rouse faded from the sight of his women and their maintenance demands. Later he would collect the insurance money on his life and his car—although how that was to be done he had apparently not worked out. For the moment only the next step mattered. He arranged to pick the man up and drive him north on the evening of November 5.

Only a matter of hours

A clear indication of the simple-mindedness behind his brash man-of-the-world appearance was given by Rouse when he added in his confession that he had not thought "there would be much fuss in the papers" about his burning car. All the more shock for him, then, when Phyllis Jenkins confronted him with the front-page headlines; all the more certain that it could be only a matter of hours before the police would be inviting him to "assist" them in their inquiries.

Rouse, who had travelled from the scene of the fire to Gellygaer by way of London—on a lorry which he stopped at the Hardingstone cross-roads—and then by long-distance bus, decided that he had better put distance between himself and Wales. By the afternoon of November 7, he was on a return bus to Victoria Terminal, London.

But his departure was not unnoticed. Gossip about his visit had reached the Cardiff police, who now had urgent information to pass on to their London colleagues.

At 9.20 that evening, Detective-Sergeant Robert Skelly of the Metropolitan Police peered through the windows of a motor-bus which had stopped, on its way to Victoria, at Hammersmith Bridge Road coach station. He picked out one passenger and signalled to him to alight. The man was hatless, wore a light raincoat and carried a small overnight case bearing the initials A.A.R.

"Are you Mr. Rouse?" Skelly inquired politely.

"Yes, that's right."

Skelly indicated a constable with him and said: "We are police officers. You are to accompany us to the police station."

Rouse replied: "Very well. I am glad

SMOOTH-TONGUED Rouse had at least 80 women on his visiting list, among them (from top left): Nellie Tucker, Helen Campbell (with their son) and Ivy Jenkins. The "real" Mrs. Rouse is pictured left.

323

it is over. I was going to Scotland Yard about it. I am responsible. I am very glad it is over. I have had no sleep."

So Rouse talked. The story he told he stuck to. He was making an overnight journey to the Leicester headquarters of his firm when a man thumbed a lift. They drove north, saying little to each other, and, having made a mistaken right turn into Hardingstone Lane, Rouse decided to stop for a brief doze.

But first he needed to relieve himself and as he left the car he told his passenger: "There's some petrol in the can. You can empty it into the tank while I'm gone."

The man had a request, too, according to Rouse. "Have you got a smoke?" he asked. Conveniently, Rouse, a non-smoker, happened to have a cigar which he passed to the man.

Rouse then walked more than 200 yards from the car, taking his case with him—he had, he said, earlier seen the man's hand on the case in the car and didn't trust him. Almost as soon as he had found a secluded place out of sight of the car he "saw a light".

He described what happened then: "I ran towards the car which was in flames. I saw the man inside and tried to open the door but could not as the car was then a mass of flames . . . I was all of a shake. I did not know what to do and ran as hard as I could along the road where I saw the two men [Brown and Bailey] . . . I lost my head and did not know what to do and really don't know what I have done since."

"A certain man"

Accident followed by panic: in someone else's case it might have seemed a satisfactory explanation. But Rouse's behaviour after the fire, his failure to seek help from Brown and Bailey, his "looks like a bonfire" cry and his lies to people he met in Wales put the seal on the police suspicions. Rouse was taken under arrest back to Northampton, charged with the murder "of a certain man whose name is unknown".

From the opening of the proceedings at the magistrates' court Rouse did himself mortal harm. His statement to the police about his "harem" and evidence from a number of young women about his private life and illegitimate children were given nationwide publicity. His defence lawyers feared that no juryman able to read or even to overhear the public gossip could judge him impartially.

But Rouse was brought to trial at Northampton Assizes on Monday, January 26, 1931, with the late Lord Birkett—then plain Mr. Norman Birkett, King's Counsel—exercising the utmost fairness, as chief prosecutor for the Crown, by eliminating all the "immorality" evidence given at the magistrates' court.

Rouse made a sad spectacle in the dock. He was, by turns, wheedling, arrogant and over-talkative. He showed no remorse for the dreadful fate of his unknown passenger.

Why, when he got to the Jenkins' home in Wales, Mr. Birkett asked, had he told lies about what had happened to his car? "Because," said Rouse, "there are many members of the family, for one thing, and I should have to tell the story over and over again, and I did not like to tell it with ladies present."

Why, for 43½ hours between the fire and being called off the coach at Hammersmith, had he made no move to report the "accident" to the police?

To the fountainhead

"My reason is that I have very little confidence in local police stations . . . If you want my candid opinion I have not much faith in them. I was going to the fountainhead. One usually goes to the fountainhead if one wants things done properly."

No, in their five-hour journey together Rouse had asked no details of his passenger. He didn't know his name, home town, job; not even where the man eventually intended making for.

"He inferred that he did not do tramping on his feet," said Rouse who, as a teetotaller, added the pseudo-fastidious comment that he soon regretted giving the man a lift because "his breath smelt of drink".

Why had he told Sergeant Skelly he felt "responsible"? Ah, Rouse replied, that was a mere technicality for "in the police eyes the owner of the car is responsible for anything that happens to that car. Correct me if I am wrong".

Rouse's case was that the man had set the car on fire himself through trying to light the generously-given cigar while

UTMOST FAIRNESS was shown by Prosecutor Birkett (near left), who eliminated Rouse's "harem" statements. His wife was loyal to the end (right).

March. 7. 1931.

I have fought to the last ditch
to save my husband's life.
But alas, I have failed, and the law
will take its course.
Those who knew him well, knew the
good that was in Arthur, I did, and
so do others.
But I knew I was fighting a lost
cause, for before he went to the
Court of Criminal Appeal, he had told
me that the Jury's verdict was the
correct one, and he was guilty.

My own opinion is that he was
not in his right mind on Nov 5th /.

Lily May Rouse

pouring petrol. Rouse, as he told it to the jury, fled in panic, said nothing at all to Brown and Bailey, just ran to the cross-roads and thumbed a lift from a lorry driven by a Mr. Henry Turner.

Some of the conversation Rouse admitted to with Mr. Turner on the journey to London gave the jury a clear idea of the real man behind the panic-stricken motorist who had just seen a man roasted alive. Rouse told Mr. Turner: "I have been expecting a mate with a Bentley but I missed him . . . That's a good idea of yours, to have the floorboards up; because of the exhaust it makes a warm cab."

Technical evidence by a fire assessor and Rouse's own actions after the fire were the two strongest weapons in the Crown's armoury. Rouse was noticed to pale when the remnants of his car's carburettor were handed to him in the dock — an apparently clear sign, if not evidence in law, that he had deliberately tampered with it to ensure a swift, consuming funeral pyre.

It was impossible for the jury to be given any proof of the man's condition at the outbreak of the fire — had Rouse already killed him? (Much was made of a wooden mallet found near the burned-out wreck, but it almost certainly played no essential part in the crime.) But most criminologists now broadly accept Rouse's post-trial "confession" in which he said the man was befuddled by whisky — supplied by Rouse for the purpose.

At the end of the six-day hearing, on Saturday, January 31, 1931, the jury took only one hour and 15 minutes to arrive at their verdict of guilty. And they had spent part of that time examining a Morris Minor similar to Rouse's, as well as having lunch.

Just to be near him

Rouse's appeal was heard and dismissed on February 23 and he was hanged at Bedford Jail on March 10. His long-suffering wife had remained loyal to the end, even taking a job in a Northampton shop to be near him during his weeks under arrest.

Apart from its other aspects of notoriety, the blazing car murder remains a classic among crimes because of that shadowy figure who featured so promin-

ALONE AND PENNILESS after the execution of her husband, the faithful Mrs. Rouse had to sell the contents of what had once been their happy home.

ently, yet so fleetingly, in it: the victim.

His identity was never discovered. Only one witness, a Hertfordshire policeman, was able to give the jury even the vaguest glimpse of him. At 11.15 p.m. on November 5 — a few hours before the murder — Police Constable David Lilley saw Rouse's car standing without lights near a small café a mile from Markyate.

He spoke to Rouse, who was sitting in the driving seat and who immediately apologized and switched the lights on. The man in the passenger seat, the constable told the jury, "appeared to me to be about 35 to 40 years of age. He was a man of small stature, had an oval, pale face and was dressed in a dark coat and trilby hat. I am not certain as to whether he had a moustache or not."

It was a meagre record, for history, of one man's life. But, for all its obscurity, that life was not too unimportant for the law to ignore its brutal and merciless end.

THE TRIANGLE FIRE

One of the most horrifying disasters in American history leaves 146 people—most of them young girls, garment workers in a 10th-floor Manhattan factory—trapped and burned to a crisp in the building or crushed and broken on the pavements below. The owners, tried for manslaughter, are lucky not to get lynched. . . .

HISTORY records little about the life of 18-year-old Margaret Schwartz, except that she was one of the teeming mass of young girls who were the mainstay of the burgeoning garment industry in New York in the early years of the twentieth century. But it does chronicle the manner of her death, as one among 146 victims destroyed in a frighteningly swift, devouring fire—for it brought two men to trial and led to reforms that helped to improve the lot of America's working women.

Public anger had rarely shown itself in such a seething form as it did that day, in the autumn of 1911, when Max Blanck and Isaac Harris entered New York's old Criminal Court Building—known as the Tombs—to answer to the charge of the manslaughter of Margaret in the first and second degrees.

Hysterical mobs surrounded the grimly hideous building, constructed in mock Egyptian style, and shrieked abuse at the two ashen-faced men. "Murderers!" they screamed. "We want justice!" It was only by the strong-willed efforts of the police that the two defendants were hustled into the court, unharmed.

Many in the roaring crowd were relatives of girls who, like Margaret, had worked for Blanck and Harris at the men's Triangle Waist Company factory— which had occupied the three top floors of the 10-storey Asch Building at Washington Place and Greene Street in lower Manhattan.

Like human torches

There, at a quarter to five in the afternoon of the last Saturday in March, 1911, 600 workers had been trapped by the inferno which reached its peak within a few short minutes of starting. Many of the victims had died leaping, like human torches, from the blaze on to the sidewalks below. All had been buried in a common grave after a five-hour-long funeral procession, watched by 50,000 silently brooding New Yorkers.

Now they sought vengeance at the trial. The preliminary proceedings had suggested that many, if not most, of the dead might still be alive had it not been for the way Blanck and Harris had operated their factory, and their allegedly inhuman treatment of their workers. The mood of the public was that it would not rest, and no city employer must be allowed to rest, until someone had paid for what had happened to the victims.

District Attorney Charles S. Whitman had assigned the leading of the prosecution's case to his two assistants, Bostwick and Rubin. As soon as Justice Thomas Crain had taken his place on the bench, Mr. Bostwick centred his argument upon one single question: what had happened to the ninth-floor exit door on the Washington Place side of the building?

MAX BLANCK.   MAX STEUER.   ISAAC HARRIS.

Defence Will Probably Be Disclaimer of Responsibility as to Conditions in Washington Place Building, Where 146 Persons Lost Their Lives by Fire.

Isaac Harris and Max Blanck, owners of the Triangle Waist Company, were placed on trial yesterday before Judge Thomas C. T. Crain, in the Court of General Sessions, on a charge of manslaughter growing out of the Washington place fire on March 25 last, when 146 men and women lost their lives. There are six separate indictments against each of the men. The specific charge on which they are now being tried is that they caused the death of Miss Margaret Schwartz, of No. 745 Brook avenue, ⸫ employe in their factory. The ⸱ day was ⸱sumed ⸱btaining ⸱⸱s. Ch⸱ F. P ⸱k and ⸱trict

building which structurally did not conform to the regulations required by the Building Department.

This is the first case of manslaughter based upon the Factory law. That law requires that lessees of a building used for factory purposes shall keep alll exits from their factory open during working hours and that such exits shall open on the outside of the building. Failure to comply with these regulations is a misdemeanor. It is alleged that Messrs. Harris and Blanck kept the doors of their factory locked during working hours and on this account the lives of their ⸱loyes were destroyed. ⸱⸱ statute ⸱ ⸱ference to homicide ⸱ ⸱th⸱ an⸱ ⸱o cause⸱

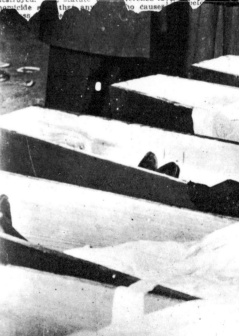

THE ASHEN-FACED defendants (above), charged with manslaughter, were the target of shrieking abuse from the hysterical mob surrounding the Tombs. Many were relatives (right, identifying the dead) of the victims.

His contention was that the two defendants had insisted on that door, like some others, being kept locked. Because of that Margaret Schwartz and many of her fellow workers had been trapped by the fire. To uphold that contention he called to the stand a 17-year-old girl named Katie Wiener, a shirtwaist worker, who had been lucky enough to escape. Katie appeared in deep mourning, for although she had lived through the appalling fire, her elder sister had died in the blaze.

She made a sad spectacle, yet she told her story to the court with a natural and moving dignity. "I heard some cry 'Fire!' but it seemed a long way off," she said. "In less time than I can tell it all became confusion about the ninth floor. Girls ran about shouting and fighting to get out.

Some crowded about the elevators and others about the Greene Street stairway.

"I rushed to the table where my sister worked and she wasn't there. Then I began to cry, but something told me that would be no good, and then I saw my sister near the window. I started to run towards her, but the smoke was so dense that it choked me, and I could not reach her. I shouted to her, but she didn't hear me, and that was the last I saw of her then. I was at a loss to know what to do for a time, but I saw many girls about the Washington Place door and ran there. Just as soon as I started to the Washington Place door someone said: 'Girls, it's no use. The door is locked and we can't get out!'"

Mr. Bostwick nodded grimly but interrupted the narrative to suggest to judge and jury: "Suppose we allow this girl to illustrate just how she tried to pull that door?" The judge inclined his head in agreement, and, with the members of the jury craning forward for a better view, Katie left the stand and walked across to the door at the side of the bench.

Licking flames

There she grasped the door handle and twisted and pulled at it with all the strength she could muster. Suddenly, it seemed, she was re-living those terrible moments when the flames licked around her and her life was in jeopardy.

Mr. Bostwick let the spine-chilling pantomime speak for itself. Then, with the hint of a bow, he ushered Katie back to the witness-stand and the continuation of her story. Softly, she began to speak again. "It seemed as though I had been standing at that door for three minutes. Again, I saw the Washington Street elevator come up. Once more I was pushed back by the crowd. All around me I saw flames spreading.

"The elevator car was crowded and was on its way downstairs again. I don't remember just how it all happened, but as the car passed the floor the door was left open and I got hold of the cable and swung myself towards the car. I think I landed on top of the car. My feet were up in the air and my head downward. My ankles were hurt. I must have landed on top of a lot of girls. In that way I made my escape and finally reached the street."

The silence in the court was intense. This palpably honest young girl was making people understand—for the first

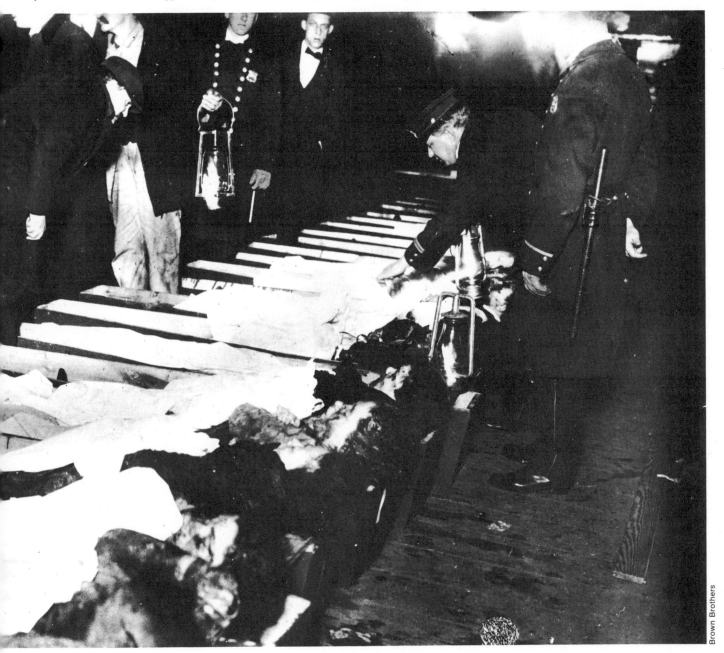

time, and beyond all the previous emotional reactions to the event—just what it meant to confront the bleakly objective face of death. Gently, acutely conscious of the atmosphere in the courtroom, Mr. Bostwick put one final question. "Did you see your sister?" he asked. "Yes," Katie replied. "Yes—but she was dead."

Slowly, Mr. Max D. Steuer, the defence counsel, rose to cross-examine. He was a notable figure of the East Side bar, but, in the atmosphere then reigning in the city, his cause was unpopular. "What was your sister's name?" he asked. "Her name was Rosie," Katie answered and added, "and she was only 18 years old."

Mr. Steuer considered that and then, abruptly, moved his case on to a tack that puzzled many in the courtroom. "Don't you know," he demanded, "that your mother has sued Harris and Blanck for a very large sum of money?" Instantly, Katie responded: "My mother never spoke to me about that."

But it was the locked door that still dominated the prosecution's line of argument. It was locked as a matter of "tradition" in the factory, Mr. Bostwick brought other witnesses to testify, showing that no girl could leave work each evening until she had been searched. Such were the labour relations at the Triangle Company that Mr. Blanck and Mr. Harris acted on the assumption that every employee was intent on stealing the materials on which

"OPEN THE DOOR! Open it! Open it!" But the locks hold as Harris and Blanck's sweatshop goes up in flames like a well-laid bonfire.

they worked—the bits of lawn, lace, muslin and even tissue paper.

Mr. Steuer leapt upon that fact. Was it not a fact, he queried, that some of the women employees habitually came to work carrying suspiciously capacious handbags? Without waiting for an answer, he reached along the lawyers' table and waved aloft such a handbag. Throwing it across to Assistant District Attorney Rubin, he commanded: "Open it and see for yourself how big it is." Mr. Rubin did so and from its interior extracted four silk shirt waists of the kind manufactured at the Triangle factory.

A little dancing

"Oh, yes," said Mr. Bostwick, blandly but somewhat taken aback. "We will concede that the bags carried by the girls were big enough at times to hold shirtwaists such as are shown here to the jury."

However, it was clear that none of this was doing the defence much fundamental good. Mr. Steuer therefore switched his efforts towards showing that the defendants were good employers whose basic decency was being unfairly impugned. He asked another employee, 17-year-old Josie Nicolosi, if she had not known that Mr. Blanck and Mr. Harris had even gone to the extent of installing a phonograph during lunch breaks so that the girls could enjoy a little dancing. But the defence counsel was disconcerted by Josie's answer.

"Oh, yes," she said, "I remember that, but the phonograph only played while there was a strike in the shop. They wanted to treat us very nicely . . . The

331

moment the strike was over that stopped.''

It was apparent to everyone in court that all this was merely a diversion, and that the main road led back to the locked door. The state did its best to keep attention centred on the door, and reserved much of its effort for the appearance of another ninth-floor employee, Kate Alterman, who had been with Margaret Schwartz at the end.

For the drama and clarity with which she told her story, in answer to Mr. Bostwick, she was as impressive as young Katie Wiener had been. She had been in a dressing-room with Margaret when the alarm was given, and she vividly recalled what had happened then:

"We ran out together and saw a great crowd near the door on the Washington Place side. I saw Mr. Bernstein, a brother of the superintendent, trying to open that door, but he couldn't budge it. I ran over to the windows, but there was nothing but flames around them.

Her hair was loose

"I saw Margaret once more — trying to open the door I had just turned away from. I pushed her aside and tried the door myself, but I couldn't open it. It was locked. Margaret was kneeling at the door when I noticed her again, a moment later. Her hair was loose and the hem of her dress was on fire. She was using all her strength to turn the knob. She was tearing at it. Then she screamed: 'The door is locked! I am lost! Open the door! Open it!' "

Kate paused and Mr. Bostwick let the silence make its impression upon the court. Then, finally, he asked, quietly: "And then what became of Margaret?" Kate lowered her eyes and all in the courtroom strained to hear her answer. "That was the last I saw of her," she said.

She continued with the story of what had then happened to herself: "I ran to the sink and wet my hair. I saw Mr. Bernstein flying around like a wildcat, putting his head out of the windows and pulling it back again. Then I took my fur coat, turned it inside out and put it on that way. I picked up some unfinished dresses from a table that had not yet caught fire, wet them and wrapped them about my head.

"Purple flames were following me along the floor. My pocketbook, which I had in my hand, caught fire, and I pressed it to my breast to put out the flames. I ran then for the door and the Greene Street side of the building. Flames were all around me, and finally my dress began to burn.

"A girl caught me around the waist as I ran. I begged her to let me go, but she wouldn't. I knew I couldn't save myself if I had to drag her along with me. I struck her, I hit her, I kicked her away from me. I don't know what became of her, but I reached the stairs and I was safe."

When Mr. Steuer opened his cross-examination, everyone waited, tensed, to hear how he would deal with this crucial witness. His approach was surprising. Ignoring, for the most part, the details of the girl's evidence, he concentrated on the suggestion that her story was, as he put it, "so pat" that she must have been carefully rehearsed in it by the prosecution. He made her relate her story over again and hammered at the fact, which he seemed to find so suspicious, that she retold in words almost identical with those she had previously used.

Mr. Steuer worried at the issue like a frustrated terrier vainly seeking to claw a rat from its hole. "Can you," he asked, almost in desperation, "tell that story in other words than those you have told it in?" Kate looked at him with innocent bewilderment. "Tell it in any other words?" she repeated. "I remember it this way, just exactly how it was done."

There were many others who remembered how it was done, such as Fire Chief Worth, who found that the extension ladders of his fire-trucks reached only to the sixth storey, and who ordered a jumping net to be spread. To his horror, three girls leapt together from the ninth floor so that when they struck the net they had gained a velocity which produced an impact equivalent to 16 tons.

"Nobody could hold a net when those girls from the ninth floor came down," the fire officer told the court. "There were so many bodies hitting the ground that it was impossible to see them. You just did not see them. You heard the impact of the bodies hitting the ground." But he and others did see one heart-tearing spectacle: a man and a girl, sheathed in flames, jumping to their deaths while tightly embraced in each other's arms.

The court was told how it was on the Washington Place side of the building. There an elevator — weighted beyond all possible limits by the frenzied girls who had packed into it and jumped onto its roof — gave way and plummeted to the foot of the shaft, shattering the bodies of many of the would-be escapers.

Shrieking down the shaft

The jury heard how one elevator man had rushed from the building in panic, and his place had at once been taken by a man passing by in the street. This gallant helper operated the elevator on a series of trips, bringing around 30 girls a time to safety, until the fire finally made any further ascent impossible. When that happened, he said, desperate girls still caught in the blaze fell shrieking down the shaft.

Beyond all else the tragedy was made poignant by the fact that, as witnesses testified, work at the Triangle factory was just finishing for the day as the blaze began. Its source, too, was known. It had

THE IMPACT of bodies hitting the ground adds to the fearful din. Relatives (below) are lucky to get $75 compensation. Most get none at all.

Brown Brothers

SCORES RESCUED AS FLAMES TAKE FEARFUL TOLL OF HUMAN

broad and strong, and at the top of the flight was a large door which was easily opened by those who went in that direction.

Theoretically the employes, well poised through frequent fire drills, should have used these methods of escape. In practice the most of them staggered over machines and chairs, cut off from flight by the flames which were converting the stairs into a fiery flue. Some there were who were stifled where they sat at their machines or were flung suffocated to the floor, to be trodden upon by panic stricken fellow workers.

Women and girls, terror maddened, raised the windows seeking air and aid. Back of them was roaring Tophet, before them death in the brick walled abyss.

Some made the choice, others were involuntarily hurled off the window ledges by the crazed and stifling throngs at their backs clamoring for air. In twos and threes the women and girls dropped from the sills, hurtled through the air and fell to the pavements, where they lay shattered masses of riven flesh and protruding bones.

The sound of the fearful impacts which came like hail of death, caused men to hide faces and women spectators to sink to their knees on the flags and moan over the calamity.

The response to the first alarm had been prompt and efficient and soon the street was gorged with engines, trucks and towers, which followed each other with precision to the fourth alarm. The firemen shouted and gesticulated and citizens pleaded with them not to leap. The ladders of the Fire Department would reach only to the seventh floor, and before the firemen could get even that far scores had gone to their deaths on the flagging of the street. It was the carnage of battle which filled those short blocks in Washington place and Green street.

Perish by Twos and Threes.

The women employes hurled themselves in twos and threes to their doom, descending with hair and clothing ablaze. Here was the valley of the shadow of death where had been a mart of humdrum trade. The clothes of the victims were blackened, which contrasted with the pallor of their faces. There was no time to perform the offices of the dead, for uncovered they lay with their faces to the sky. In one window of disaster were counted fifty-three bodies.

Three young women, fully dressed for leaving the factory, with the exception of putting on their hats, met death locked arm in arm. They were employed in the Triangle Shirt Waist factory, and evidently were close friends in the workshop. The first crowd that gathered in the street below saw them standing on the ledge of a window imploring for some one to come to their assistance. They were seen to converse with each other, as if they were advising the best course to pursue. One of them looked

MISS CLOTILDE TERRANOVA

BODIES COVERED WITH CANVAS ON SIDEWALK.

then to remove the bodies of the dead that were strewn all over the street. Part of the water played on the building was dashed back upon the bodies in the street, and the gutters were crimson. When coffins were rushed to the scene the bodies were picked up and placed in them, and a card attached with a number for the purpose of identification.

Firemen and ambulance surgeons who assisted in this work were horrified on finding two girls alive at the bottom of the heap of victims killed when the fire net proved inadequate. One of the girls was found to be breathing as she was lifted up and the other gave evidence of life just as she was laid in a coffin. The two girls had been left beneath the bodies of their dead companions for twenty minutes.

Dr. Keeffe, of St. Vincent's Hospital, hailed a passing taxicab and the two girls were hurried to the hospital. One of them revived for a few moments and tried to narrate her harrowing experience. Soon afterward she lapsed into unconsciousness and both of them died within an hour after they entered the hospital. Their bodies were not identified.

DOCTOR HUNTER ATTENDING FRED. RUTT, AN INJURED FIREMEN.

TAGGING BODIES ON PIER, FOOT OF EAST TWENTY-SIXTH STREET, WHICH WAS USED AS A MORGUE.

SCORES SAVED BY ELEVATOR RUNNERS

Joseph Zito and Joseph Gaspary Describe Scenes of Panic in the Burning Building.

Two elevator operators, their clothing burning and their faces and hands scorched by flames, staggered out of the building twenty minutes after the fire started. The conduct of each was last night acclaimed as heroic, and the police reports gave them credit for rescuing more than a hundred young domen from certain death. They were Joseph Zito, twenty-three years old, and Joseph Gaspary, twenty-five, both foreign born.

To this modest list of two names, others will be added to-day and to-morrow when more details of yesterday's disaster become known.

Zito and Gaspary were standing in their respective elevator cars, resting at the ground floor of the building, when at a few minutes after half-past four o'clock both heard shouts of "Fire!" and a shower of splintered glass rained down upon them from the shaft doors leading from the upper three stories of the building.

"The building's on fire!" shouted one of them, and a few seconds later they were at the eighth floor, where a screaming and struggling crowd of young women fought to gain entrance to the elevators and be carried to the street and safety below. Each operator made four or five trips, and ceased in their work of rescue only when the mechanism of the elevators became disordered.

Elevator Hero Describes Panic.

"At the first alarm of fire," said Zito last night, "Gaspary and myself ran our elevators up to the eighth floor, where in front of the door were hundreds of young women. Mr. Max Blancke, one of the owners of the Triangle Waist Company, was standing there, holding the young women in check as best he could. Mr. Blancke shouted to me to 'run the elevator until she falls,' and then I heard him yell, 'Let the women go down first!'

"When I opened the elevator door leading to the eighth floor all I could see were the girls and men and behind them great flames and clouds of smoke. Fully twenty women crowded into my elevator on the first trip and as many more came down with me on the second trip. When I went to the floor the third time I could see some of the girls standing on the window sills surrounded by fire, but they seemed so terror stricken that they didn't hear the shouts of Mr. Blancke and other men on the floor who called to them not to jump.

"After the third car load had been taken to the street I started up the fourth time and, hearing screams and shouts from the ninth floor, I ran my elevator there. The girls were more frightened there than were those on the eighth floor. Gaspary also made a trip to the ninth floor, but after the fourth trip I could not go by the eighth floor as the girls would jump on my elevator and I was afraid, because the door was open, that they would fall into the shaft.

"Perhaps both of us made more than five trips, but I can't say for sure."

Hundreds Escaped by Stairs.

Zito said that several hundred persons escaped by way of the stairs, which were adjacent to the elevator shaft, on both the Washington place and Greene street sides of the building. Also the elevator operators, who ran the freight elevators on the Greene street side, made several trips to the burning floors and carried scores of women to the street. The freight elevators were not so swift, however, as those on the Washington place side.

When the mechanism of the elevators became disordered there were fully three hundred young women and men still trapped on the eighth, ninth and tenth floors. Among these was Mr. Blanck, who had left his wife and two daughters in the firm's office on the tenth floor, hurrying, at the first alarm of fire, to the operating room, on the eighth floor. Caught in the struggling crowd which blocked the stairway between the eighth and ninth floors, Mr. Blanck found it impossible to get back to his office.

Describing his experience later, Mr. Blanck said that he rushed to the seventh floor, believing that perhaps his wife and

children had gone safe... low. Unable to find t... had given them up for...

Among the workers... were a number who f... to escape by way of t... those crawled to the fir... their way to the botto... where later they wer... bodies were found in t...

Slid Down Elev...

Half crazed with fri... uninjured, Hyman M... years old, of No. 332 Ea... a cutter employed by ... Company, was found a... elevator shaft shortly ... last night. For four ... clinging to the drum ... water up to his waist... the cable from the te... escape by the windows ... off. He told his rescue... eight hundred persons, ... girls, on the tenth floor ... out.

He was taken to St. ... where an examination ... had been uninjured. ... had been applied, he re... to tell a fairly coherent ... penings on the tenth f... of fire spread through th... was found by Battalion ... five men who were work... floor. Hearing feeble ... the cellar, they batte... through a door on th... side and reached Meshel... with débris, and gave th... prise of their lives whe... able to walk. For hour... been carrying the dead ... all parts of the buildin... reached the street he be...

"I was working on th... eight hundred other per... the cry of fire," said ... seem more than a few... heard it that the flame... the windowsills. The ... coming from the ninth f... who were among the firs... dows were driven bac... Women screamed and ... lunatics and then they ... see who would jump th... windows to the street.

"As I recall it now ... half a dozen trips and ... many women as we co... men in my vicinity al... when the elevator faile... was a case of each one f... could describe the horro... the tenth floor.

"It seems as if I ha... daze for weeks listenin... As a last resort, I ju... elevator shaft and grab... to the bottom. When ... pouring down on me I ... being drowned, and if th... found me that would ha... The water was ice cold ... have clung to the drum ... lot of people jumped ... shaft and their bodies m... tom of it. I thought I ... for a dozen hours."

Meshel's hands were b... the cable.

Girl Slides to ...

A miraculous escape ... related by Miss Cecilia ... years old, an operator ... shirt waist company, ... Stanton street. She is ... jured in St. Vincent's H... recover.

The young woman w... floor of the building an... get into an elevator. ... tors ceased running s... young woman leaped to ... companion, she said, ... fell. Of her own terrify... top of the elevator ca... below, she remembered...

Pathetic scenes were ... the Mercer street police ... the catastrophe. To this ... of relatives and friends ... ployed in the Triangle ... were sent by policemen, ... to send inquirers to the ... issued. Gussie Horowitz ... girl, living at No. 15... street, walked into the ... for her brother, Mauric... ployed as a shipper. Sh... the first to escape by w... from the eighth floor.

While she pleaded wi... sought their assistance ... tered the police station, ... from the burning buildi... roof.

Runs Frantic Thr...

While the fire was s... young girl, with hair di... clothing almost torn fr... through Broadway, ne... store and gave to a larg... the first intimation of th... from the scenes of deat... which she had escaped, ... out between street car... the crowd lining the st...

"Don't let them hurt m... hurt me!"

She was taken to a dru... she was quieted she sa... Dougherty, of No. 228 Ea... She said:—

"We were all ready to ... having finished our w... most of us had on our ... cried 'Fire!' and the ne... the room was filled with ... know which way to turn... ber of girls running to ... room, where I knew th... located, I followed. The... ahead of me, and knew I... to get out that way. I ... the elevator, when I he... out, 'My God, they say ... up again.'

Rescued by Of...

"I grew weak and wa... the floor when little '... office boy, took hold of m... past me, saying, 'Come ... that's the only way.' I ... found my way along, but ... two other girls who led t... stairway leading to the r... prayer when I saw the o... and fell on my knees.

"I had only been ther... another girl turned back ... me to come on. I aros... There were about twen... the Cohen boy, in the c... on the roof of another b... across. I understood aft... were college students i... University Law School. ... the street I seemed to los... ing of that horrible place ... of, and knowing that m... girls left behind would ...

Miss Dougherty was ta... in a taxicab by voluntee... story.

The Dead and the Injured

... other bills of five and ten dollar ...nations.' Surmising that other bills ...e hidden and possibly the woman's ...nd address, the searchers examined ...rt more closely and then the shoes ...ockings, resulting in discovery of ...l. Up to a late hour last night no ... identified the woman.'

...le Terranova, one of the dead, was ...ughter of Calogero Terranova, of ... President street, Brooklyn. Her ...is seriously ill and it is feared that ...ck of his daughter's death will re...ally. She was expected home early ...ay because of her father's illness.

...RT INQUIRY TO-DAY ...LEARN CAUSE OF FIRE

... Who Escapes Tells of Terror ... Cry of "Fire!" Rings Out in Factory.

...etermine the exact cause of the ...hich had not been ascertained late ...ght by several firemen working ...pecial orders of Fire Chief Croker, ...haustive inquiry will be instituted ... when women and men who es... from the building will be ques...

... Triangle Waist Company occupied ...ee upper floors of the structure, a ...y completed ten story fireproof loft ...g. From all accounts gathered ...nployes of the firm the blaze start... the eighth floor in a corner of the ...pen room nearest the elevators and ...y on the Greene street side. This ... the factory was given over entire... the shirt waist operators and cut... There were about five hundred per... work on the eighth floor when the ...rted.

... Rothen, of No. 91 Washington ..., the Bronx, a cutter, furnished ...lice with the most accurate de... ...on of the start of the blaze.

...h sixty other cutters I was at ... over long benches and tables ... were placed on the Greene street ... the room," said Rothen. "The ... had the places nearest the win... because of the necessity for light. ... best of my knowledge every man

BUILDING AT NORTH-WEST CORNER OF EAST WASHINGTON PLACE AND GREENE STREET, THE THREE TOP FLOORS IN WHICH LOSS OF LIFE OCCURRED, WERE COMPLETELY DESTROYED.

space. For a structure co... square feet in area three s... required and for 40,000 squ... stairways. Furthermore, ... stairways were required fo... exceeding the 10,000 square ...

Might Have Saved ...

If that code had been ad... garded as almost certain th... escapes would have been r... Washington place building. ... fire escapes would have bee... all buildings, of more than ... in height.

In the building code in e... entirely with the Departmen... to order such fire escapes a... factory building safe. Th... under the jurisdiction of ... Aneny, President of Manha... who appointed the present ... of the bureau, Rudolph P. ...

Section 103 of the code pr... buildings occupied by three ... lies, and including factori... and other structures, "shal... with such good and su... capes, stairways or other m... in case of fire as shall be d... Department of Buildings; an... ment shall have full and ex... and authority within the cit... escapes and other means o... provided upon or within sa...

It is further provided that ... must be kept free from encu... a fine is prescribed for pl... tions on a fire escape. An... ment is that all such build... equipped with stationary iro... ing to a scuttle opening to t...

Cyrus W. Miller, presi... Borough of the Bronx, was ... Washington place disaster ... of it by a HERALD reporter ... When told that there was ... escape for the entire ten sto... said he could not understan... condition was allowed to ex...

"One fire escape certainly ... vide sufficient egress for a b... size," he said, "and I am su... have been some other mea... well. The law provides th... ings shall have fire escape... and rear and the enforceme... is within the province of the ... ment. The fact that there ... and stairways would not al... tion.

"I recall that not long ago ... owns a building about six s... the Bronx was ordered by th... ment to place a fire es... front. There was one alread... and the owner of the building ... was enough, so he came ... whether I couldn't get the o...

...ing burned off; wore ... on left hand. Body ...rgue.

...man, about twenty-...eight five feet seven ... face, black hair, ...coat, black trousers, ...eather shoes. Body ...rgue.

...woman, twenty-four ...ght five feet two ...air, white bead ear...ist and skirt, black ...g on left hand bear...L." Body No. 11 at

...woman, twenty-five ...feet three inches in ...tton shoes; most of ... off. Body No. 34 at

...oman, twenty-seven ...aist, black stockings ...hoes; imitation gold ...d; body No. 2 at the

...oman, thirty years ... inch in height; red ...n shoes, black stock-...0 at Morgue.

...rl, fifteen years old; ...ned off except black ...ck laced shoes; body ...rgue.

...oman, about twenty-...lothing burned off; ...on left hand; appar-... body No. 20 at the

...oman, about twenty-...ve feet six inches in ...air, eyes and com-... 12 at the Morgue.

INJURED.

A.

...ee, twenty-one years ...some street; shock, ...d body. Taken home

B.

...n, twenty years old, ...her street; cut by ...aken home.

F.

... Fannie, twenty-one ...waist maker, No. 354 ...rooklyn; fell down ...s and internal in-...ne. Will recover.

G

Disastrous Fires and Lives Lost

Victims' Friends Besiege M...

broken out in a rag bin between two cutting tables, and the most likely explanation was a carelessly discarded cigarette butt. Waste was stacked knee-deep in the factory so that the whole building resembled a perfectly prepared bonfire.

It was this monstrous fire hazard that made the question of exit from the factory so important. Mr. Steuer called a series of witnesses to testify to the claim that even if the ninth-floor door had been locked, it could quickly have been opened — since a key, secured by a piece of string, was kept permanently in the lock.

Commissioner John Williams, of the Department of Labour, told the court that a factory inspection of the premises, just before the fire, had been satisfactory. But although some additional safety recommendations had been made, these were passed to a telephone operator and not directly to Blanck and Harris themselves.

Other evidence then came out which did not do any credit to the two accused men and their sweatshop. It was said that labour relations at the factory had continually been bad. When workers had turned to strike action as their only effective means of protest, the company had hired thugs to beat up pickets, and prostitutes to harass and intimidate women employees with street-corner abuse. Heavy fines, it was said, were levied against workers for material they allegedly damaged, and girls had even been charged for the needles with which they sewed.

The prosecution also contended that some "damaging witnesses" who would have been called had been blackmailed by the company by the sudden offer of pay rises. The factory superintendent, it was said, had even personally threatened some of the employees at the time of the earlier grand jury hearing.

In his summing-up Judge Crain reminded the jury that the charge was manslaughter in either the first or second degree. But, to give that substance, it had positively to be shown that culpable negligence on the defendants' part led directly to Margaret Schwartz's death. On the central issue of the locked door the judge emphasized that the jury needed to be satisfied that it was, in fact, locked. And, moreover, that it was locked with the full knowledge of the defendants.

"It was murder!"

This was the first time that the essence of the law had intruded into what had otherwise been an emotional occasion. From their expressions, it seemed that some members of the jury had only suddenly realized the extent of the responsibility they carried. They trooped thoughtfully out, and returned an hour and 40 minutes later to deliver their verdict. It came as a shock to most of the spectators, if not to some of the lawyers. Blanck and Harris, the jury declared, were not guilty.

Outside the court building the unofficial "jury" of the mob was waiting to make its own verdict known. "Not guilty!

THE SURVIVORS attend memorial ceremonies 50 years later. Among them: Josie Nicolosi (second from right), who testified at the trial that her employers' one good deed was forced by a strike.

Not guilty!" the crowd shrieked in a new wave of incredulity and rage. "It was murder, murder!" Little Katie Wiener's brother, David, collapsed with hysterics and was taken to hospital.

The howling for "justice" was heard by the two terrified Triangle company owners. The fear of a lynching was clearly etched on their faces. Accordingly, the police smuggled Blanck and Harris out through a back entrance of the court building and off to safety.

So far as the criminal law went, the Triangle fire case was over — later, the families of 23 girl victims each collected $75 in full settlement of all claims. But at least it gave rise, indirectly, to measures intended to avoid future repetitions of the sweatshop conditions.

A state commission was set up to investigate factory operations. As a result of this, radical new controls over buildings and fire hazards were introduced.

Limitations on women's hours of work came into force, and — learning from the experience of its members involved in the Triangle tragedy — the recently formed International Ladies Garment Workers' Union commenced the growth and development that was to make it one of America's foremost labour unions.

They were British diplomats with impeccable academic and social credentials. No one suspected them of dishonesty . . . until the scandal erupted of:

BURGESS AND MACLEAN
THE OLD SCHOOL SPIES

ON THE morning of May 25, 1951, diplomat Guy Burgess sat in his New Bond Street flat reading the London *Times*. He was in no hurry. A friend of his, a male dancer in a West End musical comedy, had just left, and an apparently uneventful day stretched before Burgess.

Under suspension

He did not have to report to the Foreign Office because he was under suspension after being sent home from his job at the British embassy in Washington. The complaints against him ranged from homosexual affairs to driving offences, from repeated drunkenness to "inattention to duty".

At 40, his career as a diplomat was clearly near its end. The Old Etonian, very much in favour of taking life as it came, was not particularly worried. Apart from *The Times,* his only immediate concern was the holiday he planned to take with a young American friend he had met on the *Queen Mary* a month earlier during his voyage home in disgrace. They were due to sail from Southampton at midnight aboard the steamer *Falaise,* bound for Brittany.

On that same morning, another diplomat, Donald Maclean, was working away busily at his "American desk" at the Foreign Office. It was his 38th birthday and he was in good spirits. His wife, Melinda, was expecting a baby; he had recovered from his homosexual infatuation with a Negro porter at a Soho nightspot, who had repaid his devotion by beating him up; he was looking forward to a birthday lunch with a few friends.

Crisp message

Then came the tip-off that changed everything. The source was a third "diplomat", Kim Philby. Philby worked ostensibly as a first secretary at the Washington embassy. In fact, he was the liaison officer between the British S.I.S. (Secret Intelligence Service) and its American counterpart, the C.I.A. (Central Intelligence Agency). He was also, like Burgess and Maclean, a Soviet agent.

Security men, trying to track down a whole series of atomic secret leakages, had suspected Maclean for some time. Now they were about to pounce, and, because of his job at the very heart of Anglo-American Intelligence, Philby had been informed.

His message to Burgess was short and crisp: "Warn Donald he is about to be interrogated." Burgess, although not directly under suspicion himself, panicked. He decided not merely to warn Maclean and help him to flee the country. He would flee himself as well.

One of his first steps was to arrange an assignation with the young American due

Weidenfeld

CAREER of a communist spy: Burgess (ringed left) poses with his soccer team when a bright young schoolboy at Eton. The school was generally considered as a preparation for entry into the top echelons of British society. Somehow, in the case of Burgess, the system failed and he ended up as an escapee in Moscow where he settled to a life of drinking.

to join him on a holiday that night, and explain that the trip would have to be called off. "A friend of mine at the Foreign Office is in serious trouble," he said at their meeting in Green Park. It must have sounded a reasonable excuse. But, for once, Burgess was speaking the truth.

What had promised to be an uneventful day proved to be a busy one. Burgess hired a car "for about ten days", invested in a new suitcase and some clothes, packed, and, in the early evening, climbed into the car and set out to drive to Maclean's country home at Tatsfield in Kent.

Maclean, shadowed by security men who had had him under surveillance for some weeks, caught his usual train home, the 5.19 from Charing Cross Station. It was to be for the last time. As soon as Burgess arrived with news of his impending interrogation, Maclean also packed his bags. Then, after a hasty dinner, the two spies drove down to Southampton.

They arrived only minutes before the *Falaise* was due to sail, abandoned the hired car on the quayside, and rushed for the gangway. "Hey," shouted a sailor,

Weidenfeld

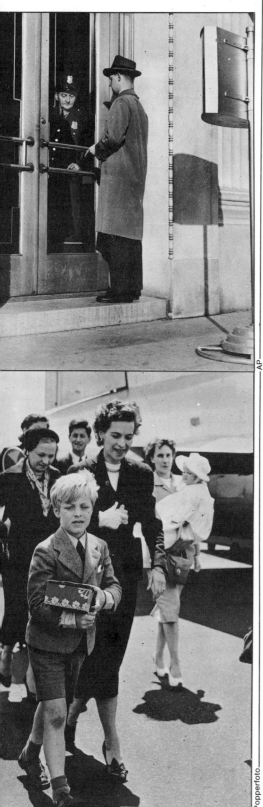

SECURITY and how to breach it . . .
Two plain clothes officers (top) at U.S.
Atomic Energy headquarters demonstrate
defensive technique against spies. Armed
with his official pass, however, Maclean
walked straight in. Later, with wife and
children (above) he fled to the U.S.S.R.

"what about the car?" "Back on Monday," called out Burgess as he boarded the cross-channel steamer—but neither he nor Maclean would ever see England again.

By a secret route they made their way to Moscow while behind them the storm broke—not only over their escape, but over the fact that two men of such unstable character had been able to betray their country over such a long period without detection.

Dilettante spy

Burgess was a talkative, once-handsome but now bloated, figure who breakfasted off benzedrine tablets washed down with brandy and port, and who never tired of boasting about his sexual excesses. "I could never travel by train," he once announced at a party. "I would feel obliged to seduce the engine driver."

His Communist sympathies, like those of Maclean and Philby, went back to Cambridge—where all three had been contemporaries in the early 1930 As an undergraduate, Burgess far outshone his two friends and "fellow-travellers". He has been described as "the most brilliant young talent of his day".

That promise was never fulfilled. He drifted from job to job, served for a brief period in the war in a minor Intelligence job, worked for the B.B.C., then finally found a niche in the Foreign Office. That he survived there from the end of the war until 1951—despite his drinking, homosexual exploits, and lack of enthusiasm for work—is a tribute to the strength of the "old school tie network".

As a spy, as in everything else, Burgess was something of a dilettante—more interested in being able to boast to his intimates that he was "working for the Reds" than actually providing his Moscow masters with information of genuine value. It is doubtful if he told them anything that changed the course of history. Maclean, however, was an entirely different prospect.

Bright young men

He was the son of Sir Donald Maclean, a staunch Presbyterian who had been Minister of Education under Liberal Prime Minister Herbert Henry Asquith. By the time Maclean arrived at Trinity Hall, Cambridge, to read modern languages, he was as staunch an atheist and Communist as his father was a Christian.

Outside of his studies, Maclean's main—in fact, almost sole—interest was undergraduate journalism, which he used to popularize Marxism. He had quite clearly accepted the whole Communist philosophy. It was therefore a surprise to his friends when he announced that he proposed to seek a career in the British Foreign Office—the very anthesis of Red belief.

"I have decided to join the oppressors instead of the oppressed," Maclean uttered. It was an uncharacteristically flip explanation which, along with his uncompromisingly Left-wing written views, should have aroused suspicion.

As it was, the Foreign Office accepted Maclean as a more than passable recruit. If the pro-Communist sympathies he had shown in the past were considered at all, they were dismissed as the not-uncommon excesses of an intellectual undergraduate. It did not occur to anyone in authority that he was already a committed Soviet agent.

Luck was to prove unusually kind to Maclean in his role as a spy. He was posted in the spring of 1944 to Washington as a First Secretary. With him went his wife, Melinda. The fact that he was only 31—unusually young for such a job—is an indication of the esteem in which he was held at the Foreign Office—who regarded him as one of the brightest of their bright young men.

It was only natural, when the post became vacant a couple of years later, that Maclean should be appointed British Secretary to the Combined Policy Committee on atomic affairs. The function of the Committee was to control the exchange of information on atomic matters between the United States, Canada, and Britain.

Privileged position

This post not only enabled him to pass on to the Soviet Union details of vital atomic secrets being pooled between the countries—he was able to lay his hands on even more important information held back by the United States for security reasons.

This came about because he managed, as part of his duties, to obtain a non-escort pass to the U.S. Atomic H.Q. in Washington. He made frequent use of the privilege—usually at night when the building was more or less deserted.

Nobody knows, or is ever likely to know, exactly how much information he managed to filch on these nocturnal visits. One secret—at a time when uranium was believed to be in critically short supply—was almost certainly a cheap American process for converting waste from South African goldmines into high-grade uranium.

Eventually, a security officer, Brian La Plante, became suspicious of the frequency with which Maclean made use of his non-escort facility and the unusual hours he kept. "I reported him and the pass was withdrawn," said La Plante. But by then the damage had been done and, with no follow-up investigation, Maclean was able to move on to his next coup.

From his privileged position he was able to monitor for his Russian task-

Popperfoto

Popperfoto

Central Press

IMPORTANT CONNECTIONS . . . two British prime ministers were involved on the sidelines of the diplomatic spy ring. Agent Philby (left) was publicly cleared of being the "third man" by Foreign Secretary Harold Macmillan in 1955. Burgess (inset right) was a personal friend of Macmillan's predecessor Eden (left), as signed letter clearly shows.

masters the top secret negotiations which led up to the signing of the Western defensive alliance – the North Atlantic Pact – in April 1949. During the negotiations, Maclean was switched to a new post, Head of Chancery at the Cairo embassy. It did not affect his efficiency as a spy because, as a Grade A embassy, Cairo was kept informed as a matter of routine about all details of British Middle East policy.

Alcoholic binge

There were signs, however, that he was beginning to feel the strain of his dual role. In Washington he had already started to drink heavily. In Cairo he drank even more, and his conduct became increasingly bizarre.

After one alcoholic binge, he broke into the apartment belonging to the United States ambassador's secretary, smashed up the furniture, stuffed some of her clothing down the lavatory, and shattered the bath with a marble shelf.

Finally, on May 11, 1950, he was sent home. Melinda had complained to the British ambassador, Sir Ronald Campbell, that it was no longer possible to control him. The official reason for his return – not far from the truth – was "a nervous breakdown".

Back in London, Maclean was given six months' leave on condition that he underwent psychiatric treatment. It was at this time, urged on by his woman psychiatrist to face up to his latent homosexuality, that Maclean embarked on his affair with the Negro porter of a Soho nightclub.

Intermittently, he still drank heavily, and friends would sometimes find him reeling about in the bar of a West End

club declaiming: "I am the English Alger Hiss" – a reference to the respected American State Department employee who had turned out to be a Soviet spy.

His friends did not for a moment believe that he was speaking the literal truth. They simply dismissed his mumblings as the ravings of a drunk. Maclean then returned to the Foreign Office in November 1950. Fortune – or official naïveté – continued to smile upon his spying activities. He was next appointed head of the American Department.

In his new position, Maclean was able to keep Moscow abreast of all the vital details of such matters as the U.S.-Japan Peace Treaty negotiations, and the Korean war strategy. For instance, it was through the services of Maclean that the Chinese learned – via Moscow – that President Truman had ordered General MacArthur not to retaliate even if China invaded Korea from the north.

But, although Melinda had by now returned to him, and they had bought a country house in Kent, his inner life was far from well. He still found his burden of guilt difficult to bear. By the beginning of

1951 he was again on the bottle. At times, it seemed as if he was almost seeking discovery so that he might have some peace of mind and conscience.

In one of his drinking bouts, he asked Mark Culme-Seymour, a friend from pre-war days: "What would you do if I said I was working for Uncle Joe?" Culme-Seymour debated with himself whether to report the conversation, but eventually decided – as had the friends whom Maclean had told he was "an Alger Hiss" – that it was merely the eccentric remark of a man who was overimbibing.

However, the net was beginning to be drawn in on Maclean. The earlier leakages of atomic secrets were known, and for two years British security men had been trying to track down the informer. The finger pointed to Maclean even at the time when he was in London on his six months' leave for psychiatric treatment.

Personal tragedy

Then, at a three-cornered meeting of M.I.5, S.I.S., and Foreign Office executives, it was decided that the time was ripe to spring the trap. The next day, a Friday, the Foreign Secretary, Herbert Morrison, gave the authority for Maclean to be interrogated. The investigation would begin on the Monday. M.I.5 ordered their top man, William Skardon, the ex-Murder Squad detective who had unmasked atom bomb spy Klaus Fuchs, to stand by.

Then onto the scene stepped Kim Philby, "The Third Man" in Washington. It was to prove a personal tragedy for him that Burgess – the go-between in warning Maclean – should have chosen this moment to make his unnecessary flight. Had he stayed put, Philby might have continued undetected for many more years as a Soviet agent.

In the quest for the man who had tipped off Maclean he would have figured as just one of several possible names.

But in lists drawn up of Maclean suspects and Burgess suspects, he was the only person to figure on both of them. Philby was recalled from Washington, where the Americans had made it clear that they would no longer work with him, and asked to resign.

In his time as a spy Philby had probably done even more than Maclean to damage the interests of the United States and her Western allies. He had occupied two offices of supreme trust which had put

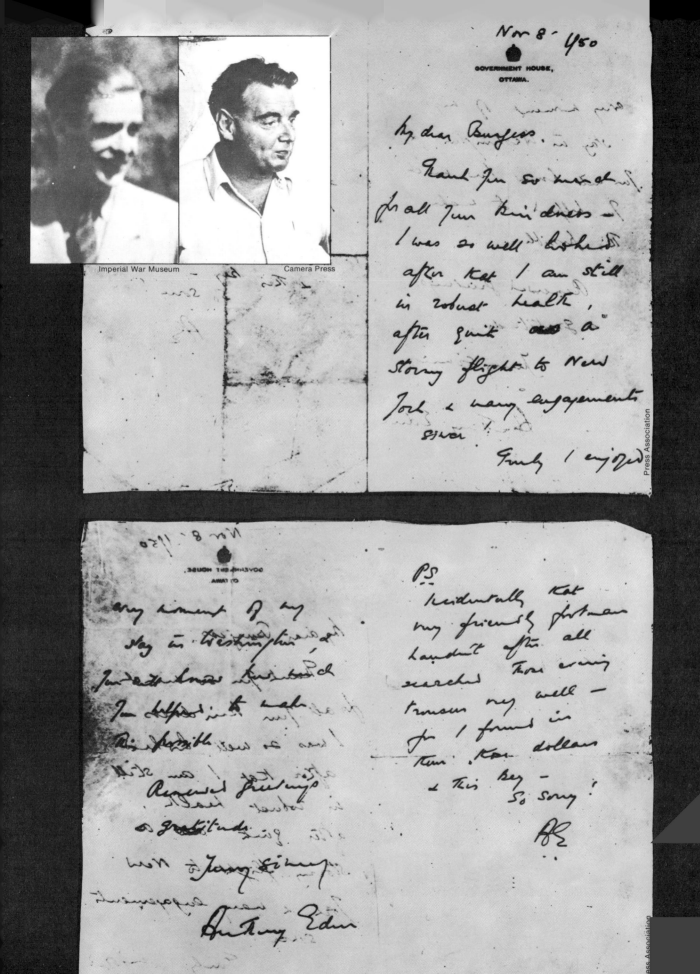

RETRIBUTION came for Guy Burgess in the form of an early death in which his heavy drinking played a large part. The funeral (left) was attended by his old partner Maclean, accompanied by Melinda and Burgess's brother Nigel. The story worked out differently for Philby – the most important and influential of the three. He fell in love with Maclean's wife and married her. News reports and photographs of the couple (below) seem to suggest that they have settled well into Soviet life styles. Meanwhile the former agent has continued to perform valuable work for Russian intelligence.

him in an ideal position from which to serve the Communist cause.

One was when – at a time that the war had not yet ended, and Russia was still officially an Anglo-American ally – he was given the task of setting up a new Soviet counterespionage section of S.I.S. The other was his key position as liaison officer between S.I.S. and the C.I.A.

No one was certain how many Western agents as well as Western secrets he betrayed. Certainly the blood of 150 Albanians was on his hands. They were men who took part, in 1950, in an American- and British-inspired attempt – at the height of the Cold War – to overthrow Russian influence in Albania through guerilla-fomented uprisings. But when the guerillas crossed the frontier the Russians were primed and waiting for them.

Yet Philby's treacherous career was a long time in dying. He managed to bluff his way through his interrogation on his return from Washington. As late as 1955 he was publicly cleared of being "The Third Man" by Foreign Secretary Harold Macmillan in the House of Commons. Afterwards, smiling and confident, he held a press conference. Some of the questions and answers at it were:

If there was a third man, were you, in fact, the third man?
No, I was not.
The Foreign Secretary said in the past that you had Communist associations. Is that why you were asked to resign?
I was asked to resign because of an imprudent association.
That is your association with Burgess?
Correct.
What about the alleged Communist associations?

The last time I spoke to a Communist, knowing him to be a Communist, was sometime in 1934.
That rather implies that you have also spoken to Communists unknowingly and now know about it?
Well, I spoke to Burgess last in April or May 1951.
He gave you no idea that he was a Communist at all?
Never.

Loose tongue

Philby then went on to work as a S.I.S. secret agent in the field – his final posting being to Beirut, Lebanon, where his cover was foreign correspondent for the Sunday *Observer*. Meanwhile, back in London, irrefutable evidence was gradually being assembled of his long connection with Communism. And the fact that he had been "The Third Man" in the Burgess-Maclean affair.

At the end of 1962, S.I.S. confronted him in Beirut. He was given the choice: come home to Britain and face trial, or disappear for good behind the Iron Curtain. The British government hoped he would choose the second alternative – thus saving the "dirt" a trial would bring to light, and the inevitable demands for an

inquiry into the Security Services.

Philby plumped for the Iron Curtain and fled "in secret" to Moscow. From there – speaking for himself *and* Burgess and Maclean – he wrote to a friend in England: "My tongue is looser now!"

Burgess and Maclean settled in Moscow after their flight and continued to serve the Russians in minor advisory roles connected with propaganda. Maclean was joined by his wife, Melinda, and their two sons.

Although the Macleans lived discreetly, Burgess still drank heavily and went on with his homosexual affairs. Western correspondents would often encounter him, usually the worse for alcohol, in Moscow hotels. He died in 1963, a few months after Philby's defection, of advanced hardening of the arteries. Before his death he added a codicil to his will, leaving a third of his estate to Philby.

Philby, with his enormous memory for facts and faces, remained an important member of Russian Intelligence. He also helped Russian agent Gordon Lonsdale, the key figure in the Portland (a top secret underwater naval base in Dorset, England) Spy Case, to write his memoirs. Later Philby fell in love with Melinda Maclean whom he married.

Did Julius Rosenberg and his wife Ethel sell the secret of the atom bomb to the Russians? Or were they the victims of a ruthless frame-up . . . ?

THE ATOM SPIES

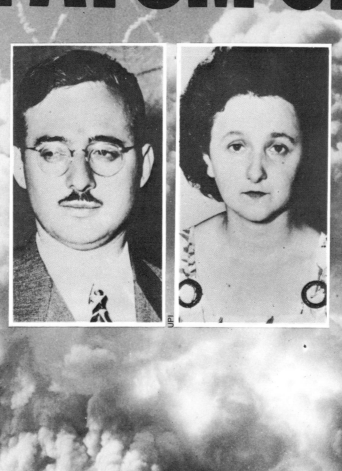

THE TRIAL which began on March 5, 1951, in the Federal Court House in Foley Square, New York City, may well prove to be the most celebrated espionage trial in American history. Certainly no case of its kind in the United States has had wider ramifications and repercussions, both nationally and internationally.

There were three defendants, Julius Rosenberg, his wife Ethel, and their confederate Morton Sobell, who had fled to Mexico but had subsequently been extradited. They were jointly charged with conspiring together with others, including Ethel Rosenberg's brother, David Greenglass; Harry Gold, a Swiss-born Russian, whose real name was Goldnitsky; and Anatoli Yakovlev, a Soviet agent who was ostensibly a clerk in the Soviet Consulate-General in New York.

The object of the alleged conspiracy was a plan to deliver information, documents, sketches, and material vital to the national defence of the United States to a foreign power—namely Soviet Russia—in violation of the Espionage Act of 1917. All these individuals had originally been charged in the Grand Jury indictment.

Deadly earnest

However, Gold pleaded guilty and was sentenced to 30 years. Greenglass and Yakovlev were ordered to be tried separately, but Greenglass, who had also pleaded guilty, had not yet been sentenced. Yakovlev was not apprehended, since he managed to escape to the Soviet Union before F.B.I. agents could catch up with him.

The Hon. Irving R. Kaufman, one of the district judges for the Southern District of New York, presided on the bench. The prosecution was led by U.S. District Attorney Irving H. Saypol, who had three assistants. The Rosenbergs were defended by Emanuel H. Bloch, a well-known criminal lawyer, and his father Alexander Bloch. O. John Rogge held a watching brief for Greenglass, who was expected to testify for the prosecution.

After the three defendants on trial had pleaded not guilty, the District Attorney opened the case for the prosecution. "The significance of a conspiracy to commit espionage," he said, speaking in deadly earnest tones, "takes on an added meaning here where the defendants are charged with having participated in a conspiracy against our country at the most critical hour in its history, in a time of war." He continued: "The evidence will reveal to you how the Rosenbergs persuaded David Greenglass . . . to plot the treacherous role of a modern Benedict Arnold while wearing the uniform of the United States Army . . . We will prove that the Rosenbergs devised and put into operation with the aid of Soviet nationals and Soviet agents in this country an elaborate scheme which enabled them, through Greenglass, to steal the one weapon which might well hold the key to the survival of this nation and the peace of the world — the atomic bomb."

Maximum sentence

The prosecutor gave due credit to the F.B.I. for breaking the spy ring. At the same time he made it clear that this could not have been done had it not been for the information revealed by a German-born naturalized British subject named Klaus Fuchs — who had pleaded guilty in England to spying for the Soviet Union, and received the maximum sentence of 14 years under the relevant British statute.

Fuchs — who was one of the senior scientific officers at the British Atomic Research Establishment at Harwell — had been sent to the United States during the war to cooperate in the development and production of the atomic bomb at Los Alamos. While there he had witnessed the explosion of the first test bomb

in New Mexico. Nothing was hidden from him, said J. Edgar Hoover, Director of the F.B.I., "Dr. Fuchs had all our greatest secrets."

After Fuchs began to serve his sentence in England, F.B.I. agents were allowed to question him, and subsequently got on to the trail of the Soviet spy ring in the United States. Fuchs was able to identify Harry Gold — a biochemist whom the Bureau had previously suspected of being active in Soviet espionage, but whom it had previously been impossible to incriminate. The British in turn had picked up Fuchs through the revelations of a Russian cypher clerk named Igor Gouzenko, who was employed in the Military Attaché's office in the Soviet Embassy in Ottawa.

The first of the star witnesses to be called to the stand was Max Elitcher, an electronics engineer who had worked in the U.S. Navy Bureau of Ordnance between 1938 and 1948. Elitcher admitted

ATOM TRIO (facing page) . . . Morton Sobell (left), Julius Rosenberg and his wife Ethel look calm as they are driven from the courtroom. But there were many unanswered questions. Why, for example, were their alleged collaborators David Greenglass and Harry Gold (below) so keen to implicate them? And how did Soviet agent Yakovlev (right) escape so easily? Was he the mastermind behind the atom secrets leak from Los Alamos (bottom)?

to being a Communist and to having become a member of a "cell" at Sobell's urging. It was also through Sobell that the witness had met the Rosenbergs and learned that they were active party members and secret Soviet agents.

Entire truth

Julius Rosenberg, Elitcher went on, invited him to help transmit secret information from the ordnance office files. Elitcher swore that he pretended to do so, but in fact he had never given Rosenberg any information classified as secret. Under cross-examination, Elitcher admitted that he lied when he took a loyalty oath. But he firmly insisted that

"ever since the F.B.I. got hold of him he had told the entire truth". Finally Elitcher admitted that he had regularly acted as a courier between Sobell and Rosenberg.

Ruth Greenglass then testified that her husband, David, had been a Communist, and described how in the autumn of 1944 Julius Rosenberg had asked her to go to Los Alamos and obtain classified information from David—a member of the United States armed forces and working on an atomic bomb project there. At first she demurred, but Julius assured her that her husband would want to help. Russia was an ally of the U.S., argued Julius, and as such deserved information about the bomb, but Communists were not getting the information which they should. Eventually, said the witness, she agreed to make the trip, as her second wedding anniversary was coming up and she wanted to spend it with her husband. Julius gave her $150 for her expenses, saying the money came from "his friends the Russians".

Jello box

At first David Greenglass was reluctant to cooperate. The next morning, however, he agreed to give his wife "the general layout of the Los Alamos project", together with the number of employees, the experiments being conducted, and the names of the scientists working there. The witness carefully memorized this information, she said, and duly passed it on to Julius Rosenberg on her return to New York.

In January 1945, she continued, her husband came to New York on leave, and they both met the Rosenbergs by appointment at the latters' apartment. They were introduced to a Mrs. Sidorovich. First, they discussed the kind of information Greenglass should look out for when he returned to Los Alamos. Rosenberg then explained that Mrs. Sidorovich might be sent to New Mexico to get this information from Greenglass, and he produced two torn halves of a Jello box top.

It was arranged that Mrs. Greenglass—who planned to return to New Mexico with her husband—should keep one part, and whoever was sent to get in touch with her and her husband would establish his or her identity by producing the other half. Ruth Greenglass remembered that when David commented on the simplicity and cleverness of this device, Julius Rosenberg remarked, "The simplest things are always the cleverest."

Subsequently, contact was made in June 1945, when the Greenglasses were living in Albuquerque, New Mexico. Early one morning a man called on them. "I come from Julius," he said, and produced the matching piece of the Jello box top. Ruth Greenglass identified him as Harry Gold, who gave her husband

$500 which David Greenglass handed over to her.

By May 1950, the witness said, she and her husband—who had then been discharged from the army—were back in New York, and their relations with the Rosenbergs were closer than ever. On May 24, according to Ruth, Julius Rosenberg burst into their apartment brandishing a copy of the New York *Herald Tribune,* which carried a picture of Harry Gold on the front page together with the news of his arrest as a Soviet spy. "You will be next," said Julius, and urged them to escape at once to Mexico.

Ruth did not think their ten-month-old baby could stand the trip. Rosenberg, however, brushed aside her objection and left $1000 with them to cover preliminary expenses, telling her to have passport photographs taken and get vaccinated against smallpox. In spite of these warnings, the Greenglasses stayed in New York. On June 15 David was arrested.

In cross-examination, Alexander Bloch tried to bring out that the witness knew she had committed a crime, and that her direct testimony had been influenced by fear of the F.B.I. "Weren't you frightened of the F.B.I.?" he asked.

"Everyone is frightened by the F.B.I.," Ruth Greenglass replied, "but it was not because I realized it was a crime that I was frightened. I didn't think the F.B.I. wanted my husband, I thought they wanted someone my husband would lead them to, someone much more important than he and much more deeply involved."

David Greenglass generally corroborated his wife's testimony when he followed her on the witness stand. However, he denied that he had known of the atomic bomb until he had learned about it from Julius Rosenberg. As a machinist at Los Alamos, he knew only that he was working on "a secret device of some kind".

Expert knowledge

The details, he insisted, he had first learned from Rosenberg in January 1945 —"fissionable material at one end of a tube and on the other end a sliding mechanism with fissionable material, and when the two were brought together under tremendous pressure nuclear reaction was accomplished." As far as it went, this description fitted the uranium bomb which was dropped on Hiroshima seven months later.

In the following September, he continued, he and his wife went to New York, where he met the Rosenbergs and handed over a sketch of the atom bomb and a ten-page analysis, which Ethel later typed out. "This is *very* good," said Julius when he read it. These particulars, said Greenglass, related to the plutonium bomb which was dropped on

Nagasaki. The witness's testimony in this respect revealed such an expert knowledge that Judge Kaufman ordered the court to be cleared, and cautioned the newspaper reporters present "to exercise discretion in what they printed".

The tension created in the courtroom by the witness's long recital of treachery was relieved by a small touch of humour at its close. He was asked in cross-examination if, when looking at the Jello box top, he had noticed the flavour. "Yes, raspberry," he promptly replied. This answer raised the only laugh in the sombre proceedings.

Harry Gold was the next prosecution witness. He told how he had been working for the Russians as far back as 1935, and how in 1944 he acted as a go-between for Russian agents and persons who procured information for them. At that time his Soviet superior was Anatoli Yakovlev, but Gold only knew him as

LAWYERS in the case: Emanuel Bloch who defended the Rosenbergs; prosecutor Irving Saypol (bottom) and (right) judge Irving Kaufman. The trial aroused great public interest. Demonstration (above right) is led by Rosenbergs' young sons.

"John". It was at Yakovlev's instruction that in June 1944 the witness first met Fuchs—who promised to give him information "relating to the application of nuclear fission to the production of a military weapon".

At a subsequent meeting in Cambridge, Mass., in January 1945, Fuchs told the witness that he was working on the atomic bomb with other scientists in Los Alamos, which he described, particularly mentioning a lens which was one of its essential parts. It was agreed between them that Gold should visit Los Alamos in June—when Fuchs hoped to have more information about the bomb and its lens.

When Gold told Yakovlev of this, the Soviet master spy intimated that he had another very "vital" job for him in New Mexico, namely to contact Greenglass in Albuquerque. At first the witness objected, he said, but when Yakovlev insisted he agreed, since he took this to be an order. After he had seen Fuchs, and obtained a sealed envelope from him,

Gold went on to Albuquerque where he met the Greenglasses and received another envelope from them.

A few days later he reported to Yakovlev in Brooklyn, handing over the two envelopes, which Yakovlev later told him contained "extremely excellent and very valuable" information. The witness's last meeting with Yakovlev took place at the end of 1946, the day before Yakovlev sailed for Europe.

Inestimable value

Gold was not cross-examined. This was good tactics on the part of Sobell's attorneys, since Gold's testimony had not implicated their client in any way. As for the Rosenbergs' counsel, they may well have decided not to cross-examine, because Gold had shown himself eager to help the government in any way he could—and answers elicited in cross-examination might only have made matters worse for the Rosenbergs.

Several other witnesses testified to the

value of the information imparted by Greenglass as being of "inestimable value to a nation which did not possess the secret of nuclear fission". If Sobell and the Rosenbergs had committed the crimes they were charged with, they said, their actions seriously jeopardised the security of the United States.

Emanuel Bloch opened the defence by calling Julius Rosenberg to the witness stand. Answering his attorney, Rosenberg admitted that he was a first-generation American of Russian parents who had emigrated to New York City. He was a Bachelor of Science, having graduated from New York City College. He told how he married Ethel Greenglass, and in 1940 became a junior engineer in the U.S. Signal Corps, from which he was dismissed five years later.

"Did you ever have any conversation with Ruth Greenglass about November 1944 with respect to getting information from David Greenglass at the place where he was working?"

"I did not."

"Did you know in the middle of 1944 where David Greenglass was stationed?"

"I did not."

"Did you know in the middle of 1944 that there was such a project known as the Los Alamos project?"

"I did not."

"Did you ever give Ruth Greenglass $150, or any other sum for her to go out to visit her husband at Los Alamos for the purpose of trying to enlist him in espionage work?"

"I did not."

Julius Rosenberg denied everything. Shown the sketch of the atomic bomb that David Greenglass had made, he denied that his brother-in-law had ever delivered such a sketch to him. "I never saw this sketch before." Apart from what he had heard in court, he could not describe the bomb. Nor had he ever taken a course in nuclear or advanced physics.

He also denied all knowledge of the Jello box top; he had never introduced David Greenglass to a Mrs. Sidorovich. Nor had he tried to induce the Greenglasses to leave the country, and he had not provided them with money for their trip. Finally, he denied that he and his wife had ever contemplated fleeing from America themselves.

Asked in cross-examination by Saypol whether he had been discharged from his job in the Signals Corp because he was suspected of being a Communist, and thus belonging to an illegal organization,

SILENT and bare, the death chamber at Sing Sing prison (facing page) where Julius and Ethel Rosenberg were executed on June 19, 1953. Huge crowds gathered in protest in New York's Union Square, some wept openly (left).

he admitted that this was so.

"Were you a member of the Communist Party?" the District Attorney asked.

Rosenberg paused for a few moments. Then he replied: "I refuse to answer on the ground that it might tend to incriminate me."

He repeated this reply when confronted with a statement he had signed on joining the Signals Corp stating that he was not then, and never had been, a member of the Communist Party. The court sustained the witness's objection to incriminating questions, and ruled that he was not required to answer them.

At the same time, in answer to further questions, Rosenberg protested his loyalty to the United States. "I will fight for this country if it were engaged in a war with any other country," he declared. On the other hand, he admitted that he felt some admiration for the achievements of the Russians—particularly in improving the lot of the underdog. "I felt and still feel," he added, "that they contributed a major share in destroying the Hitler beast who killed six million of my co-religionists, and I feel emotional about that thing."

Not an expert

Judge Kaufman intervened at this point to ask a couple of questions which the witness tried to dodge.

"Did you approve the Communist system of Russia over the capitalist system of this country?"

"I am not an expert on those things, Your Honour, and I did not make any such statement."

"Did you ever belong to any group that discussed the system of Russia?"

Again the witness took refuge behind the protective constitutional amendment. "Well, Your Honour, I feel at this time that I refuse to answer a question that might tend to incriminate me."

Ethel Rosenberg's testimony was along the same lines. She blandly asserted that she was a loyal citizen of the United States and had never engaged in espionage. Everything her brother and sister-in-law had testified to was false, she said. But when she was asked in cross-examination about her affiliations with the Communist Party, she refused to answer.

No further witnesses were called for the defence, since Morton Sobell did not testify. In rebuttal, the prosecution called a New York commercial photographer, who stated that about mid-June 1950 the Rosenbergs and their two children had three sets of passport photographs taken in his studio. Mr. Rosenberg, the witness said, told him that they were going to France to look at some property Mrs. Rosenberg owned there.

In his closing speech to the jury on behalf of the Rosenbergs, Emanuel Bloch

concentrated on the unreliability of Ruth and David Greenglass as witnesses. "Don't you think that the Greenglasses put it over on the government when Ruth Greenglass was not even indicted?" he asked the jurors. "She walked out and put Greenglass's sister in. David Greenglass was willing to bury his sister and her husband to save his life. Not only are the Greenglasses self-confessed spies, but they are mercenary spies. "They'd do anything for money."

Worse than murder

"Any man who will testify against his own flesh and blood, his own sister, is repulsive, revolting, and is violating any code of civilization that ever existed. He is lower than the lowest animal I have ever seen."

"The Greenglasses have told the truth," asserted District Attorney Saypol in winding up for the prosecution. "They have tried to make amends for the hurt which has been done to our nation and to the world."

In reality, the D.A. continued, the unreliable testimony came from the Rosenbergs—who had denied planning to leave the country, in spite of the testimony about the passport photographs. "The Rosenbergs have magnified their treachery by lying here." Furthermore, they were linked with Sobell in their espionage activities—since Sobell had flown to Mexico with his family in the same month that Greenglass had been paid by the Russians, through Rosenberg, to do likewise. "Sobell's conduct fits the pattern of membership in this conspiracy and flight from an American jury when the day of reckoning had come."

After the fairest and most impartial summing up of the evidence by Judge Kaufman, the jury retired at 4.53 in the

FAMILY TRAGEDY: distraught Mrs. Sophie Rosenberg weeps hysterically at seeing her son and daughter-in-law buried after their execution (left). Then, overcome with emotion and pain (right), she faints. Hundreds witnessed the scene.

afternoon of March 28 and did not return until 11 o'clock next morning—when they pronounced all three defendants guilty as charged.

"Your crime is worse than murder," Judge Kaufman told the Rosenbergs when they came up for sentence. "In your case I believe your conduct in putting into the hands of the Russians the A-bomb years before our best scientists predicted Russia would perfect the bomb has already caused the Communist aggression in Korea, with resulting casualties exceeding 50,000 Americans."

Flood of letters

While not doubting for a moment that Morton Sobell was also engaged in espionage activities, the judge said he was bound to recognize the lesser degree of his implication. He was consequently given 30 years, the maximum prison term provided by the statute. Next day David Greenglass was sentenced to 15 years in the light of the considerable help he had rendered in the prosecution of the Rosenbergs.

A series of appeals and petitions followed, which in the case of the Rosenbergs had the effect of delaying the execution of the death sentence for more than two years. Their petition for executive clemency was presented to President Truman on January 11, 1953. It was supported by a flood of letters mostly in favour of the sentence being commuted. Among the writers were Albert Einstein, the world-famous scientist—who had

earlier urged President Roosevelt to make sure that the United States did not fall behind in the race to make the atom bomb —and a group of 3000 lawyers who declared that "the death penalty would not conform to the great pattern of Anglo-Saxon jurisprudence". But President Truman declined to act on the petition which reached him during the last days of his term of office, and he left the decision to General Dwight D. Eisenhower, his successor in the White House.

Appeals

President Eisenhower refused to interfere with the sentence on the Rosenbergs.

Meanwhile, the appeals and motions for stays of execution continued. At the beginning of June, the Rosenbergs' counsel announced that their clients had rejected the offer which had been made to them on behalf of the Attorney-General that their sentences would be commuted to life imprisonment if they made full confessions and exposed any other members of their spy ring who had not been brought to justice.

"By asking us to repudiate the truth of our innocence," they said at the time, "the government admits its doubts concerning our guilt. We will not help to purify this foul record of a fraudulent and barbarous sentence." Shortly afterwards the Supreme Court voted by a majority of five to four against granting a further stay of execution.

At the last moment, however, it looked as if there would be a stay when Supreme Court Justice Douglas ordered it in response to an application for time to argue a point of law—namely that the Espionage Act of 1917 had been superseded by the Atomic Energy Act of 1946, under which a death sentence could not be imposed except on the recommendation of a jury. On June 19 Justice Douglas's decision was revoked by a majority of the Supreme Court. Defence counsel submitted a final petition to the President for clemency which Eisenhower again rejected.

First Americans

The Rosenbergs went to the electric chair in Sing Sing the same evening and met their end bravely, protesting their innocence to the last. The time of execution was advanced from the usual hour of 11 p.m. to 8 p.m. to avoid carrying out the sentences on the Jewish Sabbath.

Julius and Ethel Rosenberg were the first Americans to be sentenced to death for espionage by a non-military court—while Mrs. Rosenberg was the first woman in the United States since Mrs. Surratt had been sentenced for her part in the assassination of President Lincoln, to suffer death by the judgement of a Federal tribunal.

MUST JOHN DICKMAN BE HANGED?

Had he really killed that wages clerk (inset) on the
slow train from Newcastle? At first the public had howled for his blood,
but now there were certain rumours about police procedure. . . .

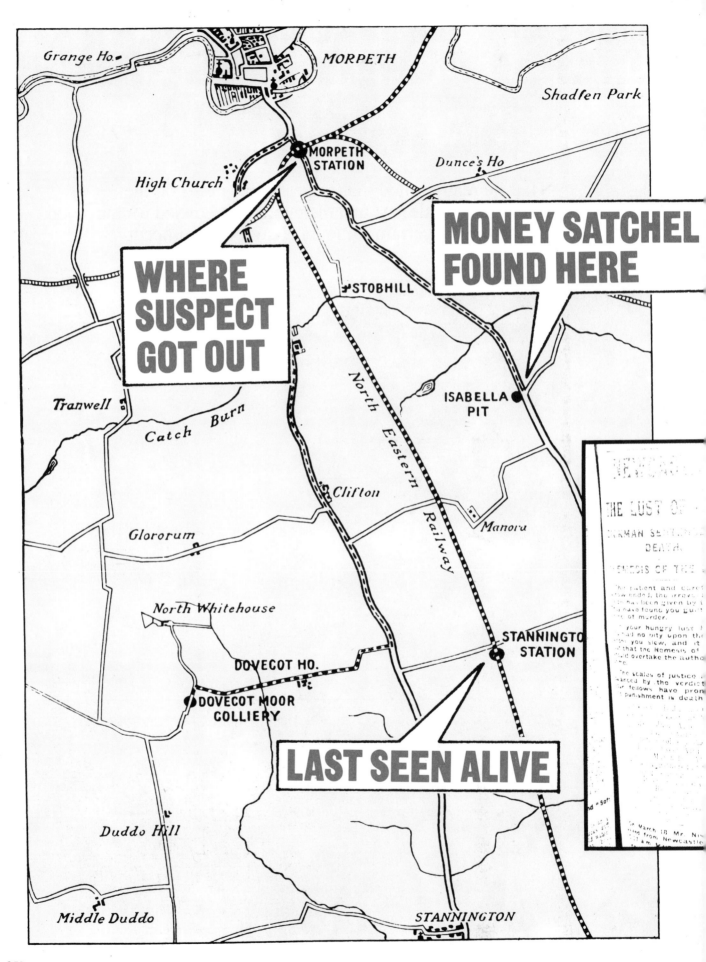

WHERE SUSPECT GOT OUT

MONEY SATCHEL FOUND HERE

LAST SEEN ALIVE

THERE was no escaping the terse, urgent handbill. It was left in restaurants all over London, distributed in public houses, thrust by demonstrators into the hands of passers-by . . .

MUST JOHN DICKMAN BE HANGED TOMORROW? NO! NO! NO! WIRE HOME SECRETARY AT ONCE AND WASH YOUR HANDS OF COMPLICITY IN THE LEGAL CRIME

It was evening on August 9, 1910. Two hundred and seventy-two miles away to the north, John Alexander Dickman sat in the condemned cell of Newcastle jail, counting the diminishing hours. It was ironic. Only a few months earlier the crowd had been screaming for his blood. They had fought to get a glimpse of him on the way to his trial for murder. They had shaken their fists, shouted threats and abuse as the police escort shouldered its way through the mob. Now they wanted to reprieve him.

"Stop the hanging!" demanded the placards carried by the demonstrators. "Dickman is a victim of circumstantial evidence and police prejudice!"

But there had been nothing circum-

stantial about the sight which had greeted railway-porter Tom Charlton when he had opened the door of the slow train from Newcastle at Alnmouth Station on a drizzly Friday, March 18.

At first, it appeared empty. Then Charlton saw the three broad streams of blood flowing across the floor from under one of the seats. Crammed beneath the seat was the body of 44-year-old John Innes Nisbet, a wages clerk for a local colliery. He had been shot five times in the head, with bullets of two different calibres, and the leather satchel containing more than £370 in wages was missing.

Crumpled paper pellet

The only clues in the compartment were Nisbet's battered felt hat and smashed spectacles . . . and a small wad of paper which was collected automatically by the police, but discarded as insignificant. Yet that crumpled paper pellet held the key to one of the strangest riddles in the case — a riddle which baffled experts, mystified the police, confounded lawyers, and even misled the trial judge.

Within a few hours, police had traced Nisbet's movements from the time he left a bank in Newcastle with the colliery wages in his satchel to catch the 10.27 a.m. train, calling at every station on the 35 miles to Alnmouth, Northumberland.

One vital point emerged straight away: there had been somebody with the murdered man. Somebody who had been seen walking with him along the platform at Newcastle, who had been seen entering the same compartment, who had been seen sitting opposite Nisbet at Heaton Station. *But who had never been seen again.*

The eye-witnesses — some of whom knew Nisbet but not his companion, and others who recognized the companion but were not acquainted with the murdered man — all told a consistent story.

Charles Raven informed the police that he had noticed Nisbet walking along Platform 5 at Newcastle with another man whom he vaguely recognized, but not by name. Mr. Wilson Hepple, an elderly artist, was more explicit. While he was standing outside his carriage, he saw Nisbet, who was a stranger, pass by with a man he had known for several years. The two men stopped at a compartment higher up the train and one put his hand on the door-handle. At that point, Hepple turned round. From his seat in the train, Percival Hall, another colliery cashier, also saw Nisbet walking along the platform with an unknown man in a light raincoat.

It was a routine journey for Nisbet. Every alternate Friday he collected the miners' wages and travelled on the same train back to the colliery. At Nisbet's home town of Heaton, his wife always

snatched the chance of a quick chat as the train passed through.

March 18 was no exception. Mrs. Cicely Nisbet was standing at the wrong end of the platform, however, and took a few seconds to reach his carriage, which was next to the engine. A shadow from a tunnel fell across the window of the compartment, but not enough to hide Nisbet's companion. He was facing the engine, with his coat collar turned up. Mrs. Nisbet caught a distinct glimpse of his profile before the train moved off and her husband waved goodbye for the last time.

Nisbet was still alive at Stannington Station, where Hall and a friend, John Spink, got out and nodded a greeting to him as they walked past. Again, they noticed he was not alone. Nisbet was never seen alive again.

The next stop after Stannington was Morpeth, 2½ miles and six minutes away. On arrival, a man in a light raincoat got out and passed through the ticket barrier. Ticket-collector John Athey remembered him clearly for several reasons. Although the man's return ticket had been valid only as far as Stannington, he already had 2½ pence in excess fare in his left hand. His other hand had been hidden inside his coat pocket.

Small-time speculator

While the train was idling at the station, a passenger glanced into Nisbet's compartment. It was apparently deserted. The man who passed through the barrier at Morpeth — and whose description fitted that of Nisbet's mysterious travelling companion — was a 43-year-old bookie named John Alexander Dickman, a former colliery secretary and a man well-known in the area as a small-time speculator.

Dickman couldn't have been more helpful when the police called. Certainly, he admitted, he had been on the 10.27 from Newcastle on the morning of the murder. Yes, he had seen Nisbet on the platform but had lost sight of him after buying his ticket and eventually entered a different compartment, near the end of the train.

Why had he got off at Morpeth instead of Stannington? Simple; as a bookie, he had been so engrossed in the *Manchester Sporting Chronicle* — it was the day of the great Grand National race — that he had been carried past his station and only realized his mistake when the train rounded the sharp bend just before Morpeth.

Why hadn't he taken the next train back to Stannington, then? Dickman had an answer for that, too. He had intended to make a few business and social calls around Dovecot Colliery, situated between the two stations, so it had been almost as quick to walk from Morpeth.

Had he made the calls? Well, no.

RAIN MURDER.

Spoke to

A ROUTINE JOURNEY for colliery clerk Nisbet ended under the seat of a train compartment with five bullets (of two different calibres) in his head and his leather satchel, containing more than £370 in wages, missing.

Dickman explained with an embarrassed shrug that he suffered from both diarrhoea and piles, and had been taken suddenly ill on the walk to Stannington. After resting in a field, he decided to return to Morpeth and catch the 1.12 back to New-castle, but he missed it and had to take the 1.40 p.m. instead.

There was something altogether too glib about Dickman's story. It also failed to agree in several important details with statements police had taken from other witnesses. Dickman was charged with the murder of John Innes Nisbet. "It is absurd for me to deny the charge," he replied coolly, "because it is absurd to make it."

A search of Dickman's home revealed a bloodstained glove and trousers, a light raincoat that had been crudely cleaned with paraffin, and a small canvas bag—identical to those handed over by the bank to Nisbet—containing £17 in gold sovereigns.

Tests on the clothes failed to establish whether the bloodstains were human or animal. Dickman's explanation was that they had been the result of a nosebleed or a slip of the scissors while he had been cutting his corns. As for the bag, Dick-man claimed that he had been using similar bags for carrying loose change for 20 years. Every time one wore out, he merely got a replacement from the bank.

Extortionate interest

But investigations gradually disclosed an unsuspected side to Dickman's char-acter. He had backed a succession of arthritic horses and was badly in debt. On February 14, he had pawned a scarf-ring, some studs, and a set of cufflinks to raise money. He had also borrowed £20 from a moneylender named Hermann Cohen, despite an extortionate interest rate of 60%. There was not even enough housekeeping money for his wife. In January, she had written to him while he was away at the races:

"Dear Jack, I received your card and am sorry that you have no money to spend. I am needing it very badly. The weather here is past description. I had to get in a load of coals, which consumed the greater part of a sovereign. The final notice for rates has come in—in fact, came in last week—which means they must be paid next Thursday. Also Harry's school account. With my dividend due this week and what is in the Savings Bank I dare say I can pay the most press-ing things, but it is going to make the

PROSECUTING counsel Tindal Atkinson (right) suggested that the defendant had been rehearsing the robbery. But the court's attention was riveted else-where . . . upon the fascinating riddle of the murder weapon.

question of living a poser, unless you can give me some advice as to what to do. Trusting to hear from you soon regarding what you think I had best do,

Annie Dickman."

Dickman denied being hard-pressed for cash. Although his joint bank-balance with his wife stood at only £4, he claimed he had a "reserve fund" of £120. He in-sisted that he hadn't pawned the jewellery but merely "put it in a place of security, in case of burglary". The visit to the moneylender had just been a "kind of experiment" to see if the man stuck to the terms laid out in his advertisements.

Not surprisingly, the police were un-convinced. Their next discovery was even more incriminating. They traced the address of a shop in Newcastle where Dickman collected business letters under the name of "F. Black". But letters weren't the only things that arrived. The shopkeeper, Miss Henrietta Hymen,

remembered receiving a parcel from a gunsmith. It was addressed to "Mr. Black" and contained a revolver. When Dickman next called at the shop, he assured her it had been sent in error and promised to post it back. She never saw the gun—or Dickman—again.

Identification parade

On March 21, an identification parade was held at Newcastle Central Police-station in which Percival Hall picked out Dickman from among nine men as being Nisbet's travelling companion on the morning of the murder. The parade, how-ever, was a shambles. Hall seemed un-sure what to do and singled out Dickman with the odd remark, "If I was assured that the murderer was in among these nine men, I would have no hesitation in picking the prisoner out."

Dickman was wearing the light rain-coat found in his home, although he

TRAIN MURDER.

DEAD MAN'S WIFE WEEPS IN COURT.

The Public Prosecutor has taken charge of the case against Jno. Alex. Dickman, who was charged at Newcastle with the murder of Jno. Innes Nesbit, colliery cashier, in a North-Eastern train between Newcastle and Alnmouth on March 18.—The Public Prosecutor, represented by Mr. S. Pearce, opened the case against accused. Every corner of the court was crowded, and hundreds of people outside saw the arrival of Dickman.—Mrs. Dickman occupied a seat in the court behind the dock.—Mr. Pearce recalled the circumstances of the crime, stating that Mr. Nesbit, who had been employed in the Stobswood Colliery Co. for 28 years, was as usual taking about £370 to the colliery for the men's wages. His destination was

Jno. A. Dickman.

Widdrington Station. He left Newcastle by the 10.27 a.m. train. When his dead body was found there were
Five Bullet Wounds
in the head and face. Prisoner made a statement to the police, counsel continued, in which he stated that he saw, but did not speak to, Nesbit at Newcastle Station. He booked for Stannington, but inadvertently passed through Stannington, and, having alighted from the train at Morpeth, began to walk back. Feeling ill, he changed his mind, and returned to Morpeth, going back to Newcastle by the 1.40 p.m. train. As against that statement, proceeded Mr. Pearce,

EXHUMED BODY.

ACCUSED CLERK AGAIN REMANDED.

The ex-railway clerk, Fdk. Geo. Beeton, who was arrested after being released from St. Albans Gaol, was again placed in the dock at Hitchin, and charged with the wilful murder of a child, whose body was dug up in an allotment at the Letchworth Garden City, which had been tenanted by accused from March, 1908, to March 25 last.—The charge was preferred against Beeton mainly on account of the dramatic evidence given at the inquest by a convict, to whom Beeton is alleged to have confessed to having killed the child while the two men were together in a cell in Wormwood Scrubs Prison.—At the last hearing before the magistrates, evidence was given by the police as to the finding of the body in the allotment, the name of the child being given as Margaret Anna Young, and it being stated that it was the illegitimate daughter of prisoner.—Prisoner, who had been incarcerated in St. Albans Prison, was brought to Hitchin in custody of two warders.

No Further Evidence.

When placed in the dock he was seen to be wearing a grey overcoat over the blue suit which he was wearing when arrested. He appeared somewhat dejected. Neither the Treasury nor prisoner was represented by counsel, and immediately Beeton was placed in the dock Supt. Reynolds, of the Herts police, said he was instructed by the Home Office to apply for another remand.—No further evidence was now offered; and after perusing the communication from the Home Office, Mr. Hill (the chairman of the bench) without comment, ordered the remand applied for, first asking prisoner whether he had any objection to that course being taken. The reply, "No, sir," was given with a shake of the head, and in an almost inaudible whisper. Prisoner was then removed to the cells, and the capacious court was rapidly emptied of the crowded people, who had gathered there to hear the proceedings. It is understood that no fur-

PEACE WITH HO

insisted that on the day of the murder he had been wearing a dark coat. He accused the police of "intimidating" Hall, and a rumour that Hall had been allowed a peep at Dickman before the parade assembled was later borne out in an extraordinary letter from the Chief Constable to the Under-Secretary of State.

Had Dickman known then of the "sneak preview", he would have played on it for all it was worth. But within a few weeks the ramshackle identification parade had been completely overshadowed by a new development which pointed even more accusingly to Dickman as the murderer.

They found Nisbet's money satchel. It was lying at the bottom of an air shaft at the Isabella Pit, only 1¾ miles south of Morpeth Station and close to the main road. It had been slashed wide open and everything emptied out except a few coppers, some of which were scattered near the entrance to the shaft. The spot could easily have been reached by Dickman on his diarrhoea-and-piles-plagued walk from the station, but he denied all knowledge of the shaft when questioned by the police.

Resting in a field

Peter Spooner, the colliery manager, had another story. He plainly recalled telling Dickman about the shaft and the problems they were having draining away surplus water. Dickman failed to produce a single witness to substantiate his movements during the "missing two hours" between arriving at Morpeth Station and returning just in time to miss the 1.12 to Newcastle. "Most of the time I was resting in a field," he told the police, rather limply.

On Monday, July 4, 1910, Dickman's trial opened at Newcastle Assizes. On the way to the court, he was mobbed by booing crowds and had to be protected by the police. At an earlier hearing, the dead man's widow, Mrs. Cicely Nisbet, had fainted at her first sight of Dickman. After she recovered, she explained, "I recognized the man I saw in the train, sitting opposite my husband. I saw that same profile, in the same position. That was the first time I had seen the prisoner's face as I saw it on the morning of March 18." Now Mrs. Nisbet faced Dickman again. "I am certain that the man I saw in that carriage is the man I now see in the dock," she told the court. "That man Dickman!"

Under cross-examination, Dickman admitted that he knew about the regular transfer of wages on alternate Fridays — a point which the prosecution used to explain a series of pointless visits Dickman had made by train to an acquaintance named William Hogg at Dovecot Colliery. Dickman had found an excuse to call on

WITH GLEE, defence counsel Mitchell-Innes took up the argument that two murderers were involved. But it turned out to be a false trail. . . .

Hogg on five occasions, usually on a Friday. In court, Dickman was unable to give an adequate explanation for the repeated visits. Mr. Tindal Atkinson, prosecuting counsel, provided a reason for him by suggesting that Dickman had been rehearsing the robbery. He needed to know exactly how long the train stopped at each station, what wages were carried and which cashier was most likely to travel alone.

But it was the riddle of the murder weapon — still untraced by the police — that fooled everyone, from the judge downwards. Thomas Simpson, a Newcastle gunsmith, was the first one to lead the court down a completely wrong turning in his description of the four bullets found in Nisbet's head.

"Two of them are nickel-capped, with a calibre of ·250," he said. "The other two bullets are leaden, they have no nickel capping, and their calibre is ·320. They are larger, of course, than the first two. The nickel-plated bullets would be fired from an automatic pistol. With regard to the other two bullets, they are larger and could not have been fired from that pistol. They are of a common calibre and it follows that the four bullets found in the man's body must of necessity have been fired from two different pistols."

It was a false trail, but it was taken up with glee by Dickman's defence counsel, Mr. Edward Mitchell-Innes, as proof that *two* murderers could have committed the crime.

"The first remarkable thing about the murder was that two pistols were used," he said. "There were five shots, with two different kinds of bullet. The reasonable inference from the presence of these shots, and two kinds of bullets, was that two murderers did the deed. If two men did the deed, the whole story of the prosecution fell to the ground."

The same basic mistake was made by the judge, Lord Coleridge, in his summing-up. Anxious to expose the flaw in Mr. Mitchell-Innes's theory of "two murderers", Lord Coleridge fell even deeper into the trap.

"One thing that is clear is this," he said, "that the wounds were inflicted by two instruments—that is, by two pistols, because they were inflicted by a small, nickel-plated bullet and by a leaden bullet, and the two classes of bullet would not fit into the same bore. The first natural inference you would derive from that is that the man must have been attacked by two persons, each holding a lethal weapon.

"As a matter of fact, it would appear upon the evidence, unless we are to disregard it in its entirety, one man and one man alone was the companion of the deceased in that compartment. If therefore you are of the opinion on the evidence that one man, and one man alone, was in the carriage with the deceased man when he was murdered, it stands to reason, does it not, that, however unusual, the murderer must have used two weapons?"

Superficial wounds

Unusual or not, the correct answer to Lord Coleridge's rhetorical question should have been "No!" For the murderer had only used *one* gun. The clue was in the wad of paper found on the floor of the compartment—a clue so obscure that its significance was not realized until after the trial. Dickman had made the smaller-calibre bullets fit into the chamber of the larger-bore revolver by wrapping them in paper. As a result, their velocity had been impaired and they had only caused superficial wounds. The fatal wounds had been made by the proper calibre bullets.

The judge was on safer—and far more telling—ground in recalling the evidence of John Athev, the ticket collector at Morpeth. "Mr. Athev has described how the prisoner had his ticket and his fare in his left hand, and it is suggested on the part of the prosecution that the exact amount of the excess fare was suspiciously ready. However that commends

"IN YOUR HUNGRY LUST for gold," pronounced Lord Coleridge, the judge, **"you had no pity on the victim whom you slew . . . the punishment is death."**

itself to you, it is a matter for you and not for me; but if the suggestion of the prosecution be correct that in his right hand, under his coat, he was carrying a bag with £370 in it, it would not leave his right hand free for getting at his ticket or finding his change. His left hand would be free; and therefore the prosecution rather suggest that the prisoner, calculating the fare beforehand, got his ticket ready and the exact amount of the excess fare so as to be able to pass the barrier, using only his left hand."

The jury took $2\frac{1}{2}$ hours to reach their verdict. It was Guilty. Lord Coleridge turned to Dickman, standing rigid in the dock. "Prisoner at the bar," he said, "the patient, careful trial is now ended, the irrevocable decision has now been given. The jury have found you guilty

of murder. In your hungry lust for gold you had no pity on the victim whom you slew, and it is only just that the nemesis of the law should overtake the author of the crime. The scales of justice are now balanced by the verdict which your fellows have pronounced. The punishment is death."

Some loose talk

But rumours had already started leaking to the defence about the irregular identification parade at Newcastle Central Police-station four months earlier—when Percival Hall was given a "helping hand" in picking out Dickman as the murderer. Eight days after the sentence, the rumours were acted upon.

In a letter addressed to the Under-Secretary of State, the Chief Constable of

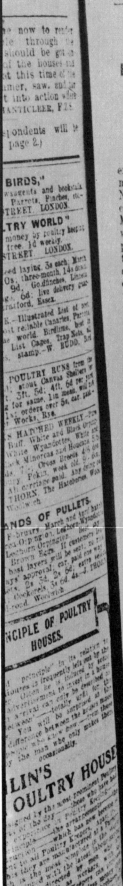

DICKMAN'S FATE.

HANGED FOR THE TRAIN MURDER.

THE LAST SCENE.

Jno. Alexander Dickman, 45, was executed in Newcastle Gaol for the murder of Jno. Innes Nisbet in a N.E. Rly. carriage, between Newcastle and Alnmouth, on Friday, March 18. Interest in the crime for which Dickman paid the extreme penalty of the law was maintained to the last. A crowd of fully 1,500 persons had assembled in the vicinity of the prison long before the execution was to be carried into effect. A number of police officers kept them at the extreme ends of Carliol-square. Every precaution had been taken to prevent the curious from attempting to obtain a view of the prison yard from adjacent buildings. To this end, a high canvas screen had been erected from the exit of the corridor leading from the condemned cell to the execution-house, some 60 yards away. Representatives of the Press were excluded from the prison.

Last Hours on Earth.

Dickman passed his last few hours calmly. The prison chaplain (Rev. W. P. Lumley) was with him till 10 o'clock the previous night. Mr. Lumley stayed in the prison overnight, and attended the condemned man shortly after six o'clock in the morning, and ministered to him. Dickman ate his breakfast of porridge, bread and butter, and tea, and calmly awaited the end. The pinioning process in the cell was quickly performed by Ellis, the executioner, and his assistant Williams. The procession was then formed, the chaplain, in his surplice, leading the way, and reciting the burial service. Then followed the chief warder (Mr. Matthews), the Governor of the gaol (Mr. H. J. Hellier), the Under-Sheriff (Mr. E. G. Harvey), and the deputy Under-Sheriff (Mr. J. W. Monk), and the prison doctor (Dr. Hardcastle). The condemned man was placed between two of the warders who had been with him since his condemnation, and the executioners came behind. The scaffold was some 60 yards distant, and Dickman walked as erect as a soldier on parade.

"I am Innocent."

Arrived at the place of ...
walked on ...

his proper sta...
placed under...
police and ch...
to which he r...
stand the pr...
for me to de...
it is absurd t...
absolutely den...
ceedings foll...
heard before...
the Moot Ha...
two day's tri...
or more wit...
magistrates ...
trial at the ...

The ...

Before the A...
quest on Nisb...
sence of priso...
Coroner Perc...
an inquiry w...
day, a verdic...
returned agai...
therefore com...
coroner's warr...
lain in prison...
man was put...
July 4, before...
jury. The cou...
half of the C...
Atkinson, K.C...
while Mr. Mi...
Lord Wm. Pe...
Edwd. Clark,...
presented pris...
defence. At t...
the evidence,...
soner himself,...
the witness-bo...
had been hea...
Innes had mad...
fence. On the...
July 6, Lord...
for two hours...
which the jury...
sent for a littl...
half. On retu...
turned a verdi...

Th...

When asked i...
say why senter...
be passed upon...
"I can only re...
innocent of th...
no complicity...
spoken the tru...
in everything I...
of death was t...
and, turning...
court, Dickma...
sonant voice:...
that I am inno...
afterwards lod...
tence, and this...
Lord Chief Jus...
rence and Phil...
it. A petition ...
warded to the H...
ground that th...

Northumberland admitted that there had been "some loose talk" among officers at the police station while Hall and Spink had been waiting in a corridor to identify Dickman. One of the policemen suggested that Hall and Spink take a peep through the window of the room in which Dickman was being interviewed. "They looked in," said the Chief Constable, "but could only see tops of heads."

Shortly afterwards the door of the interview room was opened, and another policeman invited Hall and Spink to take a quick look at Dickman. They only saw his back, but they noticed that he was wearing a light raincoat. At the parade Hall picked a man in an identical coat.

Despite this highly unorthodox method of identification, the Chief Constable was able to reassure the Under-Secretary. "Hall states, and is most emphatic," he wrote, "that the impression he got when looking through the door did not in any way influence him when he came to the identification, such as it was."

Mr. Mitchell-Innes, Dickman's counsel, was not so easily satisfied. As public disquiet mounted, he lodged an appeal. Although the Appeal Court refused to accept the Chief Constable's letter as evidence, Mr. Mitchell-Innes achieved the same effect by cross-examining Hall on the incidents at the police station. "I thought it was most irregular," said Hall. The appeal, however, was dismissed.

Must he be hanged?

In the three days immediately before the date fixed for Dickman's execution, public indignation reached its height. Telegrams were sent to public figures, demanding a reprieve. A huge petition was forwarded to the Home Secretary. "MUST DICKMAN BE HANGED TOMORROW?" shouted the placards. At 8 a.m. on August 10, 1910, the demonstrators got their answer. John Alexander Dickman walked to the gallows at Newcastle Jail, still protesting his innocence.

The proceeds of the robbery were never traced. At the end of the year, after a protracted legal battle, Mrs. Cicely Nisbet received £300 compensation from the Stobswood Colliery for her husband's death; just £70 less than the amount he had been carrying on the day he was murdered. With all his planning, Dickman had picked on the wrong day to kill John Innes Nisbet. That week, some of the mineworkers had forfeited their pay because of a strike. Nisbet should have been carrying £1000.

THE CONTROVERSY reached its height in the three days immediately before the date fixed for Dickman's execution. But despite telegrams and a huge petition, he died . . . protesting his innocence right to the gallows.

HARPER'S WEEKLY.
JOURNAL OF CIVILIZATION

SEPTEMBER 10, 1864.

FRANCIS MULLER, THE MUR-
DERER, FROM LONDON.

THE TOP-HAT MURDER

Murder most foul . . . and Franz Müller, 25-year-old tailor and would-be American immigrant, could congratulate himself on a job well done. But in the frantic death struggle on the speeding train, both killer and victim had lost their hats. Could Franz Müller also have lost his head . . . ?

IT seemed as if the whole of New York had turned out to welcome Franz Müller. The dockside was packed with craning spectators. Somewhere, a band played. Hawkers and peanut-vendors did a bonanza trade. As the transatlantic sailing-ship *Victoria* glided majestically towards the quay, a flotilla of excursion boats scurried out to meet her. "How are you, Müller?" the sightseers shouted up at the *Victoria*'s passengers.

Franz Müller, a 25-year-old tailor who had left Britain five weeks earlier to start a new life in America, was certainly being given a glad reception. On the dockside, the official "reception committee" waited for the *Victoria* to drop anchor. The group did not consist of the usual Mayor and civic dignitaries. At its head were the grim-faced figures of Chief-Inspector William Tanner and Detective-Sergeant George Clarke from London. Nor was their greeting the conventional message of welcome. Their first words to the startled Franz Müller were:

"You are charged with the murder of Thomas Briggs on the North London Railway, between Hackney Wick and Bow, on July 9, 1864."

The whole of America had been in on the drama of Müller's arrest. The case had even rivalled the Civil War in the newspaper headlines. For Inspector Tanner and Det.-Sgt. Clarke had been waiting in New York for 20 days, while Müller sailed unsuspectingly towards them on the *Victoria*.

Transatlantic race

The detectives had left London five days *after* Müller had set sail—but on the much faster New York & Philadelphia Company's steamship, *City of Manchester*. They had actually passed the *Victoria* in mid-Atlantic. All they had to do when they arrived was to sit back and wait for the sailing ship to appear.

Despite all the excitement, Franz Müller's crime had not been particularly startling. He had battered to death and robbed Thomas Briggs, the 70-year-old chief clerk of a London bank. What made it unique was *where* the crime had taken place. For Franz Müller was the first man to commit a murder on a British train.

The British travelling public had been appalled. Agitated newspaper editorials asked, "Is it no longer safe to travel alone by train?" When Müller's name had been revealed as the leading suspect, the newspapers turned on him in fury. Even before the two detectives reached New York, the British Press had Müller tried, convicted, and hanged.

But their conviction was premature. Before a real-life judge and jury, it wasn't so easy. When Müller's trial opened at London's Old Bailey on October 27, 1864, the prosecution case rested solely on circumstantial evidence, supported by an odd collection of exhibits: two hats, a watch and chain, and a cardboard box bearing the apt word, Death. Again and again, both prosecution and defence counsel were to return to those two hats and their seemingly endless implications.

The Solicitor-General, Sir Robert Collier, neatly forestalled defence objections right at the start. "Undoubtedly the evidence in this case is what is called circumstantial evidence, but I may remind you that it is by circumstantial evidence that great crimes are most frequently detected. Murders are not committed in the presence of witnesses, and to reject circumstantial evidence would be to proclaim immunity to crime. There are circumstances which give evidence that cannot be false and which cannot be mistaken. Gentlemen, I venture to think that a stronger case of circumstantial evidence has rarely, if ever, been submitted to a jury."

The hangman's noose

Not everyone agreed with the Solicitor-General's confident view. Franz Müller was still a German citizen and, convinced of his innocence, the German Legal Protection Society in London briefed Serjeant John Humffreys Parry—one of Britain's most forceful advocates—to defend him. Somehow, Parry had to convince the jury that the circumstantial evidence so confidently paraded by the prosecution was insufficient for the hangman to slip his noose over Müller's head.

Parry's first move was a master-stroke of psychology. Only too aware of the traditional British prejudice against "foreigners", he waited for the judge to make his obligatory offer to the prisoner: "Franz Müller, you are entitled to be tried by a jury partly composed of foreigners." Gravely, Serjeant Parry rose. "My Lord," he said, "my client wishes to be tried by 12 Englishmen."

The Solicitor-General then crisply outlined the bare facts of the case against Müller. The *crime* had been committed in the space of four minutes—"a marvel", commented Sir Robert—in an empty 1st-class carriage travelling between Bow and Hackney Wick stations, in London.

The *victim* had been beaten to death with his own walking-stick and robbed of a gold watch and chain and a pair of gold eyeglasses. The bloodstained stick—"a formidable weapon"—had been discovered by two young men when they entered the carriage at the next station, Hackney, at around 10-11 p.m.

The *body* of Mr. Thomas Briggs was

"HOW ARE YOU, Müller?" cried the crowd at the New York dock as the fugitive landed—to be met by a reception committee of London police.

found lying on the line between Bow and Hackney Wick stations at 10.20. He was still alive, but died shortly afterwards.

The *first hat*, with a distinctive striped-silk lining, had been found in the murder carriage, near the bloodstained stick. It had not belonged to Mr. Briggs. The *second hat* – cut down to alter its appearance – had been found on Franz Müller aboard the *Victoria* and tallied exactly with one Mr. Briggs had been wearing.

Obvious satisfaction

The Solicitor-General paused to let the facts sink in. With obvious satisfaction, he commented, "The conclusion appears to me inevitable that the murderer, in the hurry and excitement of the moment, took the wrong hat. He took Mr. Briggs's hat with him and left his own. I venture to think that one point in this case which may not be disputed is this, that the man, whoever he was, who robbed and murdered Mr. Briggs left his hat in that carriage. If you discover with certainty the

person who wore that hat on that night you will have the murderer, and the case is proved almost as clearly against him as if he were seen to do it."

The *watch-chain*, Sir Robert went on, had been exchanged by Müller for a cheaper chain and a ring at a jeweller's shop run by the macabrely-named Mr. John Death. Müller had later given the *cardboard box* bearing Death's name as a present to a friend's daughter.

All that remained was the *watch*. Sir Robert held it up for the jury to see. "It was found," he intoned, "in Müller's trunk aboard the *Victoria*, sewn up in a piece of canvas!"

When the Solicitor-General had said the circumstantial evidence was overwhelming, he had not been exaggerating. It was now up to Serjeant Parry to provide an innocent explanation for every incriminating item. But he got no satisfaction from the first prosecution witness, the jeweller John Death. Mr. Death clearly remembered "a man with a foreign accent"

ONLY TOO AWARE of traditional British prejudice against foreigners, Müller's counsel Parry chose that he be tried by a jury of "12 Englishmen".

coming into his shop on July 11 and offering him a gold watch-chain for £3. 10s. The man eventually agreed to accept a new chain worth £3. 5s. in exchange, along with a 5s. ring. Mr. Death identified both chains, and the box in which the new one had been packed.

Hopefully, Serjeant Parry suggested to the jeweller that Müller might have visited him on another occasion, with a different chain to sell. "Do you recollect in June last the prisoner offering to exchange another chain at your shop?" he asked. There was no chance of confusing Mr. Death. "No, I do not," he replied bluntly.

Mrs. Ellen Blyth, Müller's landlady, recalled her lodger showing her the new watch-chain he had obtained from Mr. Death. She also dropped the first clue to the hat found in the murder carriage.

"When he first arrived at our house, he brought a hatbox with him," she said. "It had the name Walker, of 49 Crawford Street, London, on it. After Müller left for America, I found it in his room."

Mrs. Elizabeth Repsch—whose husband was a close friend of Müller's—had even more to say about the telltale hat. "It was a plain black beaver hat, with merino rim inside and striped lining, broad brown stripes and a broad blue stripe edged with white. My attention was drawn to it by its peculiar lining. I had never seen a hat lined that way before. I have often been holding it when he visited our house."

Anticipating a raised eyebrow from Serjeant Parry at Mrs. Repsch's conveniently photographic memory, Sir Robert produced the hat—giving his witness the opportunity to comment, "Of course, I gave a description of the hat to the police before seeing it here."

Mrs. Repsch had only just started, however. "I never saw the prisoner wear any other hat but that one," she continued pointedly, "until Monday, July 11." Imagine her surprise, therefore, when Müller appeared at her house on the Monday after the murder sporting a smart new hat.

"I told him he was very extravagant in having another new hat," said Mrs. Repsch smugly. "He said that his old one was smashed and he had thrown it in the dusthole. My husband asked him how much he had given for it, and he said 14s. 6d. My husband said it looked more like a guinea hat."

A telling link

Mrs. Repsch had tellingly linked the two incriminating hats together—the one found in the murder carriage and the one missing from Briggs's body—and no needling by Serjeant Parry could shake her from her story. The more he questioned, the more indignantly definite she became. "I must have looked into that hat 30, 40 or 50 times," she told him tartly. "It was the peculiarity of the lining I noticed."

Mrs. Repsch's husband had made a perceptive remark in identifying the new hat as "worth a guinea". It had been made by Daniel Digance, a fashionable hatmaker at 18, Royal Exchange, London, who had served Mr. Briggs for nearly 30 years. "I made him his hats to order," Mr. Digance told the court, hinting that he would never have sold the inferior headwear normally worn by Müller.

Sir Robert handed him Mr. Briggs's hat from the exhibit table. Mr. Digance, with a fine show of expertise, ran his hands over the crown and round the brim. His evidence was detailed and to the point.

"This is similar to a hat I made for Mr. Briggs in September, 1863. But its appearance does not correspond to the details in my book. It has been cut down. Mr. Briggs's hat was a little too easy on the head and I placed a small piece of tissue paper round. That tissue paper is not here, but there are some small fragments of it remaining in the band of the hat."

Mr. Digance peered inside the hat and

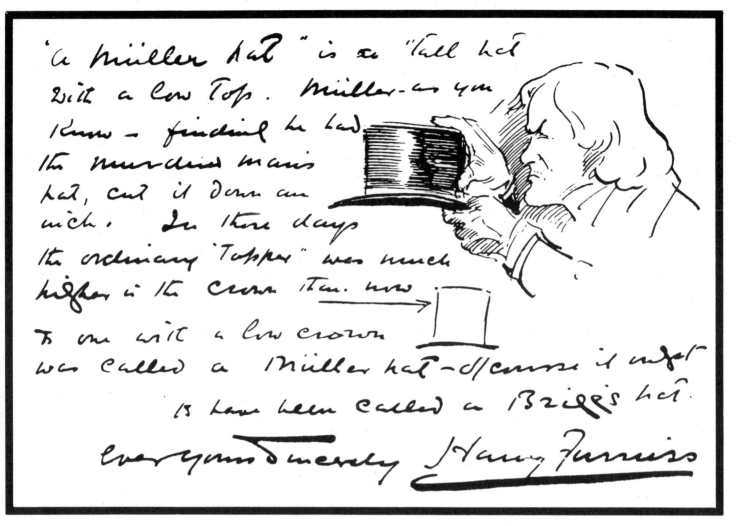

"a Müller hat" is a "tall hat with a low Top. Müller — as you know — finding he had the murdered man's hat, cut it down an inch. In those days the ordinary "Topper" was much higher in the crown than now. To one with a low crown was called a Müller hat — of course it ought to have been called a Briggs hat.

Ever yours sincerely   Harry Furniss

frowned disapprovingly. "I should say the hat has been cut down by one to one-and-a-half inches," he said. "The bottom part of the leather has been cut off and the hat has been sewn together again. The missing part would have contained the name of the customer. It has not been cut down as a hatter would do it; it is an operation I have never seen. It has been neatly sewn and the silk pasted down. I should say it was done by a person who understood sewing . . ."

By the expressions on their faces, the jury had completed the rest of Mr. Digance's sentence. ". . . *like a tailor*". The Solicitor-General had no need to press the issue. The next witness, Mr. Thomas Walker, represented the cheaper end of the hatmaking trade. But his evidence was just as useful to the prosecution, and even more unwelcome to the defence.

"Oh yes," he said, as he was handed the hat found in the railway carriage, "this is one of mine. The lining is peculiar. It was one of about 500 sample French linings in which there were scarcely more than two alike. The price of the hat was around 8s. 6d."

Nothing could have been more unhelpful to Serjeant Parry. Not only had the

EVEN HABERDASHERS cashed in on the murder, as this contemporary account of the sudden fashion for "Müller hats" explains at length.

murder hat definitely come from Walker's shop, but only two — or even one — had ever been made. All it needed now was to link Müller irrefutably with that selfsame hat. It was Müller's best friend, a cab-driver named Jonathan Matthews, who stepped into the witness box to tie the final knot. At first, Matthews — an apparently simple-minded fellow — was slow to follow Sir Robert's patiently planted signposts . . .

Matthews: At dinner one day, Müller admired a hat I was wearing and asked me if I would get a similar one for him.

Sir Robert: And in consequence of that, you got one?

Matthews: Yes.

Sir Robert: At what shop?

Matthews: The same.

Sir Robert: What same, what shop?

Matthews: At the hatter's.

Sir Robert: Of course, but where?

Matthews: Mr. Walker's, of Crawford Street.

Sir Robert: Can you remember the

lining of the hat?

Matthews: It appeared to be a striped lining.

Sir Robert: Did Müller take away the hatbox as well?

Matthews: Yes.

Sir Robert: Did Müller pay you for the hat?

Matthews: No. But he made me a waistcoat — the one I'm wearing now — in return for it.

With a look of relief, as if having safely reached the shore, Sir Robert turned and picked up the hat. Matthews nodded and said it "corresponded exactly" to the one he had bought for Müller. Serjeant Parry had already spotted a hairline crack in Matthews's evidence and hammered away at it until it got bigger . . .

Serjeant Parry: Tell me, what has happened to the hat of yours to which Müller took a liking; the one similar to the court exhibit?

Matthews: I have no idea whatever.

Serjeant Parry: Did you ever throw your old hats into the dusthole?

Matthews: Yes, occasionally I do.

Serjeant Parry: Could you swear to the colour of the lining of *your* hats?

Matthews: I cannot. Not at all.

For once, Serjeant Parry was able to introduce an element of doubt into the apparently cast-iron evidence of the exhibits. Whose was the hat found in the carriage? The Solicitor-General himself had said, "If you discover with certainty the person who wore that hat on the night, you will have the murderer." Was it Müller's? Or had Matthews had the only other hat with a striped French-silk lining?

It was dangerous ground, and Serjeant Parry knew it. At a preliminary hearing, counsel for the German Legal Protection Society had almost accused Matthews of the murder, merely as an attempt to undermine the case against Müller. Allowing the jury to take the hint without any further elaboration, Serjeant Parry contented himself with insinuating that Matthews had given evidence against Müller purely to collect the reward of £300 offered by the police, Mr. Briggs's bank, and the North London Railway.

Serjeant Parry: Are you in debt?

Matthews: Yes, sir.

Serjeant Parry: Of course, you expect a portion of the reward?

Matthews: I don't understand.

Serjeant Parry: Then you are the only person in the court who does not. Do you expect some of the £300?

Matthews: I leave that entirely to my country, if it thinks that I have done my duty.

Serjeant Parry: Then you do expect it. Why did you not answer me before? Have you ever said this, that if you had kept your mouth shut a little while longer there would have been £500 instead of £300?

Matthews: I never said so.

Serjeant Parry: Never anything like it?

Matthews: No. I said that I was given to understand when I was before the coroner that there were posters offering £500. But if it had been a shilling I should have done my duty the same.

Serjeant Parry: I do not ask you to compliment yourself.

Bearing Death's name

After this unedifying exchange—later to be ridiculed by the Solicitor-General—Mrs. Eliza Matthews, Jonathan Matthews's wife, identified the cardboard box bearing Death's name. Müller had given it to her 10-year-old daughter as a present just before he left for America. He had also shown the watch-chain and ring he had bought from the jeweller.

Sir Robert: Was there anything unusual about Müller?

Mrs. Matthews: Yes, he was wearing a carpet slipper on one foot. He said he had had an accident on the previous Thursday, when a letter-cart ran over his foot on London Bridge.

Still flushed with the success of his dramatic arrest in New York, Inspector

HIS CLIENT confessed at the gallows . . . but Serjeant John Humffreys Parry, one of Britain's most forceful advocates, had mounted a brilliant defence.

Tanner told how a search of Müller's belongings aboard the *Victoria* had revealed Mr. Briggs's watch and hat. It was the point Serjeant Parry had been waiting for. There was no question of demolishing all the circumstantial evidence against Müller. But if he could cast doubt on the credibility of at least *some* of the damaging exhibits, it could split the jury.

"Did you hear the prisoner say in New York that he had purchased the watch and chain on Monday morning at the docks?" he asked Inspector Tanner. The detective was not falling for that one, however. "That was suggested by the prisoner's counsel in the court in New York," he replied, adding rather haughtily, "*after* Müller had seen his legal adviser." All the same, Serjeant Parry had succeeded in getting over an alternative explanation for Müller's possession of the murdered man's watch. The hat could take care of itself.

The trial had reached the end of the second day when Serjeant Parry began his opening speech for the defence. Adopting the conventional "more in sorrow than anger" pose, Serjeant Parry conceded that the crime had been "atrocious" and "unparalleled in Britain"

"It is a crime which strikes at the lives of millions," he rumbled. "It is a crime which affects the life of every man who travels upon the great iron ways of this country. A thrill of horror ran through the whole land when the fact of this crime was first published. Gentlemen, this is a crime of a character to arouse in the human breast an almost instinctive spirit of vengeance. But . . ."

The "but", of course, was that the police had got hold of the wrong man.

Whether the jury believed him or not, there was no doubting Serjeant Parry's inventiveness and ingenuity. He had an innocent explanation for nearly every piece of circumstantial evidence, along with a substitute suspect, the hapless Jonathan Matthews. In a text-book example of mischievous equivocation, he commented, "I should be very sorry to charge Matthews with being a party to the murder, but I should be very wicked if I were not to say that suspicion is pointing to him."

One by one, Serjeant Parry rejected the prosecution's prize exhibits. The hat found in the murder carriage may have been the same *style* as Müller's, but need not have been his. It could have been the one Matthews so fortunately lost. As for Mr. Briggs's hat, Müller could have bought it secondhand—that would explain the cutting-down—before leaving for America. In the same way, Müller could have bought the watch and chain cheaply at the docks, eventually selling the chain to Mr. Death because he suspected it was stolen property.

Conveniently forgetting that the murdered man had been 70 years old, Serjeant

Parry pointed to his client and asked, "Do you believe that a slight and by no means muscular man could have committed that murder in that time? Compared with Mr. Briggs, the prisoner is a mere stripling." Serjeant Parry reminded the jury that Müller had not fled impulsively from Britain, but had been talking about emigrating to America for some time. "If he were a murderer," he demanded, "why did he not change his name?"

After this resounding start, Serjeant Parry's defence witnesses came as an anti-climax. They were an unconvincing bunch. Thomas Lee, a coal merchant and property-owner, claimed that on the night of the murder he saw Mr. Briggs sitting in the 1st-class compartment at Bow station. There were *two* other men in the same compartment, neither of whom looked like the prisoner.

A poor impression

Under cross-examination, however, Lee created a poor impression. He admitted that he had not bothered to inform the police until they had called on him after a tip-off. With simulated disbelief, Sir Robert asked him, "Am I to take it that during the whole of that week you, knowing, as you say, that there were two men who you could describe, gave no information to the police?"

Lee: Yes.

Sir Robert: You did not give it until one of them came to you?

Lee: I should not have given any information at all if they had not come, because I thought it unimportant and because I knew how much bother it was. I have things to do. I collect my own rents.

Worse was to come. Müller's alibi for the night of the murder was based on that flimsiest of all testimony – the evidence of a prostitute. A Mrs. Elizabeth Jones told the court archly that she had "two female lodgers, young women, who receive the visits of men". In short, she was a brothel-keeper.

At 9.30 on the night of the murder, Müller called for a regular "appointment" with one of the girls, Mary Ann Eldred. But Mary had left the house half an hour earlier. Mrs. Jones recalled the time clearly, because she had glanced at the clock. Müller, who was wearing a carpet slipper on one foot, chatted with her for about 10 minutes before leaving.

Mary Eldred did her best to shore up the ramshackle story by confirming that she had been out at that time. She had known Müller for some while, and he had told her he was hoping to emigrate to America. "He asked me to go with him," she said rather sadly. "He said that if I did not go with him, he would only stay there six months."

Maybe the pathetic Mary Eldred had been genuinely fond of Müller. In her evidence, she certainly tried her hardest to save him from the gallows. The court had listened to her with compassion, and, as she returned to the public benches, Müller gave her a look of sincere gratitude.

It was more than he gave Charles Foreman, a bus conductor whose worthless testimony did more harm than good. Foreman recalled seeing a passenger wearing a carpet slipper clamber aboard one Saturday evening . . . but he could not remember the date, the month, or even whether the man looked like Müller.

It was then scorn-pouring time for the prosecution. The Solicitor-General, referring to Serjeant Parry's "fertile imagination", demolished every one of the defence's theories. He polished up Jonathan Matthews's tarnished image.

"What is the imputation against Matthews, if there be any?" he laughed. "Why, gentlemen, it is supposed that he was actuated by a hope of reward. What is the object of advertising rewards if you do not intend that anyone should be influenced by them? The object is to induce people to come forward to give evidence; and if you are to disbelieve every man who gives evidence because of a reward, then at once and forever cease to give rewards for the purpose of detecting great offences."

He was scathing about Serjeant Parry's sorry parade of witnesses. Lee had been "extraordinary", Foreman "valueless", and Mrs. Jones had based her "unsatisfactory and dangerous alibi" on "the reliability of a brothel clock".

Three separate links

The judge's summing up seemed to foreshadow the inevitable verdict of the jury. "The facts of the history of this case, though appearing to be many, are in reality very few – the watch, the chain, and the hat Mr. Briggs lost that night. A hat was found in the carriage in the place of Mr. Briggs's hat. These are the three matters which constitute the case for the prosecution. These are three links of the same chain; but do not make the mistake which it appears to me Serjeant Parry is rather inclined to lead you into, that, if there is one link of the chain broken, you have got rid of the prosecution. There are three separate and distinct links, having each of them a separate history, and a failure on the part of one does not in the slightest degree affect the position of each of the others."

The jury took only 15 minutes to return a verdict of guilty. But if there was satisfaction among Britain's railway travellers, there was consternation elsewhere. German newspapers accused the devious British of framing Müller for political ends. The German Society presented a petition to the Home Secretary, and the King of Prussia sent a personal message to Queen Victoria. All the pleas were rejected, and the date of Müller's execution was set for November 14.

The scenes round the scaffold on the morning of November 14 were shameful. Throughout the night, a drunken, obscene rabble of more than 50,000 people had gathered to watch Müller hanged. With the utmost distaste, *The Times* reporter commented on the brutalizing effect of public executions.

Müller behaved with exemplary fortitude. Not a muscle in his face twitched as he walked to the gallows with his Lutheran pastor, Dr. Louis Cappel. Right until the last second, the condemned man maintained his innocence. But as the noose tightened round his neck, and the crowd groaned in sympathy, he choked out the words: *Ich habe es gethan* (I have done it). As the trapdoor snapped open, Dr. Cappel, who was standing at Müller's side, almost tumbled in. However, he recovered himself enough to rush excitedly from the scaffold shouting, "Confessed! Confessed! Thank God!"

Triumphant cry

The echoes of Franz Müller's crime lingered on long after Dr. Cappel's triumphant cry of "Confessed!" Every "foreign-looking" man travelling alone in a train was regarded with suspicion. Passengers travelled in groups for mutual safety, and several railway companies cut peepholes – nicknamed "Müller's Lights" – between compartments to reassure people sitting alone. Although well-intentioned, Müller's Lights proved unpopular with passengers seeking privacy . . . particularly courting couples. Even the hatmaking industry cashed in on the murder. Fashionably dressed young men started sporting hats with cut-down crowns called, naturally enough, "Müller hats".

But Müller himself remained a mystery. Why had he risked his life for a mere gold watch and chain? There is some evidence that he suffered from a "split personality". Although his landlady referred to him in court as "inoffensive and affectionate", fellow-passengers on the *Victoria* remembered him as boastful, bullying, and overbearing. The trial judge gave a simpler reason. He maintained that Müller had been worried about scraping together enough money to get to America, and had been overcome with greed at the sight of Mr. Briggs's watch and chain.

If so, the crime was a complete disaster. All Müller finally gained from the murder was 30 shillings in cash, which went towards his steerage fare of £4 on the *Victoria*. Four gold sovereigns, a silver snuffbox, and a valuable diamond ring were left on Mr. Briggs's body. In the frenzied four minutes between Hackney Wick and Bow, Britain's first train murderer had been beaten by the timetable.

THE EAST END
DESTROYERS

CHURCHILL demanded cannons . . .

THE NIGHT of Friday, December 16, 1910 was bitterly cold. The wind blew icily through the almost deserted streets of London's East End, and the few muffled figures who were about hurried on their way. As they went by, their faces showed up pale and fearful in the dim glimmer of the street lamps before vanishing once more into the blackness. Occasionally a door or shutter banged to with an echoing sound audible in adjacent streets, while overhead shop signs creaked and swayed on their rusty hinges.

If these had been the only night-time sounds, Max Weil and his sister would have slept peacefully in their dingy Houndsditch apartment over their fancy goods business. But they heard other noises—strange bangings—which appeared to be coming from Harris's, the jeweller's, next door. Max decided to investigate. He went outside, peered through the shop window, but saw nothing. As the noises continued, however, he decided to go for the police. He was sure that someone was trying to break in from Exchange Buildings—the cul-de-sac behind the main road.

Anarchist saboteurs

Max Weil was right. But this was no ordinary robbery. For the temporary occupants of numbers 9, 10, and 11 Exchange Buildings—the houses which backed onto the jeweller's—were not criminals in the usual sense but self-styled "expropriators"—Communist and Anarchist saboteurs from Eastern Europe in search of money for their "cause".

They were a strange collection of men. Most of them spoke little or no English, and had already had considerable experience of violence and revolutionary activity in their own countries. Most had also suffered terrible beatings and torture at the hands of brutal, totalitarian police. To these political fugitives, hounded out of their homelands and desperate, London was a refuge—as it was for thousands like them. But that did not signify a halt to their activities. They continued to campaign for revolution and they continued to need "funds".

Leading the group was George Gard-

367

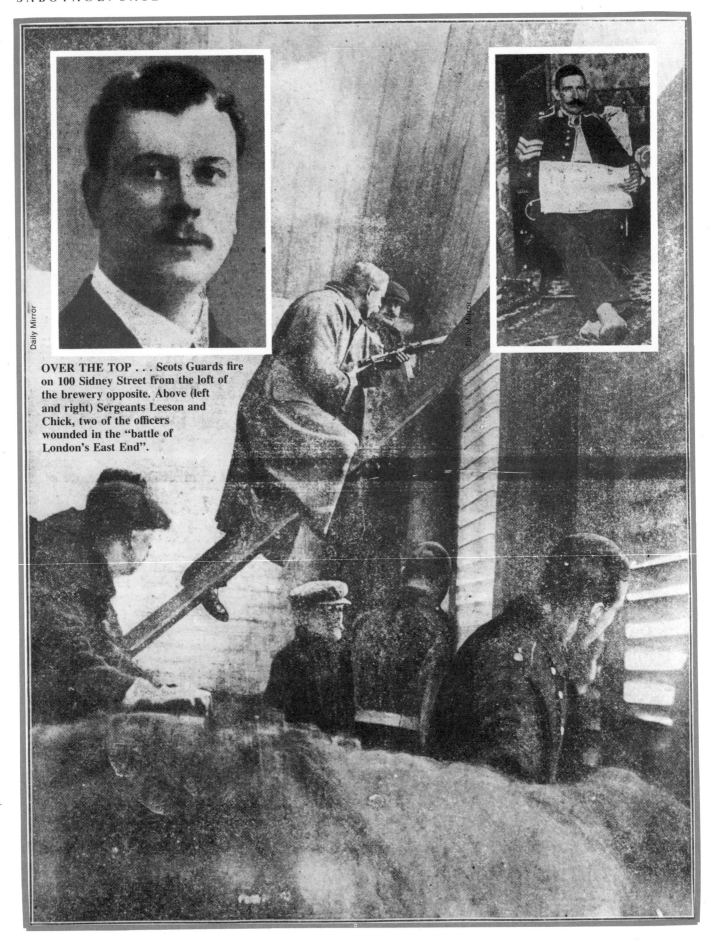

OVER THE TOP . . . Scots Guards fire on 100 Sidney Street from the loft of the brewery opposite. Above (left and right) Sergeants Leeson and Chick, two of the officers wounded in the "battle of London's East End".

Daily Mirror

Daily Mirror

stein, whose real name was Mouremtzov. He was an experienced operator, tough, unscrupulous and already wanted by the police in Germany for his part in an armed bank robbery. It was he who masterminded the plan to rob the Houndsditch jeweller's, and he carefully selected his companions from the many hundreds of foreign political agitators living in East London.

With him were Max Smoller, a notorious criminal from the Crimea, Yourka Dubof, a locksmith and expert lockpicker, and Jacob Peters, who had been severely tortured in Tsarist Russia for his fanatical belief in the Communist revolution. There was also a woman: the passionate, hot-blooded Nina Vassileva, Gardstein's mistress, who kept watch in number 11 for any sign of trouble with the police. It was her job to give warning to the men at work on the robbery.

Man-size hole

They had set themselves a difficult task. In order to reach the jeweller's safe, they had to hammer a man-sized hole through the 9-inch thick brick wall that separated the houses in Exchange Buildings from the shop. This was the noise that startled Max Weil and sent him hurrying to the nearest police station.

Within minutes the police arrived at the spot and stationed themselves at vantage points round the three houses, making it impossible for anyone to leave or enter without being seen. Nina, however, had spotted them from the first-floor window. In a panic she tore downstairs to where the men were working. "It's the police!" she hissed.

Suddenly the banging stopped and for several minutes nothing and no one stirred. The police held their positions in silence outside. They could see a thin bar of light escaping through the cracks in the door of number 11, but no light came from either of the other two houses. The atmosphere, both inside and outside, was tense with expectation. Finally Sergeant Bentley, followed by a group of other policemen, approached the buildings and knocked on the door of number 11. There was no answer. He knocked again, and this time the bar of light slowly widened as the door was pulled back. It was Gardstein.

"Have you been working or knocking about inside?" inquired the sergeant. Gardstein squinted at him suspiciously and ignored the question. "Do you understand English?" Bentley persisted. Still no reply. "Well, fetch someone who does."

Gardstein dutifully disappeared, leaving the officers outside. Bentley took his opportunity, pushed open the door and entered, followed by Sergeant Bryant.

At first they saw nothing; then they became aware of being watched from the top of the stairs—though there was insufficient light for them to make out who it was.

The two officers advanced through the main room on the ground floor towards the back of the house. Then, suddenly, the back door swung open and a man rushed in firing a pistol at the two officers. Almost at the same moment the figure on the stairs also opened fire. Bentley staggered back in the direction of the front door and collapsed on the threshold. He had one bullet in the shoulder and another in the neck which almost severed his spinal cord. Bryant was luckier. He was shot in the arm and received a minor chest wound. He managed to stumble out of the house before falling unconscious against the wall of one of the other buildings in the cul-de-sac.

Seeing Bentley fall, Constable Woodhams ran to help him, only to feel his own left leg buckle beneath him, the thigh bone shattered by a Mauser bullet. Then, firing rapidly and continuously, the gang emerged from the house. Another officer, Sergeant Tucker, was simultaneously making his way towards them. He was shot in the heart at point-blank range and died instantly.

Reaching the entrance to the cul-de-sac, Gardstein, who was in the lead, was caught by the massive figure of Constable Choat and for a few seconds they struggled. Gardstein pulled the trigger of his pistol repeatedly and finally hit Choat in the leg.

Peters and Dubof then opened fire and ploughed five more bullets into the stricken policeman. As he fell, however, he dragged Gardstein with him and a shot, fired at Choat, struck Gardstein in the back. Two of the gang pulled him to his feet. Then all five disappeared into the night, leaving behind a scene of devastation and a trail of blood coming from the dying Gardstein's body. One policeman was dead, two others were to die shortly afterwards, and the rest were wounded.

Police search

The group made its way to 59 Grove Street—the lodgings of Fritz Svaars. Svaars was a cousin of Jacob Peters and had been involved in planning the robbery. The gang then left Gardstein in his bedroom to die, and quickly separated.

The police immediately initiated a search for the criminals, but it was a difficult, if not impossible, job. London's East End was full of potential saboteurs—many living under false names and with forged passports. It was easy to locate Gardstein's body—the trail of blood had seen to that—but how were they to find the other conspirators? Various witnesses who saw the killings, or had spotted members of the group leaving and entering Exchange Buildings, helped to narrow the field and a number of arrests were made.

Among those arrested were Jacob Peters and Yourka Dubof. But Max Smoller had disappeared and was never again seen in London. Fritz Svaars had also vanished, leaving his pathetic mistress Luba Milstein to face the police.

Fritz was in a difficult position. He had taken no direct part in the murders or the attempted robbery, but one of the murderers—Gardstein—had been found in his lodgings and there was no way he could prove his innocence. Even if he escaped hanging he knew that he might be deported back to Russia, where he would have to face a capital charge. In addition, he was terrified of the London police. The Russian police had beaten him up badly earlier that year, and he had been lucky to escape to England with his life. He had no reason to believe that their British counterparts did not use the same methods. He would rather die than be caught again.

Revolutionary jeweller

For two weeks detectives searched the area in vain. The two officers in charge of the investigation, Detective Superintendent John Ottaway and Detective Inspector "Weasel" Wensley, scoured the East End of London looking for clues. They learned that Fritz was probably hiding with another revolutionary known as "Joseph", a jeweller, who was also wanted by the police for theft. But where were they?

Their own researches proved futile. But on the evening of New Year's Day, 1911, an informant arrived at City police headquarters. In return for a promise from the police not to reveal his identity, he disclosed the whereabouts of Fritz and Joseph. They were hiding, he said, in 100 Sidney Street with a woman lodger called Betsy Gershon, and would be leaving for a new hiding place between 5 and 6 p.m. on the following day. Ottaway and Wensley hurriedly called a conference and made a plan to trap the two men as they emerged into the street. This was much easier than attempting to storm the house, which could result in further loss of police lives.

Accordingly, two large horse-drawn carriages with armed police inside drove into Sidney Street on Monday, January 2, 1911, and waited. By 6 p.m. it was growing dark, the men were complaining of cold—snow was falling and there was a bitter wind—and Fritz and Joseph had not been sighted. By 9 p.m. it was obvious that the two men were staying put. It was then decided that an attempt should be made to get them out.

The house in Sidney Street was one of

In the plan: SOLDIERS FIRED FROM HERE. • BREWERY • SIDNEY ST • WINDOW FROM WHICH BURGLARS FIRED • SOLDIERS IN THESE SHEDS • SMALL HOUSES IN WHICH WERE SOLDIERS & ARMED POLICE • BREWERY YARD • BREWERY STABLES FROM WHICH SOLDIERS FIRED → • ✛ POLICEMAN SHOT HERE.

Daily Mirror

a row of ten four-storey houses, each of which had its own back yard. Police were stationed in the houses on either side in case the fugitives should attempt to break through the walls. They were also placed in the houses and shops opposite on every floor, in the adjoining yards at the back of the block, and at every other vantage point. Finally the whole block was cordoned off by 200 policemen.

Nothing more could be done, however, until the other occupants of number 100 — who, the police learned, were respectable people — had been moved out of the house. This was a delicate operation. By now it was 3.30 a.m. and the occupants would be asleep, totally unaware that in the same building were two armed and desperate men. By talking to neighbours Wensley learned that the landlord and his wife, Mr. and Mrs. Fleishmann, slept in the front room on the ground floor. He tapped on the window pane and waited. Soon the curtain parted and a woman's face appeared. It was Mrs. Fleishmann.

Not a milkman

"We don't want any milk," she said sleepily, and promptly went back to bed. Wensley tapped again, louder, and this time Mr. Fleishmann parted the curtain. "We don't want any milk," he shouted. "Go away!" "I'm not a milkman, I'm from the police," Wensley shouted back. It was a curious moment of farce in a situation which was chillingly tense.

The Fleishmanns dressed hurriedly and opened the front door to let Wensley in. They confirmed that Betsy Gershon lived there, on the second floor, but said they knew nothing of the two criminals. Wensley thought quickly. He had to get Betsy

out of the house without arousing their suspicions. He persuaded the now terrified Mrs. Fleishmann to help. She was to pretend that her husband was ill and ask for Betsy's assistance.

Trembling, Mrs. Fleishmann climbed the narrow stairs and knocked timidly on Mrs. Gershon's door. Without warning, the door of the stockroom behind her opened and Betsy stepped out naked except for a petticoat. "Help me," said Mrs. Fleishmann weakly and the two women crept downstairs. Betsy later revealed that Fritz and Joseph had removed her clothes so that she could not run away, and had made her sleep in the stockroom. She and the Fleishmanns were then quickly ushered out of the house.

Here there was a further pause. Wensley had realized when he saw the interior of the house that it was futile to attempt to storm it. The staircase leading to the second floor was so narrow that Fritz and Joseph could easily pick off anyone who tried to reach them, and thus block the passage to those who followed. It was decided to wait until dawn before making the next move.

WHITEHALL WARRIOR . . . Churchill (above opposite) in ministerial silk topper surveys the besieged house. Above, plan showing scene of the gunmen's last stand. Fritz and Joseph had a perfect vantage point from their top-floor window. Below, a detective sidles up to the house just after the fire had started. He was driven back by a hail of bullets. Below, opposite, police fire on the anarchists' hide-out.

At 7.30 a.m. on January 3, the action began. In an effort to attract the attention of the two men some police officers began hurling small pebbles at the second-floor windows. One sergeant ran across the road, banged furiously on the still-open door of the house and then ran back. Someone else aimed a brick, again at the second floor. Then, all at once, the window of the floor below shattered and a volley of shots sprayed a group of policemen waiting directly opposite. As they scattered for cover one of them was wounded in the chest. The fight was on in earnest.

Mauser pistols

For an hour the police exchanged shots with the gunmen, but, in spite of their superior numbers, they made no headway. Fritz and Joseph seemed to have virtually unlimited supplies of ammunition and both were equipped with deadly Mauser pistols — far more powerful and accurate than the Morris-tube rifles used by the police. It looked like stalemate. Fritz and Joseph could not get out. Equally, the police could not get in, and were trapped in their positions by the gun-

Syndication International

men's pin-point fire. Wensley, attempting to get the wounded officer out of harm's way, found himself stuck on the loose tiles of an outhouse roof. He lay there, flat out, for half an hour in more than an inch of sleet and water; the slightest movement was greeted with a shower of bullets.

He finally scrambled to safety during a lull in the shooting, and immediately consulted the other senior officers on the scene—who agreed that troops should be brought in from the Tower of London. This was not easy to arrange. Official permission would be needed. A telephone call was put through to the Home Office, which immediately contacted the Home Secretary, Winston Churchill.

Churchill was in his bath when he received the message, but he at once authorized the police to "use any force necessary". Within 20 minutes he was dressed and at his Whitehall office. There he discovered that no further information was available other than that the house had been surrounded and the shooting was still continuing. Almost on an impulse—as he later admitted—he decided to go and see for himself what was happening, and what more could be done.

Meanwhile Superintendent Mulvaney, who was now in charge of the police forces deployed in the area, hurried to the

Daily Mirror

371

MILITARY MIGHT . . . it took a detachment of powerfully-armed soldiers to end the fiercest gun-battle ever to take place in London's streets. Here the Scots Guards prepare to enter the fray. Above opposite, heavy artillery arrives at the end of the street as smoke begins pouring from the stricken house, and below, Guards set up a Maxim gun. Fortunately the big guns were not necessary.

Mirrorpic

WINDOW FROM WHICH BURGLARS FIRED.

POLICE FIRED FROM THESE WINDOWS

PLAIN-CLOTHES POLICE FIRED FROM THESE DOORWAYS

ARMED POLICE

Daily Mirror

Tower of London armed with his "official permission", and returned with 19 men of the Scots Guards under Lieutenant Ross. The troops quickly took up position and aimed a steady stream of shots at the house, concentrating on the windows and the open door. Breaking through the deadly sound of their rapid fire could be heard the crack of pistol and rifle shots from the police, and the high-pitched whine of the Mausers used by Fritz and Joseph.

It seemed impossible that there were only two gunmen in the house, so swiftly did they change position. One moment the sharp stabbing flash of their guns would be seen bursting through the garret window; seconds later it was coming from the window on the second floor. The house itself seemed to wilt under the withering attack as bullets spat against the walls, tearing at the brickwork and plaster, and ripping huge splinters from the door and window-frames.

Nasty job

Among the policemen called to the scene was Melville MacNaughten (later to be knighted and appointed Chief of Scotland Yard's Criminal Investigation Department). "As I approached," he wrote later, "I realized what a really nasty job we were up against. Strong cordons of police encircling, at a distance of some three hundred yards, the besieged house, kept back thousands of would-be spectators.

"Long before Sidney Street was reached reports of firing were audible . . . At the north and south ends of Sidney Street, within some seventy yards of the beleaguered house, four or five guardsmen were lying prone on advertisement boards with rifles which spoke in answer to the puffs of smoke from the Mauser pistols . . .

"On the roof of a brewery, higher up on the other side of the thoroughfare, more guardsmen were posted. It appeared . . . that the danger up and down and in around the street must be very considerable by reason of the extreme probability of ricocheting bullets."

At noon Churchill, in top hat and flourishing a cigar, arrived in his car. As he got out he found himself surrounded by part of the huge crowd which had gathered at the end of the street. "Who let them in in the first place?" someone shouted at him, referring to the government's refusal to restrict alien immigration.

Churchill ignored the remark and, with the help of the police, pushed his way through the cordon to the corner of the block – from where he had an unrestricted view of the scene. Immediately he took command, calling a conference of senior

SORE-HEADED . . . an innocent civilian, on his way for a cup of tea, is attended by a doctor after being shot.

officers. A plan was hatched to storm the building. It was dangerous and would probably have cost several lives – but it turned out to be unnecessary.

At around 1 p.m. there was a shout from the crowd followed by a sudden silence – during which not a single shot was fired. From the garret window onlookers saw a thin stream of bluish smoke rising and curling up towards the roof. The house was on fire! Soon the smoke thickened and tongues of flame could be seen flickering and leaping from the spot. Just then, one of the gunmen leaned a little too far out of the window. Every gun was turned on him and there was a furious volley of shots. The man sank back; it was discovered later that he was killed at that moment by a bullet through the brain.

Blazing inferno

By now the house was a sparkling, blazing inferno. The fire brigade stood by ready to prevent the fire from spreading. But Churchill stopped them. His orders were to let the house burn. The crackle and roar of the flames increased. Then, with a great crash, the roof of the house fell in. A gust of wind momentarily lifted the smoke pouring out of the ground floor window, and watchers opposite saw into what had been the Fleishmanns' bedroom.

There they made out a man lying on the

bed with his face buried in a pillow. Seconds later the blazing first floor caved in on him with another sickening crash. It was the end. For a short while the fire surged on, and volleys of shots continued to rain into the building. Then, at last, the firemen were given the signal to move in and soon the blaze had died to a few smoking embers.

Charred bodies

It was the firemen who found the bodies, charred and broken by the flames and falling masonry. Identification was difficult, but the evidence indicated that it was Joseph who had received the bullet in the head. Fritz had no bullet wounds. He had simply lain on the bed in despair and waited for the fire to consume him.

The so-called Siege of Sidney Street created a sensation both in Britain and other parts of the world. German and American newspapers were openly contemptuous of the "ineffectual" British police methods, and suggested that future "battles" should be conducted by the navy from warships moored in the Thames. The French press, on the other hand, was full of admiration. Many newspapers felt that international Anarchism and Communism had been dealt a severe blow by the two gunmen who had tried to injure the country which had given them asylum.

As a result of the affair, the public and Press had almost forgotten about the attempted robbery from Exchange Buildings, and the murder of the three policemen. The trial of the arrested men at the Old Bailey did little to revive interest. Incredibly, all were discharged for lack of evidence – largely due to the reluctance of the judge, Mr. Justice Grantham, to accept the prosecution case. Peters and Dubof, both of whom certainly had an active hand in the murders, were particularly fortunate to be released from custody.

"The police can hardly be congratulated upon their success in dealing with this formidable conspiracy," commented the *Daily Mail* on May 13, 1911. "But, in excuse, it must be remembered that in the vast alien population of East London it is a matter of peculiar difficulty to obtain evidence or run down the offender."

The overall official attitude to the saboteurs and anarchists, however, was expressed by Melville MacNaughten when he wrote: "The . . . men were wild beasts seeking to destroy, and it is the part, office, and duty of the police to turn the tables on all such dangers to humanity.

"I remember one hot season in Bengal we suffered from an epidemic of mad dogs. Some I shot, some were clubbed to death by my servants: surely it mattered not how the end came so long as they were finished off somehow."

EIGHT AGAINST AMERICA

HITLER sent them to destroy the industries upon which America's defence depended. They were trained to kill and devastate . . .

UPI

NAZI DYNAMITE . . . boxes containing
high explosives buried on the beach
near Jacksonville by saboteurs. Left,
Coast Guardsman John C. Cullen, who
spotted the Germans after they landed.

IN DEMOCRATIC countries such as Britain and the United States, whose legal systems stem from the English common law, it is generally accepted that not only must justice be done but it must be *seen to be done* – also that every accused person is presumed to be innocent until proved guilty, instead of the other way round. However, occasionally in times of war or other grave national emergency where the accused are tried by a military court, it is necessary to dispense with these traditional safeguards of civil liberty.

Such a trial took place in secret in Washington, D.C., during World War II, when the accused were eight Nazi saboteurs who had been put ashore from a German submarine at two separate points on the American mainland with instructions to carry out specific acts of sabotage against American war industries and other strategic targets.

Death sentence

The shorthand transcript of this extraordinary trial was kept locked up in the U.S. Justice Department for 18 years, and it was not until 1960 that it was declassified and the details became generally known. All that the public was able to gather at the time was that eight named enemy saboteurs had been captured. That they had been tried and convicted by a special military commission. And that the death sentences passed upon them by the court had been confirmed by President Roosevelt in the case of six of the prison-

ers and immediately carried out – while in the case of the other two prisoners the sentence had been commuted to long terms of imprisonment.

The court sat in a large room on the fifth floor of the Justice Department Building, normally used by the Federal Bureau of Investigation for lectures and motion pictures in the training courses which the Bureau ran for its agents. The windows were covered with heavy black curtains which completely excluded the daylight, while the motion picture screen was draped in green velvet forming a somewhat bizarre backdrop to the sombre scene. There were seven military judges, four major generals and three brigadier generals. The presiding judge was Major General Frank R. McCoy, a veteran who had commanded an infantry brigade in France during World War I, and had served on various important boards and commissions since his retirement from active service. Behind the President's chair hung an American flag.

It was the first time a military court had sat to try civilians since seven men and one woman had been charged with conspiring with John Wilkes Booth to assassinate Abraham Lincoln in 1865.

To the left of the judges was a dark mahogany chair for the use of the witnesses. Farther to the left, at right angles to the judges' bench, was a long table for the prosecution team which was led by the Attorney General Francis Biddle. A special place at the prosecutor's table was provided for Mr. J. Edgar Hoover, the F.B.I. chief. Behind this table were the eight prisoners, seated alphabetically and guarded by soldiers.

The first — corresponding with groups in which they landed — group was led by George John Dasch, and included Peter Burger, Heinrich Harm Heinck, and Richard Quirin. The second group consisted of Herbert Hans Haupt, Hermann Otto Neubauer, Werner Thiel, and Edward Kerling, who was in overall charge of both formations. Dasch was defended by Colonel Carl Ristine and the others

by Colonel Cassius Dowell and Colonel Kenneth Royall, counsel assigned by the court for the purpose. The defence counsel occupied a table to the right of the judges' bench, facing the prosecution team.

Legal device

At the outset of the trial, which began on July 8, 1942, General McCoy announced that he would preside according to President Roosevelt's order constituting the commission. Under this the court would have the right to admit evidence which in the opinion of the judges had "probative value to a reasonable man". This was a legal device, often employed in hearings before special tribunals, to permit the admission of evidence which might not be admitted in civil courts — where the rules of evidence are strictly applied.

GATHERING EVIDENCE . . . U.S. officials (below) sift through evidence and discuss the implications of the trial for American war-time security. Left to right (foreground), Attorney General Francis Biddle, F.B.I. boss J. Edgar Hoover and Colonel Carl Ristine. Right, the military judge who presided, General Frank McCoy.

The commission was then sworn and the oath of secrecy was administered to all present. The Press was excluded from the proceedings and was only to be admitted for a very short time on one occasion when the court recessed; this was to allow the newspapermen to satisfy themselves as to the existence of the prisoners and the composition of the court. They were also allowed to inspect the clothing, explosives, boxes, and other exhibits in the trial.

The prisoners were formally charged with violating, and with conspiracy to violate, the law of war, in that they were

Both UPI

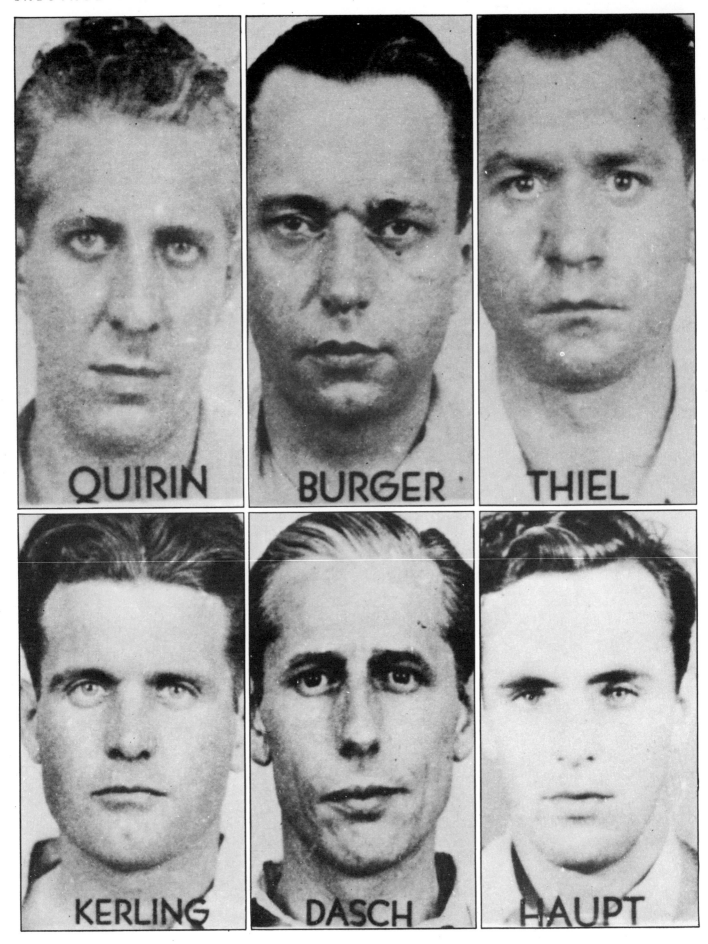

QUIRIN BURGER THIEL

KERLING DASCH HAUPT

enemies of the United States, "acting for and on behalf of the German Reich", who had "secretly and covertly", while in civilian dress, passed through American military lines for the purpose of committing sabotage and other hostile acts in order "to destroy certain war industries, war utilities, and war materials". They were also accused of spying. When all the accused had pleaded not guilty, the Attorney General opened the case for the prosecution. It was an amazing story he had to tell the court.

New York waiter

On June 13, 1942, the first group of saboteurs under the command of George Dasch, who had been a waiter in New York and San Francisco before the war, landed on Amagansett beach, at the southern tip of Long Island. They came ashore in a rubber dinghy dropped under cover of night from a U-boat, which managed to elude local U.S. destroyer patrols and also to escape the vigilance of the local Coast Guards. The saboteurs wore German naval fatigue uniforms, which they buried in the beach along with boxes of explosives and other equipment. The second unit was similarly transported and landed four days later on Ponte Vedra Beach, Florida, some 25 miles south of Jacksonville.

Each group possessed a substantial supply of TNT and other high explosives, fuses, timing devices, and detonators—which in the hold of a boat or in the baggage room of a crowded railroad station would be capable of causing untold damage and loss of life. The saboteurs also carried with them plans of key railroad centres and bridges and of the locks on the Ohio River from Pittsburgh to Louisville. Besides all this, they had the layouts of three plants of the Aluminum Company of America, of the Niagara Falls hydroelectric plant, of the New York water supply system, and of a number of key industries.

The men in the second team were to concentrate on railroads. They all possessed forged birth certificates, automobile driving licences, and selective service and social security cards. They also had plenty of cash—each man carrying $4000 in a money belt and $400 in small denominations in his wallet, while in addition Kerling and Dasch each car-

HAND-PICKED for disaster . . . six of the eight saboteurs. Under Hitler's orders they were specially trained to work in American conditions. But their long preparation proved futile and led them straight into a U.S. jail. Top (left to right), Richard Quirin; Peter Burger and Werner Thiel. Bottom, Edward Kerling, George Dasch, and Herbert Haupt.

ried a reserve of $70,000. They had all undergone a rigorous training in a sabotage school at Quentz, near Berlin, in the use of explosives; they had also been taught how to communicate with their Nazi masters in secret writing.

Although six of the sabotage team were loyal Nazis, the other two were not. Dasch and Burger both detested Hitler, and it is remarkable that the Nazis did not check their *bona fides* before they embarked on the U-boat. Burger, in particular, had no love for the Fuehrer, since he had spent 17 months in a concentration camp, and been tortured for having been a supporter of Ernst Roehm—the S.S. leader whom Hitler had had murdered in the abortive *Putsch* of June 1934. At all events they quickly combined to give their comrades away to the American authorities.

Five days after wading ashore at Amagansett beach, Dasch took the train from New York to Washington, checked into the Mayflower Hotel and next morning put through a telephone call to F.B.I. headquarters. He was interviewed at length, signed a long, rambling confession—the prison psychiatrist who later examined him considered that he was suffering from an "obsessive, compulsive, neurotic, hysterical personality disorder" —and, as the result of the information he gave, all the saboteurs were rounded up and in custody by June 27. Brief details of the landings and arrests were then released by Mr. Hoover, who was warmly congratulated on all sides for the success of the coup, and later given a "medal of honor" by President Roosevelt.

Shadowy silhouettes

The first witness called to testify for the prosecution was 22-year-old Coast Guardsman second class John C. Cullen, who had surprised Dasch and his three companions when they were burying their uniforms and explosives in the sand at Amagansett beach. He was patrolling the foggy beach at the time and he described how he saw the shadowy silhouettes of the saboteurs. "I hollered out," he said, and as he hollered one of the men walked towards him.

According to Cullen, the man said he and his companions were fishermen who had come from nearby Southampton, Long Island, and run ashore. A voice in the fog—it was Burger—shouted out something in a foreign language, and this made the guard nervous and suspicious. The man he had hollered at approached closer and said, "Forget about this and I'll give you some money and you can have a good time"—having previously told him that he would not like to kill him. He held out two 50-dollar bills. The Coast Guard refused to accept them, but after the man had reached for more

money and said, "Here's 300 dollars," he took the proffered bills.

Cullen then went off into the fog and reported his experience to his superior, Warren Barnes, the chief of the Amagansett Coast Guard Station, handing over the money—which was found to total $260. The young guard then took a party of colleagues back to the beach and pointed out the spot where the suspicious encounter had taken place. It was still too foggy to make a search, so station chief Barnes returned with some of his men, not including Cullen, when it was light. Soon they dug up the boxes with the explosives, uniforms, and other paraphernalia which the saboteurs had buried.

"Do you recognize the man in the court who walked towards you?" the Attorney General asked the witness.

"I think so, sir," replied Coast Guardsman Cullen.

"Will you stand up and identify him, if you see him in court?"

Explosive equipment

The witness did so and pointed towards Dasch in the row of prisoners. He then asked Dasch to say something so that he could identify him by voice as well as by sight. Dasch's counsel had no objection, so the prisoner asked the witness, "What is your name?" Cullen then turned towards the Attorney General and said, "That's the man." Asked about what Dasch had suggested to him if he did not go away, he replied, "He said he would not want to have to kill me." The Coast Guard went on to refer to the boxes of explosives as "this equipment they had dug up", and Colonel Royall objected for the defence that this was hearsay. The President sustained the objection, and struck the reference from the record after the Attorney General had agreed with the objection.

"Since the witness did not see the boxes dug up," said Biddle, "he cannot testify with respect to their being dug up. We shall later show that they were dug up and put the witnesses on." It was a small point, but it demonstrated how the niceties of "due process" were observed in a wartime secret trial.

Cullen's evidence was confirmed by his chief, who also identified the various articles found on the beach. He was followed by various F.B.I. agents and explosives experts—after which the articles themselves were put in evidence, and finally the statements made by the accused after they had been arrested. This led to a legal argument between the opposing counsel; the defence lawyers arguing that under the rules of common law evidence the confession of one was not evidence against another except on the point of conspiracy, since otherwise

COAL COMFORT? The innocent looking piece of coal (right) is not coal at all but a block of TNT in disguise. It was one of the devices intended for use by the saboteurs. This and many other appliances, from deadly explosives to the mundane shovel (above), were found neatly packed in the boxes found on the shore. They had planned for everything . . .

hearsay would prevail.

To Biddle it was a simple issue which involved incontrovertible facts. To deny them because of a technicality in common law was preposterous, he submitted. "Those men, not having an opportunity to confer or talk it over, on the whole made confessions entirely bearing out what each other said," the Attorney General declared.

"Dasch supports Burger, Burger supports Kerling, and so on, right down the line . . . The defendants say that in spite of that close interlocking of all those statements, all alike, all bearing the obvious marks of truthfulness, all comparable to each other, all showing this essential common intent . . . you must in some curious way take out of your minds with respect to some defendants the confessions of the others."

Virtually sealed

In the event the commission upheld Biddle and ruled that it would "admit the confessions and admissions for all purposes". With that the prosecution rested its case, and the prisoners' fate was virtually sealed.

Briefly, the case for the defence was that the eight men had no intention of going through with their instructions, there was no indication that they were spies, and there was the patent fact that they had committed no act of sabotage by the time they were arrested. Broadly speaking this was borne out by the prisoners themselves, who all testified in their own defence – though some of them were more convincing than others.

Kerling, for instance, did not plead a change of heart about Germany or the Nazis. His doubts of the success of the sabotage assignment were due to his profound disrespect for the quality of the others as effective saboteurs – if they had only been more like himself, he felt, they would not have been caught and somehow would have succeeded in carrying out their orders.

On the other hand, Neubauer and Thiel felt they had been trapped. "As a soldier you are not supposed to think," the former said in reply to his counsel. "I just got the order and I didn't know what for." Even when he was told that it was for sabotage, what could he do about it?

His superior in the sabotage school, Kappe, was a lieutenant, "which in Germany is quite a high superior above me," he explained. "There was nothing I could do. I had the order from my regiment to report to him." But he was relieved, he added, that Kappe's instructions specifically ruled out killing or harming Americans.

Nervous wreck

The seventh man to be called to the witness chair was George Dasch. His defence was based on the single, undeniable fact that he had voluntarily gone to the F.B.I. and revealed the sabotage plot. Unlike the six previous witnesses, who may have intended to do so, Dasch had acted. Asked by Biddle in cross-examination why he had delayed for a week, Dasch replied:

"First of all I was a mental and nervous

ON TRIAL . . . Attorney General Francis
Biddle questions F.B.I. agent during the
trial of the saboteurs. Colonel Kenneth
Royall (below right) arrives at U.S.
Supreme Court, Washington to plead case
for civil trial. It soon became clear
that the prisoners were going to have a
tough fight steering wide of the death
sentence. In the end, only Burger and
Dasch lived to tell the full story.

wreck. I was so glad I was here. Second,
I had to be human . . . To be a real decent
person I had to wait. I had to give every
person a chance to say what I had to say.
That's the reason."

The most effective and forthright of the
eight prisoners was Burger, who had become an American citizen of his own
choice, but who had lost his citizenship
when he was drafted into the German
army in 1941. Ever since the attempted
Putsch of 1934 he had been anxious to
leave Germany, but an illegal escape
would have meant serious trouble for his
family. The only way out was when he
joined the sabotage group.

Hitler's friend

General McCoy asked him whether he
knew Hitler. Yes, Burger replied, he
knew Hitler intimately at one time and
had taken part in his first grab for power.
But his loyalty to the Fuehrer had died
during the purge in which his friend
Roehm had been killed.

"Do you remember," McCoy finally
asked him, "whether or not Kappe told
you to confess in case one or all of you
were caught?"

"No, sir," said Burger. "On the contrary, in case anyone got caught we were
not to tell anything. That was understood from the beginning."

In the circumstances a verdict of guilty
was inevitable. The court convicted all
eight prisoners and sentenced them to
death by electrocution. However, the
judges recommended that in the cases of
Dasch and Burger, the sentence should be
commuted to life imprisonment.

This was because of the assistance they
had given the government in the apprehension and conviction of the others — Burger
had provided particularly valuable information about the operations of the
sabotage school where the men had been
trained. President Roosevelt duly commuted the death sentence to life imprisonment for Burger and 30 years
for Dasch.

If he could, President Roosevelt would
have gladly added to the punishment in a
rather old-fashioned way. When told by
the Attorney General that a total of
$175,000 had been collected from the
prisoners, he remarked with a chuckle:
"Not enough, Francis. Let's make real
money out of them. Sell the rights to

Barnum and Bailey (the circus showmen) for a million and a half—the rights to take them round the country in lion cages at so much a head!"

No appeal

There was no appeal against the sentences. Nevertheless, the defence tried to get them quashed by applying to the Supreme Court for a writ of *habeas corpus* on the ground that a military court had no right to try civilians when the civil courts were open and properly functioning.

Colonel Royall, who argued the motion, based his argument on the precedent of the case of a man called Milligan, who had been condemned to death during the American Civil War for sending military supplies to the Confederates. His sentence had been confirmed by President Lincoln, but his release was ordered by the Supreme Court—which held that the law of war "can never be applied to citizens where the courts are open and their process unobstructed".

However, in the case of the saboteurs, the court now held that the earlier decision had reference to the particular facts of Milligan's case—which were different from that of the saboteurs. It also held that as a general rule individual offenders against the law of war—such as the saboteurs—could be tried and punished by a special military court since they were not entitled to be treated as prisoners-of-war. Thus the defence motion failed and the saboteurs prepared to face the chair.

Volunteer firing squad

About 3 a.m. on Saturday, August 8, 1942, three American soldiers and a British sailor arrived at the entrance to the District of Columbia Jail—where the condemned men were being held—saying they had come to volunteer as a firing squad "to save the government some money on electricity". They were firmly turned away by the guard on duty, but not before their pictures were taken by waiting news photographers. Later the same day the executions were carried out in the electric chair, a proceeding which lasted from 12 noon to 1.20 p.m.

The six bodies were afterwards taken to Blue Plains—the District of Columbia Potters Field—and buried in nameless graves, surmounted by six unpainted wooden boards numbered 276 to 281, to correspond with U.S. Health Department records. The six graves were in a new plot which, by a grim touch of irony, was separated from the bodies of the other unclaimed dead in Blue Plains by a five-foot wire fence of a type called "anti-sabotage" by its manufacturer.

In 1948, Roosevelt's successor in the White House, President Truman, com-

PRESIDENTIAL PARDON... Truman (top), who succeeded Roosevelt, deported the two surviving saboteurs back to their own country. Roosevelt preferred cages.

muted the remainder of the prison terms being served by Burger and Dasch, and both men were deported to Germany. Nothing more was heard of Burger. But Dasch eventually erupted into print with the result that Attorney General Biddle had anticipated.

"I have no doubt," wrote Biddle, "that Dasch, one of the most unhaltingly voluble men I have ever encountered, has by now generously embellished the strange story of his capture and release as he keeps recounting it to a younger generation."

Indeed, the saboteur's account, which appeared in 1959, is much more fanciful than trustworthy. It was entitled *Eight Spies against America,* and described the operation which, according to J. Edgar Hoover, Director of the F.B.I., "would have stilled the machines and endangered the lives of thousands of defence workers ... they came to maim and kill."

THE WAKING NIGHTMARE

When he woke up, the face of a girl was etched vividly on his mind.
Something had happened during the night. A body had to be disposed of.
Three days later, they found her . . . in a field, near Lovers' Lane.

Essex Chronicle

LAST SEEN ALIVE HERE

Yesterday's picture of The Bell Public-house in Braintree, frequented by the girl who died. It was here that she was last seen enjoying herself . . . .

And this is the Jean her parents loved so well . . . pretty, fond of the family, a hard worker.

100 SPECTATORS AT THE CASTLE HEDINGHAM TRIAL

AS AMERICAN APPEARS IN THE DOCK

STAFF-SGT. WILLIS EUGENE BOSHEARS, 29-year-old United States Serviceman, charged with the murder of Halstead girl JEAN SYLVIA CONSTABLE, hid his face in the hood of his flying jacket as he was hustled into Castle Hedingham Police Station yesterday on his way to the local Court. He arrived at the police station, where more than 100 spectators lined the pavements, in the back of a police car with a Chief Inspector on either side of him.

Jean Constable, the 20-year-old party-loving girl from Abels Road, Halstead, was found dead in a roadside water-filled ditch at Ridgewell. Her body was only partly clothed.

Boshears, of The Close, Dunmow, is attached to the 20th Field Maintenance Squadron at Wethersfield—the base where Chief Det.-Supt. Ernest Barkway, of Essex C.I.D., spent 24 hours questioning servicemen about the murder.

The car in which he arrived parked in the driveway leading down to the courtroom entrance. Getting out, Boshears; short with dark crew-cut hair, was screened by police officers until the courtroom door closed. He was 30 minutes in a back room before entering court.

SUPT. H. J. WOOD, of Braintree, said that Boshear was charged with the murder of Jean Constable on or about December 31. He said that on January 3 the police received information that the body of a woman, partly clothed, had been found on the A.604 at Oaken Hill, Ridgewell.

Police officers went to the scene under the direction of DET. CHIEF-SUPT. BARKWAY. From then on inquiries were made which led the police to Wethersfield Air Base.

"LAST NIGHT THIS MAN WAS CHARGED," said Supt. Wood.

DET. - INSP. WILLIAM JEAVONS, of Braintree, said: "At 9 a.m. on Tuesday, January 3, I received information as a result of which, with Det. Chief-Supt. Barkway and other officers I went to Oaken Hill, on the A604 Halstead-Hedingham Road.

"At the side of the road I saw a partly-clothed dead body of a young woman lying head first in the ditch.

"The body was later identified as that of Miss Constable, of Abels Road, Halstead.

With Det. Chief-Supt. Barkway

wanted to say anything and he replied "No."

In reply to another question to the Clerk, Boshears said: "I have legal aid from the Air Force."

The chairman of the magistrats, LADY BEATRICE PLUMMER, said: "Boshears will be remanded in civil custody until 3 p.m. on January 13."

Throughout the whole of the hearing Boshears stood with head bowed, arms to his side. He was dressed in a denim flying jacket with a fur collar and denim trousers with black laced boots.

Also present in the court room were senior detectives and two American Air Force personnel, Col. E. Dedera, Boshears' squadron commander, and T/Sgt. James D. Geiger also from the Judge Advocate's Office at Wethersfield.

There were 40 people in the court room — normally only once a fortnight — and more 20 of them were reporters.

At the end of the hearing Boshears was led to a police which was surrounded by graphers and members public.

CLASSIFIED ADVERTISEMENTS

Too late to Classify

GIFTS F

NEW Year's Eve. Outside, people were going to parties. There was the sound of singing and distant laughter. Staff-Sergeant Willis Eugene Boshears was lonely. His wife was away with their three children at the home of her parents. He should have been with them. In fact, he would have been with them if his leave had not been cancelled at the last minute. He needed a drink. Just a little vodka at first. Only a glass or two. Then just a little more. . . .

Late the following morning he awoke in his flat at Dunmow, Essex, England, near the Wethersfield American Air Force base, with a hangover and the pervading memory of a nightmare. The face of a dead girl was etched vividly on his mind, and there was a confused connection between her and the spare bedroom. He went into the next room and there, neatly laid on the floor by the bed, was the corpse of a beautiful girl. She had been strangled.

For two days, in a torment of panic and bewilderment, he kept the body in his flat. Dimly at first, and then more clearly, he began to remember how he had hacked off her lovely, long brown hair in a pathetic attempt to disguise her. Then eventually he dumped her in a ditch six miles away. Those events led to one of the most remarkable murder cases in British legal history. They also led to the crew-cut Boshears—known as Little Mac

Essex Chronicle

because of his smallness—being recognized as a Sleep-Walking Slayer.

Boshears, at the age of 29, was an American hero. He had three rows of medals and there were 49 combat missions in Korea to his credit. When the American authorities realized he was to face a murder charge they asked Britain to hand him over—so that he could be tried at a court martial. However, the Director of Public Prosecutions refused. In February, 1961, Boshears appeared at the assize court in Chelmsford, England—pleading not guilty to murder before a jury of 11 men and a woman.

Quiet and respectable

His duties with the 20th Field Maintenance Squadron were as a jet-engine fitter, and he had eight months to serve before completing his second three-year-tour of duty in Britain. He and his Scots wife, Jean, were a happily married couple whose youngest child, a boy called George, was born two weeks before Christmas, 1960. Jean had gone to her parents' pre-fab home at Ayr, Scotland, with the two older children for the birth of George and had stayed on there to recuperate. So, on the last day of December, Boshears, who came from Michigan, was alone in their flat. He got up shortly after 6 a.m. and went to the Wethersfield base to draw his pay.

He stayed there for about five hours and had a meal at the N.C.O.s' club. He had just had a number of teeth out so he ate only one egg. Before leaving the base he had a few drinks and then bought a 40 oz. bottle of vodka to take home. But, without the family around him, the flat seemed intolerably empty. He began to feel bored and restless and he thought of all the people outside enjoying themselves. So he decided to join the noisy, cheerful crowds in the local pubs.

At about the same time a 20-year-old girl called Jean Constable was also on her way to the pubs to seek lively company. She worked in a nearby plastics factory and had a reputation as a good-time girl who "liked G.I.s". One of her favourite evening places was the Wethersfield base where she often went dancing and, according to one of her closest girl-friends, she "was always asking people to give her lifts there".

THE KOREAN-WAR HERO . . . whose fate was snatched from the United States by the arm of Britain's law. The charge is murder . . . and a rural newspaper sets the scene.

Despite this, she felt that her parents, a quiet and respectable couple, might not altogether approve so she often kept her activities a secret from them. They could hardly fail to know that she often spent complete nights away from their neat rented house in Halstead, Essex. But they assumed she was safely at the home of a girl friend.

As she left the house on New Year's Eve, wearing the black-and-white fur coat of which she was so proud, she told her parents she was going to a party in London with some girl friends—but did not mention the names of those friends. Mr. and Mrs. Constable never saw their daughter alive again.

Meanwhile, Jean tried, as she had done so often before, to find an American serviceman who would take her to the base. One of them later told the police: "She asked several of us but most of the guys had girls with them already."

In the Nags Head public house at Braintree, after failing with the Americans, she "picked-up" a 20-year-old English apprentice engineer called David Sault. They shared a few drinks before moving on to the Bell Hotel. Boshears was in the bar at the Bell, quietly drinking on his own. He was delighted when Jean and Sault arrived, for he had known her casually for some three months, and it was good to see a familiar face.

Jiving to a jukebox

"Hey! It's great to see you!" he cried. "Come and have a drink!" Jean gladly accepted the invitation—which was the first step towards her death. "I'd love a vodka and tonic," she replied, and introduced Sault to the sergeant. So the three of them had a lively evening, drinking round after round of vodka and jiving to juke-box records. When it was time for the pub to close, Boshears suggested that they should return to his flat for more drinking and dancing.

There they played records so loudly that the people living above and below complained. But still the party went on. Boshears, after dancing with Jean, left the sitting-room for a while and Sault had inter-course with her on a rug. He claimed afterwards that she had made the initial advances. Then Boshears returned and, after a few more drinks, he offered—according to Sault—to show them round.

All three went into a bedroom where, once again, Boshears left them alone. "We were left together in the bedroom and we had intercourse again on the bed," said Sault. Boshears, he added, "more or less disturbed" them, and shortly after midnight he asked the couple if they were planning to stay the night. They said that they were, and Boshears placed a mattress and some blankets in front of the sitting-room fire. The trio sat by the fire for a

Press Association

while. Then Jean undressed in front of both men before curling herself up in blankets and going to sleep.

Boshears lay on blankets by the side of the mattress and, a few minutes later, Sault undressed and settled down on the mattress beside Jean. After a while he changed his mind, decided to go home, and got dressed. The girl was then "drowsy and pretty well asleep". But Boshears, who told Sault where to get a taxi, was — according to Sault — "sober as far as I could say". So Sault left the flat somewhere between 12.30 and 1 a.m. Later, at around 1 a.m., Mrs. Clara Miller, wife of a United States Air Force sergeant, in the flat above, heard a girl crying.

"It was like sobbing and I heard something which sounded like either 'You love me' or 'You don't love me', but it was muffled as though she was holding a handkerchief," she said.

Experts later believed that it was more likely that the indistinct words heard by Mrs. Miller carried a far more sinister message. "You're hurting me", perhaps. Or even: "You're choking me." During the day Mrs. Miller challenged Boshears about the crying, but he made no reply.

Boshears' own memory of the evening was not as clear as Sault's. He remember-ed showing Sault and the girl to the main bedroom and placing a mattress on the floor for himself. There was nothing particularly unusual in that as he had put people up in that manner before. Then he remembered Jean falling asleep on the mattress where she had been sitting.

"The other fellow and I had a couple more drinks and I must have fell asleep — not fell asleep but passed out," he said. "The next thing I remember was the fellow waking me up and asking me where he could get a taxi."

Lay down beside her

When Sault had gone Boshears lay down on the edge of the mattress. "Jean was asleep and I lay down beside her," he said. "The next thing I remember was something scratching and pulling at my mouth. I opened my eyes and Jean was lying there under me and I had my hands round her throat. She was dead then. That sort of sobered me up. I got scared and did not know what to do."

So, his brain stupefied by terror and by alcohol, he panicked. He had to disguise her. He had to make sure that no one could recognize her. Her hair! Yes, that was it! He had heard people say what lovely hair she had — that would make her easy to identify.

So he hacked off her hair until it was almost as crew-cut as his own, and then he burned it. The body had to be cleaned. Yes, that was the next move. He picked up the dead girl and carried her into the bathroom. He placed the body in the bath and thoroughly washed it. The next thing was to dress her — or partially dress her — and place her on the floor of the spare bedroom.

Then, after tidying the sitting-room, he returned to the mattress and collapsed into sleep. When he awoke, suffering from a severe hangover, he had the strange half-memory of something having happened during the night . . . something — very unpleasant . . . and yet . . .

"I decided that it had been a dream, but I went to check and I saw clothes in the bathroom and Jean in the spare bedroom," he said. "I wanted to go to the police but I was scared. I figured out how to get rid of the body and I washed the sheets and blankets."

Her fur coat was too distinctive. Too many people – particularly men at the base – could hardly fail to recognize it. It had to be destroyed. He burned the coat. Then, continuing his pathetic attempt to hide his crime, he stripped Jean of her watch and ring and disposed of her handbag. But the body was still there. For two days, dreading the approaching return of his wife and children, he lived with it – puzzling how to get rid of it in safety.

That must be a Yank

Then one evening, shortly before midnight, he wrapped up the body in some of his own heavy winter clothing, carried it downstairs over his shoulder, and placed it in the back of his car. He drove through the night until he came to a lonely country spot, about five miles from his base, which was known locally as "Lovers' Lay-by". There, four yards inside a field, he pitched Jean head-first into a ditch which was partly screened by a wild rose bush. A lorry driver called Sidney Ambrose found her there on January 3 and, in view of Jean's friendships with servicemen, the American Air Force police were asked to help the team of British detectives.

A murder headquarters was set up at the Wethersfield base, and around-the-clock interrogation of scores of servicemen began. The following evening Boshears was detained and taken to

THE WIFE WHO WENT HOME for the Christmas holidays. A wedding-day smile is transformed into stunned horror . . . "My head spun. I screamed. I collapsed." And the man whose testimony was vital to the defence . . . David Sault had made love to Jean Constable that same night.

Essex Chronicle

Braintree police station by Chief Detective-Superintendent Ernest Barkway, and Chief Inspector Harry Burden. There he was charged with murder. Strangely enough, his wife Jean saw him being arrested, while watching television – but did not realize it was him.

She was at her parents' home when, only half-listening, she heard a newscaster say: "A man at Wethersfield American Air Force base has been arrested for murder . . ." She looked up and saw pictures of a man being escorted from the base with his head covered by a cape. She said casually to her brother: "That must be a Yank they've arrested." Then came a knock at the door. The local police were there to tell her that the man under the cape was her husband. "Horror took my breath away," she said later. "My head spun. I screamed. I collapsed."

Boshears spent the night in Brixton Prison, in South London. The following day he had to wait in a police cell at Braintree for five hours while urgent calls went out to assemble an unexpected magistrates' court hearing at the 800-year-old village of Castle Hedingham. A clerk had to be hurriedly brought from a court in a different part of the county and Lady Beatrice Plummer, chairman of the magistrates, had to be summoned from London.

Eventually Boshears, wearing a fur-lined parka, green combat suit, and boots, was standing rigidly to attention in the little courtroom – which was heated by a roaring coal fire – while the Americans argued for the right to try him by court martial. Major Carl B. Prestin of the United States Judge Advocate's Department asked that Boshears be remanded to a U.S. detention centre. This plea, made under the Visiting Forces Act, was vigorously opposed by the police and was subsequently rejected by Sir Theobald Mathew, the Director of Public Prosecutions. A U.S.A.F. spokesman explained the application:

"Under the terms of the N.A.T.O. status of forces agreement, the British authorities have primary jurisdiction to try this man. But, under the agreement, we are required to ask that we shall receive jurisdiction, which would mean an air force court-martial. The British authorities have the right to refuse our request and to try the man in their Courts and that is what they are doing."

N.A.T.O. observers and U.S.A.F. officers were in the crowded courtroom at Essex Assizes, Chelmsford, when the trial formally began and Boshears pleaded Not Guilty to murder. Boshears spoke in a low voice which, at times, was difficult to hear. He told the jury that he did not know how Jean Constable died and added: "There was no quarrel or argument. At no time did I make any

overtures or sexual advances to her, nor did I have any desire to kill her or harm her in any way."

He then said: "I cannot throw any light on how I came to have marks on my face. I have no more knowledge of how Jean met her death than I have told the police and the jury." Initially, when questioned by the police, he had stated: "Jean and her boy friend came into my flat. It might have been around 11 p.m. We had a few drinks in the living-room and I passed out. We were there an hour or two before that. I could not be sure."

Jean Constable and her "boy friend" had left the flat but he did not know at what time. Under cross-examination by Mr. Stanley Rees, prosecuting, he admitted that, at first, he had told lies to the police – but had done so because he had been scared. He had been sober when he threw the body in the ditch, and had not been telling the truth when he informed the police that he did not know why he had done so.

Less intense struggle

Mr. Rees: "It is a lie because you knew exactly why you took the body to the ditch?"

"Yes, sir."

"And in a sober and determined attempt to cover up what had happened you carried her body into the bathroom and then into the bedroom. This was a calculated attempt to hide the crime?"

"Yes, sir."

"What crime did you think you had committed?"

"The logical one."

"What did you think was the logical one?"

"I had killed someone."

"But you didn't think it was a crime to kill someone when you were fast asleep?"

"I thought to kill any way was a crime."

The eminent pathologist Dr. Francis Camps was then asked: "On the findings which you made on that body did you think it is possible that he could have killed her while asleep in that way?"

"I should think it is certainly within the bounds of improbability," said Dr. Camps. "My reason, from my findings, is this process would take a certain amount of time and during that period the person would go through certain phases of movement and, from the description given of finding her suddenly dead like that, I don't think it fits in with that type of crime."

When Dr. Camps was cross-examined by the defending counsel, he agreed that marks on Jean Constable's elbow and wrist were nothing to do with the activity of the death night. This indicated that the struggle could have been less intense than had earlier been supposed. The defence made great play of this statement – and of

the fact that Dr. Camps had said he would not go as far as to say that it was "impossible" for a man, while asleep, to strangle someone.

Mr. Justice Glyn-Jones, summing up, said the jury might think that, in putting his hands on the girl's neck and applying pressure for such a length of time, the strangler intended to cause grievous bodily harm or death. "He must have known what would be the result of what he was doing," he said.

He explained to the jury that there were only two verdicts possible—guilty of murder or not guilty of anything at all. "There is no lesser alternative verdict open to you," he stressed. The judge apparently had not studied the earlier cases of sleep-walking slayers, for he asked: "Have you ever heard of a man strangling a woman while he was sound asleep?" "We have no medical evidence that there exists any record in all the records of the medical profession that such a thing has happened." Dr. Camps had said that this might be possible. The judge paused and looked sternly at the members of the jury. "You use your commonsense and decide whether it happened," he instructed.

Was it within the bounds of possibility that Boshears could have moved from his position beside the girl, taken the covering from her and then, straddling himself across her, seized her throat in his hands and applied pressure resulting

SISTER AND MOTHER of the victim arrive at the headline—making trial. When it was all over, Staff-Sergeant Boshears was surrounded by a horde of women . . . some booing, some cheering. He had to be rescued by the police.

in unconsciousness, convulsion and death—without him being awakened by his own exertions?

That was the vital question. And, again, it was the duty of the jury to use its commonsense. During his 22-minute summing-up the judge also stressed that if Boshears had strangled while he was asleep, it was not a voluntary act and he was entitled to be acquitted. If the jury were in any doubt about whether or not he was asleep he was also entitled to be acquitted. The jury retired for one hour and 50 minutes. When they returned and gave a "Not Guilty" verdict, there were incredulous shouts from the public gallery.

Six weeks of hell

Fantastic scenes took place outside the court following the acquittal. As Boshears walked out a free man there was a barrage of booing and cheering. Hordes of women, hoping to catch a glimpse of him, disrupted the rush-hour traffic. The handful of U.S.A.F. officers surrounding him could not carve a way through the crowds. Finally a squad of policemen rescued Boshears, and formed a protective circle around him as he walked 400 yards through the main streets to an Air Force car. The hearing had lasted two days, and Boshears commented:

BROS.
otors) Ltd.
ORD DEALERS
MALDON
Tel.: MALDON 535'6
COMMENT COLUMN
is handed over this week to one of our regular readers. We are unable to improve on his remarks! He says:—
A HIGH STANDARD
TO THE EDITOR
SIR, — I have pleasure of renewing my 'Essex Chronicle' subscription for 1961 and thank you for the prompt despatch of your newspapers throughout the year.
May I once again compliment you upon the high standards of reporting and "Comment" which you maintain, so valuable in these days when so much that is vulgar and cheap is foist upon the public.
My mother, who is now in her eighty-fifth year, values your paper which still serves as a link with Braintree and Coggeshall, which she left nearly 30 years ago to come here.
May 1961 be happy and prosperous for you all.
With every good wish,
Yours sincerely,
NORMAN G. CRESSWELL
24 Court Drive
Croydon
SEE BACK PAGE
Frederick Hone, of Fairfield Road, Chelmsford, was fined £1 at Chelmsford yesterday for leaving his car outside his house without lights.
Bolingbrokes
74-75 HIGH STREET
and 7-9 NEW LONDON ROAD
CHELMSFORD Tel. 2193

Press Association

"It has been six weeks of hell. I'm still in a daze. I cannot believe it's true that I am a free man. British justice? It's wonderful. My wife has forgiven me. She came to see me in prison while I was awaiting trial to tell me so. I am longing to see my kids again. I kept a picture of them in my cell."

But the real torment which his wife had experienced was described more evocatively by her. She told how she felt living with the knowledge that the girl Jean Constable had been in her flat and' had died there.

"The most terrible moment was when I had to return to the flat at Dunmow where it all happened," she said. "I had vowed I would never set foot in it again. But a month after Bill's arrest I had to go back to pick up our belongings. My knees were shaking and my hand trembled so much I could scarcely get the door key into the lock. The place was in a terrible shambles.

"The police had turned out the kitchen fire in search of clues. In the bathroom the ceiling plaster had fallen. I walked down the long hall to our living-room. This is where the girl had died. I pushed open the door. I could see the mattress by the fire. The bloodstains on the carpet. I turned and ran. I remembered

"I REMEMBERED all my hopes and disappointments. My knees were shaking. My hand trembled." . . . "My wife has forgiven me. I'm longing to see the kids."

all my hopes and all my disappointments. I wept."

Twenty-four hours after being cleared of the murder, Boshears, re-united with his family, was at the Wethersfield base – preparing to go on leave. Then in July of that year—after returning to America— Boshears was dismissed from the army. The official statement said that his dismissal was "under other than honourable conditions".

In the High Court of Justiciary on 15th
July 1878

Special Defence
J. B

Trial of Simon Fraser for Murder.

The panel pleads not guilty and further
pleads that at the time the alleged crime was commit-
-ted he was asleep.

Cullen Macalford
121 West Regent Street, Glasgow

Agents.

THE BEAST IN THE BEDROOM

It was a monster that killed baby Simon. Its eyes glowed with a hideous green light and its mouth foamed with steaming saliva. The child's father saw it . . . and expert witnesses backed up his story.

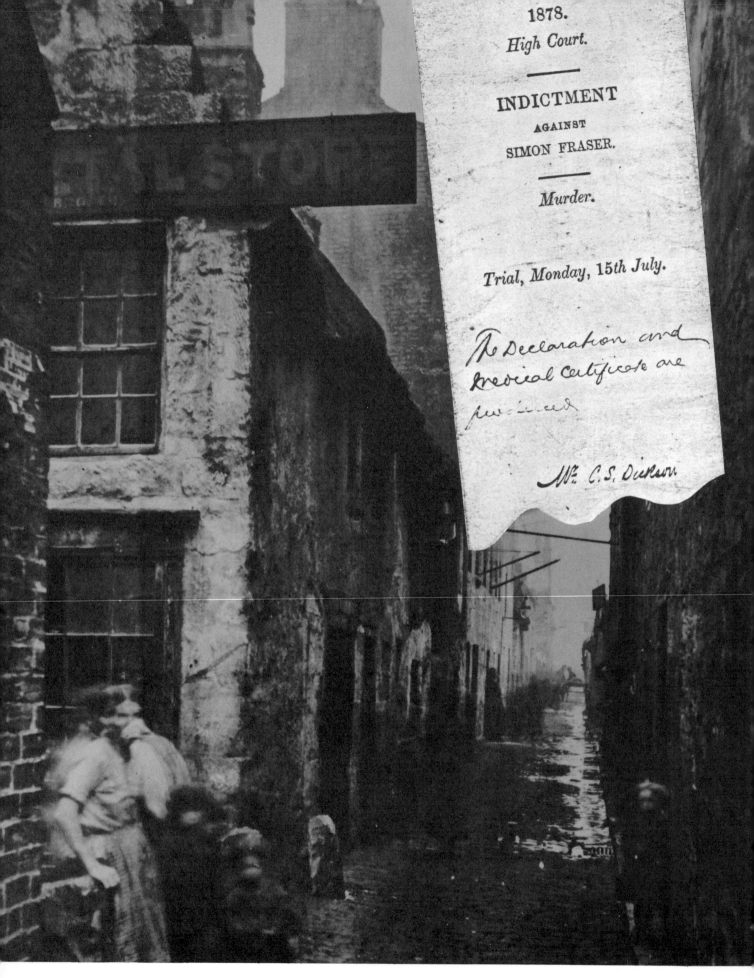

1878.
High Court.

—

INDICTMENT
AGAINST
SIMON FRASER.

—

Murder.

Trial, Monday, 15th July.

*The Declaration and
medical certificate are
produced*

Wm. C. S. Dickson.

NO FATHER could have been more loving or gentle than 27-year-old Simon Fraser, it was stated at his trial. Sometimes his wife used to protest laughingly that he might be spoiling their 18-month-old son. But that did not stop him pampering the boy . . . buying him expensive presents . . . taking such a delight in showing him off to friends and relatives.

Then one night, in a frenzy of violence, he battered the child to death—to save himself from a savage beast which did not exist. Fraser made no secret of it. He ran to fetch neighbours to the blood-spattered room. He told a doctor how he had picked up the peacefully-sleeping infant and smashed his head against a wall. He made a frank and detailed statement to the police. But he considered himself completely innocent. "You see, I was fast asleep at the time," he explained.

That night of savagery, in April 1878, was the bizarre climax to thirteen years of terror for the Fraser family. For the quiet man, the easy-going, home-loving man, who lived in the little terraced house in Lime Street, Glasgow, Scotland, was a sleep-walking psychopath. Evil forces trespassed through his sleep and goaded him to violence. And his son was not his first victim.

Wicked and felonous

On July 15 Fraser was locked in a cell below the High Court of the Justiciary in Edinburgh. As the early routine cases of the day were heard—and the sentences relayed along the warders' grape-vine—his chances of winning leniency seemed hopelessly remote.

"The old man's really hitting them up there today," said one warder. And it certainly did seem as if "the old man"—Lord Moncrieff, the Lord Justice-Clerk—was in a harsh mood. A man called Reynolds admitted having stolen three watch-chains whilst he was drunk. Seven years' penal servitude. Another called Goodwin pleaded guilty to having taken some old iron from a ship. Seven years' penal servitude. Fraser's fears grew as he heard of these sentences. These men's crimes seemed so trivial compared with what he had done.

Then it was his turn. He stared impassively ahead from the dock, not taking his eyes from Lord Moncrieff's face, as the charge was read aloud: ". . . did wickedly and feloniously attack Simon Fraser junior, a child of eighteen months, did seize him violently and did

THE NIGHT brought searing episodes of endless terror to the terraced street where the Frasers lived. Evil forces trespassed in the sleeping family's home, bringing horrific fire, flood . . . and a roaring, violent, psychopathic frenzy.

throw or push him several times against the door or floor or walls of the house and thereby did fracture his skull and lacerate his brain so that he was mortally injured and was thus murdered by the prisoner . . ."

Fraser's voice, flat and drained of emotion, was so low that his answer to the charge could not be heard at the back of the crowded courtroom. People towards the front, who had been queueing since dawn for the best seats, whispered his words back to those behind. "I am not guilty. I am guilty in my sleep but not in my senses."

The prosecution's first witness was Mrs. Janet McEwen, a capable and motherly woman, who lived near the Frasers in Lime Street. At one o'clock on the morning of April 10 she had been awakened by Fraser pounding on her door.

Seized hold of it

"He was wringing his hands and seemed to be in great distress of mind," she said. "He asked me to go and see his bairn. I went with him to his house and saw his wife who was screaming with the child unconscious on her knee. Mr. Fraser was terribly excited and kept calling the child 'my dear' and 'my dear little son'. He wasn't pretending at all. He seemed quite sincere in his distress. I asked him who had done this awful thing and he said: 'It was me that did it, mistress. I did it through my sleep.'"

The Public Prosecutor repeated the key words for the benefit of the jury: "'It was me that did it, mistress.' Now tell me, Mrs. McEwen, did you, at that time, put any further question to the prisoner?"

Janet McEwen nodded. "Aye, that I did. I asked him if he was in the habit of pacing in his sleep. He said he used to do it when he was a boy. Then he told me he thought he'd been dreaming and that he'd thought he'd seen a beast running through the room. It leaped into the bed and he seized hold of it."

She had then ordered Fraser to get a doctor while she stayed to comfort his wife. It seemed there was little she could do to help the baby. Her view was confirmed by Dr. Alexander Jamieson of Main Street, Gorbals, Glasgow, who had been roused by Fraser. "He told me he thought he had killed his child," said Dr. Jamieson. "I found the child Simon in convulsions and he was dying. There was a severe injury on his forehead, such as would be caused by the head being driven against the wall or floor. Fraser told me that, in his nightmare, he had thought the baby was a wild beast. He also said he had been violent before whilst sleep-walking—that he had used violence against his half-sister and his wife."

The baby died at 3.00 a.m. and, once

again, Fraser had rushed from the house to share his burden of grief and fear. This time he had run to near-by Rutherglen Road to wake a man called John Pritchard who worked with him at the local saw-mill. Once again he poured out the same story: "Wee Simon is dead and it is me that is the cause of it."

What sort of father then was Fraser? Pritchard, called to the box, said: "I can tell you the answer to that question without any doubt. We used to go visiting at his house quite a lot and I could see he was very fond of his child—none more so."

This opinion was endorsed by Fraser's father—yet another Simon Fraser—who told the jury: "He is of a kindly disposition and he was extra fond of his wife and child." Mr. Fraser, a big and ungainly man, was uncomfortably aware that he was helping to parade his family's secret shame before the eager public. He shuffled uneasily as he gave evidence on behalf of the prosecution. The prisoner was the child of his first marriage and had been quite well educated, not having left school until he was twelve or thirteen.

"But ever since he was a little one there has been a dullness and stupidness about him," he added. "He could not learn his lessons at school. It was a common thing for him to rise during the night and go through capers."

"Capers?" repeated the Prosecutor. "Could you be a little more specific, Mr. Fraser?"

"How d'you mean?"

"These capers—what form did they take?"

Monstrous hooves

"Well, all sorts, really. Sometimes he supposed the house was on fire and sometimes he was fighting with dogs and horses. They weren't there, if you follow me, but he was fighting with them. When he was in this condition his eyes were open but, having seen him so often in this state, I knew that he was not awake. He spoke but what he said was nonsense."

Then Mr. Fraser described the first time he had been injured by his son. Fraser, at about the age of fourteen, had a vivid nightmare in which a white stallion was stampeding through the house. It was so real, so horrifyingly real. Steaming saliva was dripping from the creature's jaws. Its eyes glowed with hideous green light and its monstrous hooves were shattering the furniture and crushing the unprotected family. Young Fraser, in an agony of desperation, had sprung from his bed to fight the beast. Seconds later, Mr. Fraser woke with blood streaming over his pillow—his demented sleeping son on top of him, punching and clawing at his face. "When he had come to his senses he used always to be ashamed of what he had done," said Mr. Fraser.

But there was always another night, another nightmare, another explosion of violence. "We lived in Norway for a while with my present wife and my daughter Elspeth – she's my daughter by this second marriage. I was over there as the manager of a sawmill. There was one night, I remember, when he went wandering from the house and into the sea in his sleep. It seemed he'd been having this nightmare about her drowning and he was trying to save her."

On another occasion Elspeth woke to find him trying to strangle her – in the belief that she was some wild monster. "He left the marks of his nails on her neck," stated Mr. Fraser.

Tortured mind

So the stories, which had never been told before by the Frasers to protect their family pride, now began to flow. Like how Fraser, in his somnambulistic state, had grabbed his wife by the legs and pulled her out of bed – convinced he was saving her from a fire which was blazing only in his tortured mind..

The Public Prosecutor then put a question which was already intriguing many people in the court. "Tell me, Mr. Fraser, did your son ever harm himself on these occasions?"

"Just once," came the reply. "That was when he was jumping over a bed and broke his toe."

But the pain, apparently, had not woken him. The only explanation seemed to be that Fraser's brain, if it registered the pain at all, translated it as being part of the nightmare. This could have made it even more imperative for him to use all the brute strength he could muster to kill whatever monster was haunting him on that particular night.

Still more evidence of Fraser's sleep-walking habits came from his step-mother, Mrs. Elspeth Fraser. She was a woman who had always treated him with great affection and understanding. Even after his attacks on her daughter she had tried to comfort him and help him. "I tried to cure him of his habit by putting tubs of water by his bedside so that when he stepped into them he might wake up."

This was not always effective. There were also times when Fraser jumped over the tubs. "On April 9, just a few hours before that . . . that thing . . . happened, he and his wife and baby came to see me," she continued. "He was quite steady and all right at that time. He is a man who can take a dram, but I've never seen him the worse for drink."

The next time she saw him was in the early hours of the following morning. He had run to fetch her after getting the doctor. All the witnesses so far – although called by the prosecution to help prove the case of murder – had shown some sympathy for Fraser. The next witness, however, did not try to disguise her loathing for Fraser. She was his mother-in-law, Mrs. Elizabeth Parker of Dundee, and she could not forgive the horror he had unwittingly brought to her daughter. She had loved her grandson, and this grotesque man in the dock had killed him.

She had stayed at the Frasers' house in Glasgow for just one night – and, during that night, Fraser had slept through one of his bouts of violence. He had thought there was a mad dog in the house and he had shrieked aloud as he had tried to kill it. "I was so frightened that I left the next day," Mrs. Parker stated.

The Prosecutor looked keenly at her. "Do you consider him to be a stupid man?" he asked.

Mrs. Parker glanced at Fraser and then picked her words with elaborate care: "Perhaps it was his want of education that made him seem a little droll."

Controversial stage

At this stage the foreman of the jury rose to say that he and his colleagues felt there was little point in hearing any more evidence. They were all agreed that Fraser was not responsible for what he had done. Lord Moncrieff considered the suggestion for a moment before replying: "I quite agree with you but I think the testimony of one or two medical men would be desirable."

It was then clear to the prosecution that they were not going to secure a conviction for murder. So the Public Prosecutor, after a hurried discussion with his advocate-deputy, decided to concentrate on a slightly different aspect.

INSANE OR NOT? If a man's whole life seems to be hypnotized by an endless kaleidoscope of nightmares, should he be judged as mad? Should he be locked up in the great grey castle of lunacy that serves as the local asylum? The evidence confounded superintendent Dr. Yellowlees.

Declaration of Simon Fraser 10ᵗʰ April 1878

At Glasgow the tenth day of April eighteen hundred and seventy eight years In presence of Alexander Erskine Murray Esquire Advocate, Sheriff Substitute of Lanarkshire Compeared a prisoner and the charge against him having been read over and explained to him and he having been judicially ad-monished and examined, Declares and says: My name is Simon Fraser, I am a native of Aberdeen 28 years of age a Saw Sharper and I reside at 44 Lime Street Glasgow. I have been subject to rising in my sleep since I was ten years old. Last night I, my wife and my child J S Fraser

N Erskine Murray

child Simon Fraser — now deceased an infant not quite 18 months old were in bed in my said house. I thought that I saw a white beast flying through the floor and round to the back of the bed where the child was. I tried to catch at the said beast, and I caught something which I believed to be the beast and I got out of the bed and dashed it on the floor or against the door. I woke up in consequence of my wife crying and then I found that it was the child I had had in my hands, instead of a beast, and that the child was very severely injured. — S Fraser

A Erskine Murray

And the trial moved into its most controversial stage.

Should a man who acts violently while in the grip of a nightmare be considered medically insane—and therefore be locked away in a lunatic asylum? That was the proposition now being put before the court. The Public Prosecutor was determined that—one way or another—Fraser would never again be free. It was a question that could only be answered by an expert—Dr. Yellowlees, the superintendent of a local asylum.

The doctor, stoop-shouldered and scholarly, told the court that he had examined Fraser. He then waited to answer the prosecution's questions.

"What do you consider to be the nature of the case from a medical point of view?"

"I think somnambulism is a state of unhealthy brain activity coming on during sleep of very varying intensity—sometimes little more than restless sleep, sometimes developing into delusions and violence and amounting really to insanity. This man labours under somnambulism in its most aggravated form."

Bluntly aggressive

"Do you attribute his condition to a mental disorder?"

"To the abnormal condition of the brain. That is the case in every instance of delusion, even where there is no insanity."

The Public Prosecutor paused before putting the next question. He wanted to get the phrasing exactly right. "I suppose," he said, "I suppose there is no doubt that a person in such a state as this is as unconscious of the actuality of the thing which he is doing as a person who is insane?"

He shouted the final, crucial word. The doctor, aware of the line of attack, did not disappoint him. "Quite as unconscious," he responded. "The word 'insane' describes his condition or nature."

Mr. C. S. Dickson, defending Fraser, was clearly concerned by the evidence. During a spirited session of cross-examination he tried to force the doctor to change his mind about the accuracy of the word "insane" in the context, and eventually won the grudging admission: "I thought him below average intelligence certainly, but he was practically sane when I examined him."

That, for Dickson, was a step in the right direction. But it was not nearly a big enough step. If he could not get Yellowlees to retract completely the damaging word, he had no alternative but to try to discredit Yellowlees himself. Was the doctor an authority on somnambulism? he wanted to know.

Yellowlees looked uncomfortable and made no reply. Let the question be put again. It was a very simple one. Was the doctor an authority on somnambulism—or was he not?

"I have no experience of somnambulism," confessed Yellowlees grudgingly. "That is to say I have not seen a man in his condition."

Dickson was satisfied. He was confident that he could now persuade the jury to discount the so-called "expert opinion". The next doctor called by the prosecution, however, was a far more dominant personality. Alex Robertson—physician and surgeon at Glasgow's City Poorhouse and at the City Parochial Asylum—was a squat and bluntly aggressive man, supremely confident in his own infallibility. His voice was loud and firm as he opened with a categorical statement which threatened to prove vital in any consideration of Fraser's future:

"I have had considerable experience of abnormal conditions of the brain. I know the facts of this case and I am of the opinion that the prisoner was insane when he committed this act."

He was equally adamant throughout his examination by the Public Prosecutor. Could he put the prisoner's condition in the category of a disease?

"Certainly. It most nearly approaches mania. The fact that he roared, that he was violent and dangerous, that he had extravagant delusions under excitement—along with the unconsciousness of the act—in my opinion constitutes insanity." Then, to ensure that the jury completely understood his viewpoint, he added: "It is my opinion that this somnambulism was just short fits of insanity that came on during sleep. In medical parlance there is no name for this particular kind of delusion. It is altogether exceptional."

Contrasted starkly

It began to look more and more certain that Dr. Robertson's Parochial Asylum would soon have one additional inmate. "Thank you, doctor," said the Public Prosecutor. "Now would you please tell the court in what respect does somnambulism differ from a dream—except in degree?"

"A dreamer fancies he sees and feels objects, but this man really *did* see and feel."

"What do you mean by 'really did see'? Do you mean that he saw a thing that was not in existence?"

"He saw and felt a child in reality and mistook it for a beast."

Robertson was too tough to be shaken by the defence. He stuck to his opinion. Fraser was a victim of insanity. So that was the case for the prosecution. Only one witness was to be called for the defence—a Dr. Clouston of Morningside, Edinburgh. He contrasted starkly with Robertson. He was a slight, anxious man who coughed nervously as he took the oath, and who glanced at his notes as he addressed the court.

"I had an interview with the prisoner for an hour yesterday and for ten minutes today," he said. "I have heard the history of the case and I could not detect any symptoms of unsoundness of mind or insanity. However, I consider that the prisoner was the subject, while asleep, of somnambulism. Intellectually I found him to be a man of fair judgment for his education. His memory is not good but he seemed a particularly affectionate man."

Clouston consulted his notes. "One thing struck me very much in my conversations with him. I asked him if he felt very much over the death of his child and he said that he had but, as his wife had felt it so much more, he had concealed his own feelings and appeared calm for her sake."

Normal, loving man

This was seized upon by the defence as an indication of the intrinsic good in Fraser. Even in his own agony of mind, he was still concerned for the feelings of those he loved. Did this sound like a man who was tainted by insanity? Or did it sound like the generous and protective response of a normal, loving man? And that time he had plunged into the sea to save the sister he had genuinely believed to be drowning—did that give the same picture of a man who was basically caring and sane? Anyway, was the case *really* so unusual? Had not other people reacted in an uncharacteristic style while under the domination of a nightmare—without being labelled as insane?

Clouston reassured the jury that Fraser was not such an exception as they might have been tempted to think. "I once had a case similar to this one," he said. "It was the case of a missionary connected with the church in Yorkshire. He was a most respectable man in every way. He had been in ill-health and on one occasion in a town whither he had gone for a change he went to see a wax-works display which made a great impression on his imagination.

"He was especially struck by the figure of some murdered person. He went home and went early to bed that night. His wife came into the room about an hour afterwards and he started up, thinking she was a robber coming to rob his house. He would have throttled her if a neighbour had not come to the rescue."

The Public Prosecutor was now eager to start his cross-examination, eager to steer Clouston towards considering the possibility of Fraser's insanity. "Why may a man not be insane although the fit only comes on him while he is asleep?" he asked.

"I should say that the condition is

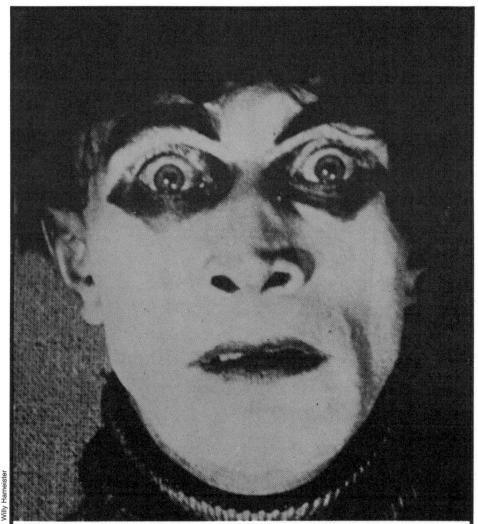

Willy Hameister

CESARE'S DEADLY DAWN

ON A mild October evening in 1913 the young Czech writer, Hans Janowitz, was strolling through a fair in Hamburg looking for a girl who had previously appealed to him. He thought he heard her laughing in some shrubbery, investigated, but only caught a glimpse of what he later called "the shadowy figure of an average bourgeois". The next day he read in the local paper of the TERRIBLE SEX CRIME AT THE FAIR—LOCAL GIRL MURDERED. Six years later—together with a young German story-editor, Carl Mayer—he used his experience as the basis for the classic film dealing with a sleepwalking slayer, *The Cabinet of Dr. Caligari*.

The film—which was a sensation in Europe, Great Britain, and North America—tells of a mysterious fairground barker, Dr. Caligari, and the somnambulist he manages, Cesare—played by Conrad Veidt. Awakened daily from his trance, Cesare predicts the time of death of anyone who asks him. Standing in an upright coffinlike box he tells one young student that he will only live "until tomorrow's dawn". Sure enough, the student is found dead early the following morning, and Caligari and Cesare—who is dominated by his master's hypnotic power—are suspected of the crime.

Seizing the girlfriend of the dead student, Cesare seeks refuge in the local lunatic asylum (the film is set in a fictitious North German town), and it is in the asylum that the story comes to a shocking, but weirdly logical, ending. Intended as an attack upon the "upside down" Germany of the years after World War One, *Caligari* is one of the few horror films to pose the question: can people kill in their sleep?

Its answer is blunted by psychiatry, the revelation of the true "madman", and a statement by the Director of the Asylum: "At last I understand the nature of his madness . . . Now I see how he can be brought to sanity again."

physiological, during which the brain rests. Hitherto the medical profession has not called anything occurring during sleep 'insanity'."

"Is there not ground for holding that the delusions of a man in a state of insanity should not fall within the category of insanity?"

Clouston coughed again and the court awaited his reply. He dabbed a handkerchief at his mouth. "It may at some future time," he said. "It has not been so reckoned yet. There is merely an abnormal condition of the brain producing delusion and violence."

"Is that not just the same as insanity?" the Public Prosecutor pursued.

The defending counsel, angered by this pressure on his witness, rose to protest but, before he could speak, the doctor was already replying: "We do not regard it as such. A sane man may have delusions during sleep which, while sleep lasts, he believes are true. In that state he is not morally responsible when that develops into action because he is not conscious of the true nature of what he is doing."

Labouring under delusion

Lord Moncrieff felt that the court had now heard quite enough. He told the jury he supposed they had "not the slightest doubt that when this unhappy and lamentable event took place, the prisoner—who is certainly to be pitied—was totally unconscious of the act". He went on: "There seems to be not the slightest doubt that when he was labouring under this delusion he was in a state of somnambulism and acting under the belief that he was trying to kill a beast.

"It is a matter of some consequence to the prisoner whether he is considered to be insane or simply as not responsible. His future might be, to a great extent, dependent on the verdict you might return on the question of whether the state of somnambulism, such as this, is considered a state of insanity or not."

There, finally, was the core of the matter. Was Fraser to be allowed to go free? Or was he to be committed to an asylum for the insane? The decision rested with the jury. Lord Moncrieff, for their guidance, suggested the verdict:

"The jury unanimously find that the prisoner killed his child when he was unconscious of the act by reason of a condition of somnambulism, and that the prisoner was not responsible for his act at the time."

The jury did not retire and, after less than a minute of whispering among themselves, their foreman announced that they were prepared to accept the terms of the verdict without any reservation. Not a word about insanity. Not a chance of Fraser going to an asylum.

The Glasgow News.

GLASGOW TUESDAY, JULY 16, 1878.

PRICE ONE PENNY.

Mr. EVANS, Inns of Court, gained the Armourers Prize ; and the winner of the Rifle Oaks is Sergeant-Major TAIT, 3rd Renfrew, with 34 points—Private CALDWELL, 1st Renfrew, being third in the competition with 33 points.

In the High Court of Justiciary yesterday, SIMON FRASER was tried for having, in his house at Lime Street, South Side, Glasgow, murdered his child by striking it against the floor or walls of the house. The contention of the defence was that accused, at the time he committed the act, was in a somnambulistic fit, and imagined that he was destroying a wild beast which had come into the room and attacked him. The jury, by direction of the LORD JUSTICE-CLERK, returned a verdict finding FRASER guilty, but not responsible, and sentence was deferred.

The show of the Royal Agricultural Society of England at Bristol closed yesterday. The aggregate attendance has been 121,851, as against 163,145 at Birmingham, and 138,031 at Liverpool.

For the first time in the trial, Fraser showed signs of emotion. Through all the evidence and the legal wrangling he had been almost expressionless. Staring straight ahead most of the time as though he were somehow detached from everything around him. Now came just the hint of a smile, and he rubbed his left eye with the back of his hand. The courtroom ordeal was over. In just a few minutes he would again be a free man.

But it was not to be quite so simple. The Public Prosecutor had the attention of the court—and he was asking for the case to be adjourned, for Fraser to be kept in custody. Fraser heard him say:

"In consequence of the verdict it seems to me that the most advisable course would be to adjourn the case for a short time so that possibly some arrangement can be come to with those who are responsible for the prisoner to see that the public are kept safe."

Lord Moncrieff agreed. When the hearing was resumed two days later he announced that the Public Prosecutor had come to "a special arrangement with the prisoner and his family which might have the effect of guarding against any possible repetition of such a disaster." He then acquitted Fraser and told him: "It is right to impress upon you that you are bound to take every possible means of curing yourself of this unfortunate and involuntary habit which has already landed you in so much misery."

And what was the special "arrange-

AN HISTORICALLY BIZARRE murder case, beasts and all, is summarily recorded for posterity in the grey type between a shooting match and a livestock show.

ment"? The lawyers refused to reveal it. So did Fraser and his family. But neighbours in Lime Street were later confident that they knew. For the rest of his life Simon Fraser was a free man by day. But he slept alone—in a room locked from the outside. His wife kept the key.

Women loved him. He was handsome, extravagant and dressed with eye-catching elegance. But the hotel he built across the street was not exactly what it appeared. For inside was a maze of secret passages and torture chambers!

CASTLE OF DEATH

TIP-OFF about the deadly activities of Holmes came from train robber Marion Hedgepath (left). The Chicago World's Fair of 1893 (top left) inspired the building of Holmes's infamous hotel. Trial judge was Michael Arnold (above).

A PROFOUND silence lay over the main hall of Moyamensing Prison, Philadelphia, despite the fact that more than a hundred people—journalists, policemen, and officials—were nervously assembled there. A shaft of sunlight, slanting through a lofty window, shone on the leaden coloured beam of the gallows which stood in the centre of the hall. Sparrows in the yard outside were clearly audible.

It was eight minutes past ten on the morning of Wednesday, May 7, 1896, and the tense crowd were waiting to witness the death of the man who had been described as "America's First Mass Murderer". He was known nationwide by his pseudonym, H. H. Holmes, and in one admission had claimed to have killed 27 people in his Chicago death house: by police estimates it was nearer 200.

Few words

Holmes stood at the railings around the raised gallows exhibiting all the calm of an after-dinner speaker. He wore an old-fashioned grey-brown tweed suit with a double-breasted waistcoat, and apart from his lack of collar and tie he might have stepped from the doorway of an exclusive men's club. His voice was low and firm when he spoke, but it echoed around every corner of the hushed hall.

"Gentlemen," he said, "I have very few words to say. In fact I would make no remarks at all at this time were it not for my feeling that by not speaking I would acquiesce in my execution by hanging."

Someone coughed, and Holmes paused in his speech. Then he went on: "I wish to say at this instant that the extent of my misdoings in taking human life con-

sists in the killing of two women. They died by my hand as a result of criminal operations. I only state this so that there shall be no misunderstanding of my words hereafter.

"I am not guilty of taking the lives of the Pitezel family, the three children or the father, Benjamin F. Pitezel, for whose death I am now to be hanged. I think that is all I have to say."

Very quietly Holmes stepped back and positioned himself immediately over the trap. His face, spectators noted, was totally impassive, and his final statement had not helped to unravel the complex skein of seduction, double-dealing, and murder which had been his life during the past few years.

Sinister stories

His trail, painstakingly uncovered by detectives, led from Fort Worth in Texas, to Toronto, through St. Louis and Philadelphia, to an extraordinary building on the outskirts of Chicago which he used as a torture house-cum-murder factory. The route was littered at every turn with tales of fraud, and with more sinister

stories of women who had been seen with Holmes only to vanish completely.

Holmes had been arrested in November 1894, following a complicated insurance swindle in which he had claimed money after the apparently accidental death of a colleague, B. F. Pitezel. Investigating the fraud, police came to the conclusion that Pitezel had been murdered by Holmes, and it was on this charge that he was tried and found guilty in Philadelphia. While in jail awaiting execution, Holmes had written his flowery "I killed 27 people" confession. Now, seconds from death, boastfulness deserted him . . .

Highly attractive

The name "Holmes" was one of several aliases used by the young man who was born Herman Webster Mudgett on May 16, 1860, in the village of Gilmanton, New Hampshire. His father, Levi H. Mudgett, had been the village postmaster, but was eager that young Herman should rise in the world. Accordingly he attended Gilmanton Academy, where he graduated with honours before becoming a schoolteacher. In 1882, Herman went to Burlington to study medicine at the University of Vermont, after which he was briefly apprenticed to a doctor, and the following year enrolled at the medical college of the University of Michigan at Ann Arbor—where he was awarded a Doctorate of Medicine in 1884.

For a few short months, Mudgett practised as a doctor in Mooers Fork, New York, and then gave it up; it was to be the first and only spell of honest and non-lethal work of his adult life.

Besides intelligence, Mudgett was blessed with wholesome, upright good looks – a vital asset for a would-be seducer and con-man. He had thick, dark hair which receded slightly as he approached 30, giving him an even more distinguished appearance; heavy, pleasantly-arched eyebrows; keen brown eyes; an aristocratic nose, and a neatly kept walrus moustache.

He habitually dressed in the manner of a Victorian family physician, choosing tweedy "gentleman's" suits with square cut waistcoats; his shoes were always highly polished and a heavy gold watch chain hung from his fob pocket. In short Herman Mudgett was a handsome figure of a man, highly attractive to women.

Mudgett married for the first time on July 4, 1878, while he was still a student. His bride, a pretty young woman named Clara Lovering, was a native of Alton, New Hampshire, not far from the Mudgett family home. For the first few years of their life together, the couple were outwardly happy and doted on their bonny baby son.

But stable married life was not for the handsome, virile doctor. In 1886 he left Clara Lovering and her child and headed for Chicago, arriving there in the late spring. Looking around for prospects in the windy city, Mudgett met a dark, attractive young woman named Myrta Belknap whose family owned considerable property in Wilmette, Illinois.

Desperate for cash

If the lady's looks were not already sufficient attraction for him, her money was, and in the following year Mudgett married Myrta – bigamously – under the name H. H. Holmes. He then set out to swindle her great uncle Jonathan Belknap.

Holmes could not, of course, practise medicine, as his diploma was in his real name. But he managed to convince Mr. Belknap that he was well-to-do, and borrowed enough money from him to build a house for himself and Myrta; a short while afterwards, Holmes began his career of fraud by forging Jonathan's check for $2500.

It was obvious that even at this juncture, Holmes's murderous instinct was coming to the fore. A short time before the fraud was discovered, he invited old Jonathan Belknap up onto the roof of the new house. "If I'd gone," recalled the old man years afterwards, "the forgery probably wouldn't have been discovered, because I wouldn't have been around to discover it. But I didn't go. I'm afraid of heights."

After the forgery there was a rift between Holmes and the Belknap family, although the latter – disliking the thought of publicity – did not prosecute. Myrta, however, was still completely under his spell, and stood by the man she called her husband. But Holmes was becoming desperate for cash, and he began casting around again for opportunities. One day he saw a job as a chemist advertised in a local newspaper and, investigating, found the prospect appealing.

The job was in a store owned by a recently widowed Mrs. Holden, on the corner of 63rd Street and Wallace, Englewood – then a suburb of Chicago across the city from Wilmette. Holmes turned on his charm with Mrs. Holden, spouted his medical knowledge to her, and was hired. He also impressed Mrs. Holden with his grasp of figures. A few months after taking the job business was booming, and the handsome young pharmacist was attracting women from considerable distances to the shop.

Long holiday

Apparently, the Englewood job began in 1888 or perhaps later – like much of Holmes's life the record is somewhat obscure – but by 1890 Mrs. Holden had become slightly less than satisfied with the way Holmes was taking over the reins of her business. She talked vaguely to friends of embezzlement, rigged books, and so on. Then, quite suddenly, she vanished. Holmes met all inquiries with a polite blandness. Mrs. Holden, he announced, had decided to take a "long holiday" in California – a holiday from which she never returned.

If the neighbours suspected anything amiss about the disappearance of Mrs. Holden, they kept it to themselves. One of the most curious features of Holmes's character was that he was able to soothe away suspicion even under the most sinister circumstances. "His" business continued to thrive, boosted by the mail order sale of worthless patent medicines of his own devising.

By this time, he had tired of the faithful Myrta Belknap – whose family fortunes were now beyond his grasp – and he moved permanently into an apartment above the store in Englewood, where he entertained various girlfriends. Soon after he had settled into the apartment, Icilius Conner came into Holmes's life.

Gothic structure

Conner, a jeweller from Davenport, Iowa, was looking for somewhere to set up in business, and Holmes accommodated him in part of the drugstore. He was motivated not by any sudden generosity, but by the fact that Conner was accompanied by two attractive women, Mrs. Julia Conner, a "comely and sportive" lady, and Conner's 18-year-old sister Gertie. The Conners also had an 8-year-old daughter named Pearl.

While Conner worked at his jewellery, his wife Julia acted as secretary for Holmes, running the mail order business and leaving the doctor free to concentrate on an ambitious construction project that had been in his mind for some time.

Opposite the drugstore in Englewood was a huge vacant plot of land, 50 feet wide by 162 feet long. Holmes knew that the Columbian Exposition – the first Chicago World's Fair – was scheduled for 1893, and that thousands of people were due to visit the city. He bought the plot at 63rd and Wallace Streets, under the pseudonym H. S. Campbell, and began to build a hotel: a Gothic structure of brick and timber which became notorious as "Holmes's Castle".

It was a prodigious undertaking, planned, in view of later events, with what the police described as "fiendish cunning". To oversee the main construction job, Holmes employed a partner, a shiftless con-man named Benjamin Fuller Pitezel, who had drifted into Englewood with his wife, several small children, and an eye open for any "operation" or "deal" which would make quick and easy money.

Through Pitezel, various building and carpentry firms were employed, one after another, each working to plans drawn up by Holmes himself. The use of numerous builders was largely for financial reasons – Holmes exhausted his credit with one company and then employed a second and a third. But it also meant that in the end only Holmes knew the exact layout of the bizarre "castle".

Winding corridors

When complete, in the spring of 1891, Holmes's castle filled the entire lot and stood two stories high, with a basement and cellar beneath. Its upper stories, topped with sham turrets and battlements, contained almost a hundred rooms interlinked by winding corridors, trapdoors and windowless alcoves. Investigation later showed that some were lined with iron or asbestos, some were airtight and fitted with gas inlets, some had bolts only on the outsides of their doors, and others were connected to the basement by chutes and elevators.

On the ground floor was a row of shops which Holmes let to local tradesmen, and his own office; a system of electric buzzers connected to the switchboard there told him of the movements of anyone in the building above him.

A number of awkward incidents during the building of the castle stretched Holmes's ingenuity to the limit. On one occasion, after having ordered loads of expensive furniture and fittings, he found himself unable to pay the bill and the company attempted to repossess its property. But bailiffs searched the building in vain; the property had vanished, and it was only after bribing a janitor that they learned the secret – Holmes had piled the furnishings into one room and then sealed the door and papered it over.

A firm of locksmiths was not so lucky. Holmes ordered a large safe from them and installed it at the castle. When payment was not forthcoming, the company demanded the safe, only to find that Holmes had made the doorway of the room in which it reposed smaller, so that the safe could not be extracted without knocking down part of the wall. Holmes threatened that if the company's workmen damaged his building while regaining the safe, he would sue. The safe stayed where it was.

Hundreds of guests

As soon as the castle and its "extras" were ready for use, Holmes moved in, taking with him Julia Conner, her daughter Pearl, and her voluptuous sister-in-law Gertie. Some time before, Holmes had had a row with Icilius Conner, the cause being Holmes's flagrant adultery with his wife. The row ended with Mr. Conner vanishing. Whether he had become the first victim of Holmes's castle, or whether he had gone back to Iowa, was not established. But in either event Holmes, as usual, glibly explained away the disappearance to inquirers.

The details of Holmes's career over the next year or two were vague, contradictory, but decidedly sinister. Police who were prompted to investigate the castle at the time of Holmes's trial found that, according to neighbours, it was Gertie Conner who disappeared next. Julia was becoming more and more possessive of Holmes, and she and Pearl vanished for good in the summer of 1892.

At about this time Holmes struck up a relationship with a girl named Emiline Cigrand, from Dwight, Illinois. Then when Emiline duly went missing, he explained to anyone interested that she had "entered a convent".

Later, witnesses testified that during the period of the World's Fair, hundreds of "guests", mostly women, had stayed at Holmes's "hotel"—and that many of them were not seen to leave. "It was as if they had spent their lives in travelling towards and then reaching the building," said one neighbour. "They did not always get out of it alive—but that was part of the fate which drew them there in the first place."

If Holmes's business dealings were deplored by those "conned" into dealing with him or his partner Pitezel, he was not generally suspected of anything more than sharp practice at this point. He was still able to put on a romantic front for the young women who fell into his

TORTURE CHAMBERS abounded in the house on 63rd Street. Searchers (shown right in contemporary prints) found room after room containing murder devices. It was like a medieval fantasy.

A TRAP IN A CLOSET

E. ALICE PITEZEL   HOWARD PITEZEL   BENJ

MINNIE WILLIAMS   H. HOLMES. THE ACCUSE

F. PITEZEL

NELLIE PITEZEL

NANNIE WILLIAMS

clutches — women such as Minnie R. Williams, an orphan from Mississippi who, along with her younger sister Nannie and her brother Harold, had in 1892 inherited a fortune of between 20,000 and 50,000 dollars.

Holmes told Minnie that he was a wealthy property dealer and she soon became a resident at the deadly castle. When he heard of her sister Nannie's share of the fortune, he invited the younger girl to stay in Chicago. As a lure he promised that he would take her and Minnie on a protracted trip to New York and Paris, as well as making arrangements for Nannie to study art.

Nannie wrote a letter to her brother Harold, excitedly recounting all these plans, and exhorting him "not to worry about her or Minnie any more". No trace of Nannie was ever discovered after the posting of the letter.

Beautiful blonde

As the Chicago Fair drew to a close, custom began to drop off at the "hotel" and Holmes again turned his hand to various frauds, juggling one deal against the other with consummate skill. Pitezel did not fare as well; on one occasion he was jailed for fraud in Terre Haute, Indiana, until a well-dressed Congressman from that state bailed him out. The "Congressman" was Holmes, and naturally enough the check was forged.

Returning to Chicago, Holmes tried to revitalize his mail order business, and also became involved for a short while in the marketing of a copying machine. But the income from these ventures was not enough to meet his numerous outgoings; he tried to claim insurance by setting fire to the roof of his castle, but an astute insurance inspector thought that the $6000 claim "smelled", and no payment was made.

By November 1893 life in Chicago had become too devious even for Holmes, and he and Minnie quit the city, heading south. En route he met a beautiful blonde named Georgiana Yoke, the possessor of a shapely figure, eyes "so big they were almost disfiguring", and money of her own. Holmes introduced himself to her as Henry Mansfield Howard, a patents broker, and married her bigamously — both his other "wives" were living — after a short courtship. Poor Minnie, like her sister before her, disappeared from record at around this time.

But Minnie's property in Fort Worth, Texas, was still prominent in Holmes's mind; he and B. F. Pitezel travelled there

JUST A FEW of the victims of mass murderer Holmes arrayed round him (left) in a sinister halo. Even his fellow-swindler and partner in crime, Benjamin Pitezel, was not safe from Holmes greed.

and launched into a highly complex deal involving bank drafts, property, and live-stock, so swindling a small firm of lawyers out of a few thousand dollars.

The main result of the Fort Worth operation was that it involved Holmes in a charge of horse stealing—the most heinous offence that a man could commit in the Lone Star state in the days when the old Frontier was still technically thriving. If Holmes had been caught he would probably have been lynched. Even at the time of his trial in Philadelphia he quailed visibly at the prospect of being sent back to Fort Worth.

Insurance swindle

Leaving Texas, Pitezel and Holmes headed for St. Louis, Missouri, where they launched into yet another swindle. This time Holmes's over-expanded luck snapped, and he was jailed on a minor check charge. Somehow he managed to convince Georgiana—a highly respectable girl who had no knowledge of her "hus-band's" skulduggery—that the whole thing had been a "dreadful mistake", and she bailed him out.

But, while languishing in jail, Holmes had in fact made the mistake that was eventually to hang him. He shared a cell with a small-time train robber named Marion Hedgepath, and told him of an insurance swindle which he and Pitezel intended to pull off. He asked Hedgepath

MODERN MAN associates "horror castles" with the fantasy world of the cinema. But Holmes turned imagination into reality—with terrifying effect.

to recommend a crooked lawyer, in return for which Hedgepath was to receive $500 on completion of the coup. When Holmes failed to pay up, Hedgepath went to the police. . . .

The basis of the scheme was that Pitezel, under an assumed name, should set up as a patents broker in Philadelphia. His wife would insure his life for $40,000 with the Fidelity Mutual Life Assurance Company, and then he and Holmes would stage an accident, using a corpse stolen from a mortuary, and claim the money.

Accordingly, in the late summer of 1894, a body, badly burnt—apparently as the result of an explosion—was found in the city. However, the victim really turned out to be Pitezel—Holmes and Pitezel's elder daughter Alice identified him. Fidelity Mutual paid up: and then Hedgepath, the train robber, came forward with his story.

Holmes's flight from the police during the next few months was, as the Phila-delphia District Attorney said later, "an inspired piece of generalship". He travel-led from city to city with Mrs. Pitezel, her five children, and Georgiana, in three groups: Holmes and Georgiana; Mrs. Pitezel and her two younger children; and

the three elder children—Alice, Nellie, and Howard. Then somewhere along the line the three elder children disappeared. Alice and Nellie were later found together in a shallow grave dug in the cellar of a house rented by Holmes, and a few charred bones—which it was claimed were Howard's—were discovered in an incinerator in a house also known to have been used by the doctor.

But the Philadelphia police—following the trail of fraud, deceit, and butchery—finally caught him. Holmes was brought back and first charged with embezzle-ment, then with the murder of Pitezel. At his trial he proved to have a shrewd grasp of the law, and masterfully questioned witnesses for the prosecution—who in-cluded Mrs. Carrie Pitezel and Georgiana Yoke. Unfortunately for him he was labouring against the detectives of more than one city.

Surgical equipment

Inspired by the example of the Philly colleagues, the Chicago police raided Holmes's deserted castle and found the bones of several women in the basement and cellar, along with trays of surgical equipment and instruments of torture. There was a modified rack, said to have been used by him in attempting to prove a theory that the human body could be stretched indefinitely.

There were vats of acid, two greased chutes connected the upper floors with the basement; there were peepholes and asbestos-padded rooms; windowless rooms lined with sheet iron. There was also the evidence of Charles Chopmen, a Chicago mechanic, who told how Hol-mes had given him the gruesome task of stripping the flesh from three bodies and articulating the skeletons for sale to medical schools. He had been paid $36 per body—all three of which, Holmes had told him, had come from the city mortuary.

The newspapers gloatingly reported all these details in full. Despite the judge's warning that Holmes was on trial for only one murder the jury was not unaffected by the lurid stories.

Holmes then embraced the Roman Catholic faith while in the death cell. Two priests accompanied him to the scaffold, and knelt with him in prayer on the trap after his address to the onlookers. He thanked them, and to the assistant chief warden of Moyamensing Prison, who adjusted the noose around his neck, he said: "Make it quick!"

The warden obliged him. An eyewitness reported: "The trap fell with a crash . . . Holmes's body dropped six feet, re-bounded in the air, and then whirled around rapidly to the right, his head lean-ing sharply over on his shoulder . . . the legs made walking movements for a while, and then were still."

DOCTOR DEATH

The ex-mayor of Villeneuve-sur-Yonne seemed a respectable doctor who had worked against the Gestapo. But his house reeked of burning flesh . . .!

Quartet

THE TRIAL of Dr. Marcel Petiot which began on March 18, 1946, was, next to the liberation, the greatest event in post-war France. People had been starved of excitement during the German occupation, and their appetite was whetted by lurid stories of Petiot's activities. All the papers carried horrific details of the discoveries at 21 rue Lesueur, which helped to create a sensational atmosphere.

When Petiot's well-groomed figure appeared at the Seine Assize Court he was greeted like a film star. Crowds pushed and fought to catch a glimpse of him and the press cameras clicked and flashed. Marcel Petiot was news and he enjoyed every minute of it, adjusting his tie and smiling for the photographers.

Foul smoke

The indictment against him contained the names of the 27 persons whose bodies had been found at Petiot's "death house", 21 rue Lesueur. The discovery had been made two years earlier, when a badly smoking chimney directed attention to the house. With the revelation that the smoke resulted from the burning of flesh, the story quickly became headline news.

On Saturday, March 11, 1944, the foul-smelling smoke belched all day from the chimney of No. 21 rue Lesueur, a side street in the fashionable Etoile district. Mme Marçais, the occupier of No. 22, was annoyed by the stench, and the greasy smuts which settled on her furniture even with the windows closed. The smoke did not lessen and by early evening her husband, fearing that the chimney might catch fire, rang the bell at No. 21. There was no reply so he telephoned the police.

Gendarmes soon arrived and they found out that the tenant of No. 21 was a Dr. Marcel Petiot who lived nearby. The doctor was contacted. He said he would come at once with the keys.

After kicking their heels for half an hour the police could wait no longer. They called the fire brigade who quickly forced an entry to the house. Guided by the appalling smell, the firemen reached the basement where they found the source of the offensive smoke—a boiler fuelled with human corpses.

The floor around the boiler was littered with bits of bodies: arms and legs, some with the flesh stripped from them, and corpses in every state of dismemberment. While the police stood about open-mouthed with shock, Dr. Petiot arrived at the house. He did not reveal his identity. Rapidly assessing the situation and gesturing towards the basement, he said to one of the gendarmes, "What you see there are Germans and traitors."

He declared that he was a member of the Resistance and was in fear of the Gestapo. The mere mention of the dreaded Gestapo made the policeman flinch and he let Petiot go without question.

A thorough search of the premises revealed an outhouse containing a heap of lime-covered corpses. Inside the house was a medical consulting room joined by a passage to a mysterious, triangular-shaped room. This had thick, soundproof walls, a false door and a spyhole. Its purpose in the death house could be imagined—but Dr. Petiot was not available to answer for it.

While Petiot was being hunted, the gruesome remains at the house were examined by doctors. They had 34 recognizable limbs to work on, a number of scalps, some with hair attached, bone fragments and 33 lbs. of charred remains.

The experts were unable to state either the time or the manner of death, but the technique for dismemberment had been the same in every case. The collar bone, shoulder bone, and arm had been removed in one piece—indisputably the work of a skilled dissector.

Petiot was not found until November 1944. It had not been difficult to lie low during the turmoil of the last days of the occupation and the liberation of France. The doctor helped the detectives by revealing himself. He wrote a letter to the paper, *Résistance,* refuting a claim that he had been a pro-Nazi collaborator. His patriotic motives led to his arrest and he was charged with 27 counts or murder.

The list of victims—which included names like Jo the Boxer, François the Corsican, and Paulette the Chinese—had

GENERAL EXECUTIONER . . . Dr. Petiot's medical practice looked harmless enough (below) but, as police discovered (left), his home was a chamber of horrors.

a ring of fantasy to it. The evidence which followed, coupled with Petiot's conduct, was equally fantastic.

Clutching a large dossier and cocksure of mood, the doctor admitted responsibility for killing 19 of those named. They were, he alleged, all traitors and German collaborators. He denied murdering the other eight, but for good measure, confessed to killing another 44 people, also traitors. He was then the self-confessed killer of 63 persons.

Mental hospital

Following French trial procedure, the President of the Court began by giving an account of the previous history of the extraordinary man standing in the dock. It was hardly a character reference. Marcel Petiot, born at Auxerre in 1897, had always sailed close to the wind. When serving in the army in 1917 he had been court-martialled for stealing drugs. The charge was dismissed but he was sent for psychiatric treatment.

In 1921, Petiot qualified as a doctor. At the time he was, incredibly, still being treated in a mental hospital. Three years later, he set up in practice at Villeneuve-sur-Yonne. He was energetic and politically active and in 1927 was elected mayor. He later married and had a son.

There followed a catalogue of skirmishes with the law. He was questioned about the disappearance of his housekeeper and faced charges of stealing, drug peddling, and murder. Asked about his relationship with his housekeeper, Petiot gave a flippant reply which was to mark his contemptuous attitude to the court. "She told everyone she was having sexual intercourse with me. In fact, I declined the honour." This brought howls of laughter from the public gallery—this was what they had come for.

In 1930, Petiot was accused of murdering a patient, a Mme Debauve, and he was also linked with the death of the chief witness, also a patient. But Petiot had the gift of avoiding trouble and he managed to slip out of these charges.

Considerable fortune

He moved to Paris in 1936, and in no time at all was caught stealing from a bookshop. Again, he balked the authorities. On this occasion the charge was dismissed provided he undertook psychiatric treatment.

Despite his unprofessional, not to say criminal, conduct, Petiot was never struck off the medical register. When he started his practice at 66 rue Caumartin, he had printed an exotic prospectus advertising the medical services he could provide. This was not illegal in France—it was a matter of conscience. The President of the Court scathingly referred to "these prospectuses of a quack". Petiot replied,

"Thank you for the advertisement."

The medical practice was such a success that Petiot soon had 3000 patients and managed to amass a considerable fortune. He used part of this in 1941 to buy the 15-roomed house at 21 rue Lesueur—near to his apartment in rue Caumartin. He had various alterations made to the interior of the house and raised the height of the wall surrounding the courtyard.

With his life history made public Petiot now faced his accusers. Advocate-General Dupin prosecuted and a number of lawyers representing relatives of the rue Lesueur victims had the right to put questions. The President of the Court conducted a great deal of the examination himself. It was a powerful array, and apart from his own aggressive conduct, Petiot was defended by Maître Floriot, an acknowledged lawyer of brilliance.

Argentine letters

The prosecution argued that Petiot had contrived a scheme to grow rich by finding wealthy Jews who wished to escape from occupied France. He lured them to 21 rue Lesueur telling them to bring as much money and valuables as they could find. There they were disposed of and their disappearance went unnoticed—for stealthy escape from France was their avowed intention. It was a situation which played right into the hands of Petiot. His victims escaped not to the free world but to oblivion. The Advocate-General decided to test Petiot on the eight victims he denied killing. To show that the doctor had murdered just one of them would send him to the guillotine.

Joachim Guschinow, a furrier, had gone to Petiot for help to escape the Germans. He took with him a suitcase containing jewellery, watches, money, and fur coats. These were intended to set him up in the Argentine. "I sent him to Robert Marinetti . . . the great expert at 'passing' along the route to the Spanish frontier," explained Petiot. He added that Guschinow had reached the Argentine, from where he had written letters to his wife.

The police had checked these letters but could find no trace of Guschinow at the hotel address given. "Of course not," snapped Petiot sarcastically. "Don't forget that the Argentine was almost a German colony. He wouldn't, in the circumstances, register under his own name."

"Why did you instruct Guschinow to remove his initials from his linen?" asked the Advocate-General. "That was elementary," replied Petiot, affecting a

PETIOT'S PIT . . . It was there that the deadly doctor kept the iron stove which he used to burn his victims. Telltale traces of lime were also found, as well as (inset) numerous human bones.

weary expression. "However little you worked with the Resistance . . ." He was cut off by the Advocate-General, "I know the Resistance better than you do." "Yes," retorted Petiot to the delight of the public, "but not at the same end of the pipe."

Petiot's tactics were a mixture of bluster and abuse. He passed off the fact that Guschinow's furs had been found in his apartment by explaining that they had been given him out of gratitude. Mme Guschinow's lawyer asked about injections given at 21 rue Lesueur.

"If you are one of those who think I administered injections to my presumed victims you have been reading the newspapers," replied Petiot. The lawyer was not easily put off. "But Mme Guschinow has said that her husband was nervous about the injections." Petiot's brief reply was, "She is lying."

Unique document

Among the exhibits in court were 47 suitcases. These had been found by the police in a private house near Villeneuve after several witnesses had testified that a large number of suitcases had been removed from 21 rue Lesueur in June 1943. Mme Marçais, who had raised the alarm about the smoking chimney, had seen the cases loaded onto a truck driven by Petiot's brother.

When the police opened the bags they found an incredible assortment of clothes. There were 1691 articles in all, including 29 men's suits, 79 women's dresses, and five fur coats, few of which bore any identification marks. The police inventory alone was a unique document of 140 pages listing item by item the garments and luggage of the death house victims.

One of the cases contained a hat and a shirt which Mme Braunberger claimed belonged to her husband Paul, one of the eight murders denied by Petiot. If the prosecution could prove beyond doubt that the clothing belonged to the dead man, Petiot's case would be severely weakened.

But hard as they tried, the prosecution could not effectively lay Braunberger's death at Petiot's door. This was partly due to the brilliant argument about sweat bands and sizes of shirt cuffs put up by Maître Floriot. He routed the opposition, revealed the shortcomings of the police and destroyed Mme Braunberger's validity as a witness by pointing out that she was almost blind.

As the roll call of witnesses continued it was clear that the prosecution was failing to drive home the nails. There was circumstantial evidence in abundance — but Petiot, as he had done all his life, slipped the net at the last moment. The Advocate-General, however, was also aware that he had plenty of tricks up his sleeve. He

had only to prove that Petiot killed one of the eight he denied, or show that any one of the 19 he admitted was not a German collaborator.

Yvan Dreyfus had been a potential escapee. Petiot had been asked to "pass" him and admitted being responsible for his death. Maître Floriot was not disposed to waste much time on him ". . . there is a German dossier," he said, "which shows that Dreyfus was a Gestapo informer." His voice trembling, and in a great state of emotion, Petiot interrupted, "He was four times a traitor. A traitor to his people, his religion, his fatherland and . . ." His outburst was only stopped short by the President of the Court who thundered at him to be quiet.

Perhaps Petiot sensed that his fortunes were beginning to change, for reliable evidence was called which showed Dreyfus to be a patriot. His bold front also foundered in the next case, that of Kurt and Greta Kneller and their small son René. They were among the group he denied killing.

The story was that Kneller, despite owing money to the doctor, was offered help by Petiot to escape from the Germans. "I provided them with false papers," explained Petiot, "which showed they were not married." "But they had a child," pointed out the President of the Court. "Yes," replied Petiot conversationally. "He was a nice little boy."

Petiot argued that the Knellers did escape, and he claimed to have received a postcard from them indicating that all

THE TRIAL . . . Petiot (below) listens to the evidence and (facing page) looks confident as he poses for photograph. The courtroom (inset) was always crowded.

Picture Post

had gone well. "How do you explain the presence of the boy's pyjamas in one of the cases?" inquired the President of the Court. "They were the pyjamas the boy slept in on the last night. There was no point in their taking dirty linen with them," answered the doctor.

On various occasions Petiot claimed to have been sent letters from people he helped to escape. These were examined by handwriting experts who without hesitation concluded that the writers were under nervous strain if not actually under physical duress. But they were not able to say that Petiot had actually written them.

It was in the matter of the letters that Petiot made a bad mistake. He had shown some of the letters to a patient saying that they came from two escapees who had got safely away to South America. But later on the doctor admitted killing the two men in Paris. Clearly they could not have sent the letters — but Petiot solved the contradiction by admitting to writing them himself.

Resistance group

Petiot's defence was quite simply that he was a member of the Resistance and acted under orders to eliminate traitors and collaborators. If he could show that he killed only the enemies of France he would be acquitted and most likely hailed as a patriot.

But throughout the trial he steadfastly refused to give the names of any of the Resistance people he had worked with. The Advocate-General assured him that any who came forward would go free if they had only been responsible for killing Gestapo agents. "I know that tune all right," shouted Petiot. "You won't arrest them, but your pals will!"

He was, however, prepared to name the group to which he had belonged — it was called Fly-Tox and he was known as Dr. Eugène. As a result of a German collaborator infiltrating the group, Petiot said that he was arrested by the Gestapo in May 1943. He was interrogated in a brutal fashion but revealed nothing.

A fellow prisoner at the time, Richard Lhéritier, was questioned in court. He stated that he had heard about Fly-Tox from Petiot with whom he had shared a cell. He spoke highly of the doctor and especially of the way he raised the morale of the prisoners by being hostile to the Germans. Lhéritier concluded, "Whatever the result of this trial, I shall always be grateful for having Dr. Petiot as a cell companion."

Petiot was visibly moved by this and Maître Floriot was quick to point out that this proved "Petiot did not invent Dr. Eugène and Fly-Tox for his defence at this trial."

At this stage in the trial Petiot lapsed

Keystone

LEA

into moody behaviour. At times he would sit quietly, doodling in the margins of his papers, at others he would throw out shafts of wit. It was a highly eccentric performance even in a French court.

He clashed several times with prosecuting lawyer Maître Véron and during questioning about his Resistance activities he shouted at Véron, "Shut up, you advocate of Jews." To which the lawyer replied, "I won't allow you to soil the Resistance purely so that you may defend yourself." Purple with anger, Petiot screamed, "You're a double agent!"

Special weapon

The Advocate-General asked Petiot for more information about his Resistance activities. "It would be quicker to ask me what I have *not* done," was his modest reply. He went on to say that he planted explosives in German vehicles, provided false papers, gathered military intelligence, and invented a special weapon. "What was this weapon?" asked Maître Véron. "Do you think I will reveal something that could be harmful to Frenchmen?" retorted Petiot.

But Maître Véron persisted: "You have boasted of having experimented with plastic explosive . . . tell us something about it; how, for example, it is used." Petiot gave a rambling answer that carried no conviction at all. Pressing the attack, Véron said, "Petiot says that it takes half an hour for plastic to explode —in fact, it takes seven seconds." Enraged, Petiot could only shout abuse. But telling points were being scored by the prosecution.

Now the President of the Court took up the questioning. "Tell us about your escape organization. Who, for example, supplied the false papers?" Putting his hands to his head, Petiot thought for a while, then said, "I think he was on the staff of the Argentine Embassy." Pressed to give names, he could only reply, "There was a man called Robert . . . at Orléans there was a man with a black beard." For the first time he seemed to be floundering.

Maître Floriot came to the rescue by trying to play down the Resistance. He argued that if Petiot, in the course of carrying out "private resistance", had killed from motives of patriotism, no one would reproach him. But even the brilliance of Floriot could not divert attention from Petiot's claim to have worked for the Resistance: it was vital to his case.

When he was released by the Germans in January 1944 Petiot said he retired to Auxerre for a while to recuperate, and because he knew he was being followed. After a while he thought it safe to reappear in Paris and he went to 21 rue Lesueur. He was shocked to find a number of partially decomposed bodies covered with quicklime. He at once wrote to

his brother asking for four hundredweight of quicklime and some disinfectant.

He concluded that while he had been in prison, members of his group had carried on business as usual. His group denied this and it was assumed to be the work of another group. At any rate they agreed to clean up the mess. As it was not feasible to transport the bodies away from the house, they lit the central heating boiler, cut up the rotting corpses, and began burning them.

Challenged to give the names of those who had carried out this grisly operation, Petiot refused, saying that it was against the principles of the Resistance. This was arguable, but it was open for any one of the group to come forward and give testimony on his behalf. But none did.

Triangular room

Early on in the proceedings, the President of the Court, Counsel, and the jury visited the death house at 21 rue Lesueur —when great interest was shown in the triangular room. Petiot said it was intended to house radio therapy equipment, hence the thick walls and observation hole. A medical expert dismissed this as ridiculous on the grounds that the room was not large enough to contain both

STAR EXIT . . . The flamboyant doctor clearly enjoyed the trial and used it as a vehicle to entertain his public. Leaving the court (below) he appears at ease even though surrounded by police and spectators. It was V.I.P. treatment.

patient and equipment. The sinister room, the boiler in the basement, and knowledge of what was in the 47 suitcases created a vivid image of evil-doing in the minds of the jury.

Hoots of laughter

As the trial drew to its close, psychiatric evidence was called to show that Petiot was considered sane and responsible for his actions. Counsel for the relatives of the victims addressed the jury and asked for the death penalty. One of these lawyers confounded everyone by launching into a complete review of the case. The President of the Court seemed unable to stop him, but Petiot lent a helping hand by shouting, "I'd like to point out that I haven't paid this advocate." After hoots of laughter, order was restored.

The Advocate-General in his closing speech drew the irresistible conclusion that Petiot had organized an escape route which began and ended at 21 rue Lesueur. It was a sure way of making money. Petiot's profits were estimated at over £1 million. But the suitcases full of clothes—what could be said of them? Perhaps Petiot anticipated a market for them in post-war France.

Maître Floriot pleaded strongly for Petiot. Many thought it the most brilliant defence speech heard in a French court for half a century. But in the end the sheer weight of circumstantial evidence crushed Petiot's reliance on showing that he worked for the Resistance. His answers—and the lack of them—damned him in most people's eyes.

Addressing the prisoner, the President of the Court said, "Petiot, have you anything to add to your defence?" Petiot replied, "Nothing. You are Frenchmen. You know I have destroyed members of the Gestapo. You know what you have to do."

The jury found Petiot guilty of 24 of the 27 murders. Amid uproar, the President of the Court pronounced the death sentence. Petiot did not hear at first, so great was the hubbub. When it became clear he resisted the guards and shouted to his wife, "You must avenge me!"

Relieve himself

Marcel Petiot waited in the Santé Prison in Paris for the result of his appeal. Both the appeal and a plea for presidential clemency failed. On May 26, 1946, he was escorted to the guillotine. He rejected the services of a priest, and smoked the traditional cigarette. It was said that he asked to relieve himself but was refused permission. He shrugged and replied, "When one sets out on a voyage, one takes all one's luggage with one."

Then, in the name of justice, the knife crashed down and severed Marcel Petiot's head from his body.

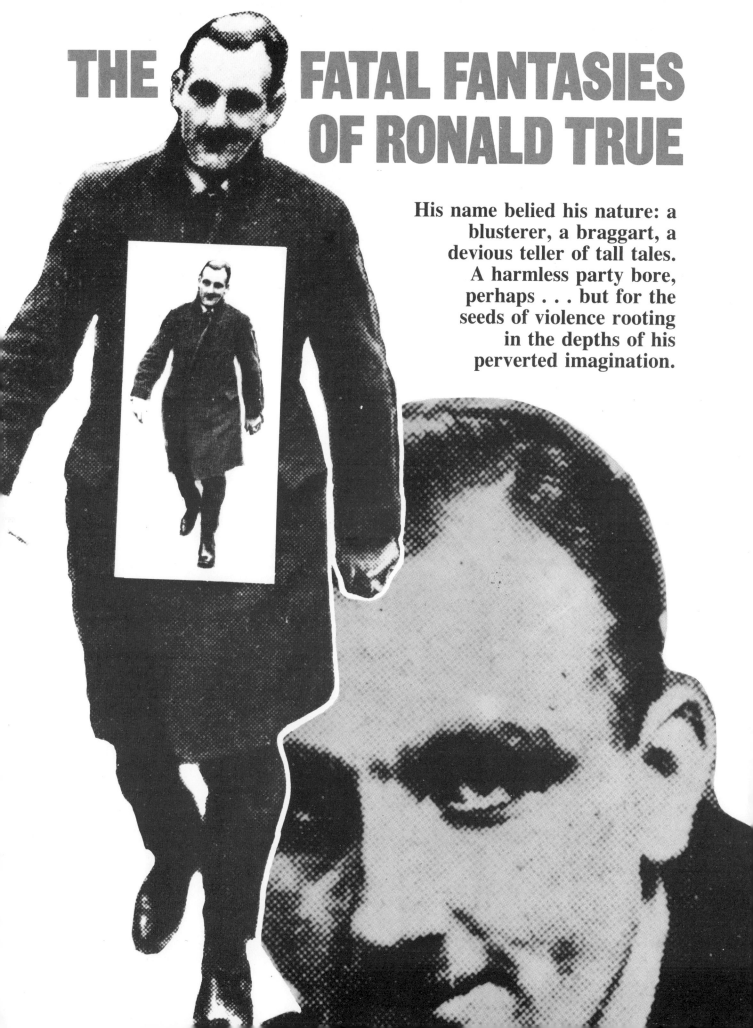

THE FATAL FANTASIES OF RONALD TRUE

His name belied his nature: a blusterer, a braggart, a devious teller of tall tales. A harmless party bore, perhaps . . . but for the seeds of violence rooting in the depths of his perverted imagination.

PUNCTUAL as always, Miss Emily Steel arrived at 9.15 a.m. at the basement flat in Fulham for her regular five hours' stint as cleaning woman to the tenant, Miss Olive Young.

She let herself in with her latch-key and was not surprised to find the bedroom door still shut, for her employer often slept late. She was equally not surprised to see a man's coat, scarf and gloves on the table in the small sitting room.

For Miss Steel was under no illusions about her employer's profession—it was, as the saying goes, the oldest in the world. Olive Young, whose real name was Gertrude Yates, was a prostitute of what some later called "the rather better class".

Many of her clients were "regulars" who could afford the cost of entertaining her to meals and staying all night with her.

So, accepting what seemed to be a routine situation at No. 13a Finborough Road, London, S.W. 10, Miss Steel went into the kitchen and began to prepare some sausages for her own breakfast.

She noticed that a teapot contained the dregs of still-warm tea, and two cups and saucers were gone from the dresser. Clearly Miss Young or her friend had been up and about in the flat not so very long before.

Impressive and sleek

Leaving the sausages to cook, Miss Steel returned to the sitting room to tidy up. She had barely begun when she saw a man appear from the direction of the bedroom. She recognized him at once as Major True, whom she had seen at the flat with Miss Young two weeks previously.

The impressive, six-foot visitor with the sleek, dark hair and neat moustache addressed her in quiet confidential tones.

"Don't wake Miss Young," he said. "We were late last night and she is in a deep sleep. I'll send the car round for her at twelve o'clock."

Miss Steel helped the Major on with his coat and received in return a tip of half-a-crown—a handsome gratuity for 1922. From the top of the basement steps she watched Major True hail a taxi and drive off down the Fulham Road.

Back in the flat, Miss Steel tapped at the bedroom door and, receiving no reply, went in. The bed was empty, but when she drew back the bedclothes she was alarmed to find two pillows laid lengthways down the middle of the bed and covered with blood. Under the eiderdown was the kitchen rolling-pin.

The dressing-table drawers were open, and it was obvious that someone had been

A PROSTITUTE of "the rather better class", Gertrude Yates, alias Olive Young, lay brutally battered about the head with a cord knotted around her neck.

As Good as Sunshine: Pip, Squeak and Wilfred up the dullest day. See Page 13.

The Daily Mirror

NET SALE NEARLY TWICE THAT OF ANY OTHER DAILY PICTURE NEWSPAPER

No. 5,724.   Registered at the G.P.O. as a Newspaper.   TUESDAY, MARCH 7, 1922

GIRL'S MURDER IN LONDON FLAT

VANISHED P

An official of Scotland Yard sketching the house in Finborough-road at which the tragedy occurred.

NEW LAW APPOINTMENTS

Mr. Leslie Scott, Solicitor-General.

The Rev. F. S. Kinder, the Baptist from Lewisham. He left his home on ruary 14, and no news has since been to have resigned his pa

EX-UNDERGRADUATE

rummaging through the contents. With growing apprehension she went to a cupboard near the bed where she knew Olive Young kept her jewel box. Some of the more valuable pieces of jewellery were missing.

There was only one room left in which Miss Steel could look for her employer—the bathroom. Fearfully she pulled open the door and there on the floor, almost completely naked and brutally battered about the head, lay Olive Young.

Not only had the 25-year-old prostitute been bludgeoned but, as the subsequent police examination showed, a piece of rough towelling had been thrust into her mouth with such force that her tongue was doubled back. And a dressing-gown cord had been knotted tightly around her neck.

The police, led by Chief Inspector William Brown of Scotland Yard, knew at once the name of the man they must

A CERTAIN SURFACE POLISH enabled True to be charming in the most unlikely circumstances . . . even at the inquest (below) after Olive Young's death.

seek to "help" them with their inquiries. Miss Steel gave the information. But, more than that, the ferocious murderer had even left his own calling card on the sitting-room sideboard "Mr. Ronald True," it said in print, and below that, in handwriting, "23 Audley Street, W.1." The name was correct, the address false.

In such circumstances most murderers would have used every ounce of energy and every second of time to disappear from public view. But not True. He behaved almost as though he were deliberately setting out to lay a trail for himself, like the "hare" in a paper-chase.

He went, by the taxi Miss Steel had seen him hail, to an outfitter in Coventry Street, just off Piccadilly Circus, and bought a bowler hat, collar and tie and a ready-made brown suit—for a total cost of £16 16s. 10½d.

Mr. James Milne, assistant in the tailoring department, noticed that True's trousers were stained in front by a large patch of blood.

To his surprise True volunteered a unique explanation. "This came from an

aeroplane accident," he said. "I'm a pilot flying the Marseilles express and I had a smash on landing this morning."

True changed into his new suit in the shop's fitting room and asked Mr. Milne to wrap his bloodstained clothes in a parcel. As True emptied the pockets of the old suit Mr. Milne saw him open a small jewel case containing a wrist-watch and a string of pearls. These, and the money he was spending, had belonged to Olive Young.

From the outfitter's he went to a barber's, where he had a haircut and shave and asked if he could leave his parcel, "while I pop across the road". He did not return for the parcel, and it was eventually retrieved by the police.

True's next call was at a pawnshop in Wardour Street, Soho, where he produced two of Olive Young's rings and asked for a loan on them of £70. The assistant, Mr. Herbert Elliet, told him that was "an absurd price" and offered him £25, which True promptly accepted.

By then it was time for True to go to the entrance to the Prince of Wales theatre, in Coventry Street, where he

was due to be met by the hired car he had been using for the past five days for a series of idle trips around London with his friends. His usual driver, Luigi Mazzola, was sitting at the wheel.

The previous night Mr. Mazzola had driven True to 13a Finborough Road and been told: "I am staying here the night. Meet me tomorrow at 11."

Now, at this next day's meeting, True's first words were: "Sorry I dismissed you last night, because I stopped only 20 minutes in the flat and left a man and woman fighting there."

But still True showed no anxiety to disappear. He picked up a friend and they were driven off on another of True's aimless wanderings—calling at Hounslow first for a drink, then driving out to Croydon and Richmond and finally to the Hammersmith Palace of Varieties.

The Palace was True's last stopping place in freedom. Detectives had traced him through the hired car company, and just before 10 p.m. four senior police officers walked quietly into the box where True was sitting with his friend.

Detective Inspector Albert Burton grasped True with both hands and ordered him out into the corridor behind the box. There another officer frisked him and found a loaded revolver in his hip pocket.

Charged with the murder of Olive Young, True denied any knowledge of the crime, but told a rambling story of

Syndication International

ONCE ARRESTED (by Detective Inspector Burton, left), True faced a line of ominous witnesses from driver Luigi Mazzola (above) to Miss Emily Steel the maid (centre left). . . .

seeing, on the night of the murder, a "tall man running along Fulham Road coming from Finborough Road".

It was the first of a series of fantasies the police were to hear from True. And when his trial opened at the Old Bailey on May 1, 1922, it was evident that he was either a schizophrenic or was trying to appear like one. His general behaviour in the weeks before the murder had been "strange", to say the least.

One of the stories he told his friends was that a man was visiting West End pubs and clubs impersonating him and using the name Ronald True. This man, so the fantasy went, was passing out dud cheques which eventually the real Ronald True's mother was having to honour.

For that reason the "real" True carried a loaded revolver which he frequently brandished, even in the company of strangers. He also produced bullets which had been cut so as to turn them into the dum-dum variety, which cause tearing wounds.

Curiously, most of the men he met seemed to believe his impossibly tall stories. The women he knew did not. Rightly they suspected that True was in fact living most of his life in a self-created never-never land.

True was born in 1891, so that by the time of Olive Young's death he was 30. He was illegitimate, but his mother, who was only 16 at the time of his birth, looked after him well and later married a prosperous businessman who was able to give young Ronnie True a good start in life.

The good start proved to be of little value, for True was shiftless and unreliable. He was sent out to New Zealand to try his hand at farming, but that failed, and for several years he drifted around the world.

He went to the Argentine and then to Canada, where he had a brief and inglorious career in the North-West Mounted Police. Then he was off to Mexico, and finally to Shanghai where, in 1914, he learned of the outbreak of war and decided to return home and become a hero.

True was by now a morphia addict, but despite the effects of that and his general fecklessness, he had a certain surface "polish".

He could be charming and observe the social graces when he wasn't being foul-tempered and moody. And it was that superficial charm that helped to get him into the Royal Flying Corps as a student-pilot with commission prospects.

To the amazement of some of his fellow trainees, True passed his pilot's examination. He immediately ordered an insignia of wings for his uniform jacket, three times the size of the regular type and worked in silks of rainbow colours.

Guy Dent, another pilot who trained with him at Gosport, Hampshire, said: "He had a feverish air about him. He was always rushing about and laughing with a loud voice, and he seemed deficient in common sense. When I saw the case in the paper I thought if this is the same True, he was unstable six years ago."

Crashing aircraft

Inevitably, and despite his "wings", the only thing True could do with aircraft was to crash them. After one accident, in which he was seriously injured, he was invalided out of the air force.

By the end of the war True had invented the "other True". In a nursing home, where fruitless attempts were made to wean him from his daily dose of 30 grains of morphia, he went into a rage when any bill was presented to him and declared: "It's not meant for me—it's for the other one."

Once out of the nursing home he adopted the title of "major" and announced that he was a wartime fighter ace who had shot down at least five German aircraft.

Exhibiting his loaded revolver, he shouted that he was "out to get the other Ronald True". If any of his friends had anyone they wanted removed he would do the job, he offered, at "a bob a nob"—a shilling a head.

He told a woman friend: "I'll murder someone one of these days. You watch the papers and see if I don't. There'll be a big case about it."

This woman decided there and then that True was insane. Yet his circle of friends increased, and many found him amusing. With his fantastic stories and sudden outbursts of maniacal anger he became something of a party clown—for the men around him, at least.

On the night of February 18, 1922, True paid his first visit to Olive Young at her Fulham flat. They had met a few days previously in London's West End. Olive Young had once been a shopgirl. She drifted into prostitution, and because

RONALD TRUE REPRIEVED.

CONVICT CERTIFIED TO BE INSANE.

Ronald True, who was found guilty and sentenced to death at the Central Criminal Court on May 5 for the murder of Olive Young, has been certified to be insane, and the death sentence has been respited.

The following official notice was issued last night:

The Home Secretary, a[...]

THE GREATEST TRAGEDY of all was that so many people who knew of his illness did nothing to help him—and so save the life of Olive Young.

of her intelligence and attractiveness had built up a successful "business". She had money in the bank and, unlike a common street-walker, could be choosey about her clients.

She quickly decided that Major True was not her type. During his first night's visit to Fulham he had frightened her by his routine with the revolver. After he had left she found that a five-pound note from her handbag had gone with him.

From then on she tried to avoid him. She made sure that each night no light was visible from her flat. She let him hammer at the door in vain. She would not speak to him on the telephone.

Close to midnight on Sunday, March 5, a near-penniless True, who was keeping his hired car until the final moment of payment arrived, ordered the faithful Mazzola to drive him to Finborough Road.

For once Olive Young had relaxed her vigilance. Through the glass of the front door True saw a light in the hallway. He knocked, and Olive opened the door.

In view of her efforts to dodge True the girl must have been dismayed when she saw the tall figure of the "major" looming in the doorway. But in her profession she could not afford to create a "scene" in the quiet, respectable street.

She had no option but to let him in and so bring about her own violent death.

The medical evidence given later show-

ed that she had died at between 7 a.m. and 8 a.m. on Monday, March 6. It was clear that, on the pretext of making tea, True had gone to the kitchen in search of a murder weapon and had found the rolling-pin.

While the girl sipped her tea he moved behind her and struck her five savage blows on the head. He then used the towel and the dressing-gown cord to ensure that she was quite dead.

The fact that True so stupidly remained in the flat until the "daily" arrived was made much of at the trial by his defence counsel, the brilliant Sir Henry Curtis Bennett. That, and the wild spending spree that followed, were clear pointers to True's insanity, Sir Henry pleaded.

Sentenced to death

All the same, a cautious jury found True guilty as charged, and he was sentenced to death. From Pentonville Prison he wrote to a friend: "If you come to the same place I'm going to I'll have a drink of nice cold water ready for you."

But True did not go to that place. Instead, on the intervention of the Home Secretary, he was sent to Broadmoor. He lived out the rest of his life there and died in 1951, at the age of 61—one of the happiest, most popular and longest-staying patients the criminal mental asylum had ever had.

The greatest tragedy of True's case is that so many people who realized how split and mentally ill he was did nothing to help him—and so save the life of Olive Young, who loathed and feared him.

SEEK POISON PLOT IN DEATH OF MICHIGAN MILLIONAIRE AND HIS WIFE HERE

...AW OF PECKS

Autopsy in Grand Rapids on Body of Mr. Peck. Who Died in Riverside Drive Home of Son-in-Law Shows Arsenic Was Administered Before Death.

WIFE TOO SEEMED WELL THE DAY BEFORE SHE EXPIRED.

Swann's Theory Is Slayer Intended by Third Crime to Gain Half of $1.500.000 Esta...

Suspect Und...

Watch...

THE HAPPY POISONER

Everybody liked the urbane Dr. Waite. Even the jurors giggled and smiled as he told his blood-curdling tale of calculated murder. . . .

A MAN being tried for double murder might be expected to show a certain degree of strain and anxiety, particularly after having pleaded not guilty. Dr. Arthur Warren Waite, 28-year-old dentist, was exactly the opposite. Throughout the hearing he remained relaxed, urbane and amused. At times during the prosecution case he laughed heartily, and when his own turn came to give evidence he admitted cheerfully – despite his not guilty pleas – that everything the prosecution had said about him was true. Not to put too fine a point on it, he added, he was really even more outrageous and contradictory a character than they had made out.

Yes, he had indeed murdered his mother-in-law, Mrs. John E. Peck, wife of a drug millionaire, when she came to visit her daughter, Clara. Waite had married Clara in September, 1915. Mrs. Peck arrived at their home on fashionable Riverside Drive, New York, just before Christmas of that year. By January 30, 1916, this apparently healthy woman was dead. A doctor certified kidney disease.

But now Waite, with the air of a man relating a diverting story at a cocktail party, was confessing: "I started poisoning her from the very first meal after she arrived. I gave her six assorted tubes of pneumonia, diphtheria and influenza germs in her food. When she finally became ill and took to her bed I ground up 12 five-grain veronal tablets and gave her that, too, last thing at night." And then? "Why, I guess I went back to sleep," he shrugged. "I woke up in the small hours. My mother-in-law was dead. I went back to bed again so that it would be my wife who would discover the body."

Tubes of typhoid

He then went on, in the same bantering manner, to outline his six-week struggle to kill his father-in-law. Mr. Peck came for a visit early in February to cheer himself up after his wife's funeral. By March 12 this sturdy old man of 71 was dead as well.

"I used to insert tubes of typhoid, pneumonia, influenza and diphtheria in his soups and rice puddings," Waite continued gaily. "Once I gave him a nasal spray filled with tuberculosis bacteria. Nothing seemed to affect him, so I used to let off the occasional tube or two of chlorine gas in his bedroom, hoping the gas would weaken his resistance like it did with the soldiers at the front. I used to put some stuff on the electric heater so that if he noticed a funny smell I could say it was something burning.

"Still nothing happened. I tried to give

"FOR THEIR MONEY," said Waite, when asked why he'd killed his in-laws (left), Mr. and Mrs. Peck. Detectives found germ cultures in the suspect's apartment.

him pneumonia by putting water in his Wellingtons [*rubbers*], damping his sheets, opening his bedroom window and wetting the seat of the automobile before taking him out for a drive. That didn't work either."

Becoming desperate, he had toyed with the idea of faking a car accident. Finally, unable to bring himself to resort to such violence, he had settled for arsenic. However, even after a full 18 grains – far more than the fatal dose – the tough old man was still alive although in a bad way.

"On the night of March 12 he was in great pain," Waite explained, "and he wanted some ammonia and ether. I couldn't find any, but in Clara's medicine chest there was some chloroform, so I gave him that. It did him good, so I gave him a second dose to make sure, and then I held the pillow over his nose and mouth until he was finished."

The jurors, who had regarded Waite with some horror at the start of his recital, had by now become infected with his *bonhomie*. They swopped smiles with him, and some even gave vent to hysterical giggles as Waite went on to reveal that the two murders were only part of the story. He had also tried to kill his wife's aunt, the rich Miss Catherine Peck – despite the fact that he was something of a favourite of hers.

Germs and arsenic

"I gave her repeated doses of germs, then some arsenic, and after that some ground glass," he related. "I also injected live germs into a can of fish before presenting it to her." He had abandoned this attempt at murder, he explained, because Mrs. Peck had come to stay for Christmas, and he couldn't see the point of murdering the aunt when there were much richer pickings to be obtained by murdering his mother-in-law.

Given time, he also confessed, he would almost certainly have murdered his wife, Clara. "She was not my equal in anything," he said. "When I had got rid of her I meant to find a more beautiful wife."

Earlier, the prosecution had filled in the background to Waite's life and the circumstances which led to his arrest. In the fall of 1914 he had returned to his birthplace, Grand Rapids, Michigan, after an absence of several years, during which he had worked as a dentist in South Africa. He had a dental surgeon's degree from Glasgow University in Scotland, a British accent, and a ferocious talent for tennis which soon made him the local champion. In the bank he also had $20,000, a useful sum in those days.

"Waite met and began his courtship of his wife almost immediately," said the prosecution, "and they were married the following September." Waite's charm and slender good looks made an immediate

hit in the New York social circles to which his new wife introduced him. Two people with whom he quickly became intimate friends were Dr. Jacob Cornell, of the Cornell Medical School, and Dr. Cornell's sister, Mrs. Henry Hardwicke.

In addition to setting himself up in dental practice, Waite began to do serious research at the Medical School where later – as the need arose – he was able to lay hands on a plentiful supply of germs to slip into his in-laws' food.

Mrs. Waite told the court of her surprise, after her mother's unexpected death, when Waite said it had been Mrs. Peck's last wish to be cremated. "It was the first I'd heard of it," she said. On the night of March 12 she heard Arthur, who had been sitting up with her father, ring the doctor. Later he came into the bedroom in his robe, looking disturbed, and said: "I don't think Dad's too good."

Already dead

She rushed to her father's room, but he was already dead. Once again she was surprised when Arthur told her: "It was Dad's wish to be cremated." Nevertheless, she accepted his word. The next day Arthur busied himself having the body embalmed and making arrangements for it to be taken, first to Grand Rapids, then to Detroit.

The only time he did not seem his normal charming, helpful, and urbane self was when Dr. Cornell called to pay his respects. Arthur was irritable and offhand with him. In fact, he refused initially to let him see the body of his old friend who, according to the death certificate, had died, like Mrs. Peck, of kidney disease. His behaviour was so uncharacteristically brusque that Dr. Cornell commented upon it that evening to his sister. That comment was to lead to Arthur's undoing.

Arthur and his wife – plus the coffin – set out by train for the Middle West at five o'clock the next morning. The family party waiting at Grand Rapids station included Percy Peck, Clara's elder brother, and Aunt Catherine Peck. Aunt Catherine – unaware at this stage that Arthur had set out at one time to kill her with germs, arsenic and ground glass – was her usual friendly self. But Percy seemed hostile and withdrawn.

Nobody thought that too strange. Percy had lost his father and mother in the space of six weeks. Over and above the natural grief and shock, he and Arthur had never really got on too well. Percy had something else on his mind, however. That morning he had received an anonymous telegram, later discovered to have come from Mrs. Hardwicke, saying: "Don't allow cremation until an autopsy has been carried out."

"Everything's fixed," Arthur announced efficiently. "I've arranged for poor Dad's body to go right on to Detroit to be cremated. I'll go with it and see this sad business finished. Would any of you folks like to come with me?'' Percy, however, wanted to do more than that. ''Just a minute,'' he said bluntly. ''I guess we aren't in all that hurry to see the last of Father. I'll see to the coffin.''

Arthur professed to be puzzled. ''I can't understand what that brother of yours is up to,'' he said to Clara, as they hurried off to see the family lawyer about her father's will. ''Why can't he let poor old Dad have his last wish carried out?'' Then, as they travelled back to New York later that day, Arthur had recaptured his customary good spirits. Dad had left more than a million dollars, including a bequest of $2000 to Arthur's father ''out of regard for his son''.

Bombshell news

Back on Riverside Drive, Arthur's high spirits did not last long. First came the bombshell news that Percy had asked for an autopsy. Newspaper reporters descended on Arthur's doorstep. Others were let loose in New York, Michigan, Glasgow, and South Africa. Gradually it emerged that Arthur was by no means the straightforward pillar of respectability that he claimed to be. There was another, and twisted, side to his personality.

As a boy he had been in trouble several times over thefts from his parents, relatives, employers, schoolmates and others. While at the dental college at the University of Michigan, Ann Arbor, he had been expelled from his fraternity for an act of dishonesty. He had used false papers to help him get a quick degree at Glasgow University, so that he could practise in South Africa.

In South Africa itself his attempt to marry an heiress had been foiled by her father on the grounds of Arthur's ''unsavoury reputation''. As the dossier built up, the New York newspapers suggested pointedly that the $20,000 he had brought home from South Africa could not have been come by honestly. Finally, the Press broke the story that—married less than six months, and in the process of murdering his father-in-law—Arthur had also been carrying on a passionate affair with a married singer named Margaret Horton.

In the middle of this trial by publicity, Arthur, beginning to feel desperate, telephoned Aunt Catherine at her New York apartment. His voice sounded strained. ''What is the best thing for a man to do who has been cornered?'' he asked. ''Do you think suicide would be the right thing?''

Aunt Catherine counselled him against it. But it was the course he decided to take when the news was ultimately released that five grains of arsenic had been found in old Mr. Peck's body after

several days of tests. On March 23 police, who had him under surveillance by now, broke into the Riverside Drive apartment and found Arthur dying from a drug overdose. He was rushed, sobbing ''not to be taken to prison'', to Bellevue Hospital, where his life was saved.

In the dock Arthur listened good-humouredly—very much the man-of-the-world—as witnesses unfolded this tale. From time to time he gave an amused chuckle. As a dentist, it was explained, he had bought the arsenic quite openly, claiming that he wanted it to ''kill a cat''. Books about the uses and effects of arsenic had been found in his flat with the pages marked. Initially, however, he had claimed buying the arsenic at Mr. Peck's request.

''He was so wretched about his own life after his wife's death that he implored me to provide him with the means of self-destruction,'' he explained. ''That was all I did. I did not administer the poison to him, nor did I see him take any. But, of course, you won't believe me. I suppose I'll go to the chair.''

Arthur, the court learned, had also been caught out in an attempt to bribe two witnesses to keep silent. One was Dora, his Negress maid. He had offered her $1000 not to reveal that she had seen him ''putting white powder into Mr. Peck's food''. The other was Eugene Kane, an embalmer, who asserted that Arthur had given him $9000 to say there had been arsenic in the embalming fluid injected into Mr. Peck's body.

Small embalmer

The appearance of the small, bespectacled embalmer clearly tickled Arthur's fancy, and he burst out laughing several times during Kane's testimony. Kane explained how Arthur had come out of a telephone booth and ''pushed a roll of notes in my pocket''.

Prosecution: Did you know what it was for?

Kane: No, I thought it must have been for something I had done.

Prosecution: He told you, though, didn't he?

Kane: He said: ''Put some arsenic in that fluid and send it down to the District Attorney.''

Prosecution: Were you nervous?

Kane: I certainly was.

Prosecution: Did you count the money when you got home?

Kane: No. I tried to, but I was too

A PASSIONATE AFFAIR with married singer Margaret Horton (far right) was to prove Waite's undoing. Her testimony demolished his hopes of pleading insanity. Was she the ''more beautiful wife'' that the killer had planned to marry after he had murdered Clara (right)?

A FATEFUL TELEGRAM from Mrs. Hardwicke (top right, with Waite's wife Clara) . . . and brother-in-law Percy (above) demands an autopsy on his father.

nervous. I saw some fifties and some hundreds and that's all.

Prosecution: Any large bills?

Kane: Yes, sir. Two five-hundred-dollar bills. I hid the money in a closet. I tried to count it two or three times. Finally, I went to Long Island and buried it. I went to Greenport, 'way to the east end of the island. I don't remember just how long I stayed. I was too nervous.

Prosecution: Did you deliver a sample of embalming fluid to the District Attorney's office?

Kane: Yes.

It was after this exchange that Arthur himself went into the witness-box. He did not refute any of the testimony given against him. Rather, with the aid of his attorney, he did everything in his power to embellish it and blacken himself still further. After he had confessed to the murder of his in-laws, the start of his attempt to murder Aunt Catherine, and his intention one day to murder his wife, his counsel asked: "Why did you want to kill them?"

"For their money," he answered laconically. "I've always needed lots of money, and it has never worried me how I get hold of it." Into his evidence he

dropped various asides about himself and the world around him. He confided that he had always considered himself "attractive and charming". "Everyone liked me," he said disarmingly.

Reincarnation was a topic to which he returned frequently. "I believe," he explained, "that, although my body lives in America, my soul lives in secret in Egypt. It is the man from Egypt who has committed these foul crimes." When the prosecution pressed him for details of his other life by the banks of the Nile, however, there was not much he could recall. He mentioned Caesar, Cleopatra, and the pyramids — to the last of which he applied the improbable adjective "voluptuous".

Streak of piety

The whole purpose of this charade — carried through with unflagging style, laced with wit and laughter — was to implant in the minds of the jury the thought: "Surely such a civilized and intelligent man could not have carried out the crimes to which he has confessed so freely and, at the same time, be sane?" One entire day towards the end of the trial was taken up with a series of witnesses paying tribute to Arthur's impeccable manners and gentle heart.

He had a strong streak of piety in him, some stated, and had attended church regularly while in the process of poisoning his relatives. An alienist told the court that Arthur had informed him: "Miss Peck said that, when she remembered how beautifully I had sung hymns in church while my wife's relations were visiting us, she could not believe that I committed the crimes. It was my real self

that appeared then."

"Whatever they may say of me," he announced on one occasion, "I pride myself on being kind and always giving water to flowers so they will not die. They are beautiful. This is nature."

There were, of course, experts for the defence to say that a man who could murder in such cold blood, and talk about it afterwards in such a carefree manner, could not be sane. And there were prosecution experts to assert that Arthur gave the normal responses and *was* sane. The judge finally ruled in favour of the prosecution. He had, in part, been swayed by his irritation over Arthur's constant smile. But far more vital was the evidence of Margaret Horton.

Between February 22 and March 18, Arthur and the singer had spent many hours together in a studio she rented at the Hotel Plaza in New York. According to her husband, Harry Horton, a 56-year-old dealer in war supplies: "They were brought together by a mutual interest in art and modern languages. She made the kind of mistake any young woman might be guilty of. I personally am ready to forgive her."

It was Mrs. Horton's disclosures that robbed him of any slender chance he might have had of escaping the death sentence. At the time when rumours and innuendos about Arthur were being voiced, she remembered his inviting her

HIS SUICIDE ATTEMPT (below) a failure, Waite lives to face damaging testimony. Among the witnesses is embalmer Kane (far right) who alleges bribery.

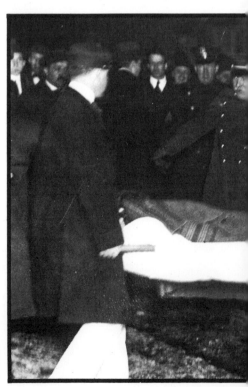

to his laboratory—where he showed her various tiny germs wriggling under a microscope.

She had brought everything out into the open by asking: "You didn't really do it, did you, Arthur?"

"Yes," he had answered. "It's true, I did."

After his arrest, Arthur had sent her a letter which she subsequently destroyed on the advice of his attorney. Under pressure, however, she had to admit that she could remember some damning words from it. "If they prove it, I suppose it will mean *la chaise,* but I hope and expect to spend a while in detention as an imbecile, and then I'll be free again to join you . . ."

It was this, more than anything else, that impelled the judge to rule that Arthur was not a moral imbecile but was fit to plead: madmen do not, as a rule, show so calculated a faith in the benefits to be derived from their insanity.

Waite was found guilty in May 1916, and sentenced to die in the electric chair at Sing Sing. The case dragged on, however, until the following spring, pending hearings in the Court of Appeals and

before a lunacy commission. In the third week of May 1917, both bodies decided that there were no grounds for interfering with the verdict of the lower court.

The condemned man responded with a gesture matching the performance he had put on in court a year earlier. He sent the following letter to Warden Moyer from the death cell:

"Dear Sir: In one of the newspapers today is the statement: 'A. W. Waite to die next week.' On inquiry I learn that you have power to name the day. I am sure you would not be averse to obliging me if you found it possible and reasonable to do so, and I wonder if we could not arrange for Monday of next week. There really is a reason for asking this, although I will not trouble you with explanations. I would be very grateful indeed for this favour. Yours respectfully, Arthur Warren Waite."

This latest touch of bravado convinced many outsiders that, despite what the experts said, he must surely be abnormal to crave as early a death as possible and show so little fear. They were even more convinced when he walked calmly to the chair on the morning of May 24, 1917, with a boyish smile on his somewhat effeminate lips. He was in full control of himself right to the end, reading the Bible and Keats before he was finally taken to the execution chamber. In his cell was later found the beginning of a poem he had started to write. The first two lines read:

Call us with morning faces,
Eager to labour, eager to be happy . . .

At the autopsy—after Waite had been killed with two shocks of 2000 volts each—doctors found the scars of an old meningitis operation on the right side of the cerebellum. This they thought could be the result of a fall or a blow on the head in childhood. But, they added, they did not think that would affect Waite's sanity. The other discovery they made was that he had an abnormally large heart.

TO THE END Waite (below, in police van) was in complete control of himself. He read Keats and the Bible and wrote poetry as he awaited execution.

GUNMEN BIND THREE AFTER HOLD-UP IN FLA

430

LANA'S LOVER

It began as a casual pick-up, this unlikely affair between the ageing movie queen and the smooth young gigolo and sometime hoodlums' flunkey. But then it grew, with the remorseless inevitability of a melodramatic tragedy, into obsessive love . . . and bloodshed. The death of Lana Turner's lover Stompanato at the hands of her precocious daughter Cheryl was just the beginning of her ordeal in an inferno of scandal.

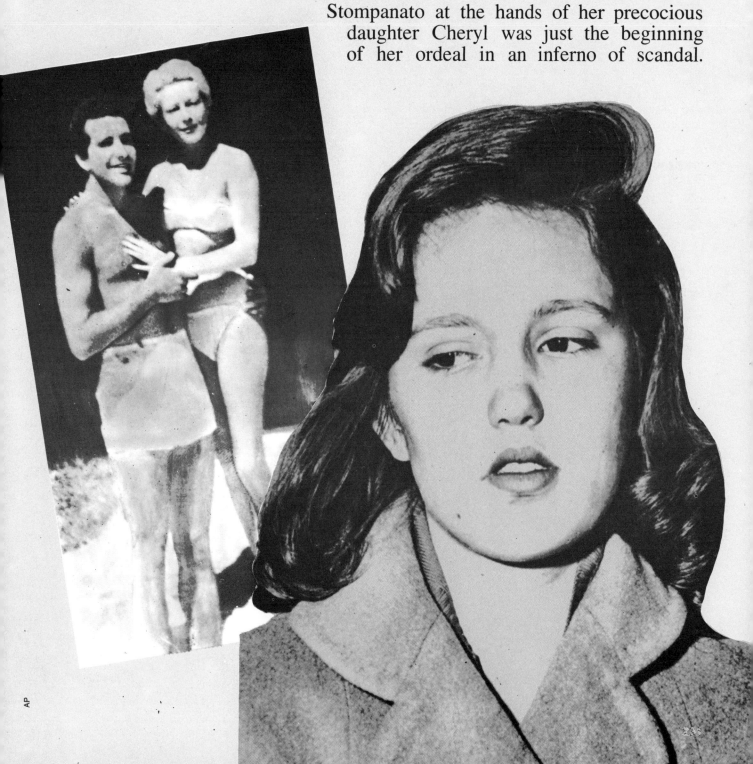

GOOD FRIDAY, 1958, was drawing to its close when two senior detectives of the Beverly Hills police arrived at No. 730 North Bedford Drive, Hollywood. Officers already on the scene led them to a pink-furnished bedroom where lay the body of a well-nourished Caucasian male, dressed in casual clothes: shirt, slacks and woolly cardigan.

The dead man, Johnny Stompanato, had received a knife-stab in the stomach —a violent and painful end that, nevertheless, had left no imprint upon the corpse's darkly handsome, Latin features.

Stompanato was known to the police as a vaguely undesirable character who lived in the half-world of gangsterdom and whose name had been linked, in the scandal mags, with many of the top women stars of Hollywood. The latest of these names was Lana Turner: in fact, No. 730 North Bedford Drive was Miss Turner's home.

The blonde star was there. Face ravaged and make-up ruined with tears, she appealed to the senior of the two detectives, Chief of Police Anderson: "Can't I take the blame for this horrible thing?"

Anderson replied stolidly: "Not unless you have committed the crime. We'll find out all the facts."

Sun-kissed and athletic

The star's 14-year-old daughter by her second husband was in her own room. This was Cheryl. Tall and grown-up for her age; a typical Californian teenager; long-stemmed, sun-kissed and athletic.

Cheryl faced the detectives. "I stabbed him," she said. "I didn't mean to kill him. I just meant to frighten him."

There was a bloodstained knife in the bathroom sink. It had a nine-inch blade that tapered to a finely honed point. A man of Anderson's wide experience may well have speculated how little effort, and how little penetration, would be needed to kill a man with such a weapon. The kid was quite likely telling the truth.

The routine investigation of a homicide —refined by long and frequent practice— was under way; and the body of Johnny Stompanato, gigolo and possible small-time gangster, was borne off to its protracted obsequies that would begin on the post-mortem slab at the Los Angeles mortuary.

Already, through the night, the wires were singing the news of a top-flight scandal that would break the following morning.

Lana Turner, the super-star, was born Julia Jean Frances Mildred Turner in 1921, daughter of a San Francisco stevedore who was murdered in an alley for the sake of his winnings in a crap game.

At the age of 15, the girl was living

Both AP

CHERYL'S father Stephen Crane (above) was sued by Stompanato's surviving brother. Ironically, Lana, pictured with lover and daughter on facing page, rose to fresh heights of stardom after the scandal.

with her mother in Los Angeles, where Mrs. Turner was working in a local beauty salon.

The day that gave Lana Turner to the world has gone down in the folk history of Hollywood. It was the day on which, dressed in skin-tight sweater, skimpy skirt and high heels, she was spotted in a soda fountain on Sunset Avenue by a journalist named Billy Wilkerson.

He should have had his face slapped for handing this truant high-school girl the oldest pick-up line in the Hollywood book: "How'd you like to be in pictures?" Except that Wilkerson was on the level: he had spotted something extra-special in the 15-year-old sweater girl.

Wilkerson fixed her up with an agent, who got her a small part in a murder drama called *They Won't Forget*, which

Mervyn LeRoy directed for Warners. She only played three short scenes; but *They Won't Forget* is only remembered for the breezy kid in the tight sweater. A star was born.

At 19, Lana Turner (the studio gave her the name) made her first venture into what was to be, for her, the familiar state of matrimony. This was to band-leader Artie Shaw. The marriage lasted two months, and drove Lana to a nervous breakdown. (Shaw fancied himself as an intellectual, and was disappointed when his bride's mind did not, in his opinion, match up with her physical endowments.)

Husband number two was a young executive of a hot dog concern named Stephen Crane. He asked her to dance at a night club, for a bet. Nine days later they were married; an impulsive act that could have led to a charge of bigamy, since Crane's divorce was not yet through.

The non-marriage was annulled, and before they could be properly joined in matrimony, Lana fell pregnant. The child was born five months after the second wedding. It was a girl, and because of the Rhesus Negative factor, its blood had to be changed every four hours by transfusion. They called the baby Cheryl. The girl who was later to admit to the killing of Stompanato.

It was some time after the break-up of her fourth marriage (to Lex Barker, the screen Tarzan; her third was to millionaire Bob Topping) that Lana became acquainted with Stompanato. In a manner that recalls Stephen Crane's pick-up, Stompanato rang her up for a dare and asked her to come out on a blind date.

It is a good indication of Lana's impulsiveness and naïvety that she responded to what she possibly regarded as a romantic and adventurous invitation. They met, and Stompanato played her along by telling her he was five years older than she; in fact he was five years younger.

At this time, Cheryl was 10, and spent her time between her maternal grandmother and various expensive private schools. Being the daughter of a superstar who was forever presenting her with new stepfathers could hardly have benefited the child's psyche, and her relationship with her mother left a lot to be desired.

"It's a meal ticket!"

At one of the schools she attended, Cheryl was told she must either write to her mother once a week or go to bed without any supper. She began her first letter: "Dear Mother, this is not a letter, it's a meal ticket."

In April, 1957, Cheryl was found wandering in a Los Angeles slum, having run away from convent school. She accosted a total stranger and begged him to help her find a hotel room, because, she said, she was being followed by three men.

This man had the decency to take the girl to the police station, where she told them she was upset because of a misunderstanding with her mother. Lana and her ex-husband Stephen Crane took her away from the station together. By now, Lana was deeply involved with Johnny Stompanato.

It was an affair that held all the elements of eventual tragedy. It began as a pick-up, and developed into a mutual obsession. There was the disparity of ages, tilted in his favour—though she did not know it till it was too late.

Believing her handsome Johnny to be older than herself, Lana cast him in the

SHE NEVER SAW THE KNIFE in her daughter's hand . . . and only when she lifted up her lover's shirt did Lana see his wound. Stompanato made a half turn and fell on his back, already in his agonized death throes, on the floor.

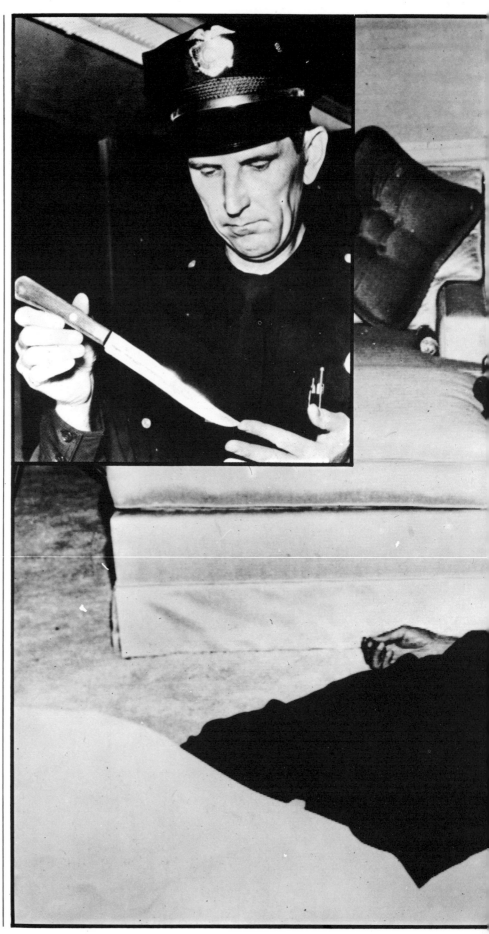

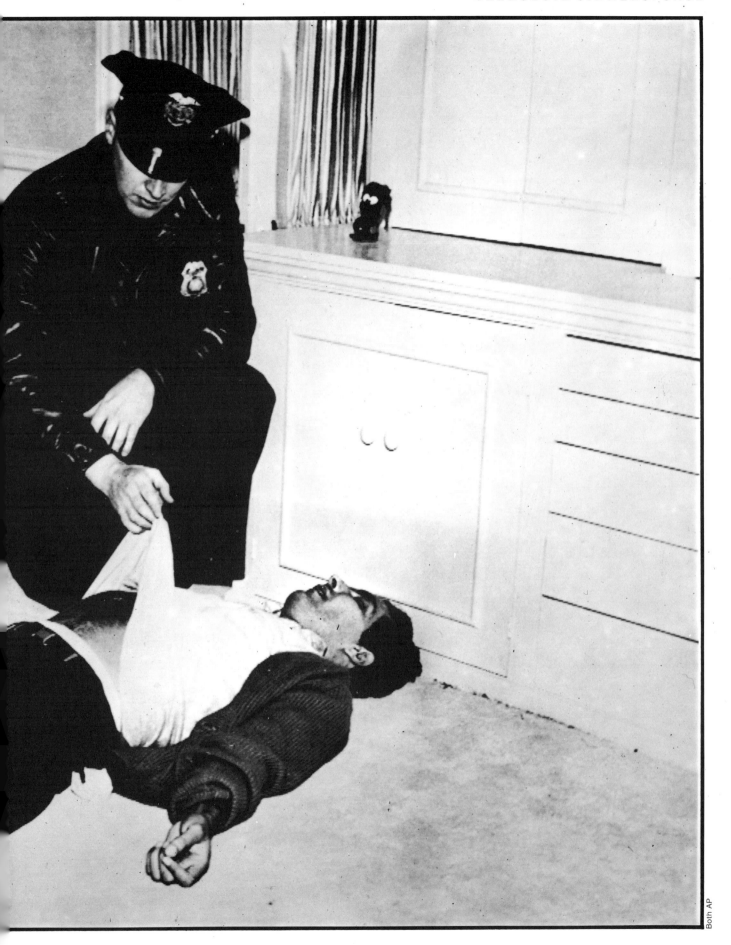

role of a father-figure: in her letters, she was always "Little Lana", and he was "Daddy" or "Papite". Her love letters, which were dragged out and splashed all over the newspapers after his killing, were innocent of eroticism or even passion. They were simply affectionate.

Stompanato's feelings for her were more complex. Whatever his intentions at the start, it is certain that, in the end, he loved Lana to obsession. No less than three women who had been in love with him have stated that "Lana was the real thing, and he loved her more than anyone in the whole world".

The trouble was, he was stuck with the lie about their respective ages. . . .

He was jealous. When she came to England to film, he was jealous of her leading man, Sean Connery—later to become famous as the screen James Bond. His violent rantings and his quarrels with Lana—he attempted to strangle her, and threatened to slash her face with a razor—led to Scotland Yard

ordering him out of England.

Notwithstanding all that, the lovers were soon holidaying together in Acapulco. The obsession was to pursue its preordained course—to tragedy. Cheryl's letters indicate that, far from disapproving, she was very happy about the relationship between her mother and the superficially personable Stompanato. She wrote to him from school, and her choice of phrases reveals a casual affection for her mother's lover: "Give my love to Mother. Write soon and be good. Love ya and miss ya loads, Cherie."

Not sentiments of which murder is usually made. But, then, the killing of a fellow human being can often be a very casual matter: 90 per cent of people who kill before midnight meet their own re-

flection in the morning mirror with no thought of the dreadful thing they are fated to do that day.

Lana and her Johnny returned to Los Angeles from Acapulco in March, and Cheryl was at the airport to meet them.

Sophisticated chignon

At 5 ft. 8 in. tall, she almost topped Stompanato. Relaxed and smiling, her hair done in a sophisticated chignon, lipsticked and wearing dark glasses, she made a mockery of her mere 14 years. She was home for the Easter holidays, from boarding school.

Still on holiday, Cheryl accompanied her mother to the Academy Award presentations at Hollywood's Platages Theatre. Lana had been nominated for her performance in *Peyton Place*.

Tragedy was only a bare week away. Good Friday, April 4, 1958, Cheryl paid a visit to her father, Stephen Crane. She returned home to North Bedford Drive around half past five, and went to her

room. She was watching TV when her mother walked in, followed by Stompanato. He was in a furious temper and abusing Lana, who turned and rebuked him for saying "such things" in front of her daughter. Some time after this exchange, Cheryl went down to the kitchen and took a carving knife. As she was to testify later, she did this "in case he tried to hurt Mother".

Terrible threats

Soon after, the row was resumed, this time in Lana's bedroom. Cheryl may, or may not, have heard the threats that her mother attributed to Stompanato. She said afterwards:

"No matter what I did, how I tried to get away, he would never leave . . . and I would have to do everything he told me or he'd cut my face or cripple me . . . he would kill me, and my daughter and my mother."

It was at this point that Cheryl opened the door and went into her mother's room. Lana pleaded with her not to listen, but to go back to her own room. After a moment's hesitation, the girl obeyed.

But soon after, the row blazed up again, and Cheryl opened the door again, to see Johnny Stompanato swinging at her mother with a jacket on a coat hanger.

Cheryl closed with the man; struck him in the stomach. Lana afterwards remembered that they came together, and then parted. She never saw the knife in her daughter's hand.

Stompanato was already dying. He made a half turn and fell on his back. Not till Lana lifted up his shirt did she see his

THE BIGGEST SHOW of the season was the televised inquest, where Lana described the horror at North Bedford Drive. "He'd cut my face or cripple me . . ."

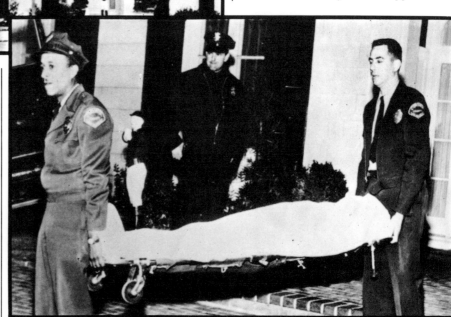

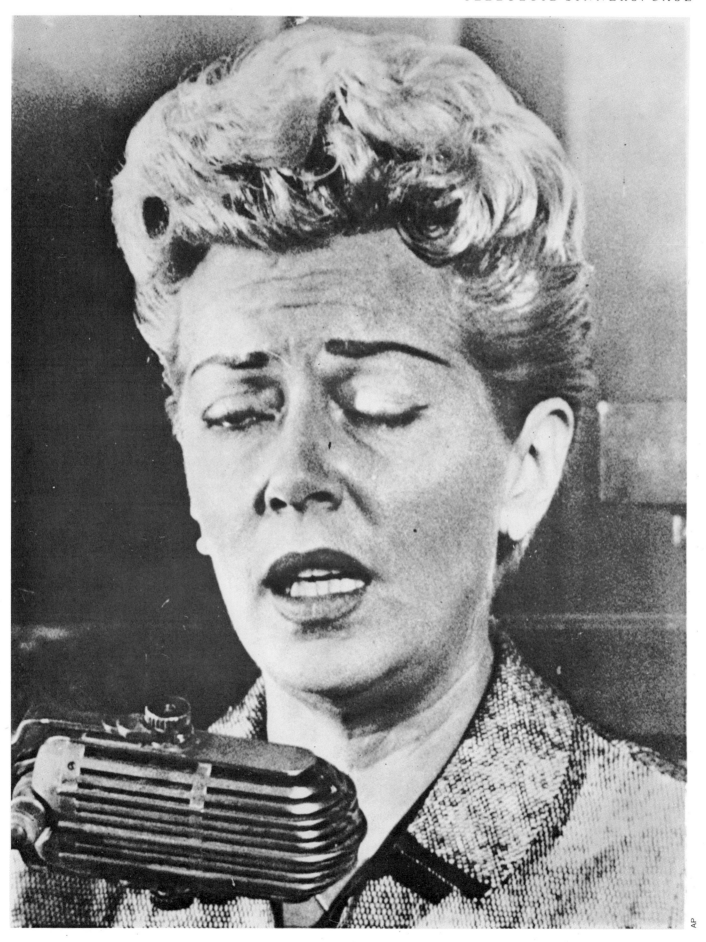

wound; and while her lover was in his death throes, the distraught star telephoned her mother.

It was Mrs. Turner who summoned the doctor, and in every way she showed an admirable presence of mind: while the doctor was giving Stompanato an adrenalin shot, she was trying mouth-to-mouth resuscitation.

It was no use. Johnny Stompanato's heartbeat faltered and faded away to nothing before the detectives arrived — and the doctor was smart enough to advise Lana to call lawyer Jerry Giesler.

Love letters

Stompanato had once been employed as bodyguard to the Hollywood gambler Micky Cohen; and Cohen was summoned to make a formal identification of the dead man. This he refused to do "on the grounds that I may be accused of this murder" — a cryptic statement that served to add an extra angle of sensation to what was already the biggest news story of the year.

Mindful that Stompanato and Cohen had always been close friends ("This was a great guy," was Cohen's epitaph on the dead gigolo), a newspaper editor asked the gambler if he knew of the existence of any love letters. Cohen came up with a pile of Lana's letters to her Johnny, from London, and also Cheryl's letters to her mother's lover.

How Cohen came by them is anyone's guess; it was suggested that his henchmen stole them from the dead man's flat. The letters were plastered all over the press of America, so that everyone was thor-

EPITAPH FOR A GIGOLO: "This was a great guy," said gambler Micky Cohen of his former bodyguard. By refusing to identify the body he added to the drama.

oughly acquainted with the relationships between the three parties before the coroner's inquest.

The inquest was held on April 11, and it was televised live on a nationwide hook-up. The biggest show of the season.

There was a sensational moment when an unnamed man got up and yelled: "This whole thing's a pack of lies! Johnny Stompanato was my friend. The daughter was in love with him, and he was killed because of jealousy between mother and daughter."

Jealous tantrums

It was Lana Turner's testimony that settled the issue. Gently guided by the skilful Giesler, she told the story of that fateful Good Friday evening. Not as Turner the super-star playing the role of her life, but as a distraught mother fighting for her child: confused, frightened, sobbing, completely broken.

Her story satisfied, for the same reason, both the requirements of the court and the criteria of good television. It was completely convincing. She gave the reason for the quarrel that evening. She had, at last, discovered his true age. The myth of the father-figure broken, she no longer needed to have around the man whose jealous tantrums caused her so much pain and embarrassment.

Stompanato, who loved his middle-aged super-star — after his fashion — could not

face up to the thought of losing her. So there was violent talk, and the beginnings of violent action. Lana told how her daughter had leapt to her aid — and all America wept.

The coroner's jury did not take long to arrive at a verdict of justifiable homicide, and Cheryl walked from the court a free person.

They buried Johnny Stompanato at his home town in Illinois. The dead gigolo's brother filed a suit for $800,000 damages against Lana Turner and Cheryl's father, alleging parental negligence; and lawyer Giesler arranged a settlement of some $20,000.

The wry coda to the Stompanato case was that Lana Turner, whose meteoric career had decidedly flattened by 1958, rose to fresh heights of stardom on the wave-crest of the scandal. And mostly in mother-and-daughter dramas with a strong autobiographical slant.

ERROL FLYNN'S FOLLIES

He had everything: fame, fortune—and a unique physique. Just how unique the world was soon to discover when teenage floozies Betty Hansen (inset) and Peggy Satterlee began to rock the boat.

ON A cool, quiet evening in the autumn of 1942 Errol Flynn—the self-styled "Hollywood Hell-Raiser"—was relaxing in the study of his sumptuous $125,000 mansion Mulholland House, overlooking the San Fernando Valley. For once in his turbulent, publicity-prone career the Irish he-man and film star was feeling at one with the world. "I couldn't have it better," he told himself contentedly.

Only the month before he had paid off most of his Government taxes; he was newly divorced from his beautiful first wife, Lily Damita; and he had just received his naturalization papers officially making him an American citizen.

Soothed by all this, Flynn eyed the originals by Gauguin and Van Gogh which gave added dignity to the panelled walls, and gazed proudly through the picture-window at the estate's swimming-pool, riding-ring, tennis-court and cock-fighting arena.

Then, as suddenly as one of the bush fires that periodically break out in the Hollywood hills, his peace was interrupted and shattered beyond repair. There was an agitated rapping on the study door and Flynn's valet, Alexandre, entered. He was white-faced and shaking.

"And stop quivering"

"There are two gentlemen to see you, sir," he said in French. "They have police badges and what looks like a warrant."

Flynn, accustomed to the police or "dicks" as he preferred to call them, grinned nonchalantly. "Show them in and stop quivering," he said. "It's me they want to see, not you!"

A couple of seconds later the two detectives—"they were quite pleasant", said the actor later—strode briskly into the room. Refusing to drink liquor, they settled for cups of coffee, and then one of them said heavily:

"Mr. Flynn, we have a very serious charge against you. Your accuser is in Juvenile Hall, and we've come to take a statement from you. The charge is of statutory rape."

Beneath his assiduously acquired suntan, Flynn paled. At the time he was uncertain as to the exact legal meaning of statutory rape. He appreciated, however, that it was a major morals offence, and soon learned that it carried a minimum sentence of five years' imprisonment.

After protesting his innocence, and submitting to some further cut-and-thrust questioning, Flynn agreed to accompany the officers to the Juvenile Hall in Los Angeles, where a teenaged vagrant named Betty Hansen was being held in protective custody.

"Among the girl's possessions," continued the senior detective, "we found your unlisted telephone number, and she claims that you had sexual intercourse with her at a house rented by some friends of yours. . . . She gave a detailed description of the act."

Despite himself, 33-year-old Flynn showed his curiosity. "What did she say?" he asked anxiously.

The policeman kept his face straight. "That you got undressed, but kept your shoes and socks on."

Various images formed in Flynn's mind. First he realized that with his film about General Custer's last stand—*They Died With Their Boots On*—currently on world-wide release, he would never be free from sexual jokes and innuendo. Secondly, he remembered the house, the party and the girl. An "over-friendly" girl who had sat on the arm of his chair and later gone with him to an upstairs bedroom.

"You don't mean that frowsy little blonde?" he gasped incredulously. "Is she a frowsy little blonde?"

The detective nodded. "Yes, that's the one."

A short while afterwards, at the downtown Juvenile Hall, Flynn and his homeless 17-year-old accuser were brought face to face. Dressed in a grey institution uniform, she was, according to the actor, "gruesome-looking".

Hanging her head and speaking as if she had been rehearsed, Miss Hansen repeated her assertions. "Yes, he took me upstairs," she said dully. "They had been playing tennis, then they played some cards. He took me upstairs, undressed me, and then he . . ."

Modesty overcame her, and she was unable to complete the sentence. "You know what I told you," she mumbled to the listening police.

Statutory rape

Although she admitted that she hadn't put up a fight, and had welcomed if not encouraged Flynn's advances, this was not held to be in her favour. Statutory rape, he heard with dismay, meant having "carnal knowledge" of any person or persons under the age of eighteen, whether they consented or not.

Eager to gain a conviction, and not certain that Betty Hansen's stilted and unconvincing story would do this, the police found another teenaged girl willing to shout "rape" and point an accusing finger at the star. The second "victim"—a night-club dancer called Peggy Satterlee—had an even more bizarre and ludicrous tale to tell.

Two days later Flynn stood confidently before a Grand Jury on four charges of statutory rape, two on each count. Due to doubts concerning the

HE GOT UNDRESSED but kept his shoes and socks on, said Betty Hansen (left). But that wasn't all. When under-age dancer Peggy added her tale, Flynn's he-man reputation was fixed for ever. No wonder the jurors were "starry-eyed".

girls' evidence, the charges were quickly thrown out of court. But for once the District Attorney decided to go against the jury's decision and to proceed with the case.

Flynn was flabbergasted and, like other Hollywoodites before him, gave the traditional cry of: "Get me Giesler!"

The lawyer Jerry Giesler had a reputation for getting the big fish of the movie industry off the hook of scandal and disgrace, and he took over Flynn's defence without even bothering to ask the star whether or not he was guilty.

Meanwhile, as the date of the trial was set, Flynn found himself in the limelight as never before. He was taken to the top floor of the Los Angeles Police Department and was fingerprinted and measured for a suit of prison clothes. "If I went to

"GET ME GIESLER!" cried Flynn. As his "victims" circled for the kill, big-fish Errol would need Hollywood's best lawyer to get him off the hook. Betty Hansen, prime witness (below).

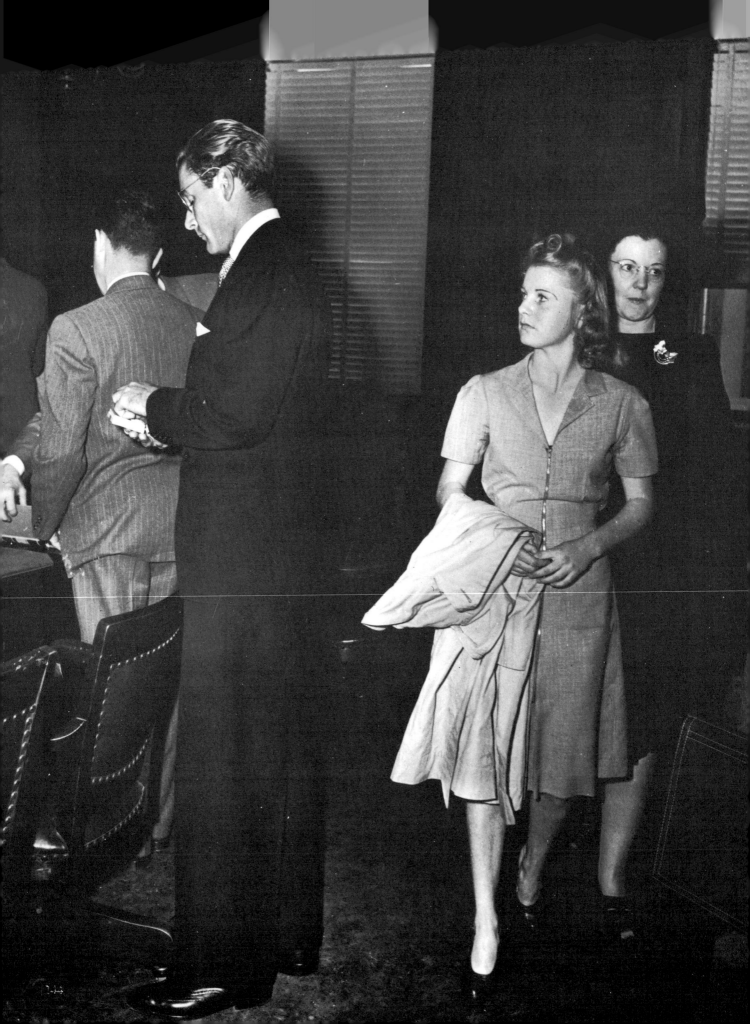

prison," he said wryly, "I was going to have a nice striped suit . . . and if I tried to make a prison break, maybe a coffin."

On his return to Mulholland House, he was under daily siege from mobs of excitable women who banged on the bolted doors "like ice-drops in a hailstorm" demanding to meet "The Great Rapist".

"I had proposals of marriage every day," complained Flynn. "I got letters from women setting up dates, hours and places where they would be waiting for me, ripe and ready, and they didn't wait for a written reply.

"They went ahead with their plans, and when I wouldn't show up I suppose they were disappointed . . . I was a big Hollywood star, and female flak burst around me all the time. So what the hell was this charge of RAPE?"

An ideal scapegoat

But despite the self-assurance which Giesler instilled in him, Flynn was ready to flee the country if the verdict were unfavourable, to avoid the time in San Quentin. He had a twin-engined plane waiting at Burbank Airport, ready at a phone call's notice to wing him to Mexico and then on to South America.

"I was known as a roisterer," he said defensively. "I was vulnerable, an ideal scapegoat."

With this fear in the front of his mind, the hard-drinking Flynn entered Los Angeles County Superior Court at the beginning of January 1943, to discover if he would be sentenced to spend the next five years of his life behind — instead of in — bars.

The trial took place before a jury of three men and nine women — who were described by an optimistic Giesler as being "starry-eyed". The jurors heard Betty Hansen's testimony first of all, and gasped collectively when she told the Deputy District Attorney, Thomas W. Cochran, that, apart from keeping his shoes on, Flynn had proved to be a most unusual lover.

"How long would you say the act of sexual intercourse took?" asked Cochran solemnly.

Without hesitation Miss Hansen answered: "A half hour. Maybe fifty minutes."

With this statement Flynn's reputation as a ladies' man *par excellence* was established for ever. Reports of the hearing made headlines throughout the world, and Flynn modestly noted that:

"The war against Nazism went on to pages two and three, and my case covered five or six or seven columns of front page space in papers all over the land . . . In New York . . . people came out . . . in queues each evening at eight o'clock to get the papers, to read the latest testimony."

BY ANY OTHER NAME Flynn was still a draw. Women (above) even packed a Senate hearing on an obscure ministerial appointment named Edward J. Flynn. Meantime (facing page) star Errol and Betty passed like ships in L.A.

But with the end of Betty Hansen's evidence there were even spicier revelations to come. The first of these arrived when night-club dancer Peggy Satterlee took the stand, and Flynn almost failed to recognize her.

"She was a beautiful girl," he said of the Peggy he had formerly known. "Her upholstery was sensational. Her waist was a lovely moulding. She had long, dark, silky hair, and could have passed for anywhere between twenty and twenty-five."

Yet the girl who stood shyly before the court was none of those things. Although her correct age was never established, she looked about 15 in her schoolgirl shoes, Peter Pan collar, and — of all things — pigtails!

"She could have looked like my kid sister," said Flynn in despair. "My heart sank when I saw her. My God, I thought, she looks like a baby. Yet a week or two earlier she had been in a chorus dressed scantily, to say the least."

In a voice that made Shirley Temple sound like a bar-room virago, Miss Satterlee told how Flynn had "seduced" her on his yacht, *Sirocco*, some 18 months previously.

One night, she said, she was standing on deck admiring the South Californian moon when Flynn approached her and said in best B-picture manner: "The moon looks even more beautiful when seen through a porthole."

Having delivered this line without laughing, Flynn took her down to his cabin where he allegedly threw her on the bed and made violent love to her. During this unwanted performance he told her to look out of the porthole at the moon . . . the moon . . . the moon.

As Miss Satterlee went into intimate details of how and what Flynn had done to her, people in court noticed that he was looking less than his usual gallant and carefree self.

Cheeks like chalk

"His eyes were red-speckled," wrote one reporter, "and his cheeks were like chalk. His smile was patent, false. There were strings in his face, taut and extruded . . . He knew exactly what was at stake. His future. Even perhaps his life."

It was true that ever since the night the detectives had visited his house the actor had been sleeping badly. Even so, this did not stop him from fancying a "very lovely looking redhead" who worked in a cigar and chewing-gum kiosk in the entrance to the City Hall.

"I didn't get a look at her figure for quite some time," said Flynn. "Finally I stopped and bought some cigarettes. I stared beneath the lovely complexion and spotted just enough freckles to make it interesting. I craned my neck a bit

over the counter, and saw that all was well.

"She had about a nineteen- or twenty-inch waist, hips to go with it and slender ankles and wrists . . . The redhead behind the counter interested me to the point where something had to be done . . ."

After establishing the girl's age (she was a "safe" 18), Flynn duly dated her at night, away from the strains of the court. During the day, however, he sat with "clammy hands", feeling he was "growing greyer" every hour, and relying totally on Giesler's supreme ability to turn hostile witnesses into benefactors of the defence.

And Giesler did not let him down. After quizzing Miss Satterlee about the "moon in the porthole" scene, he produced three expert witnesses—a harbour-master and two sea captains—who testified that the moon could not have been seen from Flynn's cabin on the right-hand side of the yacht.

On the night in question the moon was riding on the left of the *Sirocco*, and for the ravished girl to have viewed it, she must have eyes that could see through steel bulkheads.

With that fact established—and with Betty Hansen's evidence already discredited—the jury retired to consider its verdict. The trial had now stretched into the middle of February, and the jurors took an agonizing four hours to reach their decision.

Flynn hid himself from the crowd outside, and confessed that he turned numb as the three men and nine women filed back into the courtroom. "I felt Jerry's hand on my leg, gripping me like an eagle grasping a rabbit," he stated in his uninhibited autobiography, *My Wicked, Wicked Ways*.

"He didn't know, or wasn't sure, what was going to happen, any more than I, but this was his way of showing his feeling for me, and his gesture took away some of the numbness."

Until his dying day

As it turned out, they had nothing to fear. To an outburst of cheering, Flynn was found "not guilty" on all four charges. He waved to the women on the jury, heard the judge compliment them on their "fair" decision, and willingly paid Giesler the $50,000 it had cost to clear his name.

But, pleased as he outwardly was, Flynn realized that the mud that had been flung at him would stick until his dying day.

"In a way I had conquered the forces

LIKE ICE-DROPS in a hailstorm, mobs of excitable fans besieged the defendant daily, demanding a meeting with "The Great Rapist"—who was ready to flee the country if convicted.

of life—rather young," he wrote. "I had fame, fortune—and Nature had given me a unique physique . . . I had everything—ostensibly. And yet I knew I had lost.

"I knew that I could never escape this brand that was now upon me: that I would always be associated in the public mind with an internationally followed rape case."

This was still so 17 years later when —in October 1959—Flynn collapsed and died of a heart attack while holidaying in Vancouver. His companion at the time was a young actress named Beverly Aadland (she was just 15 when she first took up with the ailing star), who had appeared with him in his last and most feeble film—a sleazy semi-documentary, *Cuban Rebel Girls*.

A doctor who examined Flynn's body commented on how dissipated and worn-out it was. "He was aged only fifty, but he had the appearance and the organs of a man of seventy," he said. "He was truly one of the living dead."

THE LONELY ROAD TO DEATH

He looked a charming man to the lonely widow anxiously waiting for his first visit. But Charles and "sister" Martha were after something else. . . .

Associated Press

Popperfoto

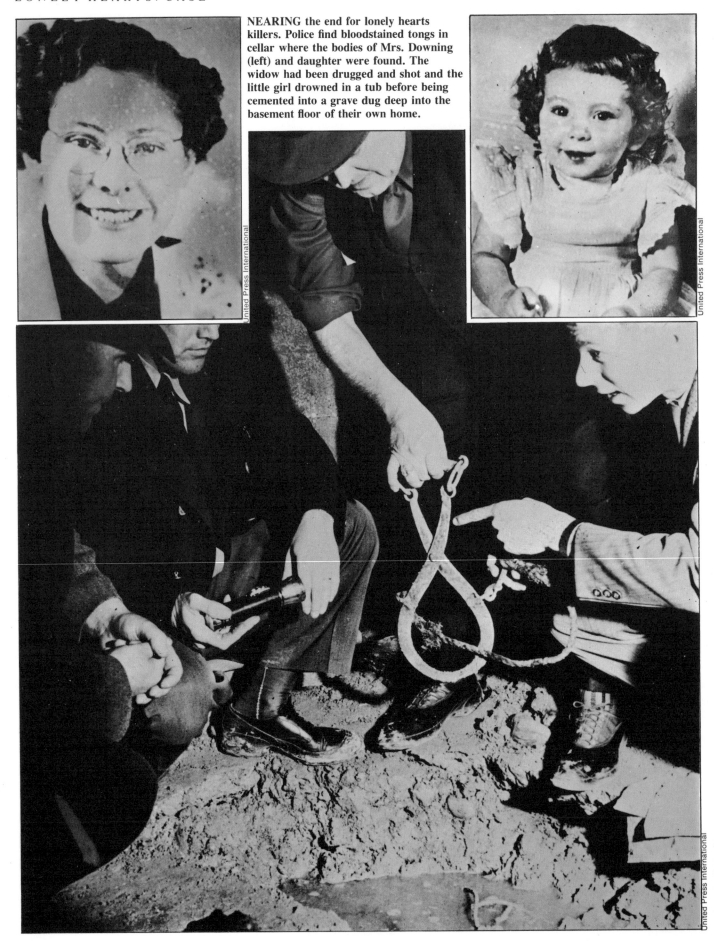

NEARING the end for lonely hearts killers. Police find bloodstained tongs in cellar where the bodies of Mrs. Downing (left) and daughter were found. The widow had been drugged and shot and the little girl drowned in a tub before being cemented into a grave dug deep into the basement floor of their own home.

United Press International

United Press International

United Press International

AT THE house in Byron Centre, a suburb of Grand Rapids, Michigan, all was excitement. Mrs. Delphine Downing, a 28-year-old widow, had led a lonely life since the sudden death of her husband a couple of years earlier. Her only consolation was her daughter Rainelle, now coming up to her third birthday, but Rainelle did not help to make the nights any shorter.

Now, however, it looked as if all that might change. She was awaiting a visit from the man she expected to fill the gap in her life. He was Charles Martin, a Hawaiian-born Spaniard who said that he had worked for British Intelligence during the war. That really did make him sound reliable. His letters—after they had been put in touch with each other through a Lonely Hearts Club—had been charming. Most important of all, he loved children, and Rainelle needed a father.

Charles proved to be everything she hoped for when he walked up the pathway to the house at 3435 Barn Centre Road on the afternoon of January 19, 1949. He was slim, young, elegantly-dressed, and romantic-looking with his thin moustache and sensuous lower lip. "Rather like Charles Boyer," thought Mrs. Downing.

Rainelle, not so certain, hid behind her mother's skirts. "Hallo, Rainelle," said Charles, bending down with a winning smile. "Don't be a shy little girl." His words and gentle manner coaxed a smile from her in return. Mrs. Downing was enchanted. He really did love children.

Sex-crazed crook

Charles had not arrived alone. With him was his big, jovial sister, 28-year-old Nurse Martha. The widow was quick to reassure Martha that she was glad of her presence. "Charles on his own might have caused a bit of scandal with the local folks," she explained. "You know what it's like in these close-knit communities."

She would have been less happy had she had any inkling of the truth—that Charles was actually a sex-crazed crook named Raymond Fernandez, who made his living by seducing lonely women and swindling them out of their savings . . . that Martha, whom he had also met through a Lonely Hearts Club, was his passionate mistress; only too willing to satisfy his lust for perverted sex . . . and that Martha's insane jealousy over Fernandez's attentions to his victims had already turned both of them into murderers.

They moved into the widow's home where to Martha's rage—he was there to work, not enjoy himself—Fernandez quickly seduced their hostess. For the next five weeks he busied himself as Mrs. Downing's financial adviser, helping her to sell up property she owned before taking her to his home at Valley Stream, Long Island, and making her Mrs. Charles Martin.

And then the widow suddenly disappeared. Charles and Martha called on neighbours to reassure them: "Delphine has gone away for a while and we're looking after Rainelle for her." But the neighbours, who had always thought there was something "peculiar" about Charles and his sister, were not satisfied. They called the police.

The squad car which sped to 3435 Barn Centre Road found the house empty. The policemen waited. Finally, Charles and Martha reappeared. "We've been to the pictures," they explained. No, they had no idea where Mrs. Downing had gone and when she might be back. In answer to further questions, Fernandez suggested: "Go ahead and search the house if you want to."

Damp spot

Deputy Sheriff Clarence Randle, one of the policemen, later said: "Somehow I had a hunch there had been a murder and that the body would be in the basement. We went down to the cellar. The first thing we saw was a damp spot of cement. It even had the outline of a grave. So we dug—and dug—and there we found them, not only Mrs. Downing but her little girl."

The widow had been forced to take an overdose of sleeping pills, then shot in the head. It was never to be established clearly who had actually pulled the trigger. Fernandez claimed at one point that he thought she was dying from the pill overdose, and had shot her as an act of euthanasia. On the other hand, it was suggested that Martha had fired the fatal shots: jealous because she believed Fernandez's "necessary" lovemaking had made Mrs. Downing pregnant.

No matter who was responsible, they were left with the problem of a disconsolate Rainelle, weeping continuously and asking over and over again: "Where's my Mummy?" In the end Fernandez couldn't stand it any longer. "You'll just have to do something about her," he said. Martha needed little prompting. She had never liked the child—and now she picked up the screaming little figure and calmly drowned her in a washtub.

Fernandez took the limp body down to the cellar, laid it on top of Mrs. Downing's in the deep pit he had dug and filled the hole in with cement. Then, their getaway planned for early the next day, he took his mistress off for a pleasant evening at the cinema.

But it quickly became clear that this was just the beginning of a horrifying story. Fernandez proved a boastful prisoner who made no attempt to hide how he had made his living. Lonely Hearts Clubs' lists of past and potential victims, found in his possession, were checked out by the police. By the night of March 2,

the Spaniard and his fat mistress had not only been charged with three murders, but were suspected of having committed another 17, and feared to have committed even more.

There was, for example, the case of Mrs. Jane Thompson, who had died at the end of a holiday with Fernandez at La Linea in Spain in October, 1947. The Spaniard, on his return, had given two versions of her death—firstly that she had been killed in a train crash, secondly that she had been the victim of a heart attack. La Linea police believed she had been poisoned, and had they been able to lay hands on him, were prepared to arrest Fernandez.

As it was, he was able to make his escape and, back in New York, produced a fake will laying claim to the apartment occupied by Mrs. Thompson's mother on 139th Street. First he moved in with her, but later he packed her off to live with a son so that he could have the flat to himself.

Then there was Myrtle Young. Fernandez, who already had a wife in Spain as well as his mistress Martha, went through a bigamous form of marriage with her on August 14, 1948, in Cook County, Illinois. Martha was, as usual, present, and—as usual—consumed with jealousy at the thought of Fernandez having to play the role of gallant lover.

When the "newlyweds" moved into a Chicago boarding-house after the ceremony, Martha moved in with them and —because of her "brother's" shyness—insisted on sharing the same bed as "the bride". When Myrtle protested, Martha, a frightening and dominating personality, fed her an overdose of barbiturates "to soothe her nerves".

She was unconscious for 24 hours. After she came to, but was still in a dazed state, the couple put her on a bus bound for her home town of Little Rock, Arkansas. She died shortly afterwards in hospital. At the time, however, the cause of death was presumed to be a liver complaint from which she suffered.

Marriage promise

Fernandez denied murdering either woman. In fact, he and Martha would admit to only one other killing apart from Mrs. Downing and her little girl. That was a 66-year-old widow, Mrs. Janet Fay, of Albany, New York. "I got 6000 dollars out of her just three weeks before moving in with Mrs. Downing," he boasted. Once he had his hands on the money, the widow was lured by the promise of marriage to her death at the new apartment Fernandez and his "sister" had rented at 15 Adeline Street, Valley Stream, Long Island. It was Martha who gave the police the details of the murder.

DEATH HOUSE . . . the apartment building where Fernandez lived with Jane Thompson and her mother. Jane died mysteriously while on holiday with Fernandez in Spain. On the murderer's return Jane's mother "disappeared".

"I bashed her head in with a hammer in a fit of jealousy," she said. "I turned to Raymond and said: 'Look what I've done.' Then he finished the job off by strangling her with a scarf."

They had cleaned up the flat at once to stop blood dripping through to the apartment below, then made passionate love while the body of the murdered widow grew cold on the floor beside them. Next day, Fernandez bought a trunk, locked the widow's body in it and took it to his sister's home—where it was left in the cellar.

It was there for some time while Fernandez and Martha made arrangements to rent a house in the Queens district of New York as a disposal place for the body. Nobody had noticed the smell of the decaying corpse when the Spaniard came back to collect it. He and Martha buried the body in the basement of the rented house, cemented it over, and waited for four days for the cement to dry. Then they went back to the agent and said that the house was unsuitable.

"What was the address?" the police asked. Fernandez had no compunction about replying. He gave them the number on 149th Street, South Ozone Park, Queens. A few minutes later, Fernandez and Martha were calmly repeating details of the murder to the New York District Attorney over the telephone. Mrs. Fay's body was found, just as they had described, wrapped in brown paper and buried four feet down in the basement.

Fernandez and Martha would not have remained so calm and self-assured had they realized what lay behind the increasing police interest in the murder of Mrs. Fay. In Michigan there was no death penalty and, if convicted of the murder of Mrs. Downing and her little girl, the worst the couple could expect was a life sentence—which would probably mean freedom at the end of 16 years or so. It was this which had led the couple to talk so freely about their crimes.

Legal battle

In New York, however, the electric chair was still the penalty for first-degree murder. The authorities therefore set about getting Martha and her lover extradited on the grounds that, although they had been arrested in Michigan, the first murder they had admitted to—that of Mrs. Fay—had been committed in New York.

The couple's first intimation that they might have talked too much came when the Michigan Attorney General ordered a delay in their trial. They began an immediate legal battle to try to avoid extradition. The police had moved too quickly for them, however. Although the legal arguments were to last for more than a year, Martha and Fernandez

MYRTLE YOUNG: She was fed barbiturates and later, still in a daze, packed off in a bus to her home town in Arkansas. She died soon afterwards; but not before Fernandez had fleeced her of $4000. She had withdrawn the money in order to get married to the man who was to kill her.

United Press International

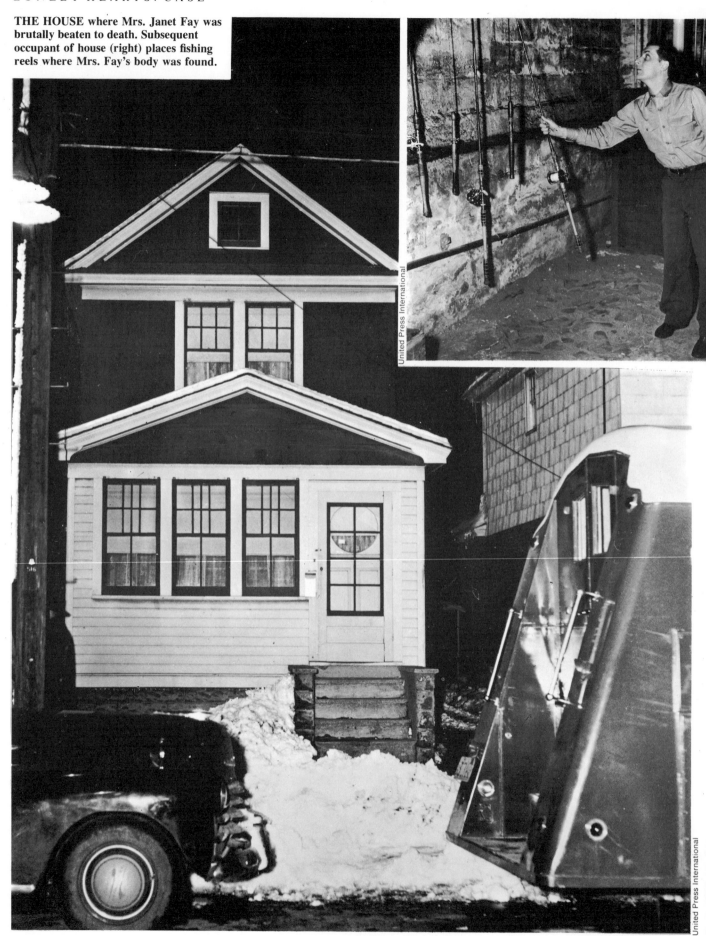

THE HOUSE where Mrs. Janet Fay was brutally beaten to death. Subsequent occupant of house (right) places fishing reels where Mrs. Fay's body was found.

United Press International

United Press International

Martha and Fernandez on their way to death house at Sing Sing prison. "Let him who is without sin cast the first stone," she said without a trace of repentance.

found themselves within a month in a Long Island prison, where Martha passed away the time by reading two crime novels a day.

They were finally brought to trial—charged for the time being only with the murder of Mrs. Fay—before Judge Ferdinand Pecora in New York at the beginning of July, 1949. The question at issue was not so much their guilt, as whether or not they were sane.

Twisted mind

The defence spared no efforts to try to prove that they were unbalanced and not responsible for their actions. Martha, it was said, had a twisted personality as a result of being repeatedly raped by one of her brothers when she was a child. Fernandez, once woman-shy, had been transformed into a sex-mad gigolo when he was accidentally struck on the head by a falling hatch while working aboard an oil tanker.

Martha—like Mrs. Fay and Mrs. Downing later—had come into his life via a Lonely Hearts Club in 1947. At the time she was a divorcee, Mrs. Martha Beck, who had just lost her job as matron of a crippled children's home in Pensacola, Florida. Not only was she lonely. She had two children to support—one

illegitimate by a West Coast bus driver who had committed suicide rather than marry her.

Fernandez picked Martha's name out of the Lonely Hearts list for two reasons. She was, unlike most addicts of Lonely Hearts Clubs, a mere 26. She had also given her maiden name, Seabrook—and he regarded this as a good omen because he was a practitioner of Voodoo and, by a coincidence, (William) Seabrook was also the name of the author of *The Magic Island,* his Voodoo "bible". So he sent her his standard letter:

Dear Martha:

I hope you'll allow me the liberty of addressing you by your Christian name. To tell the truth, I don't quite know how to begin this letter to you because, I must confess, this is the first letter of this sort I have ever written.

Would you like to know a little about me? I'm 31 and I've been told I'm not a bad-looking fellow. I am in the importing business from Spain, my mother country. I live alone here in this apartment, much too large for a bachelor,

but I hope some day to share it with a wife.

Why did I choose you for my debut friendship letter? Because you are a nurse and therefore I know you have a full heart with a great capacity for comfort and love.

Your friend,
Raymond Fernandez.

A month later she came, by invitation, to New York. It was a disappointed Fernandez who received her at the 139th Street apartment, which had once belonged to Jane Thompson's mother. Not only did Martha seem a poor bet financially: her appearance was repellent—fourteen-and-a-half stone, treble chin, mop of dark, unruly hair, heavy make-up. The long fashions of the era did nothing for her, although she usually wore black in an effort to make herself seem slimmer than she was.

Handsome lover

Fernandez tried to break with her not long after that first meeting. But Martha refused to be shaken off. To outsiders he might seem—with his long, sallow Spanish face, thin moustache, and receding hairline concealed by a toupee—like a seedy, dancehall gigolo. She saw him with

453

different eyes. He was the handsome lover she had dreamed about all her life —the embodiment of all the romantic heroes she had read about in the true-story magazines she devoured like a drug.

She was mad about him right from the beginning. At their very first meeting she allowed him the pleasure of her obese body—and when he later attempted to ditch her, she tried to gas herself. Fernandez's response was not merely to take her back. He also revealed to her how he made his living.

Her jealousy

She was not horrified. "That's all right," she told him, snuggling up to him in bed. "I don't mind, darling. We can work together. I can pretend I am your sister. We can be together always. And I can help to persuade the women to put their trust in you."

Which was how they worked, fleecing an average of one new victim a month. Even to Fernandez, the number seemed incredible. Yet the lonely women caught in his net—when, otherwise, they seemed condemned to a solitary life—were anxious to please. If they had any misgivings, the Spaniard and his "sister" proved a persuasive team.

The one factor that he could never control, however, was Martha's all-consuming jealousy. She wanted the money that meant a nice modern home with a refrigerator and all the other contemporary comforts. But the thought of her beloved Fernandez caressing the bodies of other women, and making love to them as part of the swindle, drove her mad. Eventually, it drove both of them to murder.

One of the remarkable aspects of the case is that Fernandez had any energy left to satisfy the desire of his victims. Martha had a voracious sexual appetite. Anything and everything went. As part of the defence's attempt to make them seem unbalanced, no detail of their bizarre sexual experiences together was withheld from the court. The details of their carnality and bestiality were so lurid that not even the most outspoken newspapers felt they could publish them.

Kissed him

An indication of Martha's passion for her lover was given when she appeared —wearing a silk dress, green shoes, bright red lipstick and thick rouge on her sagging cheeks—to give evidence for the first time. She rushed across the courtroom, cupped Fernandez's chin in her hands, and kissed him passionately, first on the mouth, then on his face and head. He was covered in lipstick before court officials could pull her away. "I love him, and I always will," she yelled as she was dragged to the witness-stand.

HEADLINE MURDERER . . . Fernandez reads the story of his own case as a way of passing time in jail. His only regret was separation from "sexy" Martha.

It was three weeks before the jury retired to consider their verdict, by which time the court testimony amounted to some 45,000 pages. It took the jury all night to reach a conclusion. In the middle of their deliberations they had to return to hear a confession by Fernandez. At times he had complained that Martha was the sole culprit and deserved to die. Now he pleaded for her release because he wanted to confess that he, and he alone, was the killer.

Ultimately, the jury found them both guilty of first-degree murder. They appealed, Raymond changing his plea to one of insanity, but reverting to his original response to the charge—that he had been a mere accessory after the fact—when psychiatric reports indicated that he was of perfectly sound mind.

During the long months they spent in Death Row at Sing Sing awaiting the hearing of their appeals, Martha and Fernandez corresponded regularly. One of her most treasured possessions was a letter from her Latin Romeo saying: "I would like to shout my love for you to the world."

Finally, their appeals were rejected and the date of their execution was fixed for the night of March 8, 1951. Both, at the end, seemed calm and unrepentant. Fernandez entered the execution chamber in the company of a Roman Catholic priest at 11.12 p.m. "I am going to die," he said calmly. "That is all right. As you know, that's something I've been prepared for since 1949. So tonight I'll die like a man."

Martha followed him 12 minutes later. It had been decided that she should be the last to go to the chair because she was the more unlikely to break down in the face of impending death. Her last statement to the world was an attack on everyone who had judged her harshly.

It said:

"What does it matter who is to blame? My story is a love story, but only those tortured with love can understand what I mean. I was pictured as a fat, unfeeling woman. True, I am fat, but, if that is a crime, how many of my sex are guilty?

"I am not unfeeling, stupid or moronic. The prison and the death house have only strengthened my feeling for Raymond, and in the history of the world how many crimes have been attributed to love? My last words and my last thoughts will be: Let him who is without sin cast the first stone."

THE BRIDES IN THE BATH

The notorious bigamist who preyed on lonely, unsuspecting women.
He married them, took their money . . . then he drowned them.

Thomson Newspapers Ltd

MUSTACHIOED MURDERER George Joseph Smith (right) was a skilful seducer. Women found him irresistible and gave up not only themselves but their money in response to his charm. He drowned three of his wives in the bath. Below, the two who escaped: Caroline Thornhill (top), Edith Pegler.

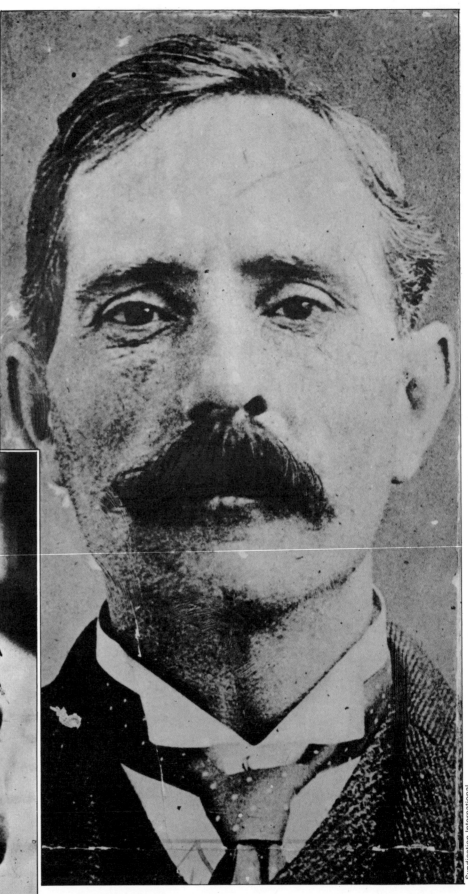

456

FOR NINE days during the summer of 1915 the attention of the British public was temporarily diverted from the bloody trench warfare in France to an amazing murder trial which took place in London's Central Criminal Court, the Old Bailey. The accused whom the police brought into the dock on June 22, 1915, was a 43-year-old criminal adventurer charged under his real name of George Joseph Smith – although he had employed a number of aliases in the course of his unsavoury sexual and criminal career.

As a youngster he had been sent to a reformatory and later went to prison twice for stealing. From an early age, in spite of a certain talent for drawing and playing the piano, he was the despair of his respectable mother – who prophesied with remarkable accuracy that he would die with his boots on. He had tried his hand at a variety of occupations: gymnasium instructor in the army, music hall songwriter, baker, junk shop owner, and finally dealer in antiques.

Lonely women

However, his principal occupation was preying upon lonely and unsuspecting women who, unfortunately for them, found him most attractive. It was one of these women, Bessie Mundy – whom he had "married" bigamously as Henry Williams in 1910 – that he was tried for murdering two years later. She died while taking a bath at the lodgings where they lived together in Herne Bay, on the English south coast.

The presiding judge at the trial was the great commercial lawyer Mr. Justice Scrutton. The prosecution was led by the senior prosecuting counsel Mr. (later Sir) Archibald Bodkin, afterwards Director of Public Prosecutions. Smith was defended by Sir Edward Marshall Hall, the most popular and successful criminal advocate of his day and then at the height of his powers. As Smith had no money, Marshall Hall provided his services for £3 5s. 6d. – the maximum fee allowed defence counsel by the Poor Prisoners' Defence Act.

After Smith had formally pleaded not guilty, Mr. Bodkin began his opening speech for the prosecution. In outlining the prisoner's career to the jury, the prosecutor drew particular attention to the fact that the accused – under the assumed name of George Oliver Love – had married Caroline Beatrice Thornhill at Leicester in 1898. A year or two later she left him, but she remained his legal wife and was alive at the time of the trial. In 1908, Smith met a young woman named Edith Pegler in Bristol and "married" her under his own name. They lived together from time to time, and though he would leave her for long periods, he always returned to her in the end. In fact he had

done so after the death of Bessie Mundy.

On August 26, 1910, the prisoner went through a ceremony of marriage, posing as Henry Williams, with 31-year-old Beatrice ("Bessie") Constance Annie Mundy in Weymouth Registry Office. She had a small fortune of £2,500 left by her late father, who had been a bank manager. She could not touch the capital sum, which was held in trust for her, but she was paid £8 a month from the trust, which she allowed to accumulate.

By September 1910 the accumulated balance amounted to £138, and this Smith obtained by applying for it to the trust solicitor in his "wife's" name. As soon as he received it, he made off, leaving her without a penny. He subsequently wrote to her explaining that his health had become "terribly impaired" as the result of an "infectious disease" which he claimed she had given him, and that a long cure was necessary before he could return.

Meanwhile, Bessie went to live in lodgings with a friend in Weston-super-Mare. There, by an extraordinary coincidence, while walking along the esplanade one day in March 1912, she spotted her errant "husband". Instead of running away or calling the police, she spoke to him and again fell completely under his charm. She immediately left her lodgings to spend the night with him, not even taking her nightdress. The reunited couple then moved together to lodgings in Herne Bay.

There was no bath in the new house, but Smith bought one secondhand and installed it in an empty room in the lodgings. This was on July 6, 1912. Next day they both made wills, the unfortunate Bessie appointing her "husband" sole executor and legatee. Four days later the couple called on a local doctor named French. Smith said that his wife had shown signs of epilepsy – although the lady described herself as being perfectly well except for occasional headaches.

Completely submerged

On the morning of July 13, Dr. French received a note from Smith: "Do come at once. I am afraid my wife is dead." When the doctor arrived at the lodgings, he found that this was so, the woman's body being completely submerged in the bath water. In one hand she clutched a piece of soap.

At the coroner's inquest, Dr. French stated that in his opinion the woman drowned as the result of a fit of epilepsy in the bath. In these circumstances it was not surprising that the jury returned a verdict of death by misadventure – "the cause of death being that while taking a bath she had an epileptic seizure causing her to fall back into the water and be drowned".

The dead woman's estate was proved at £2,571, and under the terms of her will

her "husband" inherited all of it. He first invested the proceeds in house property, and after selling out at a considerable loss, used the £1,300 that was left to buy an annuity which brought him an income of £76 a year. Clearly George Joseph Smith had an expectation of a long life.

"This case is of a very grave character," said the prosecutor after he had told the jury how Bessie Mundy had died, "and one to which you will give the most earnest attention in the interests not only of the prisoner, but also of the public." Counsel paused dramatically for a few moments. He then turned to the judge and said that he had an important point of law concerning the admissibility of certain evidence to put to him. Mr. Justice Scrutton accordingly directed the jury to retire while it was being argued.

Virtually doomed

This was a move which Marshall Hall had feared, since he knew from the documents in his brief that there was evidence that his client had "married" two other women, that the two had likewise died in their baths, and that they had previously both executed wills making the prisoner sole beneficiary. Hall realized that if once this evidence was admitted his client was virtually doomed.

Mr. Bodkin's point was that the prosecution was entitled to call evidence of any character tending to prove that this was a case of killing by deliberate design and not by accident – and that the accused in causing the death of Bessie Mundy was operating a "system". In reply Marshall Hall submitted that evidence of "system" was only admissible where it was necessary for the defence to set up a denial of intent. It was not necessary in this case, he said, since as yet the prosecution had not put forward sufficient evidence to displace the primary presumption of innocence in the prisoner.

It was a gallant effort on the lawyer's part, but it proved of no avail. The judge ruled that such evidence *was* admissible. However, he warned the jury that they must not use it to infer that the prisoner was a man of bad character and infamous acts, but only to help them to decide whether Miss Mundy's death was the result of an accident or had been deliberately engineered by Smith.

The prosecutor then proceeded to outline the facts of the two additional murders for which he suggested that the prisoner was responsible. In 1913 Smith had bigamously married a buxom young nurse named Alice Burnham whom he had seen praying in a Wesleyan-Methodist chapel in Southsea. Her father, a fruitgrower in Buckinghamshire, had been keeping a sum of £104 for her, and when Smith wrote to Mr. Burnham demanding that it should be handed over, Mr. Burnham

458

Syndication International

BUXOM BRIDE number four, Alice Burnham. Smith collected £500 insurance.

Popperfoto

replied in a letter in which he asked some questions about his son-in-law's family background. To his letter he received the following astonishing postcard:

> Sir,—In answer to your application regarding my parentage, my mother was a bus-horse, my father a cab-driver, my sister a roughrider over the Arctic regions. My brothers were all gallant sailors on a steam-roller. This is the only information I can give to those who are not entitled to ask such questions contained in the letter I received on the 24th inst.
>
> Your despised son-in-law,
> G. SMITH

In the end Smith got Alice Burnham's £104 through a solicitor. He also saw to it that she took out an insurance policy of £500 on her life, as well as making a will leaving everything she had to him. Together they visited Blackpool and stayed in lodgings—where the landlady saw water coming through the ceiling one evening when Alice was taking a bath. She was afterwards found drowned in the bath. Much to the landlady's surprise, Mr. Smith had the body put in a plain deal coffin and given a pauper's funeral. "When they are dead, they are done with," he remarked callously. The coroner's jury brought in a verdict of accidental death.

Insurance money

Shortly afterwards Smith received the £500 insurance money on Alice Burnham's life, which he prudently handed back to the insurance company in order to increase his annuity by some £30 a year. He spent Christmas with one of his former "wives", Edith Pegler, and her family in Bristol, saying he had just returned from a profitable antique dealing visit to Spain.

About a year later, under the name of John Lloyd, he contracted another bigamous marriage, this time in Highgate to a clergyman's daughter named Margaret Lofty. She was the most highly born as well as the most short-lived of his brides. She likewise made a will the day after their "marriage", and later the same evening the sound of splashing was heard coming from the bathroom, followed by the slapping of wet hands on flesh, and finally a sigh.

A short while later the landlady heard the mournful strains of the hymn "Nearer my God to Thee" being played on the harmonium in the Lloyds' sitting-room. Then she heard the slamming of the front door. Before long the male lodger returned and knocked at the landlady's door. He asked about the key which she had given him, but which he had forgotten, and added: "I have bought some tomatoes for Mrs. Lloyd's supper."

A third coroner's jury exonerated Mr. Lloyd, who showed great emotion. "We were only married on Thursday," he said. Being a Friday evening the incident attracted the attention of the national press, and on the following Sunday the *News of the World* headlined the story of a "Bride's Tragic Fate on Day after Wedding".

Under observation

Among those who read the story was the late Alice Burnham's father, and also another landlady who later turned Mr. Lloyd away when he came to engage lodgings. He could not provide a satisfactory reference after he had been shown the bath which he had complained was very small—although as an afterthought he murmured: "I daresay it is large enough for someone to lie in." Both the landlady and Mr. Burnham got in touch with the police, and as a result Mr. Lloyd was kept under observation. He was arrested on February 1, 1915, when about to enter a solicitor's office in Shepherd's Bush, London, with a view to proving the late Margaret Lofty's will.

He was first charged with causing a false entry to be made at his bigamous marriage to his third victim. Then after he had been identified by Mr. Burnham, he was remanded in custody for further police inquiries. Two months later he was charged with the murder of Bessie Mundy, Alice Burnham, and Margaret Lofty—although he was only indicted for killing the first named.

"In each case you get the simulated marriage," said Mr. Bodkin in concluding his speech to the jury. "In each case all the ready money the woman had is realised. In each case the woman made a will in the prisoner's favour. In each case the property could only be got at through the woman's death . . . In each case there were inquiries about the bathroom. In each case the prisoner is the first to discover the death. In each case the prisoner is the person in immediate association with each woman before her death. In each case the bathroom doors are either unfastenable or unfastened . . . In each case there is the immediate disappearance of the prisoner."

The only one of Smith's "brides" to testify was Edith Pegler, the only one whom he loved enough neither to desert, to rob, nor to kill. On the whole, she said, the prisoner had been kind to her. But she added a curious fact when she stated that Smith had once warned her of the danger of baths to women. "I should advise you to be careful about these things," she stated he had told her, "as it is known that women often lose their lives through weak hearts and fainting in a bath." While she was giving her evidence, the prisoner showed some signs of distress.

When a police inspector took the stand, Smith lost all control. "He is a scoundrel!" he shouted as he jumped up from his seat in the dock. "He ought to be in this dock. He will be one day!"

"Sit down," said the judge. "You are doing yourself no good." But the prisoner refused to be pacified and he banged his fist on the ledge in front of him, his face white with fury. "I don't care tuppence what you say," he roared back at Mr. Justice Scrutton, "you can't sentence me to death. I have done no murder!"

The police inspector described how he had induced a woman friend, who was a strong swimmer, to don a bathing costume and subject herself to an experiment in one of the baths, which had been filled with water. The inspector pulled up her legs at the narrow end so that her head fell under water. She immediately lost consciousness and there was considerable difficulty in bringing her round.

This testimony was corroborated by the celebrated pathologist Sir Bernard Spilsbury, who was called for the prosecution after the three baths had been brought into court as exhibits. "If a woman of the stature of Miss Mundy was in the bath in which she died," said Sir Bernard, "the first onset of an epileptic fit would stiffen and extend the body. In view of her height, 5 feet 7 inches, and the length of the bath, 5 feet, I do not think her head would be submerged during that stage of the fit . . .

Limp body

"After the seizure has passed the state of the body is that of relaxation. The body would probably be limp and unconscious. Bearing in mind the length of the body and the size of the bath, I do not think she would be likely to be immersed during the state of relaxation . . . Dr. French has described the legs straight out from the hips and the feet up against the end of the bath, out of the water. I cannot give any explanation of how a woman—assuming she had had an epileptic seizure—could get into that position by herself. *If the feet at the narrow end were lifted out of the water, that might allow the trunk and head to slide down the bath.*"

Defence counsel could do little with this formidable witness in cross-examination. However, Marshall Hall tried his best, as always. He endeavoured to get the witness to say that clutching a piece of soap lent support to the theory of epilepsy.

"It is not impossible," was as far as Spilsbury would go, "not very likely," he concluded cautiously.

When the case for the prosecution was closed—no less than 112 witnesses had been called and 264 incriminating exhibits put in—Marshall Hall rose and announced briefly: "I do not call any evidence." This gave him the last word

ONE DAY was all Margaret Lofty (above) lasted—just enough time to sign her will in Smith's favour. Opposite, Smith listens calmly to the overwhelming evidence presented against him. But he frequently interrupted the trial with passionate outbursts. Far right, Sir Archibald Bodkin, prosecuting counsel (top) and the famous Sir Edward Marshall Hall who used all his celebrated verbal skill in a vain attempt to get Smith acquitted of the ghastly charges.

with the jury, and again he exerted all his great rhetorical skill with the scanty material at his disposal.

The gist of his defence argument was that no act of violence had been proven, and that it would have been impossible for his client to have killed Bessie Mundy without leaving marks of violence and evidence of a struggle. "If you tried to drown a kitten, it would scratch you, and do you think a woman would not scratch?"

WATERTIGHT EVIDENCE . . . Home Office pathologist Sir Bernard Spilsbury arrives at the Old Bailey clutching vital evidence. It was his testimony which tied up the case against Smith. The whole trial was a fascinating and lurid diversion for Londoners accustomed to a diet of gloomy war news. Above, crowds jostle and push at the doors of the Old Bailey on the last day of the trial in tense anticipation of the verdict being pronounced.

As evidence of Smith's humanity he stressed the mutual affection between the prisoner and Edith Pegler, adding that the crimes of which Smith had been accused were outside the orbit of sane humanity.

Most dramatic moment

"Let me with all the solemnity I can," he besought the jury, "and with all the power of conviction I can put into words say to you: be fair to yourselves, be fair to the prisoner, be just to justice itself before you decide the fate of this man by saying that this terrible accusation against him has been proved."

Mr. Justice Scrutton summed up largely against the prisoner, as he was obliged by the evidence to do. With great effect he compared the knocking at the landlady's door by Smith—shortly after Margaret Lofty had died—to the knocking at the gate just after the murder of Duncan in *Macbeth*—"The most dramatic moment in English poetry," the judge called it.

"You may as well hang me at once, the way you are going on," the prisoner shouted from the dock. "It is a disgrace to a Christian country, that is. I am not a murderer, though I may be a bit peculiar."

It took the jury only twenty minutes to find Smith guilty. Before sentencing him to death by hanging, Mr. Justice Scrutton observed sternly: "Judges sometimes use this occasion to warn the public against the repetition of such crimes—they sometimes use such occasions to exhort the prisoner to repentance. I propose to take neither of these courses. I do not believe there is another man in England who needs to be warned against the commission of such a crime, and I think that exhortation to repentance would be wasted on you."

An appeal was lodged challenging the evidence of the other murders, but the Court of Criminal Appeal held that this evidence of "system" had been rightly admitted, and the appeal was dismissed. The Home Secretary refused a reprieve and the law took its course.

Holy Communion

Smith protested his innocence to the last. On the morning of his execution in Maidstone Prison, in Kent, he partook of Holy Communion. To the prison chaplain who administered the sacrament he said: "I beg of you to believe me when I say I am innocent. No one else does, except my wife. I don't care now. I shall soon be in the presence of God, and I declare before Him I am innocent."

As the hangman put the cap over his head and adjusted the noose, he again declared, "I am innocent." Then the trap-door fell and the pinioned figure disappeared into the pit below the scaffold. George Joseph Smith died like his three lonely-hearts brides—by suffocation.

THE PEDLAR WHO BOUGHT NEW YORK

Jubilee Jim Fisk began life as an itinerant trader, but he had no intention of staying that way. Smooth-tongued and ambitious, he wanted power, wealth and the most beautiful women in town — and he would stop at nothing to get them.

AS the Jersey City ferry docked on the cool, misty morning of March 11, 1868, three men stood on the deck, looking back at the city of New York from which they had just fled. James "Jubilee Jim" Fisk, and his confederates, the ageing Daniel Drew, and small, swarthy Jay Gould, had finally pulled off the most audacious "robbery" in the already murky history of the infant New York Stock Exchange.

In a battered, black valise, held firmly in Fisk's hand, were the proceeds of that robbery — $6 million in Federal currency.

Across the Hudson River, in his palatial railroad offices, sat the man whose money it was, the shipping and railroad magnate, Commodore Cornelius Vanderbilt — a ruthless genius who had sought to control the communications of the entire northeast of the United States by buying up transportation systems through any means he could, whether illegal or not.

The story of the rise of Jim Fisk — from itinerant Vermont pedlar's son to one of the richest men in the United States, and of his battles with Cornelius Vanderbilt that led at one time to his fleeing the State of New York pursued by State Supreme Court deputies — is among the most bizarre of all the histories of the robber barons.

It started more than 20 years earlier, when James Fisk began his business education at the reins of his father's mule-driven pedlar's cart, touring the back lanes of the New England countryside of Vermont. The Fisks sold anything, from silks and satins to patent medicines. By the age of 14, young James, already showing signs of the stout, florid figure which was to become all too familiar to the 1860s and 1870s New York financial community, had taken charge of the family business.

Six years later he had sold out at a profit to a rival Boston concern, Jordan, Marsh and Company, for whom he became their Washington agent. In Washington the pedlar's son soon made his mark. By now a tall, well-built man, with a shock of blond hair, and sporting great side-whiskers, Jim Fisk used his earlier pedlar's experience to advance the cause of his employers.

By the time of the Civil War Fisk had in his pocket enough prominent officials and politicians to ensure hefty war-supply contracts for Jordan, Marsh, and a healthy profit for himself.

The weapons he used to gain favour over rival business interest he was never to discard: personal charm, wine, women, and bribery. When the war ended, Jim Fisk had become such a powerful Washington lobbyist that he was a danger to his employers. With the $60,000 with which they had paid him off, Fisk made his way to New York, and to fortune, and eventual tragedy.

The ruler of the New York business community, which had profited greatly from supplying the vast needs of the Federal Army in the recent war, was Daniel Drew. Drew had risen from an early life as a cattle drover to become the controller of the 800-mile-long Erie Railroad, and the major manipulator of the booming stock market. Any young man wishing to go places, Jim Fisk reasoned, would be well advized to gain the confidence of Daniel Drew.

As he stood before Drew, in his mahogany-panelled office, on the afternoon of their first meeting, even Jim Fisk was in awe. That morning he had dressed carefully, setting off his blue frockcoat and smart, narrow trousers with a white, frilled shirt and cravat, complete with diamond stick-pin. The shabby, corpulent Drew lolled back in his chair, mopping his sweating brow with a red, drover's bandana.

"I've heard of you from Boston," he drawled. "It seems that you're a smart operator. But Boston's no New York, young man. To survive here you must be more than smart: you've got to be tough —damned tough. What have you to offer me this time?"

Fairground huckster

It was the opportunity that Fisk had been waiting for, the reason he had sat for a week in Drew's outer office. Now was his chance. He had to talk fast; he had to talk persuasively, and few could do that better than ex-pedlar Jim Fisk.

He smiled. "I hear you want to sell the Stonington Railroad." Drew sat up, and took a closer look at the young man. The Stonington had been a side gain in a bigger railroad deal that he had recently concluded. It was widely considered unsaleable, even in the railroad mania that was gripping the New York investors of the time. Without allowing Drew to interrupt him, Fisk continued.

"I guarantee that I can sell it for you, provided that my cut is 40 per cent of the deal." Half an hour later, the millionaire Drew was convinced. Jim Fisk, using all his persuasive powers, flashing a ready smile here, looking suitably grave there, had won the confidence of the hardest mind in New York. He would act as Drew's agent, and sell the railroad to a group of Boston financiers whom he knew had money to invest.

The careful, flamboyant dressing had paid off. When, within a week, the deal

SLIGHTLY STOUT, but with the manners and appearance of a dude, Jim Fisk managed to acquire just about everything he could ever have wanted . . .

was concluded, both Drew and Fisk had made a massive profit.

It was the start of an association which was to prove disastrous to Drew—for behind the larger-than-life image of Fisk was a ruthlessness and cunning that threatened to crush all who stood in his way. This man who had been let loose on Wall Street was a fairground huckster for whom there were no rules. The name of the game was money; the object, to win and enjoy as much of that money as possible.

Daniel Drew had made his fortune through speculation with other people's money, much of it coming from the pockets of the British investors who had caught the fever of the chance of quick profits from the railroads and other enterprises of the rapidly expanding American economy. Like many a millionaire before and after him, his prosperity had brought Drew little happiness. Obsessed with the power that riches could bring, his life had become an 18-hour-a-day drive for more.

Similarly, the small mercurial Jay Gould, a sinister financial wizard with whom Drew and Fisk were early associated, had only one aim in mind—to make money, and, having made it, to make more. They and their competitors had this characteristic in common. They seldom smoked or drank, many were intensely religious, and the idea of enjoying whatever fortunes they made was a heresy.

Alone, Jubilee Jim Fisk stood out as the exception among the wheelers and dealers who were rightly to earn the collective epithet of "the Robber Barons". His very shape and style of life set him apart. Always well-dressed, usually to be found in the company of women rather than in the drab, all-male clubs of downtown New York, indulging to excess in most of the vices of modern man, Fisk fought his financial battles for the excitement of the chase rather than for the power that success brought.

Court injunctions

Nowhere is this more clearly shown than in the long and protracted battle that he, Gould, and Drew fought with Cornelius Vanderbilt for the control of the Erie Railroad in the later 1860s and early 1870s. Vanderbilt was a man with a dream—to control the communications of the north-east United States, and through them the newly opened coalfields of Pennsylvania, the steel industry, oil, farm produce, and, eventually, the economy of the country.

The Erie Railroad stood in his way, and he was determined to wrest it from the control of the triumvirate of Fisk, Drew,

TYCOON Daniel Drew (above right) was the man who gave Fisk his first opportunity to enter big business—and the crooked world of the robber barons.

Both Culver

465

and Gould. Through a series of complicated financial manoeuvres, the more shares of the Erie that Vanderbilt bought on the market, the more Fisk ordered to be printed on the press he had installed in that company's basement.

Vanderbilt lost a fortune. It was this, and State Supreme Court injunctions demanding that they return Vanderbilt's estimated $8 million loss, that had brought Fisk and his companions to the New Jersey shore of the Hudson—beyond the jurisdiction of the New York courts.

Cocky statement

Though Drew and Gould had been the financial brains behind the "battle for the Erie", it was at this point—in March, 1868—that Jim Fisk revealed his true strength. No sooner had the party landed than Fisk took firm control. Outside the Taylor's Castle Hotel, his red-lined cloak swirling in the mist, he issued his instructions. The ramifications of dubious business dealings were forgotten; Jubilee Jim now had a new role.

He had crossed the river well prepared. In the violent world of post-Civil War America it was advisable to do so. To protect the $6 million cash, and the lives of himself and his partners, he had brought with him men, rifles, and even cannon.

"Get those cannon in position," he roared, shortly after landing. The small army of thugs and helpers he had brought with him sweated and strained as they trundled three 12-lb. cannon to their sites overlooking the hotel's river approaches. Four hours later Fisk was at the head of a well-armed force of 48 men, equipped with Springfield rifles and lifeboats. As a direct insult to business rival Commodore Vanderbilt, Jubilee Jim issued an order that, for the duration of their stay, he be known as "Admiral" James Fisk.

Incredibly, he was prepared to defy the whole of the State of New York—and the ransom of $25,000 that Vanderbilt had put on his head—to defend the battered black valise and the 6 million greenbacks that it contained. As he prepared his defences at the hotel, he issued a cocky statement to the press:

"The Commodore owns New York," he said. "The Stock Exchange, the streets, the railroads, and most of the steamships there belong to him. As ambitious young men, there was no chance there for us to expand, and so we came over here to grow up with the country."

In the weeks that followed, Fisk strengthened his position. The local police chief was "lubricated" with some of the cash into augmenting Fisk's "army" with an official force of his own, and several attacks from across the river were repelled. Meanwhile, Drew and Gould kept to their rooms, bewildered.

As March moved into April, Jim Fisk became increasingly irritated with his companions. In the smoke-filled rooms of New York clubs and meeting-places they had been in their element. With corrupt local politicians, or on the floor of the Stock Exchange, their word had been law. Now, Jay Gould sat locked up with the company ledgers, while the shattered Drew spent most of the day praying.

Sitting in the bar of Taylor's Castle—his recently acquired mistress, the buxom Josie Mansfield at his side—Fisk called for Gould. As the small, dark man shuffled into the room, Fisk put aside his half-full champagne glass.

"I do not intend to stay in New Jersey for ever," he bellowed. "You are to go to Albany [the New York State capital] and contact the following people." Here Fisk produced from his pocket a list of "friendly" politicians. "Tell them that they must pass legislation to correct our position with the Erie. Here is $500,000 to help them decide."

MILITARY MAGNATE . . . Fisk bedecked in uniform was, perhaps, a slightly ridiculous figure. But it symbolized his ruthlessness and love of power perfectly.

Gould protested in vain that he would be arrested once he set foot across the river. Nevertheless, Fisk insisted—and that evening Jay Gould was rowed across the darkness of the Hudson, bound for Albany with half a million dollars to corrupt the State legislature. Fisk returned to the more important business of the day, the charms of white-skinned, brunette Josie Mansfield and the effervescence of champagne.

Jay Gould did his work well. From the confines of his hotel bedroom, where he had been put in the custody of the sheriff, he began to apply pressure on Fisk's contacts. Simultaneously, Senator William Tweed, New York's corrupt political boss, arranged with his cronies that they would take money from both sides in the dispute.

Whichever group finally offered most was to get its way. Fisk's money held out longer against the low offers of the miserly Vanderbilt. By the September of 1868 a bill releasing Fisk and his partners from any criminal or civil proceedings was passed by the New York senate. Freed from his hotel bedroom, Gould—together with Fisk, and Drew—returned in triumph to New York.

On the morning of September 3, 1868, peace was finally declared in what had become known as the Erie War. Meeting in Vanderbilt's hotel bedroom, with the defeated railroad magnate sitting dejected on the bed, Jim Fisk agreed that they should pay him a fraction of the money they had stolen through the "printing press" shares.

For $4½ million, Cornelius Vanderbilt agreed on his part to make no more trouble. As Fisk swaggered from the room, Vanderbilt threw a final, bitter retort at the broad, retreating back: "I've never been involved with such a bunch of gangsters before," he spat, "and I never want to again!"

Jim Fisk was in his element. Though now nominally the vice-president of the Erie Railroad, he ruled it in a style that captured the popular imagination, and earned him the title of "The Prince of Erie".

To the horror of the more staid members of the Stock Exchange, he moved the headquarters of the Erie Railroad Company to the most unlikely building in the city, Pike's Grand Opera House. Here, on the corner of 23rd Street and 8th Avenue, amid the chandeliered splendour and marbled halls of the theatre, Jim Fisk set up his office.

On the second floor, protected by iron grills and armed guards, he plotted further financial wars—while in the theatre below fashionable New Yorkers flocked in their thousands to see the operettas that the versatile Fisk staged in the auditorium.

It was a mixture unique in business history. On the one hand, the hard, ruthless Fisk was the terror of the money market; on the other he was a jovial theatrical impresario who satisfied the city's thirst for entertainment. On days when he did neither, he would remain in the public eye by riding in his blue and red carriage through Central Park, his mistress or one of his theatrical ladies seated beside him.

Secret passage

There was, however, solid Yankee sense in choosing Pike's Grand Opera House as a base for operations. First, it was relatively secure against the armed attacks that Fisk's business methods invited. Secondly, it had a strongroom larger than the average bank. Finally, in the basement, among the theatrical props,

PARTNER IN CRIME Jay Gould was unquestionably a financial genius who understood only too well how to go about manipulating less gifted speculators . . .

was the printing press which had brought Fisk such rewards.

The gossip that followed him around did not light upon such matters. Outside the business quarter, the city was more fascinated by Jim Fisk's outrageous private life than by where he found the considerable sums of money needed to support it. Behind the Opera House was the mansion that the Prince of Erie had built for himself. The rumour was that a secret passage connected this with the theatre, so that Fisk could conduct his hectic lovelife in private. The rumour was true.

Audacious campaign

Attired in a variety of uniforms designed to his own fancy, Jim Fisk was the talk of New York. He bought his way into becoming the Colonel-in-Chief of the local militia. He affected cloaks, high hats, gave away money at whim, and, it was said, never did anything to harm the poor. For Jubilee Jim Fisk, Prince of Erie, ex-pedlar and travelling menagerie attendant, life was what it had always been — a three-ringed circus.

There was still day-to-day business to conduct, officials to bribe, rivals to crush, and deals to manipulate. Fisk and Gould — James Drew having by now been ousted by his own lieutenants — swept through the market looking for fresh targets. Fisk's interest was simply that he delighted in the fight; Gould's because the vast sums the railroad had accumulated from speculation were wasted unless invested further. Friday, September 24, 1869, saw their greatest coup to date.

Black Friday — so called because it was the day that saw many of America's speculators ruined — was the climax to an audacious campaign to gain control of the Federal gold reserves by cornering the gold market. Put simply, the mathematical genius of Jay Gould had calculated that a sufficient shortage on the open market of gold would force the Government of President Grant to release Federal stocks to lower the market price.

Fisk, Gould, and their agents conspired to buy as much gold as they could. Unknown to the market, however, Jim Fisk, as charming and plausible as ever, had gained the confidence of members of the President's cabinet in Washington. Grant, himself, had been a frequent guest on Fisk's yacht, the *Providence*.

For Jim Fisk, that yacht was wellnamed indeed. For as the price of gold tightened that Friday, he received word — if not from Grant then at least from someone very close to him — that the Government was about to intervene. As the commodity hit a new high price, Fisk, Gould, and their undercover agents sold their vast stocks.

Ten minutes later, the official news of the Grant administration's intervention became known. The price dropped dramatically. The only winners were Fisk and Gould — who had sold their gold at a far higher price than they had paid for it.

In the uproar that followed, Jim Fisk denied all knowledge of what had happened. As far as he was concerned, the gold dealings had been legitimate, rather than corrupt. It did not occur to the supershowman that his closeness to Grant's

PLUMP AND PRETTY Josie Mansfield loved Fisk's money but preferred the amorous attentions of Ned Stokes (below right). For a time she enjoyed both . . .

administration verged upon the illegal, that his use of independent brokers had hidden his own role in the affair, or that suspicions would inevitably be aroused by there being no written record kept by his office of any gold dealings whatsoever.

However, there *was* an inquiry, in which Fisk called into question the loyalty of the President's brother-in-law—with whom he had formed a close association—of the President's wife, and of many of the Administration. To the unknown, but undoubtedly high-ranking, conspirators he let fall a clear warning. "Let everyone carry out his own corpse," he cried. In return for his silence, Jim Fisk was granted immunity from investigation.

All too soon, the prophetic quality of his words was to become clear. The equally crooked but more conventional Jay Gould decided that Fisk's flamboyant conduct was drawing unwelcome attention to the company's activities. He suggested that the time had come for Jubilee Jim to bow out of the circus ring.

In addition, Fisk was involved in a personal scandal concerning his mistress Josie Mansfield. Installed in luxury, in a house close to Fisk's own, the ageing Josie had taken a fancy to a young man, the well-bred but penniless Ned Stokes. Using information that she had provided behind Fisk's back, Stokes had blackmailed him for large sums of money which the young lover had then lavished upon Josie. Jim Fisk was not a man to be blackmailed—at least not for long.

Eventually, his patience exhausted, he took the faithless couple to court. In a spectacular civil action, in which Stokes was cast as the gilded youth, Josie Mansfield as the wronged mistress, and Jim Fisk as the villain, the drama would have graced the Grand Opera House.

On November 25, 1871, the comic drama unfolding in the courts took a tragic and fatal turn. For, on that morning, the jury voted in favour of Jim Fisk. Ned Stokes had been blackmailing him.

On that afternoon, as Jubilee Jim Fisk arrived for a business appointment at a New York hotel, he played out the final act in a life that had been full of acting. Striding up the hotel's main staircase, he came face to face with the young, beaten adversary. In his hand, Stokes held a revolver. "Help me—won't somebody help me?" But Jim Fisk's cries were in vain. Before the shocked bystanders could move, he fell mortally wounded, with a bullet deep in his abdomen.

Carried upstairs to an empty bedroom, Fisk breathed his last. Even dead, the great showman's last act was not finally concluded. For some days his body lay in state in the foyer of the Opera House, his handsome, embalmed face calm in the open-topped coffin. The Ninth New York Militia accorded their dead Commander-in-Chief a military funeral, and solemnly buried him with full military honours, complete with a rifle salute.

Josie Mansfield disappeared from history, and her lover Ned Stokes into Sing Sing for six years.

A cartoon published on the day of the funeral showing Gould, Tweed and other business cronies by the grave read "Dead men tell no tales".

NOBODY needles Ned Stokes . . . The young man found the only way of winning out against Fisk. Jay Gould (left) wept openly beside his dead friend's coffin.

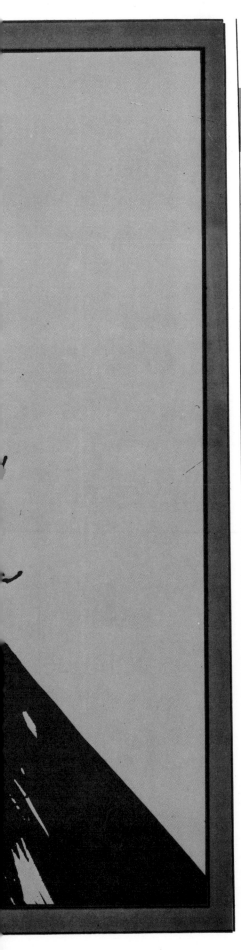

THE BLOODSUCKING COLONEL

With his red face, bushy white whiskers and booming voice, Colonel William d'Alton Mann looked like a jovial Father Christmas. But his scandal sheet *Town Topics* was hated and feared in New York high society. And when a wily District Attorney tricked him into court, the genial Colonel was revealed as a master blackmailer—who robbed the "robber barons".

IT was as if some highly selective plague had struck the state of New York, removing in a stroke all its wealthiest and most influential citizens. In the most fashionable houses along the North Shore telephones rang unanswered. On Newport's exclusive Bellevue Avenue some of the most luxurious homes were deserted, silent behind barred windows and locked doors. Virtually overnight the rich and famous had fled.

Like hunted foxes, New York society itself had gone to ground, and the man they were most definitely "not at home" to was the crusading District Attorney, William Travers Jerome. Not that the smart set had been involved in some vast communal felony; all that Jerome wanted was a little moral support in bringing to trial one of the most bare-faced, audacious, and hypocritical scoundrels of all time.

In a devious legal manoeuvre District Attorney Jerome had managed to lure America's most successful blackmailer into court. All he needed to clinch the case were sufficient witnesses from among the upper crust to testify that Colonel William d'Alton Mann—publisher and editor of the scurrilous *Town Topics* magazine—had shaken them down.

Only the "top people" weren't playing. Even with the chance of getting the bloodsucking Colonel Mann off their backs, the thought of rattling family skeletons and exposed dirty linen had sent them scurrying out of New York, away from the District Attorney's bombardment of subpoena writs.

After rigging the most transparently spurious trial to get Colonel Mann into the courtroom, District Attorney Jerome faced a bitter disappointment. For want of evidence it looked as though Colonel Mann might get away with a career of outrageous extortion—which had cost the erring members of New York society hundreds of thousands of dollars.

A pity, for the plot had been as perfect in its way as the Colonel's method of putting the bite on his victims. For a start, the wily Colonel wasn't in the dock. He was the main prosecution witness in an action for criminal libel against *Collier's Magazine,* which had run a deliberately defamatory campaign exposing him as a blackmailer. The Colonel had been forced to sue, and in court he was represented by none other than District Attorney Jerome himself. But the whole thing had been a set-up, an ingenious trick to confront the Colonel with enough evidence to result in his arrest for extortion.

The cunning legal contrivance was jeopardized, however, by the reluctance of the victims to show their faces. It was January 15, 1906, the first day of the trial at the New York Criminal Court. The 66-year-old Colonel, dressed in a top hat, frock coat and sporty waistcoat, his purple face wreathed in venerable whiskers, sat sanctimoniously in the courtroom, a picture of injured innocence. The conspiracy had gone wrong.

Eyebrow-raising paragraphs

Although the proof was so thin on the ground, everyone knew how the Colonel used his magazine to threaten his victims.

"Not for Babes, Prudes, Idiots or Dudes" was the motto of *Town Topics,* whose weekly circulation of 130,000 was based more than anything else on the first 14 pages—a ragbag of poisonous society gossip, phoney piety, and

aggressive opinionizing under the heading "Saunterings" and signed by "The Saunterer". "Viewed from every aspect," claimed the Colonel, "there is no feature of my paper of which I am more proud than its informative and regenerative influence. To save the sinner by rebuking the sin is an achievement over which the angels rejoice."

New York's *bon ton* certainly didn't rejoice. It was with trembling hands that they turned to the Saunterer's garnerings each week. Scattered among the deferential reports of tea-dances, dinners, weddings and parties were the most eyebrow-raising paragraphs.

Extortion payments

"Harry Lehr's proud parade of his many sissy qualities, his pink complexion and golden hair, his thin voice, his peculiar gestures, the feminine prettiness of his general make-up has gone beyond the limits of tolerance by decent society" . . . "Miss Van Alen suffers from some kind of throat trouble. She cannot go more than half an hour without a drink" . . . "The erotic southern novelist, Amelie Rives, has a kink in her hair that extends well into her brain."

When the name of the "sinner" was dropped it was the signal for even more alarming revelations. New York society, it appeared, included anonymous perverts, drunkards, swindlers, transvestites, thieves, nymphomaniacs, adulterers, lesbians and committers of incest. There was no problem in identifying this weekly crowd of fashionable degenerates. The Saunterer gave readers a helping hand.

"The young man's name," he would write, "is the same as the title of the leading primate of the Church of Rome." Or, "The lady in question is the daughter of a leading shipping magnate to which this city is particularly indebted".

Regular readers noticed, however, that there were certain exceptions to the Saunterer's roll-call of moral turpitude. Names which always appeared, bathed in a fulsome and flattering light.

Among the Saunterer's rebukes would appear deferential references to "Mrs. Potter Palmer, whose latest party confirmed once again that she is among the city's most outstanding hostesses", or "Mr. Ogden Armour's tireless efforts for charitable causes elevate him to an exemplary position among our most generous philanthropists".

They were the ones who had put their hands in their pockets when the Saunterer had rattled the collecting-box. Or, as District Attorney Jerome put it, yielded to blackmail. The Saunterer was Colonel William d'Alton Mann himself, and the method he had devised to make his magazine pay was effective, if unorthodox.

For a small financial consideration the Saunterer would drop the brickbats and start presenting the bouquets. Nothing so vulgar as blackmail, of course, or as crude as a bribe. There was a delicate routine to be observed. It started with a visit by one of the Colonel's employees, usually bearing a galley-proof of a future edition of Saunterings. The attention of the victim was directed to a paragraph which would cause him embarrassment, ostracism, or social death the instant it appeared.

This unnerving introduction would be followed by a discreet invitation to offer a loan to the company, to purchase shares or "invest" in a series of advertisements. Sometimes, as an added refinement, the emissary might invite the victim to subscribe to a "forthcoming" Who's Who of American society, to be called *America's Smart Set*. No publication date was ever mentioned, and the hapless victim knew that *Smart Set* would never appear.

The Colonel fixed a sliding scale for extortion payments, according to the wealth and social standing of the victim. The standard rate for ensuring editorial goodwill was $500, though several subscribers for *America's Smart Set* forked out $1500, and one woman—with either more to hide or headier social aspirations—was relieved of $10,000.

The stratagem worked every time, bearing out the Colonel's much-repeated claim that "I've never met a big businessman yet who wasn't a coward at heart". Some of America's most ruthless robber barons meekly reached for their wallets when the Saunterer rang their doorbell. Among the known victims who contributed their loans, investments or subscriptions were:

MILLIONAIRE William K. Vanderbilt (below) was just one of many rich victims. Right, cartoonists saw Judge Deuel as Mann's dupe . . .

J. Pierpont Morgan, Colonel John Jacob Astor, Mrs. Collis P. Huntington, William K. Vanderbilt Jun., Reginald Vanderbilt, Alfred Vanderbilt, Clarence Mackay of Postal Telegraph, Judge Elbert Gary, Isaac Guggenheim of United States Steel, Harold McCormick of International Harvester, the architect Stanford White, Charles M. Schwab of Bethlehem Steel, Harrison Drummond of the Drummond Tobacco Company, Ogden Armour of the meat-packing family, corporation lawyer James W. Gerard, silver czar Thomas Walsh, Mrs. Potter Palmer of the Chicago department store millions, Theodore Shonts, the chairman of the Panama Canal Commission, Henry Huntington of the Central Pacific Railroad, banker H. P. Whitney and—according to rumour—even President Theodore Roosevelt.

The Colonel robbed them all. In his 30 years as publisher of *Town Topics* he fleeced the rich of hundreds of thousands of dollars. The Colonel had his principles, however. "I never collected from anybody who wasn't rich enough to pay out," he said. There was moral justification for his depredations, too. "I believe," he wrote in Saunterings, "that the possession of great wealth, the presence of continual luxury and an existence of sybaritic ease are sufficient to lead voluptuous natures into a system of sensual gratification more intensely and ingeniously base than is found in humbler walks of life. The Four Hundred Leading Families of New York is an element so shallow and unhealthy that it deserves to be derided constantly."

Free drinks

Not surprising in someone who gained such complete fulfilment from his work, the Colonel was a jaunty and ebullient figure for his age. "A rousing, bouncing, noisy, vigorous, open-hearted, choleric old man" was how one of his staff described him. His office was open house to any pretty girl, and there was nothing the rumbustious Colonel loved more than being surrounded by what one reporter called "a wreath of fluttering girlhood". There was a kiss for everyone and a constant supply of free drinks, which he stored in the office safe.

Even his worst enemies agreed that Colonel William d'Alton Mann was several sizes larger than life. In 1863, while fighting for the Union forces, he had led a daring cavalry charge at the Battle of Gettysburg. After leaving the army, he floated a phoney oil company and managed to milk $57,000 from his fellow-officers before being arrested on a charge of obtaining money by false pretences.

The only oil any of his investors had ever seen, it had been alleged, was the small sample he kept in a phial in his pocket. A legal technicality saved him from jail, and a year later he turned up in

473

Mobile, Alabama, having somehow secured an appointment as Federal tax assessor. It was like giving a cat-burglar the key to Fort Knox. With the money he managed to misappropriate, the Colonel bought out all Mobile's four newspapers and opened his own, the *Mobile Register*.

First mistake

It was a huge success and provided enough capital for the Colonel to launch into his biggest — and most honest — venture, the Mann Railway Sleeping Carriage Company Ltd. By 1876 the Colonel had 58 of his patented "boudoir cars" running on half-a-dozen European railway systems — including those of Russia, Germany, Austria, France and Belgium. He founded the *Compagnie Internationale de Wagons-Lits*, which still operates, and built special sleeping-cars for England's King Edward VII, King Leopold II of Belgium, actress Lily Langtry, and the opera star, Adelina Patti.

The Colonel made a fortune — only to lose the lot when he sold out his valuable European interests and returned to America to challenge the powerful Pullman Company. The Mann Railway Sleeping Carriage Company Ltd. left the rails in a cloud of debts. Pausing only to write a remarkably far-seeing military treatise on mobile armoured warfare, the indefatigable Colonel started *Town Topics*. Within a couple of years he had cleared debts of more than $100,000, thanks mainly to his novel editorial policy of "buy one and stop me".

As the Saunterer genially dispensed booze, bonhomie and brickbats in the summer of 1905, it seemed nothing could stop the endless flow of greenbacks, prised from the wallets of New York's Frightened Four Hundred. But two things happened which were to addle the Saunterer's golden egg. One of his vituperative campaigns over-reached itself . . . and one of his employees fumbled the collecting-box.

The Colonel's first mistake was to embark on a vendetta against Alice Roosevelt, the 20-year-old daughter of President Theodore Roosevelt, whose fun-loving escapades had already caused pursed lips in high society. Alice had just made her debut at Newport, and the Saunterer had caught the noxious scent of "sensual gratification". Describing the debut in his column, the Colonel wrote:

"From wearing costly lingerie to indulging in fancy dances for the edification of men was only a step. And then came a second step — indulging freely in stimulants. Flying all around Newport without a chaperone was another thing that greatly concerned Mrs. Grundy. If the young woman knew some of the tales that were told at the clubs in Newport, she would be more careful in future. I was really surprised to hear her name mentioned

openly there in connection with certain rather unmentionable doings.

Alice's name was not disclosed, but readers were given their customary do-it-yourself clue. "She is the daughter of a figure on the highest level of national life, and her host is a man named after a distinguished American to whom the world of steam navigation is deeply indebted."

This time many people thought the Saunterer had gone too far. Among them was 28-year-old Robert Collier, the lively publisher of *Collier's Magazine*. There was no love lost between the Collier family and the Saunterer. Collier's father, Peter Fenelon Collier, who had emigrated from Ireland at 17 and built up the entire magazine empire, had frequently been the butt of the Saunterer's sarcastic wit. For young Robert Collier it was a chance for revenge. That day Robert Collier steamed into the magazine's office and threw the *Town Topics* cutting on the desk of editor Norman Hapgood.

"This is the most vicious paragraph that ever appeared in a magazine," he snapped. "I want you to write an editorial for next week's issue, attacking Mann and his miserable publication." Hapgood rose to the occasion magnificently. "The most degraded paper of any prominence in the United States," he wrote, "is a weekly of which the function is to distribute news and scandal about society. The mind which guides such a publication tests credulity and forces one to take Swift's Yahoo as unexaggerated truth."

A public service

Warming to the subject, Hapgood continued: "The editor in question leads a somewhat secluded life, and well he may. A recent issue of his sewer-like sheet contains as its leading feature an attack on a young girl who happens to be the daughter of the President. It uses her first name only. That is a little way it has. It charges her with all the errors that hurt a woman most, and it makes these charges in the most coarse and leering way. That any steps could or should be taken to suppress such unclean sheets we do not believe. Official regulation can go too far.

"We can only say that whoever refuses to read the journal we refer to or advertise in its columns performs a public service. As to personal recognition, we can hardly imagine that many decent men would consent to meet the editor." Just before the article went to press, Robert Collier added the words, "The editor's standing among the people is somewhat worse than that of an ordinary forger, horsethief or second-story man."

Gnawing his whiskers in fury, the Saunterer fired back in characteristic style in the following issue of *Town Topics*, mistakingly picking Collier senior as his target. "The man is lecherous, leprous

and unable to write his name," sneered the Colonel — who went on to refer to a jewel theft which had taken place after a party in Collier's neighbourhood. "The police might solve the case," he wrote, "if they cared to take a close look at Pat Fagin's new scarf pin." Pat Fagin, as everyone knew, was the Saunterer's contemptuous nom-de-plume for the elder Collier. Chortling triumphantly, the Colonel then departed on a European holiday, leaving *Town Topics* in the charge of an old crony, the corrupt Judge Joseph M. Deuel. He couldn't have picked a worse time to take a trip.

In the last week of June 1905 Mr. Edwin Main Post — a distinguished New York stockbroker and husband of the high priestess of social etiquette, Emily Post — received a visit from Charles Ahle, a young employee of *Town Topics*.

Gentlemen's lavatory

It was the old "stand and deliver" routine. Ahle smilingly handed over a galley-proof of a Saunterings paragraph scheduled for the next issued of *Town Topics*. The write-up dwelt at embarrassing length on Post's marital affairs and referred to "a little white studio in Stamford" which it claimed that the broker had shared with "a fair charmer with a liking for white shoes with red heels and patent leather tips". This awkward information, Charles Ahle assured Post, could be withheld if the broker cared to take advantage of a bargain-price subscription of $500 to *America's Smart Set*. The fee would also cover an obsequious article on Mr. Post in the proposed Who's Who.

But for once the Saunterer had met his match. Promising to call Ahle in a few days, Mr. Post reported the pay-or-be-pilloried threat to District Attorney William Travers Jerome. For 10 years the District Attorney had been trying to scratch together enough evidence to stop the Colonel in mid-saunter. For the first time one of New York's Four Hundred was willing to stand up in court and testify. Mr. Post agreed to play along with the Colonel's messenger, and on July 11, 1905, the two men met by arrangement in the gentlemen's lavatory of Holland House, at the corner of 30th Street and 5th Avenue. The purpose of the meeting was for Mr. Post to hand over $500.

Charles Ahle was in a talkative mood. "You're getting off easy," he told Mr. Post. "We've had scandals worth $20,000." Ahle patted his black briefcase meaningfully. "In fact," he beamed, "*Town Topics* makes most of its money from the suppression of stories." Exactly

CARTOONIST F. T. Richards was foreman of the jury in the Mann case. His sketch of the Colonel threatening the rich with a sabre appeared in the *American*.

one second later the smile vanished from his face. Like the Demon King in a pantomime, Detective-sergeant Bernard Flood of the New York Police Department leaped from one of the cubicles and fastened the handcuffs on Ahle.

The surprise arrest fell right into the lap of the campaigning Robert Collier, who sent Norman Hapgood to interview District Attorney Jerome. Together, the two men cooked up the conspiracy which was to goad Colonel William d'Alton Mann into court. *Collier's Magazine* had to make its campaign against the Colonel so defamatory, said District Attorney Jerome, that he would be forced to sue for criminal, as opposed to civil, libel. In that way the Colonel and Judge Deuel would have to give evidence, and — although they were testifying for the State — the District Attorney would gladly leave them to be torn apart by defence counsel.

Defiant figure

In the August 5 issue of *Collier's Magazine* Hapgood took the Colonel and his judicial crony to the cleaner's. After repeating all the original accusations, this time fully identifying the Colonel as the culprit, Hapgood turned his attention to Judge Deuel. "He is paid $9000 a year by the people and is clothed with an honour that should be worth more to him. What is his return? He is part owner and one of the editors of a paper of which the occupation is printing scandal about people who are not cowardly enough to pay for silence. What kind of public opinion would allow him to remain upon the bench until 1913? Every day he sits upon it is a disgrace to the State that endures him."

The immediate result was a two-way traffic in blackmailers. Before he could be tried for extortion, Charles Ahle skipped his $3500 bail and fled to Europe — passing on the way the irate Colonel, who had cut short his holiday and was steaming back home at full speed. It was a defiant figure who stepped from the liner *Zeeland* to confront a crowd of waiting reporters. The Colonel refused to comment on the accusations, but insisted:

"I have often kept out a story I thought might work serious injury to some person or family." In a menacing tone he added, "As a matter of fact at this very moment I have cartloads of stories locked up in my safe that would turn New York upside-down if they were published."

The air was already thick with denials. Both the Colonel and Judge Deuel disowned Charles Ahle and his black brief-case. But, as *Collier's Magazine*'s campaign continued unabated, *Town Topics* found itself propelled inescapably towards legal action. The canny Colonel started by pushing Judge Deuel into the firing-line first. On September 11 the Judge swore out a warrant for criminal libel and police formally arrested *Collier's* editor Norman Hapgood in his office. But Robert Collier was determined to join his editor behind bars.

"The principal villain is Colonel Mann," he told reporters. "It is not our fault if Justice Deuel chooses to lay his body athwart the track. I challenge the *Town Topics* publisher to swear out a warrant in my name."

The jibe was too much for the ex-cavalry Colonel. On October 30 the Saunterer swore out the warrant, and Robert Collier, along with his father, was arrested for criminal libel. Meanwhile the "criminals" from *Collier's* had been gathering together their witnesses. One of them was James Burden, the young heir to the Troy ironworks millions. At the preliminary hearing Burden told the court that, four years earlier, the Colonel had asked him to see a *Town Topics* employee named Robert Irving.

It was the usual story. When Irving showed up, he "invited" Burden to subscribe $1500 to *Fads and Fancies* — another spurious society Who's Who. Irving had advised him to "consider the matter very carefully, as the Colonel wields a trenchant pen". Just how trenchant, Burden was soon to find out. A week after turning down the offer, Burden opened *Town Topics* to discover himself labelled as a drunkard and whoremonger.

In his chair in the centre of court, the Colonel glowered at the witness. His expression darkened further still when Robert Irving — who had been promised immunity from extortion charges if he testified for the defence — took the stand and repeated the story.

Virtuoso performance

The Colonel jumped to his feet, quivering with wrath. "I don't even know this fellow!" he boomed, and strode out, complaining of a toothache. The trial of the *Collier's* trio was fixed for January 15, 1906. From his bed of pain that night the Colonel told reporters, "I am 66 years old, and with the career I have made as open as the day, if there has been any testimony given in this case that reflects upon my honour, I must fight to the end."

Although most of New York's Four Hundred had discreetly left town, the courtroom was packed with spectators on the first day. What seemed like the city's entire middle-class was there, agog to hear what its betters had been up to. They were treated to a virtuoso performance by the wronged Colonel. As each defence witness took the stand he reacted like a ham actor, groaning, grimacing, glaring, stamping his feet, hammering his chair with his fists and snatching at his whiskers. On the other side of the witness box for once, Judge Deuel was given a rough ride by Defence Counsel James Osborne. Osborne reminded him of the City Charter which stipulated that "No Justice shall receive any fees or perquisites nor carry on any business or practice as an attorney". Judge Deuel knew what was coming.

Counsel: Do you appear in the office of *Town Topics* every week for the purpose of reading over the galley-proofs for possible libels?

Deuel: No.

Counsel: Do you make any additions to these proofs?

Deuel: I might put in a few exclamation marks.

Counsel: Have you a desk at the magazine?

Deuel: Yes. But this is because I have been writing a series of articles for *Town Topics* on New York crime, and the office was a convenient place for research on the subject.

"Services rendered"

Judge Deuel's answer was almost drowned in a howl of laughter from the court, in which Osborne and Judge James Fitzgerald joined in. The Colonel turned a deeper shade of purple. Defence Counsel picked up a copy of the *Town Topics* accounts ledger — which had been seized from the magazine's offices — and read out details of payment after payment made to the Judge for "services rendered". As the litany continued, Judge Deuel put his hand over his eyes and his mouth twitched nervously.

Counsel: Do you admit the record?

Deuel: I'll have to.

Well into his stride, Osborne produced a letter from Deuel to a *Town Topics* "collector" who was about to leave on a subscription-raising tour. "I hope you will have not only pleasant weather but pleasant people to see and to meet," the Judge had written. "I hope that all of them will be like Davy Crockett's 'coon — all you need to do is point your gun and every high-toned desirable citizen at Palm-Beach may tumble into your basket."

"As the day wore on," wrote a reporter in the *American,* "Judge Deuel appeared to shrink and age before the very eyes of the crowd." Acting as a kind of legal "double agent", District Attorney Jerome was now ready to feed his fattest witness to the defence lions. But not before he had gone through the motions of establishing the Colonel's innocence of the gross libel perpetrated against him.

Jerome: Does *Town Topics* print scandal?

The Colonel: No!

CONQUERING HERO. Colonel Mann led a gallant cavalry charge of Union soldiers at the Battle of Gettysburg in 1863. But when the war was over, he turned embezzler.

Jerome: Has it ever been guilty of levying blackmail or publishing anything in consideration of money being paid?

The Colonel: Absolutely not!

With those two questions satisfactorily answered, District Attorney Jerome handed his witness over to the mercies of Defence Counsel Osborne, who began by reading a series of Saunterer paragraphs concerning a Mr. Reginald Ward, a well-known Boston socialite. They were hardly complimentary. The first hinted at "a scandal that savours strongly of the Oscar Wilde type". Another read, "I hear from London that Reginald Ward is more of a dandy than ever and affects the dress and manners of the fops of the last century. He wears his fingernails long, and each finger is loaded with rings. He is a great friend of Mrs. Ronalds, who, I hear, arranged his coming marriage with a widow of title who has seen at least 65 winters."

The final paragraph, however, was far more deferential in tone. "Mr. Reginald Ward has returned to this country, where he has received notable social attention. His old friends in the Union and Metropolitan Clubs, where he has always been very popular, were glad to have him with them. Few men have gone from the States to London and established themselves more successfully in both the social and financial worlds than Reginald Ward."

Abusive paragraphs

What miraculous transformation had occurred to Mr. Reginald Ward to soften the heart of the Saunterer within the space of a few paragraphs? Osborne provided the answer.

Counsel: Do you deny that shortly before the appearance of the last paragraph Ward transferred to you 10,000 shares in the Rico Syndicate, a copper-mining enterprise?

The Colonel: I do not recall.

Darting to the pile of documents on his desk, Osborne read several letters detailing the change-over of shares, ending with a nervous note from Ward saying, "I am looking forward with much interest to the paragraphs to which you refer. I wish you would please put my name down on the regular list of *Town Topics* so that I will get it regularly, if not too much trouble." The letter was countersigned "OK—W.D.M." The Colonel denied ever seeing or signing the letter.

By the fifth day of the trial District Attorney Jerome's subpoenas were beginning to take effect. Several distinguished New Yorkers appeared to accuse the Colonel of sinking his teeth into their wallets. Banker Oliver Belmont testified that the Saunterer had asked him for sums of $5000 and $2000, one as an "investment" in *Town Topics* stock, the other as a straight loan. After he refused, the magazine had printed more than 50 abusive paragraphs about him and his family.

The Colonel's cockiness in the witness box had vanished. He was in full retreat. The turning point came when Osborne asked him about loans from broker E. Clarence Jones.

Counsel: Did you ever borrow money from Mr. Jones?

The Colonel: I don't want to answer.

Counsel: You'll have to answer.

The Colonel: Yes, I borrowed $10,000 from Jones.

Counsel: Have you repaid it?

The Colonel: Probably not.

Counsel: Now let us turn to —

The Colonel: I do not wish to answer further.

Counsel: On the grounds that it would degrade you?

The Colonel: Yes.

The following day the Colonel appeared to have regained some of his composure, if not defiance. He blandly admitted having failed to pay back "loans" totalling more than $187,500, including $25,000 from William K. Vanderbilt, $14,000 from Dr. Seward Webb, $2500 from J. Pierpont Morgan, $3000 and $2500 from George and Howard Gould, $5000 from Mrs. Collis P. Huntington and $76,000 from James R. Keene. Pressed for further details on his borrowing, the Colonel replied airily. "I have borrowed so much money that I can't remember it all."

Counsel: How can you explain the reason for Pierpont Morgan — who is known to be virtually unapproachable — lending $2500 without security to a comparative stranger?

The Colonel: I went to Mr. Morgan the same as I did to the other men of prominence, and asked them because I felt they were of such standing that if they accommodated me there would be no occasion for me to criticize them.

With that equivocal answer the Colonel stomped from the witness box, his jaw clenched and his whiskers bristling. Assistant-Counsel Edward Shepard then summed-up for the defence. "Colonel Mann and Judge Deuel are a vile pair," he said. *Town Topics* has been proved to be not a literary publication but a conspiracy to produce money in large sums, making use of sneaks in the clubs, sneaks in the kitchen, sneaks in the churches. Deuel is a corrupt judge and Mann the master craftsman of blackmailers."

Not even the much-chastened Colonel expected anything different. But it was the closing speech of District Attorney Jerome that shook the court, and reduced the cruelly libelled Colonel to near-apoplexy. He managed to present Judge Deuel and Colonel Mann as unprincipled blackguards, while at the same time maintaining they were innocent and aggrieved parties.

"I have never listened to such a story of weakness and degradation," he said. "And I regard my own two witnesses with loathing and contempt." While the courtroom wondered just whose side he was supposed to be on, the District Attorney continued:

"I will admit that Judge Deuel violated the city charter — but, as everyone knows, nearly all other judges in town are similarly guilty. Don't say a man is a vampire and sucks human blood just because he has violated the city charter. With the shadows lengthening in his life, broken in health, his back to the wall, Judge Deuel may have broken the law only to provide for himself in his old age. But the point to remember is that Colonel Mann never borrowed money from anybody who hadn't got any. He simply cashed in on the knowledge that the titans of American industry were spineless men with more money than brains and more vanity than either."

The only point District Attorney Jerome omitted to make involved the very reason for the trial. He somehow forgot to call for the conviction of the criminal libellers. Compared to Jerome's 1½-hour speech, the jury's deliberations were completed in a twitch of the Colonel's whiskers. They took just seven minutes to return a verdict of Not Guilty, which was greeted by thunderous applause.

"A magnificent triumph for public decency!" proclaimed Assistant-Counsel Shepard, as District Attorney Jerome clapped Hapgood on the back and laughed. "Get out of here, you criminal — you've had your day in court." The Colonel, who had fallen back into his chair with a thud at the verdict, gave short shift to the reporters. "Why should I say anything?" he bristled. "*I* wasn't the prisoner!"

At the *Town Topics'* offices the recriminations fell over each other. While the *New York Evening World* topsy-turvily headlined the verdict "TOWN TOPICS GUILTY", the Colonel rumbled, "I was tricked — it was a frame-up."

But District Attorney Jerome hadn't finished with the Colonel. At that very moment he was putting the rubber-stamp to a charge of perjury against the Saunterer, based on his "wilful, corrupt and false testimony" that he had not written "OK — W.D.M." on the letter from Reginald Ward.

When news of the new charge reached the Colonel he gamely volunteered to stay at the *Town Topics* office to await arrest. But by 4.45 in the afternoon his patience had worn thin. "By George," he complained to a crowd of reporters who were there to watch the fun, "unless they hurry up they will seriously interfere with my dinner!"

In the weeks before the new trial the Saunterer's column exuded nothing but sweetness and light. The Colonel had not lost his taste for self-righteous humbug, however. A regular reminder that "every accused man is innocent until proved otherwise" was accompanied by the sermon, "This fundamental precept of right is forgotten only when an epidemic of injustice, born of fanaticism and made contagious through an overheated consciousness of one's own tendency to moral obliquity, sweeps over the land, twisting and distorting for the moment the people's usual sanity and calmer judgment."

Maybe all the world secretly loves a rogue, particularly one plausible and audacious enough to rob the robber barons. At the trial, on December 18, the Colonel's counsel, the barnstorming Martin Littleton, delivered a panegyric more suited to a national hero than a bare-faced blackmailer.

"Colonel Mann," he throbbed, "is widely known as an exemplary citizen, a brave soldier and a loyal friend." The only other sound in court during this impassioned speech were the elephantine sobs of the deeply moved Colonel. After four hours the jury returned a verdict of Not Guilty, which was received by more monumental weeping from the Colonel.

The Colonel was so proud of Littleton's hymn of praise that he had it reprinted and expensively bound in gold-tooled leather. He was still delightedly giving away copies of the book in 1920, when he died, aged 81, having outlived nearly all his accusers . . . the robber barons whom he so brazenly robbed.

AVENGING ANGEL. Mann justified his scandal-sheet by claiming that he was of moral value to the country in exposing the follies and vices of the very rich.

INDEX